Terry Miller

The New
EXPLORING
A
CHANGING
WORLD

The New
EXPLORING
A
CHANGING
WORLD

Melvin Schwartz
John R. O'Connor

GLOBE BOOK COMPANY INC.

NEW YORK/CHICAGO/CLEVELAND

MELVIN SCHWARTZ

B.S.S. and M.S., the City College of the City University of New York
Ed.D., Teachers College, Columbia University

Dr. Schwartz began teaching social studies in the New York City school system more than twenty-five years ago and is currently a school principal. He has authored several other Globe social studies textbooks, including *Exploring the Non-Western World, Exploring the Western World, Exploring Africa, South of the Sahara,* and *The New Exploring American History.*

JOHN R. O'CONNOR

B.A., St. Francis College
M.A., University of Pittsburgh

Mr. O'Connor taught social studies for many years before becoming a principal in the New York City school system. He is widely known for his lectures and for his articles on reading skills in the social studies. Mr. O'Connor co-authored the textbooks *Exploring World History, Exploring the Urban World,* and *Exploring Urban New York.* In addition to this textbook, he has edited *Exploring the Non-Western World, Exploring the Western World, Exploring Africa, South of the Sahara,* and *The New Exploring American History.*

Editors: Alexandra Lyons, Lois Bredhoff, and Gerald Bagner

Cover design: Oscar Liebman
Text design: Nancy Dale

Illustrations:
Maps and Pictographs by Dyno Lowenstein, Pictograph Corporation
Text Illustrations by Joseph Forte
Unit Openers by Harry Schaare

Photo Editors: Adelaide Garvin Ungerland and Gerald Bagner

Our thanks to Mr. Robert Gritz for reading the manuscript of this text and making many helpful suggestions.

ISBN: 0-87065-556-6

Copyright © 1975 by Globe Book Company, Inc.
New York, N.Y. 10010

PRINTED IN THE UNITED STATES OF AMERICA   6 7 8 9 0

TABLE OF CONTENTS

Unit 4: LATIN AMERICA

Unit 5: WESTERN EUROPE

Unit 6: THE SOVIET UNION

MAPS AND PICTOGRAPHS

LIST OF MAPS

LIST OF PICTOGRAPHS

READINGS FROM OTHER SOURCES

Environment, Race and Culture

1 PEOPLE AND THEIR CULTURES

Reading For A Purpose: What is culture?

1. There are more than 3½ billion people living today on the planet Earth. They live all over the earth's surface—on plains, on hillsides, in jungles and deserts. Some even make their homes on the waters of the earth. There are places where as many as 20,000 people live crowded together on one square mile of land. In others, there is not a soul for miles. In some places, people make thousands of dollars a year from their work. In others, they barely scratch out $200 a year. There are places where houses have heat in the winter and air-conditioning in the summer. In other places, mud walls are the only protection against the weather.

2. Wherever people live, they have developed ways of working, playing and governing themselves. How people live day by day, how they work, the songs they sing, the god or gods they worship, the sports they enjoy—all these things make up their *culture*. The culture of a people is passed on to their children and their children's children. It may change greatly or very little over the years. Ours is a fast-changing culture. Among the Tasadays of the Philippines, ways of living have changed little since

All people need protection from the weather, but the kinds of shelters they build vary from place to place, from culture to culture. In these photos are typical shelters of three different cultures. Which shelter is likely to be the home of a hunter or herder? Of a fisherman? Of a factory or office worker?

the dawn of history. These people still hunt with stone weapons and gather food from trees.

3. Culture depends in part on a people's surroundings, their *environment*. Soil, climate, minerals, the kind of land surface, power resources—all of these make up a people's environment. Ways of living may vary greatly among different environments. Nevertheless, no matter where people live, they have a great deal to say about *how* they live. Our culture depends less on the natural environment than that of the Eskimo. Through science we have been able to change our surroundings to make life more comfortable for ourselves.

4. Let us look at some things that are part of the culture of Western Europe. (In this book we shall be studying the countries of Western Europe as one *culture region*—an area throughout which the way of life is much the same.) In most of Western Europe, soccer is the most popular sport. It is part of the culture of the region. Most people of Western Europe are Christians. Religion is part of their culture, too. Careful farming on small plots is also important. In Western Europe there are many fine churches, forts and palaces hundreds of years old. They have been saved and cared for because respect for the past is part of the culture of Western Europeans.

5. In the United States and Canada, some people play soccer. Most Americans belong to one of the Christian religions. Some Americans like caring for small gardens. Some Americans do not want to see old, historic buildings torn down. This does not mean that the culture of the people of North America is the same as that of the people of Western Europe. It does mean that there is a kinship. It also means that Americans have borrowed from Europeans and vice versa. People may take things from another culture and use them as their own. Spaghetti is a favorite dish of many Americans, yet it began as a part of the culture of Italy, where it was brought from China. Automobiles, which were at first a feature of American cul-

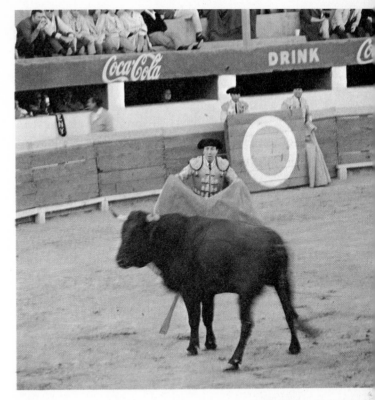

Football and baseball are two of this country's favorite sports. Our Mexican neighbors enjoy bullfighting, a sport they borrowed from Spain. What have we borrowed from our Spanish-speaking neighbors?

ture, soon became a feature of the culture of many European countries.

6. Cultures of one place are often a mixture of the cultures of people of many places. People have come to the United States from all over the world—from Spain, France, England, Holland, Africa, Sweden, Italy, Poland, Ireland, Russia, China, Japan. The list runs even longer. The first people in America were the Indians. Almost every part of the world has given something to the culture of Americans today. In Canada, the English and French cultures can easily be noticed. Within the same country, some areas are chiefly English in their culture. Others are chiefly French.

7. Once the culture of a people did not spread far. Mountains and oceans kept people apart. People developed their own ways of living, their own language, and often their own religion, separate from others. Now, however, ideas spread quickly. TV and the airplane have had much to do with breaking down the "walls" between people. Rapid communication and transportation help to bring people together. They help to wipe out differences in cultures. Will the time come when everyone on Earth will live in the same way, when everyone will have the same culture? What do you think?

A people's culture includes its forms of play and recreation as well as work. Here musicians accompany a Kathakali dancer, whose dance tells a story about India of long ago. What kind of picture would you choose to show a form of recreation in our culture?

UNDERSTANDING CHAPTER 1

Which statements below are true?

1. The cultures of different peoples are all pretty much the same.
2. How people live, work and play depends in part on their environment.
3. Our religion is part of our culture.
4. All people depend on their natural environment, but some people depend on it less than others.
5. The foods people eat have little to do with their culture.
6. Americans have borrowed from other cultures.
7. In today's world, cultures of one people rarely mix with the cultures of others.

DEVELOPING IDEAS AND SKILLS

In paragraph 1 of this chapter, we mentioned the number of people living on one square mile of land in some areas of the world. We call this *density of population*. Look at the two pieces of land below and see if you can tell the difference in the density of population. Density comes from the word *dense*, which means thick or crowded.

LAND A

1 SQUARE MILE

LAND B

1 SQUARE MILE

EACH DOT REPRESENTS 20 PEOPLE

4

1. How many people live on the square mile in Land A? In Land B?
2. Which has the greater *density of population?*
3. What reasons might explain why A is more crowded than B?

The People's Republic of China has more people than any other country in the world. In land area it is about the same size as the United States. Look at these drawings.

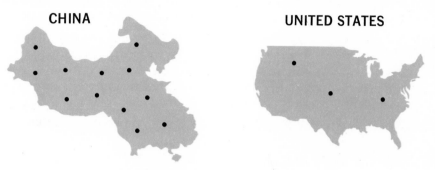

EACH DOT REPRESENTS 20 PEOPLE ON EACH SQUARE MILE OF LAND

1. How many people live on a square mile in China? In the United States?
2. Which country has the greater *density of population?* Which one is more crowded?
3. What reasons might explain why China is more crowded than the United States?

2 RACE AND CULTURE

Reading For A Purpose: How is race different from culture?

---

1. What is meant by a *race* of people? Some people say that there are three main races, and that all people belong to one race or another, depending on the color of their skin. If the skin is white, the race is Caucasian. If the skin color is black, the race is Negro. If yellow, the race is Mongolian. Can we accept this idea? If we do, where can we place the American Indian or people from India? The American Indian really has brown skin, but he looks more like people from China than people from Africa. The people of India have brown skins, but they are really more like people from Europe than people from Africa. Skin color, then, is not enough to tell us what race is.

2. Can we tell race by height or weight? Among the black-skinned people of Africa are the Watusi—the tallest people in the world—and pygmies—the shortest people. Some white Americans are over 7 feet tall and some are less than 5 feet. No, we can't tell race by height. Or weight either. Can we tell race by blood type? Among people of all skin colors, we find all types of blood—O, A, B and AB. The same can be said about color of eyes and type of hair—straight or curly, fine or coarse.

3. Can we tell race by language or nationality? A person of any race can speak any language. A black person can speak Swahili or Malay or French or any other language he may choose to learn. People with white skins can speak French, Malay or Swahili or a great many other tongues. A person of any race can

be a citizen of any country. One cannot make race mean the same as nationality or language.

4. Perhaps one can tell race by religion. All people are free to choose their religions, though people generally choose the religion of their parents. A Christian can be American, Brazilian or Congolese. He can speak English, Portuguese or a Bantu dialect. He can be blue or brown-eyed, curly or straight-haired, tall or short. It is hard to say what a Christian, a Jew or a Moslem will look like, if you haven't any particular one in mind.

5. What, then, is race? A race is a group of people who have similar bodily characteristics. Their children inherit these characteristics. Language, religion, nationality, customs, dress, are not passed on in the same way as race. A person may choose them as he wishes. They are part of his culture, not his race. They are learned. His race is inherited.

6. Is everyone a member of the black, white or yellow race? Experts cannot agree on how many races there actually are. Some say there are as many as 30. Races have been mixing since man began on this earth. Is a person who had a white European grandfather and an American Indian grandmother white or yellow or brown or some other color? Is a person whose ancestors were black and white, black or white or some other color?

7. Some people say that one race is superior to another. Even some who do not say it, act as if they believe it. We call such people "racists." Today, however, many scientists believe that the thinking abilities of all races are the same. There are bright people of all nationalities, religions and races. All groups of people can point to their brilliant thinkers, builders and artists.

8. Culture seems to make the difference among people. But many say that anyone can learn any culture. Can the ideas of different cultures be brought into harmony so that all people can live together in peace? As you read in this book about the different cultures of the world, think about this question.

Peoples of the world. False notions about race are fairly common. Has this chapter helped to rid you of some? If so, which notions were they?

I. Finding the Main Idea

One of the most important skills you can learn is how to find the *main idea* of a paragraph or chapter. In good writing, each paragraph has one main thought. Together these main thoughts add up to the main idea of the chapter. The title of the chapter is a clue to the main idea of the chapter. Let us look at Chapter 2 and see if we can find the main idea of the paragraphs and the chapter.

The main idea of a paragraph may be expressed in a sentence. The sentence may be at the beginning or end of the paragraph, or it may be in the middle. Sometimes the main idea is not stated, but we can tell what it is if we read all the sentences in the paragraph.

In *paragraph 1*, we learn that some people say there are three races: white—Caucasian, black—Negro and yellow—Mongolian. But the color labels can be misleading. For example, some people who have light skins are actually Negro. Is there a sentence that gives us the main idea of the paragraph? Yes, the last sentence says, "Skin color, then, is not enough to tell us what race is." This is the main idea of the paragraph.

In *paragraph 3*, we learn that any person can speak any language or be a citizen of any country. Language and nationality are not determined by race. The main idea is the last sentence of the paragraph, "One cannot make race mean the same as nationality or language."

In *paragraph 5*, the main idea is in the second sentence. The rest of the paragraph develops the idea by comparing race to culture. Race is inherited at birth from the parents. Culture is learned after birth.

The main idea of the chapter is the summary of the main ideas expressed in the paragraphs of the chapter. In Chapter 2, we learn that it is not easy to place everyone in three races, that color alone does not tell us race, that language and nationality are not the same as race, that some ways in which people are alike are the results of their culture, that any person can learn any culture, that no race is superior to others. We have learned about *race and culture*. This is the title of the chapter, the main idea. We could express the title in a sentence, too, as "Race is different from culture."

II. Separating Race From Culture

Make two headings on a page of your notebook. Head one column RACE and the other CULTURE. Then place each item below in the correct column.
1. The language a person speaks.
2. The clothing a person wears.
3. The religion a person has.
4. The shape of a person's head.
5. The kind of hair a person has.
6. The government a person chooses.
7. The color of a person's skin.
8. The home a person lives in.
9. The country a person is a citizen of.
10. The color of a person's eyes.
11. The job a person has.
12. The games a person plays.
13. The bone structure of a person's body.

Conclusions: What makes a person what he is? Is it race or culture or both? Which is more important in your opinion? Why do you think so?

Tell whether you *agree or disagree* with these statements. Explain why.

1. The American Indian is a member of the yellow race.
2. Knowing whether a person is tall or short helps us tell to which race he belongs.
3. Religion and language help us to decide a person's race.
4. The people of the world are divided among three races.
5. A person's race cannot be told by his blood type.
6. A member of any race can learn any culture.
7. Many people throughout the world are a mixture of races.

UNIT 2
The Earth

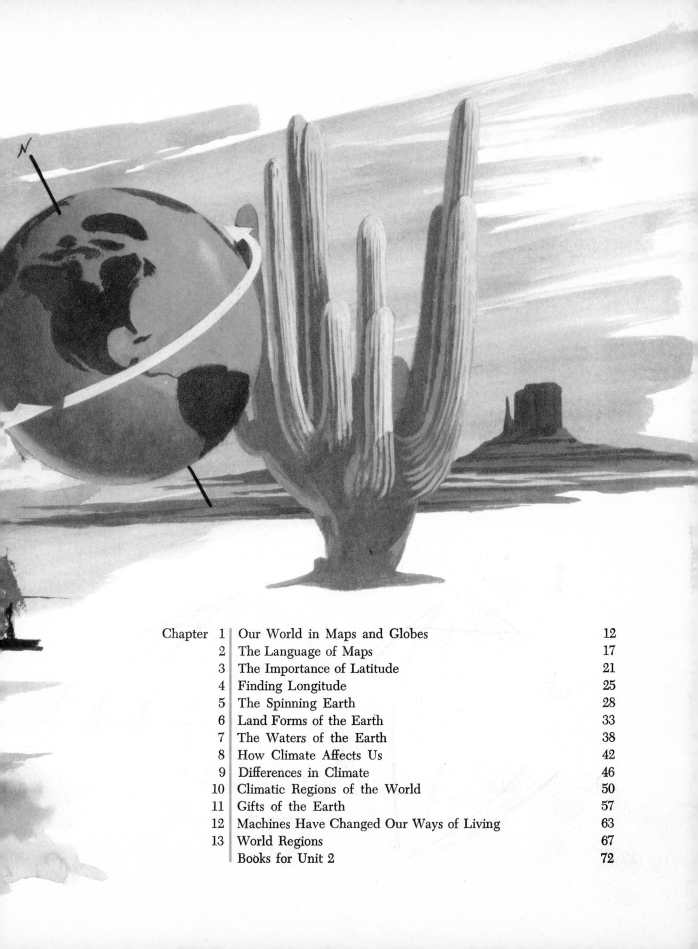

1 OUR WORLD IN MAPS AND GLOBES

Globe map.

Reading For a Purpose: What different kinds of maps are there?

1. We live on the planet Earth. It is one of nine planets that travel around our sun. Our planet is shaped like a ball or *sphere*. Since most of us cannot travel into space to look at our planet, the next best way to study it is through maps. The best map of the earth is a *globe*. A globe is round, so it shows us the earth almost as it is. (The earth really is slightly pear-shaped.) It is the only map that shows us the correct size and shape of the land and water areas on the earth.

2. There are some disadvantages to a globe, though. A globe is not easy to carry with you; it can hardly be kept in your pocket. When we are learning about our planet in school, we can't keep a globe inside our book. Therefore, map makers have had to make other maps that show how the earth looks on a flat surface.

3. There are many such maps, some of which are shown in this chapter. All are ways in which map makers have tried to show the roundness of the earth on a flat surface. There is a problem, however. Flat maps cannot be made without some *distortion*, or changing of the accurate shapes of things. For example, a map that can show the correct directions on

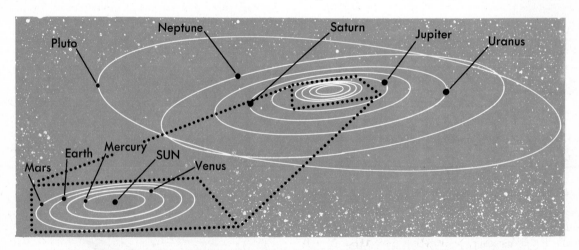

Planets traveling around the sun. The term "planet" comes from an old Greek word meaning "wanderer." Why do you suppose the Greeks chose this name?

the earth's surface probably will not show the true size and shape of land areas. If the correct size and shape of land areas are shown, the water areas may not be correct. In any flat map of the earth, the map maker decides which things he wants to show correctly. (The globe photograph is an attempt to show the roundness of the earth on a flat surface.)

4. The *Mercator* map is one of the most common of flat maps. Mercator was a Dutch map maker who lived about 300 years ago. He was interested in making a map that would help sailors. His map uses only straight lines. This map has been useful for sailors. However, it cannot be used if you want to find correct distances. The land and water areas are not shown in their true size. On a Mercator map, the continent of North America looks larger than the continent of Africa, and Greenland is

Polar map.

south.) The polar map shows clearly how close Europe, Asia and North America are to each other across the Arctic Ocean. On this map, it is easy to mark some of the air routes that connect these continents. However, there are distortions here too. The lands far from the center of the map appear too large and have strange shapes.

6. The *Lambert* projection is sometimes called the "flier's map." This map is good for

Mercator map.

Lambert projection.

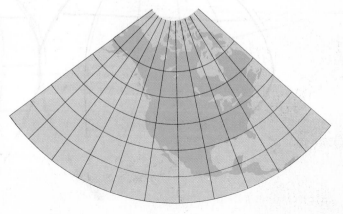

as large as South America. A globe would show that this is wrong.

5. With the coming of the airplane, it became possible to travel over the "top" of the earth rather than "around" it. As a result, distances between certain countries became much less. The *polar* map shows this fact. The North Pole is the center of the polar map. (The North Pole is the northernmost point on the earth. The South Pole is the farthest point

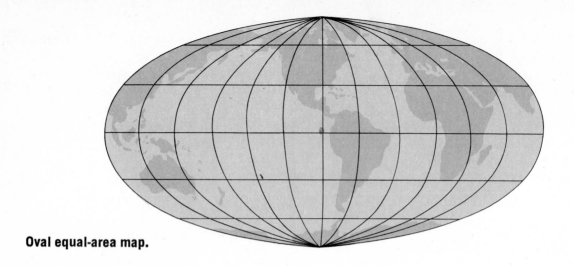

Oval equal-area map.

showing land areas that extend in an east-west or right-left direction. The shapes of these land areas are true. The distances and directions are almost accurate. Therefore, this map is used by pilots.

7. In order to compare the sizes of land and water areas, the *Mollweide* or *equal-area* map is used. This is a map in the shape of an oval. The land and water areas are shown in true size, but the land shapes are not true. To correct this distortion, the oval is broken into several parts. The continents now show their correct shape, but the oceans are distorted. This is called a *broken projection* map.

8. There are many other kinds of maps. There are maps that show us highlands, lowlands and bodies of water. These are called *physical* or *relief* maps. These maps also show us the altitude or height of land above sea level. (Sea level is the level of the ocean when it is still.) Maps that show the boundaries between countries and states are called *political* maps. *Product* maps show us the things made from a country's resources. *Rainfall* maps tell us how much rain a place receives at certain times. Some maps tell us how many people live in one area. These are *population* maps. *Climate* maps show us the climatic regions of the

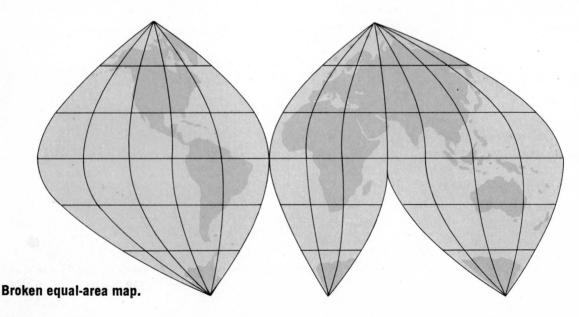

Broken equal-area map.

14

earth—where it is hot or cold, wet or dry. We will use many of these maps as we study our world.

9. As we have seen, each type of map has its good and bad points. However, we will always need maps, because we cannot study or travel without them. When we travel by car, we need a road map. We may have a large map of a section of the United States, another of the particular state we are interested in, and still another of the city or community in the state. In the subways of our large cities, we must look at a map to find our station. At sea, a captain must use a map to plot the course of his ship. We use maps on planes and in the armed forces. We may even use a map to look for buried treasure, as men have done for hundreds of years. Whatever the reason, maps are a part of our lives. And they make easier the job of exploring our changing world.

UNDERSTANDING CHAPTER 1

As you read *Exploring a Changing World*, you will find some words that you do not know. Sometimes it is easy to tell the meaning of a word from the way the word is used in a sentence. You will often find *clues* to the meanings of words. It is important that you learn to recognize some of these clues.

Let us look for some of the new or difficult words·in Chapter 1 and see the clues that tell us what they mean:

In paragraph 1, a new word is *sphere*. The clue to the meaning of sphere is the smaller word before it, *or*. The sentence states that "Our planet is shaped like a ball *or* sphere." The word *or* tells us that sphere means "shaped like a ball." *Or* is therefore one of our clues.

In paragraph 3, the new word is *distortion*. Again, you will notice the use of the word *or* as a clue. The sentence says there is ". . . some distortion, *or* changing of the accurate shapes of things." We know then that *distortion* means "a twisting out of shape."

Sometimes the clue to the meaning of a word appears *in the sentence before the word*. In paragraph 8, there is an example of this kind of clue. The third sentence tells us about *physical maps*. The sentence before it tells us that these are maps that show highlands, lowlands and bodies of water. Therefore, we know that a *physical map* shows us the surface of the earth.

The clue may appear *in the sentence following the word*. In paragraph 5, the third sentence tells us about a *polar map*. The next sentence states that this map has the North Pole at the center. Thus, the word *polar* refers to the *North Pole*, or to the poles of the earth.

In paragraph 8, there is another example of the clue to the meaning of a word appearing in the sentence before the word. The sentence says, "Some maps tell us how many people live in one area." The next sentence states, "These are population maps." We know, therefore, that the word *population* refers to the number of people living in a certain area.

You will meet other clues to word meanings as you read the other chapters in this book. Some of these clues are explained for your help:

A *dash* (—) is often a clue to the meaning of a word. Example: "The *llama*—a woolly animal of the Andes—can carry heavy loads." The word *llama* is explained by the words set off from the rest of the sentence by dashes.

The meaning of a word may be shown by the use of *parentheses*, ( ). Example: "Inventions brought about many changes in farm *implements* (tools used in farming).” Parentheses ( ) are used to show that “implements” means “farm tools.”

The meaning of a word *may be given in a sentence* for you. When that happens, the meaning of the word is very clear. Example: “*Canyons* are long narrow valleys surrounded by high cliffs.”

The words *that is* are often good clues. Example: “The earth *revolves*, that is, travels, around the sun.” The words *that is* show us the meaning of *revolves*.

In your study, you will often be asked to tell the meanings of words. You will have to know their meanings if you are to understand the important facts about our changing world. Remember the clues that may help you:

1. *Or*
2. *Dash* —
3. *Parentheses* ( )
4. *That is*
5. The *sentence before* the word
6. The *sentence after* the word
7. The *definition in* the sentence

SUMMING UP
Tell whether these statements are true or false. The underlined words make the statement true or false. If the statement is false, what words would you place in the statement to make it true?

1. The only true picture of the earth is the <u>Mercator map</u>.
2. A <u>Mercator map</u> has straight lines.
3. A <u>polar map</u> will show us how close land areas are to the North Pole.
4. A “flier’s map” will show us true <u>shapes and land areas</u>.
5. <u>Physical maps</u> will usually show us the number of people living in one place.
6. Boundaries between countries are shown on a <u>political map</u>.
7. Land areas will have strange shapes near the center of the earth on a <u>polar map</u>.
8. Highlands, lowlands and bodies of water are usually shown on a <u>rainfall map</u>.
9. The sizes of land and water areas are best shown on a <u>globe</u>.
10. Another word for “a twisting out of shape” is <u>distortion</u>.

16

2 THE LANGUAGE OF MAPS

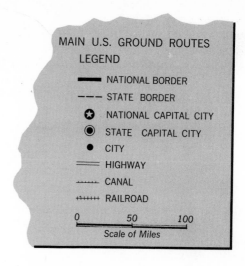

MAIN U.S. GROUND ROUTES
LEGEND

▬▬▬ NATIONAL BORDER
--- STATE BORDER
✪ NATIONAL CAPITAL CITY
◉ STATE CAPITAL CITY
● CITY
═══ HIGHWAY
┈┈┈ CANAL
╫╫╫╫ RAILROAD

0   50   100

Scale of Miles

Reading For A Purpose: How do maps show what is on the surface of the earth?

1. No map can show us real things on the earth—farmlands, hills, mountains, rivers, oceans, cities, crops and minerals. Those things are shown on a map by using special marks. These marks are called *symbols.* Most map makers use the same kinds of symbols: lines, dots, special colors and small pictures. No map shows everything, but every map will show a few things.

2. In order to understand what a particular map is trying to tell us, it is necessary to read the map *legend.* The legend, usually found in one corner of the map, explains what the symbols on the map mean. It is sometimes called the *key* to the map. You should first look for the legend before you begin to read any map. The title or name of the map is usually part of the legend.

3. The map on page 18 shows the North American continent and part of South America. A thin black line is used to show where the land and water meet. This line is the symbol for the coastline. The black line can also be called the shoreline. Coastline symbols may be crooked or irregular, showing places for harbors or seaports. (A seaport is a city by the water where people and goods go in and out by boat.)

4. The large land areas on the map are called *continents* or mainlands. There are also smaller land areas on the map. A small land area entirely surrounded by water is an *island.* A *peninsula* is a piece of land *almost* entirely surrounded by water. An *isthmus* is a narrow strip of land joining two larger bodies of land.

Mountains are shown on maps by little pictures or symbols that look roughly like mountains.

5. There are many kinds of bodies of water on the earth. The largest bodies of water are the *oceans.* Bodies of water are sometimes shown by the use of wavy lines. *Lakes* can be seen easily because they are completely surrounded by land. A thin black or blue line that winds through land is usually a *river.* Still other lines join the river. These are the *tributaries,* or branches of the river. The land that is drained by a river and its branches is called a *basin.*

6. Lines are also used to show the boundaries of countries. Many countries are divided further into smaller areas called states and provinces. (Sometimes these boundary lines are broken lines: - - - .) The map symbol for a city is a dot. The symbol that stands for the capital city of a country is a star or a dot with a circle around it. The name of the city is usually given with the dot or star to show what the symbol stands for.

7. The map maker also uses colors for many reasons. Colors can be used to show the difference between land and water areas. Water is usually colored blue. Colors also make it easier for the reader to see the boundaries of different countries. Maps that show differences in climate use a color for each kind of climate.

The map legend on a climate map will tell you what each color means. The height of land—the elevation above sea level—is shown in color on relief maps. Sometimes different shadings of

Map #1—Map of Geographic Terms

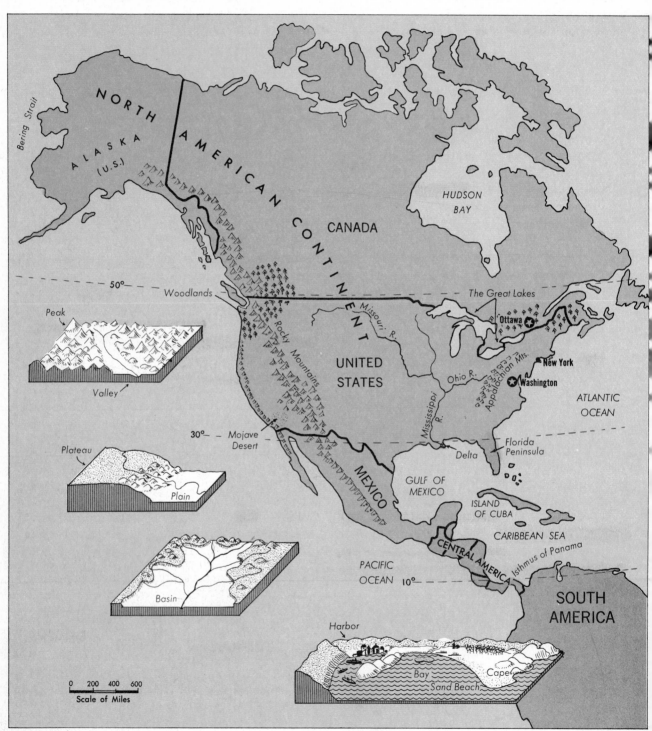

the same color are used on these maps. Again, you must look at the legend to find out what each color stands for.

8. Map makers use still other symbols. For example, they use dots and circles of different sizes to show the number of people, the amount of cattle, or the kinds of minerals that may be found in the places shown on the map. *Picture symbols* can also be used to show these things. Many of the small pictures look much like the items they represent or stand for. You may see small stacks of wheat or oil wells, horses or lumps of coal, depending on what facts must be given about an area.

UNDERSTANDING
CHAPTER 2

I. Finding the Main Idea

In Chapter 2 of Unit 1, you learned how to find the main idea of a paragraph or chapter. See if you can answer the following questions about the main ideas of paragraphs in Chapter 2 of Unit 2.

1. In paragraph 1, we learn that special marks called symbols are used on maps to show us real things. Is there a sentence that tells us this idea? Which sentence is it?
2. After you read paragraph 2, you know that it is about a map legend. We learn what a legend is and that it is important in map reading. Is there a sentence that tells us these ideas? Which sentence is it?
3. Read the six sentences in paragraph 4. Each one tells us about a land area on a map. No sentence exactly states the main idea. Put all the sentences together and you have a main idea. In your own words, what would you say the main idea is?
4. The main idea of the chapter is the summary of all the ideas presented in the paragraphs of the chapter. In Chapter 2 of this unit, we learn about map symbols, the map legend, lines on a map, how land forms are shown, colors used on maps and other markings. Do you think the title of Chapter 2 tells us the main idea of the chapter? Can you think of another good title?

II. Knowing Words

In Chapter 1 of this unit, you learned how to tell the meanings of words by using clues in each paragraph. Look at each paragraph for the words listed below. What are the meanings of these words? Can you tell the *clues* you used to know the meanings of these words?

Paragraph 1—symbols	Paragraph 5—tributaries
Paragraph 2—legend	Paragraph 5—basin
Paragraph 3—irregular	Paragraph 6—provinces
Paragraph 4—peninsula	Paragraph 7—elevation above sea level
Paragraph 4—isthmus	Paragraph 8—represent

In the list below, each term is followed by an explanation. Tell which explanations are correct. Then give a correct explanation for each incorrect one.

1. Legend—key to a map.
2. Peninsula—entirely surrounded by water.
3. Isthmus—narrow body of water.
4. Continent—largest land area.
5. Symbols—special map marks.
6. Tributaries—lakes.
7. Political map—shows boundaries of states.
8. Climates—dots of many sizes.
9. Map Symbols:
    a. Dots—cities.
    b. Lines—boundaries of countries.
    c. Dot with a star—harbor.
    d. Winding lines—rivers.
    e. Blue color—mountains.

3 THE IMPORTANCE OF LATITUDE

Reading For A Purpose: How can we find places on the earth's surface, using latitude?

1. There are three main kinds of information that a map can give you: *location*—where are certain places on the earth?, *distance*—how far is it from one place to another?, and *direction* —what route would you take to get from one place to another?

2. The actual size of any place on the earth cannot be shown on a map. It would be impossible to bring such a map into your home or classroom. Even a map that is made to be 1/100 of the size of a country would be far too large to handle. It would cover as much room as a large city. For a map to be small enough to use, it must be drawn *to scale.* This means that a map is drawn to a definite *proportion*, or part of the true size. For example, one inch on a map might stand for 500 or 1,000 miles. The scale would then be written as 1:500 or 1:1000. This *scale of miles* would be part of the map legend. The scale is a clue to how distant or far one place on the map is from another. It can also be used to find out the sizes of the areas shown.

3. Directions on maps are indicated by the words *north, south, east* and *west*, or combinations of these words, such as *northeast, northwest, southeast* and *southwest*. North means toward the North Pole; south means toward the South Pole. When a person faces north, south is behind him, east is on his right and west is on his left. On most flat maps, north is placed at the top of the map, south is at the bottom, east is at the right and west is at the left. While it is easier to have most maps alike in this way, there is actually no top or bottom to the earth; it is almost a perfect sphere. One could draw a map with any direction at the top and still be correct. (*Down* means toward the center of the earth and *up* away from the earth; they are not the same as north and south.)

4. To show location, map makers use lines that crisscross the map. Some of the lines are drawn across the map in an east-west direction; others go north and south. These lines do not really appear on the earth's surface. They are imaginary lines invented by the map maker. The lines form a pattern called a *grid*. With them, it is possible to locate any place on the earth.

5. The east-west lines on a map are called lines of *latitude*. The imaginary line of latitude that circles the earth at its center is called the *equator*. It goes 25,000 miles around the middle of the earth. It gets its name from the fact that it is halfway between, or equally distant from, the North and South Poles. The equator is the longest line of latitude on the earth.

6. The equator divides the earth into two parts, the *northern hemisphere* and the *southern hemisphere*. (*Hemi* means "half," so a hemisphere is half a globe or half a sphere.) The northern hemisphere lies between the equator and the North Pole. The southern hemisphere lies between the equator and the South Pole.

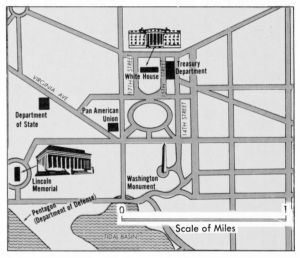

Differently scaled maps showing Washington, D.C. How does a map's purpose determine its scale?

Most of the land areas of the earth are in the northern hemisphere. Most of the water areas are in the southern hemisphere. (Look at the world map on pages 584–585, and you will see that this is true.)

7. Lines of latitude are *parallel* to the equator. That is, each line of latitude remains the same distance from the equator for its entire length around the earth. These lines or parallels are numbered. Through the numbers we can tell how far north or south of the equator the lines are. Their numbers are called *degrees*. One degree of latitude is about 70 miles on the earth's surface. (Figure this out by dividing 25,000 miles, the circumference of the earth, by 360, the number of degrees or divisions in any circle.) Instead of saying that a city is about 70 miles north of the equator, we say that it is one degree north, or 1° N.

8. The lines of latitude or *parallels* are numbered from 0 degrees to 90 degrees. The equator is 0 degrees, the North Pole is 90 degrees north latitude and the South Pole is 90 degrees south. The numbers of the latitudes grow larger the farther you go from the equator— from 0° to 90°. In writing degrees of latitude, you must add the word "North" (N) or

"South" (S) to tell whether the line is north or south of the equator. For example: Seattle, Washington, is located at 47° N. Latitude. Lima, Peru, is at 12° S. Latitude.

9. New York City is about 41° north of the equator. New Orleans is 30° North. Washington, D.C. is about 38° North. We know then that Washington is farther from the equator than New Orleans, but not as distant from the middle of the earth as New York City is. Cities that are 40 degrees north of the equator and cities that are 40 degrees south are the same distance from the equator, but in opposite directions.

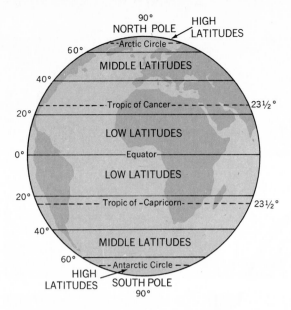

Lines of latitude (parallels) of the Earth.

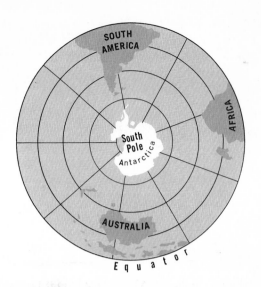

The Earth from the South Pole.

10. A few lines of latitude are specially marked on the map. Two of these are 23½° north and 23½° south of the equator. All places between these two lines of latitude have the noonday sun directly overhead twice a year. Places farther north or south never have the direct rays of the sun overhead. The area between 23½° north and 23½° south is called the *tropics.* (These two lines of latitude have names that will give a clue to their meaning: The Tropic of Cancer is north of the equator; the Tropic of Capricorn is south of it.) The tropics is an area of direct sunlight. This same region is often called the *low latitudes.* They are called "low" because they are marked with the lowest numbers, 0 to 23½ degrees.

11. Other special lines of latitude are found at 66½° north and 66½° south of the equator. In the northern hemisphere, 66½° is known as the Arctic Circle. In the southern hemisphere, the same distance from the equator is called the Antarctic Circle. Between the tropics and these lines of latitude are the *middle latitudes.* Beyond 66½° north and south of the equator are the *high latitudes.* The low, middle, and high latitudes do not have completely different climates. Their special parallels are marked to show a separation between areas that get different amounts of sunlight. You will read more about the effect of the sun on these areas when you study the movement of the earth around the sun.

UNDERSTANDING
CHAPTER 3

I. Finding the Main Idea

Finding the main idea of a paragraph or a chapter is an important skill, for it helps you to know the important ideas in any lesson. It helps you to remember what you have learned. See if you can answer the following questions about the main ideas of paragraphs in Chapter 3. Is there a sentence in each paragraph that helped you to choose your answers?

1. In *paragraph 2,* the main idea is that:
    a. many maps are too large to use in the home.
    b. the scale of miles is part of the map legend.
    c. maps are drawn to a scale of the true size of an area.

2. The main idea of *paragraph 3* describes how:
   a. most maps are alike.
   b. directions are shown on maps.
   c. flat maps are made.
3. The main idea of *paragraph 4* describes:
   a. the largest line of latitude.
   b. lines that crisscross maps.
   c. the imaginary lines of latitude.
4. The main idea of *paragraph 8* describes:
   a. how lines of latitude are numbered.
   b. latitude south of the equator.
   c. the use of grid lines.
5. The main idea of *paragraph 10* describes:
   a. the region of low latitudes.
   b. places that never get the direct rays of the sun.
   c. names for special lines of latitude.

II. Knowing Words

Look at each paragraph in Chapter 3 for the words listed below. What are the meanings of these words? What clues, if any, helped you know the meanings of these words?

Paragraph 2—proportion
Paragraph 4—grid
Paragraph 5—latitude
Paragraph 5—equator
Paragraph 6—hemisphere
Paragraph 7—degrees
Paragraph 8—parallels
Paragraph 10—tropics
Paragraph 11—middle latitudes

SUMMING UP

Tell whether these statements are true or false. The underlined words make the statements true or false. If a statement is false, what words would you place in it to make it true?

1. You can measure distance on a map by using the <u>scale of miles</u>.

2. Bogotá, Colombia, is 4° North Latitude. This means that is located in the <u>high latitudes</u>.

3. Lines of latitude on a map are <u>real</u> lines on the earth's surface.

4. Columbia, South Carolina, is located at 34° North Latitude. This means that it is located in the <u>tropics</u>.

5. 0° latitude is shown on the map by the line called the <u>equator</u>.

6. Between 23½ ° North Lat. and 23½ ° South Lat. are the <u>low latitudes</u>.

7. If one inch on the map stands for 500 miles, cities that are 2,000 miles apart would be <u>3 inches</u> apart on the map.

8. The number of degrees <u>grows higher</u> as we travel away from the equator.

4 FINDING LONGITUDE

Reading For A Purpose: How can we "pinpoint" places on the earth's surface?

1. It was easy to begin at the equator to measure distances north and south. But where do we begin to measure distances in an east-west direction? This beginning line has been placed at Greenwich, Great Britain, by agreement among the nations of the world. Greenwich is near the city of London. Greenwich is the line of 0 degrees (0°) *longitude*. This line is called the *Prime Meridian* or *First Meridian*. All distances east and west of the Prime Meridian are measured in lines of longitude or meridians. These lines are numbered in degrees just as lines of latitude are.

2. Lines of longitude run north and south from North Pole to South Pole. They all meet at the two poles. Thus they are *not* parallel—that is, the same distance apart for their whole length—as are lines of latitude. At the equator, where the meridians are farthest apart, the distance of one degree is about 70 miles on the earth's surface, the same as between lines of latitude. Near the poles, the meridians or lines of longitude may be only a few miles apart.

3. Using the map at the lower right, place your finger on the line showing 0° longitude that passes through Greenwich. Place another finger on the line to the right or east of 0°. This line is 20° east of the Prime Meridian. Try the same thing in the opposite direction. This line is 20° west of the Prime Meridian. Find Los Angeles, California, on the map on page 27. Note that it is almost 118° west of the Prime Meridian. In reading degrees of longitude you add "East" (E) or "West" (W) to tell whether the line of longitude is located east or west of the Prime Meridian.

4. When we put latitude and longitude together, we can accurately locate any place on the globe. Find St. Louis on the map on page 27. On what line of latitude is it located? Is it north or south latitude? What is its longitude? Is it east or west longitude? We can tell anyone how to find St. Louis on a map or globe of the earth simply by saying that it is at 38° North Latitude and 90° West Longitude. Can you imagine the value of these lines to a ship at sea or an airplane in the sky? A ship in trouble can radio its exact position by giving its

Lines of longitude (meridians) of the Earth.

25

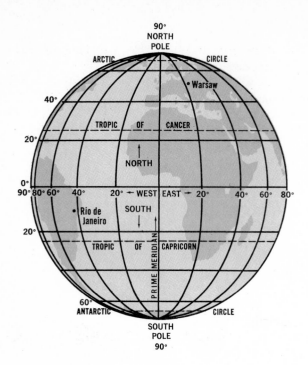

latitude and longitude. Ships that speed to the rescue will know exactly where the troubled ship is.

5. There are 360 degrees in a complete circle. If you travel halfway around the earth from the Prime Meridian, in either direction, you will come to the 180° Meridian. This line is the International Date Line and is located in the middle of the Pacific Ocean. Like the other lines we have studied, it is imaginary, but it is always a "talking point" for travelers who go across the Pacific. You will learn the reasons for travelers' interest in the International Date Line in Chapter 5.

Put lines of latitude and longitude together and they look like this. Of what value are lines of latitude and longitude to ships at sea?

UNDERSTANDING CHAPTER 4

I. Finding the Main Idea

Below are listed the main ideas of each of the paragraphs in this chapter. After reading the main ideas, *choose the two best titles* for the chapter from the list that follows.

Main Ideas:

Paragraph 1—0° Longitude is the Prime Meridian.

Paragraph 2—Lines of longitude run from North Pole to South Pole.

Paragraph 3—In reading lines of longitude, it is necessary to say whether the lines are east or west of the Prime Meridian.

Paragraph 4—Any place on earth can be located by using latitude and longitude.

Paragraph 5—The International Date Line is the 180th Meridian.

Titles:

1. Measuring Distance from the Equator.
2. Parallels on a Map.
3. Longitude and Latitude Equals Exact Location.
4. Longitude of Large Cities.
5. Longitude Helps Us to Find Places on the Earth.

II. Choose the Best Answer

1. Lines of longitude are called:
   a. meridians.   b. parallels.   c. east-west lines.
2. Lines of longitude:
   a. are always the same distance apart.
   b. are measured from the equator.
   c. run in a north-south direction.

3. 0° longitude is called the:
   a. equator.　　　　　　b. Prime Meridian.　　　　　c. First Parallel.
4. When we know latitude and longitude, we:
   a. can accurately find any place on the map.
   b. know the distance from one place to another.
   c. know areas of sunlight.
5. In paragraph 2, the word *parallel* means:
   a. meeting at the poles.
   b. closer together.
   c. the same distance apart.

DEVELOPING IDEAS AND SKILLS

Map Study

Map #2—The United States

Study the map. Then answer these questions.

1. What are the latitude and longitude of:
   a. Cleveland, Ohio?　　b. Montreal, Canada?　　c. Great Falls, Montana?
2. What cities are located at:
   a. 30° N. Lat. and 95° W. Long.?
   b. 34° N. Lat. and 118° W. Long.?
   c. 42° N. Lat. and 88° W. Long.?
3. Which *two* of these cities are located at 90° West Longitude?
   Cincinnati, St. Louis, Kansas City, New Orleans.
4. Which *two* of these cities are located at 39° North Latitude?
   Baltimore, Denver, Los Angeles, Detroit.

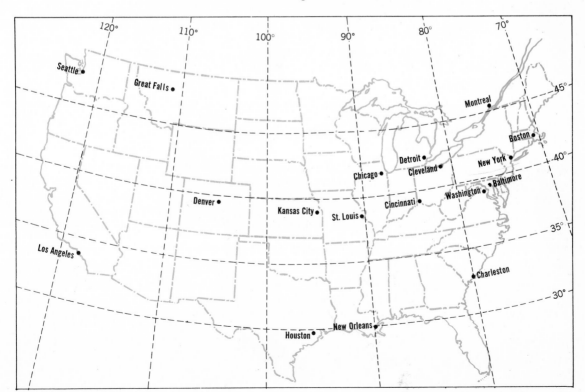

5 THE SPINNING EARTH

Reading For A Purpose: What are the effects of the earth's movements?

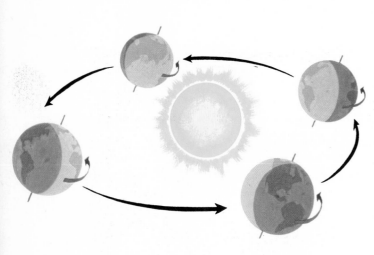

1. The earth is always spinning. It is always turning or spinning in the same direction, from west to east. Of course, only one side of the earth can face the sun at a time. The side of the earth that faces the sun receives light and heat. When that happens, it is day on that side of the earth. On the part of the earth that is away from the sun, it is dark or night. If the earth did not spin, one half of the earth would always be lighted and the other half would always be dark.

2. The earth spins on an *axis*, an imaginary line through the earth from one pole to the other. This spinning of the earth on its axis is called *rotation*. *The rotation of the earth causes our day and night.* Since the earth makes one complete turn in a 24-hour period, we say that the earth rotates once each day. At the same time that the earth rotates, it is also *orbiting*, or moving around the sun. This movement of the earth around the sun is called *revolution*—the earth *revolves* around the sun. Once every year, 365¼ days, the earth makes a complete trip around the sun. At the same time, it is spinning on its axis, once every 24 hours.

3. If you should someday travel in space, you would see that the earth is not standing straight up and down facing the sun. It is leaning at an angle. The earth leans or tilts at an angle of 23½ degrees. It is always tilted in the same direction. As it revolves around the sun, the earth tilts so that the North Pole points toward the North Star. For part of this revolution, the northern hemisphere is tilted toward the sun and catches the direct rays of the sun. At this time, the southern half of the world gets only the indirect or slanting rays of the sun. This is the period of spring and summer in the northern half of the earth, March 21 to September 22, while the southern hemisphere has fall and winter.

4. As the earth continues on its path or orbit around the sun, the southern hemisphere is then tilted toward the sun and gets the direct rays. At this time, the northern half of the earth receives the slanting rays. It is now spring and summer in the southern half of the earth and fall and winter in the north. The lands near the equator receive the direct rays of the sun during the earth's entire trip. This is why the tropics are warm all year round.

5. The leaning of the earth and its orbit around the sun cause our four seasons—spring, summer, fall and winter. When the people of New York, Detroit, Chicago and San Francisco are receiving the more direct rays of the sun, the people of Argentina, Chile and Australia are receiving the indirect and weaker rays. Thus, when it is summer in the middle and high latitudes north of the equator, it is winter

in the same regions south of the equator. The reverse is also true. If you are a sports fan, you may have noticed that tennis championships are played outdoors in Australia near Christmas time. You may also have heard that the skiing in Chile is excellent in July!

6. On March 21st and September 22nd, days and nights are equal in length all over the earth. At noon the rays of the sun strike the earth directly at the equator. Each of these days is called an *equinox* or equal night. March 21st marks the beginning of spring in the northern hemisphere and the beginning of autumn in the southern hemisphere. On September 22nd, autumn begins in the northern hemisphere and spring begins in the southern hemisphere.

7. After March 21st, the sun's rays move a little farther north of the equator each day. Summer is on its way to the northern half of the world and winter to the southern half. Since the earth's axis is tilted 23½ degrees, the direct rays move north 23½ degrees to the Tropic of Cancer. They reach this point about June 22nd. This date is the beginning of summer north of the equator. On this date, the rays of the sun strike the earth directly at the Tropic of Cancer. This is the farthest point north at which the sun will shine directly overhead. On this date, too, all places within the Arctic Circle will have 24 hours of sunlight. As you may have guessed, this date also marks the beginning of winter in the southern hemisphere.

8. The movement of the earth around the sun continues. The sun's rays move again steadily south until they reach 23½ degrees south of the equator, the Tropic of Capricorn. This point is reached on December 22, the beginning of summer south of the equator. This is the beginning of winter in the northern hemisphere.

9. Even if you have not traveled, you may have noticed a difference in time from one part of the country to another. For example, if you

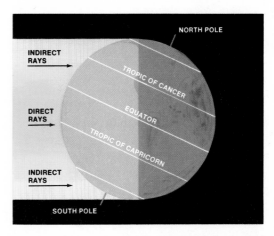

The Earth in its orbit. How do the Earth's tilt and its orbit around the sun cause the change of seasons?

live in Kansas City and want to see a swimming meet on television from Boston, it may start at 9:00 in Boston, but you will see it at 8:00. This difference in time is caused by the *rotation* of the earth. In its spinning on its axis, the earth turns through 360 degrees of longitude in 24 hours. It thus turns 15 degrees of longitude in one hour. (The 360 degrees of the earth divided by 24 hours equals 15 degrees each hour.) Therefore, there is one hour's difference in time between places on earth for each 15 degrees of longitude. The world is di-

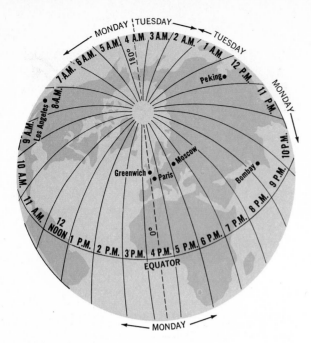

Map #3—Time Zones of the Earth

lier at places that lie farther east. For example, when it is 8:00 A.M. in New York City, it is also 8:00 A.M. in Boston, Philadelphia and Cleveland—they are in the same time zone. However, it is then 7:00 A.M. in Chicago and New Orleans because they are 15 degrees *west* of New York City. It is only 6:00 A.M. in Denver, Colorado, because Denver is about 30 degrees west of New York. Los Angeles and San Francisco are still in darkness because they are still farther west. In Fairbanks, Alaska, and Honolulu, Hawaii, it is only 3:00 A.M. People in these cities will not see daylight in summer until three hours after Denver and five hours after New York.

11. The *International Date Line*, halfway around the world from the Prime Meridian, is a special problem. Look at the map of time zones at the top of this page. Starting at Greenwich, Great Britain, where it is 4 o'clock on Monday afternoon, count 12 hours in an easterly direction. You will see that it is then 4 o'clock in the morning on *Tuesday*, at the International Date Line. Now begin at Greenwich again and count 12 hours in a westerly direction. You will see that it is 4 o'clock in the morning on *Monday*. Yes, it is Monday west

vided into 24 time zones about 15 degrees apart from each other. In the United States alone there are six time zones.

10. The earth turns or rotates from west to east. As a result, the sun "rises" or appears ear-

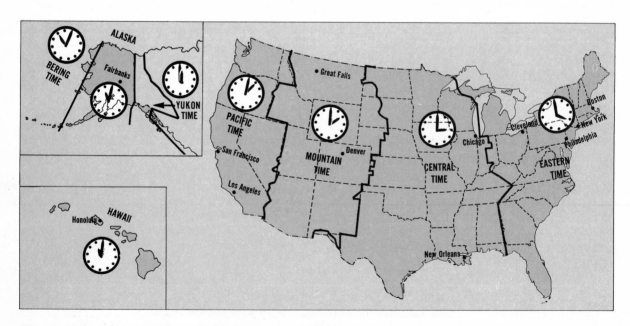

Map #4—Time Zones of the United States

of the Date Line, but it is Tuesday east of the line. A traveler who is going west across the Date Line will "skip" a day in his trip, but one who is going east across it will repeat the same day. The winter Olympic games of 1972 were held in Sapporo, Japan. People in New York City saw the games on live TV at 11 o'clock in the evening. It was then 1 o'clock in the afternoon in Japan. If they were watching on February 10, it was February 11 in Japan. Technically, they were seeing the games "before they took place!"

UNDERSTANDING
CHAPTER 5

1. The main idea of *paragraphs 5 through 7* describes:
   a. why we have differences in seasons.
   b. the reasons for the tilt of the earth.
   c. the results of the earth's rotation.
2. If the earth did not spin:
   a. we would have no seasons.
   b. half of the earth would always be in sunlight.
   c. there would be no summer in the northern hemisphere.
3. The differences in seasons are caused by:
   a. the revolution and tilting of the earth.
   b. the rotation of the earth.
   c. the spinning of the earth.
4. The earth orbits around the sun:
   a. once each day.
   b. once each season.
   c. once each year.
5. The earth rotates on its axis:
   a. once each day.
   b. once each month.
   c. once each year.
6. When do the direct rays of the sun strike the city of Chicago?
   a. on June 22.
   b. on September 22.
   c. never.
7. The earth *orbits* the sun. The best meaning for *orbit* is:
   a. rotates.
   b. travels around.
   c. spins.
8. Some people say that a storm will take place on the *equinox*. This refers to:
   a. 6 months of daylight at the South Pole.
   b. the time when days and nights are the same length.
   c. the season when the southern hemisphere is tilted toward the sun.

Agree or Disagree   Decide whether or not each of the following statements agrees with what you have read. If the answer is *disagree*, explain why.

1. All places north of the equator have summer at the same time.
2. The tropics always receive the most direct rays of the sun.
3. When the sun's direct rays are striking the earth north of the equator, the North Pole is in darkness.
4. High latitude regions never receive the direct rays of the sun.
5. On the hottest day of the year in the middle of the United States, the direct rays of the sun are directly overhead.
6. If the earth did not lean on its trip around the sun, sunlight could never reach the poles of the earth.
7. The *tropics* means low latitudes.
8. The slanting rays of the sun are not as hot as the direct rays of the sun.
9. In our summer, there are more hours of daylight than there are of darkness.
10. At the equator, the length of the hours of sunlight changes greatly during the year.

6 LAND FORMS OF THE EARTH

Reading For A Purpose: What are the varieties of land surface on the earth? How do differences in land surface affect the ways people live?

1. Although water covers 75 per cent of the earth's surface, the 25 per cent land area is most important to us. The reason, of course, is that we live on the land. Land areas are called either continents or islands, depending on their size. There are seven continents on our planet. Asia is the largest and Australia is the smallest. After Asia, in size, comes Africa, then North America, South America, Antarctica, Europe and finally, Australia. Antarctica is a huge mass of land covered with a thick layer of snow and ice.

2. Look at the globe. Look at the earth from the North Pole. Then look at it from the South Pole. You will see that most of the land on the earth is in the northern hemisphere. About 85 per cent of the earth's surface below the equator is water. (You will see that all the oceans are connected here.) The important trade routes of the world are north of the equator. It may not be surprising, then, to find that the most powerful nations of the world are in the northern hemisphere.

3. There are four chief kinds of land forms on the earth. These are mountains, hills, plateaus and plains. Most of the land surface of the earth is made up of one of these four land forms. These lands are also crossed by rivers. When geographers write or talk about land forms, they use the word *topography*.

4. *Mountains* are masses of land that rise high above the surrounding areas. They come to a top or peak. Mountains are grouped into ranges or chains. There are two great moun-
tain chains on the earth. One borders the Pacific Ocean. You can trace an almost continuous line of mountains through the lands around the Pacific Ocean. Most of these are high, and many have *volcanoes*. (A volcano is an opening in the earth. Through this opening, melted rock or lava from the center of the earth escapes.) The tops of these mountains form islands, such as the Philippines, Indonesia, Japan and the Aleutians. A huge mountain chain extends from Alaska in the north to the southern tip of South America. This mountain system is called the Rocky Mountains in North America and the Andes in South America.

5. The other great mountain chain spreads across Africa and Eurasia. (We group Europe and Asia together and call them Eurasia be-

These mountains are in the Canadian Rockies. They are part of the long mountain chain that circles the Pacific Ocean. What features of mountains mentioned in the chapter are illustrated in this photo?

cause they are really one great land mass.) The western end of this chain starts in Spain and North Africa. It stretches across southern Europe as the Alps and the Caucasus. It extends into inner Asia as far as the Himalayas. The Himalayas are the highest mountains in the world. Mt. Everest, the highest peak on earth, is in the Himalayas. These mountains separate India on the south and China and Siberia (Soviet Asia) on the north. Moving eastward, this range begins to spread out. Some mountains run north into Siberia and others stretch eastward across China and southeastward across the Southeast Asian peninsula.

6. *Hills,* in general, are lower than moun-

tains. It is often hard to tell the difference between high hills and low mountains. Hills are usually no higher than 1,000 feet above sea level. More people live in the hills than in the mountains because hills are lower and flatter. They are easier to reach.

7. Hill and mountain regions are often called highlands. Highlands are not heavily populated. The chief occupations of mountain people are mining, lumbering, cattle raising and sheep grazing. It is difficult to farm hillsides because the soil is thin and rocky and rains wash away the seeds and the soil. In the hilly regions of the Far East and southern Europe, farmers cut *terraces* (steps in the hillsides) to increase the amount of land they can farm.

8. Mountains are a source of *minerals* such as coal, iron ore, lead and manganese. (Minerals are useful materials that can be mined or dug up from the earth.) Streams that tumble down the mountainsides are used to make electric power. However, mountains have often separated people from one another and made transportation difficult. People who live in the highlands of the Andes in South America and of the Himalayas in Asia often know little of what happens outside their villages.

9. *Plateaus* are land forms that rise sharply above the level of the land around them. Many are level on top. They are also called *tablelands* or *mesas*. In the high latitudes, the plateaus are very cold. In the low latitudes, they may have a cool and healthful climate. The Bolivian Plateau of South America is an example of a cool climate in an area that would otherwise be very warm. Some plateaus are surrounded by mountains that shut out rainfall. The plateaus that extend northward from Mexico through the western United States and into Canada are very dry. In the high latitudes, plateaus are likely to be covered with snow and ice. This is true in Greenland and Antarctica.

10. *Plains* are areas of broad level land. The land is never completely flat, but slightly rolling. These land forms are sometimes called lowlands. Plains support most of the world's people. The lowland area of North America reaches from the Gulf of Mexico northward to the Arctic Ocean and from the Appalachian Mountains westward to the Rockies. Another lowland area extends from Great Britain east through Central Europe into Siberia. Although the Far East is hilly and mountainous, there are several lowland areas of good size.

11. Many plains throughout the world have been formed by large rivers. Great numbers of people live in these river valleys because they are usually fertile—that is, good for growing crops. One of the most thickly populated regions on earth is the Yangtze River Valley in China. Great industrial cities are located along the Rhine River in Europe. The Nile River Valley of Egypt is the only fertile area in a land that is mostly desert. The Mississippi drains the great farm lands of the United States. However, the hot lowland of the Amazon River in South America has few people. The great heat, thick jungles, poor soil and millions of insects make it hard for large numbers of people to live there.

12. Our earth is a restless, living thing. It is always moving beneath our feet, even though we cannot feel it. It is continually being changed by heat, cold, rain, snow, winds and rushing water. It is disturbed by volcanoes and rumbling earthquakes. (An earthquake is a terrible trembling that causes buildings to fall and great cracks to open in the ground.) There are still glaciers or large masses of ice in the far north of our planet. Because of these forces, our land forms are still changing, sometimes slowly and sometimes quickly.

Yellow wheat from the fertile soil of the North American plains. Why do so many of the world's people live in plains areas?

Making an Outline

An outline is like the bones of the body. It is the skeleton of a chapter. The sentences of each paragraph are like the body built around the skeleton. Once we are able to pick out the main ideas of a paragraph or a chapter, we are able to *outline*. It is as easy as that. Let us see how we can outline Chapter 6. We have to read the chapter first. Then we pick out the main idea for each paragraph. Let us see what these main ideas are:

Paragraph   1—Land is important to us.
Paragraph   2—Most of the land is in the northern hemisphere.
Paragraph   3—There are four chief kinds of land forms.
Paragraph   4—Mountains are masses of land that rise above the land around them.
Paragraph   5—There are great mountain chains on the earth.
Paragraph   6—Hills are lower than mountains.
Paragraph   7—Not many people live in the highlands.
Paragraph   8—Mountains have good and bad features.
Paragraph   9—Plateaus rise sharply above the land around them.
Paragraph 10—Plains are areas of broad level land.
Paragraph 11—River valleys have many people.
Paragraph 12—Our earth is continually changing.

After listing these main ideas, we can easily see the important thoughts of the chapter. These main ideas are a good *summary* of the chapter, too. If you were *taking note*s for this chapter, you would have a fine set of notes simply by listing these main ideas.

In making an outline, we first choose our *headings*. We collect some of the thoughts that are about the same topic and see if we can find one heading for them. The title of the chapter is "Land Forms of the Earth." What does this chapter say about land forms? It tells us that there are four main kinds: mountains, hills, plateaus and plains. We can make these our headings.

A. Mountains   B. Hills   C. Plateaus   D. Plains

Next, we locate the paragraphs that tell us about these headings. You will note from our list of main ideas that paragraphs 4, 5 and 8 tell us about mountains; paragraphs 6 and 7 tell about hills; paragraph 9 is about plateaus; and paragraphs 10 and 11 are about plains. (A river valley is a kind of plain.)

Now take one of our headings, "Mountains," and look in the paragraphs about mountains to see what is said about this land form. We can begin our outline with these facts about mountains:

A. Mountains
  1. There are two great chains of mountains.
  2. Some islands are the tops of mountains.
  3. The highest mountains are the Himalayas.
  4. Many mountains have minerals.
  5. Mountains have made travel difficult.

This can be our outline on mountains. We can then go on and do the same thing with our other headings. When we finish, the rest of our outline may look like this:

B. Hills
  1. Hills are lower than mountains.
  2. More people live in the hills than in the mountains.
  3. Farming is difficult on hillsides.

C. Plateaus
  1. In high latitudes, plateaus are cold; in low latitudes, they are cooler than the lowland around them.
  2. Some plateaus are dry because the mountains around them shut off rainfall.
D. Plains
  1. Most of the world's people live on the plains.
  2. There are great plains areas in North America and in Europe.
  3. Rivers have made large plains.
  4. Fertile soils are often found in plains.
  5. Rivers have brought people together rather than separating them.

This could be your outline. You will find that outlining is not hard if you can pick out main ideas. The outline helps you to jot down important information in such a way that you can remember it. It helps you to take notes when you look for information. It helps you to put the ideas of a chapter into a small form—to make a summary.

SUMMING UP   Tell whether these statements are true or false. The underlined words make the statements true or false. If a statement is false, what words would you place in it to make it true?

1. Most of the land surface of the earth is found south of the equator.

2. The great mountain system of South America is called the Andes.

3. Africa is the largest continent.

4. Most of the world's people live on the plains.

5. Europe and Asia are really one large mass of land.

6. The Nile River flows through a jungle where few people live.

7. The highest mountains in the world are the Rockies.

8. Mountains have often had the effect of keeping people from meeting and exchanging ideas.

9. Farmers often cut steps or terraces into hillsides so that they can farm the land.

10. Another word for plains is mesa.

11. Topography is a word that we use when we talk about land forms.

12. River valleys are very often a source of minerals.

7 THE WATERS OF THE EARTH

Reading For A Purpose: How has man made use of the earth's waterways?

1. "Water, water, everywhere!" This is what you might say if you were on a spaceship looking at the earth. The fact is that if we divided the earth into four equal parts, three of those parts would be made up of water. Therefore, we should know more about the kinds of bodies of water that are found on our planet.

2. The earth's largest bodies of water are called *oceans*. There are five oceans: the Pacific, the Atlantic, the Indian, the Arctic and the Antarctic. The largest of these is the Pacific, separating North and South America from Asia and Australia. The Pacific Ocean covers almost one-third of the whole earth's surface. It covers more area than all the land on earth put together! The Atlantic Ocean is about one-half the size of the Pacific. However, it is more important because of the many trade routes that cross its waters. The smaller

Indian Ocean touches Africa on the west, Asia on the north and Australia and Indonesia on the east. The ice-filled Arctic Ocean extends to the North Pole. The Antarctic Ocean surrounds the ice cap of Antarctica, in which the South Pole is located. In every ocean there are many swift-flowing "streams" of water that always move in the same direction. These are called *ocean currents.* You will learn more about ocean currents and how they affect us in Chapter 9.

3. While there are only five bodies of water that are called oceans, there are many other large bodies of water in the world. Most of these are called *seas.* A sea is a body of water almost completely surrounded by land. The Mediterranean Sea has long been important, for it lies between the large land areas of Africa and Eurasia and was once the center of all that was known of the world. The Caribbean Sea, east of Mexico, the Arabian Sea and the Sea of Japan are all important water routes for trade.

4. *Gulfs* and *bays* are also large bodies of water. It is sometimes difficult to tell the difference between a sea, a gulf and a bay. The Gulf of Mexico is really larger than the Sea of Japan or the North Sea. Hudson Bay is also larger than either of them.

5. Rivers are the "lifeblood" of many nations. Rivers are formed by rainfall and melting snow. They begin as small streams. The place where a river begins is called its *source.* The movement of a river is called its *current.* Rivers flow from higher land to lower land. They may be joined by other rivers and streams as they flow "down" into a larger body of water. The place where a river empties its waters is called its *mouth.* Larger rivers usually build a *delta* at their mouth by carrying bits of rock and soil along their course and depositing them. These deltas are often very fertile.

6. It is not easy to tell which rivers are important, or whether one river is more important than another. Each great river is important to so many people. However, as you study the world and the people in it, you will learn

about the rivers listed below. They are among the most important in the world.

River	Region of the World
1. Missouri-Mississippi	Anglo-America
2. St. Lawrence	Anglo-America
3. Amazon	Latin America
4. Danube	Europe
5. Nile	North Africa
6. Tigris-Euphrates	Middle East
7. Congo	Africa, South of the Sahara
8. Ganges	Far East
9. Hwang	Far East
10. Yangtze	Far East

7. Transportation by water has always been important for trade. It was the earliest and cheapest means of moving from one place to another. Water transportation is still used in many places where heavy loads must be moved. When it is possible to go from one body of water to another without unloading, shipping goods is easy.

8. Sometimes, two larger bodies of water are connected by a narrow water passage. This narrow body of water is called a *strait*. In passing from the Atlantic Ocean to the Mediterranean Sea, ships travel through the Strait of Gibraltar. Ferdinand Magellan found a strait in sailing from the Atlantic to the Pacific Ocean at the southern tip of South America. It now bears his name. The Soviet Union and Turkey have argued over control of the Dardanelles for years. This strait provides an opening between the Black and Mediterranean Seas.

9. Man sometimes has to dig his own water passage to connect two larger bodies of water. Such a man-made passage is called a *canal*. There are several important canals in the world. The Suez Canal connects the Mediterranean and Red Seas. It is a sea-level canal. The Suez Canal shortens the trip from Great Britain to India by almost 5,000 miles. Because of the importance of this canal in world trade, it is an often disputed spot in the world. Once controlled by Great Britain, it is now run by Egypt.

Map #5—Water Trade Routes of the World

10. The Panama Canal was opened in 1914. It connects the Atlantic and Pacific Oceans through the narrow country of Panama. It belongs to the United States. Before it was built, ocean-going ships had to travel all the way around South America to go from New York to San Francisco. Because the Isthmus of Panama is mountainous, locks had to be built to move boats from one level to another. The Soo or Sault Sainte Marie Canals are three canals that connect Lake Superior and Lake Huron at the United States-Canada border. This canal chain carries a huge traffic in iron ore and manufactured products.

11. Not all canals are used for ocean-going ships. There are many important inland canals. In Western Europe, the canal system connects rivers with other rivers. This canal system is an important means of shipping farm and factory goods for short distances. In the Far East, too, canals connect rivers in order to make travel and communication easier.

UNDERSTANDING
CHAPTER 7

1. A good title for *paragraph 8* is:
   a. Making Water Transportation Easy.
   b. Important Straits of the World.
   c. The Strait of Magellan.
2. The greatest water trade routes of the world are found on the:
   a. Pacific Ocean.
   b. Atlantic Ocean.
   c. Gulf of Mexico.
3. A large body of water that has three narrow entrances to it is the:
   a. Mediterranean Sea.
   b. Indian Ocean.
   c. Caribbean Sea.
4. An example of a canal inside a large continent is the:
   a. Soo Canal.
   b. Panama Canal.
   c. Suez Canal.
5. The largest of the oceans is the:
   a. Pacific.
   b. Atlantic.
   c. Indian.
6. Great inland canal systems are found in:
   a. the Soviet Union.
   b. North Africa.
   c. Western Europe.
7. Water transportation has long been important because:
   a. it is the fastest means of transportation.
   b. it is the cheapest means of moving heavy goods.
   c. goods can be delivered directly to factories.
8. Straits and canals are important in water routes because they:
   a. are sometimes as large as seas.
   b. have the best seaports along their routes.
   c. are often short cuts to larger bodies of water.

Making an Outline

In Chapter 6, you learned how to develop the outline of a chapter. Now try to make a short outline of part of Chapter 7. From the chapter, choose *one* of these two sections: paragraphs 2 through 4 or paragraphs 9 through 11. Follow the steps you learned in the previous chapter:

1. Find the main ideas of the paragraphs you choose.
2. After you have seen the three main ideas, choose a title for the outline that includes all the main thoughts of the three paragraphs.
3. Use each of the main ideas of the paragraphs as your *headings*: A, B and C.
4. See what *details* there are in each paragraph for each of the headings.
5. List two or three of these details under each heading. Choose the ones that you think are most important.

When you have finished these five steps, you will have made an outline of the paragraphs you selected.

Match each item in Column A with one of the descriptions in Column B.

COLUMN A	COLUMN B
1. strait	a. Swift-flowing stream in the ocean.
2. current	b. Large body of water almost completely surrounded by land.
3. source	c. Where a river begins.
4. delta	d. Soil and rocks piled up at a river mouth.
5. mouth	e. Man-made waterway.
6. canal	f. Where a river empties its water.
	g. Narrow body of water connecting larger bodies of water.

8 HOW CLIMATE AFFECTS US

Reading For A Purpose: How does climate affect the ways people live and work?

1. A class was about to begin a lesson on Latin America. One of the students asked, "Why don't bananas grow in the United States?" When the class looked for answers, they found that bananas need a long growing season. It must be hot and rainy most of the time. There is hardly any place on the mainland of our country where such a climate can be found. Therefore, we must bring bananas in from other lands if we want them. In short, bananas grow where the *climate* is right for them.

2. Climate and *weather* do not mean the same thing. The weather report on the radio or in the newspaper tells you what each day will be or was like. The report tells you how hot or cold it is during a day or over a short period of time. It tells you whether to expect rain or snow. This is weather. Climate, on the other hand, means the kind of weather a region has over a long period of time—year after year.

3. Therefore, when you read about climate in any place on the earth, there are three questions you should ask: How hot or cold is it over a long period of time? How much rain falls throughout the year? How long is the growing season? The answers to these questions will give you a good idea of an area's climate.

4. The earth is surrounded by a "blanket" of air called the *atmosphere.* This air can be hot or cold. Geographers call the amount of heat or cold in the air *temperature.* Temperature is measured by a thermometer, which is marked in degrees. (Thus, 70 degrees is written as 70°.) Temperatures can change rapidly. It can be very hot in the daytime and cold at night. However, one who studies geography is more interested in temperature throughout a season than in daily changes. For example, the *average* daily temperature of New York City during the winter months is 34°. The average tem-

perature during the summer months is 76°. This tells you that New York City has warm summers and cold winters. In San Francisco, the average winter temperature is 52° and in summer, 63°. You can tell from these temperatures that San Francisco is neither too hot nor too cold the year round.

5. The *average rainfall* of any place is also measured over a long period of time. Rainfall is measured in the number of inches of rain that falls in a given time. Ten inches of rainfall is recorded as 10″. It is possible to measure rainfall during a season or during a year. For example, the average rainfall for six summer months in Charleston, South Carolina, is 30″. The winter average is only 15″. This tells us that the summer months receive a great deal of rain. By comparison, the winters are dry. The average rainfall for the year, then, can also be found.

6. Another factor in climate is the *length of the growing season.* This is the length of time that a place is free from frost. This is very important to the farmer. He can plant only the kinds of crops that can be grown in the particular growing season of his area. He plants his crop after the last frost in the spring and harvests before the first frost in the fall. In general, the farther one travels from the equator, the shorter the growing season.

7. Throughout your study of our changing world, climate will be mentioned many times. You will find that climate is important in understanding how people live and work. (For example, the people of the Sahara live and think differently from the people who live in the Amazon Basin.) In many cases, people are making good use of a favorable climate. In other regions, they are struggling against the problems caused by a difficult climate.

8. Climate explains, in part, the kind of homes people live in. The Eskimo in northern Canada lives in an igloo made of blocks of ice. People of the cold northern forests live in log

On the left, a worker in Nicaragua's rain forest area carries a stem of bananas from the fields. On the right is a shot of the Jordanian desert. What are the differences in climate between the two areas shown? What similarities, if any, are there? How does climate affect the way in which the people in each of these areas live and work?

cabins. Rain-forest peoples live in huts made of straw and grass. Some people in the dry lands of the earth live in homes made of sun-dried brick or mud.

9. Climate affects the clothes we wear. The desert people of the Middle East wear loose-fitting cotton clothing to keep themselves cool while they travel in the hot desert. In the highlands, shepherds wear clothing made of wool or leather in order to keep themselves warm. In places such as the Amazon rain forest, the natives wear little clothing because it is always hot and wet.

10. As you have learned, climate also determines the kinds of crops that are grown in an area. Differences in climate mean differences in temperature, rainfall and length of growing season. Some parts of the world have plenty of rain, while other parts are dry. Farmers cannot always grow the same crops in both wet and dry regions. For this reason, you would not find rice being grown in Michigan or oats in Indonesia. If a country is located near the equator, it would be safe to guess that it might export bananas but not furs. Wheat can be grown in a great variety of climates, whereas olives need a dry climate.

11. *Trade*, or the exchange of goods among nations, is also the result of differences in climate. Our country, except for Hawaii, does not have the climate for growing rubber, coffee or bananas. Thus, we buy coffee from Brazil and Colombia. We get rubber from Indonesia and Malaysia. We may be able to grow silk and olives, but we can grow other crops better, so we import those things as well. We grow what suits our climate best. Hawaii's climate is perfect for growing sugar cane and pineapples. The Midwest of the United States is good for growing corn and wheat. Just as we cannot grow all kinds of products, so do other nations face the same problem.

UNDERSTANDING CHAPTER 8

1. The main idea of *paragraphs 4 through 6* describes:
   a. the meaning of temperature.
   b. how we figure average rainfall.
   c. what we mean when we speak of climate.

2. On the mainland of the United States, we do not have the climate to grow:
   a. cotton.   b. rubber.   c. oats.

3. A "growing season" refers to:
   a. weather.   b. rainfall.   c. climate.

4. Growing seasons become shorter as we:
   a. travel toward the equator.
   b. travel away from the equator.
   c. travel toward the Prime Meridian.

5. Climate causes a difference in the:
   a. minerals nations have.
   b. amount of steel a nation can make.
   c. amount of water for farming.

6. When the newspaper says that "Tomorrow will be cloudy and warm," it is telling us about:
   a. weather.   b. climate.   c. rainfall.

7. Which figure refers to rainfall?
   a. 30°   b. 25″   c. 61° N. Lat.

8. Climate will affect the kinds of clothing we wear, the crops we grow and:
    a. the sports we enjoy.
    b. the television programs we see.
    c. the newspapers we read.

Understanding the Difference Between FACT and OPINION

One of the most important things you can learn as a citizen is to be able to distinguish (to tell the difference) between statements that are *facts* and those that are *opinions*.

A *fact* is a true statement. It can be proven. An *opinion* is what a person or a group of people think about a subject. An opinion cannot be proven to be true. An opinion may tell:
    a. what a person thinks *will happen*.
    b. what someone thinks *should happen*.
    c. the *feeling* that a person has about a subject.
    d. what a person *believes* about a subject.

It is from your knowledge of facts that you arrive at a good opinion. There is nothing wrong with having an opinion. Good citizens will think about the facts they know and try to make judgments about problems in their lives. The important thing is that we are able to tell when a thought that is expressed is a fact—is true—and when it is someone's feeling about a subject.

Notice the difference in these examples:

FACT: The Pacific is the largest ocean.

OPINION: The Pacific Ocean will have more trade than the Atlantic Ocean in a few years.

FACT: The United States has taken part in two world wars.

OPINION: The United States should not go to war unless it is attacked.

FACT: Transportation has improved in the last hundred years.

OPINION: It is nonsense to say that we will travel to Mars by the year 2,000.

Now see if you can tell which of these are *facts* and which are someone's *opinion*:

1. Temperatures may change quickly from day to night.
2. Chicago will have more snow than Denver next year.
3. A farmer will plant a crop that he can raise in his growing season.
4. The clothing people wear will depend upon the climate of the place in which they live.
5. Climate is the kind of weather we have over a long period of time.
6. People who live on the desert are not able to govern themselves.
7. The United States should use all the cotton it grows instead of selling some of it to other countries.
8. Some farmers find that they can grow several different crops on the same farm.

9 DIFFERENCES IN CLIMATE

Reading For A Purpose: What are the reasons for differences in climate?

Altitude as well as latitude determines climate. How is this so?

1. Throughout the world, there are differences in climate from place to place. Even within our own nation, there is a variety of climate. Why is this so? There are five good reasons for differences in climate, and we ought to know them.

2. The most important factor that influences climate is *latitude*, or distance from the equator. If two places in the world are the same in all ways and they are the same distance from the equator, they will have the same climate. At the equator, the sun's rays are direct. Thus, they are stronger and hotter. As you travel away from the equator, the sun's rays slant and become weaker. You will find that it gradually becomes cooler.

3. *Altitude*—the elevation or height of land above sea level—also affects climate. Air grows cooler as we travel upward, away from the surface of the earth. For example, Quito, the capi-

tal of Ecuador in South America, has 500,000 people. Yet this city is almost on the equator. Not too far east, the city of Manaus, Brazil, has a lot fewer people. How do you explain the fact that so many people live in one city and so few in another? Part of the answer is that the Andes Mountains cross the equator. Quito is located in the highlands and Manaus is in the lowlands. Quito has a pleasant climate. Manaus is hot and wet. In general, the *higher* a region is, the *colder* it is. Most people prefer to live in a cool climate.

4. *Winds and mountains* also determine climate. If the winds blow in from a warm sea, they will carry moisture with them. Rain will fall when the air cools. If the winds blow from the land out to sea, they will be dry winds because they have had little chance to pick up moisture. The winds that blow from the Pacific Ocean toward the United States are a good example of this factor in determining climate. The Pacific winds carry moisture with them, for they come from the ocean. As the winds meet the mountains along the west coast, the air rises and is cooled. When the air is cooled, the moisture drops as rain on the western side of the mountains. Here are found thick, green forests and fertile land. After the air has crossed the mountains, it is drier. Thus the land east of the mountains receives little rainfall. The rainy side of the mountains is the *windward* side. The dry side is called the *leeward* (or sheltered) side.

5. Not all the winds of the earth blow continually from the same direction. There are shifting local winds caused by the heating or

Winds and mountains also determine climate. How is this so?

46

cooling of land. The *monsoon* winds of Asia are an example of this. When the winds blow from the land, they are dry and cold. These dry winds cause great hardship for the farmers of India. However, when the winds blow from the Indian Ocean, they are warm and wet, bringing humid weather and heavy rains.

6. *Nearness to water* is another factor that affects climate. Water has the effect of making temperatures "even." Water neither heats nor cools as fast as land. Places near large bodies of water (oceans, seas and large lakes) have a more "even" temperature than other places in the same latitude. When it is a hot summer day and you go swimming to cool off, the temperature of the water may be 20 degrees cooler than the land temperature. At night the sun's rays disappear and the land cools. You can feel the cold and dampness if you lie on the ground. But the water may have dropped only a few degrees in temperature, if it has dropped

at all. If you went swimming in the evening, you would find the water almost the same temperature as during the day.

7. This difference in land and water temperature explains the fact that although New York City and Omaha, Nebraska, may have almost the same latitude, there is a difference in temperature throughout the year. Omaha is not near a large body of water. Summer temperatures there often reach 100° and winter temperatures may drop to 10° below zero. New York City is on the Atlantic Ocean. The temperature seldom reaches 100° in the summer or 0° in the winter. Omaha may have a difference of 110 degrees in temperature during a year. New York is likely to have a difference of only 80 degrees throughout the year.

8. *Ocean currents* affect climate in many parts of the world. Ocean currents are like fast-flowing "streams" of water within a larger body of water. Some of these currents are cold

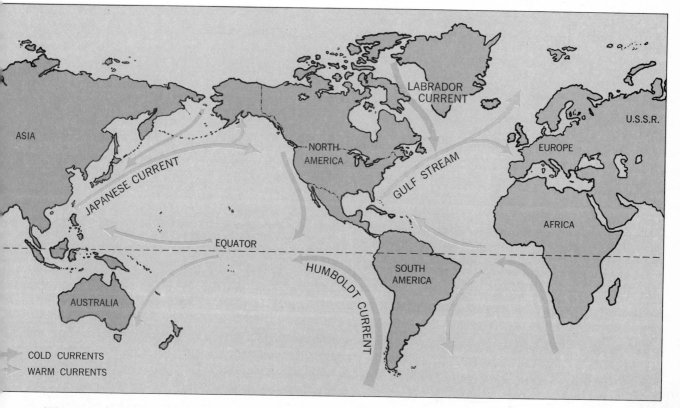

What are the patterns in the flow of warm and cold currents above and below the equator?

and others are warm. The winds that blow over them, therefore, are affected by the temperatures of the currents. The Gulf Stream is a warm current that begins in the warm waters of the Gulf of Mexico. It flows northward along the eastern coast of the United States toward Newfoundland. Then it turns eastward across the Atlantic Ocean. This current brings warm waters to the British Isles. The winds blowing over the current are warm winds. These warm winds blow across Great Britain and Western Europe. As a result, the people of those lands enjoy a warmer climate than that of Hudson Bay, Canada. Yet Great Britain is about the same distance from the equator as that cold region of Canada.

9. The Japanese Current is another warm current. Warm winds from this ocean stream make it possible to farm along the southern coast of Alaska. This current also warms the coasts of Oregon and Washington. On the other hand, the Labrador Current brings masses of floating ice from the north polar region into the Atlantic Ocean. When the cold air from the Labrador Current meets the warm air of the Gulf Stream in the North Atlantic, dangerous fogs result. The southwest coast of South America is colder and drier because of the Humboldt Current, which flows northward from the Antarctic Ocean.

10. These, then, are some of the important facts about the causes of different climates:
1. In general, the farther a land is from the equator, the colder its climate.
2. As you climb higher above sea level, temperatures become cooler.
3. As you move farther from large bodies of water, there is a greater difference in temperature throughout the year.
4. Rainfall is greatest where land borders a warm part of the ocean.
5. Winds that blow from the land are dry winds. Winds that blow from the sea are wet winds.

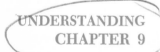

UNDERSTANDING CHAPTER 9

1. The main idea of *paragraph 7* describes:
    a. the weather of cities in the same latitude.
    b. the temperatures of New York City.
    c. how nearness to water affects temperature.
2. When wet winds blow toward mountains, the side that gets the most rain is the:
    a. northern side.
    b. windward side.
    c. leeward side.
3. *Monsoons* are winds of Asia that:
    a. blow from the ocean.
    b. are sometimes wet and sometimes dry.
    c. always blow from the same direction.
4. Midwestern United States has hot summers and very cold winters because:
    a. this land is far from large bodies of water.
    b. the land is thousands of feet above sea level.
    c. cold ocean currents bring cold winds.
5. Large cities, like Quito, Ecuador, can be found in the mountains because:
    a. it is cooler there.
    b. it is the only place with fertile land nearby.

c. sheep are raised in the mountains and manufacture of clothing is important.

6. Great Britain is warmer than other places of the world the same distance from the equator because of:
   a. its nearness to water.
   b. its altitude.
   c. the warming effects of the Gulf Stream.

7. Our states of Oregon and Washington are warmer in winter than other American states at the same latitude because of the:
   a. Japanese Current.
   b. warm winds that blow from the east.
   c. altitude of land along the coast.

8. The western side of the mountains along the Pacific Coast receives more rain than the eastern side because:
   a. the Gulf Stream brings warm winds.
   b. the western side is nearer the equator.
   c. winds from the Pacific bring rain.

DEVELOPING IDEAS AND SKILLS

Making an Outline

Using the headings below, write at least two topics under each heading for your outline of the factors that affect climate.

   A. Latitude
   B. Altitude
   C. Winds and Mountains
   D. Nearness to Large Bodies of Water
   E. Ocean Currents

SUMMING UP

Fact or Opinion

Read each statement carefully. If the statement is a fact, write F in your notebook. If it is an opinion, write O.

1. The climate of Oregon is better than the climate of South Carolina.
2. Some places in the world get rain during only one season of the year.
3. Ocean currents have changed the climates of many places in the world.
4. As the population of the world grows, lands with cool climates will become crowded, while lands with warm climates will have fewer people.
5. People who live in a cool climate are harder workers than those in a hot climate.
6. There are many different climates in the United States.
7. Farmers can grow crops even in parts of Alaska.
8. No country having a hot climate will ever be a leading nation of the world.

10 CLIMATIC REGIONS OF THE WORLD

Reading For A Purpose: What are the different kinds of climate in the world?

1. There are many kinds of climate in the world. Very rarely does a single country have only one kind of climate. In this chapter, we will make a summary (give the main points) of the different kinds of climatic regions found throughout the world. We have divided the climatic regions into the latitudes at which they will probably appear: low latitudes—0° to 23°, middle latitudes—24° to 66° and high latitudes—67° to the poles.

2. The low-latitude climates are the *rain forest*, the *savanna* and the *desert*. The tropical rain forest is the hot, wet climate of the lowlands near the equator. Large rain forests are located in South America, central Africa and Southeast Asia. In the rain forest, the sun shines overhead all year and it is hot throughout the year. Some rain falls almost every day.

The coastal lowland of Venezuela has a rain forest climate. What kind of climate is this?

Temperatures seldom rise above 90°, but it is always damp and sticky. The thick jungles keep the sun from reaching the ground. If the jungle is cut away, it grows back quickly.

A house in the savanna of Colombia. Why is the roof sharply slanted rather than flat?

3. North and south of the rain forests are the tropical savannas or grasslands. These are the "lands of two seasons." There is a winter dry season and a summer wet season. During the dry season, the grasses turn brown as the hot sun burns the earth. The water in the streams gets lower and lower. During the rainy season, the rain pours down day after day. River beds fill up with muddy water. After a while, the water floods the land. The ground becomes soft and muddy. Now the climate is like that of the tropical rain forest, hot and sticky. When the rain stops, the process begins again.

4. North and south of the grasslands are the deserts. (The change from the savanna to the desert is gradual, not sharp. This area of change from heavier to very light rainfall is called the *steppe* zone.) These are lands that receive less than 10 inches of rainfall a year. Among the large desert areas of the low latitudes are the Sahara Desert in Africa; Arabia; parts of the Middle East; and the desert that covers most of Australia. The Sahara is almost as large in area as the mainland of the United States. Deserts are the driest and hottest parts of the earth. The difference in temperature between day and night is very great. The land cools off quickly when the sun goes down, and the temperature may drop as much as 50 degrees. Although few people live in the desert, desert soils are not poor. They can come to life if they are irrigated or watered.

5. In the middle latitudes there are several kinds of climate: *Mediterranean, humid-subtropical, humid-continental, marine, steppe* and *desert.* The Mediterranean climate areas are pleasant, sunny lands. Five areas in the world have this kind of climate: the lands that border the Mediterranean Sea, southern California, central Chile, southwestern Africa and southwestern Australia. This type of climate is found on the western coast of countries between 30° and 40° latitude, both north and south. The growing season in these lands is usually twelve months long, with mild winters and hot, dry summers. The little rain that falls

The lonely Libyan desert of North Africa. Why is there a sharp drop in temperature from noon to night on the desert?

comes in the winter months. Los Angeles, California, has an average rainfall of less than ⅓ of an inch in the summer months! About 10 inches fall from November through February.

6. The humid-subtropical climate is just what its name tells us. *Sub* means under. This is the moist region just north and south of the tropics. This climate is found along the southeastern coasts of the United States, South America, Australia and mainland China and Japan. All areas with a humid-subtropical climate are located on the eastern side of their continents. Warm ocean currents flow along these coasts. Winds blowing across these currents bring warm, moist air to the land in all seasons. Summers are long and rainy; winters are short and mild. Many different crops are grown, not once but several times a year. This climatic region supports more people than any other.

7. The marine climate gets its name from its location. Marine, of course, refers to water. Western Europe, the British Isles, our own Pacific Northwest, western Canada, southern Chile and some of the islands of the Pacific have a marine climate. All of these lands are near water or are surrounded by water. The winds that blow from the ocean are warm and

Winter snow settles over a farm in the humid-continental climate belt in Canada. Which of our states are in the same climate area?

wet. They bring a mild, rainy climate to these areas. Summer temperatures in marine lands average below 70°. In the winter, the warming effect of the ocean water usually keeps the temperature from falling below freezing.

8. The humid-continental climate is the kind of climate found in northern and central United States, the central part of the Soviet Union, northern China and southern Canada. This is the "climate of the four seasons"—autumn, winter, spring and summer. Summers are hot, and winters are cold. As you move inland, away from the coasts, there is a greater difference in temperature throughout the year. It is called humid because there is enough rainfall for a variety of crops. In the areas of the humid continental climate are some of the greatest farm lands in the world. In each of the areas where this climate is found, mining and trading are important.

9. In the interior of large continents like North America and Asia, far from the ocean breezes, are the dry flatlands. These regions are called *prairies* or Great Plains in the United States and Canada. They are called *steppes* in Asia. Summers are hot and winters are cold in these regions as in the humid-continental climate, but there is a big difference. Rainfall is light and uncertain in the steppe climate. Ten to twenty inches of rain a year is normal, falling chiefly in spring and summer. Grass grows where there is enough rain, but there are also deserts where it rains very little. These steppes gradually become deserts as in our own Southwest, the Gobi Desert of Asia and smaller deserts in Peru, Chile and Africa south of the equator.

10. High-latitude climates are of two kinds, *tundra* and *taiga*. "Tundra" is a Russian word meaning "marshy plain." This climate is found in the northern areas of Canada, Europe and the Soviet Union. Here winters are very cold. The ground is frozen for most of the year and is mushy during the short summer months. Less snow falls, however, in the tundra than in the eastern United States. Because of the cold, no crops can be raised and few people live there. But although the tundra is empty of

human life, it has many land animals and plants that grow during the short summer. (In the very far north and in the far south, it is cold the year round. This is the *ice cap*. There is no summer in Antarctica or Greenland away from the ocean.)

11. South of the frozen tundra is the northern forest region or taiga. "Taiga" is also a Russian word, meaning "forest." The taiga stretches from Alaska and northern Canada across Norway, Sweden, Finland and the Soviet Union. Most of this land is covered with swamps and marshes. Temperatures in the taiga are usually colder in winter and hotter in summer than in the tundra. This is because the taiga is farther from the waters of the Arctic Ocean. Here also, the growing season is too short for crops, and few people live here because of the extreme climate. But the region is very important in spite of these facts. It contains the largest forest lands in the world. It is also rich in minerals and valuable fur-bearing animals.

12. High mountains form a climate of their own, often different from their surroundings. At the foot of a mountain, the climate may be hot and rainy and many lowland crops may be grown. As you go higher up the mountain, the air becomes cooler. The climate changes sharply and different activities must be performed, such as growing corn and grazing sheep. At the very top, many mountains have

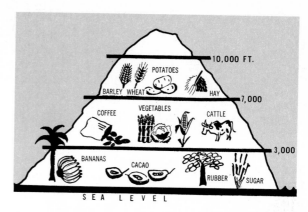

Cold- and warm-climate crops can be grown in the same region, providing the region has a vertical climate. What kind of climate is required for growing sugar?

snow on them all year round. This is called a *vertical* climate.

13. You can tell a lot about the climate of any region by knowing what natural plant life or *vegetation* grows in that area. In general, there are three kinds of vegetation: trees, grasses, and bushes. Trees are found, of course, in the forest areas (rain forest, taiga); grasses are found in the grasslands (savanna, humid subtropical, steppe) where there is not enough rain to support too many trees; and bushes and other low plants are found in the deserts and tundras of the earth.

DEVELOPING
IDEAS AND
SKILLS

Map Study

There are many ideas and much information that we can find out from maps. It is not even necessary to know the name of the map we are studying. If we know about land forms, latitude, longitude, the factors that affect climate and the ways in which climate influences people, we can gather a great deal of information.

On p. 55 is a map of a land we will call "Solaria." It does not really exist. It is imaginary. Yet we are going to study this map and see how much we can learn about this land.

See if you can answer each question about the map. If you can't, the answer is explained after the question. Check yourself. See how much you can learn from the map without reading the answers.

1. Is the land north or south of the equator? *Answer:* It is north of the equator. The degrees of latitude grow higher as we go north. We know that 0°, the equator, is south of 10°. Therefore, the land must be north of the equator.

2. Is Solaria in the low, high or middle latitudes? *Answer:* The southern part—the smallest part—is in the low latitudes. Above 23½° is the middle latitudes. Most of the land lies in the region of the middle latitudes. None of Solaria is in the high latitudes.

3. Is Solaria east or west of the Prime Meridian? *Answer:* It is west of the Prime Meridian. 0° longitude must lie to the east of Solaria because the degrees of longitude are increasing as we go west.

4. Where will most of the seaports be? *Answer:* On the west coast, probably. The western coastline is rough—it has many inlets and harbors. The other coastlines are smooth and probably have few harbors.

5. Where will the largest city be? *Answer:* Probably at C. This city is located a small distance below the place where the rivers have joined to empty into the sea, a good location for trade. The harbor looks as though it will have a wide mouth, and it is sheltered from the ocean.

6. What kind of land form is shown by letter A? *Answer:* An isthmus, a narrow piece of land connecting two larger bodies of land.

7. What land form is shown by letter B? *Answer:* A peninsula—a body of land almost completely surrounded by water.

8. What are the latitude and longitude of city D? *Answer:* About 55° north latitude and 43° west longitude.

9. What city is located at 47° north latitude and 59° west longitude? *Answer:* E.

10. In which direction does River 2 flow? *Answer:* It flows almost directly west. It rises in the mountains and flows to the ocean—to the west.

11. Which side of the mountains will have the most rain? *Answer:* The western side. The winds blow from the west in the middle latitudes, and they have come from the ocean. Therefore, they bring moisture with them. Notice that the rivers are on the western side.

12. What is the difference in climate between cities R and L? *Answer:* City L will probably be hotter in the summer and colder in the winter since it is not near the ocean. Remember that water has the effect of keeping temperatures even.

13. What might keep city F from being a large city? *Answer:* It does not have a good harbor. Also, it lies in the low latitudes in a lowland. It no doubt has a very warm and wet climate.

14. If you flew in an airplane from E to F, in what direction would you fly? *Answer:* Southeast.

15. If you traveled by air from D to F, how far would you have traveled? *Answer:* About 4000 miles. Measure 2,000 miles on the scale of miles. From D to F is about twice that distance. Two times 2,000 miles is 4,000 miles.

16. When it is 8 o'clock in the morning at D, what time is it at C? *Answer:* 7 o'clock. There is a difference of one hour in time for each 15 degrees of longitude. Since the earth is moving toward the east, D has daylight earlier than C. So, D will always be one hour ahead in time.

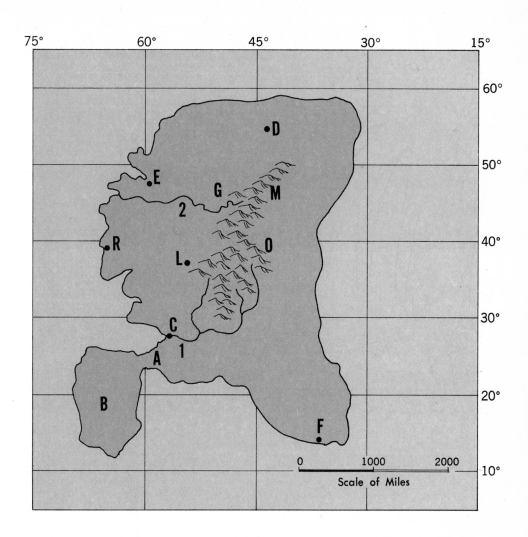

Map #6—
Solaria

SUMMING UP

I. **Match each item in Column A with one of the descriptions in Column B.**

COLUMN A

D 1. marine
F 2. humid-subtropical
A 3. taiga
E 4. rain forest
C 5. savanna
G 6. humid-continental
D 7. Mediterranean

COLUMN B

a. High-latitude forests.
b. Sunny lands with dry summers.
c. Grassland north of the rain forest.
d. Wet, cool lands of Western Europe.
e. Less than 10″ of rain a year.
f. Good farm lands on the east coast of continents in the middle latitudes.
g. Climate of the four seasons—cold winters and hot summers.
h. Always hot and wet.

55

II. True or False

Tell whether these statements are true or false. The underlined words make the statement true or false. If a statement is false, what words would you place in the statement to make it true?

1. Most of Australia is rain forest. _False Desert_
2. The tundra is a climate of the middle latitudes. _False High_
3. Day and nighttime temperatures differ greatly in the desert. _True_
4. Part of the United States has a Mediterranean climate. _True_
5. A humid-subtropical climate is found along the southeastern coast of _Tr_ China.
6. A great part of the taiga is found in the United States. _False Canada_
7. The wet and dry seasons are a feature of the savanna climate. _True_
8. Temperatures that are mild in both winter and summer are a part of the _N_ marine climate.

11 GIFTS OF THE EARTH

Reading For A Purpose: What are natural resources? How are they divided among the peoples of the earth?

1. Our planet Earth has been very good to us. The surface of the earth is covered by water, soil and forests. Beneath the surface of the earth is its crust. In it are rich minerals, such as iron, gold, silver, copper, lead, tin and aluminum ore. The earth's crust also contains layers of coal, petroleum (oil) and natural gas. These are all natural resources. Without the gifts of the earth, man could not live.

2. The *soil* that covers our earth is very valuable to us. The earliest civilizations on earth (China, India, Egypt) started where there was fertile soil—where people could grow crops. The topsoil throughout the world is only about 8 inches deep. This thin layer of topsoil is made up chiefly of minerals and living things. The topsoil contains plants and insects as well as water, air and minerals. The minerals are called *nutrients.* As long as the nutrients remain, the land is useful and provides us with food to eat and raw materials for clothing and shelter.

3. There are many different kinds of soil throughout the world. The soils in the rain forests and savannas are very poor. The heavy rains *leach* or wash out the minerals or nutrients from the soil. In the dry lands, one finds gray desert soils. These soils are very fertile when *irrigated* because they have had little rain to wash away the nutrients. (When we irrigate, we bring water to dry land through ditches and canals in order to grow crops.) In the humid-subtropical lands, the soils are a reddish-yellow. If they are *fertilized*, they can give rich harvests for many years. (Soil is fertilized when minerals are added to make it richer.) The best farming soils are found inland on the prairies of North and South America and the steppes of the Soviet Union. They are the rich black soils. They have plenty of minerals and need little fertilizer. These "black belts" are the great wheat-growing regions of the world.

4. *Water* is another natural resource that most of us accept without much thought. We need water to drink, to keep us clean and to wash our food. A city of one million people may use as much as 50 million gallons of water a day! We also need water for growing crops. (Where not enough rain falls, we must irrigate dry fields.) Water also gives us a means of travel and carrying goods, and it is an important source of power. Power plants near rivers and waterfalls use water to turn machines called turbines that produce electricity. We call this *hydroelectricity.*

5. *Forests* are one of the valuable resources of the world. They still cover about 1/5 of the earth's surface. Most of the large forests are

POWER LINE

DAM

STORAGE LAKE

DAM

CONTROL ROOM

TRANSFORMER STEPS UP POWER

POWER HOUSE

TURNING OF GENERATOR MAKES ELECTRICITY

FALLING WATER TURNS TURBINE

TURBINE

RIVER

This drawing shows how important the power of falling water is in making hydro-electricity. What do you think the prefix hydro- **means?**

found in the northern taiga (Canada, Alaska, Norway, Sweden, Finland and Siberia) and in the rain-forest regions of South America, central Africa and Southeast Asia. There are many kinds of trees, from the hardwoods of the rain forest to the evergreens of the taiga. Our forests provide us with raw materials for building homes and for many other things that we use in our daily lives. Wood is used as fuel for heating and cooking. Trees help save our soil resources. They keep the soil on steep hillsides from being washed away. Newsprint, turpentine, maple sugar, cellophane and many medicines are but a few of the products of our forests. Lastly, forests provide a home for wildlife and a place of beauty and recreation for millions of people.

6. *Coal* is the world's chief source of power. It is important as a heating fuel. But of greatest importance is the fact that with coal we can make steel from iron ore. The largest deposits of coal are found in the United States, Great Britain, West Germany and the Soviet Union. As a result, all of these countries have great mills and factories. Most of the world's known coal deposits are in North America and Europe. Little coal has been found in Africa and South America. In Asia coal has been mined only on a small scale.

7. *Petroleum*, or oil, provides power for farms and factories. Petroleum is a liquid mineral found in layers of rock deep below the surface of the earth. It is a heating fuel for millions of homes. After petroleum is refined—that is, its impurities are removed—one of its products is gasoline, the chief fuel for automobiles and airplanes. Chemists have learned how to change petroleum into many useful things. Like other natural resources, petroleum is not found everywhere in the world. Some nations have large deposits of oil, while others have none at all. The great oil countries are the United States, Venezuela, the Soviet Union and the countries near the Persian Gulf (Arabia, Iraq, Iran, Kuwait).

8. *Iron ore* is more valuable than any other mineral. Without iron ore, great industrial nations could never have developed. When iron

is smelted or separated from rock and mixed with other minerals, steel is made. Iron ore is often hard to remove from the earth's crust, but in some places it lies near the surface. The ore of the great Mesabi Range of Minnesota is soft and easy to mine. It is simply scooped up by large steam shovels and loaded in railroad cars.

9. About ¹⁄₁₀ of the world's supply of iron ore comes from the Lake Superior district of the United States. In Europe, France and Sweden are the chief iron-mining centers. The Soviet Union has large deposits of iron ore, coal and limestone. Large deposits are also found in India, China and Indonesia. Other countries have some iron ore, but it is not mined because it is expensive to carry the ore to smelters where it is refined.

10. There are other minerals that are very useful to man. *Copper* can easily be made into wire and can carry electricity. At the present time, the United States is the largest miner and user of copper. A large copper supply also comes from Chile (in South America), central

Pictograph #1—Important Mineral and Food Resources of the World

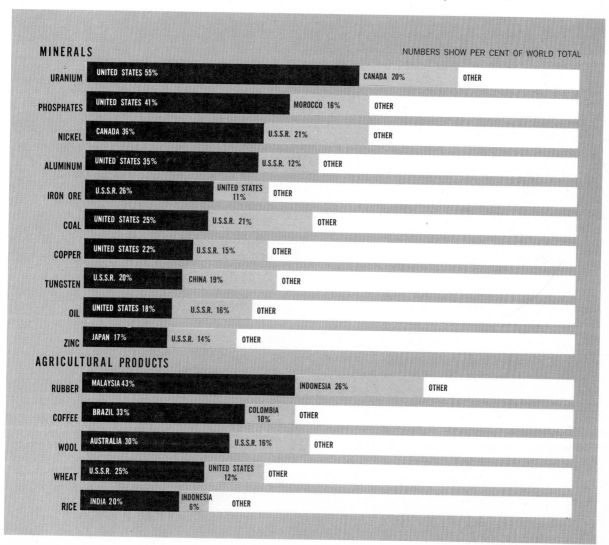

MINERALS — NUMBERS SHOW PER CENT OF WORLD TOTAL

Mineral			
URANIUM	UNITED STATES 55%	CANADA 20%	OTHER
PHOSPHATES	UNITED STATES 41%	MOROCCO 16%	OTHER
NICKEL	CANADA 36%	U.S.S.R. 21%	OTHER
ALUMINUM	UNITED STATES 35%	U.S.S.R. 12%	OTHER
IRON ORE	U.S.S.R. 26%	UNITED STATES 11%	OTHER
COAL	UNITED STATES 25%	U.S.S.R. 21%	OTHER
COPPER	UNITED STATES 22%	U.S.S.R. 15%	OTHER
TUNGSTEN	U.S.S.R. 20%	CHINA 19%	OTHER
OIL	UNITED STATES 18%	U.S.S.R. 16%	OTHER
ZINC	JAPAN 17%	U.S.S.R. 14%	OTHER

AGRICULTURAL PRODUCTS

Product			
RUBBER	MALAYSIA 43%	INDONESIA 26%	OTHER
COFFEE	BRAZIL 33%	COLOMBIA 10%	OTHER
WOOL	AUSTRALIA 30%	U.S.S.R. 16%	OTHER
WHEAT	U.S.S.R. 25%	UNITED STATES 12%	OTHER
RICE	INDIA 20%	INDONESIA 6%	OTHER

Africa and Canada. The demand for a light, strong metal has made *aluminum* important. Today it is being used more and more in buildings, automobiles, trucks, boats and airplanes. The United States makes more aluminum products than any other nation. The aluminum comes from a mineral called *bauxite*. It must be refined in order to make aluminum. Electric power, chiefly water power, is used to manufacture aluminum. Bauxite is imported from France, Italy, India, Yugoslavia and Surinam.

11. *Tin* is used in cans because it does not rust. We import it from Malaysia, Indonesia and Bolivia. *Uranium* is one of the newest and most important minerals of our time. Leading producers of uranium are the United States and Canada. This ore is the source of our newest form of power, atomic energy!

12. As you study these chapters, you will learn how natural resources differ from region to region throughout the world. You will see that they are not found in the same amounts in every region. Even such large countries as the United States and the Soviet Union do not have all the resources that their people need. You will find out how people make use of natural resources, whether as farmers, miners, fishermen or lumbermen. You will learn how much you depend on these people even though you live far from them. You will learn how people turn to trade in order to provide themselves with the raw materials they don't have.

13. Finally, you will learn that many of these great resources are being used so rapidly that man is searching for new materials to take the place of the ones that are being used up. Every year, man is trying to find ways to conserve, or save, his resources. Conservation is a very important part of our government's responsibilities. The valuable gifts of nature must be used wisely if we hope to keep the standard of living we now enjoy.

UNDERSTANDING CHAPTER 11

1. The main idea of *paragraph 3* describes the:
   a. great farm regions of the world.
   b. different kinds of soil on the earth.
   c. problems of rain on soil.
2. Minerals such as iron and coal are usually found in the:
   a. earth's crust.   b. topsoil.   c. sea.
3. We get all these products from trees EXCEPT:
   a. paper.   b. maple sugar.   c. cotton.
4. The most valuable minerals for use in industry are:
   a. copper and coal.
   b. tin and iron ore.
   c. coal and iron ore.
5. Uranium is a mineral used in making:
   a. atomic energy.   b. steel.   c. aluminum.
6. The United States and the Soviet Union have large supplies of all of these EXCEPT:
   a. oil.   b. iron ore.   c. tin.
7. Aluminum has become important in many kinds of work because:
   a. it is found almost everywhere in the world.
   b. there is a demand for a strong light metal.
   c. it can be used as a fuel.

8. Desert lands may still have good soil because:
   a. rains have not washed away the minerals from the soil.
   b. beneath the surface, there is black soil.
   c. they have been farmed for thousands of years.

DEVELOPING
IDEAS AND
SKILLS

Map Study

Map #7—Carmania

Getting Information From Maps

This is another map of an imaginary land, like the map in Chapter 10. You will be able to get information about this land in the same way that you did in Chapter 10. Study the map. Then see if you can answer the questions that follow on this page and at the top of page 62. You should be able to find all the answers from information given in the map.

1. Is Carmania located in the low, middle or high latitudes?
2. Is Carmania north or south of the equator?
3. Which city is nearest to the Prime Meridian: C, R or O?
4. What is the distance from R to O by railroad: 1050 miles, 1350 miles or 1680 miles?
5. Which city looks as though it would be the biggest seaport: B, R or O?
6. What kind of climate would you expect to find around R: marine, subtropical or rain forest?

7. What kind of climate would you expect to find around F: desert, rain forest or Mediterranean?
8. What city is located at 40° S. Lat. and 57° W. Long.?
9. Which direction is upstream in River 3: north, northeast or southwest?
10. Which city would have the greatest change in temperature during a year: B, D or O?
11. When it is 3 o'clock in the afternoon at R, what time would it be at E: 2 o'clock, 3 o'clock or 4 o'clock?
12. What do we call A: a peninsula, a strait or an isthmus?
13. Where would you expect to find minerals: P, D or S?
14. Which place is northwest of D: S, E or O?
15. Which place would probably have the most rainfall: F, C or B?

SUMMING UP   *Knowing Words*   Review the word clues you learned in Chapter 1 of this unit. Then see if you can find the meanings of these words in Chapter 11. What *clue* helped you to know the meaning of each word?

Paragraph   1—petroleum
Paragraph   2—nutrients
Paragraph   3—leach
Paragraph   3—irrigate
Paragraph   4—turbines
Paragraph   9—smelter
Paragraph   10—bauxite
Paragraph   13—conserve

12 MACHINES HAVE CHANGED OUR WAYS OF LIVING

Reading For A Purpose: How have machines changed some nations of the world but not others?

1. The greatest change in the way men use the resources of the earth took place in the seventeenth and eighteenth centuries. This change was called the Industrial Revolution. (A revolution is a basic change that brings about a new way of life for many people.) New kinds of machines were invented and new kinds of power were developed to run these machines. Many goods were now made by machines instead of by hand, in factories instead of at home. New forms of power such as steam began to do some of the work once done by men and animals. This "revolution" changed the face of the earth. It divided the world into those countries that have many industries and those that do not. Let us see what an *industrial society* looks like.

2. With the use of machines it was now possible to produce large amounts of goods of many kinds. These products of the factories could be sold for lower prices than handmade goods because they were cheaper to make. As more and more people came to work in the factories, they earned more money to pay for these goods than they had had before. They became a *market* for the products of the factory. (Factories will not make goods unless there are people who will buy them.)

3. Because the factories made so many more goods, more raw materials to make these goods were needed. Coal and iron ore were needed to make steel. New uses for oil were discovered. As factories grew, there was a demand for more and more workers. Thousands left their farms and moved near the factories. Cities grew around the great industrial centers. In a large city many were factory workers, but many found jobs filling the needs of their neighbors. For every person who worked in the factory, two people could earn a living by working in "services"—storekeepers, teachers, doctors, policemen.

4. How could all these city people be fed? New machines began to be used on the farm. With improved methods of farming and machinery, it was possible for farmers to grow more food with fewer workers. Farmers not only grew food for themselves, but they were able to feed people throughout the nation and the world as well. They now grew *money crops*—crops they could sell at a profit. The farmer was now in business just as much as the factory owner.

5. Steam took the place of wind as the source of power in water transportation, and the great sailing ships were replaced by steamships. (In time, there were other sources of power: water, oil and atomic energy.) The automobile and airplane were invented; as a result, goods could be carried swiftly and cheaply almost anywhere in the world. The invention of the telephone, telegraph and radio

during this period meant that people from one corner of the world to the other could communicate with each other.

6. Today, countries like the United States, Great Britain, Canada, Japan, West Germany, France and the Soviet Union are *industrial societies.* An industrial society or region is one in which many people make a living by manufacturing or making things in factories. They have power-driven machinery and make great use of the raw materials of the earth. Their factories produce goods for their own people and have enough to sell to other nations as well. They have the means to ship goods from one place to another. Many other countries are also beginning to have mills and factories.

7. On the other hand, there are many countries in the world that the Industrial Revolution still has not reached to any large extent. These countries have not made full use of their natural resources. They still depend on hand labor in the fields and at home. They do not manufacture goods in great amounts and must buy them from other nations at high cost. Many of the people are farmers who work all day just to provide simple food, clothing and shelter for their families. They have nothing left over to sell to other peoples. This is known as *subsistence farming.* Such countries are often called "underdeveloped" or "agricultural" or "developing" countries. The people usually are poor. The average yearly income for people in some of these low-income areas is hard for us to believe: Latin America—$300; the Middle East and North Africa—$150; Africa, South of the Sahara—$120; the Far East—$100.

8. However, the people in many of these countries no longer feel that they must be poor and have undeveloped resources. They want the changes brought about by the Industrial Revolution. There are reasons for this growing demand for change. First, such nations feel that having factories will bring them the many comforts of life that people of industrial countries seem to have. They too want better schools and hospitals, radios and television

In the picture above, a husband and wife use a simple sieve-like basket to irrigate their rice paddy in India. In the one below, Canadians test a communications satellite (a complex machine used in space to speed communication between distant parts of the earth). What ideas of the chapter do these pictures point out?

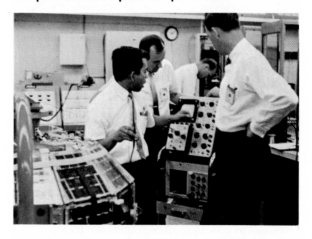

sets, refrigerators and washing machines. Second, the population of the world is growing fast. There are more people to be fed. Many feel that this means more jobs are needed, chiefly in factories. Finally, all people, whether rich or poor, have pride in themselves and their country. They want to be free of the need to sell their raw materials to other countries. They want to use these resources for their own benefit.

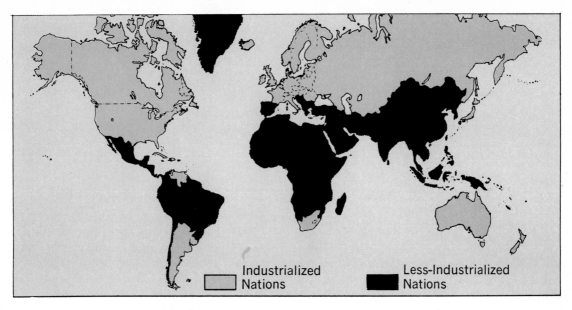

Map #8–Industrial Development Throughout the World

Industrialized Nations

Less-Industrialized Nations

UNDERSTANDING CHAPTER 12

1. The main idea of *paragraph 7* describes:
   a. underdeveloped countries.
   b. problems of the Industrial Revolution.
   c. poor natural resources.
2. A high standard of living can be found in:
   a. most of North Africa.
   b. Canada.
   c. all of southern Africa.
3. All of these are problems of underdeveloped countries EXCEPT:
   a. they have little money to buy goods.
   b. they have few people.
   c. few feople have had an education.
4. A change in farming caused by the Industrial Revolution was that:
   a. fewer machines were used on farms.
   b. the farmer did not raise food beyond the needs of his own family.
   c. fewer workers were needed on farms.
5. Which of these kinds of power was first used?
   a. Electric.   b. Oil.   c. Steam.
6. The *Industrial Revolution* refers to the:
   a. use of machines to do work once done by men.
   b. discovery of oil.
   c. rise of independent countries.
7. An *underdeveloped country* is one that has:
   a. few water resources.
   b. made little use of its natural resources.
   c. most of its workers in factories.

8. When there are people who will buy a product or places where it can be sold, we say that the product has:
   a. an industrial center.
   b. a market.
   c. been developed.

Making Inferences

Whatever you read, you gain ideas not only from the words you read, but often from what is *not* said. You read "between the lines." This is true in your study of the world, too. You know some things even though they are not stated. You are able to understand because some things are "inferred." One of the skills in reading social studies is to be able to *infer* meanings from what you have read. Here is an example:

The five o'clock whistle meant that the rush of workers had begun. Off they went in their shiny cars. Others poured into the subways nearby. The bright street lights were already lit.

What can we *infer* from these few sentences? First, *this is probably a city.* There are subways and street lights. *It is probably winter*, too, for the lights are already on at 5 o'clock, the end of the working day. And *the people probably have a high standard of living*, since the workers have their own cars.

In this exercise, see if you can infer from each paragraph whether it is written about *low*, *high* or *middle* latitudes.

1. Across the vast lowland, we see farm after farm. Corn and wheat can be seen for miles. Next to the farms, the hogs and cattle stand out against the green trees in the background.
2. A trip down the river is like going through a fairyland. Coconut palms, banana trees and all kinds of flowering trees and bushes line the shore. The monkeys never seem to stop chattering as they swing through the long vines.
3. The heat goes on and on. It wouldn't be so bad if it weren't for that rain! I'll never come here to build a road again. The bushes grow back as fast as I cut them, and the insects don't stop biting for a moment.
4. It could be worse in these winter months. I don't mind the darkness. After a few weeks you get used to it. I even enjoy melting the ice so that I can wash and make hot coffee.
5. Most of the farms look brown now, but some rain will come soon. The sheep seem to get enough food in the mountains, even though it is winter.
6. All the streams seem to be bordered with trees. The small fields were yellow with grain a month ago. Some workers are weeding potatoes; others are harvesting the ripe oats and wheat.
7. Everything is made of wood here because there is so much of it around. There's no use trying to farm. These trees are our wealth. When the summer comes, the ice will melt and we'll float the heavy logs downstream.

13 WORLD REGIONS

Reading For A Purpose: How will we explore our changing world?

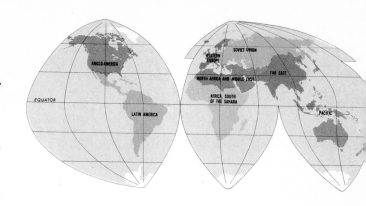

1. After this unit, each unit of this book tells about one of the eight regions of the world. Each region has features that make it a single region. The people and countries may be tied together through climate, land features, history, religion or ways of making a living. One region is made up of only one country, the Soviet Union. The other regions have from a few to a great many countries. Here are a number of questions to guide you as you prepare to study each of the eight world regions:

1. Why are we interested in this region?
2. How do the land and climate of the region explain, in part, the way the people live?
3. How has the geography of the region influenced the history of the people?
4. Who are the people of the region? What are their problems?
5. What are the resources of the region? How do the people make use of these resources?
6. What is the standing of the region in the world community?

2. The first region we will study is *Anglo-America*. This includes the countries of the United States and Canada, two of the largest nations of the world. Only the Soviet Union is larger than Canada. The United States ranks fourth in land size after China. Both the United States and Canada are located in the middle and high latitudes of the northern hemisphere. They have many things in common. They have the same language and the same ideas of government. They have great industries and a high standard of living. Both countries have been friendly and have cooperated with each other for more than 150 years. They are the richest region of all in natural resources. The people of the United States and Canada make great use of these resources for farming, manufacturing and trading.

3. Our southern neighbors in *Latin America* make up the next region of study. Most of the countries in Latin America were colonies of Spain, Portugal or France. They are studied together because most of them are Catholic in religion and Spanish or Portuguese in the language their people use. This is largely a region of tropical or subtropical climate, although mountains provide a cooler home for many people. Most of the people are descendants of Europeans, Indians and Negroes. Small farms and farming on large estates are the chief kinds of work. The countries of Latin America export many raw materials to other parts of the world.

4. The countries of *Western Europe* (other than the Soviet Union and its satellites) are our next area of study. While Western Europe is the smallest region we will explore, there are a large number of countries within this region. These countries have a marine climate. The leading countries are thickly populated. The people have made good use of their resources —the level and fertile lands, the iron and coal from the earth, the forests and the nearby seas. Their factories make iron and steel goods that are sold all over the world. The people of Western Europe have a high standard of living. The lands of Europe that border the Mediterranean Sea are poorer. Most people here make a living through farming.

A view of the Rhine River in West Germany. What signs of industrialization do you see in this picture?

5. The *Soviet Union* will be studied as a separate region. This giant country extends across great parts of Europe and Asia. It is the largest country in the world. Its land has vast plains, many resources and large areas in which few people live because of the cold climate. The Soviet Union was once a farming nation only, but today it is the second leading industrial nation in the world, following the United States. (The countries of Eastern Europe will be studied here too, since they are under Soviet influence.)

6. The lands of *North Africa and the Middle East* are combined into one region in this book for several reasons. This area, stretching across northern Africa and southwest Asia, is almost all a desert region. Few people live in it because of the lack of water. Except for oil, there are few mineral resources. It is a region of oasis farmers, city people and herdsmen who travel from place to place. Most of the people are Moslem in religion. Many are very poor and unable to read or write. This region is divided into many small countries.

7. *Africa, South of the Sahara* is studied as a region apart from North Africa. It is a region of rain forests, grasslands and desert. Most of the people are black. Since 1945, many small countries in Africa have won their freedom. Although Africa is making much progress, many of its mineral resources have scarcely been used. Most of the people are either poor farmers or herders.

8. The *Far East*, or Orient, has been included as one region. This region is made up of the countries of southern and eastern Asia. It is the home of almost half the people of the world! Most of these people live on small farms, on which they grow rice. As in Africa, there are new nations in the Far East. These nations are trying to make better use of their resources, but they face many problems.

9. To complete our study of the regions of the world, we will look at the land areas of the *Pacific*. Included in this region are the continent of Australia and the islands that are scattered throughout the Pacific Ocean. Except for Australia, New Zealand and Western Samoa, these islands are governed by other nations. The people of Australia and New Zealand have a high standard of living. They depend largely upon sheep and dairy farming and some manufacturing. Most of the island peoples are simple farmers who depend upon the coconut palm.

An anti-malaria team works in a field laboratory in Togo, in Africa. How have people been helped by such medical programs?

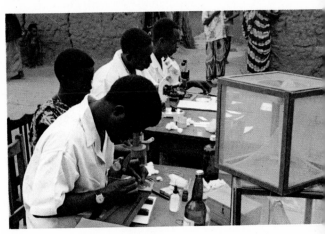

Match each item in Column A with one of the descriptions in Column B.

COLUMN A

i 1. Anglo-America
g 2. Latin America
h 3. Western Europe
c 4. The Soviet Union
e 5. North Africa and the Middle East
b 6. Africa, South of the Sahara
f 7. Far East
a 8. The Pacific World

COLUMN B

a. Many islands; simple farming.
b. Large region with large black population.
c. Region of one country.
d. Smallest region; high standard of living.
e. Largely desert and oil.
f. Half the world's people.
g. Spanish-speaking people; large area of warm climate.
h. One of the highest standards of living; divided into many small nations.
i. English-speaking people; high standard of living.

Map Study

Map #9—The Regions of the World

Locating Our World Regions

Locate each of the regions on the map of the world shown on this page. This will help you to prepare for the first region that you are to study.

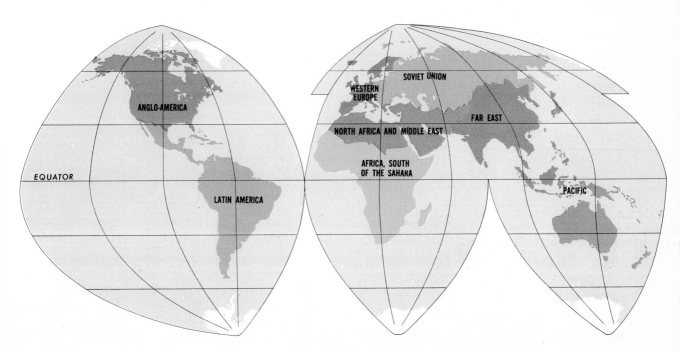

Making Inferences   In our reading, many facts are given to us. From these facts, we draw conclusions. Here are some conclusions or inferences that you might make after reading Chapter 13. Tell whether these conclusions are correct or incorrect. Give reasons for your answers.

Paragraph 2—There will be some places in Anglo-America with very cold climates.

Paragraph 3—Manufacturing is an important work in Latin America.

Paragraph 4—There are large areas of land in Western Europe where few people live.

Paragraph 5—The Soviet Union has large mineral resources, including coal and iron ore.

Paragraph 6—Many cities of millions of people are found in North Africa and the Middle East.

Paragraph 7—The climate and the surface of the land have hurt the development of Africa, South of the Sahara.

Paragraph 8—Much of the Far East is a region of desert, mountains and rain forest.

Paragraph 9—The standard of living of most of the people of the Pacific islands is rather low.

We Americans hear and read about other people in the world, but often we don't have the slightest idea of the hardships which millions face daily. The following selection gives us a clear picture as to what some of these hardships are.

What Is Life Like in the Developing Countries?

It is not easy to make this mental jump. But let us attempt it by imagining how a typical American family, living in a small suburban house . . . , could be transformed into an equally typical family of the underdeveloped world.

We begin by invading the house of our imaginary American family to strip it of its furniture. Everything goes: beds, chairs, tables, television set, lamps. We will leave the family with a few old blankets, a kitchen table, a wooden chair. Along with the bureaus go the clothes. Each member of the family may keep in his "wardrobe" his oldest suit or dress, a shirt or blouse. We will permit a pair of shoes to the head of the family, but none for the wife or children.

We move into the kitchen. The appliances have already been taken out, so we turn to the cupboards and larder. The box of matches may stay, a small bag of flour, some sugar and salt. A few moldy potatoes, already in the garbage can, must be hastily rescued, for they will provide much of tonight's meal. We will leave a handful of onions, and a dish of dried beans. All the rest we take away: the meat, the fresh vegetables, the canned goods, the crackers, the candy.

Now we have stripped the house: the bathroom has been dismantled, the running water shut off, the electric wires taken out. Now we take away the house. The family can move to the toolshed. It is crowded, but much better than the situation in Hong Kong where (a United Nations report tells us) "it is not uncommon for a family of four or more to live in a bedspace, that is, on a bunk bed and the space it occupies—sometimes in two or three tiers—their only privacy provided by curtains. . . ."

And still we have not reduced our American family to the level at which life is lived in the greatest part of the globe. Communication must go next. No more newspapers, magazines, books —not that they are missed, since we must take away our family's literacy as well. Instead, in our shantytown we will allow one radio. . . .

Now government services must go. No more postman, no more fireman. There is a school, but it is three miles away and consists of two classrooms. They are not too over-crowded since only half the children in the neighborhood go to school. There are, of course, no hospitals or doctors nearby. The nearest clinic is ten miles away and is tended by a midwife. It can be reached by bicycle, provided the family has a bicycle, which is unlikely. Or one can go by bus—not always inside, but there is usually room on top.

Finally, money. We will allow our family a cash hoard of five dollars. This will prevent our breadwinner from experiencing the tragedy of an Iranian peasant who went blind because he could not raise the $3.94 which he mistakenly thought he needed to secure admission to a hospital where he could have been cured. . . .

. . . And so we have brought our typical American family down to the very bottom of the human scale. It is however, a bottom at which we can find, give or take a hundred million souls, at least a billion people. . . .

Abridged from pp. 33-37 (hardcover edition) in *The Great Ascent* by Robert L. Heilbroner. Copyright © 1963 by Robert L. Heilbroner. Reprinted by permission of Harper & Row, Publishers, Inc.

1. What, if anything, surprised you in this description of poverty in developing countries? Why?
2. From the description of world regions in this chapter, in which regions would you be likely to find such conditions?
3. What do you think are the most important needs of people who live in poverty-stricken areas of the world?
4. A *generalization* is a general statement that is based upon a number of facts. Here is an example of one. "Most people in developing regions live in poor homes with only a few household goods." Write three generalizations of your own about life in developing regions.

BOOKS FOR UNIT 2

Author	Title, Publisher	Description
1. Barnes, Malcolm	THE MOUNTAIN WORLD, Rand McNally	The stories of several mountain expeditions.
2. Barnett, Lincoln, and editors of *Life*	THE WORLD WE LIVE IN, Golden Press	The story of the earth from its beginnings.
3. Beach, Edward L.	AROUND THE WORLD SUBMERGED, Holt	The cruise of a nuclear submarine around the world.
4. Brown, Lloyd	MAP MAKING, Little, Brown	The history of cartography.
5. Carson, Rachel	THE SEA AROUND US, Golden Press	How the seas work and move.
6. Deacon, G. E. R., editor	SEAS, MAPS, AND MAN, Doubleday	Articles about the sea with maps and illustrations.
7. Doss, Helen	THE FAMILY NOBODY WANTED, Little, Brown	The story of a little "U.N." family.
8. Liversidge, Douglas	ARCTIC EXPLORATION, Franklin Watts	The greatest contribution in the exploration of the Arctic—"over the ice" and "under it."
9. Werner, Elsa J.	GOLDEN BOOK OF GEOGRAPHY, Golden Press	An exciting and well-illustrated introduction to geography.
10. Werner, Jane	THE LIVING DESERT, Golden Press	The life of desert plants and animals.
11. White, Anne Terry	ALL ABOUT ARCHAEOLOGY, Random House	How we learn about ancient civilizations.

BOOKS IN SERIES (useful for many units)

Title	Publisher
1. The "Challenge" Books	Coward-McCann
2. The "First Book of" Series	Franklin Watts
3. The "Getting to Know" Books	Coward-McCann
4. The "Keys to the Cities" Series	Lippincott
5. The "Landmark" Books	Random House
6. The "Lands and Peoples" Series	Holiday
7. The "Let's Read About" Series	Fideler
8. The "Let's Visit" Series	John Day

9. The "Made In" Series   Knopf
10. The "Meet the World" Books   Harper
11. The "My Village" Series   Pantheon
12. The "Other Lands" Series   Life Publications
13. The "Picture Stories of Other Countries" Series   David McKay
14. The "Portraits of the Nations" Series   Lippincott
15. The "World Background" Series   Scribner
16. The "World Neighbors" Series   John Day

UNIT 3
Anglo-America

1 NORTHERN GIANTS

Reading For A Purpose: Why do we study the United States and Canada together?

Montreal, Canada, is similar to many American cities. The buildings are tall; the streets form neat, well-ordered patterns; people and cars move busily up and down the streets. What typical city problems do you suppose the people of Montreal face?

1. Stretching north of Mexico as far as the Arctic Ocean is a vast region that covers nearly all of the continent of North America. It is called Anglo-America. This area is shared by two countries, the United States and Canada. These two countries are called Anglo-America because most of their people speak English. (*Anglo* is the Latin word for "English.") French is also spoken in Canada, but not as much as English.

2. Canada takes up most of the northern half of the North American continent. It covers an area of almost 3,900,000 square miles. As such, it is the second largest country in the world. South of Canada is the United States. It covers more than 3,600,000 square miles, including the Hawaiian Islands in the Pacific Ocean and the state of Alaska northwest of Canada. It is the fourth largest country in the world. Both nations border the two largest oceans, the Pacific Ocean on the west and the Atlantic Ocean on the east.

3. The United States and Canada share a common border that is more than 3,000 miles long. There are no guns or forts along this border. The eastern part of the border is made up of two great waterways—the Great Lakes and the St. Lawrence River. Farther west the border stretches along the 49th parallel until it reaches the Pacific Ocean. For over 150 years, Americans and Canadians have crossed this common border without difficulty.

4. In many ways the Canadian and American ways of life are alike. Often it is as if there were no border between the two countries. For example, the farming lands just north of the St. Lawrence River are very much like the farming region of our New England states. Along the St. Lawrence River, factories on both sides of the border turn out machinery and manufactured goods.

5. If you were to visit the large cities of Montreal and Toronto, they would remind you of our own large cities. Most of the people speak English. They use many of the same products we do and eat many of the same things. The children go to school and play such games as hockey and baseball. Both peoples, Canadian and American, have a high standard of living.

6. In the Central Plains region, there are large wheat farms on both sides of the border. The farmers of both nations use large machinery to plant and harvest their wheat. Farther west, on the prairies, large herds of cattle and sheep are raised. Cowboys on horseback take care of the cattle in both countries.

7. The Rocky Mountains extend north and south through both countries. In both countries miners dig for gold, silver, lead and zinc. Farther west, on the Pacific coast, fishermen on both sides of the border bring in salmon. Lumberjacks cut down trees in the western forests of both the United States and Canada.

8. The relationship between the United States and Canada was very well described by President John F. Kennedy. On a visit to Canada in 1961 he said, "Geography has made us neighbors. History has made us friends. Economics has made us partners; and necessity has made us allies." In the next few chapters, we will explore the meaning of this statement and learn how these two nations are using their great resources for the benefit of both their peoples.

A west-coast logger begins the task of sawing this giant tree. In what ways is his work important to us?

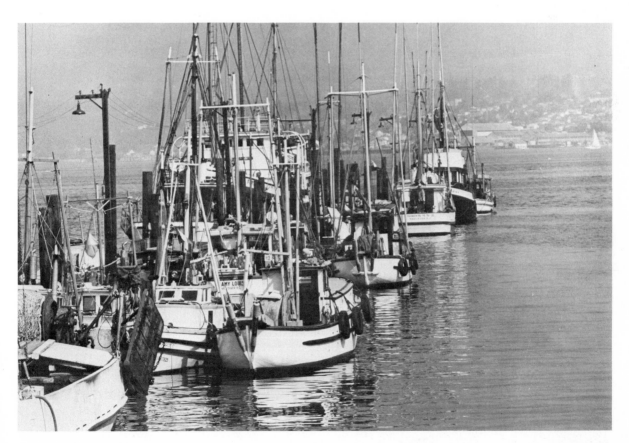

Pacific fishing fleet. Salmon is an important catch in Canada's west-coast fishing grounds.

1. Which questions are answered in this chapter?
   a. What kinds of work do many people do in the United States and Canada?
   b. What does *Anglo-American* mean?
   c. What two languages do the Canadians speak?

2. The main idea of *paragraph 3* is that:
   a. people of the United States and Canada trust each other.
   b. two great waterways form the boundary between the United States and Canada.
   c. the United States and Canada have a common border.

3. The United States is the:
   a. largest country in the world.
   b. smallest country in the world.
   c. fourth largest country in the world.

4. On both sides of the St. Lawrence River you are likely to find:
   a. forests.
   b. farms and factories.
   c. fisheries.

5. We are studying the United States and Canada as one region because:
   a. both countries lack natural resources.
   b. most people in both countries are farmers.
   c. English is the language of most people in both countries.

6. People in both countries do much the same kinds of work because:
   a. both are located in the middle latitudes.
   b. both are located in the high latitudes.
   c. both lands are surrounded by water.

**DEVELOPING
IDEAS AND
SKILLS**

Map Study

Map #10—Anglo-America

Study the map on page 79. Then answer these questions.
1. Is the region north or south of the equator?
2. Is the region east or west of the Prime Meridian?
3. What region or regions are near it?
4. What are the chief bodies of water that border the region?
5. What are some of the important rivers in the region?
6. What waterways form part of the boundary between the United States and Canada? The United States and Mexico?
7. What is the capital city of each country? How do you know they are the capitals? Is either a sea or river port?

Map #10—Anglo-America

SUMMING UP

Picture Symbols

The pictures on this page should help you to recall parts of the chapter you have read. What is the main idea of each picture?

FOLLOW UP

Our northern neighbor Canada is often in the news. The class may start clipping articles about Canada from the newspaper. Perhaps one of the pupils has visited Canada. He should report on his experiences there.

2 GEOGRAPHY HAS MADE US NEIGHBORS

Reading For A Purpose: How are the land forms of Canada and the United States alike?

At harvest time, the plains of Canada look like a patchwork quilt of brown and gold. What is the chief work of people who live in this area?

1. In many ways, the United States and Canada share the same topography or land features. Looking at the map on page 84, you will see that a large coastal plain stretches north and south along the Atlantic Coast, around the Gulf of Mexico into Texas. It is narrow in the north but widens in the south. The Atlantic Coastal Plain is bordered along its western side by the Appalachian Mountains. The Appalachians are low mountains whose peaks were smoothed by the ice of the glaciers. The Appalachians extend northward over most of eastern Canada. These mountains are a great source of wood, coal and water power.

2. Most of the continent between the Appalachians in the east and the Rockies in the west is covered by a vast lowland, the Central Plains. This area is one of the world's richest farming regions. Here the soil is very fertile. The eastern part of this gently rolling land was once covered with forests. West of the 100° meridian, the inner plains become the prairies or dry grasslands. These grasslands begin to rise slowly toward the Rocky Mountains. The plains spread north and northeast through Canada to the Arctic Ocean. They include the St. Lawrence River Valley.

3. The inner plains of the United States are drained by the Mississippi River and its tributaries or branches. The Mississippi River begins near the border of the United States and Canada. As it flows south, the Mississippi is joined by other rivers. Two of these are almost as large as the Mississippi—the Ohio River

from the east and the Missouri River from the west. The Mississippi flows southward, emptying into the Gulf of Mexico at Louisiana. The Mississippi River and its tributaries form the longest river system in Anglo-America. The lowlands drained by these rivers of the plains form the greatest farming region of North America.

4. The snowy peaks of the Rocky Mountains mark the end of the Great Plains and the beginning of the western highlands. The Rocky Mountains are higher than the eastern Appalachians. They begin in Alaska and run southeast and then south the length of our continent. The Canadian Rockies are part of this chain.

5. West of the Rockies is a dry, rough area of plateaus and basins. (A basin is a low area in the middle of the mountains.) Great rivers like the Colorado and the Columbia cut across the plateaus, making deep canyons. Many of the streams in this area flow into lakes that have

The wrinkled mountains are foothills of the Grand Canyon. The snake-like river is the Colorado.

Death Valley, California. Why is its name well chosen?

no outlet to the sea. The streams bring salt and other minerals with them. When the water evaporates or dries up, the salt is left in the lakes. The largest and most famous of these lakes is Great Salt Lake in Utah. Many rivers rise in the highlands of the American Rockies. Some flow toward the Atlantic Ocean or the Gulf of Mexico. Others flow westward to the Pacific Ocean. This division is called the Continental Divide. Near the southwestern edge of the Rockies' Great Basin lies Death Valley. This is the driest and hottest desert in North America. It is in the state of California.

6. Farther west are the coastal ranges or mountains that border the Pacific Ocean. They extend southward from Alaska into Mexico. These ranges change names from place to place. Between the coastal ranges are valleys, some of which are very wide. The great Central Valley of California is the largest of these. There is no great coastal plain along the Pacific Ocean as there is along the Atlantic.

7. Canada has one topographical region that is different from any place in the United States. It is called the Laurentian Shield. The Laurentian Shield is an upland that encircles Hudson Bay like a giant horseshoe. It covers more than half of Canada and extends into the United States near Lake Superior. This vast area of hard, old rocks was once scraped by glaciers. As they moved southward from the Arctic Ocean they created valleys, low hills and thousands of lakes and rivers. The Laurentian Shield is rich in forests, minerals and fur-bearing animals. However, only a few people live in this cold northern region. They earn their living mainly by trapping and fishing.

Far back in time, glaciers ground the area called the Laurentian Shield into a gentle, rolling plain. What are the land forms of your state?

1. Which questions are answered in this chapter?
   a. How did the glaciers affect the lands of the United States and Canada?
   b. How do the people of Anglo-America use these lands?
   c. What land form is found in Canada but not in the United States?
2. The main idea of this chapter describes the:
   a. land surface of Anglo-America.
   b. effects of the glaciers.
   c. Laurentian Shield.
3. The longest river system in Anglo-America is the:
   a. St. Lawrence.   b. Mississippi.   c. Colorado.
4. The highest mountains in Anglo-America are the:
   a. Rockies.   b. Appalachians.   c. Ozarks.
5. Few people live in the Laurentian Shield because:
   a. the land is filled with streams and lakes.
   b. there is a lack of wood and minerals.
   c. the climate is too cold.
6. The inner plains of the United States are valuable because:
   a. they have a wonderful climate for tropical fruits.
   b. the soil is easy to plow.
   c. the land is good for farming and grazing.
7. A *glacier* is a large mass of:
   a. ice.   b. land.   c. hardened minerals.
8. A branch is to a tree as a *tributary* is to a:
   a. person.   b. river.   c. mountain.
9. In paragraph 5, the word *evaporates* means:
   a. "carries salt."
   b. "cuts deeply."
   c. "dries up."
10. The word *topography* refers to:
    a. climate.   b. crops.   c. land features.

Map Study

Map #11—Land Forms of Anglo-America

Study the map on page 84. Then tell whether these statements are *true* or *false*. Be able to explain your answers.

1. Plains stretch from north to south through the center of Anglo-America.
2. A great mountain system of Anglo-America lies along or near the western coast.
3. A large lowland area is located along the southeastern coast.
4. A long plain borders the Pacific Coast of Anglo-America.
5. There are more hills than mountains in Anglo-America's eastern highlands.
6. When you compare the map on page 84 with the map of Anglo-America on page 89, you will find that the plains all over Anglo-America have the same climate.
7. Plateaus are an important land form of our Far West.
8. Alaska has a mix of all four kinds of land forms.

LAND FORMS OF ANGLO-AMERICA

Mountains

Plateaus

Hills

Plains

0 200 400 600 800 1000
Miles

Map #11

84

SUMMING UP

Agree or Disagree   Decide whether or not each of the following statements agrees with what you have read. If the answer is *disagree*, explain why.

1. The land forms of both the United States and Canada have been changed by volcanoes.
2. Both countries have chains of low mountains in the east.
3. A vast plateau runs north and south through the heart of North America.
4. The Mississippi River drains the inner plains of the United States and Canada.
5. The longest river in Anglo-America is the St. Lawrence.
6. Much of Canada is a land of old rock, rivers and lakes.

7. Both the United States and Canada are bordered by oceans.
8. Many of the same mountains, plateaus and plains are found in both countries.
9. The western highlands cover about one-third of the United States.
10. Both the United States and Canada have ports open throughout the year.

FOLLOW UP   Match the items in Column A with those in Column B.

COLUMN A	COLUMN B
1. Prairies	a. Western highlands.
2. Rockies	b. Area of hills, lakes and rivers.
3. Appalachians	c. Grasslands.
4. Laurentian Shield	d. Canyons of North America.
5. Central Valley	e. Eastern highlands.
	f. Found in California.

3 THE COLD AND THE WARM REGIONS

Reading For A Purpose: What are the many climates of Anglo-America?

1. Anglo-America covers a vast area on the earth's surface. Because of its great size it has many different climates. There are a number of reasons for these different climates. The most important reason is latitude, or distance from the equator. All of Anglo-America lies in the middle and high latitudes.

2. In the far north of the continent is the cold, treeless area called the *tundra*. Because of its climate, this "upstairs" of Anglo-America is not a desirable place to settle. The tundra stretches across northern Canada from Alaska and the Bering Sea to the Atlantic Ocean, including the island of Greenland. The winds from the Arctic Ocean blow far southward across the tundra bringing cold air to Canada and the United States.

3. South of the tundra is the *taiga*, or northern forest climate. Forests cover most of northern Canada. The climate of the northern forest land is also harsh. The cold, icy winter lasts from six to seven months a year. In the spring, the snow and ice melt. The surface of the ground thaws or "unfreezes." However, the soil underneath remains frozen so that the water stays on the surface. As a result, swamps and marshes form, making travel in the taiga almost impossible. When summer arrives the weather becomes warmer and many insects appear. The few people who live in this climate depend upon hunting, fishing and trapping for their living.

The tundra of Anglo-America is the home of the Eskimo. What is the climate of the Tundra region?

A cold, snowy winter in Vermont, which lies inside the humid-continental climate belt. What are summers like in Vermont?

4. Most of the eastern part of Anglo-America has a *humid-continental* climate. The northeastern part of the United States and the southern border of Canada have this climate. The humid-continental climate is mainly the result of two things: distance from the equator and wet winds that blow from the Atlantic Ocean. Farther north in this region the winters are cold. As you go south, the summers become warmer and longer. Westward, or inland, the winters are colder and the summers hotter because there are no large bodies of water nearby to "even" the temperature. In the central part of the United States, farthest from the effects of the ocean, temperatures may be as low as 30° below zero in winter and as high as 110° in summer. There is plenty of rainfall in the humid-continental climate. Most of the people of Anglo-America live in this climate area. They live and work in large cities for the most part. However, there are also rich farmlands devoted to corn, wheat and dairying.

5. The southeastern part of the United States has a *humid-subtropical* climate. There is a long, hot summer and a mild winter. Plenty of rain falls throughout the year. The growing season is at least seven months long. No part of Canada has a climate like the humid-subtropical section of the United States. About 25% of our people live here. The area is a rich farmland with fields of cotton, tobacco, peanuts and rice.

6. There is enough rainfall for farming westward as far as the 100° meridian. At this point the climate gradually becomes drier and the prairies or dry grasslands begin. This is the steppe zone of the North American continent. If you travel westward you will find there is less and less rainfall until you reach the deserts of the southwest, where there is almost none. The lands west of the 100° meridian are drier because of the Rocky Mountains. The Rockies stop the rain-filled winds as they blow inland from the Pacific Ocean. The rain falls on the western side of the mountains, but the eastern slopes are dry. (The Gulf Coast plains, farther south, have more rainfall because of winds that blow from the Gulf of Mexico.)

Tables of rock in Monument Valley, Arizona. Why does this region have so little rain?

7. These dry lands make up about one-third of our nation's land area, yet they contain only about 5% of our people. At one time, great herds of buffalo roamed these plains. Now they are shared by cattle and sheep herders and dry farmers. In the highlands, the few who live there work chiefly at mining and raising sheep.

8. The wettest part of Anglo-America is a section along the Pacific coast stretching from northern California to the southern tip of Alaska. This strip of coastal land gets plenty of rain throughout the year, and its winters are cool. A warm current flows along it causing warm winds to blow over the land. The coastal mountain ranges force these winds upward, where they cool and drop their moisture as rain. This is the *marine* climate area of Anglo-America. Because of the heavy rainfall, this land is rich with forests. The many inlets and rivers along its coast are good fishing grounds.

9. While northern California has a marine climate, southern California enjoys the warm, sunny *Mediterranean* climate. In southern Cal- ifornia the summers are hot and dry and the winters are mild. Nearly all rainfall takes place in the winter months. The population of California is growing rapidly, partly because the climate is so pleasant. While this climate area covers only 2% of our land, it has 7% of our people. In its irrigated valleys, all kinds of crops can be grown.

10. Hawaii is famous for its climate. Because it is surrounded by the warm waters of the Pacific Ocean, it is always warm. Summer temperatures are always near 80°, and it is never cold in the winter. Like the people of Miami, Florida, Hawaiians need not worry about having heat in their homes. In their fertile fields the farmers of Hawaii raise sugar cane, pineapples and other tropical fruits.

UNDERSTANDING CHAPTER 3

1. Which questions are answered in this chapter?
   a. Why is the Pacific Coast climate so wet?
   b. What is the tundra?
   c. Where does the Gulf Stream begin?
2. The main idea of *paragraph 6* is that:
   a. the Rockies extend a great distance from north to south.
   b. the Rockies affect rainfall in western states.
   c. wet winds blow from the Gulf of Mexico.
3. The Pacific Coast has a:
   a. marine climate.
   b. humid-subtropical climate.
   c. humid-continental climate.
4. Most of northern Canada is:
   a. taiga.   b. steppe.   c. desert.
5. The inner plains have cold winters and hot summers because they are:
   a. close to the equator.
   b. open to the winds from the Arctic.
   c. far from the effects of the oceans.
6. The western part of the Great Plains is dry because:
   a. it lies too far north.
   b. it lies near the cold Pacific currents.
   c. rain-bearing winds are blocked by mountains.
7. In *paragraph 2*, the expression " 'upstairs' of Anglo-America" refers to:
   a. northern Canada.
   b. the top of the Rocky Mountains.
   c. the winds from the Gulf of Mexico.
8. "The spring *thaw* brings floods to the mountain streams." Refer to paragraph 3. What is the best meaning of *thaw*?
   a. unexpected snows.
   b. warming of lands.
   c. frozen soil.

Map Study

Map #12—Climates of Anglo-America

Agree or Disagree Study the map carefully. Then decide whether or not each of the following statements agrees with the information on the map. If the answer is *disagree*, explain why.

1. Both the United States and Canada have an area of vertical climate.
2. The marine climate is located on the western coast of Anglo-America.
3. Large water areas of Canada are found in the tundra climate.
4. The humid-continental climate is found only in Canada.
5. The steppe is found largely west of 100° longitude.
6. The smallest climate area in Anglo-America is the Mediterranean climate.
7. The southeastern coast of the United States has a humid-subtropical climate.
8. The marine climate is found only in the high latitudes.
9. The humid-subtropical climate is found mainly north of 50° latitude.

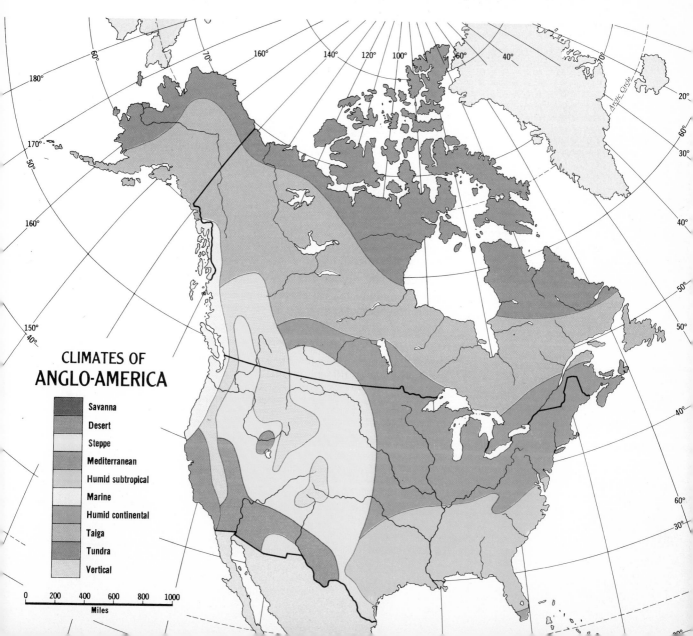

CLIMATES OF ANGLO-AMERICA

- Savanna
- Desert
- Steppe
- Mediterranean
- Humid subtropical
- Marine
- Humid continental
- Taiga
- Tundra
- Vertical

0 200 400 600 800 1000
Miles

A. Below are the names of seven climatic regions. Tell whether these regions are found in: 1) Canada only, 2) the United States only or 3) both the United States and Canada. Write "C" for Canada, "U.S." for United States or "B" for both. Do not write in this book.

tundra   Mediterranean

humid continental   taiga

desert   humid subtropical

marine

B. Match each item in Column A with one of the descriptions in Column B.

COLUMN A	COLUMN B
1. marine	a. Cold land without trees.
2. tundra	b. Wettest part of the United States.
3. Mediterranean	c. Where most people of Anglo-America live.
4. humid continental	d. Temperatures are rarely below 80°.
5. taiga	e. Region of great forests.
	f. Dry summers, mild and moist winters.

Plan a trip to one of these places in Anglo-America: Quebec, Canada; Fairbanks, Alaska; Denver, Colorado; New Orleans, Louisiana; Chicago, Illinois; Los Angeles, California. In your plan, try to include these items:
1. The season in which you would make the trip.
2. The clothes you would take.
3. The sports you would expect to play.
4. Differences in homes that you might see.
5. The best kind of travel, if you went by land.
6. The kind of climate you would find.
7. How people of that area probably make a living.
8. What products could be bought.

4 HISTORY HAS MADE US FRIENDS

Reading For A Purpose: How have we grown from colonies to free nations?

1. Tribes of Indians and Eskimos lived in Anglo-America long before white men came. The Indians lived along the great rivers, on the plains and in the woodlands. The Eskimos lived far to the north along the shores of the Arctic Ocean. As white settlers came from Europe in greater and greater numbers, they pushed the Indians off the land to a point where most Indians now live on small reservations. The Indians could not hold their hunting and farming grounds against the guns and machines of the newcomers. The Indians, however, did make many contributions to farming in Anglo-America. They gave the white man Indian corn or maize, the white potato, tobacco, beans, pumpkins, tomatoes and other foods.

2. When Columbus came to the New World in 1492, the news led other explorers to come to Anglo-America. The first European power to explore the new country was Spain. The Spanish explorer Ferdinand de Soto marched across the southeastern part of the United States in 1539. He discovered the Mississippi River. Francisco de Coronado explored the mountains, deserts and plains of our southwest in 1540. The city of St. Augustine, Florida, was founded in 1565; Santa Fe, New Mexico, was settled in 1609. The Spanish left their ways of living in these and other parts of our country.

3. French interest in the New World began in the sixteenth century. In 1524, Giovanni da Verrazano sailed under the flag of France, exploring the coast of North America. He was looking for a short route to Asia. In 1534, Jacques Cartier sailed up the St. Lawrence River, finding land that was rich in fur-bearing animals. In 1608, Samuel de Champlain founded Quebec, the first permanent French settlement in the New World. The colony was known as New France. The French explored the nearby waterways in search of furs and claimed all the lands surrounding them. In 1682, La Salle reached the mouth of the Mississippi and claimed the river valley for France.

This mission in San Antonio, Texas, stands as a reminder that the Spanish were the first Europeans to colonize the New World. What other reminders of the Spanish are there in our Southwest?

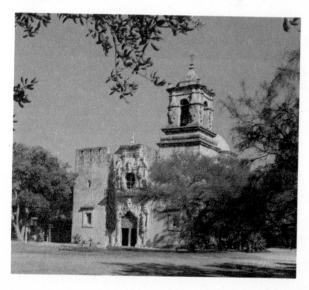

4. Only five years after Columbus' voyage, John Cabot sailed from England and explored the eastern coast of North America. British settlers came to stay in America in the early 1600's. The first settlement was made farther south along the Atlantic Coast in the present state of Virginia. The British gradually established thirteen colonies along the eastern coast of the United States. Most people in these colonies were farmers. The farms were small in the northern part of the colonies, but they were much larger in the South where tobacco was grown. In order to help work the tobacco fields, blacks were brought to the South in 1619. In 1670, the English explored the land around Hudson Bay in northern Canada. They set up trading posts . They wanted a share of the fur business as well.

5. The French built forts and trading posts along the Great Lakes and in the Ohio and Mississippi River valleys. The English colonists also wanted to settle the fertile farm lands of the Ohio Valley. Before long, there was a war between England and France over the Ohio Valley. After several years of fighting, the French were forced to give up their claim to New France, or Canada, and all the territory east of the Mississippi River. Although New France became a British colony, the French settlers were allowed to keep their own language and religion and the laws they brought from France.

6. In 1775, the thirteen American colonies began their fight for freedom from Great Britain. When they finally won, a new nation was formed, the United States of America. The Americans thought that Canada would also fight against Britain for its freedom. An American army invaded Canada for this reason but was not successful. At this time, those colonists who remained loyal to England left for Canada. The English-speaking people in Canada now began to outnumber the French.

7. There was peace between the United States and Canada until 1812. At that time some of our lawmakers accused the British in Canada of giving guns to the Indians and urging them to attack our frontier in the West. In the war that followed, the United States forces again invaded Canada, and again they were turned back. Shortly after the war ended, the United States and Canada signed a treaty. They agreed not to build any forts along the Great Lakes. Later this agreement was extended to include the entire length of the 3,900-mile border between the United States and Canada. Such trust and friendship between neighboring nations cannot be found anywhere else in the world.

8. From 1803 to 1853, the American frontier moved westward until it reached the Pacific coast. In 1803, the United States bought the Louisiana Territory from France. In 1819, Florida was acquired from Spain. Great Britain and the United States agreed in 1846 to divide the Oregon Territory at the 49th parallel. Two years later, the United States gained a large area of land in the southwest from Mexico. In 1853, the government bought a small strip of land in southern New Mexico and Arizona, the Gadsden Purchase. At that point, our westward movement was slowed by the Civil War.

9. After the Civil War, the growth of our nation continued. Everywhere men were busy building factories, railroads and bridges. Steel mills were busy trying to keep up with the demand for steel. The mills were worked by people who had come to this country from other lands. Cities grew larger as people moved to homes near their work. Factories turned out more goods. The United States began to reach beyond her borders. Alaska was bought from Russia in 1867. In 1898, as a result of war with Spain, the United States obtained colonies in the Atlantic and Pacific Oceans.

10. About that time, Great Britain decided to give more freedom to Canada. In 1867, the British government created the Dominion of Canada. This was a union of four eastern provinces—Quebec, Nova Scotia, Ontario and New Brunswick. They joined to form a new nation that had the right to govern itself. The eastern

provinces wanted Canada to reach to the Pacific coast like the United States. After a transcontinental railroad was built, more settlers began to move westward. In 1931, Great Britain allowed Canada complete self-government.

11. The United States and Canada have become fast friends. Soldiers of the two countries fought together in World War I. Canada declared war on Japan when the United States' base at Pearl Harbor was attacked in 1941 and was our strong ally throughout World War II. Both nations are members of the North Atlantic Treaty Organization (NATO) and the United Nations. Canada and the United States cooperated in building the St. Lawrence Seaway, which makes it possible for ocean-going ships to reach the Great Lakes. Both nations are also working together to keep the Anglo-American region safe from enemy attack.

The St. Lawrence Seaway alongside the St. Lawrence River near Montreal, Canada. What purpose does the seaway serve?

UNDERSTANDING CHAPTER 4

1. Which questions are answered in this chapter?
   a. Where were the early French settlements in Anglo-America?
   b. Who was John Macdonald?
   c. Why did the first Europeans come to the New World?
2. The main idea of *paragraph 9* describes:
   a. the growing demand for steel.
   b. how the United States reached the Pacific coast.
   c. the growth of the United States after the Civil War.
3. The French came to the New World in search of:
   a. furs.
   b. religious freedom.
   c. a place to build a canal from the St. Lawrence.
4. The French lost Canada as a result of:
   a. the American Revolution.
   b. a war with England.
   c. the War of 1812.
5. Why did the United States invade Canada during our war for freedom from Great Britain?
   a. We wanted to annex Canada to the United States.
   b. We wanted complete possession of the St. Lawrence River.
   c. We thought Canada would join us in our fight for freedom.

6. Canada became completely self-governing:
   a. about the same time the United States became independent.
   b. in 1931.
   c. shortly after our Civil War.
7. Another meaning for *maize* as used in paragraph 1 is:
   a. corn.   b. guns.   c. vegetables.
8. In paragraph 10, the word *transcontinental* means:
   a. long and difficult.
   b. across Canada from coast to coast.
   c. modern and western.

Picture Symbols

These pictures should help you to recall parts of the chapter you have read. What is the main idea of each picture?

SUMMING UP

In each group below are listed three events in the history of Anglo-America. Arrange the three events in each *in the order in which they took place.*

A. 1. British and French want the Ohio Valley.
   2. British gain Canada.
   3. British and French fight a war, 1756-1763.
B. 1. The United States acquires Florida.
   2. The United States obtains territory from Mexico.
   3. The United States purchases Louisiana.
C. 1. Canada gains her full freedom.
   2. The Dominion of Canada is established.
   3. The Canadian transcontinental railroad is built.
D. 1. The United States buys Alaska.
   2. The United States goes to war with Spain.
   3. The United States and Canada take part in World War II.

Using a history book or other reference work, find the answers to these questions about the history of the United States and Canada.

1. What European nations explored the east coast of both the United States and Canada?
2. Where in each country are there signs of French ways of living?
3. What ideas about government did both the United States and Canada get from Europe?
4. How did immigrants help each nation grow?
5. How did each nation grow in size? What explorers reached the west coast in each country?
6. How did both countries treat the Indians?
7. How was railroad building helpful to both countries?
8. In what other ways have these two nations cooperated, in addition to those mentioned in this chapter?

5 THE PEOPLE OF THE UNITED STATES AND CANADA

Reading For A Purpose: Who are the Anglo-Americans?

The United States has been called a "melting pot" of many different people. What is meant by this term? Do you agree that this nation is indeed a "melting pot"? Why?

1. There are now over 200 million people living in the fifty states of the United States. Our country ranks fourth in world population. While there are great cities in the Far West and in the South, most of the people live in our northeastern states. Our population is growing very fast today because the high standard of living allows us to live longer. However, our nation is not overcrowded because it is so large.

2. People have come to the United States from all over the world. These immigrants have settled throughout the entire nation. In our Pacific Coast states, there are many Chinese and Japanese. In the Southwest and in southern California, people from Mexico have come to live. In the cities of the East are large numbers of people from Puerto Rico. There are 22 million nonwhite people in the United States, most of whom are black. There are Protestants, Catholics, Jews—members of every religion.

3. For a long time most Americans lived on farms. Today most of our people (about 75%) live in towns and cities, where they can work in factories, offices and stores. This movement to the cities is called *urbanization*. It has caused many problems. There is a growing need for more housing; many cities have overcrowded slum areas. Many of our colored peoples have been crowded into poor sections of large cities because of discrimination against them in housing and jobs. Enough water must be provided for people to drink and for factories to use. There is a need for more schools. People who are out of work must have help. Much of the air in the cities is poisoned by gases that come from the thousands of autos and factories. Crime is also a serious problem of the cities.

4. The people of the United States have the highest standard of living in the world. Our people are working shorter hours, receiving higher pay and gaining better working conditions. We have more radios and television sets, refrigerators, automobiles, washing machines, telephones and other labor-saving machines than any other nation. We have a great supply of good food of all kinds. Most of our people have enough pure water. Because of our health and medical care, the average person in the United States can expect to live to be 70 years of age.

5. We have free public schools for all our people because we know that a nation governed by its people must have educated citizens. Anyone who does not understand what he is voting for cannot make wise decisions. Schooling is free so that the children of poor families can have the same opportunities as those of rich families.

6. Compared with the United States and most other nations of the world, Canada has very few people. There are slightly more than

Read

20 million people in Canada. This number is about the same as the number of people in New York State. Compare this, too, with the more than 200 million people living in the United States, which is smaller in size than Canada!

7. Most Canadians live in large cities in the southern part of the country near the border. The soil is fertile here and the climate warmer than in the rest of Canada. Aside from the land near the United States, Canada is largely a cold wilderness inhabited by a few Indians, Eskimos, fur trappers, loggers, miners and fishermen. All of the large cities of Canada are in the southern part of the country. Toronto, Montreal, Ottawa and Quebec are large cities of the St. Lawrence-Great Lakes region.

8. One-half of Canada's people are of English descent. One-third of the people of Canada are of French descent. Most French-speaking people live in the province of Quebec. Most are Roman Catholics, while the majority of the English are Protestants. The rest of the Canadian people are Indians and immigrants from different countries of Europe. The Indians live on lands set aside for them by the government. In the far north is the land of the Eskimo.

9. More Canadians work in mills and factories than on farms. Many work in mines, in the

Canadian Eskimo women share a joke. What do you think life is like for these people of the far north?

forests and on fishing boats. The manufacture of wood pulp employs the most workers. Like most Americans, most Canadian people enjoy a high standard of living.

10. Most Canadian boys and girls go to school, as in the United States. Nearly all the people enjoy the benefits of free public education. The towns and cities have large modern schools. The subjects taught are like those that a child in the United States might study. In Quebec there are two kinds of tax-supported schools: the Roman Catholic in which the children may speak French and the Protestant schools in which English is spoken. Both French and English are official languages in Canada.

UNDERSTANDING
CHAPTER 5

1. Which questions are answered in this chapter?
   a. How did the French and English come to settle Canada?
   b. What religions are practiced by the people of Anglo-America?
   c. Why is free education important to the people of Anglo-America?

2. The main idea of *paragraphs 7 through 9* describes:
   a. where Canadian people live and work.
   b. the religions of the Canadian people.
   c. the workers of northern Canada.

3. The United States and Canada are different in that there is a large:
   a. French population in the United States.
   b. Negro population in the United States.
   c. Indian population in Canada.

4. The United States has:
   a. a larger population than Canada.
   b. a smaller population than Canada.
   c. about the same population as Canada.

97

5. The majority of the people of Canada live near the United States border because:
   a. few large cities are located there.
   b. the climate is milder.
   c. the northern part of Canada has few resources.
6. Education is important to the people of the United States and Canada because:
   a. people who have come from other countries have had no education.
   b. in the past, only the rich have had education.
   c. it is necessary if the people are to run their governments wisely.
7. *Immigrants* are people who:
   a. come from other lands.
   b. work in factories.
   c. work in the government.
8. In *paragraph* 3, the word "discrimination" means:
   a. joining together.
   b. treated differently.
   c. opportunity for.

DEVELOPING IDEAS AND SKILLS

Pictograph #2—Population, Area and Standard of Living of Anglo-America

Study the pictograph. Then answer the following questions.
1. Is the standard of living in Canada high or low compared with that in the United States?
2. Is Canada more or less crowded than the United States?
3. Are the people of this region literate?
4. How long may the average Canadian expect to live?
5. What facts tell you the standard of living of the people of Canada and the U.S.?
6. How does Canada compare with the United States in size?

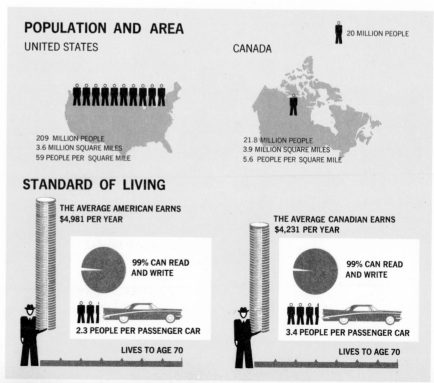

POPULATION AND AREA

UNITED STATES   CANADA   20 MILLION PEOPLE

209 MILLION PEOPLE
3.6 MILLION SQUARE MILES
59 PEOPLE PER SQUARE MILE

21.8 MILLION PEOPLE
3.9 MILLION SQUARE MILES
5.6 PEOPLE PER SQUARE MILE

STANDARD OF LIVING

THE AVERAGE AMERICAN EARNS $4,981 PER YEAR

THE AVERAGE CANADIAN EARNS $4,231 PER YEAR

99% CAN READ AND WRITE

99% CAN READ AND WRITE

2.3 PEOPLE PER PASSENGER CAR

3.4 PEOPLE PER PASSENGER CAR

LIVES TO AGE 70   LIVES TO AGE 70

We don't discover new ideas only by reading. Often ideas are to be found through maps and photographs, charts and graphs. Here is a chart. It tells us something about immigration to the United States today. See what ideas you can discover from it.

NUMBERS OF IMMIGRANTS TO THE UNITED STATES

Country of Birth	1970	1971	1972	1973
Canada	13,804	13,128	10,776	8,951
China	14,093	14,417	17,339	17,297
Cuba	16,334	21,611	20,045	24,147
Dominican Republic	10,807	12,624	10,760	13,921
Greece	16,464	15,939	11,021	10,751
India	10,114	14,310	16,926	13,124
Italy	24,973	22,137	21,427	22,151
Jamaica	15,033	14,571	13,427	9,963
Korea	9,314	14,297	18,876	22,930
Mexico	44,469	50,103	64,040	70,141
Philippines	31,203	28,471	29,376	30,799
Portugal	13,195	11,692	10,343	10,751
United Kingdom	14,158	10,787	10,078	10,638
West Germany	9,684	7,519	6,848	6,600
Yugoslavia	8,575	6,063	5,922	7,582

Source: United States Immigration and Naturalization Service. Annual Reports for the years 1970, 1971, 1972, 1973.

A. Tell whether these statements are *true* or *false*. If there is not enough information on this chart to help you decide on an answer, say *not enough information*.

1. In 1970 more immigrants came to the United States from Italy than from any other country.
2. More immigrants came to the United States from the Dominican Republic in 1972 than in 1971.
3. The number of people coming to the United States from India increased from 1970 to 1973.
4. More Canadians than Chinese came to the United States in 1970.
5. In 1972 more people came to the United States from Mexico than from Korea.
6. People are coming from Cuba because jobs are scarce in their own country.
7. More than twice as many Korean immigrants came to the United States in 1973 than in 1970.

6 TWO DEMOCRATIC GOVERNMENTS

Read

Reading For A Purpose: How are the United States and Canada governed?

Red-jacketed Canadian Mounties parade before Canada's Parliament Building in Ottawa. Which branch of our government has the same kinds of functions as the Canadian Parliament?

1. Canada is divided into ten provinces and two territories, the Northwest and the Yukon. Each province has its own government. The capital of the Canadian national government is the city of Ottawa. While our government is based on our Constitution and its amendments, Canada's form of government is based on the British North America Act of 1867 and its changes since then.

2. The laws for the people of Canada are made by Parliament. The Canadian Parliament is made up of two lawmaking houses. One of these is called the Senate and the other is the House of Commons. The House of Commons is the more powerful body. Its members serve for five years unless an election is called sooner. Their chief duty is to make laws. Members of the Senate are named for life by the prime minister. They have little power in making laws.

3. The chief officer of the Canadian government is the prime minister. The House of Commons chooses the prime minister. He is usually the leader of the political party that has the most members in the House. The prime minister selects members of his party to be his advisors, his "cabinet." Unlike an American President's cabinet, they plan most of the bills that are brought before Parliament.

4. The prime minister stays in office only so long as most of the members of the House of Commons support him. If a majority of the House votes against him, he and his cabinet must resign or leave office. He can call for a new election; then the Canadian people may vote for new representatives in the House of Commons or re-elect the same members. Most of the time the prime minister can depend on the support of Parliament. (A President of the United States cannot always count on the support of Congress to pass the laws that he wants.)

5. The courts of Canada explain and uphold the laws and protect the rights of the people. The highest court in Canada is the Supreme Court. It meets at Ottawa. Each province has its own governor and lawmaking bodies.

6. While Canada has its own government and makes its own laws, it is also a member of the British Commonwealth of Nations. The king or queen of Great Britain is also king or queen of Canada. The people of Canada are citizens of both Canada and the British Commonwealth. The Queen appoints a governor-general who represents her in Parliament. He has little power.

7. The United States is divided into fifty states. Each state has its own government. The capital of our national government is Washington, D.C. The basis for our government is the Constitution, which was written in 1787. It set up a *federal* system that divided power between the national government and the states. Unlike the Canadian government, the powers of our national government are divided among three separate branches: the legislative, the executive and the judiciary. Each branch has certain powers.

8. The President is the head of the *executive* or law-enforcing branch of the U.S. government. He is elected for a term of four years. He may be elected only twice. The executive branch enforces the laws passed by Congress. The President is commander in chief of the Army, Navy and Air Force. He may either sign or *veto* (disapprove) bills passed by Congress. He is helped in his duties by a cabinet, which he appoints. The members of the cabinet do not have to be members of Congress.

9. Congress is the *legislative* or lawmaking branch of the government. As in the Canadian Parliament, there are two houses of Congress, the Senate and the House of Representatives. There are two Senators from each state. They hold office for six years. Every two years, one-third of the Senate is elected. The House of Representatives has many more members. They are elected for two-year terms. Congress has some very important powers, such as the power to tax, the power to borrow money and the power to declare war.

The United States Capitol, where the two houses of Congress hold session. What are some of the important powers of Congress?

10. The third branch of our national government is the *judiciary*. This branch is made up of the Supreme Court and lower courts. They help explain the laws passed by Congress and protect the rights of the people. Each state also has its own lawmaking bodies and courts.

11. Both peoples, American and Canadian, believe in democracy. Our citizens have the right to choose the officials who make our countries' laws. Each citizen has the right to speak out without fear. He can worship God in a church of his own choice. His children can go to free schools. He can choose his own job and his own home. This is the opposite of a *totalitarian* government. A totalitarian government is run by a few men who control the activities of the people. Under such a government the individual is important only as he serves the state. He does not have many of the rights that we have.

UNDERSTANDING
CHAPTER 6

1. Which questions are answered in this chapter?
   a. How can our Constitution be changed?
   b. How does the Canadian government work?
   c. What are the powers of the President of the United States?
2. The main idea of this chapter describes:
   a. the powers of the prime minister.
   b. how power is divided among different branches of government.
   c. how the United States and Canada are governed by their people.

3. The head of the Canadian government is the:
    a. Queen of Great Britain.
    b. governor-general.
    c. prime minister.
4. The lawmaking branch of the Canadian government is called the:
    a. Congress.   b. Parliament.   c. Supreme Court.
5. How are the powers of the prime minister of Canada different from the powers of the President of the United States?
    a. The prime minister is the chief executive of his country.
    b. The prime minister is a member of the lawmaking body of his country.
    c. The prime minister appoints his own cabinet.
6. Why are both the United States and Canada called "democratic" countries?
    a. In neither country can the national government tax the people.
    b. In both countries the national government has little power.
    c. In both countries the people vote for the officials who make their laws.
7. Canada is divided into *provinces.* These are somewhat like our:
    a. states.   b. cities.   c. counties.
8. *Parliament* is the branch of government that:
    a. makes the laws.   b. explains the laws.   c. enforces the laws.

DEVELOPING IDEAS AND SKILLS

Pictograph #3—The Government of the United States

Study the pictograph. Then tell whether these statements are true or false.

1. Our national government is divided into three parts.
2. The President is the head of the branch that enforces the laws.
3. The President has twelve departments to help him.
4. The Senate has more members than the House of Representatives.
5. The Supreme Court is our highest court.
6. The Senate and the House of Representatives make the laws.
7. The powers of our government come from the people.
8. Matters concerning war and preparations for war are handled by the Defense Department.

Pictograph #4—The Government of Canada

Study the pictograph. Then tell whether these statements are true or false.

1. The working head of the Canadian government is the prime minister.
2. Canada's Supreme Court has more members than the Supreme Court of the U.S.
3. Both the Senate and the House of Commons share in making laws.
4. Members of the prime minister's cabinet cannot be members of Parliament.
5. Members of the Senate are probably closer to the people and their needs than members of the House of Commons.
6. The cabinet of the prime minister has fewer departments than our President's cabinet.
7. Members of the House of Commons may serve terms of less than five years.
8. Of the entire Canadian government the highest authority is the ruler of Great Britain.

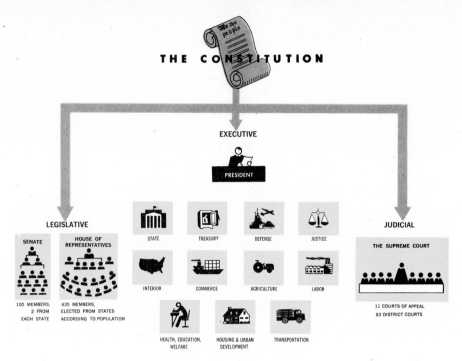

Pictograph #3—The Government of the United States

Pictograph #4—The Government of Canada

103

Fact or Opinion Read each statement carefully. If the statement is a fact, write F in your notebook. If it is an opinion, write O.

1. All nations should have the same form of government as we have in the United States.
2. The President is the head of the government of the United States.
3. Canada should not continue as a member of the British Commonwealth.
4. The Canadian system of electing the prime minister is better than our method of electing the President.
5. The Canadian governor-general has less power than the prime minister.
6. Only people who are able to read and write should be allowed to vote.
7. The powers of our national government are divided among three separate branches.
8. The provinces of Canada and the states of the United States have the power to make their own laws.

Complete the following chart in your notebook.

	UNITED STATES	CANADA

1. Chief Executive
  a. Term of office
  b. How he is chosen
  c. How cabinet is chosen		

2. Lawmaking Body
  a. Houses
  b. How chosen		

3. Highest court		
4. Capital	Ottawa	WASHINGTON D.C

7 SOURCES OF OUR STRENGTH

Reading For A Purpose: How did the United States become an industrial leader of the world?

The world's largest open-pit copper mine at Bingham, Utah. Copper is one of the world's most valuable metals. What uses for copper can you name?

1. About 160 years ago, the United States was a country of farms, villages and towns. Most Americans were farmers living in small cabins. The whole family worked hard all day to provide the things that were needed. Today the United States is a leading industrial nation of the world. The American people have the highest standard of living in the world. Let us look at some of the reasons for this change.

2. First, we have many raw materials for industry, such as minerals and forest lands. The United States is first in the production of such minerals as copper, lead and sulphur and second in iron ore. Our greatest sources of iron ore are the open-pit mines of the Mesabi Range, near Lake Superior in Minnesota. This ore is easy to remove because it is near the surface of the earth. Alabama and Michigan are other iron-ore-producing states. But we use so much iron that we must import more from Canada, Venezuela and Sweden as well.

3. The United States produces about a fourth of the world's copper. Major copper mines are in Arizona, New Mexico, Utah and Montana. Lead, zinc, gold and silver are found in the Rocky Mountains. Most of our sulphur comes from two southern states, Texas and Louisiana. We also have large quantities of phosphate and potash, useful in making fertilizer. The United States is the world's leading manufacturer of aluminum. This modern metal is made from an ore called bauxite. Some of the bauxite we need is mined in Arkansas and Georgia. Most of it is imported from the South American countries of Surinam (Dutch Guiana), Guyana and Venezuela.

4. Those who live in our great cities may not realize just how much of the United States is still covered with forests. When America was settled, its great forests were cut down as the need for farm land grew. Wood was used for homes, ships and furniture. Despite this rapid removal, forests still cover almost a third of the country! Our richest forest lands are found in the Pacific Northwest, the South and New England. Most of the wood is used to make paper, plastics, furniture and houses. We use so much lumber for these products, however, that we must import more from our northern neighbor, Canada.

5. Second, the United States has many resources that provide power for its machines: coal, oil, natural gas and falling water. The United States produces more coal than any other nation. Most of our coal is mined in the Appalachian Mountains of Pennsylvania, Ohio, West Virginia and Kentucky. Coal is used to

heat homes and to supply power for factories. It is used to smelt iron ore in the manufacture of steel. The leading nations of the world are those that are able to make large amounts of steel products.

This oil field, near Wilmington, California, has produced millions of barrels of crude oil. What happens to oil after it is taken from the ground?

6. Our chief source of power is oil. The United States has long led the rest of the world in oil production. About a fifth of the world's oil comes from the United States. This oil is found mainly in Texas, California, Oklahoma and Louisiana. Oil must be treated after it comes from the ground in order to remove the impurities in it. This process is called refining. One of the products of refining is gasoline. Gasoline is used, of course, to power automobiles, trucks and airplanes. Diesel locomotives, which pull our long freight trains, are fueled with oil. In spite of our great supply, we need more than we produce in our own country. We import oil from Venezuela and the Middle

East to make up the difference.

7. From the oil fields also comes our great supply of natural gas. When this gas first appeared along with the oil, it was wasted. Now, however, giant pipelines bring the gas from the southwestern states all the way to the northern and eastern parts of the country. Homes in Chicago and New York are heated with natural gas that comes from thousands of miles away.

8. The first factories in our nation were run by the waterfalls of New England. Since that time we have built dams on our leading rivers in order to make greater use of the power of falling water to make electricity. (The invention of turbines and generators has made it possible.) The TVA (Tennessee Valley Authority) has built a series of dams on the Tennessee River to provide electricity for people in seven states. The great Hoover Dam on the Colorado River has brought electric power to western states. On the Columbia River, the Grand Coulee and Bonneville Dams produce electricity for the farmers of the Northwest. The Niagara Falls Power Project is just one of the many hydroelectric plants throughout the country that provide light and heat for our great cities.

9. Since World War II, another source of power has been developed. This is the atom. Atomic energy comes from a mineral called uranium. The United States has been a leader in the development of atomic energy. The United States now has ships and submarines that use atomic power instead of oil, gasoline or electricity. These ships can travel for months without coming into port for refueling. Industries are now trying to find ways to use atomic power in manufacturing. We can expect that in the future our cities will be lighted and heated with power from the atom. This new source of energy will make our industrial strength even greater.

10. A third reason for our industrial leadership is the American people. They are the people who have invented our machines and have

shown us how to make good use of our resources. They are the people who have provided money to build factories, buy machinery and start new businesses. They are the skillful men and women who work in the factories, in mines and on the farms to turn out the goods we need. They are the ones who build and run our system of railroads, airlines and highways and make it possible to distribute our raw materials and finished goods. Lastly, they are all of us who buy the goods that are sold in our stores and supermarkets and thus keep our industries going.

The gigantic man-made wall of Hoover Dam holds back the waters of the fast-flowing Colorado River. How else has this dam helped the people of the western states?

UNDERSTANDING
CHAPTER 7

1. Which questions are answered in this chapter?
   a. How is iron made into steel?
   b. What are our most important minerals?
   c. Where are our great water power projects?
2. The main idea of *paragraphs 6 through 9* describes:
   a. the importance of water power.
   b. the widespread use of oil and oil products.
   c. our great power resources.
3. Our greatest source of iron ore is found in the:
   a. Mesabi Range.
   b. Appalachian Mountains.
   c. Rocky Mountains.
4. The United States leads the world in the production of:
   a. tin.   b. coal.   c. bauxite.
5. Our great oil fields are located largely in the:
   a. Northeast.   b. Southwest.   c. Southeast.
6. The United States is a leading steel-manufacturing nation because:
   a. coal and iron ore are found near each other in this country.
   b. we produce more coal than any other nation.
   c. we had an early start in the use of water power.
7. Our water resources are useful because:
   a. they are a source of power for homes, farms and factories.

107

b. they are a source of floods.

c. they are a source of atomic energy.

8. When oil is *refined*:

   a. it is made into plastics.

   b. impurities are removed.

   c. it is used as fuel.

9. A *turbine* uses the power of falling water to make:

   a. ice.　　　　　　　　b. steam power.　　　　　　　　c. electric power.

DEVELOPING IDEAS AND SKILLS

Map Study

Map #13—Iron, Coal and Oil Resources of the United States

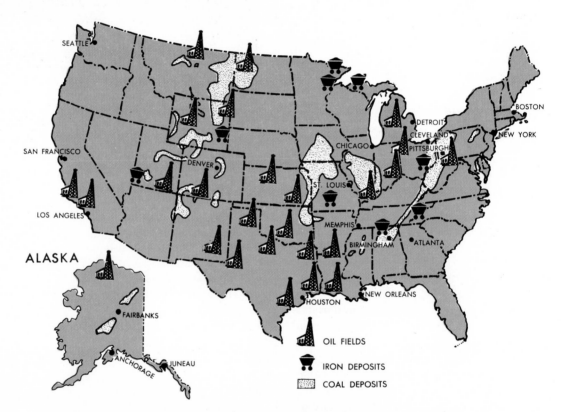

Study the map. Then tell whether these statements are *true* or *false*.

1. The largest deposits of iron ore are found near the Great Lakes.
2. The chief coal fields are east of the Mississippi River.
3. The largest oil fields are in the Southwest.
4. There are no oil fields on the West Coast.
5. Coal is found in almost every state in the union.
6. Texas has large reserves of both iron and oil.
7. Iron deposits are found in the Southeast.
8. Many coal fields are found in mountain regions.
9. Most of the large cities are near mineral resources.

SUMMING UP Complete the following outline in your notebook. Enter *three* topics under each of the headings.

How the United States Became a Leading Industrial Nation

A. The United States has great natural resources.
B. Our sources of power are highly developed.
C. Human resources are our great strength.

FOLLOW UP Tell whether these statements are true or false. The underlined words make the statements true or false. If a statement is false, what words would you place in it to make it true?

1. Our leading gold and silver mines are located in the Appalachian Mountains.
2. Aluminum is made from an ore called bauxite.
3. Oil must be smelted to get gasoline.
4. Giant hydroelectric plants have been built along the Tennessee River.
5. The United States imports much wood and wood products from France.
6. Most of our coal is mined in the western highlands.
7. Our chief source of power is oil.
8. Iron ore and coal are most important in manufacturing steel.
9. Our greatest iron ore pits are found in the state of Pennsylvania.
10. Arizona is a leading state in the production of copper.

8 GETTING AND SPENDING

Reading For A Purpose: How do we satisfy our needs and wants? How is our economic life organized?

1. Raw materials, much power and skilled workers are needed for manufacturing. But these alone would not make the United States the leading industrial nation of the world. With only 6% of the world's people and 7% of the world's resources, we produce more goods and make greater use of our resources than any other people in the world. We believe this is caused by our way of making and selling goods to satisfy needs and wants. Our way of doing this is called *capitalism* or *free enterprise.*

2. Under capitalism the land, mines, factories and resources of the nation are owned by individuals—not by the government. They are *private property.* The person who owns property uses it as he sees fit, provided he does not interfere with the rights of others. He may buy any goods he wants. He may sell any goods he produces. The prices he pays for the goods, and the prices at which he sells the goods, are decided by agreements he makes with other persons. The government does not tell him the cost of the goods he uses.

3. The American people have a *freedom of choice* in the kinds of work they want to do. A person may run his own business or work for another person. He may try to become a doctor, a lawyer, a plumber or a carpenter. The choice is his to make. He can quit his job, and he does not have to give any reason for doing so. This freedom to choose one's life work is not found everywhere in the world.

4. Capitalism is a way of life in which a person runs a business or a shop with the idea of making a *profit.* Workers in a capitalist system try to get the most money for their labor. Owners of land and buildings try to get the best rentals. Businessmen try to sell their products for more than the cost to produce or obtain them. Americans believe that the desire to make a profit encourages people to work hard, to invent better methods of doing many kinds of work and to discover new products that people will buy.

5. When many people are working to make the same goods, *competition* is the result. For example, many factories make the same kind of product. Each manufacturer wishes to sell his product. These factories are in competition with each other. Americans believe that competition results in goods of high quality and low price. (The manufacturer who makes radios and sells them at a higher price than other manufacturers ask will not sell many radios. Either he must take less profit or he must learn how to make them at a lower cost. This helps the people who buy products.) Manufacturers *advertise* their goods because they want people to buy them. Our radio, television and billboard advertising are all attempts by manufacturers to sell their products. Advertising is necessary to the capitalist system.

6. Capitalism also depends upon *mass production*. This is a method that makes use of the *assembly line, division of labor* and *standardized parts.* Let us look at a modern automobile factory to see how mass production works. A line or belt runs from one end of the building to the other. At the beginning of this line are the frames of cars. The line is moving. As each car moves along, new parts are added to it by the workers. By the time the car reaches the end of the line, it has been put together or "assembled." Each worker along the assembly line has a separate job to do. This is called "division of labor," since the work is "divided up" among workers. In mass production the parts for a particular model of car are exactly alike for each car. These are called standardized parts. Today, most factories use the methods of mass production to make all kinds of goods. It is the fastest and cheapest way to make many things.

7. Because of mass production, America's workers are paid more than those in any other country. For example, if a worker is paid $40 a day for an eight-hour day and turns out a hundred items, he is actually a cheaper worker than one from West Germany who is paid $20 a day and turns out forty items. In the first case the cost of each item is 40¢; in the second case it is 50¢. American workers turn out more and cheaper goods because of their skill and their greater use of machines. Because they are paid higher wages, they are able to buy more goods.

Assembly line work in a Ford Motor Company plant. How does the assembly line system operate? What are its advantages? Disadvantages?

8. Capitalism has also succeeded because of government help to different groups. From the beginning our government placed a tariff or tax on goods brought into the country. There are no taxes, however, on goods moving from one state to another. As a result there is a free flow of goods from one part of the nation to another. In the nineteenth century, the government encouraged railroad building. The government makes sure that all agreements or contracts are kept. In recent years, farmers have been paid to control their crop production. The government protects the rights of workers to join labor unions in which they can fight for better wages and working conditions.

9. At the same time the government has passed laws that affect the practices of industry. Laws have been passed to protect the American people from unsafe foods and medicines. The government has passed laws to end children's working in factories and to establish a basic level of wages. The communications industries such as radio, movies and television are carefully watched for fairness and decency. In this sense, free enterprise is not as "free" as one might think. It is not free to harm the people living under it.

10. As you can see, there is no one reason for our country's becoming the greatest manufacturing country in the world. We have a rich store of natural resources, power, skillful and inventive people and a vast system of transportation. All of these are brought together through capitalism. Americans believe this system to be the best in the world. Other peoples may not think so. They may think their system is better. We must learn to understand one another's choices. We will see that each nation's system grows out of its geography, history and its people's hopes for the future.

UNDERSTANDING CHAPTER 8

1. Which questions are answered in this chapter?
   a. What is mass production?
   b. How is planning carried out in the United States?
   c. What is meant by "freedom of choice"?
2. The main idea of this chapter describes:
   a. how capitalism works.
   b. how resources have made our nation strong.
   c. the freedoms that Americans have.
3. Our workers are able to turn out many goods because of the greater use of:
   a. machinery.
   b. atomic energy.
   c. hand labor.
4. Goods flow freely from one state to another because of:
   a. government planning.
   b. lack of tariffs.
   c. airlines.
5. Our workers receive high wages because they:
   a. are highly skilled.
   b. have private property.
   c. hope to make a profit.
6. Mass production is important because:
   a. more goods are now made at home.

b. new minerals have been discovered.

c. more goods are produced at lower prices.

7. Another example of *competition* as described in paragraph 5 would be:

a. actors preparing to put on a play.

b. two basketball teams playing against each other.

c. workers doing different jobs on an assembly line.

8. Under *capitalism* there is:

a. private profit and competition.

b. government control over prices of goods.

c. control over manufactured products by the government.

<table>
<tr><td>DEVELOPING
IDEAS AND
SKILLS</td><td>

Pictograph #5—The Flow of Money and Goods Through Free Enterprise

Study the pictograph. Then answer the following questions.

1. In this pictograph, people are receiving money as wages from government and business. The people must then give part of the money to the government. This is called paying ‾‾‾‾‾‾

2. What government services do we receive in exchange for the money we pay the government?

3. What private services can we buy with our money?

4. Businesses make goods that people want. How do the people obtain these goods?

5. What part do banks play in helping businesses and stores?

6. Where do banks get their money?

</td></tr>
</table>

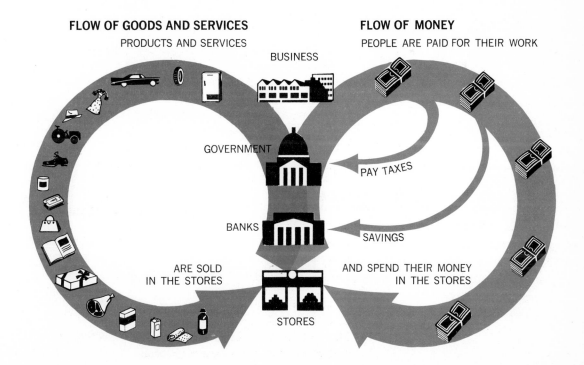

FLOW OF GOODS AND SERVICES
PRODUCTS AND SERVICES

FLOW OF MONEY
PEOPLE ARE PAID FOR THEIR WORK

BUSINESS

GOVERNMENT

PAY TAXES

BANKS

SAVINGS

ARE SOLD
IN THE STORES

AND SPEND THEIR MONEY
IN THE STORES

STORES

Pictograph #6—The United States and the World

Study the pictograph. Then tell whether these statements are true or false.
1. The United States has about half of the world's land area.
2. The United States has less than 10% of the world's people.
3. The United States produces more automobiles than the rest of the world.
4. The United States produces twice the amount of oil that the rest of the world does.
5. The United States has as much coal as all other countries in the world combined.
6. The United States has less than half of the possible electric power in the world.
7. The United States is a nation of both farms and factories.
8. For size, the United States has a small share of the world's resources.

THE UNITED STATES AND THE WORLD

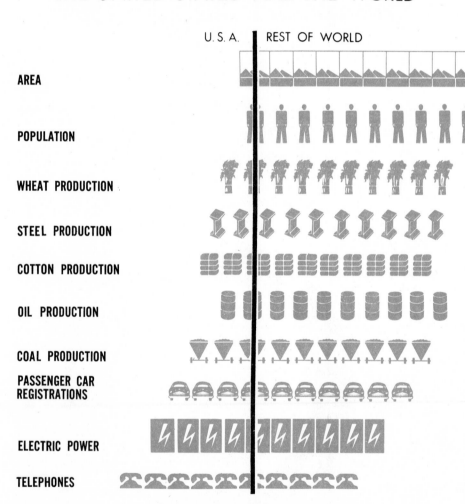

EACH SYMBOL EQUALS 10% OF TOTAL

Making Inferences In our reading, many facts are given to us. From these facts we can draw conclusions. The following are some conclusions or inferences that you might make after reading this chapter. Tell whether these conclusions are correct or incorrect. Give reasons for your answers.

1. A storekeeper may keep his workers from joining a union.
2. There is one chief reason why the United States has the greatest factory system in the world.
3. Any person may start a factory on his property if he wants to do so.
4. Nearly all of our soap products are made by one large company.
5. The United States has a small share of the world's resources, but it has made greater use of its resources than any other nation.
6. The government cannot keep a person from becoming a doctor if he wants to be a doctor.
7. Freedom of choice does not always exist in a totalitarian society.
8. Many inventions are the result of a person's desire to make a profit.

9 OUR FACTORY CITIES

Reading For A Purpose: Where are the great manufacturing areas of the United States?

1. As you have learned, an industrial region is an area in which many people make their living by manufacturing or turning raw materials into useful goods. The largest and most important manufacturing area in the United States—and in the world—is in the Northeast. This area reaches from Illinois to the Atlantic coast. In it are some of the largest coal mines in the world. In nearby Minnesota are the world's greatest iron mines. Throughout this area are supplies of coal and falling water for power. In addition, oil and natural gas are easily obtained from the Southwest.

2. The manufacturing region of the Northeast has excellent transportation facilities. The area is crisscrossed by highways, railroads, rivers, canals and lakes. (More than half the railroad track in the country is in the Northeast.

The Great Lakes–St. Lawrence Seaway and the Ohio and Mississippi Rivers are heavily used water highways.) Boats, barges and freight trains carry raw materials from mines to factories. Motor trucks, trains and riverboats carry the products of farms and factories to the cities and towns.

3. For all these reasons, there are both "heavy" industries and "light" industries in this area. (Iron and steel mills, auto and other factories that turn out heavy goods are known as "heavy" industries. Industries in which the products are light and not bulky are known as "light" industries.) The products of the factories in this region are almost endless: farm machinery and children's toys, railroad cars and finished clothing, ocean-going ships and pocket-sized cameras.

4. The largest cities in the United States are located in the Northeast. There are always reasons why a city grows up in a certain place; it does not happen by accident. The cities in the Northeast are of different kinds. Some are mining towns, some are factory cities or trading cities, some are capital cities and some are so large that they have many purposes. A few of the great industrial cities in the Northeast are New York, Chicago, Detroit, Cleveland and Pittsburgh. Farther south is Baltimore, while to the west is St. Louis.

5. New York is the largest city in the nation. It has the busiest harbor in the world. Because of its location on the Atlantic Ocean it has long been the best place to bring in goods from many parts of the world. From New York the products are carried to all parts of the nation by river, railroad or airplane. In addition to its being a trading center, New York is a leading factory center. The chief industries in New York are printing and the manufacture of clothing and leather goods.

6. In the Northeast, Pittsburgh, Chicago and Cleveland are leaders in the making of steel. Pittsburgh, where the Ohio River begins, is the greatest iron and steel center in North America. Most of its iron ore comes from Minnesota

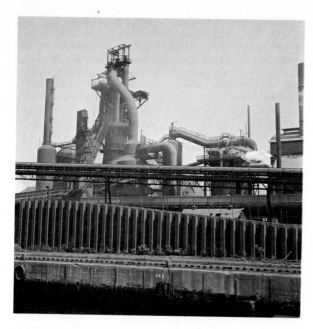

These blast furnaces in Cleveland, Ohio, produce ton after ton of steel. What parts of the country provide the coal and iron ore used to make steel?

by huge ore boats and rail; coal is mined close by in the Appalachian highlands and is brought by river barges to the mills of Pittsburgh. The Chicago-Gary area, located on Lake Michigan, is another great iron and steel center. Iron ore and coal are brought to these cities over the Great Lakes. Because it is near the corn, wheat and cattle regions, Chicago is also a leader in flour milling and meat packing. From that city, grain, livestock and farm machinery are sent (usually by railroad) to all parts of the nation.

7. Cleveland, on Lake Erie, is a heavy steel producer. More iron ore is brought into Cleveland each year than into any other city in the world. Its coal comes from the Appalachians. Baltimore, on Chesapeake Bay, has one of the largest harbors in the world. The Appalachians supply the coal, but iron ore is imported. Baltimore is the only seacoast center that is also a leader in iron and steel manufacture. Detroit is

the "auto city." It makes about half the cars of the entire world! Detroit is located on the Detroit River, which is part of the Great Lakes waterways. Heavy materials like coal, iron and steel can be moved cheaply to Detroit by water.

8. Another important industrial region in the United States is in the South. The South has many advantages for industry. It has cheap water power, plenty of workers and large supplies of minerals such as coal, iron and oil. For a long time, there have been iron and steel mills in Alabama. Birmingham, Alabama, is sometimes called the "Pittsburgh of the South" because coal, iron and limestone for making steel are found nearby. There are also many new textile factories that turn the raw cotton of the South into ready-to-wear clothing. Many articles are also made of rayon, a silk-like fiber made from cotton and wood pulp. There is a growing number of chemical plants, oil refineries and other factories around the Gulf Coast. The chief cities in this area are Houston and New Orleans. Cotton, oil, rice and sugar cane are among the many products shipped from the port of New Orleans. Along its docks can

A Baytown, Texas, oil refinery. The oil storage tanks look like pill boxes arranged in neat rows. The tall shafts, like upright cigarettes, are refining towers. In what ways do you and your family depend on oil products?

be found banana and coffee boats from Latin America and oil tankers from the Middle East.

9. The western region of the United States, between the 100th meridian and the Rocky Mountains, is large in area but has few people because it is so dry. Since mining and cattle and sheep grazing are the chief occupations, there are few cities of great size. Denver, Colorado, at the foot of the Rocky Mountains, is the largest city in the area. Because of the ways people make a living near this city, Denver's industries include flour milling, meat packing and the manufacture of mining equipment and tools.

10. When we think of California we think of the movies. Hollywood, a section of Los Angeles, is the center of the American motion-picture industry. However, aircraft factories and oil refineries are also located in Los Angeles. California is now the third largest oil-producing state. Farther north is the port of San Francisco. This city with its famous bay is a leading port for trade with Asia.

11. In the states of Oregon and Washington, forests provide the raw materials for paper manufacture. Fish canneries are found in many cities there and in northern California. Seattle is the leading seaport of the Pacific Northwest. This city is closer than any other large port to the Far East and Alaska.

UNDERSTANDING CHAPTER 9

1. Which questions are answered in this chapter?
   a. Why is the northeastern United States important?
   b. How have we wasted our resources?
   c. Why are industries found in certain places?
2. The main idea of this chapter describes:
   a. the resources of the Northeast.
   b. how goods are carried from place to place in the United States.
   c. our great manufacturing centers.
3. The most important manufacturing area in the United States is located in the:
   a. Far West.   b. South.   c. Northeast.
4. The most important industry in the United States is:
   a. the manufacture of iron and steel products.
   b. meat packing.
   c. the manufacture of clothing.
5. The Northeast is an important manufacturing area because:
   a. it is near the Pacific trade routes.
   b. it has large deposits of coal, iron and limestone.
   c. this is the leading oil and natural gas area of the nation.

DEVELOPING IDEAS AND SKILLS

Map Study

Map #14—The Northeast: The Leading Industrial Region of the United States

Study the map on page 119. Then tell whether these statements are true or false.

1. Almost every northeastern state has an important industrial area.

2. One area extends from Massachusetts all the way to Baltimore.
3. Pittsburgh and Wheeling are both steel cities.
4. Auto industry is centered around Philadelphia and Baltimore.
5. Waterways are close to the big industrial areas.
6. Textile manufacturing is most important near Chicago.

Can you answer these questions?
1. Why is machinery manufactured near Cleveland and Chicago?
2. Where are meat-packing plants located in the Northeast? Do you know why they are located there?
3. Where are the centers of the chemical industry?

Map #14—The Northeast: The Leading Industrial Region of the United States

FOLLOW UP   In Unit 1, we learned that the natural environment plays a large part in deciding where and how people live. But people can also change the natural environment. The giant St. Lawrence Seaway, built jointly by the United States and Canada, is one example of such a change. The following two articles discuss other ways in which people have changed their environment to improve their lives.

> **AIR-COOLED HOUSTON RUNS**
> **AND GROWS ON OIL**
>
> Houston, June 3. "The heat is so severe in the middle of the day that most of us just lie in the shade and pant," Ashbel Smith, Houston's first doctor, wrote in a letter 132 years ago.

Since then, Houston has learned to live with one of the most brutal climates in the world. Often the temperature and humidity are both at 90 before mid-day. The answer is air-conditioning. Texans say that Houston has enough air-conditioners to cool off hell.

Almost all cars are air-conditioned. If you want a car without it, you must have a special order in Houston. Houstonians prefer to drive to work rather than stand in the heat and wait for buses. The result is a million cars, most being driven at breakneck speed.

No one knows how many air-conditioners there are in Houston. But there must be several million. Homes, offices, schools, shopping malls—the Astrodome—all are air-conditioned. More than 1,100 Houston businesses depend upon air-conditioning sales and service. In the Houston telephone book, the list of air-conditioning contractors, repairmen and stores takes up more than 25 pages.

Refreshed by all the refrigerated air, the almost 2 million Texans who live in and around Houston are busy building what they feel will be the greatest city in the world.

The New York Times, June 4, 1971. © 1971 by The New York Times Company. Adapted by permission.

WHAT? OKLAHOMA A "COASTAL" STATE?
Reprinted from *U.S. News & World Report.*

TULSA, Oklahoma. This inland city is now, for all practical purposes, a "seaport" for ocean-borne cargo.

And the predictions are wholesale that a just-completed navigable waterway which made it possible is going to change a lot of things in a vast area from the Mississippi River to the Rockies.

The waterway is the Arkansas Navigation Project, built over the last 12 years by the U.S. Army Corps of Engineers at a cost of 1.2 billion dollars.

Running a total of 440 miles, the channel—on which cargo-laden barges are now moving the full length—extends from the Mississippi across Arkansas to the outskirts of Tulsa. It links the Arkansas and Oklahoma cities of Fort Smith, Little Rock, Muskogee and Tulsa with 11 other states and gives them access to the sea through New Orleans. . . .

. . . Lakes created by the construction of the waterway and parks along its banks provide recreation for millions each year.

Four dams on the Arkansas River and six on its tributaries will generate electric power. The 10 power plants will produce more than 3 billion kilowatt-hours of electricity—enough to supply the annual needs of a million persons. . . .

> ... The Army Corps of Engineers estimates that the present channel will move 13.2 million tons of cargo annually once the river ports are fully developed. This is more freight than is handled by such river ports as St. Louis, Memphis or Pittsburgh.
>
> Cargo on the waterway is expected to consist primarily of petroleum products, iron and steel, coal, fertilizer, wheat and other agricultural products. . . .
>
> ... Of course, deep-water vessels cannot enter the channel. But most traffic capable of moving on the Mississippi can be accommodated on the new waterway, which boasts a minimum depth of 9 feet. . . .
>
> *U.S. News & World Report*, February 22, 1971.
> Copyright 1971 U.S. News & World Report, Inc.

Which of the following statements are true? In each case, give a reason.

1. Without modern technology, Houston might not be the booming area it is today.
2. Tulsa's population will probably increase in the next ten years.
3. Business and trade are likely to increase in the cities of Little Rock, Fort Smith and Muskogee.
4. People have not been able to solve the problem of living and working in warm climates.
5. People can do little to change their surroundings in the present day.
6. As people discover new ways of changing their surroundings, new and different kind of jobs will be created.

Answer these questions.

1. What other places and other ways do you know of in which people have made great changes in their natural environment? Have there been such changes where you live?
2. It is said that the solution to any problem creates new problems. What new problems may be created by the new inland waterway from Tulsa to the Mississippi? By air conditioning in Houston?

10 THE AMERICAN FARMER

Reading For A Purpose: How are the farmlands of the Northeast and South used?

1. As you know, the United States is so large that the climate and land are not the same in all parts of the country. As a result, there are different farming regions. A farming region does not have a definite boundary like a state. The change from one kind of farming to another is gradual. Because of the differences in climate and soil, there are different ways of living and different farm products.

2. The United States has four main crop-producing regions: the Central Plains, the Great Plains, the southern coastal plains, and the valleys of the Pacific coast. The Central Plains are among the finest farm lands of the world. Many valuable crops are grown in this region. Food from these farms helps to feed people in the United States and in other parts of the world. Some farmers grow wheat; some grow corn; others raise dairy cows.

3. In the eastern part of the Central Plains the chief crop is corn. This is because the growing season is hot and moist. The soil is black and fertile. The almost flat land makes it easy for farmers to use machines to plant, cultivate and harvest their crops. The corn belt extends through the states of Indiana, Illinois, Iowa and parts of Ohio, Missouri, Kansas, Nebraska, South Dakota and Minnesota.

4. The farmer does not sell most of his corn. He feeds it to his animals—hogs and beef cattle. Then he sells the animals. The farmer uses his corn as feed because he expects to make more money from the sale of the meat than from the sale of the corn. Many of the beef cattle may not have been raised on the farms of the Central Plains. They probably came from the grasslands farther west. On the western ranches the cattle feed on grass which makes them grow large and strong. Then they are shipped to the corn belt for fattening. Wheat, oats, soybeans and alfalfa are often grown along with or rotated with the corn. (By rotating his crops, the farmer keeps the minerals in the soil.)

5. In the western part of the Central Plains is the great wheat belt. Here there is less rainfall. The wheat-growing region is divided into two parts. In the southern part of the wheat belt, winters are not so cold as they are nearer Canada. Wheat is planted in the fall, stays in the ground all winter and is harvested in July. This is called winter wheat. Kansas is the center of the winter-wheat belt. In the northern part the winters are very cold. Wheat is planted in the spring and it grows all summer long. This is the spring-wheat belt. The farmlands of North Dakota and Minnesota and the wheat farms of Canada north of these states form the greatest spring-wheat area in the world. Wheat farms are much larger than the farms of the corn belt. Farm machinery can be used easily. This is *extensive* farming—farming with machines on a large scale. The United

States is second only to the Soviet Union in wheat-growing.

6. Across the northern states, from Minnesota to New England, is a belt of dairy farms. The growing season here is short and cool. This cool, wet climate is good for growing hay. Farmers in this area keep herds of cattle and feed them the hay. As a result, milk, cheese, cream and butter are leading dairy products. Wisconsin alone produces half the cheese in the United States! Large cities in the northeastern states are a giant market for the products of dairy-belt farms.

7. The second of the great farming regions is found along the Atlantic and Gulf Coastal Plain. In the northern part of the Atlantic Plain the soils are rocky and sandy. This has made farming difficult. The early settlers turned to fishing, trading and shipbuilding to make a living. Today New England farmers grow fruit and raise dairy cattle. In the southern part of the plain the days are warmer and the growing season is longer. In the early history of our nation, tobacco, cotton and rice were the chief crops of the southern plain. Tobacco and cotton are still the leading farm crops of the South today.

8. The cotton belt reaches from the Carolinas west to the coastal lowlands of Texas. Cot-

A Texas farmer irrigates young cotton plants. Why is it important to rotate cotton with other crops?

123

ton is our nation's most valuable cash crop. The best-known cotton farms are the large plantations along the lower Mississippi River Valley and the plains of Texas. Along these lands there is plenty of rain and sunshine, and the soil is fertile. The leading cotton-growing state is Texas. Mississippi and Arkansas rank behind Texas in the South. (California, using irrigated lands, is the second leading cotton-growing state.)

9. For a long time, the large cotton farms of the South were worked by tenant farmers and *sharecroppers.* A tenant farmer paid rent for the use of the land. A sharecropper, however, gave a share of his crops as rent to the owner of the land. The sharecroppers were both white and Negro. Under this system, the land was used year after year for the same crop so that the soil "wore out." Nutrients or minerals used up by the cotton were not replaced. This meant a smaller harvest and poorer crop each year. As a result, southern farmers had the lowest income among farmers in our country.

10. Today most of the large cotton farms are worked by people who receive wages as in a factory. Large machines such as the "cotton-picker" are used in the fields. The plantation owner uses more fertilizer and plants fewer acres of cotton. In addition to cotton he may plant corn, soybeans, peanuts or other crops. He may also use some of his land as pasture for beef cattle. All these things keep his soil from "wearing out"; they put back the precious minerals so that the land can continue to be used.

11. Southern farmers are learning that they should not depend upon one crop for sale. With one crop, a bad harvest or low market price can bring ruin to a farmer. If he grows more than one crop, his chances for making money are better. Thus, along the hot, rainy coastal lands of Texas and Louisiana, rice and sugar cane are being raised. Tobacco, an important crop since 1619, is still a leading crop in North Carolina, Kentucky and Virginia. Like the cotton plant, tobacco wears out the soil. Therefore, peanuts are often rotated with tobacco. In Florida and southern Texas, large amounts of citrus fruits—oranges, grapefruit and lemons—are raised. With the coming of frozen foods and refrigerated railway cars and trucks, it is now possible to ship the produce of the South to markets thousands of miles away.

UNDERSTANDING CHAPTER 10

1. Which questions are answered in this chapter?
   a. How is cotton grown?
   b. How is southern farming changing?
   c. How is corn used by the farmers of the Midwest?
2. The main idea of *paragraph 5* describes:
   a. the winter-wheat areas of the United States.
   b. extensive farming in the United States.
   c. the wheat belt of the United States.
3. The leading farm crop of the South is:
   a. peanuts.   b. cotton.   c. citrus fruit.
4. The leading crops of the inner plains are:
   a. rice and soybeans.
   b. corn and wheat.
   c. potatoes and sugar beets.
5. Corn is raised on the Central Plains because:
   a. there is a warm and moist growing season.
   b. it is the chief food of the American people.
   c. money is made from the sale of corn oil.

6. Different kinds of wheat are grown in the Central Plains because:
   a. land is more fertile than it is in the South.
   b. factories that supply machinery are found in the cities of the plains.
   c. there are differences in climate.
7. A farmer who depends on *extensive farming* will:
   a. grow one crop.
   b. raise crops and animals.
   c. use a great deal of machinery.
8. *Citrus fruits* include:
   a. pears and apples.
   b. oranges and grapefruits.
   c. peaches and strawberries.
9. In *paragraph 11* a sentence states, "Therefore, peanuts are often rotated with tobacco." This sentence means that:
   a. peanuts are planted among the tobacco plants.
   b. peanuts are planted in place of tobacco.
   c. peanuts are planted some years, tobacco in other years.

SUMMING UP   Complete the following chart in your notebook.

Central Plains			*Southland*
	Climate		
	Chief Crops		
	Methods of		
	Farming		
	Other Products		

FOLLOW UP   Great changes have occurred in farming methods since the early settlers first cleared away the forests to plant their crops. Farming today is rapidly becoming a "big business" in the United States. The following news article will help you to understand this change.

American Farms, Fewer and Bigger

To many Americans, a farmer is a man with a pitchfork in hand, standing in front of a white house, with a red barn in the background. But farming hasn't been like this for years in the United States. No farmer could carry his fruits and vegetables to market, wrap them all in cellophane or quick-freeze them on little trays so that millions of city folks can eat, and watch TV at the same time.

125

Today's farm is as mechanized as a factory. It is just as likely to be run by a corporation as by an individual farmer. In fact, there are fewer and fewer farmers and more and more large corporations in farming today. In 1969, there were about 3 million farms in the United States, each averaging about 360 acres.

One-fifth of all farm output was produced under a contract with individual farmers in 1970. Under this system, a feed manufacturer, for example, makes a contract with a chicken farmer. The farmer agrees to raise chickens according to the manufacturer's plan. The manufacturer often supplies both the feed and the chicks. The farmer is given a fixed price for his chickens. Most of the nation's chicken farmers have signed contracts with one of the twenty or so big corporations that deal in poultry.

One company, claiming to be the world's largest producer of fruits and vegetables, owns or rents over 100,000 acres of land. It also controls thousands of other acres through its contracts with farmers. This company owns 14 can companies, an ocean terminal and processing plants in the United States and overseas. This is an example of the corporation in farming. It grows, harvests, processes, transports and sells its own products.

Adapted from Frank Jackman, "American Farms, Fewer and Bigger," *New York News*, April 7, 1972.

1. The main idea of the selection is that:
   a. Americans eat more poultry than people of any other country.
   b. farming today is a big business.
   c. small farmers specialize in growing one product.
2. Large businesses:
   a. may pay a farmer not to raise a certain crop.
   b. may control production of food from growing to selling.
   c. cannot make money in farm products.
3. *Processing* food means:
   a. preparing and packaging it for sale.
   b. gathering it from farms to ship to cities.
   c. taking it to stores for sale.
4. Now that farming has become in many instances a "big business," what problems do you suppose are presented to the thousands of small farmers in this country?

11 THE GOLDEN WEST

Reading For A Purpose: How is farming done on the dry and sunny lands?

A potato field in bloom in an irrigated field in Idaho. Where does the water come from?

1. West of the 100th meridian (Central Plains) are the dry grasslands or steppes. Most of the area receives between ten and twenty inches of rain each year. Some parts receive more rainfall than others. The eastern part of the steppes is known as the Great Plains. It extends north and south through the United States and into Canada. On the western edge of the Great Plains lie the Rocky Mountains. Not too many people live in this region because of its dry climate.

2. Since it has so little rainfall, most of the Great Plains is better suited to grazing than farming. Huge herds of cattle roam the Great Plains. The land has been fenced off into ranches. The largest ranches are found in the southern part of the Great Plains. Texas is the leading cattle-raising state. There, cowboys care for the large cattle herds.

3. There are a few farmers on the Great Plains. The farms are scattered throughout the area. The farmers draw water from rivers and streams that flow from the Rocky Mountains— the Colorado, Arkansas and Platte. The government has built dams along these rivers to hold the water back. Many canals carry water from these reservoirs to the fields. The chief crops grown on these irrigated lands are alfalfa, wheat, sugar beets, vegetables and fruits. The United States is one of the world's leading producers of sugar beets. The Idaho potato is also grown on irrigated land.

4. West of the Great Plains are the drier lands of the Colorado Plateau and the Great Basin, west of the Rockies. This is sheep-raising country. In fact, there are more sheep than people in Montana, Wyoming and Utah! Sheep can get along without much water for long periods of time. Because sheep have "split" lips, they can eat the shorter grasses and shrubs that grow there. Sheep ranches in the highlands are very large because the animals must roam over a larger area in order to find enough to eat.

5. Farther north is the Columbia Plateau. This is a grazing and farming area. Herds of sheep and cattle graze on the grasslands. There are also farmers who raise their crops by two methods: dry farming and irrigation. The dry farmer plants crops that can be raised with little rainfall. He lets some of his fields lie *fallow* (not planted) every year. The farmer waits a year or two before planting a new crop. During the time that a field is fallow, the rain that falls is stored in the ground. Dry farmers usually plant wheat and alfalfa.

6. The fourth great farming region is the coastal area of the Pacific. Because of the different climates, there are two main farming areas, the valleys of California and the rainy lands of Oregon and Washington. In the coastal valleys of southern California the sum-

mers are long, hot and sunny. The winters are mild and rainy. Much of the soil is fertile and many different kinds of crops can be raised. In many places the land is easy to cultivate with machinery because it is almost flat. California has two important farming sections: the Great or Central Valley in the central part of the state and the coastal valleys, mostly in the south.

7. The Great Valley forms an oval 450 miles long. This valley has become one of the richest farming areas in the world. Valley farms get their water from streams rising in the Sierra Mountains. These streams have been dammed. The valley farmers raise almost every crop known in the United States: citrus fruits, nuts,

A vineyard in the Napa Valley near San Francisco. The grapes may be dried to make raisins, or crushed and fermented to make wine. Many people who pick grapes are "migratory workers." Why have they been given this name?

vegetables, grains and cotton. Some farmers specialize in growing grapes that are dried to make raisins.

8. The Imperial Valley in the southernmost part of California was once a desert. It gets practically no rain. However, irrigation from the Colorado River has made it a rich farming land. A great variety of crops is grown here: lettuce, alfalfa, cotton, dates and grapes for wine. A large part of the oranges and lemons eaten in the nation comes from the valleys southeast of Los Angeles. Beets are another product of the irrigated valleys of California.

9. While there are many small farms, most of the fruit is grown on large farms with 1,000 or more acres. They are like "factories in the field." In the past, workers have come from other parts of the nation and from Mexico to help during the busy season. In the winter, these workers may pick lettuce in the Imperial Valley near the Mexican border. In the summer, they may move northward to pick oranges on the ranches near Los Angeles. From there they travel farther north and by fall are returning southward again for the cotton harvest in the Central Valley. The workers take their families with them. The families usually live in a camp set up for them near the farms where they find work. The children have very little schooling because the family is always on the move. These people are called *migratory workers.*

10. Farther north along the Pacific coast are the marine lands of Oregon and Washington. While much of the land is covered with mountains and forests, there are fertile farming areas. The cool, rainy climate is good for growing apples and berries and raising dairy cattle. Grains and vegetables are also grown.

11. Some 2,000 miles across the Pacific, the farmers of Hawaii produce two main crops: sugar cane and pineapples. These crops are grown on plantations. The climate is warm all year round and there is plenty of rainfall. Most of the pineapples we eat come from our fiftieth state, Hawaii.

1. Which questions are answered in this chapter?
   a. Where are cattle and sheep raised?
   b. How are our dry lands used?
   c. Why are cattle branded?
2. The main idea of *paragraph 9* describes:
   a. the life of California families.
   b. cotton-picking in the Central Valley.
   c. the migratory workers of California.
3. The Great Plains are best suited for:
   a. farming.   b. grazing.   c. lumbering.
4. Most of the crops on California's large fruit farms are picked by:
   a. sharecroppers.
   b. migratory workers.
   c. students.
5. The Central Valley of California is important because:
   a. desert soils were made fertile through irrigation.
   b. a large part of our citrus fruits is raised there.
   c. berry-growing has given work to thousands of people.
6. The cattle ranches of the West are large because:
   a. much machinery is used in harvesting crops.
   b. cattle need large areas of land in order to find enough grass to eat.
   c. fences keep cattle from roaming over the plains.
7. A *dry farmer* worries about the problem of:
   a. building terraces on hillsides.
   b. using his animals as a source of labor.
   c. storing water in the soil.
8. A *migratory worker*:
   a. owns his own fruit farm.
   b. moves from ranch to ranch.
   c. works the land for a share of the crops he raises.

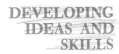

DEVELOPING
IDEAS AND
SKILLS

Map Study

Map #15—Agricultural Regions of the United States

Study the map on page 130. Then tell whether these statements are true or false.
   1. Irrigation is carried out chiefly in the western part of the United States.
   2. The New England states are shown to be a great farming region.
   3. Grazing is found in the drier areas of the United States.
   4. Cotton growing is found largely in the southern states.
   5. Most of the land in the United States is suited for growing corn.
   6. Spring wheat is grown in a cooler climate than winter wheat.
   7. Cattle are raised chiefly in the western part of the country.
   8. Cotton is the only important crop of the southern states.
   9. Fruits are important only in the western United States.
   10. Dairy farming is located near the area of large cities.

AGRICULTURAL REGIONS

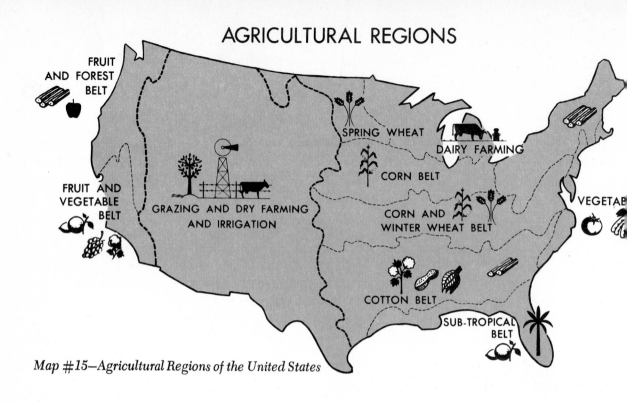

Map #15—Agricultural Regions of the United States

SUMMING UP   Complete the following chart in your notebooks.

Dry Grasslands		California Valleys
	Climate	
	Occupations	
	Farming Methods	
	Source of Water	
	Crops	

FOLLOW UP   *Farming Regions*   Tell whether these statements are true or false. The under-lined words make the statements true or false. If a statement is false, what words would you place in it to make it true? (Refer to Chapters 10 and 11 for your answers.)

1. Texas is the leading cattle-raising state in the United States.
2. <u>Cotton</u> is grown on irrigated lands of California.
3. Many workers in the valleys of California have traveled from <u>Canada</u> for the harvesting season.
4. North Dakota is in the heart of the <u>winter-wheat</u> belt.
5. The <u>United States</u> grows more wheat than any other country in the world.
6. Most of the corn grown in the corn belt is used for <u>feeding animals</u>.
7. The dairy belt lies <u>south</u> of the corn belt.
8. Sharecroppers are workers in the <u>cotton</u> fields of the South.
9. Citrus fruits are raised in Florida, California and <u>Arkansas</u>.
10. <u>Sugar beets</u> are a crop grown on irrigated land in the West.

12 TRADE, AT HOME AND ABROAD

Reading For A Purpose: Why is trade important to the people of an industrial nation?

1. In our society, we do not live by our own work alone. The farmer in North Dakota harvests his wheat with a reaper made in Chicago, Illinois. The rancher in Texas wears a shirt made from Alabama cotton and perhaps manufactured in New York City. The miner in West Virginia takes his family for a drive in an automobile from Detroit, Michigan. We all depend on others in different parts of the country for things we need and want.

2. For example, most of our oil is found in Oklahoma, Texas, the Gulf Coast and California. Coal is mined chiefly in Pennsylvania, West Virginia, Kentucky and Ohio. Iron is taken from the open pits of Minnesota and copper from the mines of Montana. Yet all of these products—in fact, all our products—go to people across the nation who need them.

3. Each section of our country exchanges its riches with another. Millions of North Americans live in cities; they work in factories or stores or provide needed services for other people living there. These people turn the raw materials of our farms, mines and forests into thousands of useful products. The materials for these are supplied by others who work close to our natural resources—the farmer, miner, lumberman, rancher and fisherman. Likewise, those people who make their living far from the city depend on the products and services of city workers. This is called *interdependence.* Our vast, swift system of transportation makes this exchange of goods possible.

4. The exchange of goods is called *trade.* Trade takes place when people produce more goods than they need so that they have some left over to sell. Other people buy goods they need from those who have them to sell. People who use the goods that are grown or made are called *consumers.* (You are a consumer. So are your parents, your friends and everyone else who has ever bought and used anything.) The process by which goods are sent from producer to consumer is not a simple one. When you buy a cotton shirt, many people are involved. The product passes from the cotton grower and picker to the baler, shipper, designer, manufacturer, salesman, wholesaler and retail store. And these are only a few of the stops on its journey from raw material to consumer product.

5. Not only is there trade between sections of our nation, but there is also an exchange of goods among nations. Trade with other nations —foreign trade—has several causes. First of all, no nation—not even the United States or the Soviet Union—has all the goods it needs. (We have little tin, for example. We must get this important mineral from countries that mine it.) Second, some countries have the right climate or soil to raise one kind of crop: coffee in Brazil, pepper in Malaysia, and so on. It is cheaper for us to import these products than it is for us to try to grow them ourselves.

The harbor in Toronto, Canada. The streetcars being loaded onto this vessel are bound for Egypt. Why do nations find it necessary to trade with one another?

6. Third, people of different nations have developed different skills. The people of Switzerland are famous for making fine watches. They sell their valuable product for goods they cannot get in their own small, mountainous country. Japan, famous for its cameras, toys and instruments, does the same. Fourth, some countries are able to produce more than they need. For example, our farmers grow more wheat and cotton than the people of this nation use. We sell these products abroad. By selling our extra cotton and wheat, we obtain money to buy goods that we need. (When we say that *we* are buying and selling goods, we mean that individual persons or companies are trading, not our national government. Only in countries where there is no free enterprise, such as the Soviet Union, does the government do the actual buying and selling.)

7. The foreign trade of a nation is measured by the amount of its imports (goods bought from other nations) and exports (goods sold to other nations). The United States is the largest trading nation in the world, followed by West Germany and Great Britain. The greatest amount of world trade is carried on between nations that are industrialized, because people in underdeveloped lands have little money with which to buy. They also have few goods to sell. Therefore, much of our trade is with Canada and the nations of Western Europe. However, we do carry on trade with some underdeveloped areas because they have products we need—tin from Southeast Asia and Bolivia, palm oil from Nigeria, cacao from Ghana.

8. The endless flow of materials and finished goods from one part of the world to another is one of the striking features of our modern world. The needs of any one group in our nation can set in motion businesses, mines and plantations in far corners of the earth. And, as our advances in science increase, the needs of people change. The discovery of how to make nylon almost ended our purchase of silk from Japan. As we have found greater uses for oil, gas and electricity in our daily lives, the coal industry has suffered.

9. Since trade affects our lives in so many ways, it is important that the flow of goods continue without difficulty during a war or when people are not able to buy goods offered

for sale. A revolution or change in the government in a foreign country can affect business there. Since our nation is the world's largest seller of goods, we want people to be able to buy them—the more the better. This is another reason why we wish to help improve the living conditions of the people in underdeveloped nations of the world. Through trade, all people work for each other to achieve a better way of living.

UNDERSTANDING
CHAPTER 12

1. Which questions are answered in this chapter?
   a. How does each section of the country help all our people?
   b. How does transportation affect trade?
   c. What will stop trade among peoples?
2. The main idea of *paragraph 5* is that:
   a. the United States must get tin from other countries.
   b. coffee cannot be grown in the United States.
   c. nations trade with each other because they cannot produce all the things they need.
3. Most of our trade is carried on with:
   a. underdeveloped nations.
   b. other industrial countries.
   c. people who make a living by hunting and fishing.
4. Goods that are sent out of the country are called:
   a. exports.   b. imports.   c. free-trade articles.
5. People trade with each other because they:
   a. like to travel to different places.
   b. have more of some goods than they need and not enough of others.
   c. help to develop new products.
6. Trade is important to a nation because it:
   a. helps poor nations to receive goods from richer nations.
   b. provides the nation with goods that it cannot always produce.
   c. makes wars and revolutions less likely to happen.
7. Which of the following best gives the meaning of *interdependence?*
   a. A farmer depends upon good soil and rainfall.
   b. An underdeveloped nation needs help from an industrial country.
   c. People in each section of our country depend upon people in many other sections.
8. *Consumers* are people who:
   a. produce goods.
   b. use goods.
   c. transport goods.

DEVELOPING
IDEAS AND
SKILLS

Pictograph #7—Foreign Trade of the United States

On the next page you'll find a pictograph and a list of statements about it. In your notebook, write the numerals 1 through 10. Beside each numeral, write T if the statement bearing that numeral is true. Write F if it is false. Write N if no information is given for that statement.

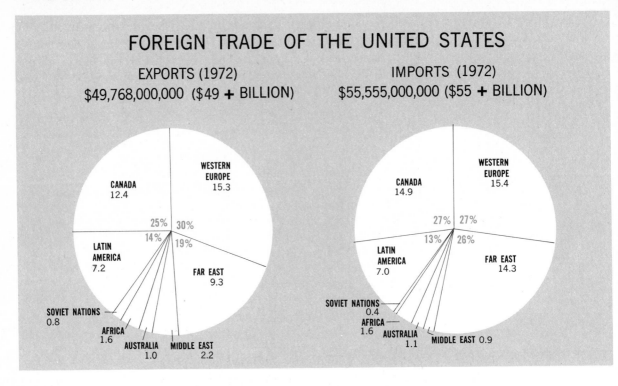

FOREIGN TRADE OF THE UNITED STATES

EXPORTS (1972)
$49,768,000,000 ($49 **+** BILLION)

IMPORTS (1972)
$55,555,000,000 ($55 **+** BILLION)

1. Exports of the United States are greater than its imports.
2. The Soviet nations rank lowest of all regions in trade with the United States.
3. We sell more goods to Western Europe than we buy.
4. People of the Middle East have little money to buy our products.
5. We have a larger trade with Canada than with all of Latin America.
6. More than half our imports come from Canada and Latin America.
7. Our trade with Africa makes up a very small part of our total trade.
8. We probably buy more goods from Great Britain than we do from West Germany.
9. These graphs show us how our trade has grown in the past twenty years.
10. Our trade with the Far East is more than $17 billion a year.

SUMMING UP *Fact or Opinion* Read each statement carefully. If the statement is a fact, write F in your notebook. If it is an opinion, write O.

1. Our country should place taxes or tariffs on all goods coming into the country that are cheaper than American-made goods.
2. No nation has all the goods it needs.
3. The standard of living of the American people depends upon its trade with other countries.
4. The work of scientists often results in the discovery of new products.
5. The United States should trade only with the countries of North and South America.

6. Our nation would have more friends if we bought more goods and sold fewer goods.
7. People of "low-income" countries are the poorest customers for trade.
8. The person who manufactures is the most important person in the process of producing goods for the consumer.
9. One of the important parts of trade is good transportation.
10. It is cheaper for us to buy some products than to try to grow or make them ourselves.

FOLLOW UP

I. If you live in a port city, visit the port and see all the activities of people working there. If you do not live near a port, you might visit a factory that sends goods out of your community. As part of your visit, try to find out the following:
   a. Which goods are shipped to foreign countries?
   b. Where do the raw materials for them come from?
   c. How are the raw materials brought to your community? How are the finished products sent out?
   d. Where are the factory products shipped?

II. Look at a mail-order catalog in which goods from foreign lands are advertised. Make your own catalog of goods from other countries: a Japanese camera, French perfume, German binoculars, and English china, for example.
   a. Why are Americans interested in buying these goods?
   b. Why are some foreign-made goods cheaper than our own?
   c. Why are these products sold here?
   d. Which products are the result of special skills by people in a foreign land?

13 THE RESOURCES OF CANADA

Reading For A Purpose: What are Canada's resources?

1. Like the United States, Canada is rich in natural resources. Minerals are the most valuable of her gifts from nature. Canada supplies most of the world's nickel and asbestos. Iron ore, cobalt, lead, zinc, copper, gold, silver, potash and platinum are other riches of Canadian mines. The discovery of large deposits of uranium has made Canada a leading producer of this valuable ore. Coal, oil and natural gas are also plentiful. Many of these minerals have been found in the Canadian or Laurentian Shield, once thought to be a wasteland.

2. Canada leads the world in the production of asbestos. This is a mineral that is made up of fibers. These fibers can be woven into many materials. Asbestos has one important quality —it is fireproof. Therefore, it is used in firemen's suits and in shingles for homes.

3. Before World War II, Canada produced little iron ore. Afterward, valuable iron ore deposits were found near the Quebec-Labrador border. The ore there is easy to mine but at first was not easy to bring to the cities. Then a railroad was cut through the wilderness. The ore can now be taken to distant industrial centers. Another rich source of iron is located near the northern shore of Lake Superior. The discovery of iron in Canada is important to the United States. There is danger that our own iron reserves may one day be used up. Rich supplies of this mineral in Canada mean that the United States will be able to import iron ore from its neighbor.

4. Canada has many power resources. The most important source of power is falling water. Most of its industries (such as aluminum and paper) are run by hydroelectric power. Water power projects on the St. Lawrence River supply electricity to the nearby parts of Canada and the United States. In 1964, the United States and Canada reached an agreement for building dams on the Columbia River. This project is to provide electricity for new factories in British Columbia, Washington, Montana and Oregon.

5. Two other important sources of power are petroleum and natural gas. Canada once had to import oil. Now the nation exports it. Discoveries of oil in the Alberta province have made the oil industry in Canada important. Research is still going on to find more sources of oil. Where there is oil, there is usually natural gas. Giant pipelines now carry gas and oil to many parts of the country.

6. Although there are large coal fields in Canada, only a few of the nation's factories use coal. Much of the coal is not very good. Then, too, the coal mines are located far from Canada's mills and factories. Because many of Canada's industries are near the coal fields of the United States, it is often cheaper for Canada to import coal than to mine it.

7. Canada's other resources include the three

"F's"—fish, forests and furs. Canada's Atlantic and Pacific coastal waters are among the world's best fishing grounds. The Grand Banks, off the coast of Newfoundland, are the world's richest source of fish. Fishing boats from many nations of Europe use these waters, catching as many fish as the Canadian fishermen do. Cod, herring and lobster are the chief fish of the Atlantic waters. On the west coast, salmon fishing is most important. Canada's many inland lakes and streams provide a large supply of freshwater fish. Canada's fisheries provide food not only for its own people, but for the people of other countries as well, through export.

8. A great belt of forest land stretches across Canada from the Atlantic to the Pacific. Over half of Canada's land is covered with forest. All ten provinces have forest regions. The most valuable product of the forests is wood pulp, from which paper is made. Nearly all the wood pulp is exported, and the largest buyer is the United States. The western province of British Columbia is the home of the tall Douglas fir.

9. Canada was first settled as a fur-trading colony. Fur-bearing animals are still a valuable resource. But fur-trapping is not so important as it was two hundred years ago. Mink, fox,

On the western coast, trucks are the chief means for hauling timber from the forests. What products are made from timber?

beaver, ermine and other fur-bearing animals are still plentiful in the northern woods. However, many of these animals are now raised more easily on fur farms.

10. Canada is now one of the few industrial nations of the world, even though it has a small population. Its industries draw materials from the nation's mines, forests and fisheries. The greatest industrial region of Canada is found in the provinces of Quebec and Ontario,

Toronto, on Lake Ontario. Why has this city become a chief trading and industrial center of Canada?

A Saint John, New Brunswick, paper mill. Why is the mill so close to the water?

near the Great Lakes and the St. Lawrence River. Industries are located here for the same reasons as in the United States. Minerals are brought from the Canadian Shield; the nearby Great Lakes and St. Lawrence are useful for transportation; sources of water power are available; and there is a large market for selling goods. Most of the large Canadian cities are found here.

11. Pulp and paper manufacture is Canada's leading industry. The industry depends upon rivers and streams to carry the logs to mills and to furnish power to run the factory machines. It uses about a third of all the electrical power produced in Canada. Another of Canada's major industries is aluminum production. Only the United States manufactures more aluminum products. One reason for Canada's importance in aluminum is its large supply of water power. Canada imports bauxite ore from Latin America and manufactures the aluminum near the sources of water power.

UNDERSTANDING CHAPTER 13

1. Which questions are answered in this chapter?
   a. Why are Canada's forests important?
   b. How is paper made?
   c. Where are Canada's sources of water power?
2. The main idea of *paragraph 10* is that:
   a. Canada is a leading industrial nation of the world.
   b. Canada has excellent water transportation.
   c. mines, forests and waters feed Canada's industries.
3. Canada's most important source of power for industry is:
   a. coal.   b. water power.   c. wood.
4. Canada's storehouse of minerals is located in the:
   a. St. Lawrence River Valley.
   b. western highlands.
   c. Canadian Shield.
5. Canada's forests are important as a source of:
   a. wood pulp.   b. rubber.   c. asbestos.
6. Canada imports coal because:
   a. much Canadian coal is not of the highest grade.
   b. there is no coal in Canada.
   c. its coal mines are found in the frozen north.

7. *Bauxite* is the ore used in producing:
    a. copper wiring.
    b. aluminum.
    c. fireproof clothing.

Map Study

Map #16—The Resources of Canada

Study the map. Then tell whether these statements are true or false.
1. Canada has few mineral resources, except for coal and iron ore.
2. Much of Canada's industry is located in the northern part of the country.
3. Large cities are grouped together near the St. Lawrence Valley.
4. Canada has many forest resources.
5. Little use is made of Canadian lumber.
6. Most of Canada's mineral wealth is found in the far north.
7. A fishing industry is located on both the eastern and western coasts.
8. Wheat-growing is important on the western plains.
9. Wheat fields and oil fields are located in widely separated parts of Canada.
10. Asbestos is found chiefly near Quebec.

SUMMING UP

Do You Agree or Disagree?   Give the reasons for your answers.

1. One of Canada's problems is that there are few places where it can sell its manufactured goods.

2. The publishing industry in the United States would suffer if it could not get materials from Canada.
3. Canada and the United States have helped each other to improve power resources.
4. Canada has several mineral resources that the United States needs.
5. Furs are Canada's most important forest product.

FOLLOW UP   Tell whether the following items refer to the United States, Canada or both countries. If the item applies to the United States only, use the letters "US"; if the item applies to Canada only, use the letter "C"; if the item applies to both the United States and Canada, use the letter "B."

1. Large area and large population.
2. Great use of coal as power for industry.
3. Large aluminum industry.
4. Fur-bearing animals plentiful in the northern forest.
5. Leading producer of asbestos.
6. Imports large amounts of wood pulp.
7. Resources of oil and iron ore.
8. World's largest producer of nickel.
9. Industrial area near the Great Lakes-St. Lawrence River.
10. Power projects along the St. Lawrence and Columbia Rivers.

14 COMPARING FARMING IN THE UNITED STATES AND CANADA

A dairy farm in the St. Lawrence lowlands. Why is so little of Canada's land useful for farming?

Reading For A Purpose: In what ways are the farms of Anglo-America alike?

1. Only a small part of Canada is useful for farming or grazing. In the north, forest and tundra cover more than half the land. Along the western coast is a chain of high mountains and plateaus as in the United States. Most of the Canadian Shield is too rocky or hilly to be farmed. (As the glaciers moved southward they scraped away the fertile topsoil.) In many parts of Canada the growing season is too short for raising most crops. Except for the Pacific coast, the farming land of Canada is within a few hundred miles of the United States border.

2. The western plains are Canada's richest farming region. These plains are an extension of the Great Plains of the western United States. The good soil, summer rains and dry harvest season are good for wheat. The farmers of the plains use machines to cut and thresh their crop. Canada is the fourth largest producer of wheat. Farther west, Canadians also graze cattle and sheep on the dry prairies.

3. The other important farming area of Canada is the lowland of the Great Lakes in southern Ontario. The winds from the lakes make it warm enough to grow hay, oats, potatoes and various fruits. Dairy farms provide milk, cream and cheese here and along the St. Lawrence River. Since this is the region of the greatest population in Canada, the dairy products find a good market in the cities of the lowlands.

4. Although only a small part of Canada is useful for farming, Canada is one of the world's great food-producing countries. As you remember, Canada's population is small. Canadian farmers grow much more food than the people need. Therefore, they export the sur-

Harvesting wheat in Canada. Why is Canada a leading exporter of wheat?

141

plus to other parts of the world. For example, Canada leads the world in exporting wheat.

5. What are some of the conclusions we can reach regarding farming in both countries of Anglo-America? In the United States there are vast areas of fertile farm land. The farming area is much smaller in Canada. Nevertheless, both countries raise more than their people need. Both countries are large exporters of food.

6. The farms in both countries vary in size from very small to very large. Most of the farmers own their own land. These farmers live in farmhouses in the middle of their fields. They do not live together in small villages as farmers do in many other parts of the world.

7. In both countries the farmers make great use of machinery, fertilizer, good seed and the latest farming methods. The great use of machinery has made it possible for fewer workers on a farm to turn out larger crops. Since World War II, science has helped farmers to grow larger and better crops. Without adding to the amount of their land, the farmers of Anglo-America have almost doubled the amount of food they are able to produce. Because the need for farm workers is not so great now,

many have left the farms to work in cities.

8. Most farms in the United States and Canada are *commercial* farms, or farms that raise a *cash* crop—a crop for sale. This means that our farmers produce enough for their own needs and still more to be sold in markets in Anglo-America and throughout the world. Many farms specialize—that is, they depend upon one main cash crop. Others raise a variety of vegetables, fruits and grains.

9. Where land is too dry for farming, as on the dry plains, rivers have been dammed to provide water for irrigation. These dams store water until it is needed. A *reservoir* is formed. To get the stored water to the farms, many miles of canals have been built. The sheep and cattle industry is carried on in both nations on the drier lands of the West.

10. Because of the great size of the United States and Canada, a variety of crops is grown. Yet there are a number of crops that cannot be grown in Anglo-America because of its northerly location. These are the tropical crops such as bananas, coffee, cocoa, rubber, spices and tropical vegetable oils. Such crops are imported by the United States and Canada from other nations all over the world.

UNDERSTANDING
CHAPTER 14

1. Which questions are answered in this chapter?
   a. Why is only a small part of Canada used for farming?
   b. How are Anglo-American farms alike?
   c. Where are apricots grown in Canada?
2. The main idea of *paragraphs 1 through 4* describes:
   a. the farming regions of Canada.
   b. wheat farming on the plains.
   c. the growing seasons of Canada.
3. Canada's chief farm crop is:
   a. potatoes.   b. rice.   c. wheat.
4. Canada's chief farming areas are located:
   a. in the western highlands.
   b. on the plains of the Pacific coast.
   c. on the plains of the southern border.
5. Only a small part of Canada can be used for farming because:
   a. most of the land is forest and tundra.
   b. mining is a more important industry.
   c. the government controls the use of land.

6. Canada is a leading exporter of food because:
   a. its people have a low standard of living.
   b. much of the land is used for farming.
   c. Canadian farms grow more food than its people need.
7. When we say that a farmer *specializes*, we mean that he:
   a. raises one main crop.
   b. divides his land among several crops.
   c. uses machinery at harvest time.
8. A *reservoir* is used for:
   a. storing food for farm animals.
   b. storing water.
   c. storing wheat once it has been cut.
9. A *commercial* farm, as mentioned in paragraph 8, is one that:
   a. is probably a wheat farm.
   b. raises a crop for sale.
   c. raises what is needed for the farmer and his family.

SUMMING UP

Write the numerals 1—10 in your notebook. After each numeral, write either *Many, Much, Some* or *Few* to make that numbered statement correct.

1. ———— land in Canada is not suited for farming.
2. ———— farms in Anglo-America are small in size.
3. ———— wheat farms in Anglo-America use modern machinery.
4. ———— people of Canada are farmers.
5. ———— wheat grown in Canada is exported.
6. ———— bananas eaten by the people of Anglo-America are imported.
7. ———— Anglo-American farmers have learned to irrigate dry land for farming.
8. ———— Anglo-American farmers raise a cash crop.
9. ———— Canadian farmers raise corn.
10. ———— Canadian farms are close to the United States.

FOLLOW UP

Read the statements in the chart below. Then check the correct column in your notebook:

WHY ANGLO-AMERICAN FARMERS ARE SO PRODUCTIVE	YES	NO
1. Extensive use is made of machinery.		
2. Farm plots are very small.		
3. Great use is made of fertilizer.		
4. Most farm lands belong to a few people.		
5. There are large areas of level, fertile soil.		
6. There are no areas of desert.		
7. Rivers are dammed to provide irrigation.		
8. Everything is planned by the government.		
9. Farmers make use of scientific discoveries.		
10. All kinds of fruits can be raised.		

15 NORTH AMERICAN PARTNERS

Reading For A Purpose: How do the United States and Canada work together and help each other?

1. You have studied many things about the two giant nations of Anglo-America. To make sure that we understand the many ways in which the United States and Canada are alike, let us review the things they have in common.

2. Great Britain was the mother country of both nations. As a result, English is spoken throughout the United States and in most of Canada.

3. Both peoples believe in democratic government. The citizens of each country have the right to elect representatives to make the laws that govern each country. Both believe in such rights as freedom of speech, assembly and religion.

4. Both countries are rich in natural resources. Among the most important are oil, iron ore, coal and falling water. These have been used to make the two nations of Anglo-America leading industrial nations. Much of the work in factories, farms and homes is done by machines.

5. Both peoples, American and Canadian, have a high standard of living. The food, clothing, shelter and general way of life of the peoples of both countries are very much alike. If you were to meet a Canadian for the first time, you probably could not tell him apart from an American.

6. The two countries are tied together by great transportation systems. Autos, trains, trucks and planes travel back and forth freely between Canada and the United States. The good transportation system of Anglo-America makes it possible to exchange many products. The United States imports wood pulp, nickel, uranium, asbestos and fish from Canada. Canada buys farm machinery, fertilizers, textiles, chemicals and household machinery from the United States. More than half of Canada's imports come from the United States. Almost 2/3 of its exports go to the United States.

7. The people of the United States and Canada use their resources to help each other. In 1959, the two countries opened the St. Lawrence Seaway. This made it possible for ocean-going ships to reach ports on the Great Lakes. The St. Lawrence Power Dam provides more electric power than any other plant in the world. In 1964, both countries signed an agreement to use the Columbia River for flood control and electric power.

8. Both the United States and Canada are interested in the Arctic region. A polar map will show you that the shortest route from northern Europe and Asia lies across the frozen north. With modern planes it is no longer necessary to travel around the North Pole. Now we can fly over it. As a result, the two nations have cooperated in building strings of radar stations across Canada. These stations will give the Anglo-American nations

an early warning in the event of an air attack from across the Arctic.

9. While there are many things that we have in common, there are some ways in which the two countries are different. For example, Canada is a large country, but it does not have many people. Therefore, it is not able to raise large sums of money. Many of its industries were started with the help of American money. Because of these investments, Americans now own large parts of Canadian industry. Canadians cannot be pleased that so much of their industry is owned by Americans rather than by Canadians. Because of this ownership, a great deal of money leaves Canada and goes to the United States. Canadians do not like to see this money leave their country.

10. There have been some disagreements, too, over foreign policies. Both nations are members of the North Atlantic Treaty Organization (NATO). But the United States and Canada do not always agree on ways to deal with other nations. Canada began selling food to communist nations some years before the United States opened up trade with communist countries.

Americans and Canadians work together to build the St. Lawrence Seaway. Why is cooperation such as this important to both the United States and Canada?

1. Which questions are answered in this chapter?
   a. Why are both Anglo-American nations interested in the Arctic?
   b. What products do both countries lack?
   c. How are both countries sharing their resources?
2. The main idea of *paragraphs 1 through 6* describes:
   a. ways in which Canada and the United States are alike.
   b. what makes an industrial nation.
   c. the standard of living in Anglo-America.
3. Canada trades chiefly with:
   a. Latin America.
   b. The United States.
   c. Japan.
4. In 1959, Canada and the United States opened the:
   a. Missouri River Valley Project.
   b. World's Fair.
   c. St. Lawrence Seaway.
5. Both Canada and the United States are interested in the Arctic region because it:
   a. has many minerals.
   b. is the shortest route to Asia.
   c. is rich in fur-bearing animals.
6. Canada and the United States are important to each other because:
   a. Canada trades with communist countries.
   b. the two nations share many resources.
   c. the two nations share the Panama Canal.
7. In paragraph 9, the word *investments* refers to:
   a. industries in Canada.
   b. discoveries of Canadian minerals.
   c. money used to begin industry.

**DEVELOPING
IDEAS AND
SKILLS**

Look at the cartoon. Then answer the questions at the top of page 147.

1. Who are the two figures at the top of this cartoon?
2. What is happening in the cartoon?
3. Give two examples of Anglo-American cooperation.
4. What continents are shown in the cartoon?
5. What is a good title for this cartoon?

SUMMING UP   *The United States and Canada*   Below are some headings for your *outline*. Following them are topics to be placed under these headings. In your notebook, see if you can make the correct outline.

A. Ways in Which the United States and Canada Are Alike.
B. Common Interests of the United States and Canada.
C. Where Canada and the United States May Disagree.

1. Radar warning stations.
2. NATO.
3. American investments in Canada.
4. Belief in democracy.
5. Standard of living.
6. Building of power projects.
7. Trade with communist countries.
8. Trade of raw materials for manufactured goods.
9. Use of machinery to do man's work.
10. Use of the English language.

FOLLOW UP   Tell whether the following items refer to the United States, Canada or both countries. If the item applies to the United States only, use the letters "US"; if the item applies to Canada only, use the letter "C"; if the item applies to both the United States and Canada, use the letter "B."

1. Two official languages.
2. Members of NATO.
3. Vast Arctic region.
4. Large Negro population.
5. Many pulp and paper mills.
6. Divided into provinces.
7. Most people live in the Northeast.
8. Once a colony of Great Britain.
9. Great Lakes are an important waterway.
10. Great railroad system.
11. Exports textiles.

16 TOWARD A BETTER AMERICA

Reading For A Purpose: What are some of the problems facing Anglo-Americans?

Poverty in the inner city. In addition to poor housing, what other problems do you think the people in this neighborhood face? What should be done to help them?

1. Compared with other lands of the world, ours is a land of plenty. Americans as a whole make more money, eat better foods, have more labor-saving machines than any other people in the world. However, not all Americans enjoy a comfortable living. There are many poor homes and many poor Americans—unskilled workers, migrant farm workers, coal miners, some of the aged and some minority groups. Many of these do not have proper homes, schooling or medical care. There are close to *fifty million* Americans living in this "other America."

2. Black Americans make up the largest minority group in the United States. Before the Civil War, most of the Nation's black people were slaves. In 1863, slavery ended in the United States. However, many states passed laws that kept black people "second-class citizens." They were not allowed to vote; they were kept apart from whites in buses, restaurants, schools and other places. For a long time a number of organizations have fought for equal rights for black people. In 1954, the Supreme Court of the United States ordered an end to separate public schools for blacks and whites. In 1964, a Civil Rights Act was passed by Congress. As a result, all Americans have the right to go where they wish, to eat where they please and to vote if they are qualified.

3. However, unfair laws alone have not kept black people or other minority groups—Puerto Ricans, Mexican-Americans, Indians—from gaining a higher standard of living. In our larger cities there are areas where only these groups live. Often this is because people in other areas will not rent or sell homes to them. Our country faces the problem of integrating *all* Americans in one society. All minority groups must be able to attend schools with their fellow Americans. All must have the chance to obtain jobs for which they are qualified and to raise their standard of living.

4. Canada, too, has a minority problem because of the large French population living there, chiefly in the province of Quebec. There are fewer French-speaking people than English-speaking people in Canada. Since 1960, the French people of Canada have been asking for a larger share in the government. Some French in Quebec have talked of making Quebec a separate nation. Although only a third of the Canadians are French, some of their leaders are asking for equal representation in the Canadian Parliament.

5. As in other regions of the world, the population of the United States is increasing rapidly. Since 1960 alone, our population has increased by more than 25 million! This means there will have to be more jobs, schools, housing and trained workers. In the future, ma-

chines will do even more of the work now being done by people. Machines will even tell other machines what to do! We call this process *automation.*

6. As our population continues to grow, we will have to use our great resources more wisely. Up to now we have been wasteful in the way we have cleared our land and used our minerals. We have carelessly dumped wastes into our streams and rivers. The amount of pure water has been reduced a great deal as a result. Yet we need more water than ever! We also may not have enough fuel for our machines. Will we be able to keep a high standard of living as our population grows so rapidly?

7. For a long time, most Americans lived on farms or in small towns and villages. Today, most people in the United States live in or near cities. As the cities grow, so do their responsibilities. Cities are expected to do many things for the people who live in them. They must provide schools, housing, health care, transportation and recreation. They must keep people

A scene showing Chicago's Lake Michigan shoreline strewn with dead fish. What do you think caused the mass death of these fish? What should be done to prevent further tragedies such as this?

safe and help them if they are out of work. Today, the cost of these services is very high. At the same time, city (and state) money is running low. Many cities and states are calling for more aid from the federal government. Without this aid, they feel that city services will break down.

8. Other dangers face both Americans and the rest of the world's people. There is a danger from nuclear warfare and the testing of nuclear weapons. The United States and the Soviet Union have agreed not to explode atomic bombs in the air or under water. In 1972, they also agreed to put limits on some kinds of nuclear weapons. Still the threat that these terrible weapons will be used hangs over all the people of the world.

9. The United States and Canada are concerned with what goes on in other countries. After World War II, the United States feared the spread of communism throughout the world. To hold back communism, the nations of Anglo-America joined with other countries to form the North Atlantic Treaty Organization (NATO). NATO is made up of the United States, Canada and twelve countries of Europe. The United States is also a member of the Southeast Asia Treaty Organization (SEATO). It also belongs to the Organization of American States (OAS). OAS includes all the nations of North and South America, except Canada.

10. After World War II, the United States began a program of helping other countries. At first this foreign aid went to countries that had been badly damaged in the war. But soon, the United States was sending billions in food and military aid to many other countries. In spite of the huge sum spent ($150 billion), there are many who question what this aid has accomplished. How much aid other countries should receive, which nations should receive it, and what the United States should expect for the aid given are questions that Americans are now asking and trying to answer.

1. Which questions are answered in this chapter?
   a. Why has the United States joined organizations with other nations throughout the world?
   b. Why must our resources be used wisely?
   c. What is automation?
2. The main idea of this chapter is that:
   a. the United States faces many dangers in the world today.
   b. fresh water and clean air are our biggest problems.
   c. Anglo-America faces many unsolved problems.
3. The United States has signed a treaty with the Soviet Union to:
   a. increase trade between the two countries.
   b. help each other in exploring space.
   c. stop the testing of nuclear weapons in the air and under water.
4. We must use our resources wisely because:
   a. they cannot be replaced.
   b. they will be used up very soon.
   c. more people will mean a greater need for resources.
5. The process by which machines give orders to other machines is called:
   a. division of labor.
   b. automation.
   c. competition.
6. The "other America" refers to:
   a. the French people in Canada.
   b. people in our large cities.
   c. the poor people of America.
7. *In paragraph 2*, "second-class citizen" means:
   a. a person who does not have the same rights as other citizens.
   b. unfair laws passed by many states.
   c. a person who is forced into slavery.

Look at the cartoon. Then answer the questions at the top of page 151.

1. Who is the man in the cartoon?
2. What do the tree stumps represent?
3. What is the man trying to do?
4. What would be a good title for the cartoon?

A. Graph Reading

Congress started the Office of Economic Opportunity (OEO) to carry out the fight against poverty. The graph shows the amount of money spent each year since 1965 by the OEO. Tell whether these statements about the graph are *true* or *false*. If the graph provides no information on which to base an answer, say *no information*.

The Fight Against Poverty Since 1965

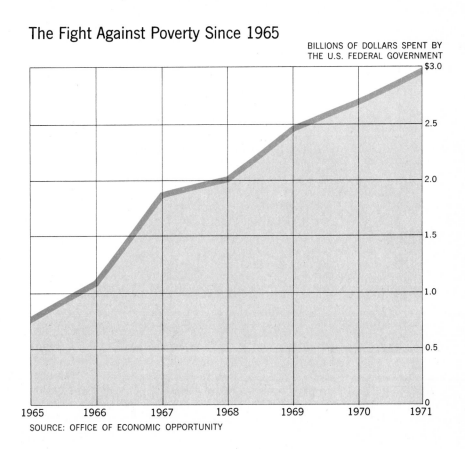

BILLIONS OF DOLLARS SPENT BY THE U.S. FEDERAL GOVERNMENT

SOURCE: OFFICE OF ECONOMIC OPPORTUNITY

1. The amount spent by OEO has increased each year.
2. Over a billion dollars has been spent every year since the beginning of the program.
3. The greatest increase in spending took place in the first two years of the program.
4. The problems of poverty are worse now than in 1965.
5. 1968 was the first year in which 2 billion dollars was spent.

B. Who Are the Poor?

In 1971, it was reported that over 25 million Americans—1 in every 8—were living in poverty. (The government defined poverty as an income of $4,000 or less for a family of four people.) Who were the poor?

10% of whites were poor.
34% of blacks were poor.

Among people 65 years of age and over:
23% of whites were poor.
50% of blacks were poor.

Among heads of working families:
2.7% of whites were poor.
9.7% of blacks were poor.

Among families in regions of the country:
7% of families in the Northeast were poor.
8% of families in the North Central states were poor.
15% of families in the South were poor.
9% of families in the West were poor.

1. What generalizations can you make about poverty in America?
2. Where do most of the poor live in your part of the country?
3. In 1971, there were about 205 million people in the United States. Of these, slightly more than 22 million were black. How many could be called poor?
4. Find out about the poor in your community or your city. Are the figures different from those throughout the country?

BOOKS FOR UNIT 3

	Author	Title, Publisher	Description
1.	Bontemps, Arna	THE STORY OF THE NEGRO, Knopf	The history of black people in the United States.
2.	Burlingame, Roger	MACHINES THAT BUILT AMERICA, Harcourt Brace	Inventions that helped America to grow.
3.	Colman, Hila	THE GIRL FROM PUERTO RICO, Morrow	The problems of a Puerto Rican girl living in New York City.
4.	Green, Constance M.	THE RISE OF URBAN AMERICA, Harper	How and why American cities grew— and why some did not.
5.	Hayes, Florence	JOE POLE, NEW AMERICAN, Houghton	The story of an immigrant to the United States.
6.	Havighurst, Walter	VOICES ON THE RIVER, Macmillan	A history of the mighty Mississippi River.

7. Hoag, Edwin	AMERICAN CITIES, Lippincott	Simply told story of the growth of American cities and the life of people in them.
8. Judson, Clara	ST. LAWRENCE SEAWAY, Follett	The great river valley from Cartier's discovery to the opening of the Seaway.
9. Lent, Henry	MEN AT WORK IN NEW ENGLAND, Putnam	Shows the wide range of jobs and skills in this region.
10. Lent, Henry	MEN AT WORK IN THE SOUTH, Putnam	Gives the wide range of industry in the southern states.
11. McNeer, May	THE CANADIAN STORY, Farrar Straus	From the Vikings to the Seaway, the story of Canada.
12. Shippen, Katherine	THE GREAT HERITAGE, Viking	The development of our natural resources.
13. Smith, Frances	MEN AT WORK IN ALASKA, Putnam	The marvels of the forty-ninth state, revealed through those who work to uncover its great resources.
14. Stull, Edith	UNSUNG BLACK AMERICANS, Grosset and Dunlap	From exploration through slavery to the rise of invention and industry.
15. Wilburn, Doug	LAND OF THE LONG DAY, Holt	The everyday life of an Eskimo family.

ARTICLES FOR UNIT THREE	"Boom in Canada's Far West," *U.S. News and World Report*, May 17, 1971	Canada's rapid growth in the west.
	"Drive to Clear Up The Lakes," *U.S. News and World Report*, April 24, 1972	Anglo-America's Great Lakes water pollution problem.
	"A New Empire Rises in Canada's West," *U.S. News and World Report*, July 17, 1967	More about Canada's western growth.
	"U.S. and Canada: Good Neighbors, But—," *U.S. News and World Report*, July 3, 1972	The problems between two longtime friends today.

UNIT 4
Latin America

1 OUR SOUTHERN NEIGHBORS

Reading For A Purpose: Why are we interested in Latin America?

1. Many of us have used the word "America" or "Americans" in speaking of the United States. This is not accurate. There are others who are Americans, too—the people of Latin America. They often resent our calling ourselves Americans as though the title belonged to us alone. It is common in Latin America to refer to us as "North Americans."

2. Latin America is made up of several parts. South of the United States is the country of Mexico. From Mexico a "bridge" of land extends to the southeast. This land, sometimes called Central America, contains six small countries. East of Central America is the Caribbean Sea and its many islands. Cuba, Haiti and the Dominican Republic, Puerto Rico, Trinidad and Jamaica are among the largest and most important of the Caribbean islands. Stretching southeast from Central America is the continent called South America. This continent is connected to Central America by a narrow strip of land, the Isthmus of Panama. All of these parts together—Mexico, Central America, the Caribbean Islands and South America—make up Latin America.

3. This region has twenty-four independent nations and small areas that are colonies of nations of Europe. Some are very large, like Brazil. This country is almost as big as the United States. Others are quite small, like El Salvador and the other nations of Central America and the Caribbean area. Some of the countries are our close neighbors like Mexico or Cuba. Others are a great distance away. Buenos Aires, the capital of Argentina, is farther from Washington, D.C. than any capital of Europe. It is even farther from Washington than is Moscow in the Soviet Union.

Taking a census among Indians of Peru. As in other parts of the world, the population of Latin America is growing rapidly. Why are census counts taken?

4. We call this large region south of us Latin America because the people who first settled there—the Spanish, Portuguese and French—spoke languages that came from Latin. (Latin was the language of the ancient Romans.) All but five of the twenty-four republics were once colonies of Spain or Portugal. The five that were not are Haiti, which belonged to France, and Guyana, Trinidad and Tobago, Jamaica, and Barbados, which belonged to England. Brazil was a colony of Portugal. The other eighteen republics were Spanish colonies.

5. We are interested in Latin America for many reasons. First, a friendly Latin America is important to the safety of the United States. If an enemy country had bases in Mexico, Central America or the Caribbean Sea, the United States would be in danger of attack. Likewise, the nations of Latin America know that an attack upon any one of them would be dangerous to the freedom of the others. That is why the United States has joined with the countries of Latin America to form the Organization of American States (OAS).

6. Second, the countries of Latin America send us products that we need. Important minerals such as oil, tin, copper and bauxite come to us from Venezuela, Bolivia, Chile and Surinam. Coffee, sugar, bananas and chocolate are foods that are eaten daily by the people of the United States. We import them from Latin America because they cannot grow in our climate. Beginning with the "Good Neighbor Policy" in the 1930's, our trade with Latin American countries has grown so that it is now $10 billion a year. Except for Argentina and Cuba, the people of Latin America buy more from the United States than from any other nation in the world.

7. Third, like countries in other parts of the world, the governments of Latin America are trying to raise the living standards of their people. We want to help them in this effort. Young people of our Peace Corps are now working and teaching in Latin America. The "Alliance

Workers in Ecuador carry bananas from the fields. Ecuador leads the world in the export of bananas.

for Progress," also for this purpose, was started by President John F. Kennedy in 1961. Under this plan, Congress has provided millions of dollars to help the Latin American people. Through this aid, it is hoped that Latin America will have more factories, more productive farms and better schools.

8. Fourth, the Panama Canal is of great importance to the United States. The canal is located on the Isthmus of Panama—in an area or zone we have "rented" from Panama. The canal was completed in 1914 by the United States. It is important to the defense of the United States. With it, warships can move from the Atlantic to the Pacific Ocean in a short time. The United States has built a chain of naval and air bases to protect the canal from attack. In times of peace the canal is open to all the nations of the world.

1. Which questions are answered in this chapter?
    a. Why are we interested in Latin America?
    b. What is the "Alliance for Progress"?
    c. How did the "Good Neighbor Policy" begin?
2. The main idea of this chapter describes:
    a. how the United States built the Panama Canal.
    b. why we trade with Latin America.
    c. why the American nations need each other.
3. Our nearest neighbor in Latin America is:
    a. Mexico.   b. Brazil.   c. Argentina.
4. All of these Latin American nations are Spanish-speaking countries EXCEPT:
    a. Mexico.   b. Brazil.   c. Argentina
5. This region is called Latin America because:
    a. the first settlers were Latins.
    b. the people speak Latin languages.
    c. Rome once conquered this part of the world.
6. The Panama Canal is important because it:
    a. shortens the distance between two great oceans.
    b. is a sea-level canal.
    c. is the center of trade between Latin America and the United States.
7. A narrow strip of land connecting two larger bodies of land is a(n):
    a. island.   b. strait.   c. isthmus.
8. In paragraph 2, a sentence reads, "From Mexico a *bridge* of land extends to the southeast." The best meaning for the words in italics is:
    a. a chain of islands.
    b. land that connects larger areas of land.
    c. wet, swampy land reaching into the ocean.

Map Study

Map #17—Latin America

Study the map on page 159. Then answer these questions.
1. Is the region north or south of the equator?
2. Is the region east or west of the Prime Meridian?
3. How far north and south does the region extend?
4. What is the largest country? The smallest?
5. What are the chief bodies of water that border the region?
6. Which countries have no outlets to the sea?
7. What are some of the important rivers in the region?
8. What are the capital cities of each country? How do you know they are the capitals?
9. Which countries are island nations?
10. Which countries are located on a peninsula?
11. Which lands are colonies of other nations?

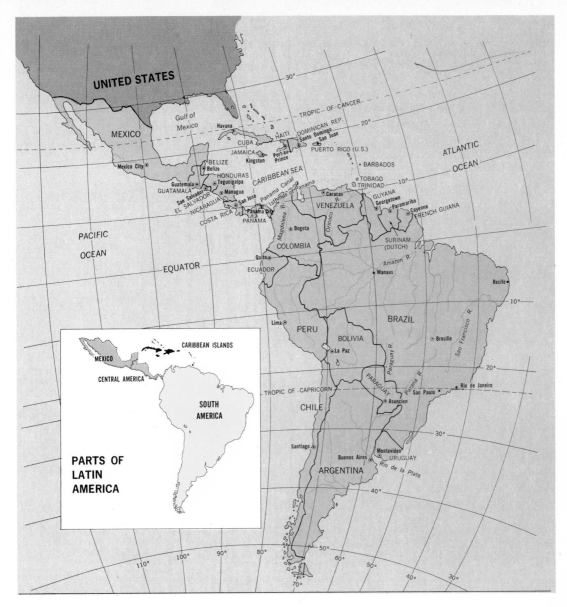

Map #17—Latin America

I. In the following, tell which reasons are correct.

We are interested in Latin America because:
1. the Panama Canal is important to us.
2. we get tropical foods from Latin America.
3. most people in this region speak English.
4. we can use Latin America's tin and copper.
5. rich farm lands supply us with corn and wheat.
6. the Latin American people are now fighting for their freedom.
7. we want these people to have a better life.
8. we are Argentina's biggest customer.

II. Tell whether each statement is a fact or an opinion.

1. Many countries of Latin America are independent.
2. The United States should buy more products from Latin America.
3. Latin American nations can improve their standard of living without help from the United States.
4. There are many reasons why the United States and the Latin American countries should be friendly.
5. Latin American countries will help the United States in defending the Panama Canal.
6. The United States would surely be attacked if a Communist country were near our borders.
7. Products of Latin America are important to the United States.

FOLLOW UP   Latin American news often appears in our newspapers. You can find many articles and pictures about Latin America in newspapers and magazines. Bring to class the news articles that you find and arrange them in a bulletin-board display. Make several headings for these news items: Government, History, Relations With Other Countries, Problems, Farming, Industry, etc.

2 THE HOLLOW CONTINENT

Reading For A Purpose: What is the surface of Latin America like?

1. The region of Latin America is about 8,000,000 square miles in area, slightly larger than the United States and Canada together. The continent of South America makes up more than 80 per cent of this land mass. A look at the map on page 159 will show you that nearly all of South America lies southeast of the United States. The eastern bulge of the continent that is part of Brazil brings South America closer to Europe and Africa than to our northeastern states. During World War II, the United States sent planes to Africa by flying them south to Brazil. Then they were flown across the Atlantic to Africa. Making two shorter flights was a safer way of delivering them to the battle areas.

2. The northern part of South America is crossed by the equator. (This is also the widest part of South America.) Therefore, Latin America lies partly in the northern hemisphere and partly in the southern hemisphere. As a result, the seasons in most of Latin America are the opposite of our seasons. When we have winter, the people of Latin America (south of the equator) have summer. When we have summer, they will be having winter. Furthermore, the largest part of Latin America is in the low latitudes. In general, this means that a large part of Latin America has a hot climate. Most of the people of this hot region live along the seacoast or in the mountains where it is cooler.

3. Latin America has many mountains. The Andes Mountains, or western highlands,

This helicopter is flying over the rain forest, or jungle, of the Oriente River. The Andes Mountains can be seen in the background. How do you think the mountains and rain forest affect travel in this part of Latin America?

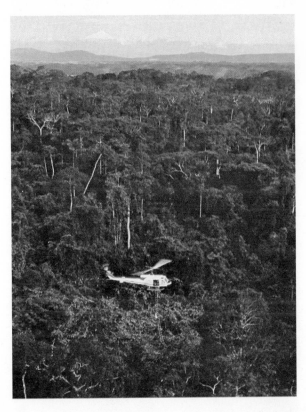

161

stretch from the southern border of the United States to the very tip of South America. The Andes are the second highest mountain range in the world. Some of the peaks are more than 20,000 feet high. These mountains are very hard to cross. On the east coast there are lower mountains or hills known as the Guiana and Brazilian highlands. The islands in the Caribbean Sea are really the tops of underwater mountain peaks of these highlands. Because of the mountains, travel by land from one part of South America to another has always been a problem.

4. Between the eastern and western highlands are the great inner plains or lowlands of South America. In Venezuela and Colombia the plains are called the *llanos*. In Argentina, the rich grassy plains are known as the *pampas*.

5. The plains are drained by great rivers.

The largest and longest is the Amazon River of Brazil. The Amazon rises in the Andes Mountains of the west. It flows eastward across the continent to the Atlantic Ocean. The Amazon flows through the hot, thick rain forest like a mighty inland sea. The river and its branches are so vast that they drain nearly half of South America. Along its path, the Amazon's shores may be as much as sixty miles apart! The mouth of the Amazon is 200 miles wide. The Amazon is so powerful that the mud that it carries along with it colors the water for fifty miles out into the ocean!

6. Two other great rivers of South America are the Orinoco and the Plata. The Orinoco flows through northern South America. It drains the lowlands of Venezuela. The Rio de la Plata ("River of Silver") is in the southeastern part of the continent. The two branches of the Plata begin in Brazil and flow southward

An Argentine cowboy herds cattle on the pampas. Why are the pampas well suited to raising cattle?

through the pampas. The river empties into the Atlantic Ocean near the city of Buenos Aires, Argentina. For the most part, the rivers of South America are *navigable.* (This means that ships can sail upstream from the ocean for long distances.)

7. In many ways, the land forms of North and South America are very much alike. Both continents have high mountains along their western coasts—the Rockies and the Andes. Both have an inner plain drained by mighty rivers. Both have highlands in the east, the Appalachians and the Guiana and Brazilian Highlands. Both have great seaports along the eastern coast.

8. There are also differences between the two continents. First, our largest river, the Mississippi, flows from north to south. The Amazon flows from west to east. The Mississippi flows through the most fertile part of the United States. The Amazon flows through a tropical rain forest where few people live. (We might call the Plata the "Mississippi" of South America. It flows in a north-south direction, through the rich grasslands of the pampas. It is also a great highway for trade like the Mississippi.) Second, the Rocky Mountains are not as high as the Andes. It has been easier to build roads and railways through the Rockies. (In South America there is no railroad across the continent from east to west because of the mountains.) Third, Anglo-America is blessed with a great inland waterway system, the Great Lakes. There is no such water highway in South America.

9. The geography of South America has caused it to be called the "Hollow Continent." The mountains of South America border the coasts, while inland are the plains. Therefore, the surface of South America makes it "high on the outside, low on the inside," like a saucer. The inland plains are also very hot, and part of the plains is tropical jungle. As a result, most of the people of South America live along the rim or coastline, and little is known about the middle of the continent.

UNDERSTANDING CHAPTER 2

1. Which questions are answered in this chapter?
   a. Where does the Amazon River begin?
   b. How do the mountains affect Latin America?
   c. When was South America discovered?
2. The best title for paragraph 5 is:
   a. Mighty River of the Rain Forest.
   b. Lowland River of South America.
   c. The "Mississippi" of South America.
3. A river of South America that flows through fertile land is the:
   a. Amazon.   b. Plata.   c. Madeira.
4. The highest mountains in Latin America are the:
   a. Rockies.   b. Andes.   c. Guiana Highlands.
5. How have the mountains affected Latin America?
   a. Most of Latin America is dry.
   b. Most of Latin America is cold.
   c. Travel is difficult from one part to another.
6. The large rivers of Latin America are useful because they:
   a. provide water power.
   b. all drain fertile farm lands.
   c. are used by ships for long distances.

7. The *llanos* and the *pampas* are both:
   a. mountains.   b. deserts.   c. lowlands.
8. A river that is *navigable* is one that:
   a. is used to supply water power.
   b. can be used by large ships.
   c. carries with it a large amount of soil.

DEVELOPING IDEAS AND SKILLS

Map Study

Map #18—Land Forms of Latin America

Study the map on page 165. Then tell whether these statements are *true* or *false*. Be able to explain your answers.
1. A high mountain area extends almost the length of South America, from north to south.
2. Hills occupy only a small part of South America.
3. Most of the central part of the continent is mountainous.
4. All of the land at the southern tip of South America is at sea level.
5. The western coast of South America is a broad lowland.
6. Plateaus are located near the northeastern coast.

SUMMING UP

Complete the following outline in your notebooks.

Land Forms of North and South America

A. How They Are Alike
   1.
   2.
   3.

B. How They Are Different
   1.
   2.
   3.

FOLLOW UP

Complete the following sentences in your notebook.
1. The largest river of Latin America is the _____.
2. The _____ Mountains extend along the west coast of South America.
3. The equator crosses the _____ part of South America.
4. The central part of South America is a vast _____.
5. The river in South America most like our Mississippi River is the _____.
6. The best seaports of South America are on the _____ coast.
7. The Caribbean Islands are really part of the _____ highlands.
8. The continent of _____ makes up most of Latin America.

LAND FORMS OF
LATIN AMERICA

Mountains
Plateaus
Hills
Plains

0   200   400   600   800   1000
Miles

Tropic of Cancer

Equator

Equator

Tropic of Capricorn

3 A REGION OF MANY CLIMATES

Reading For A Purpose: Why are there differences in climate in Latin America?

1. If you were asked to plan a trip to Latin America, what clothing would you take with you? For several reasons, this would not be easy to decide. First, Latin America extends over a great distance from north to south. This means there is a great range in latitude. Second, Latin America is mountainous. It may be cold in one place only a few miles from another place that is very hot. Third, because of the differences in wind direction, it may be very rainy or very dry. Fourth, in parts of Latin America the seasons are opposite from ours, so you would have to know whether it is winter or summer at the time you wish to travel.

2. A large part of Latin America is near the equator. This area is hot and wet throughout

A typical scene in an Indian village in Peru. Judging from the clothing these people usually wear, what is the weather like in the Andes Mountains of Peru?

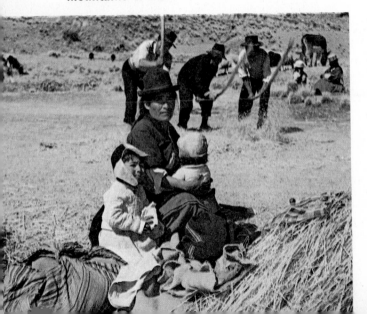

the year. It is a tropical rain forest. The rain-forest climate is found in the Amazon River Valley, along the Caribbean coast of South and Central America and along the Pacific coast from Ecuador to Panama. The average temperature throughout the year is 80°. It is never as hot as the hottest summer days in the midwestern United States. (In Kansas, Nebraska and South Dakota, temperatures of more than 100° are sometimes recorded in the summer months.) At night, one sleeps under a light blanket. But some rain falls almost every day. There is no dry season, and every day is sticky and damp.

3. Knowing that so much of Latin America is in the tropics, you might think that the entire region is hot. This is only partly true. There are differences in temperature between places only a few miles apart, even in the tropics. There are parts of Ecuador, Peru and Bolivia that are very cold, although they are located near the equator. How is this possible? These places are high in the Andes Mountains. Therefore, they have a *vertical* climate. As you have learned, this means that the climate grows cooler as you travel higher up into the mountains, away from the lowland.

4. At sea level the climate is tropical or hot. The people of Latin America call this the *tierra caliente* or hot country. As you go higher, the climate becomes somewhat cooler. You are in

the *tierra templada* or cool country. Near the peaks of the mountains, you are in the *tierra fria* or cold country. Because mountains are found in many Latin American countries, the vertical climate (up and down) is common.

5. North and south of the rain forest are the tropical grasslands or savannas. There are two seasons in the savannas—wet and dry. The rainy season brings floods and the dry season bakes the land. The soil and grasses of the savannas are tough. There are also many insects that carry diseases. Because of these conditions, few people live in the savannas.

6. South of the savannas in South America is the humid-subtropical climate. More Latin Americans live in this kind of climate than in any other. Here winters are mild and summers are warm. The pampas of Uruguay and Argentina lie in the humid subtropics. Buenos Aires, Argentina, is about as far south of the equator as Charleston, South Carolina, is north of it. Therefore, you can see that the southeastern part of the United States and the southeastern part of South America have the same kind of climate—although they have opposite seasons.

7. The winds and ocean currents affect the climate of South America as they do that of the United States. In our West, the Rocky Mountains shut off the wet winds from the Pacific Ocean, and the eastern side of the Rockies is dry. In much of South America the rain-carrying winds blow from the Atlantic Ocean. These winds are warm and wet. The West Indies and the northern part of South America get much rain. These winds move westward across South America until they reach the Andes Mountains. There the winds rise; the air is cooled and the rain falls on the eastern side of the mountains. When the air passes to the western side of the mountains, it is dry. Therefore, the narrow coastal area on the west has little rain. The Atacama Desert of Peru and northern Chile is the result. The winds from the Pacific Ocean are of little help. They blow from the cold Humboldt Current and bring little rain.

8. Much farther south, the winds over South America come from the southwest. These winds travel until they reach the Andes Mountains. The mountains force the winds to rise and rain falls along the coast. East of the mountains it is dry. This causes a dry plain in western Argentina.

9. Chile is a long, narrow country in the southwestern part of South America. Since it is 2500 miles long, it has several kinds of climate. Northern Chile is a desert, the Atacama Desert. South of the desert is a 600-mile strip of Mediterranean climate. Summers are hot and dry and winters are mild and rainy. Most of Chile's people live here. Farther south, the climate is marine, like that of the coasts of our states of Oregon and Washington.

The Atacama Desert. During the late 1800's, Chile defeated Peru and Bolivia in a war to gain control of this region. Although the desert is not suited to farming, it has rich deposits of copper and nitrate. Would you expect to find many people living here? Why?

UNDERSTANDING CHAPTER 3

1. Which questions are answered in this chapter?
   a. Why is it cold in some places near the equator?
   b. What animals live in the rain forest?
   c. Why are parts of South America's west coast a desert?
2. The main idea of this chapter describes:
   a. how the winds affect Latin America.
   b. the vertical climate of Latin America.
   c. the different climates of Latin America.
3. The largest part of Latin America is in the:
   a. low latitudes.
   b. middle latitudes.
   c. high latitudes.
4. The mountains of Latin America cause a climate that is called:
   a. rain forest.   b. vertical.   c. subtropical.
5. A reason for the desert of northern Chile is that:
   a. lowland areas in a vertical climate have little rain.
   b. the Andes Mountains cut off rain from the east.
   c. the seasons are opposite from ours.
6. Some of the large cities of Latin America are located in the highlands because:
   a. disease-carrying insects are found in all the lowland areas.
   b. all of Latin America is near the equator.
   c. the climate is more pleasant there.
7. The best meaning for *subtropical* is:
   a. near the tropics.
   b. grassland.
   c. rain-carrying.

DEVELOPING IDEAS AND SKILLS

Map Study

Map #19—Climates of Latin America

Study the map on page 169. Then tell whether these statements are true or false.

1. There is no marine climate north of the equator in Latin America.
2. Only the rain-forest is found along the equator.
3. An area of vertical climate stretches the length of South America.
4. The largest region of good rainfall is found along the north and eastern coasts.
5. South America has deserts both north and south of the equator.
6. Latin America has a marine climate along the western coast.
7. The savannas lie both north and south of the rain forest.
8. Nearly all of Brazil lies in a region of heavy rainfall.
9. The subtropical climate of Latin America is found much farther from the equator than it is in Anglo-America.
10. Although Mexico has some dry areas, none of it can be called a desert.

CLIMATES OF
LATIN AMERICA

- Tropical rain forest
- Savanna
- Desert
- Steppe
- Mediterranean
- Humid subtropical
- Marine
- Vertical

0   200   400   600   800   1000
Miles

Tropic of Cancer

Equator

Tropic of Capricorn

EQUATOR

Agree or Disagree   Decide whether or not each of the following statements agrees with what you have read. If the answer is *disagree*, explain why.

1. All of Latin America is hot and wet.
2. It is always hot near the equator.
3. Dry grasslands are found north and south of the rain forest.
4. South America has no deserts.
5. Temperatures along the equator are the hottest on the earth.
6. Chile is a land of different climates.
7. Most people live in the tropical lowlands.
8. The Caribbean and Atlantic coasts are dry.

Making Inferences   In our reading, many facts are given to us. From these facts we can draw conclusions. The following are some conclusions or inferences that you might make after reading this chapter. Tell whether these conclusions are correct or incorrect. Give reasons for your answers.

1. Mexico City, the largest city in Latin America, is probably located on a lowland near the sea.
2. In flying from New York to Rio de Janeiro, Brazil, your plane would fly almost directly south.
3. Latin Americans grow some crops that we do not have and some that are the same as ours.
4. Latin American countries trade more with Europe and Africa than they do with Australia.
5. There are few cities in the valley of the Amazon.
6. Buenos Aires, Argentina, would have the same kind of climate as Seattle, Washington.
7. Some countries of Latin America can grow crops that are suited to different climates.
8. The airplane has become an important means of travel in Latin America.

4 FROM COLONIES TO FREE NATIONS

A model of the main plaza of the Aztecs at Tenochtitlan. A pyramid with two temples was the main structure of the plaza. The temples were dedicated to the sun god and to the rain god. Why do you think the Aztecs worshipped the sun and the rain?

Reading For A Purpose: How has Latin America changed in four hundred years?

1. Long before Columbus came to the New World, there were people living on the American continents. These were the Indians. The first Americans probably came from Asia. They crossed the Bering Strait into Alaska. Then they moved southward, exploring the land and settling it. Three of the most famous Indian peoples in Latin America were the Mayas, the Aztecs and the Incas.

2. The Maya Indians lived in southern Mexico and Guatemala. They built many beautiful cities in Central America before the arrival of Columbus. They studied the skies and learned about the movements of the sun, moon and stars. They learned to keep time and made a calendar. They built huge pyramids and other buildings of stone. They painted pictures and wove cotton cloth. Around 1300, for some unknown reason, the Mayas disappeared. Many of their villages were overgrown by the tropical forest.

3. The Aztecs lived in a valley in the central highlands of Mexico. Their capital city was Tenochtitlan. It was built on islands in the middle of a lake. The Aztecs conquered the other tribes living around them. They forced these tribes to work for them and to pay taxes in gold and silver. Their temples were built on the tops of great stone pyramids. The Aztecs wove cotton cloth and made beautiful pottery and jewelry. For food, they planted corn, beans and potatoes.

4. The Inca empire was in the Andes Mountains, from Ecuador to Chile. The ruler was called the Inca and the people he ruled were called Incas. The leaders lived in stone palaces or fortresses on the tops of mountains. The capital of the empire was at Cuzco, in Peru. The people lived on the hillsides or in the valleys below. They lived chiefly by raising corn, beans and potatoes or by herding llamas and alpaca. The Inca farmers learned to terrace—that is, to build steps on the mountainsides for farming. They irrigated their farm lands with water from the highlands. The Incas were sun worshipers and made many objects in the form of a round golden disk. They were also excellent road builders and had a fine communications system.

Inca terraces at Pisac, Peru. In some areas of the Andes, the Incas built steps, or terraces, on the mountainside for farming. How did these terraces help protect the farmland?

5. Some of the lands of Latin America were discovered by Columbus while sailing westward from Spain. During his second voyage to the New World, he began the first European settlement there. Before long, both Spain and Portugal claimed lands in America. These countries asked the Pope—the head of the Catholic Church—to divide the New World between them. In 1493, the Pope drew an imaginary line running north and south on the map. This was called the Line of Demarcation. All lands west of this line would belong to Spain. All lands east of this line would belong to Portugal. Because of this settlement, Portugal later claimed the land that is now Brazil.

6. By 1500, there were a number of Spanish settlements in the islands of the West Indies. The Spanish brought horses, cattle and sheep to the New World. From their island forts, soldiers were sent to explore the nearby coasts in search of riches. In 1519, Hernando Cortez landed with a small force on the coast of Mexico. With the help of guns and horses, he was able to conquer the Aztec Indians. In 1532, Francisco Pizarro sailed southward along the west coast of South America and discovered the Inca empire. He captured the Inca chief and killed him. The Incas were soon defeated. The Spanish were now masters of two treasure houses in Latin America—Mexico and Peru.

7. By 1600, the Spaniards had explored and conquered most of Latin America. They divided their conquered lands into two kingdoms. The kingdoms were ruled by viceroys, or governors, who were appointed by the king of Spain. The viceroys divided the best lands into huge estates or *haciendas.* These were given to friends of the king. The Indians had to work in the mines or on the farms and ranches. Missionaries also traveled to the New World. They brought the Catholic religion, set up schools and missions and taught the Indians.

8. Brazil was discovered in 1500 by Pedro Cabral, who was sailing for the Portuguese. The lands along the coast were divided into

Simón Bolívar, one of South America's greatest heroes in the struggle for independence. Why did the colonies want independence from Spain?

large farms or *plantations.* Sugar was the chief crop of the plantations. The planters found there were not enough Indians to work in the sugar fields, so they brought blacks from Africa. The blacks became slaves on the plantations. As time went on, the Portuguese kept moving westward until they had conquered nearly half the continent.

9. For 300 years Spain ruled its colonies with an "iron hand." The colonies could not make their own laws. But after the success of the American and French Revolutions, the colonists wanted their freedom. However, the first revolt in Latin America was not in a Spanish colony. It took place in Haiti, which was ruled by the French. Many blacks had been brought to Haiti by the French to work in the sugar fields. Toussaint L'Ouverture, a former slave, led them in their fight against French rule. Shortly after his death in 1803 the colony was given its freedom.

10. The ideas of freedom spread throughout Latin America. In 1810, Father Hidalgo, a Mexican priest, led the Mexican Indians in the first revolt against Spain. The Mexicans finally won their freedom from Spain in 1821. Before long, other people in Latin America began to

rebel against Spain. Simón Bolívar, the "George Washington of South America," led the fight for freedom in Venezuela, Colombia, Ecuador and Bolivia. José de San Martín helped to win freedom in Chile and Peru. In 1822, Brazil became free. By 1824, most of the countries in Central and South America were free from Spain and Portugal.

11. For a time, it seemed that the freedom of the new nations might be lost. Some rulers of Europe wanted to give back the nations of Latin America to Spain. The American people were glad to see the Spanish colonies win their freedom. They did not want the powerful nations of Europe helping Spain. In 1823, President James Monroe made a statement concerning the new nations that became known as the Monroe Doctrine. He said that Europe was to keep "hands off" the new governments in the Americas. Any attempt to help Spain to regain its colonies would be thought of as an unfriendly act against the United States.

12. When the people of Latin America became free, they did not unite like the people of the United States. Communications were poor. It was difficult for people to reach one another. Separate little nations were formed. In the beginning, many of the new countries tried to draw up constitutions or plans of government like that of the United States. However, most of the people were poor. They could not read or write and could not understand what their leaders were doing. After a while the new nations came to be ruled by strong men or dictators. The people had few rights even though they were free from their European rulers. We will learn more of the later history of Latin America in Chapter 10.

UNDERSTANDING CHAPTER 4

1. Which questions are answered in this chapter?
   a. Who was Juárez?
   b. How did Spain govern its colonies?
   c. How was the New World discovered?
2. The main idea of *paragraphs 9 through 11* describes:
   a. how the United States treated the countries of Latin America.
   b. the Latin American struggle for freedom.
   c. the European rule of Latin American colonies.
3. Brazil was settled by the:
   a. Spanish.   b. French.   c. Portuguese.
4. The Inca Empire was destroyed by:
   a. Cortez.   b. Pizarro.   c. Columbus.
5. The Spanish came to the New World for all of these reasons EXCEPT:
   a. the desire for silver and gold.
   b. to convert the Indians to the Catholic religion.
   c. to get the rich furs from the animals in the forests.
6. Blacks were brought as slaves to Latin America from Africa chiefly to:
   a. work in the mines.
   b. work in the sugar fields.
   c. settle the inland plain of Brazil.

7. A *viceroy* is the same as:
   a. a governor.
   b. an explorer.
   c. a missionary.
8. In a country ruled by a *dictator*, the people:
   a. enjoy freedom of speech.
   b. choose their own leaders.
   c. have little voice in their government.

DEVELOPING
IDEAS AND
SKILLS

Picture Symbols

These pictures should help you to recall parts of the chapter you have read. What is the main idea of each picture?

SUMMING UP

Place each topic below under the proper heading. Be sure to list the topics according to their correct order in history.

Headings

A. Indian Civilizations
B. Colonies of European Nations
C. Period of Independence

Topics

1. Black people imported for work on farms.
2. Land divided into two kingdoms.
3. Hillsides terraced for farming.
4. Monroe Doctrine announced.
5. Cuzco was an important city.
6. Line of Demarcation established.
7. Many small nations.
8. Leadership of Simón Bolívar.
9. Building of pyramids of stone.
10. Gold and silver sent to Europe.

Reviewing Chapters 1 Through 4. Choose the item that does not belong with the others in each group.

1. Reasons for our interest in Latin America:
   a. Panama Canal
   b. trading for each other's goods
   c. source of machinery
   d. source of tropical foods
2. Climates of Latin America:
   a. tundra   b. rain forest   c. vertical   d. desert
3. Land forms of Latin America:
   a. mountains b. plains c. plateaus d. large inland lakes
4. Indians of Latin America:
   a. Incas   b. Seminoles   c. Mayas   d. Aztecs
5. Settlers in Latin America:
   a. Swedes b. Spanish c. Portuguese d. French

5 THE PEOPLE

On market day, one can see villagers in traditional dress. Why do you think these people continue to keep the customs of their ancestors?

Reading For A Purpose: Who are the people of Latin America?

1. The population of Latin America is growing at a fast rate. Latin America is one of the fastest growing regions of the world. About 300 million people live in the lands south of the United States. There are three main groups of people—Indians, blacks and Europeans.

2. The Indians were the first people in this region. They were conquered by the Spanish and forced to work in mines and on farms. Today the Indians live mainly in nine of the region's twenty-four countries: Guatemala, Ecuador, Bolivia, Peru, Paraguay, Mexico, El Salvador, Panama and the Amazon valley of Brazil.

3. Black slaves were brought to Latin America from Africa in the 16th century. They were the chief source of labor on the large sugar plantations. The black population of Latin America is found mainly on the Caribbean Islands and the wet coastal lowlands of Colombia and Brazil. Most of Haiti (90 percent of the people) and large parts of Cuba and the Dominican Republic are inhabited by blacks.

4. Most of the white people in Latin America are descendants of the early Spanish and Portuguese settlers and other immigrants from Europe. In the 19th century many people came to Latin America from Italy, France and Germany. They settled chiefly in the milder climates of Argentina, Uruguay and Chile.

5. Since the Spanish explorers came to Latin America, there has been much mixing among these three groups of people. As a result, a large number of people are a mixture of races. A *mestizo* is a person who is partly Indian and partly white. A *mulatto* is partly black and partly white. A *zambo* is partly Indian and partly black. Because of this great mixing of races, the people of Latin America have not been greatly concerned with the color of a person's skin.

6. The official language in eighteen Latin American nations is Spanish. In Brazil the people speak Portuguese; in Haiti, French; in Guyana, Jamaica, Barbados and Trinidad and Tobago, English. Many Indian tribes in far valleys still speak their own languages. But

Historians generally agree that slaves in Brazil got better treatment than in many other places, but today many Brazilians feel that slavery is a stain on their nation's history. How do people in the United States feel about the slavery which existed in this country for more than two hundred years?

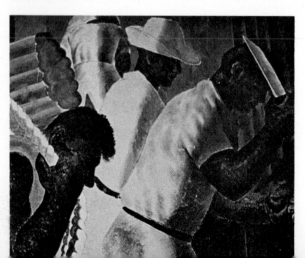

more people speak Spanish than any other language in Latin America. All languages have been changed slightly. Indian words have been added to the Spanish, and in the south Spanish may also be spoken with Indian words or accent.

7. Religion is another tie that brings Latin Americans together. More than 80 per cent of the people are Catholic. The Spanish and Portuguese brought Catholic missionaries with them to the New World. They converted many of the Indians to the Catholic religion. The Catholic Church is important in the everyday life of the people. Even in tiny Indian villages in the mountains there are churches. While there are Protestants and Jews in Latin America, they are small in number compared with Catholics.

8. Most Latin Americans are farmers who work on large farms. These large farms are called *plantations* in the Caribbean Islands. They are called *haciendas* in Mexico, *estancias* in Argentina and Uruguay and *fazendas* in Brazil. Many of the large farms are owned by

The "casa grande" (big house) on a present-day plantation near Recife, Brazil. Workers on Latin American plantations are called "peons." What are such workers called in the United States?

one man or one family. The farmers who work on the land of other people are called *peons*.

9. Besides the peons, there are many Indians who own their own small farms. They raise corn on small plots of land, farming in the same way their ancestors did. They do not speak Spanish. They do not know of the modern inventions that would make their work easier. They have little knowledge of methods of farming that would help them to grow a larger amount of crops on their land. Many herd llamas and sheep on grassy mountain slopes or work in mines.

10. While Latin America is big in size and is growing in population, it does not have a large share of the world's people. Large areas of South America such as the rain forest, the mountains and the dry plains and deserts cannot support many people and are not pleasant to live in. Except for the Caribbean Islands, most Latin Americans live in the eastern and western highlands where it is cooler than in the hot lowlands.

11. One out of three Latin Americans now lives in the growing cities. These cities are modern, and tourists find that they look like cities in the United States. There are wide streets, tall buildings and beautiful homes. There are soft drinks, neon lights and plenty of traffic. The large landowners, the government leaders and the heads of business and industry usually live in the cities as do the growing class of factory workers. Most of the people are of European background. In the cities the children have the best chance for an education. But there are poorer sections of the large cities too. The slums in Latin America are as bad as those in some of our large North American cities.

12. There are 14 cities with more than a million people in Latin America. (Anglo-America has 8 such cities.) In the urban areas of both Mexico City and Buenos Aires, Argentina, there are more than 8 million people. Only the urban areas of New York, Tokyo and London have more people. Buenos Aires is the great

port and railroad center of the southeast. São Paulo is another city that has grown fast. It is now Brazil's largest city as well as its leading industrial center. Rio de Janeiro, once the largest city in Brazil, has one of the most beautiful harbors in the world.

13. The governments in Latin America vary from democracies to dictatorships. The oldest democratic governments are found in the countries of Uruguay, Mexico and Costa Rica. In many others, the people are gaining a greater voice in their governments. Some Latin American countries are dictatorships—ruled by one or a few powerful men. These men have often been supported by the army or by the large landholders who do not want to share their power.

Buenos Aires, Argentina's capital and cultural center, is a busy, modern city. On the right we see the nation's monument to independence. What monument in our country does it remind you of?

UNDERSTANDING
CHAPTER 5

1. Which questions are answered in this chapter?
   a. What is a mestizo?
   b. Where do most Latin American people live?
   c. What do the city people of Latin America wear?
2. The main idea of *paragraphs 1 through 6* describes:
   a. the mixture of people in Latin America.
   b. people who have come from other lands.
   c. the small population of Latin America.
3. A country with a large black population is:
   a. Argentina.   b. Haiti.   c. Mexico.
4. The great seaport of southeast South America is:
   a. Buenos Aires.   b. São Paulo.   c. Bogotá.
5. Many people of Latin America live in the highlands because:
   a. there are many winter sports.
   b. gold and silver are mined there.
   c. it is cooler.
6. Latin America does not support more people because:
   a. there is a lack of machinery.
   b. much of the land is rain forest or mountains.
   c. cows and other farm animals cannot live there.
7. A *peon* is the same as a:
   a. factory worker.
   b. tenant farmer.
   c. ranch owner.
8. A *mestizo* is partly Spanish and partly:
   a. black.   b. French.   c. Indian.

Pictograph #8—Population, Area and Standard of Living of Latin America

Study the pictograph. Then answer these questions.

1. Is the standard of living of this region high or low compared with that of the United States?
2. Is the region more or less crowded than the United States?
3. Are the people of this region literate compared with the people of the United States?
4. How long may the average person in this region expect to live?
5. What facts tell you the standard of living of the people of the region?
6. How does this region compare with the United States in size?

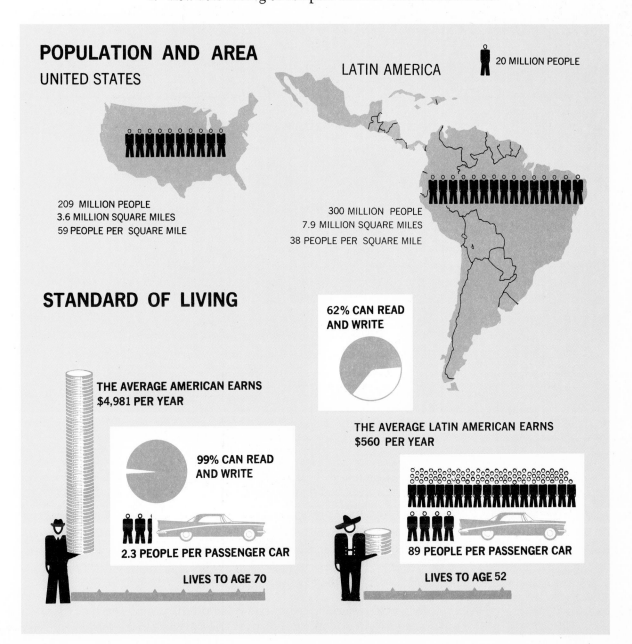

POPULATION AND AREA

UNITED STATES

LATIN AMERICA

20 MILLION PEOPLE

209 MILLION PEOPLE
3.6 MILLION SQUARE MILES
59 PEOPLE PER SQUARE MILE

300 MILLION PEOPLE
7.9 MILLION SQUARE MILES
38 PEOPLE PER SQUARE MILE

STANDARD OF LIVING

62% CAN READ AND WRITE

THE AVERAGE AMERICAN EARNS $4,981 PER YEAR

THE AVERAGE LATIN AMERICAN EARNS $560 PER YEAR

99% CAN READ AND WRITE

2.3 PEOPLE PER PASSENGER CAR

LIVES TO AGE 70

89 PEOPLE PER PASSENGER CAR

LIVES TO AGE 52

La Paz, Bolivia, is a city of over a half million people. It is one of the largest cities of Latin America. It is also one of the most unusual cities in the world. A traveler tells his impressions of La Paz in the selection below.

A Visit to La Paz, Bolivia

We knew we were going to land at the highest commercial airport in the world (altitude 13,358 feet). We were going to spend days in the highest capital in the world and see the highest ski run in the world. Perhaps we would play nine holes on the highest golf course in the world. And, when it came time to leave Bolivia, we would sail across the highest navigable body of water anywhere (altitude 12,500 feet).

... Imagine a teacup with a very wide rim. The La Paz airport is perched on the rim. The city is down at the bottom of the cup ... The ride into town was around and around the inside of the teacup, and down and down. The driver didn't have to use a bit of gas until he got to city traffic. He just coasted down.

... We knew we had to be careful about walking too far or eating too much at this altitude. But we were not really worried until we read this notice pasted on the mirror of our hotel room:

IF YOU HAVE EMERGENCY NEED OF OXYGEN,
THE HOTEL IS PREPARED TO SERVE YOU QUICKLY.

... On Sunday afternoon, we found the big Indian market. (95% of the people of Bolivia are either pure Indian or mestizo.) It sprawls over many city blocks. ..... Seldom have we seen such crowds, such movement. Most of the buying and selling was being done by women. The dress of the Indian women of Bolivia begins with a brown or black derby. Their feet are covered with two pieces of soft leather—one for the upper, one for the sole. The legs are bound tightly with brown cloth. The Sunday skirt is velvet, worn over many petticoats that make them look huge from the waist down. The Indian woman's black hair is always in neat braids.

There were few men in sight. Everywhere there were women. They were buying and selling, spinning wool, fringing shawls with silk thread, measuring out pieces of goods. Some were tying babies on their backs. Most smiled as they answered questions so that their bad teeth showed. All had red cheeks, not from the use of makeup, but from windburn.

Do you agree or disagree? Give reasons for your answers.

1. La Paz must be one of the most unusual cities in the world.

2. American visitors from the southwestern part of the United States feel at home in La Paz.
3. Bolivians expect visitors may have trouble at La Paz's high altitude.
4. One can tell from the work at the market that herding is important in the Andes.

Answer these questions.
1. La Paz is located only 17° from the equator, yet the average temperature in summer is 52° and in winter, 45°. Can you explain why this is so?
2. Why do you think a half million people have chosen to live in such a high altitude as is found in La Paz?

6 VILLAGE LIFE

Reading For A Purpose: How do people live in the villages of Latin America?

A village home in Ecuador. What household conveniences that you take for granted seem to be missing from the home of this family?

1. In Latin America most farmers do not live on their own farms, but in small villages. The center of the village is usually a small square or *plaza.* Around the plaza may stand the church, the school and a few small stores. The plaza is also the market place.

2. Near the plaza are the homes of the villagers. These homes are built differently throughout Latin America. In the dry climates they may be made of *adobe* (sun-dried bricks of mud). The roofs of the houses may be covered with tile or straw thatch. In the rainy areas, the houses or huts are often made of reeds with thatched roofs. Corrugated iron roofs are also used. In the colder areas of the highlands, there are few trees and bushes, so houses are made of stone.

3. Most of the houses are small and simple and have only one room. The furniture may be only a bed, some sleeping mats, a table and a few chairs. There may be no windows in the house. The family spends a lot of time outside, the father working in the fields and the mother cooking, sewing and taking care of the children. There is probably no electricity and certainly no plumbing.

4. The whole family works hard each day to raise the things it needs in order to live. The chief crops are corn and beans. Most of the work is done by hand. The grains of corn are planted by hand. The field is cultivated with a hoe or a digging stick. When the corn is full grown, the ears are gathered by hand. The cornstalks are then cut down with large knives called *machetes.* For several reasons, it is very hard for the farmer to raise more than his family needs. The plot is small. Sometimes the soil is dry; sometimes it is too cold. The farmer has no fertilizer, so the soil wears out. There is no machinery. Many of the farmers have poor seeds. Little is done to stop erosion (the flowing or washing away of the soil.)

5. Some families may have a vegetable garden and a few fruit trees of their own. These and the corn and beans from the fields provide nearly all that the villagers get to eat. They eat little meat because very few can afford to have large meat animals. The corn flour is often made into flat cakes called *tortillas.* On the islands of the West Indies and in the Amazon Basin, *manioc,* or starch from the root of the

A thatch-covered house in the rain forest. Why is this house built of reeds and straw thatch rather than of adobe, stone or brick?

cassava plant, is eaten. Coffee and tea are favorite drinks. Villagers seldom drink milk, for they do not keep milk cows.

6. Almost everything the people need is made at home, for the family has little money. In most parts of Latin America, the farmers and their families wear plain clothes that are made at home. The men wear shirts and trousers of coarse white cotton, and the women wear simple cotton dresses. The women also weave a *rebozo* or shawl that serves as a head covering or baby sling. The men have *serapes*. A serape is a hand-woven blanket with a slit in the center for the head. The farmer uses the serape as both a blanket and a coat.

7. To add to their income, many farmers make other things. They make and sell clay pots and bowls, jewelry of silver and turquoise, colorful wool blankets, sandals and straw hats. Many villages may have a shoemaker, a basket weaver, a hat maker and a brick maker to fill the needs of the people.

8. Once a week the people take their handwork, some pigs and chickens, and some fruits and vegetables to the nearest market place. They may sell these goods for other things they need. Several times a year there are village *fiestas*, where there is plenty of drink, food and dancing.

9. The farmer we have just described is a subsistence farmer. He probably cannot read or write because many of the poor villages or farm areas cannot afford to build schools.

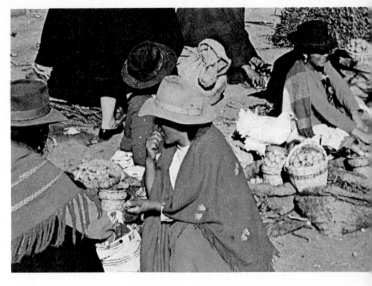

People at the market in Pisac, Peru. Why is market day especially important for farm families?

Many of his children do not attend what schools there are because they are needed at home to help with the work in the fields.

10. This farmer is probably not well. In many villages there are no sewers, and the drinking water is unhealthy. The water for cooking or washing clothes may come from a ditch alongside the road. The same water may later be used to irrigate a vegetable garden. There are many villages without a doctor or nurse. The people in some villages still go to "village wizards" who use herbs and charms to treat diseases.

Villagers in Ecuador wash clothes in the river. What does this scene suggest about the lives of these villagers?

1. Which questions are answered in this chapter?
   a. How does the Latin American farmer live?
   b. Why are many farmers in poor health?
   c. What games do the children play?
2. The main idea of this chapter describes:
   a. how the village farmer meets his daily needs.
   b. goods manufactured in the home.
   c. the meals of the small farmers.
3. The chief crop of the village farmer is:
   a. corn.   b. wheat.   c. rice.
4. Village people sell their handwork:
   a. to the large department stores.
   b. to buyers in the cities.
   c. in the nearby market.
5. Many farm families have poor health for all of these reasons EXCEPT:
   a. lack of sunshine.
   b. lack of pure water.
   c. poor diet.
6. Meat is not an important part of the diet of the village farmers because:
   a. the cattle are needed to supply milk.
   b. very few meat animals are raised on the farm.
   c. farmers sell their meat to the nearby cities.

Photograph Study

The photograph below should help you to recall parts of the chapter you have just read. What is the main idea of the photograph?

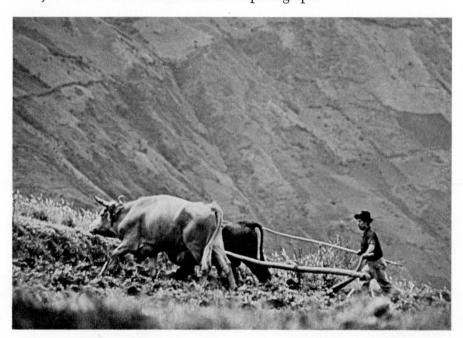

Complete the following chart in your notebook.

	SMALL VILLAGE FARMER OF LATIN AMERICA	CORN-BELT FARMER OF THE UNITED STATES
1. Homes		
2. Machinery		
3. Crops and animals		
4. Standard of living		
5. Markets for their products		

FOLLOW UP In your notebook, match each item in Column A with one of the items in Column B.

COLUMN A

1. peon
2. fiesta
3. adobe
4. mestizo
5. plaza
6. tortilla
7. hacienda
8. serape

COLUMN B

a. Blanket.
b. Festival
c. Village square.
d. Farm worker.
e. Flat cakes of corn bread.
f. Large knife.
g. Part Indian, part Spanish.
h. Large estate.
i. Sun-dried brick.

7 THE PROBLEM OF LAND

This field has been burned so that crops can be planted. Why do farmers find it necessary to make new clearings such as this every several years?

Reading For A Purpose: How do the people of Latin America make use of the land?

1. In the great region of Latin America, only a very small part of the land can be used. Much of the land is covered by mountains, jungle and desert. The Andes Mountains are too high and cold for large-scale farming. The soils of the rain forest and dry grasslands are poor. The deserts cannot support life. Nevertheless, most people in this region make their living by using the land. Let us see how the people of Latin America meet the challenge of these difficult conditions.

2. A large part of Latin America is rain forest. In the forest a few Indian tribes live in villages near the rivers. They are always crowded by trees and plants that grow fast in the hot and wet climate. There are many insects that carry diseases such as malaria. People cannot travel far because there are few paths through the thick jungle. Growing food is a problem because the soil is poor. Keeping the food from spoiling is also difficult in this hot climate.

3. The Indians in the rain forest live simple lives. They grow most of their food in small clearings in the forest. The men clear the land by chopping down trees or burning away the thick brush. Once the land has been cleared, the women start planting. The men go into the forest to get more food by hunting and fishing.

4. The chief foods in the rain forest are bananas, yams and tapioca (manioc). Every two or three years, the Indians have to move and make a new clearing because the soil in the old one has worn out. Heavy rains wash out or leach the minerals in the soil that food crops

need in order to grow. Most travel is by canoe along the rivers and streams because the forest is so thick.

5. The Indians make nearly everything they use from the products of the forest. They make their houses out of thatch—straw, grass and leaves. These are cone-shaped so as to shed water. The men make fish traps, bows and arrows and blowguns from which they blow or "shoot" small poisoned darts. They also make canoes or dugouts by hollowing out the trunks of large trees. The women weave clothing, mats and baskets out of grasses and leaves. Some of these are sold.

6. The rain forest has many products that are useful to people in other parts of the world. These products include mahogany and other hardwoods, chicle for chewing gum and cinchona bark from which a medicine called quinine is made. The products are gathered by the Indians and brought to trading posts at Belém or Manaus. (These port cities also supply the people of the rain forest with the

things they need from the outside world.) Only a small part of its riches is brought out of the jungle. Few people live there and it is hard to ship goods through the thick forest.

7. As you remember, grasslands are found north and south of the Amazon jungle. Thus, the southern half of Brazil and the llanos of Venezuela in the north have a tropical savanna climate. This means there are two seasons, one rainy and one dry. How do the people make a living in this climate? Cattle raising is very important in the llanos. The land is divided into large cattle ranches or *haciendas*. The cattle are always on the move. The herds are guarded by cowboys called llaneros. These cattle are raised for their hides and rarely for their meat.

8. In the dry season the rivers become little more than streams. Cattle are grazed near the streams where the grass is still moist and green. In the rainy season the rivers flood their banks. Then the cowboys drive the cattle to higher lands or mesas between the swollen rivers. When they have eaten all the grass on one mesa, they wade through the waters to another.

9. The savannas are not the best land for growing crops. The soil is poor because the minerals have been washed out by the heavy rains. However, a number of cash crops are grown in this climate. Sugar cane is the chief crop of the tropical grasslands. The hot weather, the rainy growing season and the dry harvest time are good for growing sugar. Sugar cane is grown on large plantations in the islands of the West Indies, particularly Cuba. Another wet and dry crop is *henequen*, or sisal, from which rope is made. Henequen is raised on the Yucatan Peninsula in Mexico.

10. As you have learned, an important feature of the climate of Latin America is that it is vertical. That is, the climate changes as you

A sugar cane field. In many parts of Latin America, sugar cane is a cash crop. What is meant by the term "cash crop"?

travel upward in the mountains. Farming is also vertical. In the hot and damp lowlands of Central America there are plantations of bananas and cacao beans. (Cacao is the bean from which chocolate is made.) These crops need the wet, rainy weather and long growing season of the tropics. Bananas need more than a year to ripen. Most of the workers are black people and mestizos. They live on land owned by the plantation or in villages near the plantations.

11. As you travel higher into a cooler climate (tierra templada), the most common crop is coffee. Coffee is grown in the highlands of Brazil and Colombia. In Brazil, coffee is grown on large estates, the fazendas. At first the coffee beans are green. During the hot, rainy summers, the little beans turn red and open. During the dry, cooler winters, the beans turn brown and are picked. Coffee is the chief export of both Brazil and Colombia. It is our chief import from those countries.

12. Many Indians live in the higher altitudes (tierra fria). They farm on the steep mountainsides. They raise the crops that fill their needs—wheat, barley, beans, potatoes and Indian corn or maize. They graze herds of sheep, llamas and burros. The llamas and burros are used for riding and for carrying heavy loads. The temperature may be from 40° to 50° all year round. Some Indians also work in the tin, copper, lead and zinc mines found at this height.

A modern Inca herds llamas. How are these animals useful to the Indians who live in the mountains?

13. In South America the humid-subtropical area is found along the southeastern coast. This includes part of Brazil, Paraguay and Argentina and all of Uruguay. Because of the climate and soil, the best cattle-grazing lands are found there. There is a long, hot summer and a short, mild winter. The famous grazing lands are the pampas or plains of Argentina.

14. The pampas are divided into large ranches or estancias. The wealthy owners live mainly in Buenos Aires. The cattle are cared for by colorful cowboys called *gauchos.* Most of them are Indians. The cattle are raised chiefly for their meat. Large amounts of alfalfa are grown on the pampas as food for the cattle. Corn and wheat are grains grown on the rich, black earth. Argentina exports the riches of the pampas—beef, corn and wheat—to other parts of the world. Unlike the rest of Latin America, most of Argentina's trade is with Europe.

15. Two important crops of Latin America are corn and cotton. Corn is a basic food in the diet of millions of Latin Americans. It had been raised by the Indians long before Columbus' voyages. In Mexico corn is largely eaten by the people. In Brazil it is an important food for animals. In Argentina it is an export. (You will note that Argentina has large amounts of farm products that are the same as the farm products of our own country. This is because our climates are similar.) Since we grow large amounts of corn and wheat and raise millions of beef cattle, the U.S. cannot be a good customer for Argentina's farm products. Therefore, Argentina looks to Europe to sell her important goods for export.

16. Cotton has become an important product of the dry lands. In her northern deserts, Mexico has used the waters of the Rio Grande to grow cotton. (Mexico ranks first in cotton production in Latin America.) In the desert of Peru, cotton is also grown. The water is brought from the mountains near the coast. All over the world, it has been found that the finest cotton can be grown in dry areas through water supplied by irrigation.

1. Which questions are answered in this chapter?
   a. What are the chief crops of Latin America?
   b. Why are the pampas good for grazing cattle?
   c. How does the banana tree grow?
2. The main idea of this chapter describes:
   a. the many farming areas of Latin America.
   b. how people live in the rain forest.
   c. the crops of the vertical climate.
3. The chief crops of the lowland plantations are:
   a. rice and pineapples.
   b. bananas and cacao beans.
   c. palm oil and corn.
4. The chief crops of the pampas are:
   a. cotton and coffee.
   b. wheat and corn.
   c. sugar cane and bananas.
5. A country of Latin America that produces much the same kind of crops as the United States is:
   a. Brazil. b. Chile. c. Argentina.
6. Life in the tierra fria is difficult because:
   a. it is too far above sea level to grow any crops.
   b. the forests must be cleared before planting.
   c. the steep hillsides must be terraced before planting.
7. A *mesa* is the same as a:
   a. lowland plain.
   b. small high plateau.
   c. mountainside.
8. *Cacao* is a small tree whose beans are used in making:
   a. medicine. b. rope. c. chocolate.

Match each item in Column B with one of the farming regions in Column A. Each farming region may be used several times.

COLUMN A

A. Rain-forest farming
B. Savannas
C. Highlands
D. Pampas

COLUMN B

a. Small clearings in the jungle.
b. Coffee plantations.
c. Home of the gauchos.
d. Houses of straw and grass.
e. Barley and maize.
f. Cattle, corn and wheat.
g. Sugar plantations.
h. Raising sheep and llamas.
i. Flood season and dry season.
j. Banana trees.

Tell whether these statements are true or false. The underlined words make the statements true or false. If a statement is false, what words would you place in it to make it true?

1. Bananas are a product of a <u>hot and wet</u> climate.
2. The chief export of Brazil is <u>coffee.</u>
3. <u>Colombia</u> is a leading exporter of wheat and beef.
4. Very dry lands that have water from irrigation are best for growing <u>cotton.</u>
5. The great farming region of Uruguay and Argentina is called the <u>llanos.</u>
6. <u>Malaria</u> is a disease carried by an insect of the rain forest.
7. A rain-forest Indian may make his house of <u>thatch</u>.
8. One of the hardwoods found in the jungle of South America is the <u>maple</u> tree.
9. Gauchos are the famous cowboys of <u>Mexico</u>.
10. An important part of the diet of the people of Mexico is <u>coffee.</u>

8 MINING AND MANUFACTURING

Reading For A Purpose: Why have industries grown slowly in Latin America?

1. Compared with the number of people who work on farms in Latin America, there are not many people working in the mines. Yet minerals are an important resource for Latin America. The earliest Spanish explorers found riches in silver and gold. Silver is still mined in Mexico, Peru and Bolivia. Mexico mines more silver than any other country in the world.

2. Even more important than silver and gold are other minerals that play a great part in all our lives. Bolivia has rich tin mines. The tin is located high in the plateaus, more than 10,000 feet above sea level. Working in the tin mines is very difficult. Workers breathe in the dust from the ore. The life of a tin miner is a short one. The Atacama Desert in northern Chile is rich in copper and nitrates. Nitrates are used for fertilizers. The people who work in the desert also lead a hard life. Everything they need must be brought in from the outside—food, clothing and even water. These important minerals—tin, copper and nitrates—are found in areas that are hard to reach.

3. Our entire modern world depends upon oil. One of the richest oil reserves in the world is at Lake Maracaibo in Venezuela. Wells have been sunk into the lake itself. Venezuela is one of the leading oil-producing nations of the world. Much of the oil is sent to the United States. Because of oil, the average income of Venezuelans is higher than that of any other people in Latin America.

4. Since World War II, Venezuela has also become a leading producer of iron ore. And in Peru, iron ore production has grown so that it now ranks second to Venezuela's. Ore deposits are not easy to reach. However, the world needs more and more iron for building and machinery. As a result, foreign countries have supplied Latin America with the money needed to find this valuable mineral and bring it to factories where it can be used. Steel mills are growing in Latin America. (Steel mills in the United States also import Venezuela's iron ore.)

5. Aluminum is much in demand for making airplanes, buildings and hundreds of other products. Aluminum is made from an ore called bauxite. A great share of the world's bauxite is found in Jamaica, Surinam and Guyana. It is shipped to the aluminum mills of the United States and Canada.

6. There are factories in Latin America, but most of them do not make use of the region's mineral wealth. Most of them depend on the products of the farm. For example, there are meat-packing plants near the grazing areas of Argentina. There are textile mills in Mexico

A textile mill in Cuenca, Ecuador. How can industry help improve the lives of Latin Americans?

and Peru turning out cloth from raw materials nearby. Despite these beginnings, Latin America exports most of the raw materials of its farms and mines to other parts of the world. The United States and the nations of Western Europe are its best customers. In turn, the United States sends Latin America all kinds of machinery.

7. Industry has not grown rapidly in Latin America for various reasons. First, there is a lack of coal. Coal is important as a source of power for mills and factories. It is needed as fuel in the making of steel. There are great possibilities, however, in the use of falling water for power. The heavy rainfall and snows in the mountains provide plenty of water. Less than ten per cent of the possible water power is used, however. This is because the sources of water power are far from the centers of population and industry.

8. Money is also needed. Money used to build factories and power plants is called *capital*. Latin America has lacked capital for several reasons. First, changes in government have taken place often in most of its countries. Businessmen from foreign nations are not eager to invest their money in countries that have revolutions all the time. They are afraid that their property will be damaged or taken away. Second, the people who settled Latin America came from Spain and Portugal. These are farming countries. The settlers kept the way of living they had learned in their homeland. Their wealth was measured in how much land they owned. Perhaps some of this wealth will now be used to start factories. Third, the profits that do come from the mines or plantations go outside the country, since they are owned by people or businesses of foreign countries in many cases.

9. Transportation and communication in Latin America have been poor. Transportation is necessary to bring raw materials to factories. Because of the mountains and jungle, it has been easier to ship raw materials by water or air than to send them overland from one port of Latin America to another. (This meant, of course, that industry in Latin America was held back even more before the coming of the airplane.)

10. Skilled workers are needed for factory work. You have learned that a large number of Latin Americans are unable to read or write. There have been only a small number of schools. However, some improvement has taken place. The leaders of Latin America know that education of the people is most important in bringing them a higher standard of living.

Clearing land to lay the trans-Andean pipeline. This pipeline now carries crude oil from the jungles of Colombia over the mountains to the Pacific coast of Colombia. The pipeline crosses rocky peaks, canyons, timberland and wide rivers. What problems do you think the pipeline workers had to face?

UNDERSTANDING CHAPTER 8

1. Which questions are answered in this chapter?
   a. Why are there so few factories in Latin America?
   b. What power resources does Latin America need?
   c. How is tin mined?
2. The main idea of *paragraphs 1 through 7* describes:
   a. the mineral resources of Latin America.
   b. the hard work in the mines of Latin America.
   c. Latin American trade with other lands.
3. Latin America has some minerals, but it lacks:
   a. coal.   b. oil.   c. tin.
4. Venezuela is one of the leading producers of:
   a. gold and silver.
   b. copper and nitrates.
   c. oil and iron ore.
5. A reason why Latin America has been slow to develop industry is that:
   a. most of her trade is with Europe.
   b. lack of rain means that there is little water power available.
   c. there has been a lack of skilled workers.
6. The desert of Chile is valuable because it is a source of:
   a. irrigation.   b. minerals.   c. oil.
7. "The machinery in the factory was poor because the owner had no *capital* to replace it." The best meaning for *capital* is:
   a. new property.
   b. money to buy new machines.
   c. useful ideas.

Map Study

Map #20—Exports of Latin America

Study the map. Then tell whether these statements are true or false.

1. A great share of Latin American trade is with the United States.
2. Bananas are an important export of countries along the east coast of South America.
3. Peru and Chile both have a supply of raw copper.
4. Argentina's exports are chiefly food products.
5. Venezuela is rich in both iron ore and oil.
6. Mexico sends a large share of her exports to the United States.
7. Latin America's trade with Asia is a small amount of her exports.
8. Chile's resources are largely minerals.

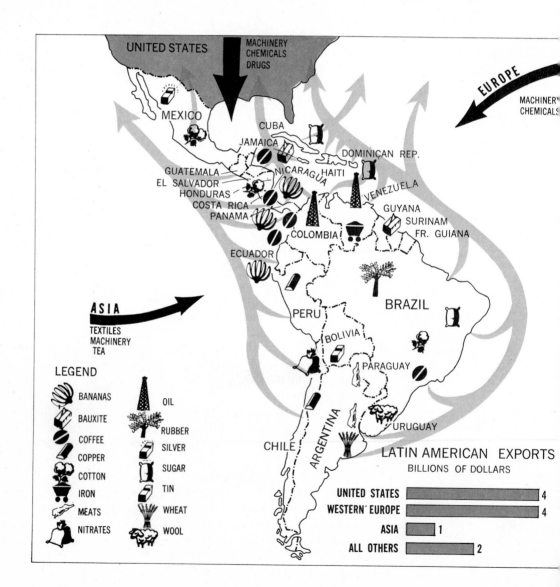

A. Where am I?

Which country or part of Latin America is described by the person speaking in each of the following paragraphs?

1. "Work here in the highland is hard. My family is poor and I have poor health. If only I didn't have to go back into that mine tomorrow. I cough so much now I know it will never stop. I live in ⸻."
2. "The ore is near the surface and the machines do the hard work. I'm glad of that because it is so hot every day. My family has a good home. But I wish we weren't so far from other people. If that pipeline breaks, where will we get water? Yet we stay because we have work. I live in ⸻."
3. "That sun shines all day, even when it rains. I know it's the rain that makes it seem so hot. And I had to come here in the season of the big rains! It's green all the time, but I can't see the color because the huge trees block out the sun. I am in ⸻."
4. "It is warm even on the side of the hill. But the sun won't hurt my precious beans here in the shade. I like to look at the rows and rows of trees. The people of the United States can't seem to do without my trees and my family at picking time. I live in ⸻."
5. "Look at the food on these docks! That wheat and corn will feed a lot of people in Europe. Funny, some people feed that corn to hogs. They should export it as my country does. I live in ⸻."

B. Looking Ahead

In Column I are listed some of the resources that bring wealth to Latin America. In Column II, list the problems that must be overcome to make full use of these resources.

COLUMN I	COLUMN II
1. copper	
2. iron ore	
3. nitrates	
4. oil	
5. tin	

Fact or Opinion Read each statement carefully. If the statement is a fact, write F in your notebook. If it is an opinion, write O.

1. A change in the system of land ownership is the greatest need in Latin America.
2. Silver is an important mineral resource in Mexico.
3. Latin America has many minerals that the United States can use.
4. Many valuable products cannot easily be brought out of the jungle.
5. Without oil and iron ore, Venezuela would be a poor country.
6. The land system in Latin America will be very slow to change.
7. If it is used, Latin America could have a large amount of electricity from water power.
8. Latin America will never industrialize because it lacks coal.
9. Control over the mines of Latin America is necessary for the safety of the United States.
10. U.S. trade with Argentina will double in the next ten years.

9 THE NEEDS OF LATIN AMERICA

Reading For A Purpose: What are the problems of Latin America?

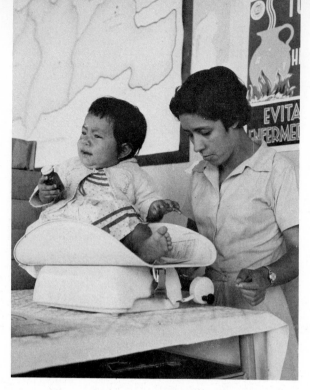

A medical center in Guatemala. What kinds of services do you think are provided by medical centers?

1. The poverty of many people in Latin America is the biggest problem of the region. There are thousands of Indian farmers who live on tiny plots of the poorest land. They are barely able to grow enough food for their families. The money they make from farming each year is very small. Many make less than $100 per year. Their health is poor. They do not eat the right kind of food. Many cannot read and write. Their needs are simple, but everywhere they are the same: more and better land, pure water, better roads, electricity, public schools and health services.

2. The number of people in Latin America is growing so fast that the population may double in twenty years! Most of this growth in population is taking place among the poorer families. Thus, there will be more mouths to feed where there is the least ability to feed them. There is already a problem of raising enough food for the present population.

3. Much of the fertile land is occupied by huge plantations. Many of these plantations are owned by foreign businessmen or by a few wealthy families of Latin America. The plantations have become like factories. Workers are housed and fed like armies in large buildings. Crops raised on the plantations—coffee, sugar and bananas—are raised for export to other countries. They are not an important part of the diet of the Latin Americans. Therefore, a large amount of food must be imported by these countries for their people.

4. As you learned in Unit 2, the kind of farming that causes a country to depend upon one chief crop may cause problems. Latin America has sometimes been called a region of "one-crop countries." For example, Brazil and Colombia have long depended on one crop—coffee—for their income. The countries of Central America depend upon their sale of bananas. Guatemala and El Salvador get more than half their export sales from coffee. Cuba has depended upon sugar cane. This kind of farming is called "monoculture." If the crop is a poor one or there is a drop in its market price, the whole country suffers greatly.

5. The need for more land for the small farmers is being faced in several ways. Governments are opening new lands for the people. For example, Brasília, the new capital of Brazil, has been built inland to attract people to a new area. There is a growing demand that the large estates be broken up and given to small farmers. People like to own their own land. The chance to have a farm of one's own is the dream of many people all over the world.

6. While the number of large factories is still small, the demand for factories is growing. The new steel mills of Cerro Bolivar in Venezuela are an example of what Latin Americans can do. With more factories, the Latin Americans

America. There are two chief classes of people in this region. The wealthy class, usually of Spanish descent, owns much of the land and the factories. The poorer class, usually Indians and black people, have small farms or work on

The contrast of old and new housing in Costa Rica. What ideas can you suggest for improving the living conditions of the people in this picture?

will be able to use more of their own resources for their own benefit. People will be hired to work in these factories. They will receive more pay than they could get from working on the farms. They will be able to buy goods that are manufactured. If they are able to buy more, the factories will make more goods and there will be a need for even more jobs.

7. More jobs and better pay will help a great deal in getting rid of another problem of Latin

the large estates. There is no real "middle class." The poorer classes are being heard more often in Latin America. They want more land, more jobs and a better education for their children. They want the opportunity for a higher standard of living for themselves and their families.

8. There have been frequent "revolutions" and changes in government in Latin America. One group after another has tried to gain

power in many countries. Many of these revolutions have been supported by the army. Others have been caused by a few strong men who want power. They become dictators. There are still countries in Latin America today that are ruled as dictatorships. Because most of the people have not received an education, it has not been easy to have democratic governments. Education of the people is an important step in the improvement of life in Latin America. It is hoped that as the countries develop, their governments will grow to be the kind that allows the people to make their own laws and choose their own leaders.

Town meeting in Salasca, Ecuador. Why are town meetings held?

UNDERSTANDING
CHAPTER 9

1. Which questions are answered in this chapter?
   a. How are some Latin Americans governed?
   b. What are the problems of Latin America?
   c. How does the United Nations help Latin America?
2. The main idea of *paragraph 8* describes:
   a. revolutions in Latin America.
   b. dictators of Latin America.
   c. some problems of government in Latin America.
3. Most Latin American nations obtain money by:
   a. manufacturing goods.
   b. selling raw materials abroad.
   c. dairy farming.
4. Which is a correct matching of country and crop?
   a. Brazil—cotton   b. Cuba—sugar   c. Colombia—wheat
5. Latin American countries import food because:
   a. plantations grow crops for export.
   b. Indian farmers grow only for their own needs.
   c. corn and wheat are not grown in Latin America.
6. More factories will help Latin Americans because:
   a. they will provide more raw materials.
   b. education will be improved.
   c. Latin Americans will be able to use their own raw materials.
7. In *monoculture*, a country depends upon:
   a. exports.
   b. one crop.
   c. many farm products.

8. The *middle class* refers to:
   a. the very rich.
   b. those who are neither rich nor poor.
   c. the very poor.

Look at the cartoon. Then answer the questions below.

1. Who is the running figure?
2. What is the meaning of this cartoon?
3. What is monoculture?
4. What is being done to overcome some of the problems shown here?
5. What is a good title for this cartoon?

Pretend you are at a meeting of the Organization of American States in which all the Latin American nations are represented. You are the representative of a Latin American country. What would you say were your greatest problems?

If you were a representative of the United States, what kind of help would you offer to Latin America?

Outline In the following outline, some topics are filled in, but the proper headings are missing. Which headings would you choose for each list of topics in the outline?

HEADINGS

A. _____
1. Little machinery.
2. Small plots of land.
3. Little medical care.
4. Impure water.

B. _____
1. Colombia—coffee
2. Brazil—coffee
3. Honduras—bananas
4. Uruguay—wool

C. _____
1. A few people own most of the land.
2. Peons work on large plantations.
3. The very rich and the very poor.

a. One-Crop Countries
b. Problems of Government
c. Land Ownership
d. Need for Education
e. Poverty of the People

10 THE UNITED STATES AND LATIN AMERICA

Reading For A Purpose: How can the United States improve her relations with Latin America?

1. In 1823, President Monroe stated that the United States would defend the freedom of the new countries of Latin America. His statement was greeted with approval by our southern neighbors. However, this friendly feeling toward the United States has changed from time to time.

2. In 1846, the United States went to war with Mexico over the boundary between Texas and Mexico. Many Latin Americans thought that the United States had "picked on" her smaller neighbor. This bad feeling caused by the war lasted for many years.

Ships pass through the locks of the Panama Canal. Why did the United States build a canal across Central America?

3. About fifty years later, the United States went to war with Spain, the "mother country" of Latin America. Our people were aroused by newspaper stories of Spanish cruelty toward Cubans. Americans sympathized with the Cubans. After the war, the United States gained possession of the island of Puerto Rico from Spain. The United States also became Cuba's "protector." Our government watched over Cuba's affairs until 1934, when Cuba was finally given complete freedom. To this day, however, the United States has a large naval base at Guantanamo Bay, though the leaders of the island are no longer our friends.

4. In 1903, the United States openly favored Panama's desire to become free from Colombia. Shortly after Panama became free, the United States got permission and land from Panama to build the famous Panama Canal. The canal was important to the United States. A quicker way was needed for ships to go from the Atlantic to the Pacific. There were those in Latin America who felt the United States had used its power to help Panama revolt against Colombia.

5. In 1902, President Theodore Roosevelt sent warships to Venezuela to stop European

nations from occupying that country. Venezuela owed money to these countries. President Roosevelt did not want any European nation landing troops in Latin America. Three years later, he sent Americans to Santo Domingo to make sure that that nation paid its debts. At other times, the United States Marines were sent to Nicaragua to keep order and to protect American property there. The people of Latin America did not want this kind of help. They resented the power of the United States. They felt they could take care of themselves.

6. But as early as 1889, an effort was being made to improve relations between the United States and the Latin American nations. The Pan American Union was formed. Twenty-one nations were members. They agreed to settle their disputes peaceably. This Union has grown into the Organization of American States (OAS).

7. President Franklin Roosevelt helped to bring about a better understanding with our Latin American neighbors. In 1933, he announced the "Good Neighbor Policy." Our troops were brought home from the Caribbean. The United States agreed that it had no right to interfere in the affairs of other countries. A spirit of cooperation grew during World War II. The nations of all the Americas worked together to defeat their enemies. In 1947, at Rio de Janeiro, the American nations agreed that each would help the others in case of attack.

8. At the present time, the Organization of American States is trying to find ways of improving the life of all Americans. The United States has offered to help many Latin American nations. In 1961, President Kennedy announced the Alliance for Progress. Through it, the United States has given money to Latin America to provide more land, schools and jobs for the people. Our Peace Corps, also started by President Kennedy, has helped farmers in Latin America. Some of its workers have taught in schools. These workers for peace

have tried to improve living conditions in the poorer nations.

9. However, not all the problems in our relations with Latin America have been solved. The control of the Panama Canal is one of these problems. The government of Panama wants to have a greater share in the management of the canal. Some Americans feel that the United States should let Panama run the canal. They feel that this would show our faith in our Latin American neighbors. Besides, we have only leased or rented the Canal Zone from Panama. We may not always be able or want to control it. The canal is already too narrow for use by our largest ships. Travel through it is slow, since it is not a sea-level canal but must use a system of locks. Many feel that the canal cannot be defended in case of an atomic war. Therefore, new routes for another canal are now being studied.

10. Another problem for the United States in Latin America is Cuba. Cuba is an island about ninety miles southeast of the Florida coast. In 1959, Fidel Castro became the leader of Cuba. In a short time he brought his government into close friendship with the Soviet Union and the People's Republic of China. In

This photo of Fidel Castro was taken when he spoke to students at a university in Chile. Why do you think political leaders are interested in sharing their opinions with young people?

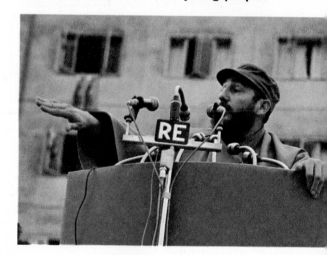

October, 1962, it was revealed that the Soviet Union was building missile bases in Cuba. President Kennedy ordered a "quarantine" of the island. Our ships were sent to keep military supplies from reaching Cuba. President Kennedy said that our ships would stay until the missile bases were broken up and the missiles returned to the Soviet Union. The world was close to war. But the Soviet Union agreed to the President's demands and withdrew its missiles. However, there is still great concern over the fact that an unfriendly state is so close to our shores.

11. How to make needed changes in the life of the people of Latin America in a peaceful manner is a problem that remains to be solved. In 1965, a civil war broke out in the Dominican Republic. Fearing that the Communists would gain control, President Johnson sent U.S. troops to the island. Not everyone agreed with the President's action. It was hoped that an understanding could be reached through the OAS.

12. *Nationalism* is growing among the Latin American peoples. (Nationalism is the feeling of pride that one has in his nation and his government.) In all countries, people desire to be free and equal instead of dependent upon others for their safety or their prosperity. This nationalism may take many forms. Latin Americans may resent North Americans who work in their nation or gain profits from it. They may demand that their government take over the mines, factories and plantations that belong to foreign companies. They may demand more land and more schools. It is understandable that this nationalism may take forms with which we do not always agree.

UNDERSTANDING CHAPTER 10

1. Which questions are answered in this chapter?
   a. Who is Fidel Castro?
   b. How did the United States help Mexico in 1864?
   c. Why was the Pan American Union formed?
2. The main idea of *paragraphs 6 through 8* describes:
   a. why some Latin American people did not trust the United States.
   b. how the United States has helped Latin America to solve its problems.
   c. efforts of the United States to cooperate with Latin America.
3. After the Spanish-American War, the United States obtained:
   a. Cuba.   b. the Virgin Islands.   c. Puerto Rico.
4. A plan suggested by President Kennedy was the:
   a. Pan American Union.
   b. Alliance for Progress.
   c. Good Neighbor Policy.
5. The Pan American Union was formed to:
   a. improve trade between the United States and Latin America.
   b. carry out the defense of the Americas in World War II.
   c. work together on common problems.

6. The United States would like another canal through Central America because:
   a. the Panama Canal is not fitted for modern transportation.
   b. Latin American states have agreed to take over the canal.
   c. it is too close to Russian missile bases.
7. President Kennedy's *quarantine* of Cuba means that:
   a. ships were kept from reaching Cuba.
   b. sugar shipments from Cuba were stopped.
   c. the United States sent soldiers to help Cuba.
8. The Pan American *Union* was formed. This means that the countries agreed to:
   a. separate.
   b. join together.
   c. take part in something.

DEVELOPING IDEAS AND SKILLS

Look at the cartoon. Then answer the questions below.

1. Who are the figures around the table?
2. What progress has been made on the problems they are considering?
3. What other problems would you suggest be added?
4. What is a good title for this cartoon?

Below are three headings for your *outline*. Sub-topics follow the list of headings. In your notebook, make the outline, placing the sub-topics under the correct headings.

HEADINGS:

A. Why Latin America Distrusted the United States

B. Cooperation Between the United States and Latin America

C. Problems in Latin America Today

SUB-TOPICS:

1. The events of World War II.
2. Panama becomes free from Colombia.
3. Good Neighbor Policy.
4. Poverty in Latin America.
5. The Panama Canal today.
6. The Organization of American States (OAS).
7. Mexican War of 1846-48.
8. Work of the Peace Corps.
9. United States Marines in Nicaragua.
10. Rise of Fidel Castro to power in Cuba.

Special Reports

Now that you have completed your over-all study of Latin America, you should be prepared to make a special report. Select one of the countries of Latin America for special study. In your report, try to answer some of these questions:

1. What does the farmer want in the country you have chosen? What is his day like?
2. What stands in the way of his getting what he wants?
3. What hopes do his children have?
4. What do they know of their country? Of ours?
5. What does the farm family do in its spare time?
6. What part does religion play in its life?

Try to answer the same questions for a factory worker or a large landowner in the country you have chosen.

11 MEXICO--A NEIGHBOR MOVING AHEAD

Reading For A Purpose: How has Mexico become a leading nation of Latin America?

1. Much of what we have been learning about Latin America is true of Mexico, the country south of the Rio Grande. Mexico is a mixture of old and new, partly Indian and partly Spanish. There are villages where the Indians live and work much as their ancestors did long ago. Here are the remains of Indian pyramids and temples. One can buy pottery and jewelry made from Indian designs hundreds of years old. The Spanish part of Mexico can be seen in the language, churches, homes and family life in the growing cities.

2. Mexico is one of the larger countries of Latin America, about one-fourth the size of the United States. The country is partly in the low latitudes and partly in the middle latitudes. Most of the land is covered by a broad central plateau or highland. On each side of the plateau are narrow lowlands. These coastal plains border the Pacific on the west and the Gulf of Mexico on the east.

3. Because of the highlands, much of Mexico has a vertical climate. Northern Mexico is very dry. As you travel southward the land rises; the climate is cooler and there is more rain. This is the *tierra templada*. Still higher, it is colder—the *tierra fria*. The lowlands on the Gulf Coast are hot and rainy. These lowlands are covered with a thick jungle. This is the *tierra caliente*. The Pacific coast is hot, but drier.

4. The central and eastern parts of Mexico were once ruled by the Aztec Indians. The Aztecs were conquered by the Spanish under Cortez in 1519. They were put to work in the gold and silver mines by the Spanish conquerors. Spain ruled Mexico for 300 years.

5. In 1810, Father Miguel Hidalgo led the first revolt against Spain. In 1821, Mexico finally became free. The new government, however, was run by only a few people. The land was divided into large estates called haciendas. Most of the workers on these farms were Indian *peons*. In 1848, Mexico lost a large part of her northern lands in a war with the United States. In 1900, the Indian peons revolted. They wanted a better government that would treat them more fairly. In 1917, a new constitution or plan of government was adopted. Some haciendas were divided up and the land given to the Indian farmers. Also, the people could now vote for their own leaders. (Later Mexican governments have been gradually giving more land to the small farmers.)

6. Most of Mexico's 52 million people live in the plateau around Mexico City, the modern, rapidly growing capital of the country. Most of the people are farmers who live in small villages. They either own their own farms or work lands belonging to the whole village. Their plots of land are small. Many farmers cannot afford machinery. They use oxen or

horses to pull their plows. They plant, cultivate and harvest their crops largely by hand. The harvest is small. Most of the food that is raised must be used at home. The Mexican government is trying hard to encourage the use of more machinery.

7. The chief crops of the highlands are corn, wheat, coffee and tobacco. A favorite food is *tortillas*, flat pancakes made from corn meal. Cotton is grown on the irrigated lands of the north. Bananas, sugar cane and sisal hemp (for making rope) are grown in the tropical lowlands. The drier northern region is also used for raising cattle.

8. The highlands of Mexico are rich in mineral wealth. Mexico exports 40% of the world's silver. It is second to the United States in the production of sulphur. Gold, copper, lead and zinc are other products of its mines. There are large oil fields on the east coast. Mountain streams are used to supply electricity and water for irrigation. Much of this mineral wealth is exported to the United States. In turn, we send Mexico machinery for its mines, farms and factories.

9. Mexico is a changing land. Its leaders are using its resources to build industry. More and more people have moved to the cities where

A farmer plows his fields in the Oaxaca Valley in Mexico. How is this man's method of farming different from methods used on many large farms in the United States today?

207

Workers making palm furniture in a Mexican village. Why is the Mexican government interested in developing such industries?

they work in steel mills, chemical plants and oil refineries. There are many new housing projects and office buildings in the big cities. Health conditions have improved. Now the average Mexican can expect to live to 68 years of age. The tourist trade is also becoming a large source of income for the country. The Mexican government has built many schools, both in the cities and in the rural areas. Good roads are being built throughout the land. The people are playing a larger role in making their government's laws and in choosing their own leaders. Because of these efforts, Mexico is becoming one of the most prosperous nations in Latin America.

UNDERSTANDING CHAPTER 11

1 Which questions are answered in this chapter?
   a. Who was Juárez?
   b. What is the occupation of most Mexican people?
   c. How is Mexico making progress?

2. The main idea of *paragraphs 6 and 7* describes:
   a. farming in Mexico.
   b. the lowlands regions.
   c. the meals of a Mexican family.

3. Mexico carries on most of its trade with:
   a. Brazil.   b. the United States.   c. Spain.

4. Mexico leads the world in the production of:
   a. silver   b. lead.   c. tin.

5. Most people live in the highlands of Mexico because:
   a. the climate is cooler.
   b. large plantations provide work for the people.
   c. this is the best grazing land.

6. Only a small part of Mexico's land is used for farming because:
   a. it is located in the middle latitudes.
   b. most people work in mines.
   c. much of the land is mountains or desert.

7. A *tortilla* is:
   a. an old Indian temple.
   b. hand-made clothing.
   c. a kind of corn pancake.

Map Study

Map #21a and b—Mexico

Study the maps. Then answer the questions at the top of page 210.

Map #21a—Mexico

*Map #21b—Mexico
and the
United States*

UNITED STATES	MEXICO
POPULATION: 209 MILLION	POPULATION: 52.6 MILLION
LAND AREA: 3.6 MILLION SQUARE MILES	LAND AREA: 759,000 SQUARE MILES
59 PEOPLE PER SQUARE MILE	69.1 PEOPLE PER SQUARE MILE

1. Does Mexico lie in the high, middle or low latitudes?
2. Does Mexico extend farther from north to south or east to west?
3. What bodies of water border on Mexico?
4. What is the approximate longitude and latitude of Mexico City?
5. Is Mexico more or less crowded than the United States?
6. How many "Mexicos" could fit inside the territory of the United States?
7. Why do you think there are few large seaports in Mexico?
8. How would you describe the topography of Mexico?
9. What does the latitude of Mexico tell you about its climate?
10. How many degrees of longitude is Mexico City from the community in which you live? (Use the map on page 27, as well.)

SUMMING UP

Agree or Disagree   Decide whether or not each of the following agrees with what you have read. If the answer is *disagree*, explain why.

1. Mexico is mostly a mountainous country.
2. Mexico has a civilization that is partly Indian and partly French.
3. Most Mexicans are small farmers who work land near their villages.
4. The chief foods of Mexicans are rice and beans.
5. Mexico is rich in mineral resources; the chief mineral is silver.
6. Mexico has little trade with the United States.
7. Many of the Mexican people make handcrafts.
8. More and more of the Mexican people are living in the cities.
9. Mexico is a changing land whose people live under a democratic government.
10. Much of Mexico's climate is vertical.

FOLLOW UP

Tell whether these statements are true or false. The underlined words make the statements true or false. If a statement is false, what words would you place in it to make it true?

1. The border between Mexico and the United States is the Rocky Mountains.
2. The United States imports minerals from Mexico.
3. Irrigation provides water for crops in northern Mexico.
4. Early Indians in Mexico were the Incas.
5. An important part of life in modern Mexico is an increase in industry.
6. Much of Mexico's power for industry comes from coal.

12 PUERTO RICO--OUR PRIDE IN THE CARIBBEAN

Reading For A Purpose: Why is Puerto Rico important to the United States?

1. Puerto Rico is an island about 300 miles southeast of Florida. It belongs to the United States, but the United States is not the only country interested in this beautiful island. People from all over the world come to Puerto Rico to see how her hard-working people have developed their land. Tourists from the United States pour into Puerto Rico for their vacations. The growth of industry has changed it from a poor land of small farms to a modern one of small factories and towns.

2. Puerto Rico is only about 100 miles long and 35 miles wide. It is smaller than any of our states except Delaware and Rhode Island. It is located between the Caribbean Sea and the Atlantic Ocean. A visitor coming by air to Puerto Rico first notices the green, hilly land. It has a warm, rainy climate throughout the year. The rain-bearing winds blow from the northeast. When the winds hit the mountains, they rise and drop their moisture on the northern half of the island. The southern coastal plain—the leeward side—is drier.

3. Puerto Rico was discovered in 1493 by Columbus on his second voyage to the New World. The Spanish began to settle the island in 1508. They divided the land into large sugar farms, first worked by Indians and then by Negro slaves. Puerto Rico was not rich in gold and silver, but it was still valuable to the Spanish. Because of its location, it helped to guard Spanish treasure houses in the New World.

4. In 1898, the United States went to war with Spain. Spain was defeated and gave up the island of Puerto Rico to the United States.

Since that time, the Puerto Rican people have won many rights. In 1900, they gained the right of free trade with the United States. In 1916, Puerto Ricans became American citizens. By 1947, the people were electing their own governor and making their own laws. Luis Muñoz Marín was the first native governor elected by the Puerto Ricans. In 1952, the people adopted their own constitution and set up a "commonwealth" with ties to the United States. Under this form of government, the Puerto Rican people have remained Americans. But they have wide powers in making their own laws.

5. This is a crowded island. There are over 2½ million people in Puerto Rico. There are nearly 800 people for each square mile of land —one of the most crowded lands in the world. For hundreds of years, most of the people were small farmers. Now many are moving to the cities for jobs in the new factories. Many have left the island for the mainland of the United

Tool and die training center in Puerto Rico. What effect have such training centers had on the lives of many Puerto Ricans?

States in order to find better jobs. While most of the people are Catholics, there are also a large number of Protestants. Most Puerto Ricans are white, black or of mixed descent.

6. The Puerto Rican people are proud of their Latin and Spanish culture. Spanish is the language used in schools. But all Puerto Rican children are taught English as a second language. It is not surprising, therefore, to find that so many Puerto Ricans speak two languages. Puerto Ricans are proud of their families too. The family is very important in the life of the people. The family is expected to take care of all its members.

7. Under Spanish rule, most of the land in Puerto Rico was owned by a few persons who raised sugar cane, tobacco and coffee. Today, more people own their own small farms. However, two of the chief crops are still sugar cane and tobacco. While some coffee is grown, land is now being used more for dairy farming. As the people move to cities like San Juan and Ponce, the demand for fresh milk for the city people grows. Citrus fruits and pineapples are grown too. Nevertheless, Puerto Ricans must still import much food from the mainland of the United States.

8. Puerto Rico has no oil, coal or iron ore, but this has not stopped it from becoming a land of small factories. Puerto Rican leaders have used what they have: water power for electricity and their hard-working people. Because of low taxes, factories have been encouraged to come to the island. These factories turn out textiles, paper, cigars, cement and other products. Puerto Ricans also advertise their wonderful climate, beaches and modern hotels and have a successful tourist trade.

9. Their next most important resource, besides themselves, has been their relationship with the United States. The Puerto Ricans, as American citizens, can move to the mainland if jobs are scarce on the island. American armies protect the island. American businessmen have invested money to help develop industry. The people of the island do not have to pay taxes to the United States government. They can trade with the United States without paying tariffs on their imports.

10. Today, through their own efforts and their relations with the U.S., many Puerto Ricans are healthy, go to school and have good jobs on farms and in factories. They have pure water and electricity throughout the island. While many people once lived on a diet of corn, beans and dried meat, today the people eat more wholesome foods. They enjoy radio and television. Low-cost houses are being built

Cane cutters play an important role in Puerto Rico's sugar industry. Where else is sugar cane a chief crop?

in the cities and in the country. All children go to school and receive free lunches daily. The standard of living of Puerto Ricans has risen until it is one of the highest in all of Latin America.

11. What will the future bring to the island? Most people want to keep their present relationship with the United States. There are those who want the island to become a state in the Union, although this would mean paying federal taxes. There are other Puerto Ricans who want complete independence from the United States, despite the loss of free trade and other forms of aid from the United States.

12. Puerto Rico is important to the United States for various reasons. We have military bases there, and they are more important now that the United States does not have friendly relations with Cuba. However, Puerto Ricans are more important as Latin Americans who are successfully raising the standard of living in their country. In this manner, the Puerto Ricans are pioneers in an experiment that may affect all the Americas.

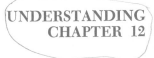

UNDERSTANDING
CHAPTER 12

1. Which questions are answered in this chapter?
   a. Who is Luis Muñoz Marín?
   b. How was Puerto Rico acquired by the United States?
   c. Why have some Puerto Ricans left the island?
2. The main idea of *paragraphs 9 and 10* describes:
   a. how Puerto Rico has used its resources.
   b. the tax problem of Puerto Ricans.
   c. trade between Puerto Rico and the United States.
3. The chief cash crop of Puerto Rican farms is:
   a. coconut.   b. sugar cane.   c. citrus fruits.
4. Puerto Rico is now:
   a. a commonwealth.
   b. a state of the Union.
   c. an independent country.
5. Puerto Rico is important to the United States because it:
   a. supplies our factories with raw materials.
   b. is rich in mineral resources.
   c. guards the United States in the Caribbean.
6. Many Puerto Ricans have come to the mainland of the United States to:
   a. look for better jobs.
   b. find religious freedom.
   c. work on the farms of our Southwest.
7. In paragraph 2, the *leeward* side means the side that:
   a. receives the wind.
   b. is away from the wind.
   c. receives the winds from the sea.

Map Study

Map #22a and b—Puerto Rico

Study the maps. Then answer the questions below.

Map #22a—Puerto Rico

Map #22b—Puerto Rico and Connecticut

CONNECTICUT
POPULATION: 3 MILLION
LAND AREA: 4,900 SQUARE MILES
612 PEOPLE PER SQUARE MILE

PUERTO RICO
POPULATION: 2.7 MILLION PEOPLE
LAND AREA: 3,400 SQUARE MILES
785 PEOPLE PER SQUARE MILE

1. Does Puerto Rico lie in the high, middle or low latitudes?
2. How wide is Puerto Rico at its widest point? How long is the island?
3. Where are the most important cities on the island located? Why do you think this is so?
4. What is the approximate latitude and longitude of the city of Ponce?
5. Why do you think San Juan is the largest city on the island?
6. In what direction do the streams of Puerto Rico flow? Can you give reasons for this?
7. Which has the greater population, Puerto Rico or the state of Connecticut?
8. Which is more crowded, Puerto Rico or Connecticut?

Making Comparisons Choose the correct word for each statement.

1. Puerto Rico is (larger, smaller) than the state of New York.
2. Since World War II (more, fewer) people have come from Puerto Rico to the United States than before World War II.
3. (More, Less) rain falls on the northern half of the island than on the southern half.
4. The standard of living of the Puerto Rican people is (higher, lower) than that of most of the people of Latin America.
5. Puerto Rico has (greater, fewer) mineral resources than Mexico.
6. (More, Fewer) people are members of the Catholic religion than of any other religion.
7. The climate of Puerto Rico is (cooler, warmer) than that of our southeastern states of Georgia, North and South Carolina.
8. Puerto Rico is (closer to, farther from) Florida than it is from Texas.
9. (More, Fewer) Puerto Rican children attend school now than did in 1940.
10. (All, Some) Puerto Rican people speak two languages.

November 19th is observed by our fellow Americans in Puerto Rico as the anniversary of Christopher Columbus' discovery of the island on his second voyage. To mark this event, prepare:

a. a chart of the second voyage showing the lands he discovered and the names given to them;
b. a map showing the regions of the island of Puerto Rico and their products;
c. letters to pupils in a school in Puerto Rico telling them how you are going to celebrate their Discovery Day.

13 BRAZIL: THE TROPICAL GIANT

Reading For A Purpose: How has geography limited the growth of Brazil in spite of her great riches?

Life in the small inland towns of Brazil is difficult, much as it was a hundred or more years ago. This is the village of Carajú, in the Northeast. During which period in our country's history were similar scenes common?

1. Brazil is the giant country of South America. Brazil has more farm land than all of Western Europe. It is rich in minerals, and forests cover more than half the land. It has a large, hard-working population. Yet much of the land is empty and many of the people are poor. Let us see the reasons for this condition.

2. With an area of more than 3 million square miles, Brazil occupies half the continent of South America. It is the fifth largest country in the world. Only the Soviet Union, Canada, the People's Republic of China and the United States are larger. (Brazil would be larger than the United States if Alaska were not included.) Every nation in South America except Chile and Ecuador borders this giant country. To the east, Brazil faces the Atlantic Ocean. The equator crosses the northern part of the country. Most of the nation lies in the low latitudes. The country is so large, however, that the southern part extends into the middle latitudes.

3. Along the Atlantic Coast, there is a narrow lowland that stretches from the Amazon River south to Uruguay. West of the coastal strip are the Brazilian Highlands, reaching far inland to the Amazon Basin. These highlands are made up of hills, low mountains and large areas of plateau. The other major land form is the lowland of the Amazon. The huge plain of the Amazon reaches from the Atlantic Ocean into Peru and Colombia. It is fed by a thousand rivers and drains almost two-thirds of the nation. The Amazon can be used by ships as far as Peru. Except for this mighty river, most of the rivers of Brazil have rapids and are not useful for transporting goods.

4. Along the low coastal area and in the valley of the Amazon, the climate is hot and rainy throughout the year. It is the rain forest. Inland, where the land is higher, the climate is cooler, but it is still warm. This is the savanna climate with its wet and dry seasons. In the southern part of the country, the humid subtropical climate is found—mild winters and long, warm and rainy summers.

5. In 1500, Brazil was claimed by Portugal. The colony was set up to grow sugar cane on large plantations worked by black slaves. In the 18th century, sugar was replaced by gold as the main source of riches. Brazil led the world in gold production for a hundred years before the supply ran out. When the world first needed natural rubber, Brazil's forests filled the need. Today the chief crop is coffee.

6. In 1822, Brazil won its freedom from Portugal. However, the country continued to be ruled by an emperor until 1889. Slavery was ended in Brazil in the same year and the country became a republic with an elected president and congress. Despite the rule of a few "strong men" and several revolutions, Brazil still has a government under a constitution. Because Brazil was settled by Portugal, the people of Brazil today speak Portuguese and are

largely Catholic. Brazil is the largest Roman Catholic country in the world!

7. Brazil's government is like ours in many ways. There is a president, and the lawmaking body is made up of two houses. Everyone past the age of 18 years who can read and write can vote. The president is elected every five years. The capital is now located in Brasília, about 500 miles in the interior. The capital was built there in the hope that people would move to the inland areas and help to develop them.

8. With over 98 million people, Brazil is the eighth largest country in the world in population. There are a large number of whites, descendants of immigrants from Portugal and other countries of Europe. Indians and black people also make up much of the population. The black population is the largest of any South American country. There has been much intermarriage among these groups, so the color of one's skin is not important in Brazil. Eight out of ten people live in the narrow lowland along the Atlantic Coast. Most of the people make a living from the land. Because the inland region is a difficult place in which to live, workers have crowded into the cities. São Paulo, Rio de Janeiro and Recife are the largest cities.

9. Brazil has many riches. There is fertile land on which to grow crops and feed animals. Around São Paulo are the large plantations or *fazendas* where coffee is grown. Brazil grows and sells more coffee than any other nation in the world. In addition, Brazil is the world's second largest grower of sugar cane. Brazilians also raise cotton, cacao, bananas, tobacco, corn and rice. In the southeast, there are large cattle ranches tended by cowboys on mules.

10. The highlands produce many minerals, chiefly iron ore and manganese. Brazil has some of the largest deposits of iron ore in the world. As in most Latin American countries, however, coal is lacking. There are good supplies of chromium, nickel, tungsten and bauxite—important metals for the modern world. Large iron and steel plants are located near Rio de Janeiro. São Paulo is the leading in-

dustrial city and is one of the fastest-growing cities in the world.

11. Forests cover about half the country of Brazil. Hardwoods are a product of the Amazon rain forests. There are great pine forests in the milder south. Carnauba wax is obtained from the oil palm. This product is used in our finest waxes and in coating phonograph records. Brazil nuts are also gathered in the tropical forests.

12. In spite of its resources, Brazil is still a poor country. Only 4 per cent of its farm land is used. Much of its mineral wealth has not been mined. Industry has been slow to develop, although since 1950 manufacturing has been growing at a rapid rate. What are the problems that slow the development of this nation? Transportation along the coast is very good, but there are not enough highways and railroads that lead inland. Secondly, Brazil has depended for a long time on one product for its income—coffee. Thirdly, many people cannot read or write and do not receive proper medical care. Many others have not been trained for skilled jobs. In an industrial nation, people with skills and knowledge are necessary. In the fourth place, a country with little coal needs other sources of power. Brazil has great water resources. But the rivers must be dammed to produce electricity for industry. Finally, there is a need for leaders who are willing to take steps to use the resources of the nation properly.

13. Relations between the United States and Brazil have been friendly. During World War

A coffee "fazenda" near São Paulo. What kind of climate is necessary for growing coffee beans?

II, Brazil fought on the side of the Allies. Its airfields were used by the United States to send planes to the battle areas of Africa and the Middle East. In the first years of the Alliance for Progress, the United States sent more than a half-billion dollars in aid to Brazil. Our trade with Brazil is greater than our trade with any other South American nation. We import coffee, cacao, waxes, hides and manganese from Brazil. The nation buys our machinery, autos, trucks, wheat, oil and coal. At times the government of Brazil has not been stable, yet our businessmen have invested much money in its industries. The giant of South America has a long way to go to reach its goals. But there is little reason why Brazil cannot become a great source of riches for its own people and for the rest of the world.

1. Which questions are answered in this chapter?
   a. What produced wealth for Brazil early in its history?
   b. What are some problems that face Brazil?
   c. Where are cacao and sugar cane grown?
2. The main idea of this chapter is:
   a. Brazil has great resources, yet it is a poor land.
   b. Brazil has a democratic form of government.
   c. forest products are Brazil's greatest wealth.
3. The chief industrial city of Brazil is:
   a. Brasília.   b. Recife.   c. São Paulo.
4. The chief export crop of Brazil is:
   a. coffee.   b. wheat.   c. sugar.
5. One reason why industry has been slow to develop in Brazil is that:
   a. the small population means few workers.
   b. the country has almost no minerals.
   c. transportation inland is poor.
6. Forests are valuable in Brazil because they:
   a. provide wood for the shipbuilding industry.
   b. are a source of hardwoods, waxes and nuts.
   c. are the world's only source of rubber.

DEVELOPING IDEAS AND SKILLS

Map Study

Map #23a and b—Brazil

Study the maps on page 219. Then answer these questions.
1. Does Brazil lie in the high, middle or low latitudes?
2. How wide is Brazil at its widest point?
3. What is the approximate longitude and latitude of the city of Manaus?
4. In what direction would you be traveling if you flew from your community to the city of Belém? (Use the map on page 159 to help you answer this.)
5. In what parts of Brazil are large cities located? Can you give reasons for this?
6. Which direction is *upstream* on the Amazon River?
7. Which city would have the greater differences in temperature from one part of the year to another—Brasília or Manaus?
8. What countries on the map border Brazil?
9. How can you explain the large number of rivers in central Brazil?

10. Would it be possible to fit all of Brazil inside the boundaries of the United States?
11. Which is the more crowded country, Brazil or the United States?

Map #23a—Brazil

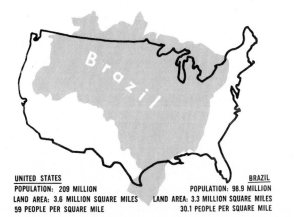

Map #23b—Brazil and the United States

UNITED STATES
POPULATION: 209 MILLION
LAND AREA: 3.6 MILLION SQUARE MILES
59 PEOPLE PER SQUARE MILE

BRAZIL
POPULATION: 98.9 MILLION
LAND AREA: 3.3 MILLION SQUARE MILES
30.1 PEOPLE PER SQUARE MILE

In which region would you find the following? (Refer to the map of Brazil on page 219 and to the climate map on page 169.)

1. cattle ranches.
2. hardwood and rubber trees.
3. cacao and sugar plantations.
4. world's largest river.
5. coffee plantations.
6. manufacturing cities.
7. iron-ore mining.
8. cotton growing.

FOLLOW UP I. Choose one of the following topics. Refer to the books in your library for information about the topic. Use these questions as guides.

1. *Coffee*—Where is it grown? What care is given the coffee trees? What happens to the beans after they are picked? Where do most of the coffee-drinking people of the world live?
2. *Rubber*—How is it grown? How is the rubber collected? Why are Brazilian rubber trees no longer so valuable?
3. *Cotton*—Where is grown in Brazil? Why is it grown there? How can the crop be developed further? How can it improve the life of the Brazilians?
4. *Iron*—Where is it found? Why is it not more fully developed? How will steel change the ways of living in Brazil?

II. Find the missing words.
1. The capital city of Brazil is _____.
2. Brazil was first explored and settled by people from _____.
3. Brazil is thought to have some of the world's largest deposits of _____.
4. Most of the cities are located along the _____ coast.
5. Most of the people of Brazil belong to the _____ religion.
6. Most of Brazil's coffee is exported to _____.
7. The _____ River flows through Brazil's rain forest.
8. Most of Brazil lies in a _____ direction from the equator.
9. In general, the people of Brazil have a _____ standard of living.
10. The head of Brazil's government is the _____.

BOOKS FOR UNIT 4

Author	Title, Publisher	Description
1. Baker, Nina B.	HE WOULDN'T BE KING, Vanguard	The story of Simón Bolívar, South America's "Liberator."
2. Burland, Cottie A.	FINDING OUT ABOUT THE INCA, Lothrop	History, achievements and downfall of the Incas of Peru.

3. Considine, Robert	THE PANAMA CANAL, Random House	How the great canal was built.
4. McGuire, Edna	PUERTO RICO—BRIDGE TO FREEDOM, Macmillan	The interesting story of the small, crowded island.
5. Malkus, Alida	THE AMAZON: RIVER OF PROMISE, McGraw Hill	An explorer describes the treasures in space, water, forests and gems in the valley of this mighty river.
6. May, Charles Paul	CENTRAL AMERICA: LANDS SEEKING UNITY, Nelson	Background of seven countries with a great variety of customs.
7. Nevins, Albert J.	AWAY TO MEXICO, Dodd, Mead	History and present-day problems of Mexico.
8. Niggli, Josephina	A MIRACLE FOR MEXICO, New York Graphic Society	The history of Mexico as a Spanish colony.
9. Radau, Hanns	ILLAMPU, Abelard	Excitement on a long and dangerous search for a llama in Bolivia.
10. Scherman, Katherine	THE SLAVE WHO FREED HAITI, Random House	Biography of Toussaint L'Ouverture, leader of the Haitian revolt.
11. See, Ingram	JUNGLE SECRET, Doubleday	The story of a rubber plantation in Brazil.
12. Sterling, Philip and María Brau	THE QUIET REBELS, Doubleday	Four Puerto Rican leaders and their contributions to their island.
13. Waldeck, Theodore	THE WHITE PANTHER, Viking	Adventure in the jungles of British Guiana (now Guyana).
14. Weeks, Morris, Jr.	HELLO WEST INDIES, Grosset and Dunlap	History, problems and everyday life of the people.

ARTICLES FOR UNIT FOUR	"An Ailing Giant Starts Its Comeback," *U.S. News and World Report,* August 30, 1971	How Brazil is trying to solve its present-day problems.
	"Finally: Last Link for the Pan-American Highway," *U.S. News and World Report,* March 8, 1971	Problems in finishing the road from Alaska to Argentina.

UNIT 5
Western Europe

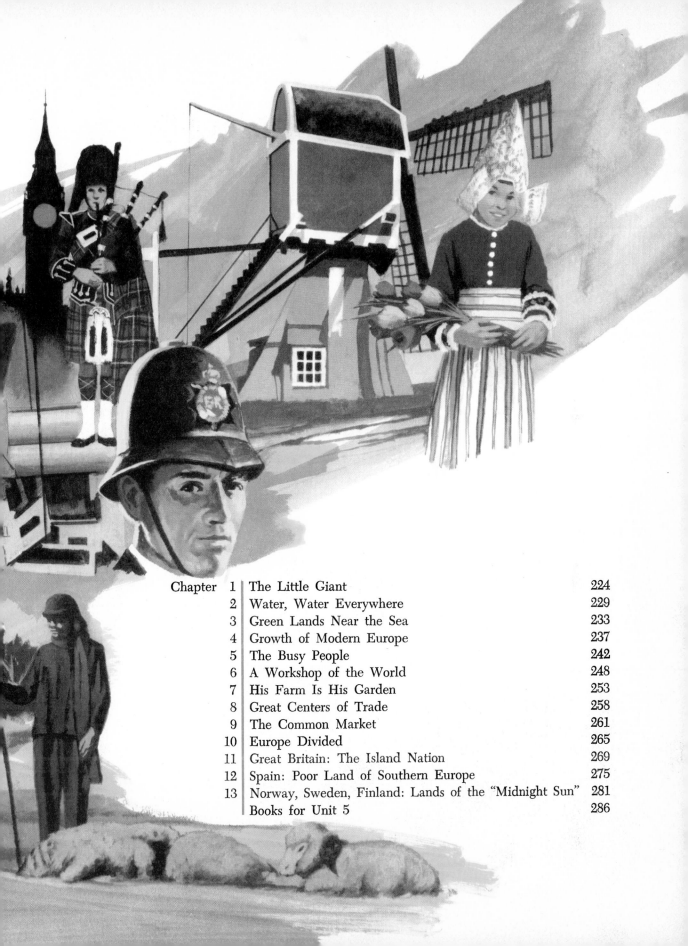

1 THE LITTLE GIANT

Reading For A Purpose: Why is Western Europe important to the United States?

A German worker uses his skills to weld metals. What processes are involved in welding? Why is welding a particularly difficult job?

1. The map of the world does not show a separate land area called Europe. Europe is really part of a great land mass called Eurasia. If you look closely at a map, you can see that Europe is a large peninsula on the west of this vast stretch of land. As such, it is bordered by the Mediterranean Sea on the south, the Arctic Ocean on the north and the Atlantic Ocean on the west.

2. There are eighteen independent countries in what we call Western Europe. All of these nations together make up an area that is less than half the size of the United States! France, the largest nation of Western Europe, is not as large as Texas. Great Britain is about the same size as Oregon. Belgium is only half the size of West Virginia!

3. The nations of Western Europe fall into two groups. There is an outer circle of nations that are chiefly agricultural. The northern part of this circle is sometimes called Northern Europe or Scandinavia. It includes the countries of Norway, Sweden, Denmark and Finland. The southern part of this circle is sometimes called Southern or Mediterranean Europe. It includes Portugal, Spain, southern France, southern Italy and Greece.

4. In the center of the circle is a group of nations to whom manufacturing is most important. These "inner" countries are sometimes called Western Europe. This area includes Great Britain and Ireland, France, the Netherlands, Belgium, Luxembourg, West Germany and northern Italy. Austria and Switzerland are landlocked countries whose customs and standards link them with the countries of Western Europe. Hereafter, when we speak of Western Europe, we refer to *all three* parts, north, south and west. There is another group of countries located in Eastern Europe. They will be studied in the unit on the Soviet Union.

5. For hundreds of years, the countries of Western Europe were the leaders of the world. While this leadership is now shared with other regions, Europe is still a very important area to the United States. Let us find out why.

6. First, our way of life owes much to Europe. The United States was settled largely by people who came from Great Britain and other parts of Europe. They brought their ways of living and learning to our land. As a result, Americans speak English, live under a democratic form of government and are mostly Christians.

7. Second, Western Europe is a center of music, art and literature. The books written by authors of Western Europe are read all over the world. Millions of tourists from the United States visit Europe each year to see its art galleries, museums and cathedrals.

8. Third, the Industrial Revolution that be-

came so important in the United States first began in Great Britain and spread throughout Europe. Over the years, the people of this region developed a high standard of living. Because of their high standard of living, the people of Western Europe can afford to buy many things. Today they are the best customers for our goods—more than 14 billion dollars' worth a year. We also buy more from these countries than from any others.

9. Finally, we thought that the Atlantic Ocean would keep us out of European wars. But two world wars have ended this belief. We now realize that what happens in Western Europe affects us in America. We need a friendly Western Europe as a place for military bases and other defenses. (About 300,000 American troops are now stationed there.) We also need Western Europe because it is still the second greatest industrial area in the world. It has many natural resources. It is a leader in making steel. It has large factories and many goods, and its people are among the most skilled in the world. If Western Europe should fall to enemies, they would be the mightiest powers on earth.

Above, students browse in an Amsterdam bookstore. On the left, a visitor enjoys the treasures of a Brussels museum. Which European authors and artists do you know of?

1. Which questions are answered in this chapter?
   a. Why is a free Europe important to the United States?
   b. Why are we interested in the people of Western Europe?
   c. What are the important cities of Europe?
2. The main idea of *paragraph 9* is that:
   a. Western Europe is an important trading partner in peacetime and a powerful ally in war.
   b. Western Europe is important to our defense.
   c. Western Europe is threatened by enemies.
3. The largest country of Western Europe is:
   a. France.   b. Belgium.   c. Spain.
4. The northern part of Europe is called:
   a. the Alpine region.
   b. Scandinavia.
   c. Benelux.
5. To Western Europe we owe:
   a. our style of buildings.
   b. our public schools.
   c. our form of government.
6. We have a large amount of trade with Western Europe because:
   a. there are no tariffs in Europe.
   b. these countries use our money system.
   c. their people have money to buy goods.
7. In an *agricultural* region, people make their living through:
   a. farming.   b. mining.   c. fishing.
8. In an *industrial* region, people make their living through:
   a. lumbering.   b. farming.   c. making goods in mills and factories.

Map Study

Map #24—Western Europe

Study the map on page 227. Then answer these questions.
1. Is the region north or south of the equator?
2. Is the region east or west of the Prime Meridian?
3. How many miles north and south does the region extend?
4. What region or regions are near it?
5. What are the chief bodies of water that border the region?
6. Which countries in Western Europe have no outlets to the sea?
7. What are some of the important rivers in the region?
8. What are the capital cities of each country?
9. Which countries are island nations?
10. Which countries are located on a peninsula?

Map #24—Western Europe

FOLLOW UP   Western Europe is always in the news. Bring in newspaper or magazine articles relating to Europe. Look for answers to these questions in particular: What are the Nobel Prizes? Who are the leaders of Western Europe? Why is Western Europe important to us?

2 WATER, WATER EVERYWHERE

Reading For A Purpose: How does Europe's topography explain the activities of the people?

The beach at Nazaré, Portugal, on the Atlantic Ocean. In what ways is the ocean important to the Portuguese?

1. As you remember, Europe is a huge peninsula on the great land mass known as Eurasia. Reaching out from Europe's mainland are a number of smaller peninsulas. These peninsulas of Europe are the most striking feature of Europe's shape. Spain and Portugal, Italy, Denmark and Scandinavia are all peninsulas. If you look closely you will see that these peninsulas have even smaller peninsulas! As a result, the coastline of Western Europe is very long and is broken into bays and smaller seas. These bays are fine natural harbors for ships.

2. Almost all the people of Western Europe live near water. No part of the entire region is more than a day's automobile drive from the sea. Therefore, it should not surprise you to learn that the nations of Western Europe have been great sea powers. They have explored distant lands. Some of the nations—Great Britain, France, Spain, Belgium and the Netherlands—have owned colonies in almost every corner of the world. As you might also expect, many people of Western Europe make their living through sea trading, fishing and boatbuilding.

3. There are important bodies of water around Western Europe. The Mediterranean Sea in the south was an important waterway long before America was discovered. The Italian cities of Venice and Genoa were great trading centers for products from the East. This sea is still the center of water travel from Western Europe to the countries of eastern Asia. The Strait of Gibraltar at the western end of the sea controls the entrance to the Mediterranean from the Atlantic Ocean.

4. The North Sea is a busy trade route from Great Britain to the Scandinavian countries and the Baltic Sea. The Baltic Sea is the main trading route for Sweden, Finland, Poland and East Germany. Most of the Baltic Sea freezes, however, during the winter months and is not as useful for trade as the more southerly Mediterranean. The English Channel, scarcely 21 miles wide at its narrowest point, separates Great Britain from the mainland of the continent.

5. Although all parts of Western Europe are near the sea, not every country has an entrance to the large bodies of water. Switzerland, Austria and Luxembourg are "landlocked." That is, they have no coastline. For Switzerland this has been a blessing. There is no entrance to Switzerland except through the mountains. This tiny nation has therefore been able to avoid war for hundreds of years.

6. Much of Western Europe is a great lowland or plain that stretches from southern Great Britain across the Germanies, Poland and the Soviet Union. It grows wider toward the east. It is known as the Great European Plain. North of the plain are highlands or

mountains that stretch from northern Great Britain through the countries of Scandinavia.

7. South of the plains the land is also hilly and mountainous. The mountains of southern Europe are high and rugged. The Pyrenees Mountains separate Spain from France. They extend from the Atlantic Ocean to the Mediterranean Sea. The Alps and Balkans stretch across southern France to Yugoslavia and Greece. These mountains separate Southern Europe from the rest of the region.

8. There are many rivers in Western Europe. The most important ones rise in the Alps—the Rhine, Rhône, Po and Danube. Compared with other rivers we have studied, the Mississippi and the Amazon, these rivers are small. However, they are generally navigable. They are joined by many canals to help carry goods such as iron ore from mine to mill. Except for the Rhine, these rivers flow south or east. The Rhône flows into the Mediterranean; the Po leads into the Adriatic Sea; the Danube flows east into the Black Sea. Each runs through fertile valleys where many people live. Many of Western Europe's great cities and seaports are located on these rivers.

UNDERSTANDING CHAPTER 2

1. Which questions are answered in this chapter?
   a. Why did Western Europeans turn to the sea?
   b. What is the topography of Western Europe?
   c. How long is the Danube River?
2. The main idea of this chapter describes:
   a. how people of Europe use the sea.
   b. the land forms of Western Europe.
   c. the southern chain of mountains.
3. Much of Western Europe is a:
   a. plateau.   b. desert.   c. plain.
4. Most of the rivers of Western Europe rise in the:
   a. Pyrenees Mountains.   b. Alps.   c. northern highlands.
5. "There are many bays and seas ..." This tells you that:
   a. there are many harbors.
   b. people travel a great deal.
   c. there are many sandy beaches.
6. The rivers of Western Europe are useful because:
   a. goods are shipped on them between ports and inland cities.
   b. most of them flow toward the east.
   c. they are a source of minerals.
7. Land that is surrounded by water on three sides is called:
   a. a peninsula.
   b. an isthmus.
   c. an island.
8. Venice was a great *trading center*. This means that the city was well known for:
   a. training soldiers.
   b. printing books.
   c. buying and selling goods.

Map Study

Map #25—Land Forms of Europe

Study the map. Then tell whether these statements are *true or false*. Be able to explain your answers.

1. Almost every country of Western Europe may be described as a plateau.
2. The Islands of Western Europe are chiefly plains.
3. Plains make up a small part of the far northern part of Western Europe.
4. Mountains are found in both the northern and southern parts of this region.
5. Some mountains appear to separate Western Europe from countries along the Mediterranean Sea.
6. Italy and Spain in southern Europe are chiefly one vast plain.
7. Most of Western Europe is part of a large lowland area.
8. In the far north, mountains line the Atlantic Coast.

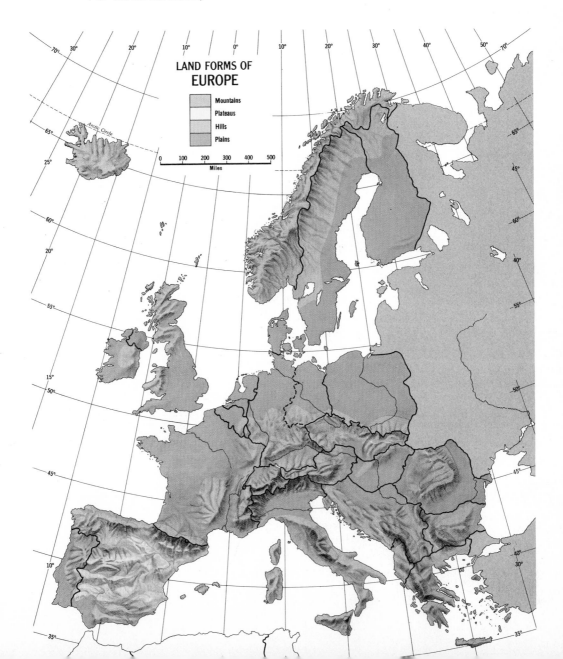

LAND FORMS OF
EUROPE

Mountains
Plateaus
Hills
Plains

0   100   200   300   400   500
Miles

Complete the following chart in your notebook. You may find it helpful to use an atlas or an almanac to find some of the information.

Comparing Rivers

	MISSISSIPPI	AMAZON	DANUBE	RHINE
1. Length:				
2. Body of water it flows into:				
3. Area drained:				
4. How it is used by the people around it:				

Tell whether these statements are true or false. The underlined words make the statements true or false. If a statement is false, what words would you place in it to make it true?

1. Europe has great areas of deserts.
2. Central Europe has a broad inner plain.
3. The Mediterranean Sea is an important water route south of Europe.
4. Almost all of the people of Western Europe live in mountain areas.
5. The Alps separate Spain and France.
6. Europe is actually a peninsula on the vast land area of Eurasia.
7. Switzerland is one country that has no outlet to the sea.
8. The main trading route for countries of northern Europe is the Baltic Sea.

3 GREEN LANDS NEAR THE SEA

Reading For A Purpose: How does Western Europe's climate help to explain its high standard of living?

Fertile plains have helped make farming an important way of life for the French. Although many farms are modern and prosperous, scenes like this are not uncommon. People farmed like this hundreds of years ago. What do the women in this picture seem to be doing?

1. Nearly all of Western Europe is nearer the North Pole than the United States is. Rome is farther north than New York. London is almost as far north as Hudson Bay in Canada. These cities ought to be very cold, but they are not. The countries in Western Europe have a mild and rainy climate. They have a marine climate.

2. The climate of Western Europe is much warmer than we would expect because of a current of warm water known as the North Atlantic Drift. The Drift begins far away in the warm waters of the Gulf of Mexico. There, it is called the Gulf Stream. The Gulf Stream travels eastward. As it nears Europe, it becomes wider and weaker. Eventually, the Gulf Stream current becomes the North Atlantic Drift. The Drift moves eastward until it reaches the shores of the British Isles and much of Western Europe.

3. The winds that blow over the countries of Western Europe come from the west. Because these winds blow over the Drift, they bring its warmth to Western Europe. Since no part of the region is more than 400 miles from the sea, the warm winds are felt through much of Western Europe. Farther inland, the winds begin to lose their warmth. The winters become colder and longer and snow falls. The summers are shorter. But the presence of water on all sides of Western Europe still tends to keep the winter milder and the summers cooler than they would be otherwise. Because of the rainy winds, the plains of Europe are green with crops.

4. Southern Europe has a Mediterranean climate. The southern coast of France is about the same latitude as Montreal, Canada. Yet this coastal area, far from being cold, has long hot summers. The winters are mild. Rain falls mainly during the winter. Why is this climate so different? The Alps keep out the blasts of cold air from the north. The winds that blow over Southern Europe come from the deserts of Africa. They are hot and dry. As a result, the climate is the same as that of southern California. The long growing season makes it possible to grow all kinds of citrus fruits. Vegetables grown in Southern Europe are sent to the colder areas farther north.

5. Much farther north is the taiga or northern forest lands. The taiga extends through Norway, Sweden and Finland—lands of the "midnight sun." Here summers are short and

winters are long and very cold. During the cold winter days, there are only a few hours of sunlight. Rivers and lakes are icy, and the ground is frozen. While the soil is poor and stony, there are many evergreen forests.

The coastal landscape in Scandinavia is known for the breathtaking beauty of the fiords. A fiord is a narrow sea inlet between high cliffs or mountains. Norway is eleven hundred miles long, but it has a coastline of more than twelve thousand miles. Why is this so?

UNDERSTANDING
CHAPTER 3

1. Which questions are answered in this chapter?
   a. Why is Western Europe mild and rainy?
   b. How are fogs caused?
   c. Why do many tourists visit Southern Europe?
2. The main idea of *paragraph 4* describes:
   a. the climate of Southern Europe.
   b. the effects of the westerly winds.
   c. the farm crops of Southern Europe.
3. Most of Western Europe is:
   a. farther from the equator than New York City.
   b. in the region of the taiga and the tundra.
   c. about the same distance from the equator as the United States.
4. The Gulf Stream begins:
   a. at the Arctic Circle.
   b. in the Gulf of Mexico.
   c. in the Pacific Ocean.
5. Much of Western Europe has a mild, rainy climate because:
   a. it is near the equator.
   b. the winds are warm and wet.
   c. high mountains shut off the eastern winds.
6. Southern Europe has a sunny climate because:
   a. it is located far from large bodies of water.
   b. it is located near the Atlantic Ocean.
   c. cold northern winds are blocked by the Alps.
7. A feature of the Mediterranean climate is:
   a. frequent rain and fog.   b. a long growing season.   c. hillside farming.
8. Winters are longer and colder inland because:
   a. the land receives breezes from Africa.
   b. the mountains bring cold winds to the plains.
   c. these lands are far from the effects of the ocean currents.

Map Study

Map #26—Climates of Europe

Agree or Disagree   Study the map. Then decide whether or not each statement at the top of page 236 agrees with the information on the map. If the answer is disagree, explain why.

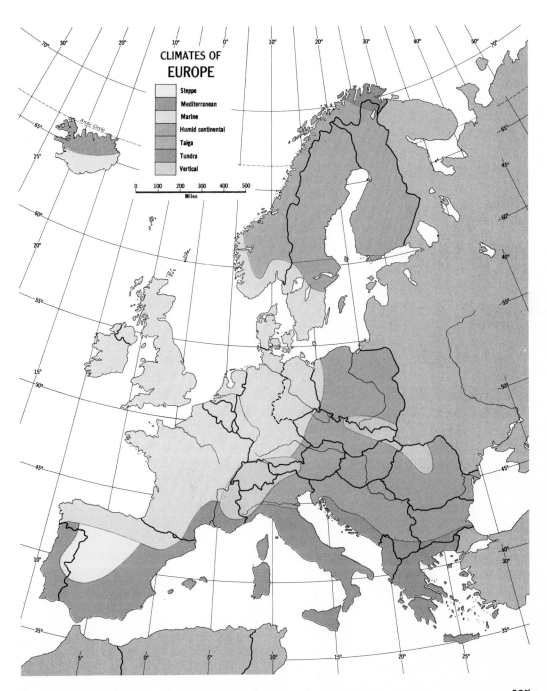

1. The taiga occupies all of Western Europe north of 50° latitude.
2. Spain and Italy are the only countries in Western Europe with an area of Mediterranean climate.
3. The climate of Europe's Atlantic coast is like the climate of the northeastern United States.
4. Nearness to large bodies of water has an effect on the climate of much of Western Europe.
5. The northern part of this region probably has the fewest number of people for each square mile of land.
6. The greatest part of Western Europe lies in an area of marine climate.
7. There is no region in Western Europe where cocoa, cane sugar or rubber can be grown.
8. Mountains have an effect on the climate of all the countries of Western Europe.

SUMMING UP
Obtain travel posters from a travel agency in your community, from an airline or from a steamship line. Plan a trip to Western Europe, keeping in mind the following questions:
   a. Where are the places described on the posters?
   b. How would you travel to each place?
   c. How long might your trip take?
   d. What kind of clothing would you take with you?
   e. What kind of work do the people do in each place?

FOLLOW UP
Tell whether these statements are true or false. The underlined words make the statements true or false. If a statement is false, what words would you place in it to make it true?
1. The rain-bearing winds blow from the east.
2. The North Atlantic Drift is a cold water current.
3. A Mediterranean climate is found on the southern coast of France.
4. Plenty of rain and mild winter temperatures are found in a marine climate.
5. Lands of the "midnight sun" have a winter in which there is almost continuous sunlight.
6. The northern countries have a short growing season.

4 GROWTH OF MODERN EUROPE

Reading For A Purpose: How have the people of Europe changed the world?

1. The lands around the Mediterranean Sea were once part of the great Roman Empire. Even before this huge and powerful empire broke up, people settled wherever there was a good piece of farm land. Later, when Roman rule was replaced by *feudalism*, these settlements were called *manors*. Under feudalism, a lord controlled the life of the manor from his castle. *Serfs* worked for the lord. They lived on the crops they raised on the land. They gave part of their crops to the lord in return for the protection he gave them. These farmers were not free to come and go as they pleased, but had to stay on the land where they were born.

2. In time this way of life changed. As people began to travel and meet other people, trade began and cities grew. The growth of the cities helped to weaken the power of the lords. Sometimes the people in the cities paid the feudal lord for their freedom. Some lords became stronger than others. Wars were fought for control of a large territory. The stronger lords began to call themselves princes or kings. This was the beginning of the nations of Europe.

3. Countries like France and England were brought together by strong lords. The people who lived in the territory of a strong lord or king came to think of themselves as part of his "kingdom"—his nation. At the beginning, this feeling of belonging to a nation was weak. By the end of the 19th century it had become very strong. This feeling of belonging to a nation, and of pride in that nation, is known as *nationalism*.

This picture shows a scene of life in one of the many cities that developed as trade grew. What do you see that is similar to city life today? What is different?

4. One of the reasons for the development of strong nations was the great period of exploration and discovery. After Columbus made his famous voyage, France, Holland, Great Britain, Spain and Portugal all sent explorers to every corner of the world. The coasts of Africa and the islands of the Far East were explored. Because of these voyages, Europe became rich from the gold, silver, furs and foods found in these lands.

5. As a result of these and later travels, the lives of millions of people in the New World, Africa, the Far East and Australia were changed. The early settlements in the Americas and Australia were made by people from Europe. The European nations set up trading posts along the coasts of Africa to supply the New World with Negro slaves. This traffic in slaves uprooted the African tribal world for 300 years. In the islands of the Far East, Europeans set up plantations to get more of the products they wanted.

6. At the same time there was a great religious change in Europe. Some kings and princes who were Catholics changed their religion. In the 16th and 17th centuries new churches were started. Because these new churches were started in protest against some of the teachings of the Catholic Church, they were called "Protestant." One of the leaders of this Protestant movement was Martin Luther of Germany.

7. While some learned more about the land and waters of our earth, others studied the heavens. In 1543, Copernicus of Poland stated that the earth revolved around the sun. For thousands of years men had believed the opposite. They had believed that they were the center of the whole universe. Now Copernicus said that they were wrong. Other men looked at the stars and developed new instruments for the study of *astronomy*. Men like Galileo and Sir Isaac Newton tested or experimented with such new ideas as gravity. Many facts concerning the world were discovered. This was the beginning of modern science.

8. The advances in science also led to the Industrial Revolution. This great change from man-made to machine-made goods began in Britain during the early 1700's. It began first in the making of cloth. New machines for spinning and weaving cloth were invented. Goods could be made faster by machine, so they became cheaper. Factories grew and people moved near them to get jobs. Cities grew where there were sources of power to run the machines. At first, machines were run by water power. Then the coal-fed steam engine was invented. In it, coal was burned to heat water to make the steam for power. The steam engine caused a change in methods of manufacturing and transportation. Britain, where the steam engine and other machines were invented, soon became the first great industrial nation. Its ships carried goods from its factories to people all over the world.

9. At the same time, a different kind of revolution was taking place in France. In 1789, the people of France overthrew their king. The

In 1609 Galileo demonstrated his first telescope. Why was this invention an important scientific advance?

A 19th century British factory. How did the Industrial Revolution change the lives of factory workers?

nies became frequent. Large armies and navies were built. Finally, in the 20th century, two great world wars were fought on the European continent. The great world-wide power of the Western European nations was broken. Winners and losers both gave up their colonies, one by one. The United States and the Soviet Union became the most powerful nations in the world.

12. After World War II in 1945, the United States tried to help the nations of Europe recover from the damages of war. Secretary of State George Marshall announced his plan to lend money to the nations of Europe. The Marshall Plan restored farm lands and rebuilt railroads and factories in Europe. In a few years the factories and mills of Western Europe were busy again. In 1949, the United States and some of the countries of Western Europe formed NATO, the North Atlantic Treaty Organization. These nations agreed to help each other in case of attack. The nations of Western Europe also learned another lesson.

new government divided the large estates of the nobility among the peasants. A few years before, in 1776, there had been a revolution in America out of which the United States was formed. Both revolutions were part of what is called the Democratic Revolution. Before these revolutions most people had few rights. The desire of men to be treated equally was one of the causes of the revolutions. The Democratic Revolution is still going on today. It is based on the desire of all men for the right to "life, liberty, and the pursuit of happiness."

10. The Industrial Revolution spread to other countries of Europe and to the United States. The machines proved to be "hungry." No one country seemed to have all the resources it needed to feed the machines. Then, too, the goods had to be sold. So industrial nations began to look for materials and markets in other parts of the world. Africa and Asia proved to be areas where the nations of Europe could find the materials they needed. In the 18th and 19th centuries, European countries took control of some of these lands. This was called *imperialism* or *colonialism*.

11. It was bound to happen that in the race for colonies, one nation would desire the territory another country wanted. Wars over colo-

The French Revolution began in 1789 with the storming of the Bastille, the state prison. The king was overthrown and land was given to the peasants. What influence do you imagine the American Revolution of 1776 had on the French revolt?

They found that only by working together could they achieve the best life for their people. Through the Common Market they have begun to cooperate with each other in supplying needed raw materials and products to each other at low tax rates. By this and other means, they have built up their industries, their trade and their standard of living.

UNDERSTANDING CHAPTER 4

1. Which questions are answered in this chapter?
   a. Why did Western Europe want colonies?
   b. Who was Adolf Hitler?
   c. How did the nations of Europe become rich after 1492?
2. The main idea of this chapter describes how:
   a. the Marshall Plan helped to restore Europe.
   b. Europe has influenced the history of the world.
   c. changes in science began.
3. One of the leaders of the early Protestants was:
   a. Martin Luther.   b. Mohammed.   c. Copernicus.
4. The Industrial Revolution began in:
   a. the Soviet Union.   b. France.   c. Great Britain.
5. One of the causes of the French Revolution of 1789 was that:
   a. the King of France wanted to explore in America.
   b. people did not have religious freedom.
   c. the people of France wanted more rights.
6. One of the most important reasons why European nations wanted colonies in the 19th century was the need for:
   a. raw materials for factories.
   b. large armies and navies.
   c. spreading the idea of equality throughout the world.
7. Under *feudalism*, wealth was measured in:
   a. factory-made goods.   b. land.   c. water power.
8. When a country obtains colonies as a source of raw materials, this is known as:
   a. imperalism.   b. feudalism.   c. liberalism.

DEVELOPING IDEAS AND SKILLS

Picture Symbols

These pictures should help you to recall parts of the chapter you have read. What is the main idea of each picture?

In each group there are three events in the history of Europe. Arrange the events in each group *in the order in which they took place.*

1. Feudalism develops.
   Kings begin to form nations.
   The Roman Empire ends.
2. The Industrial Revolution begins.
   New scientific discoveries are made.
   Nations want colonies in distant lands.
3. The race for colonies with raw materials begins.
   The world wars are fought.
   European nations lose their leadership in the world.
4. Columbus discovers the New World.
   Nations find riches in gold and silver.
   Settlements are made in Africa.

FOLLOW UP *Which Does Not Belong?* In each group, select the item that does not belong with the others.

1. Feudalism
   a. wealth gained through buying and selling.
   b. serfs work the land.
   c. lord protects the serfs.

2. Colonialism
   a. weaker lands occupied by stronger nations.
   b. African people have self-government.
   c. large nations control raw materials.

3. Industrial Revolution
   a. growth of cities takes place.
   b. new sources of power are found.
   c. greater use of hand labor is made.

4. Democratic Revolution
   a. more people can vote.
   b. new constitutions are written.
   c. fewer newspapers are printed.

5. Revolution in Science
   a. new ideas are tested.
   b. the sun revolves around the earth.
   c. new inventions are made.

6. Protestant Reformation
   a. Catholic religion spreads throughout Europe.
   b. new religions are formed.
   c. Martin Luther announces his beliefs.

7. 20th Century Wars
   a. great loss of life and property.
   b. European nations grow in strength.
   c. United States and Soviet Union become leading powers in the world.

8. Plans for Recovery of Europe after World Wars
   a. NATO is organized.
   b. Marshall Plan is put into effect.
   c. Industrial Revolution begins.

5 THE BUSY PEOPLE

Reading For A Purpose: Who are the people of Western Europe?

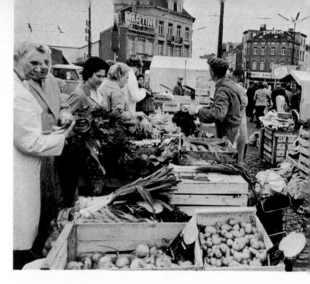

An open-air market in Holland. What products can you identify?

1. Western Europe is the smallest of all the regions in our study, but it is one of the most heavily populated. Almost 340 million people live there. This is more than in Anglo-America or Latin America. Only in the Far East are people more crowded together. In Belgium and the Netherlands there are about 700 people for each square mile of land. In West Germany and Great Britain there are over 500 people for each square mile of land. By comparison, the United States has 59 people per square mile. Only in Scandinavia, where the northern winters are cold, are there areas of few people.

2. Because of the large population, there is very little empty land in crowded Europe. Europeans try to make use of every part of their land. Throughout Western Europe, swamps have been drained and soil improved by careful fertilizing. In the Netherlands the people have built dikes, pumped out sea water and added thousands of new acres of rich soil to their country.

3. Most of the people (three out of five) live in or near large cities. In Great Britain, 80% of the people are city dwellers. In West Germany, 70% of the people live in cities. Millions of people work in factories making goods that are sold all over the world. The workers of Western Europe are highly skilled. Even before the beginning of factories and the use of machines, the people of Western Europe were making goods to sell. Others work in offices, warehouses and docks, preparing goods for shipment to distant parts of the world.

4. In many ways, the life of the people of Western Europe is like that of the people of the United States. Except for Southern Europe, the standard of living is very high. Western Europeans eat and dress much as we do. Potatoes, cheese, milk, butter and rye bread are important in their diet. They eat more fish and less meat than we do. Automobiles, telephones, radios and television sets are a growing part of their daily lives.

5. Education is important to Europeans and most children attend school. In Sweden and Denmark, over 99% of the people are literate —that is, able to read and write. This is a higher percentage than in the United States. The people of Europe are great readers. More books and magazines are printed in Western Europe than in any other region in the world, including our own.

6. The health care of many Europeans is very good. There are modern hospitals served by well-trained doctors and nurses. Government support of medical services is common in Western Europe. This means that both the poor and rich may enjoy good health care.

7. Many different languages are spoken in this region. Most of the languages come from two main sources. The *Romance* languages come from Latin. These are the languages of France, Spain, Portugal, Italy and parts of Bel-

gium and Switzerland. (Different languages may be spoken within the same country. In Switzerland, French, Italian and German are each spoken in a different area.) After the fall of Rome, many German tribes occupied different parts of Europe. They left their *Germanic* languages in such countries as West Germany, Austria, Luxembourg, parts of Switzerland and Belgium, the Netherlands, Great Britain and Scandinavia.

8. There are many different religions in Europe, but most of the people are Christians. The Christians are divided into two main groups: Roman Catholics and Protestants. Ireland, France, parts of Switzerland, Italy, Spain, Portugal and southern Germany are largely Catholic. Scandinavia and Denmark, Great Britain, northern Germany, the Netherlands and part of Switzerland are largely Protestant. For some time, many Jewish people lived in Western Europe. But during the rule of Adolf Hitler in Germany, millions of Jews were killed. Thousands have since moved to Israel and the United States.

9. Most countries in Western Europe have

A church in the French town of Morlaix. This church dates back several centuries. Why do you think Europeans take pride in churches which are hundreds of years old?

Britain's Parliament is made up of the House of Commons, shown here in session, and the House of Lords. What are the names of the two bodies that make up our Congress?

established democratic governments. In most, the laws are made by representatives of the people. In these nations the people enjoy the same freedoms as Americans—freedom of speech, religion and the press. Although kings and queens still "rule" such nations as Great Britain, Norway, Sweden and Belgium, they have little or no real power.

10. The *parliamentary* form of government is most common among the nations of Europe. In such a government there are two lawmaking bodies, but one "house" has most of the power. (In our country both houses of Congress have great power.) European countries may have presidents, but, except for France, these presidents have little power. The chief officer is the prime minister. He and his cabinet are the real leaders of the government. In most of these governments the prime minister and his cabinet are members of the parliament. They take part in passing and carrying out laws. (In our country there is a separation of the powers held by the President and Congress.)

1. Which questions are answered in this chapter?
   a. What do the people of Western Europe eat?
   b. What are the crowded countries of Europe?
   c. Who is the ruler of Spain?
2. The main idea of *paragraph 3* describes:
   a. the kinds of work in Western European cities.
   b. how Western Europeans use machines.
   c. the importance of trade in the life of the people.
3. The religion to which most of the people of Western Europe belong is:
   a. Christianity.   b. Judaism.   c. Islam.
4. Dikes have been built to reclaim land in:
   a. France.   b. the Netherlands.   c. Norway.
5. In which country would you be most likely to hear a *Romance* language spoken?
   a. West Germany.   b. Portugal.   c. Austria.
6. The people of Europe must use their farm land wisely because:
   a. there is little fertile land.
   b. there is a need to feed a large population.
   c. Europe exports food to other nations.
7. The majority of the nations of Western Europe:
   a. have parliamentary governments.
   b. are ruled by kings or queens.
   c. are governed by dictators.
8. The title of the chapter, "The Busy People," refers to the fact that:
   a. Europeans are chiefly farmers.
   b. Western Europe has a high standard of living.
   c. the people work hard and are highly skilled.
9. In the last sentence of paragraph 10, the term "separation of powers" means that:
   a. the President and Congress have different powers.
   b. our President has more power than Congress.
   c. the President and Congress have the same powers.

DEVELOPING
IDEAS AND
SKILLS

Pictograph #9—Population, Area and Standard of Living of Western Europe

Study the pictograph on page 245. Then answer these questions.

1. Is the standard of living of this region high or low compared with that of the United States?
2. Is the region more or less crowded than the United States?
3. Are the people of this region literate compared with the people of the United States?
4. How long may the average person in this region expect to live?
5. What facts tell you the standard of living of the people of the region?
6. How does this region compare with the United States in size?

POPULATION AND AREA

UNITED STATES

20 MILLION PEOPLE

WESTERN EUROPE

209 MILLION PEOPLE
3.6 MILLION SQUARE MILES
59 PEOPLE PER SQUARE MILE

337 MILLION PEOPLE
1.4 MILLION SQUARE MILES
240 PEOPLE PER SQUARE MILE

STANDARD OF LIVING

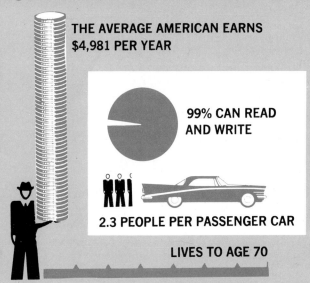

THE AVERAGE AMERICAN EARNS
$4,981 PER YEAR

99% CAN READ
AND WRITE

2.3 PEOPLE PER PASSENGER CAR

LIVES TO AGE 70

THE AVERAGE WESTERN EUROPEAN EARNS
$3,100
PER YEAR

99% CAN READ
AND WRITE

6 PEOPLE PER PASSENGER CAR

LIVES TO AGE 70

Pictograph #9—Population, Area and Standard of Living of Western Europe

SUMMING UP *Agree or Disagree* Decide whether or not each of the following statements agrees with what you have read. If the answer is *disagree*, explain why.

1. Western Europe is a region small in size and population.
2. A visitor from one of our large cities would be "at home" in Great Britain.
3. The farmlands of Europe cover a vast area, much like our midwestern states.
4. Owning a bookstore would be a good business in Sweden.
5. The health standards of Western Europeans are probably very high.

6. Most people in Western Europe live and work in cities.
7. The religions of the people of Europe are much like the religions of the people of the United States.
8. The Prime Minister of Great Britain and the President of the United States have the same powers.

FOLLOW UP   Some of the largest cities in the world are located in Western Europe. Many are at the center of large *metropolitan* areas. (A metropolitan area is a city plus the smaller towns surrounding it.) As you read, think about the kinds of problems that are presented by the growth of big cities. Also ask yourself what kinds of benefits can come to the people in urban areas.

The Big City Problem

It has never been easy to tell where London ended and the rest of Britain began. London is the biggest metropolitan area in Europe. There are close to 8 million people in the city itself. In downtown London, there is an increasing amount of traffic on streets that were not built to handle it. The crowding in streets, in restaurants, and on trains during rush hours keeps growing.

The great problem of the city of Paris is also crowding—crowding of people, of traffic, of buildings. In Paris, there are 114 people for each acre of ground, to say nothing of the roads, railways, factories, warehouses and theaters that have to be fitted in.

Rotterdam, the Netherlands, is the first port of the world in the tonnage it carries. It is a city of 700,000 people. Nearby are the capital city of the Netherlands, the Hague, with a half million people, Amsterdam with 800,000, Utrecht with 280,000 and Haarlem with 200,000. Today the cities and towns of the Netherlands have grown so close together that they actually form one city. Millions of other people live just outside these cities, forming one of the largest metropolitan areas in all of Europe. The Dutch call it *Randstad*, the Ring City. It has the shape of a great horseshoe. If the horseshoe were straightened out, it would be 110 miles long. The growth in population means that there is little open land left in the western Netherlands for farms, industry, homes and recreation.

In West Germany, within a 40-mile radius, are 10 cities with 200,000 people apiece, and another ten with between 100,000 and 200,000 people. Around these cities are suburbs, which in most cases join one city to the next. Dutch planners see a real danger in this situation. They predict that by 1980, the Dutch Randstad and the cities of the German Rhine and Ruhr rivers will have joined into one gigantic city, 180 miles long.

The real problem of this vast region is one that is the same the world over—a demand for space. Unfortunately, there is little space left.

Adapted, by permission, from Peter Hall, *The World Cities* (New York: McGraw-Hill Book Company, 1966).

1. Locate the countries mentioned in this selection. Use the map on page 227.
2. Name the different problems of large European cities mentioned in this selection.
3. Which problems seem to be the same for all the cities mentioned?
4. Are the problems mentioned different from problems faced by cities in Anglo-America? Explain.
5. Why have people been moving to cities and the areas around them?
6. From what you have learned about Western Europe, what would you predict for this region in the next twenty years?

6 A WORKSHOP OF THE WORLD

Reading For A Purpose: Why is Western Europe a great industrial area?

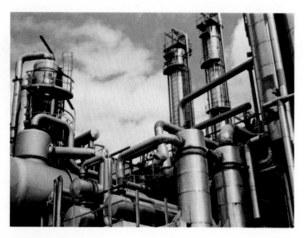

An oil refinery in Belgium. What does the term "to refine" mean? What happens to oil in a refinery?

1. Western Europe is one of the world's workshops. Many raw materials for manufacturing are found in the countries of this region. What they do not have, Europeans import from all over the world. Their factories turn these raw materials into machinery, textiles and chemicals. Great ships carry these goods to markets everywhere. With the profit from the sale of manufactured goods, Western Europe can pay for the food needed by her large population.

2. There are many reasons why industry became so important in Western Europe. This group of nations had an early start. The Industrial Revolution began in Great Britain. The first machines and factories were built by Englishmen. By the early 1800's, the use of machines and the factory system spread across Western Europe. Only in the 20th century has the change from man-made to machine-made goods become important in the Soviet Union, India, China and Africa.

3. The people of Western Europe are highly skilled. For a long time, Europeans made things to sell at home or in small shops. When the first factories were started, these people were able to work at the new machines.

4. Western Europe is rich in the sources of power for factories. Europe mines about 45% of the world's coal. Coal is the chief source of power in Great Britain, West Germany, France and Belgium. Other European nations depend upon water power. Western Europe has about one-third of the world's developed water power. France, Switzerland, Sweden, Italy and Norway make the greatest use of this power source. Oil is also used, but it must be imported from the fields of the Middle East.

5. There are great amounts of coal and iron in the region for making steel. Although most countries in Western Europe have some coal or iron ore, the main mining areas are in France, Great Britain, West Germany and Sweden. The richest coal and iron area is a small triangle of land that includes Belgium, northern France and southwest Germany.

6. Western Europe has an excellent transportation system. This region is like a spider's web of rivers, canals, highways and railroads. The chief rivers for trade—the Rhine, Rhône and Elbe Rivers—are connected by canals. It is therefore possible to carry goods easily to any inland city or seaport. Moreover, Western Europe's long, irregular coastline provides many ports. Ocean-going ships can pick up Europe's products close to where they are made or grown.

7. There is another reason for Western Europe's early industrial development. Whatever the nations of Europe did not have, they could get from their colonies. Western Europe has no cotton, no rubber and little oil. But Great Britain, France, Germany, the Netherlands and Belgium used to have great colonies in far-off lands. They depended on their colonies to sup-

Barges in a harbor on the Rhine River in West Germany. Of what importance have rivers been to the development of industry in Europe?

and Luxembourg, and the Ruhr and Saar Basins of West Germany. Here the iron ore deposits and the coal mines are close to each other. There are many rivers, canals and railroads within the Triangle. They connect the iron ore, coal and steel centers with the nearby seaports. These steel mills with their huge furnaces and smokestacks supply steel not only to Europe, but also to the rest of the world.

10. Europe's factories make use of this steel to produce many goods. Machine tools, farm machinery, electrical equipment, ships, barges and automobiles are only a few of the products. In addition, there are textile and chemical industries. All these goods are carried to world markets by Western European ships. These many products tell the story of Europe's leadership in manufacturing.

ply the raw materials they needed for their factories. Moreover, profit from this trade gave the Europeans money to build more factories. It also helped to supply them with machinery and equipment.

8. Workers from the northeastern United States feel at home when they visit the great cities of Western Europe. This is because the making of steel and mining are the chief industries. There are two main centers of steel manufacture and mining in the region. Great Britain is one, and the area of the continent known as the Vital Triangle is the other. Britain's great iron and steel district is located in the Midlands in central England. Birmingham and Sheffield are two of the great steel cities in Great Britain.

9. The Vital Triangle, continental Europe's most famous steel area, includes the Lorraine Valley of northern France, parts of Belgium

A West German factory in which locomotive parts are built. How has geography helped West Germany to become a leading industrial nation?

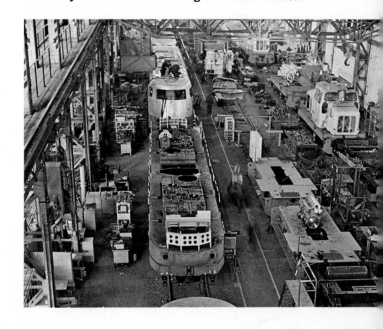

1. Which questions are answered in this chapter?
   a. What is the Vital Triangle?
   b. Why is Western Europe a leader in manufacturing?
   c. How is steel made?
2. The main idea of this chapter describes:
   a. how Western Europe makes use of its resources.
   b. the chief industries of Western Europe.
   c. why Western Europe's workers are skillful.
3. Western Europe's chief industry is the making of:
   a. steel.   b. paper and paper products.   c. food products.
4. Western Europe is called a "workshop of the world" because this region:
   a. turns raw materials into finished goods.
   b. makes nearly everything by hand.
   c. ships goods to all parts of the world.
5. The chief source of power in Western Europe is:
   a. oil.   b. natural gas.   c. coal.
6. The Ruhr Valley has become a center of industry because:
   a. rich coal mines are located there.
   b. it has good transportation.
   c. farm land is too poor and people have moved to the cities to live.
7. In paragraph 6, the term "a spider's web of rivers" means that:
   a. ships rush back and forth over many great waterways.
   b. rivers bring goods far inland.
   c. the rivers seem to flow out in all directions.
8. In paragraph 10, "chemical industries" might include the manufacture of:
   a. cotton goods.   b. light bulbs.   c. fertilizer.

Map Study

Map #27—The Vital Triangle

Read each of the following statements about the map of the Vital Triangle on page 251. Write *true* if the statement is correct. Write *false* if the statement is wrong. Write *not given* if the map does not give you the information needed to decide on the statement.

1. Belgium has much coal but little iron ore.
2. The high production of steel in Western Europe is the result of great coal fields.
3. Coal and iron ore are found near each other around the border of France and West Germany.
4. Aluminum production has been growing and steel production has been falling in Western Europe.
5. Most of the Netherlands but only a small part of Belgium lies in the Vital Triangle.

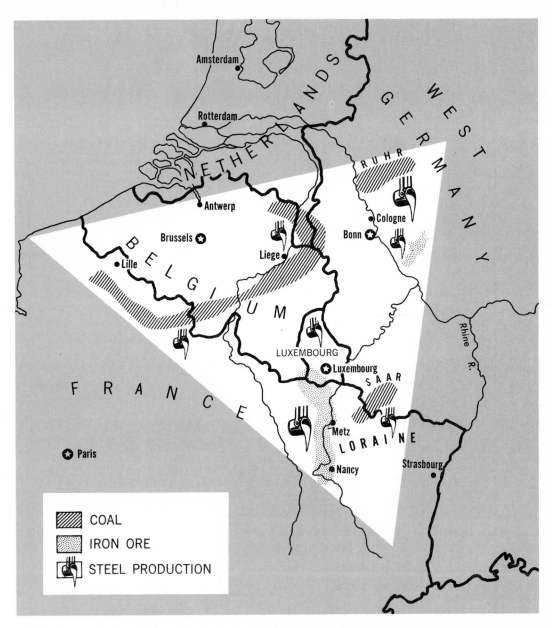

Map #27—The Vital Triangle

The map shows the region with these labels: Amsterdam, Rotterdam, NETHERLANDS, WEST GERMANY, Antwerp, Brussels, Lille, BELGIUM, Liege, RUHR, Cologne, Bonn, Rhine R., LUXEMBOURG, Luxembourg, SAAR, FRANCE, Metz, LORAINE, Paris, Nancy, Strasbourg.

Legend:

- COAL
- IRON ORE
- STEEL PRODUCTION

SUMMING UP   *Manufacturing in Western Europe*   Use these three headings to make an *outline* of the industries of this region. From what you have read, enter three statements under each heading.

A. Reasons for the Growth of Industry
B. Resources of Western Europe
C. How Europe's Resources are Used

Tell whether these statements are true or false. The underlined words make the statements true or false. If a statement is false, what word or words would you place in it to make it true?

1. The Vital Triangle is an important area of steel manufacturing.
2. Western Europe does not have a supply of rubber.
3. The chief source of power in Italy and Switzerland is water.
4. One of the mining areas of the Vital Triangle is located in Sweden.
5. Most manufactured goods in Western Europe are made from copper.
6. The Industrial Revolution began in Great Britain.
7. Britain's great manufacturing district is located along the northeastern coast.

7 HIS FARM IS HIS GARDEN

Reading For A Purpose: How does the European farmer use his land?

1. The skill of the European farmer matches the skill of the worker in Europe's factories. But in most of the Western European nations, only a small part of the population lives on farms. France has an almost even balance between those who farm and those who live in cities. Ireland is one of the few nations that has a large majority of farmers. But in Great Britain, West Germany, Belgium and the Netherlands, not even one person in four is a farmer.

2. Most farmers in Europe own their own land. They do not work for others. They live in villages near the fields. Each farmer works his small lands with great care. That is why we often say that his farm is his garden. He cares for his land much as an American might care for his garden crops. Because most farms are small, most of the work is done by hand or animal labor. However, the European farmer is gradually using more machinery.

A farm in West Germany. Why do many European farmers still use animal labor instead of modern machines?

3. Because great care is given to the land, an acre will provide a greater yield or amount of crop than in other regions. The European farmer raises about three times as much wheat on an acre of land as the American farmer! Because there is a shortage of good farm land, every acre that can be farmed is put to use. In the Netherlands, much land has been reclaimed from the flooding sea. The great dikes that hold back the Atlantic Ocean have given Netherlands farmers a large area of fertile soil that they could not otherwise have had.

4. Science, hard work and experience have also helped the farmer of Western Europe to grow large amounts of food. He rotates or changes his crops from year to year. He uses

Windmills such as the one seen here were originally used to help irrigate the land. Water pumping stations most often do that job today. But windmills continue to serve one centuries-old purpose. Farmers send messages to one another announcing events such as births and deaths by arranging the windmill sails in various positions.

fertilizer to enrich his soil. He cultivates the land carefully. He plants crops that grow best in a marine climate. The chief crops are root crops like potatoes, sugar beets and turnips. They are rotated with wheat, rye and barley. (Rye bread or dark bread is more common among the Europeans than white or wheat bread. Barley soup and potatoes are an important part of the diet of many Europeans.)

5. Marine Europe is also one of the great dairying regions of the world. The cool, wet summers provide grass for pasture. The mild winters mean that there is grass for the animals throughout the year. Oats, hay and sugar beets are also used as food crops for the animals. As a result, many countries have an important dairy industry in which cows are raised for milk, butter and cheese. The Netherlands and Denmark are leaders in this area. Switzerland is an example of the good use of mountain land. Despite its mountains, more than three-fourths of the land is used for crops or pasture for cattle, sheep and goats. (Where grass is plentiful and land is flat, cattle are raised. Sheep are found in areas of shorter grass and hillier land. Where grass is thinnest and land is very rugged or mountainous, the hardier and more sure-footed goats are raised. Goat's milk and goat cheese are very popular in many parts of Europe!)

6. Many European farmers raise hogs, chickens and sheep. Sheep are raised in especially large numbers. Great Britain alone has almost half as many sheep as the United States. The sheep supply both wool and meat for the people of Europe.

7. As rich as the farms are, and as carefully as they are worked, they cannot feed all the millions of city dwellers. Western Europe must depend upon other regions for food. Wheat, corn, animal and vegetable fats, cane sugar, cocoa, coffee and tea are a few of the foods that are imported. More wool is imported too.

8. Many European farmers have joined together to form *cooperatives.* These are organizations of farmers who agree to sell their farm

Sheep graze on the West German countryside. What areas of the United States are also well suited for raising sheep?

crops together. A cooperative sells all the crops at a certain price. Each farmer who is a member of the cooperative shares in the costs and the profits. The cooperatives also buy goods in large quantities to supply cheaply the farmers' needs for fertilizers, feed, tools and clothing. By buying in large amounts, the farmers can save money. In the Scandinavian countries, almost all farmers belong to cooperatives.

9. In the countries of Southern Europe—Spain, Portugal, Italy and Greece—most of the people are farmers. Farming is different here from that of marine Europe. There is little rainfall during the summer. Much of the land is rough and hilly. Because of this, the Mediterranean farmer has a more difficult time in raising good crops.

10. The average farm family along the Mediterranean is poor. There are many farmers and not enough good farm land. The farms are small and machinery is seldom used. Some of the farming methods have not changed in hundreds of years. Wooden plows, hoes and hand sickles are used. The farmers of the Mediterranean are also "gardeners" because they cultivate their small plots of ground very carefully. Most of the crops are grown for their own use.

11. The farmers of Southern Europe have learned how to farm the steep hillsides. At sea level they grow citrus fruits, if there is water from irrigation. Higher up, they build terraces or steps on the sides of hills. Terracing creates more usable farm land. The olive trees and grape vines that are planted here do not need much water or very rich soil. Their roots reach far down into the ground for water. (More than any other crop, the olive tree is a sign of the lack of water.) Wine is used for drinking instead of water and olive oil is used instead of animal fat for cooking. Wheat and vegetables are also planted among the vines and trees. On the higher rocky slopes, sheep and goats graze in pastures.

12. The seas of Western Europe are another source of food. Fish are an important part of the diet in lands of the marine climate. Fish and fish oils contain vitamins and other things necessary for good health. The North Sea in particular has many shallow waters and narrow areas. These fishing banks are rich in tiny plant and animal life. The larger fish come here to feed on the plants and smaller animal life in the water. Herring, cod and mackerel are found here. The fishermen of Western Europe catch thousands of tons of fish every year. Some is eaten by Europeans, and the rest is sold to other regions of the world.

UNDERSTANDING CHAPTER 7

1. Which questions are answered in this chapter?
   a. Why does the Western European farmer use little machinery?
   b. How are the hillsides farmed in Southern Europe?
   c. What foods are important in the diet of the Europeans?
2. The main idea of this chapter describes:
   a. the importance of fishing.
   b. how Europeans get their food.
   c. the importance of dairying.
3. Important crops of the farms of Europe are:
   a. sugar beets and potatoes.   b. rice and beans.   c. cotton and tea.
4. In the Mediterranean countries, farmers face the problem of:
   a. little rainfall.   b. unbearable heat.   c. heavy summer rains.

5. Western European farmers are able to raise large crops per acre because:
   a. dikes are used for irrigation.
   b. machinery is widely used.
   c. fertilizing and crop rotation are practiced.
6. Olives, grapes and wheat are farm products of which of these regions?
   a. Italy.   b. Ireland.   c. Belgium.
7. A good farmer *rotates* his crops—that is, he:
   a. waters them daily.
   b. changes them from year to year.
   c. uses minerals to enrich the soil.
8. In an agricultural *cooperative:*
   a. people work with others on the farm.
   b. farmers buy and sell goods together.
   c. people rent machinery to their neighbors.

DEVELOPING IDEAS AND SKILLS

Photograph Study

This photograph should help you to recall parts of the chapter you have just read. What is the main idea of the photograph?

SUMMING UP

Complete the following chart in your notebook.

Farming in Western Europe

	MARINE EUROPE	SOUTHERN EUROPE
1. Climate		
2. Surface of land		
3. Chief crops		
4. Farm animals		
5. Methods of farming		

Agree or Disagree   Decide whether or not each of the following statements agrees with what you have read. If the answer is *disagree*, explain why.

1. Most European farmers live on their own farms.
2. The skill of the European farmer matches the skill of the worker in Europe's factories.
3. The countries with a marine climate have a large dairying industry.
4. There are few animals on European farms.
5. France is probably better able to provide all the needs of her people than any other country of Western Europe.
6. The farmers of Western Europe have been slow to join farm cooperatives.
7. The farmers of Southern Europe have learned to farm the hilly lands along the coast.
8. The seas around Western Europe provide much food for the large population.

8 GREAT CENTERS OF TRADE

Reading For A Purpose: Why does Western Europe need trade with other regions?

Cargo freighters at Rotterdam, in the Netherlands. Rotterdam is one of the busiest ports in the world. What are some other leading ports in Western Europe?

1. Western Europe depends upon trade more than any other region in the world. There are not enough farmers to raise food for all the people of this small region. There are not enough raw materials and minerals to feed the "hungry" machines. All of these things must come from other parts of the world. Many of them come from the United States. Our trade with the nations of Western Europe amounts to 25 billion dollars a year.

2. Among Western Europe's important imports are oil from the Middle East, South America and the United States; wheat from Canada and Argentina; cotton from the United States and Egypt; tin and rubber from Malaysia and copper from Chile. In return, ships carry away coal, machinery, automobiles, chemicals and farming tools. The rest of the world benefits from the factories of Western Europe, for they get the finished products in return for their raw materials. Western Europe shows how people help each other through trade.

3. Nearly everywhere you look in Western Europe there are busy harbors. Among the largest and most important are London and Liverpool (Great Britain), Belfast (Ireland), Copenhagen (Denmark), Marseille (France) and Genoa (Italy). Paris (France), third largest city in Europe, is a busy trade and fashion center on the Seine River. Amsterdam and Rotterdam (Netherlands), Antwerp (Belgium) and Hamburg (West Germany) are also important. Day after day, shiploads of raw materials are unloaded at these ports. The empty ships are reloaded with goods to be shipped all over the world. The many bays and harbors of Western Europe have helped the people to use the nearby waters as highways for trade.

4. The leading nation in trade in Western Europe is West Germany. Together, the countries of Western Europe account for almost half of the world's trade. (While the United States leads the world in foreign trade, we are only one nation.) The imports of foods and raw materials are usually balanced by the export of manufactured goods. If it should happen that the Europeans import more than they export (buy more than they sell), the difference is sometimes made up through the millions of dollars spent by tourists.

5. Still, there are trade difficulties in Europe. The countries are small. None of them is as large as the state of Texas. (In some cases, a trip of less than 100 miles will take you all the way across one country and into another!) There are differences in language and money systems. Passports are needed as you move from one country to another. There are tariffs

or taxes on goods going from one nation to another.

6. In the United States these difficulties do not exist. A manufacturer in New York can sell his goods in California with little trouble. There is no tax, no passport, no difference in money from one state to another. An American who drives from coast to coast, almost three thousand miles, has few problems. But if you drove from Italy to Belgium (just a few hundred miles) you might pass through three different countries. Oranges can be shipped from Florida to Illinois more easily than from Spain to Belgium, even though the distance is greater. Iron ore from Minnesota is carried over the Great Lakes to Cleveland quite easily. Iron from the Lorraine district in France must cross at least one border to get to the Ruhr Valley where it is used. By the time these goods reach the customer in a European country, they are higher in price because of the tariffs that must be paid.

7. As you can see, Western Europe has a problem in using its resources wisely. The resources are divided among many nations and must support many people. In the next chapter, we will see what is being done to overcome this difficulty.

UNDERSTANDING CHAPTER 8

1. Which questions are answered in this chapter?
   a. Why is the Suez Canal important to Western Europe?
   b. Why have many cities in Western Europe become important?
   c. What does Western Europe export?
2. The main idea of this chapter describes:
   a. how Western Europe depends on trade.
   b. imports and exports of Western Europe.
   c. how many people there make a living.
3. Western Europe imports large quantities of:
   a. machinery.   b. coal.   c. oil.
4. Food imports to Western Europe are paid for by:
   a. the sale of manufactured goods.
   b. the sale of food products.
   c. income from tourists from foreign countries.
5. Western Europe imports food because:
   a. the quality of farm products is higher in the United States.
   b. the food is bought in order to carry on trade.
   c. farms in the region cannot raise all the food the people need.
6. There are difficulties in trading among the nations of Europe because:
   a. the mountains are too high to cross easily.
   b. there are many tariffs to pay.
   c. there is a lack of good transportation.
7. A tariff is a tax on:
   a. imports.
   b. exports.
   c. goods made and sold within the country.
8. In paragraph 2, the term "finished products" refers to:
   a. highly polished goods.
   b. high-priced goods such as linens and watches.
   c. manufactured goods of all kinds.

Pictograph #10—Industry in Western Europe

Read each of the statements below the graph of industry in Western Europe. Write *true* if the statement is correct. Write *false* if the statement is wrong. Write *not given* if the chart does not give you the information needed to decide on the statement.

MERCHANT
FLEET

STEEL
PRODUCTION

ALUMINUM
PRODUCTION

COAL
MINING

OIL
PRODUCTION

1. Western Europe depends heavily on trade.
2. Western Europe's chief source of power is oil.
3. Many people in Western Europe work in coal mines and steel mills.
4. The U.S. produces more steel and aluminum than Western Europe.
5. Boats from the nations of Western Europe can be seen in harbors all over the world.

SUMMING UP

Indicate whether the following items are *imports* or *exports* of Western Europe.

1. oil
2. fish
3. dairy products
4. wheat
5. meat

6. textiles
7. machinery
8. rubber
9. bananas and pineapples
10. chemicals

9 THE COMMON MARKET

Reading For A Purpose: How have some European nations planned to overcome some of their problems in trade with each other?

1. As you learned in the last chapter, Western Europe is divided into many small nations. Each nation has different resources. For example, France has iron and West Germany has coal. By the time the iron ore and coal are brought together in a steel mill, the price of steel is higher because of tariffs. Since World War II, however, the nations of Western Europe have learned that their resources can be used more wisely if they cooperate with each other.

2. After World War II, the power of Western European countries in world affairs had declined. The people were exhausted from the wars that had divided and ruined them. They realized that the United States and the Soviet Union were the new powers in the world. They knew they could not be important in world affairs unless they regained their strength. The idea of sharing their resources through free trade spread in Western Europe.

3. The agreement to lower tariffs among nations has become known as the Common Market. This movement may have started in 1948. At that time, Belgium, the Netherlands and Luxembourg formed a trade union. These nations are called the Benelux Nations because their beginning letters are BE-NE-LUX. Through the plan, each country was able to send its goods to the others without paying a tax or tariff. Trade grew so quickly that the idea began to spread. Other countries decided to try it also.

4. In 1957, Jean Monnet and Robert Schuman of France drew up a plan for pooling Western Europe's coal and iron resources. Six countries accepted this plan: the Benelux countries, France, Italy and West Germany. All of these nations had been hurt in World War II. All of them were willing to give up a little of their national power to join in the plan. This plan led to the idea of the Common Market. The leaders of the plan looked to the day when the countries of Western Europe would be united as a single nation.

5. These countries began to lower tariffs on goods going back and forth among their nations. Trade could flow as though there were no borders between them. This meant that a manufacturer in France would make things not only for the people of France, but also for the people in all six countries of the Common Market. For purposes of trade, these countries would be one nation.

6. The results of the Common Market pleased all members. Trade among the member nations doubled. Tariffs dropped lower and lower. Businessmen thought in terms of sales to all six nations rather than to only their own country. The standard of living in all member nations rose. People had more money and were able to buy more goods. Trade between Common Market countries and foreign lands also grew.

7. Because the Common Market plan was so successful, other nations wanted to become

A view of the port at Hamburg, West Germany. Why are ports such as this one important to Common Market trade? What have been some benefits of the Common Market to its member nations?

part of it. Great Britain asked to join, but France blocked its request for membership. (Each country has the right to *veto* or prevent the admission of a new member) Finally, in 1972, France agreed to British membership. Soon after, the English people voted to join. Now they hope to share in the benefits that the first six member countries have received. Along with Britain, Ireland and Denmark have also been admitted to the Market. This group of nine nations adds up to a market of 250 million people.

8. The success of the Common Market has some advantages for the United States. It brings the nations of Europe closer together. It should make them stronger and better able to defend themselves. With more money to spend, Western Europeans may buy more from us. How much more will depend on whether our businessmen and farmers can produce the goods Europeans want at prices they are willing to pay.

UNDERSTANDING CHAPTER 9

1. Which questions are answered in this chapter?
   a. Who is Jean Monnet?
   b. What are the benefits of the Common Market?
   c. Why did France block Great Britain's entry into the Common Market?
2. The main idea of this chapter describes:
   a. how the Common Market is changing Western Europe.
   b. how the Common Market affects the U.S.
   c. the work of Monnet and Schuman.
3. How many countries now belong to the Common Market?
   a. 3. b. 6. c. 9.
4. The Common Market began:
   a. after World War I.
   b. after World War II.
   c. at the urging of the United Nations.
5. The Common Market was formed to:
   a. share water power resources among the member nations.
   b. increase trade with the Soviet Union.
   c. share resources and skills of Western Europe.
6. The Common Market has been successful in that:
   a. fewer farms are needed.
   b. more and cheaper goods are available.
   c. tariffs on exports have been raised.

7. The "Benelux Nations" are:
   a. Poland, Czechoslovakia and Yugoslavia.
   b. Belgium, the Netherlands and Luxembourg.
   c. England, France and Germany.
8. Which country led the opposition to Great Britain's request for membership in the Common Market?
   a. France.   b. Belgium.   c. West Germany.

Map Study

Map #28—The Common Market

Study the map. Then tell whether these statements are *true* or *false*. Be able to explain your answers.

1. Austria and Yugoslavia are members of the Common Market.
2. France is the largest nation in the Common Market.
3. All the nations of Western Europe are Common Market members.
4. The Common Market nations together have more people than the United States.
5. The United States leads the Common Market nations in steel production.

THE COMMON MARKET MEMBERS

263

Complete the following *outline* in your notebook.

The Common Market

A. How It Started
   1.
   2.
   3.

B. How It Works
   1.
   2.
   3.

C. Results
   1.
   2.
   3.

Making Inferences   In our reading, many facts are given to us. From these facts we can draw conclusions. The following are some conclusions or inferences that you might make after reading Chapters 6, 7, 8 and 9. Tell whether these conclusions are correct or incorrect. Give reasons for your answers.

1. (Chapter 6) Many of the stoves in the kitchens of Western Europe are probably gas stoves.
2. (Chapter 6) In many parts of Western Europe, water takes the place of coal in making electricity.
3. (Chapter 6) Coal mines, factories and large cities of Western Europe are often found in the same place.
4. (Chapter 6) Western Europeans have made good use of their rivers and have developed a large system of canals.
5. (Chapter 7) Wheat bread or white bread is commonly found on the dinner tables of Europeans.
6. (Chapter 7) Europeans eat many kinds of soups made from vegetables, barley and potatoes.
7. (Chapter 8) Europe has a great many large cities on a small area of land.
8. (Chapter 9) At the present time there is a movement of the small nations of Europe to join together to solve common problems.
9. (Chapter 9) A manufacturer in Europe can succeed in business by selling his goods only within his own country.
10. (Chapter 9) As a result of World War II, the ability of Western Europe to produce a great amount of goods was weakened.

10 EUROPE DIVIDED

Reading For A Purpose: Can Western Europe solve its problems and become strong again?

1. You know that Western Europe is a region of many mills and factories. These factories use raw materials. The raw materials come from Europe or abroad. Oil, rubber, tin, cotton and copper are a few of the raw materials that have always been imported. However, Western Europe is using up its own natural resources, such as iron and coal, at a rapid rate. More and more, these must be imported at high cost from other regions of the world in order to keep the factories going.

2. The Industrial Revolution led Western Europe to obtain colonies all over the world. The raw materials from the colonies helped to feed the great factories. Moreover, Western Europe could sell the products of the factories to their colonies. After World War II, the colonies in Asia and Africa were freed. These new nations want to develop their own resources and use more of the goods for themselves. They are trading less with their "mother countries" and more with such countries as the United States and Japan. In short, the nations of Western Europe have lost many of their former markets to other parts of the world.

3. The countries of Southern Europe—Italy, Spain, Portugal and Greece—are different in many ways from the countries of marine Europe. These nations are poorer than their neighbors to the north. Their populations are growing and their small areas of fertile land are hard pressed to produce enough food for the growing population. When the people are poor, the governments are also poor. There is not enough money to provide the public schools, hospitals and health services that are needed. Moreover, the people of Spain, Portugal and Greece have had less chance to take part in democratic governments than their brothers to the north.

4. One of the big problems facing Western Europe and the entire world is the division of Germany. After World War II, Germany was divided into four parts. The Soviet Union occupied Eastern Germany. England, France and the United States occupied Western Germany. Berlin, located in the Soviet zone, was occupied by all four nations. In 1948, the three Western nations combined their zones of occupation into one. One year later, a new government of West Germany was formed with Bonn as its capital. The Soviet Union followed by establishing the "German Democratic Republic" in East Germany. Whether or not Germany will be reunited as one nation is a problem facing Western Europe and the world.

There are many poor people in Southern Europe. In what ways is this poor section of a town in Italy similar to poverty-stricken areas in this country?

5. Berlin has been a big problem for the West. It lies about 100 miles inside the Soviet zone. Two million people live in the sections occupied by England, France and the United States. They depend upon West Germany for the goods they need in order to live. These goods must be brought through part of East

The Berlin Wall was built in 1961 to stop East Germans from having free access to the West. What effect do you imagine this wall has had upon the lives of the people in East and West Germany?

Germany. In 1948, the East Germans, supported by the Soviet Union, closed the roads leading from the West to Berlin. No food or fuel could come into the city. The United States decided to fight the blockade. Food and supplies were sent into Berlin entirely by air. This airlift was a success. The East Germans gave up the blockade after a year.

6. However, in 1961, the East Germans built a wall in Berlin to stop their people from going over to the West. It is still an aim of the East German government to add all of Berlin to its own territory. It does not like to see a free city inside East Germany. However, the United States has made it clear that Berlin will stay a free city as long as we can help.

7. Events in Berlin aroused the Western nations. They feared the spread of communism from Eastern Europe into their nations. In 1949, the United States, Canada and ten nations of Europe formed the North Atlantic Treaty Organization or NATO. These nations agreed to help each other in case of attack. They formed a NATO army. Dwight D. Eisenhower was the first commander of the NATO forces. There are now fourteen nations in NATO.

8. As the Western European nations continue to grow in strength through the Common Market, they will follow a course of their own choosing. This has worried many people in the United States. Our nation would like Western Europe to follow the same policies that we do. However, we know it is more important that Western Europe be strong. A strong Europe standing between us and the Soviet Union is in our interest, even if there is not always complete agreement. Freedom in Western Europe helps the people of America to remain free.

UNDERSTANDING CHAPTER 10

1. Which questions are answered in this chapter?
   a. Why is Berlin important to the free world?
   b. How is Spain governed?
   c. What are Western Europe's chief problems?
2. The main idea of this chapter describes:
   a. the spread of communism in Europe.
   b. the current problems of Western Europe.
   c. how Western Europe lost its colonies.

3. At present, Germany is divided into:
   a. four parts.   b. three parts.   c. two parts.

4. Berlin is located in:
   a. West Germany.   b. East Germany.   c. Switzerland.

5. NATO was formed because:
   a. there was a fear of the spread of communism in Europe.
   b. the United States needed support in Europe.
   c. the United States wanted to increase her trade in Europe.

6. The loss of colonies hurt the countries of Western Europe because:
   a. immigrants no longer came.
   b. markets for goods were lost.
   c. raw materials were no longer needed.

7. In paragraph 2, the term "mother countries" refers to:
   a. England, France and the Netherlands.
   b. China, India and Japan.
   c. the United States and Canada.

8. In 1948, the East Germans blockaded:
   a. Berlin.
   b. West Germany.
   c. France.

DEVELOPING IDEAS AND SKILLS

Look at the cartoon. Then answer the questions below.

1. What are some problems dividing Western Europe?
2. For what reason was NATO formed?
3. How is the Common Market helping to overcome some of these problems?
4. When was the Berlin Wall put up?
5. What is a good title for this cartoon?

Fact or Opinion   Read each statement carefully. If the statement is a fact, write F in your notebook. If it is an opinion, write O.

1. The United States should join the Common Market.
2. Western Europe is divided into many small nations.
3. Warm ocean currents give Western Europe a mild, rainy climate.
4. The United Nations can guarantee the freedom of the city of Berlin.
5. Manufacturing is more important to the people of France than it is to the people of the United States.
6. The nations of Western Europe are going to unite into one large nation in a few years.
7. The division of Germany presents a problem that threatens the peace of the world.
8. The United States should not trade with any Communist country.

Reviewing Western Europe   Complete the following statements by using the words or phrases listed below.

Vital Triangle	coal and iron
factories	rivers and canals
peninsula	finished goods
food	food and raw
natural harbors	materials
northerly	North Atlantic
large cities	Drift
Common Market	

1. Europe is a _____ on the land mass of Eurasia.
2. Europe has many fine _____.
3. The coast of Western Europe is warmed by an ocean current, the _____.
4. Europe has great mineral wealth in _____.
5. The great steel-making area of Western Europe is known as the _____.
6. Western Europe is a web of _____.
7. Western Europe imports _____; in turn, it exports machinery and other _____.
8. Most people in Western Europe work in _____ and live in _____.
9. Nine nations of Western Europe have increased their trade through the _____.
10. Today, the farms of Western Europe do not supply enough _____ for the people.

11 GREAT BRITAIN: THE ISLAND NATION

Reading For A Purpose: How has Great Britain become a world power despite its small size?

Freedom of speech is one of the many democratic ideas brought to the United States from Britain. At Speaker's Corner in London's Hyde Park, anyone can speak his or her mind on any subject. Why is this freedom to speak out a necessary part of open government?

1. Great Britain is a narrow island west of the mainland of Europe. It is made up of three parts: England, Scotland and Wales. A fourth part of the nation lies on the northern coast of Ireland. Great Britain is about 94,000 square miles in area, a little smaller than our state of Oregon. The population is about 55 million. This makes Great Britain one of the world's most densely populated countries. Generally, ten times as many people live on each square mile in Britain as on each square mile in the United States.

2. The northern and western parts of Great Britain are hilly and mountainous. The eastern part is a lowland plain. This is part of the Great European Plain. The coastline is long and irregular. There are many fine harbors.

3. The island of Great Britain has a marine climate. This mild, rainy climate is caused by the warm current (North Atlantic Drift) and winds that come from the west. The weather of London is much like the weather of Seattle, Washington, and other cities of our Northwest. The ocean winds bring rain. The heaviest rains fall on the western side of the island. The fogs of London are world-famous. We sometimes talk about fogs so thick that we can hardly see in front of us. In London this is often true!

4. The British have always used the seas around them. In the 17th and 18th centuries they began to build a great empire. They started colonies in the New World, India, Africa and Australia. At the same time the Industrial Revolution was taking place. The British were the first to use machines run by steam engines. Their colonies furnished raw materials. The machines turned these raw materials

Rugby is a popular sport among the British. A favorite American sport has developed from this game. Which one?

into finished goods. The goods were shipped to all parts of the world. The sea has meant life to the British people.

5. After World War I, four of Great Britain's former colonies—Canada, Australia, New Zealand and South Africa—joined with Great Britain in a new relationship called the British Commonwealth of Nations. They agreed to help one another by lowering tariffs on goods sent to each other. During World War II, Great Britain fought with the Allies against Nazi Germany. Germany was defeated, but Great Britain had used up much of its resources in the process. Later, Britain had to give up colonies in Asia and Africa. Many joined the Commonwealth as free and equal partners.

6. Most Britons live in cities and towns. The largest city is London, the capital, home of 8 million people. Many of the British ways of living are like those of the people in the United States. Our language came from Great Britain. Our clothing is in the same fashion. We use many British products. Britons go to the movies, listen to the radio and watch television as much as we do. Almost everyone can read and write. Medical care is given to the people as a government service. The British standard of living is among the highest in the world.

7. Most of our ideas of law and government came from Great Britain, although in Britain there is no written constitution. The king or queen is the head of state, but holds little power. The lawmaking body of the British government is Parliament. Parliament is divided into two houses, the House of Lords and the House of Commons. The chief official is the prime minister. He is the leader of the political party that has the most representatives in the House of Commons. He chooses his cabinet to help him pass and carry out laws. (You will recall that Canada's government is a parliamentary one too.)

8. The Britons depend on their farm lands and surrounding seas for part of their food. The best farm land is on the eastern part of the island. Here farmers plant wheat and barley. Machinery is used where it is possible, and the yield per acre is high. In the northern highlands they also raise dairy cattle and sheep.

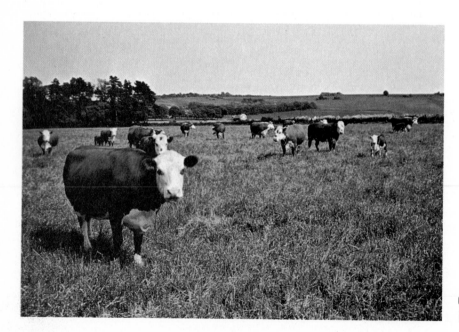

Cattle graze on the English countryside.

The wool is used in the textile factories. Besides their farm and grazing land, the British obtain a large supply of herring, cod and other fish from the nearby waters.

9. The farms and seas do not provide enough food for Great Britain's millions of people. The British must, therefore, buy more food from abroad. To pay for this food, Great Britain turns to her factories. Raw materials are imported. The raw materials are turned into finished goods and sold in world markets. These goods pay for the materials and foods that must be imported.

10. Great Britain has become a leading manufacturing nation for many reasons. Because Britain is surrounded by water, it has been able to avoid invasions from Europe for centuries. Thus, it has been left alone to develop its industries without interference. Its people are hard-working, skilled and inventive. It has had great resources of coal and iron ore. (Many British are miners. Coal is the chief source of power. The chief coal and iron fields are in Wales and eastern England.) Using these resources, Britain's skilled workers turn out a great variety of products: woolen and cotton goods, steel products of all kinds, automobiles, airplanes, farm machinery, chemicals, electrical equipment and films.

11. These manufactured goods are Britain's exports. Because of its great need for trade, Britain has long been a leading shipbuilding nation. Its ships sail the seas, trading with nations all over the world. Its greatest trade is with the members of the Commonwealth of Nations. However, Great Britain has also long been one of our best customers.

12. Great Britain has a number of problems. Its well-being depends upon its selling goods abroad. This is becoming harder because of the growing number of industrial nations that also want to sell goods abroad. The loss of colonies after World War II means that Great Britain no longer controls the raw materials or markets of its former colonies.

13. Great Britain lacks some important re-sources. It does not have oil, copper, cotton or wood pulp. It must import food at high cost. Its coal resources also may be "wearing out." The United States, Soviet Union and West Germany have now passed it in steel production. The British have been trying to develop a cheaper source of power. They were the first people to use atomic energy to operate machines.

14. Despite its weakened resources, Britain still plays a leading part in world affairs. It is a

"Bloody Sunday," February 2, 1972. In Londonderry, Northern Ireland, Catholic protest marchers became violent and British troops began firing at them. Thirteen people, all civilians, were killed.

member of the NATO alliance with the United States and nations of Western Europe. It is a member of SEATO (Southeast Asia Treaty Organization) with the United States, Australia and New Zealand, among others. It has joined with Turkey, Iran and Pakistan in forming CENTO (Central Treaty Organization). All of these agreements with nations in many parts of the world have one chief purpose—to stop the spread of communism.

15. Great Britain has faced problems in Northern Ireland. In 1920, the island of Ire-

land was divided. Southern Ireland, the larger part, became an independent country, Eire. The smaller part, Northern Ireland, remained part of the United Kingdom. Two-thirds of the people in Northern Ireland are Protestants; the rest are largely Catholics. Because they are in the minority, Catholics feel that they have suf-fered discrimination in voting, housing and jobs. They want Northern Ireland to be part of Eire. In 1970, fighting broke out between the Catholics and Protestants. Since then, hundreds of people have been killed. British troops have occupied Northern Ireland to try to stop the bloodshed.

UNDERSTANDING CHAPTER 11

1. Which questions are answered in this chapter?
   a. How are the British people governed?
   b. Where are the coal mining areas?
   c. What are some of Great Britain's problems?
2. The main idea of *paragraph 10* describes:
   a. the variety of British products.
   b. how Britain became a great industrial nation.
   c. the skill of British workers.
3. Most of the British people work:
   a. on farms.   b. in mines.   c. in industry and trade.
4. The leader of the British government is the:
   a. prime minister.   b. premier.   c. chancellor.
5. Britain has become a leader in manufacturing for all of these reasons EX-CEPT:
   a. it had an early start.
   b. it has a large supply of cotton.
   c. there have been large coal and iron resources.
6. Some of Britain's problems are now caused by:
   a. the loss of population since World War II.
   b. the loss of former colonies.
   c. problems of wheat farmers on the island.

DEVELOPING IDEAS AND SKILLS

Map Study

Map #29a and b—Great Britain

Study the maps on page 273. Then answer these questions.
1. Does Great Britain lie in the high, middle or low latitudes?
2. What is the distance from the coast of Britain to the coast of France?
3. How do you explain the presence of the large cities of Liverpool, London, Glasgow, Dublin and Belfast?
4. If you flew from your community to London, you would fly in which direction? How do you know this without looking at a world map?
5. Locate the Prime Meridian. Which city is it near?
6. Name two cities that are not seaports.
7. How many different bodies of water can you find on the map?
8. How does the map tell you that the climate of Great Britain will be milder than the mainland near it?
9. Which is larger, Oregon or Britain?
10. Which more crowded, Oregon or Britain?

Map #29a—Great Britain

OREGON
POPULATION: 2.2 MILLION
LAND AREA: 96,200 SQUARE MILES
23 PEOPLE PER SQUARE MILE

GREAT BRITAIN
POPULATION: 55.8 MILLION
LAND AREA: 93,900 SQUARE MILES
592 PEOPLE PER SQUARE MILE

Map #29b—Great Britain and Oregon

SUMMING UP   *Great Britain*   Use these four headings to make an outline of the important facts and ideas concerning Great Britain. From what you have learned, write three statements under each heading.

A. How Great Britain Compares With the United States in Size and Population
B. How Great Britain Compares With the United States in Government and Life of Her People
C. Sources of Great Britain's Strength
D. Britain's Weaknesses and Problems

FOLLOW UP   *Cause and Effect*   In Column A are six statements. In Column B are some results of the facts stated in Column A. See if you can match the causes in Column A with the effects or results in Column B.

COLUMN A

1. Warm ocean winds
2. Coal and iron resources
3. Need for raw materials
4. Lack of farm land
5. Fear of communism
6. Need for trade

COLUMN B

a. gave an early start in the manufacture of steel.
b. caused the development of atomic energy.
c. led to growth of shipbuilding.
d. bring rain and fog to the island.
e. led to defense agreements with nations all over the world.
f. led to a great empire of colonies.
g. led to the sale of manufactured goods in trade for food.

12 SPAIN: POOR LAND OF SOUTHERN EUROPE

Reading For A Purpose: Will Spain be able to regain her place as a world leader?

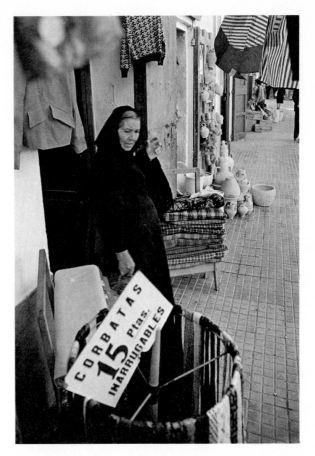

A woman selling neckties in Spain.

1. Spain occupies the Iberian Peninsula, sharing it with the small country of Portugal. The Pyrenees Mountains in the north separate her from the rest of Western Europe. Portugal and the Atlantic Ocean form her western boundary. Aside from the mountains in the north, all of the remaining boundaries are water—the Bay of Biscay on the north and the Mediterranean Sea on the east. Her long coastline of 1500 miles is regular and provides few natural harbors. The narrow Strait of Gibraltar separates Spain from North Africa.

2. Spain's 34 million people live in a land somewhat larger than California. Unlike most Western Europeans, most Spaniards are poor. Their average yearly income of $275 per person is the second lowest in Western Europe. Moreover, they do not have a democratic form of government. For years they had been ruled by one man, Francisco Franco.

3. Most of Spain is a wide, treeless plateau called the *meseta* (or little table). The plateau is crisscrossed by low hills and mountains called *sierras*. Madrid, the capital, is in the middle of the meseta. A number of small rivers, such as the Ebro and Guadalquivir, drain the plateau. In the north, the high Pyrenees have few passes through them to France.

4. Spain's climate is varied. In the north it is cool and rainy—the marine climate. The central plateau is hot and dry in the summer and very cold in the winter. Along Spain's Mediterranean coast the summers are hot and dry, but the winters bring some rain.

5. About 2000 years ago, Spain was part of the Roman Empire. The Romans controlled this land for about 600 years. They gave the Spaniards Christianity and the Roman language, Latin. The Moors, a Moslem people from North Africa, then crossed the Strait of Gibraltar and ruled most of Spain for 800 years. They were finally driven out in 1492.

6. In that same year Christopher Columbus, sailing from Spain, discovered the New World. Spanish conquerors—de Soto, Cortez, Pizarro, Coronado—soon explored and claimed large areas of this New World. Magellan made his famous voyage around the globe and claimed Guam and the Philippines. Spanish ships brought in gold and silver from Mexico

275

and Peru and silks and spices from the Orient. Spain became the richest nation in Europe!

7. In 1588, Spain's great navy or Armada lost a great sea battle to England. At that time, Spain began to lose its power. By 1825, most of its colonies in the New World had won their freedom. Then it suffered a defeat by the United States in the Spanish-American War of 1898 and lost more territory. Cuba became independent. Puerto Rico and the Philippines were given to the United States.

8. A terrible civil war from 1936 to 1939 ruined Spain. More than a million people were killed as Spaniard fought Spaniard. The winners were the "Nationalists" led by Francisco Franco. Franco became the ruler of the nation.

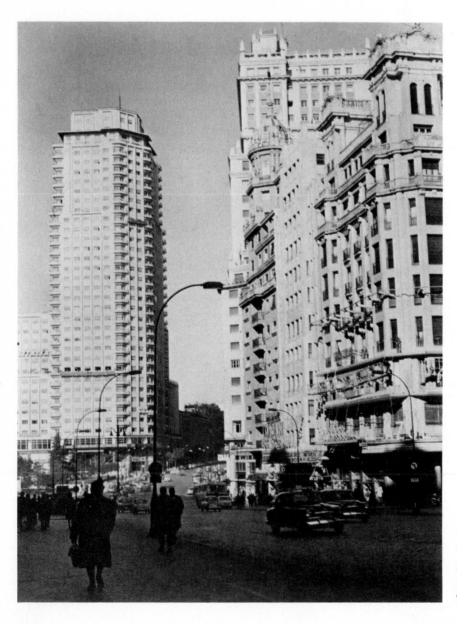

Downtown Madrid. In what ways does Madrid appear to be typical of modern cities all over the world?

9. Although there is a lawmaking body called the Cortes, the real power in Spain for many years was Franco. He was the head of the government, the armed forces and the Falange, the only political party. Spain did not take part in World War II. Since 1953, the United States has given help to Spain in return for the right to build air bases on Spanish soil. In 1975, Franco died. No one person now has his power.

10. Most of the Spanish people are farmers or herders. They live in the irrigated river valleys and along the coasts where there is more rainfall. The Catholic religion is the official religion of the country. There is no separation of Church and government as in our nation. Madrid, Barcelona and Seville are the large, important cities of Spain. Only Madrid has more than two million people. In the cities, many people are poor. Farmers, too, show the poverty of Spain.

11. Most Spanish farmers rent their land from wealthy landowners. They live in small villages of adobe (sun-dried brick). Many of the country people are not able to read and write. Their farm work is done by hand or with the simplest tool, a wooden plow drawn by a donkey. Unlike most of the farmers of Western Europe, the Spaniards do not use a great amount of fertilizer, nor do many rotate their crops. As a result, harvests are small.

12. The chief farm crop is wheat. However, not enough is raised to feed the people, so more must be imported. There is so little rainfall in some wheat-growing areas that farmers plant their fields only once in two years. In this way, they use the rainfall gathered in two seasons for one crop. Much of the meseta is also used for grazing sheep. Large herds of goats graze in the foothills of the Pyrenees as well. (When a country raises large numbers of goats —as in Spain, Italy and Greece, for example—it is often a sign that the land is poor.)

13. Olives and grapes are the chief export crops of Spain. Both of these crops can grow in land that is rocky and where there is little water. They are raised on the hillsides along the Mediterranean coast in the south and east. Spanish farmers also grow oranges near the city of Valencia.

14. Spain is rich in minerals but has few large industries. Iron ore is mined along the Atlantic Coast. It is the chief mineral export of Spain. Copper, zinc, silver and lead are also mined. Spain is one of the world's chief sources of mercury, a silver-colored metal used in thermometers. The chief industrial region lies in the north and northeast near the city of Barcelona. The main source of power is falling water, because coal and oil are lacking in large amounts.

15. Although it has valuable minerals, Spain has remained a poor country. Much of the land is in the hands of a few wealthy people. Farming methods are old-fashioned and the lack of water is a problem. The government had been run by one man for many years. However, Spain is "coming to life." New factories have been built to make use of the country's own iron. Dams are being built to irrigate more land. Electricity from these dams is now being brought to more villages. Spain is also trying to build its tourist business, and more people from Europe and the Americas are visiting the country every year.

UNDERSTANDING CHAPTER 12

1. Which questions are answered in this chapter?
   a. What are Spain's chief crops?
   b. Who are some of Spain's great writers and artists?
   c. Where do most of the Spanish people live?

2. The main idea of *paragraphs 5 through 7* describes the:
   a. government of Spain.
   b. great power that was once held by Spain.
   c. history of Spain.
3. Spain was once ruled by people called the:
   a. Mongols.   b. Moors.   c. Mayans.
4. Most of the land in Spain is:
   a. a fertile river valley.
   b. a dry, treeless plateau.
   c. covered with high, rugged mountains.
5. Farms of Spain do not produce a great amount of crops because:
   a. the land is poor and it is worked by hand.
   b. there are few farm workers.
   c. there are few farm animals.
6. Olives and grapes are grown because they:
   a. do not need much water.
   b. grow best in the cool highlands.
   c. are easy to take care of.
7. *Adobe* refers to:
   a. the lawmaking body of the Spanish government.
   b. shawls worn by Spanish women.
   c. sun-dried brick.
8. In paragraph 15, the expression "coming to life" means:
   a. going to be old-fashioned for a long time.
   b. giving birth to new ideas.
   c. beginning to develop industries.

DEVELOPING IDEAS AND SKILLS

Map Study

Map #30a and b—Spain

Study the maps on page 279. Then answer these questions.
1. What countries border Spain?
2. How would you describe the land formation of Spain and Portugal?
3. How is Spain separated from France?
4. Is your community farther north or south than the city of Madrid?
5. Why do you think there are few large seaports in Spain?
6. Which direction is *upstream* on the Ebro River?
7. What is the distance from the Pyrenees Mountains to the Strait of Gibraltar?
8. How does Spain compare in size with the United States? with the state of California?
9. Which is more crowded, Spain or California?

Map #30a—Spain

CALIFORNIA
POPULATION: 20.0 MILLION
LAND AREA: 156,500 SQUARE MILES
128 PEOPLE PER SQUARE MILE

SPAIN
POPULATION: 34.5 MILLION
LAND AREA: 194,900 SQUARE MILES
176.4 PEOPLE PER SQUARE MILE

Map #30b—Spain and California

Tell whether these statements are *true* or *false*. The underlined words make the statements true or false. If a statement is false, what words would you place in it to make it true?

1. Spain is located in southern Europe.
2. The Bay of Biscay separates Spain from North Africa.
3. From 1939 to 1975, Spain was ruled by Francisco Franco.
4. The chief grain crop of Spanish farmlands is rice.
5. Sheep are grazed on the plateaus.
6. The chief export crops of Spain are olives and grapes.
7. The chief industrial region is near Barcelona.
8. The capital of Spain is Seville.
9. Puerto Rico was once a Spanish colony.
10. The Pyrenees Mountains separate Spain and Portugal.

13 NORWAY, SWEDEN, FINLAND: LANDS OF THE "MIDNIGHT SUN"

Reading For A Purpose: How have the people of these lands reached such a high standard of living in spite of their problems of climate and topography?

Skiing originated in the Scandinavian lands. Hundreds of years ago, Norwegian soldiers wore skis on snowy batlefields. What advantages do you think a soldier wearing skis had? What disadvantages?

1. Norway, Sweden and Finland are northern lands. Except for Sweden, these countries have few minerals. Much of their soil is poor. Yet in all three countries the people have made good use of the resources they have. They have a very high standard of living. Let us see why.

2. Norway and Sweden share the Scandinavian Peninsula. To the east is Finland, a country with many of the same problems. To the west is the Atlantic Ocean; to the south are the Baltic and North Seas and to the east is the Soviet Union. These three countries are among the northernmost nations on earth. They are about as far north as Alaska. About one-fourth of each country is above the Arctic Circle. As a result, the sun shines 24 hours a day for about two months in the summer. That is why this area is sometimes called "Land of the Midnight Sun." During the winter the sun does not appear at all for about two months. The lands lie in almost total darkness during these winter months.

3. Compared with other countries of Western Europe, Norway, Sweden and Finland are both big and little countries at the same time —large in size but small in population. Sweden's 8 million people live in an area slightly larger than California. Finland's small population of 4½ million occupies an area about the size of the state of New Mexico. Norway is slightly smaller than Finland and has a little more than 4 million people.

4. Most of Norway is mountainous. To the east of these highlands is rough, hilly Sweden. Sweden's land ranges from rolling plains in the south to rugged mountains and plateaus in the north and northwest. Much of Finland is a low plateau. All three countries have countless lakes, rivers, streams and canals. The Atlantic coast of Norway is lined with inlets called *fiords*. These narrow bodies of water reach far inland and are surrounded by high banks. They were carved out of the mountains ages ago by glaciers and are very beautiful. There are still glaciers in the mountains.

5. The climate of these northern countries is not as cold as you might think. The Atlantic coast of Norway and the southern parts of Sweden and Finland have milder climates than the rest of this region. During the summer the temperature is like that of San Francisco. During the winter it is as cold as Chicago or Detroit. The mild climate is due to the North Atlantic Drift, which brings warm waters and

winds from the ocean. Much of Sweden and Finland, however, is shut off from the warm, westerly winds by the mountains. Because of this the winters there are much colder than in Norway.

6. The Scandinavian peninsula was once the home of a fierce people, the Vikings. Between 800 and 1000 A.D., the Vikings raided and occupied many parts of Western Europe. They settled Iceland and Greenland and some believe they may have reached North America about 1000 A.D. By the 14th century, Norway, Sweden and Finland were ruled by Denmark. Sweden gained its freedom and had a period of power ending shortly after 1700. Sweden and Norway were united for a while until Norway became free in 1905. Russia controlled Finland until the Russian Revolution of 1917. Now all three nations are free and, except for fighting between Russia and Finland in 1939 and in World War II, they have kept their freedom in peace.

7. Norway and Sweden both have governments in which a king rules but a parliament makes the laws. The prime minister is the chief officer of the government. The parliaments are elected by the people. Finland also has a democratic form of government. Finland, however, has no king. Its chief officer is a president.

8. The remarkable thing about these countries is their high standard of living. Schooling is important and the people read widely. Their health, old age and child care programs are paid for by the government. The people of these countries live long, healthful lives. They enjoy most of the comforts that we have—radios, telephones, automobiles and electric kitchen appliances. Until 1900, most people were farmers, fishermen and woodsmen. Today most are workers in industry. The largest number of people live in the southern part of their countries, where the climate is milder. Their largest cities are the capitals—Oslo, Norway; Stockholm, Sweden; Helsinki, Finland. Most of the people are followers of the Protestant religion.

9. Above the Arctic Circle lives a small tribe of people called the Lapps. They live in the bare northern parts of all three nations. The Lapps are nomads. They raise reindeer and follow their animals as they move from place to place in search of food. The reindeer provide Lapps with meat, milk and hides for tents and clothing.

10. Except for Sweden, few mineral resources are found in these northern countries. Only Sweden has iron ore. Coal and oil, two power resources, are lacking. There is little fertile farm land and the growing seasons are short. Despite this lack of resources and favorable climate, the people have learned to make the best use of what they have: the forests, the swift-flowing streams and the fishing grounds. All three countries are rich in forests. For years the swift streams have been used to float logs and run saw mills. Today the rivers are more important as a source of electricity for industries. Wood pulp and paper are the leading exports of all three countries.

11. Because the land and climate make farming difficult, Norway has long turned to the sea

A Lapp woman in the far north of Finland.

There are many villages such as this on fiords along the Norwegian coast. Why do many Scandinavians live close to the water?

for food and for a living. The nation borders the Atlantic Ocean. The ocean waters are filled with cod and herring. Fishermen of Norway are famous as whale-hunters as well. The modern whaling ships are like floating factories. The whale is caught and prepared for market right on the ships. Norway catches more fish than it can use and the surplus is exported. Because of this interest in the sea, Norway has one of the largest fleets of ships in the world. Fishing is less important to Sweden and Finland.

12. Lacking coal and oil, these northern countries have made great use of the electricity provided by waterfalls. This electricity is a source of power for their factories. Factories use the products of Scandinavia's mines, forests and seas. Sweden uses its own iron ore to make fine steel goods. In Finland, copper from its mines is made into wire. In Norway, there are plants for refining copper and nickel.

13. The amount of fertile farm land in each country is small. The growing season lasts only a few months. Yet the people have done re-

markable things with what they have. Swedish farmers get very high yields from each acre of land. Finland's farmers have shown the world how to grow wheat in the coldest climates. The chief crops are hay, rye, wheat, barley and oats. All three countries are now raising more dairy cattle. Sweden is one of the great milk-producing nations of the world. While the use of machinery and great care of farm land have brought good crops, Sweden and Norway must still import food for their people.

14. Because these nations need to import food and raw materials from other countries, they must depend upon foreign trade. Their chief exports are paper, wood products, fish, steel and iron ore. Norway's ships may be found all over the world.

15. These three countries of northern Europe are located between the Soviet Union and the Free World. The three nations have tried to remain neutral in world arguments. Norway has joined NATO, but not the Common Market. Neither Sweden nor Finland has joined NATO or the Common Market of Europe.

1. Which questions are answered in this chapter?
   a. What is the climate of Norway, Sweden and Finland?
   b. What are the Nobel Prizes?
   c. Why do the three nations of Northern Europe depend upon foreign trade?
2. The main idea of this chapter describes:
   a. the land and climate of the Scandinavian Peninsula.
   b. how the Lapps live.
   c. how the people of three northern nations use their resources.
3. A good description of these northern lands would include mention of:
   a. rivers cutting through plains.
   b. mountains covered with great forests.
   c. cold, treeless tundra with large areas of fertile farm land in the north.
4. The source of food of the Lapps is the:
   a. reindeer.   b. goat.   c. buffalo.
5. A reason why farming is difficult in Scandinavia is that:
   a. the growing season is short.
   b. there is a small population.
   c. there is a lack of water.
6. These nations carry on much foreign trade because:
   a. their lumber supplies materials for shipbuilding.
   b. they do not have much to sell.
   c. they need to buy food and raw materials.
7. A *fiord* would be most important to a:
   a. sailor.   b. miner.   c. farmer.
8. When a nation has a *surplus* of goods, it has:
   a. more goods than are needed for its own use.
   b. large industries using coal and iron.
   c. farm products grown on small farms.

Map Study

Map #31a and b—Norway, Sweden and Finland

Study the maps on page 285. Then answer these questions.
1. Do the Scandinavian countries lie in the high, middle or low latitudes?
2. Locate the capital cities of each country on the map. What do all these cities have in common?
3. If you flew from your community to Norway, in what direction would you be traveling?
4. What city is located near 60° N. Lat. and 5° E. Long.?
5. About how far is the distance from Copenhagen in Denmark to Stockholm in Sweden?
6. Where are the large cities of Norway located?   Why is this so?
7. Into what body of water do the great number of streams in Finland flow? In Sweden?
8. Why do you think the Gulf of Bothnia is not so important a waterway as the North Sea?
9. What country borders Finland on the east?
10. The city of Hammerfest in the extreme north is located in what country?

Map #31a—Norway, Sweden and Finland

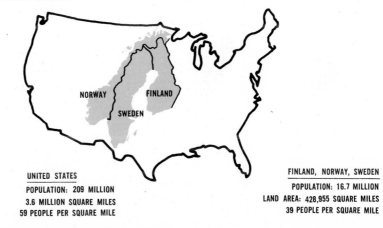

Map #31b—Norway, Sweden, Finland and the United States

285

SUMMING UP *Agree or Disagree*   Decide whether or not each of the following statements agrees with what you have read. If the answer is *disagree*, explain why.

1. All three of these northern nations are mountainous.
2. Part of each nation lies above the Arctic Circle.
3. The climate of the three countries is affected by the North Atlantic Drift.
4. Norway, Sweden and Finland have many mineral resources.
5. The northern frontier of Scandinavia is settled by nomads called Eskimos.
6. These northern lands are closer to the United States than they are to the Soviet Union.
7. Much of the land is covered with forests and rapid mountain streams.
8. Rich soils make these nations the greatest wheat-growing countries of Europe.
9. Sweden has iron-ore deposits.
10. Electricity is a great source of power in these northern lands.

FOLLOW UP In your notebook, place the following items under one of these three headings: *Norway, Sweden* and *Finland.*

1. The largest population of the three.
2. The largest nation of the three.
3. Owner of one of the world's largest fleets of merchant ships.
4. Headed by a president.
5. Famous for whaling ships.
6. Large producer of iron ore.
7. Successful in wheat-growing.
8. Fiords are part of the coastline.

BOOKS FOR UNIT 5

	Author	Title, Publisher	Description
1.	Benary-Isbert,	THE ARK, Harcourt Brace	The story of a divided family in the Germanies.
2.	Booth, Arthur H.	THE TRUE STORY OF SIR WINSTON CHURCHILL, BRITISH STATESMAN, Children's Press	The biography of a person sometimes called the "greatest man of the twentieth century."
3.	Clement, Marguerite	IN FRANCE, Viking	France's history, people and their ways of living.
4.	Crane, William D.	THE MAN WHO TRANSFORMED THE WORLD: JAMES WATT, Messner	Watt, his steam engine and the great changes it brought about.
5.	Daly, Maureen	SPANISH ROUNDABOUT, Dodd	The history and geography of Spain.

6.	DeJong, Meindert	WHEEL ON THE SCHOOL, Harper	The life of children in a Dutch fishing village.
7.	Dobren, Arnold	ITALY, MODERN RENAISSANCE, Nelson	Pleasures, customs and economy of Italy today.
8.	Geis, Darlene, editor	LET'S TRAVEL IN ENGLAND, Children's Press	One of a series that introduces the reader to life in European countries.
9.	Holbrook, Sabra	GERMANY EAST AND WEST, Meredith	The two Germanies today and how they came to be divided.
10.	Hürlimann, Martin	ETERNAL GREECE, Viking	Illustrations of Greek art and architecture.
11.	Lobsenz, Norman M.	DENMARK, Franklin Watts	The land and customs of the people.
12.	Rothery, Agnes	SCANDINAVIAN ROUNDABOUT, Dodd	The story of Norway and Sweden.
13.	Shirer, William	THE RISE AND FALL OF ADOLF HITLER, Random House	The story of Nazism and World War II.

UNIT 6
The Soviet Union

1 THE GLOBAL GIANT

A family from the Urals region on a visit to Moscow.

Reading For A Purpose: Why should we know about the Soviet Union?

1. The Union of Soviet Socialist Republics, or U.S.S.R., stretches across two continents, Europe and Asia. We often refer to this vast nation as the Soviet Union. What does the name of the country mean? "Soviet" is the Russian word for "council" and "socialist" means that the government owns the land, resources and industries of the country. (A Soviet citizen may own such personal property as a car or a home.) It is not altogether correct to use the name Russia when referring to the Soviet Union because Russia is only a small part of the Soviet Union. It is only the part west of the Ural Mountains.

2. There are many reasons why we should learn about the Soviet Union. The U.S.S.R. is the largest nation in the world. Reaching from Europe through Asia, it takes up about one-sixth of the land surface of the earth. The western part of the country is called Soviet Europe, while the eastern part is known as Soviet Asia or Siberia. This huge country is closer to us than most people think. Alaska, our northernmost state, is only about 55 miles from Siberia! And only Canada lies between the United States and the Soviet Union across the North Pole.

3. There are about 247 million people in the Soviet Union, making it the third largest nation in the world in population. Its people are made up of many different races and national groups. (A national group is any group of people who share the same customs, language and traditions.) Most of the people live in Soviet Europe.

4. Since World War II, the Soviet Union has become one of the two most powerful nations in the world. One of the reasons for its great growth in strength is that it has a wealth of natural resources. Much of the land is covered by vast forests. There is a fertile farming belt in Soviet Europe, and modern farming methods are being extended into Soviet Asia. The Soviet Union is a storehouse of minerals for use in making steel. The Communist Party is using these resources to turn the Soviet Union into a land of mills and factories. Today, the Soviet government keeps one of the world's largest armies. Like our own forces, this huge army is equipped with all the terrible weapons of modern warfare—tanks, missiles, rockets and atom bombs.

5. The Soviet Union has a government that is very different from that of the United States. This government was begun in 1917. The government is controlled by members of the Communist Party. This is the only political party in the nation. In a Communist state, the government runs all the factories and farms. It decides what goods are made. It controls the

This rocket carrier and spaceship were displayed at a recent Moscow fair. What achievements of the Soviets in space exploration have you read about?

schools and all the means of communication, such as newspapers, radio and television. In a Communist nation, people are taught that they live to serve the government. In a democracy, the government is formed to serve the people.

6. The leaders of the Soviet Union have tried to spread their way of life throughout the world. At the end of World War II, the Soviet Union occupied many countries in Eastern Europe—Poland, Hungary, Rumania, Bulgaria, Yugoslavia and East Germany. Communist governments still rule these countries, as well as Albania and Czechoslovakia.

7. In the United Nations, the Soviet Union has used its "veto" to block action by that organization more than 100 times. (Each of the five permanent nations who are members of the Security Council has this power, but no other nation has used it nearly so often.) The country has posed difficulties in other ways as well. In 1948, the Soviets blockaded Berlin to try to force the Western nations out of that city. In 1961, a wall of concrete and barbed wire was built in Berlin to keep the people of East Germany from fleeing to West Berlin. And in 1962, the Soviet Union established missile bases in Cuba, only 90 miles from our shores.

8. The spread of communism in Eastern Europe, in the Western Hemisphere and in the Far East has caused much concern among the people of the West. The government of the Soviet Union is controlled by a few powerful men. It is hard for us to know what they think, how they will act and how much they will use the great strength of their nation to spread their political ideas. Do they want to bring Communist rule to more peoples of the world? Are they interested in putting more nations under the control of the Soviet Union? The future of our country and of the world may depend to a large extent upon the answers to these questions.

UNDERSTANDING CHAPTER 1

1. Which questions are answered in this chapter?
   a. Are there forests in the Soviet Union?
   b. Why is the Soviet Union important in the thinking of Americans?
   c. Who are the leaders of the Soviet Union today?

2. The main idea of *paragraph 7* is that:
   a. the Soviet Union is an important member of the United Nations.
   b. the Soviet Union has caused a number of problems for the United States.
   c. only Soviet people are allowed in Berlin.

3. The Soviet government first took power in:
   a. 1917.   b. 1946.   c. 1964.

4. The Soviet Union placed missiles in:
   a. the Congo.   b. Cuba.   c. Spain.

5. The Soviet Union is a powerful nation today because it has:
   a. a large standing army.
   b. the most power in the United Nations.
   c. the largest navy in the world.

6. Communism has spread to all these countries EXCEPT:
   a. Poland.   b. Hungary.   c. India.

7. In a *Communist* state:
   a. the government owns all the farms and factories.
   b. there are many political parties.
   c. the people choose their own leaders.

8. "The President *vetoed* the bill; everybody was disappointed." The word *vetoed* means:
   a. "approved."   b. "disapproved."   c. "delayed."

Map Study

Map #32—The Soviet Union and Eastern Europe

Study the map. Then answer the questions at the top of page 293.

1. Is the region north or south of the equator?
2. Is the region east or west of the Prime Meridian?
3. Does the region extend farther from east to west or from north to south?
4. What region or regions are near it?
5. What is the largest country? The smallest?
6. What are the chief bodies of water that border the region?
7. Which countries in this region have no outlets to the sea?
8. What are some of the important rivers in the region?
9. Are there any island nations?
10. Are there countries that are located on peninsulas?

FOLLOW UP The Soviet Union is in the newspapers daily. Keep a scrapbook of newspaper clippings about events that are taking place in the world in which the Soviet Union is involved.

2 THE HEART OF EURASIA

Reading For A Purpose: How does the nature of the land affect the Soviet Union?

Time out for workers on a state farm near Rostov. Which area of our country is similar to this flat farming area of the Soviet Union?

1. The Soviet Union is more than twice the size of the United States. It covers 8,600,000 square miles. From the border of Poland on the west to the Pacific Ocean on the east is a distance of almost 6,000 miles, or nearly twice the distance across the United States! This is about a twelve-hour difference in time from one side of the Soviet Union to the other. (In the United States, there is a three-hour difference in time from the Atlantic to the Pacific coast.) Thus, when the sun is "rising" on the Baltic Sea in the Soviet Union, it is already "setting" over the Bering Strait. The U.S.S.R. borders twelve different nations and has the longest coastline of any nation in the world. (Much of it is useless, however, because it borders on the frozen Arctic Ocean.)

2. This huge country is located a great distance north of the equator. The southernmost point of the country is only 35° north latitude. This means that the *entire nation* is farther north than our cities of Memphis, Tennessee and Los Angeles, California. Moscow, the capital and largest city, is as far north as Hudson Bay, Canada.

3. A vast part of the U.S.S.R. is a lowland plain. This plain, part of the Great European Plain, stretches across Europe and into Asia as far as the Yenisei River in Central Siberia. The Ural Mountains divide the plain between Europe and Asia. These mountains are low, like the Appalachians of the eastern United States, and are easy to cross. The lowland of Soviet Asia is one of the flattest in the world, and much of it is swampy.

4. West of the Yenisei River, the land rises to the plateaus and mountains of the Far East. In the south, a range of high mountains and plateaus runs from west to east across the Asian continent. These mountains separate the Soviet Union from its southern neighbors. Soviet Asia is landlocked on the south.

5. The Soviet Union has many large rivers. The longest rivers are in Siberia, or Soviet Asia. These are the Ob, Yenisei, Lena and Amur. The Ob is the longest river in the Soviet Union. These rivers rise or begin in the higher lands to the south. Except for the Amur, they drain toward the ice-filled Arctic Ocean in the north. This means that ships cannot travel down the rivers to the ocean and to ports around the world. The Amur is the only river that reaches the warmer waters of the Pacific Ocean. This lack of warm-water trade routes is an important problem for the Soviet Union.

6. West of the Ural Mountains, the lowland drains mainly to the south. The largest rivers are the Dnieper, the Don and the Volga. The Volga is the longest river in Europe. It empties into the Caspian Sea, which is really a landlocked "lake." The Dnieper and Don Rivers empty into the Black Sea. However, the Black Sea is separated from the busy Mediterranean Sea by narrow straits called the Dardanelles. These straits are controlled by Turkey. Another outlet for Soviet shipping is the Baltic

The Yenisei River flows into the Kara Sea, an arm of the cold Arctic Ocean. What problems for Soviet shipping and trade are pointed out by this picture?

Sea. However, this body of water is partly frozen during much of the year.

7. As you can see, the Soviet Union is really isolated from the great trade routes of the world even though it is the largest nation in the world. In the southern part of Soviet Asia, high mountains separate the nation from warmer lands. In the north, the icy waters of the Arctic Ocean make the rivers almost useless for trade. Furthermore, the Baltic Sea is partly ice-bound. The Black Sea is separated from the Mediterranean by straits controlled by a foreign country. And the ports on the Pacific Ocean are far from the major trade routes of the world, and from Soviet industries.

UNDERSTANDING
CHAPTER 2

1. Which questions are answered in this chapter?
   a. Why are the Soviet rivers not very useful for trade?
   b. Which countries border the Soviet Union?
   c. Why is the Soviet Union called a landlocked country?
2. The main idea of *paragraphs 4 through 6* describes the:
   a. use of Soviet water resources.
   b. rivers of the Soviet Union.
   c. problems of the inland seas.
3. The vast Soviet lowland plain is divided by the:
   a. Caucasus Mountains.   b. Ural Mountains.   c. Alps.
4. The chief rivers of Siberia flow toward the:
   a. south (mountains).
   b. north (Arctic Ocean).
   c. east (Pacific Ocean).
5. Why are the rivers of Siberia not highly useful for trade?
   a. They are very short in length.
   b. Rapids prevent boats from using them for long distances.
   c. They empty into frozen waters.
6. The Ural Mountains:
   a. make travel from Europe to Asia almost impossible.
   b. guard the Soviet Union against invasion from the south.
   c. are low and easily crossed.
7. A *landlocked* country is one that:
   a. is surrounded by land.
   b. is large in area.
   c. borders the seas.
8. "In spite of its size, the Soviet Union is very much *isolated*." The word *isolated* means:
   a. "borders few countries."
   b. "its geography keeps it apart from other countries."
   c. "there are few varieties of land forms."

Map Study

Map #33—Land Forms of Eastern Europe and the Soviet Union

Study the map. Then tell whether these statements are *true* or *false*. Be able to explain your answers.

1. Comparing the climate map of the Soviet Union on page 301 with the map of land forms on this page, you will see that nearly all the tundra is mountainous.
2. The eastern part of the Soviet Union has several different land forms.
3. The western part of this region is largely lowland.
4. The Great Plains of the Soviet Union cover thousands of miles from east to west.
5. The plateau is the most important land form along the southern border.
6. Most of the mountains of this region are near its outer edges.

LAND FORMS OF
**EASTERN EUROPE
AND THE SOVIET UNION**

Mountains   Hills

Plateaus   Plains

0   500   1000   1500

Miles

Complete the following chart in your notebook. You may have to refer to your earlier notes on other countries for some information.

COUNTRY	SIZE	LOCATION	LAND FORMS
Soviet Union			
United States			
Canada			
Brazil			

Tell whether these statements are true or false. The underlined words make the statements true or false. If a statement is false, what word or words would you place in it to make it true?

1. Three large rivers of Soviet Asia flow toward the Arctic Ocean.
2. The best "warm-water" outlet for the Soviet Union is the Bering Strait.
3. Soviet Asia is landlocked on the southern border.
4. The Volga River flows into the Caspian Sea.
5. The longest river of the Soviet Union is the Don.
6. The Soviet Union is so wide that there is a six-hour difference in time from east to west.
7. The great plain across the Soviet Union is divided by the Ural Mountains.
8. The nearest part of the United States to the Soviet Union is the state of Alaska.

3 THE COLD LAND

Reading For A Purpose: How is Soviet life affected by its climate?

1. In general, the climate of the Soviet Union is much like that of Canada. This cold climate has helped the Soviet people on many occasions. For example, the cold winters have turned back invaders. In 1812, the armies of Napoleon had to retreat after a bitter winter in Moscow in which thousands of soldiers froze or starved to death. In World War II, the winter again proved to be a terrible enemy for the armies of Adolf Hitler. However, not all of the Soviet Union has a cold climate. Because of its vast size, the country has many climatic regions.

2. In the far north of the U.S.S.R. is the *tundra*. It extends along the Arctic coast as much as several hundred miles inland. This land is flat and treeless. Cold winds from the Arctic Ocean blow across it and reach the lands farther south. The year-round temperature of the tundra is always low, with temperatures below freezing as much as eight months of the year. The ground is never completely warm. As a result, there is a layer of frozen ground a few inches beneath the surface all year long. This frozen ground is called "permafrost." The permafrost allows only a short growing season for crops and prevents trees from growing on the tundra.

3. The land of the tundra climate is a place where few people live. Those who do live there make their living by hunting, fishing and herding reindeer. These people move from place to place as their reindeer herds graze the tundra. The reindeer furnish the people with nearly everything they need. They eat reindeer meat and drink the milk. They make tents and clothing from reindeer skins. The reindeer also carry burdens on their backs. Many wild animals such as the ermine and fox are hunted in the tundra for their valuable furs.

Reindeer herder of the Russian tundra. How is his way of life similar to that of the Lapps in Scandinavia?

4. South of the tundra are the forest lands or taiga. *Taiga* is a Russian word for forest. The Soviet Union has more acres of forest than any other nation in the world. The Soviet taiga is about as large as the whole United States! It has many rivers, lakes and ponds. A greater range of temperature is found here, for the land is farther from the waters of the Arctic Ocean. (As you remember, large bodies of water help to keep the climate even.) Sixty degrees below zero is common in the winter. During the summer the temperatures may reach eighty or ninety degrees. At that time the frozen waters melt and the land becomes soft and marshy. Few people live in the taiga because of the very cold winter climate.

5. South of the taiga is the humid-continental climate. It is similar to the continental climate of the United States, but colder. Temperatures are lower in the winter, and it is not as warm in the summer. The large, important Soviet cities—Moscow, Leningrad and Kiev—have this climate. The soil is fertile and much of the land has been cleared for farming. The growing season lasts five months or longer.

6. Southward the climate is drier and the summers are longer and warmer. Here the dry grasslands are found. The Soviet people call this area the *steppes*. The steppes reach from the Black Sea eastward into central Asia. Rainfall is only from ten to twenty inches a year. Despite this lack of rain, the steppes are a great farming area. The soil is rich and black. Part of the western steppes lies in the Ukraine, the great wheat belt of the Soviet Union. The steppes may be compared with the dry prairies of the United States that are west of the 100th meridian.

7. In the south, from the Caspian Sea eastward to Lake Balkhash, the land is largely a desert. There is little rain and it is very hot. The mountains provide water for irrigation so that cotton and tobacco can be grown. As you can imagine, few people live here because it is very hard to make a living from the dry land.

Hotel at Sochi, on the Black Sea. Even though Sochi is as far north of the equator as is New York City, its climate is more like that of Los Angeles. Why?

8. In the northern part of the Black Sea lies the Crimean Peninsula. This peninsula has a climate like that of the Mediterranean countries and southern California. It is the great vacation spot of the Soviet Union. There are hot, dry summers and mild, wet winters. Many fruits are grown here—oranges, figs and grapes. Large hotels provide for thousands of tourists. Because of the extreme cold in much of the nation, this warmer spot is a favorite vacation land for many people.

9. As you can see, most of the Soviet land consists of frozen wastelands, forests and mountains. Much of the Soviet Union is free from frost and snow for only about 150 days a year. This is too short a growing season for many crops. There are many areas in which there is not enough rain for farming. For these reasons, there is much unsettled land in the Soviet Union. Most people are crowded into the few areas that are fertile and more comfortable to live in.

1. Which questions are answered in this chapter?
   a. Why is most of the Soviet Union cold?
   b. In what climatic region are the large Soviet cities?
   c. What crops are grown on the steppes?
2. The main idea of this chapter describes:
   a. how people live in northern lands.
   b. the different climates of the Soviet Union.
   c. where the steppes are located.
3. The best farm lands of the Soviet Union are found in the:
   a. taiga. b. steppes. c. irrigated desert.
4. The people of the *tundra* herd flocks of:
   a. reindeer. b. llamas. c. caribou.
5. The Soviet Union has no climate in which the farmer can grow:
   a. wheat. b. cotton. c. bananas.
6. The summer climate near the city of Moscow is:
   a. warmer than that of New York City.
   b. colder than that of Chicago.
   c. much like the climate of New Orleans.
7. A *taiga* is a:
   a. treeless plain. b. northern forest. c. tropical rain forest.
8. On a *steppe*, people usually make a living by:
   a. farming. b. fishing. c. lumbering.

Map Study

Map #34—Climates of Eastern Europe and the Soviet Union

Agree or Disagree Study the map on page 301. Then decide whether or not each of the statements below agrees with the information on the map. If the answer is *disagree*, explain why.

1. The great distance in the Soviet Union from east to west causes great differences in climate throughout the country.
2. The largest climatic region in the Soviet Union is the taiga.
3. The best farm lands are located in the western part of the Soviet Union.
4. The 180° longitude of the eastern part of the Soviet Union has a great effect on its climate.
5. Only a small part of this region has a Mediterranean climate.
6. Altitude has little effect on the climate of most of the Soviet Union.
7. Most of the eastern part of the region has a climate much like our states of Oregon and Washington.
8. Most people in the Soviet Union probably live between 120° and 150° longitude.

CLIMATES OF
EASTERN EUROPE
AND THE SOVIET UNION

▨	Desert	▨	Marine
▨	Steppe	▨	Taiga
▨	Mediterranean	▨	Tundra
▨	Humid continental	▨	Vertical

0   500   1000   1500
Miles

SUMMING UP   *Are these statements true or false?*   Give reasons for your answers.

1. The tundra has many people.
2. The people of the tundra depend on the reindeer for many things.
3. Most of the Soviet Union is hot.
4. The tundra and taiga climates are found in most of the Soviet Union.
5. The Soviet Union has no deserts.
6. The Soviet Union has a great deal of fertile land.
7. People from California would feel "at home" in the Crimea.
8. The Ukraine is the great farming area of the Soviet Union.
9. Even the cold Arctic Ocean may warm the lands near it.
10. Rubber, cocoa and sugar cane are leading farm crops of the Soviet.

Generalizations to Watch Out For

Even the most careful thinkers sometimes make *sweeping generalizations*. ("Everyone was watching the ball game on TV." "Absolutely the best movie in town is ▬▬▬!") Such statements seem very definite and clear, but they are seldom true. Some kinds of sweeping generalizations are called *stereotypes*, because people use them over and over again. ("The British eat the dullest food." "Italians love spaghetti.") They are used so often that people believe they must be true. Below are some often repeated stereotypes about the Soviet Union. With which do you agree? With which do you disagree? Keep them all in mind. We'll come back to them in a later chapter.

1. All Soviet people are members of the Communist Party.
2. There are no rich people in the Soviet Union. Everyone's income is the same.
3. No one believes in any religion in the Soviet Union.
4. The Soviet system of education is better than ours.
5. The Soviet Union has a cold, unbearable climate.
6. The Soviet people are suspicious and warlike.

HOW RUSSIA BECAME THE SOVIET UNION

Reading For A Purpose: How did Russia grow in size and strength?

1. Some of the earliest settlers of Soviet Europe were Slavic-speaking people. About the 9th century, these Slavic peoples were conquered by the Vikings from the north. The Vikings set up a kingdom near the city of Kiev. They became Christians. In the 13th century, this kingdom and other lands were overrun by Mongols who came from Central Asia.

2. The Mongols ruled the small Russian kingdoms for 300 years. In the 15th century, Ivan III (known as Ivan the Great), ruler of a small kingdom near Moscow, began to fight the Mongols and enlarge his kingdom. The new country thus beginning was called Russia. The next great ruler, Ivan IV, destroyed the Mongol settlements in the Volga River valley. Now the Russians were able to push on to the Ural Mountains. Ivan IV was the first Russian ruler to be called *czar*, which means "caesar" or "emperor."

3. As early as 1581, Russian soldiers, traders and merchants moved into Siberia. They were looking for gold and furs. They built forts and trading posts along the rivers. By 1639, the Russians had reached the Pacific Ocean. One hundred years later, the Danish explorer Vitus Bering crossed the narrow strait from Siberia to Alaska (now called the Bering Strait). He had been hired by Russia to find out if there was a land connection between Asia and North America. Next the Russians turned south along the Pacific Coast almost to San Francisco Bay. By 1812 they had established trading posts in California. However, these posts were hard to reach, so the Russians gave them up. In 1867, Russia sold Alaska to the United States.

Ivan IV was also known as Ivan the Terrible. How do you suppose he earned this name?

4. Two other rulers continued to extend the land of Russia. Peter the Great (1682-1725) fought a long war against Sweden, gaining some territory on the eastern shore of the Baltic Sea. There he built a new city called St. Petersburg as his capital and chief seaport. Today this city is called Leningrad. Peter wanted to make his country modern, so he brought thousands of skilled craftsmen from Western Europe to Russia. He even wanted his people to dress and act like Westerners. Catherine the Great (1729-1796) moved the Russian boundaries farther south and west. In the south, a war against the Ottoman Turks gained land on the coast of the Black Sea. Russian ships were now free to sail to the Mediterranean. In the west, Catherine took part in dividing Poland, adding more territory to Russia's growing empire.

5. The czars were the supreme rulers of Russia from the 17th century to the 20th century. Most of the land was owned by nobles or friends of the czars. Most of the people were poor peasants called serfs. They had to live and work on the land of the nobles and pay them taxes. Serfs had little education. They could not leave the land on which they were born and were often taken to serve in the czar's armies. Meanwhile, the Industrial Revolution was taking place in Western Europe and

Catherine the Great of Russia. How did Russian boundaries change under her reign?

changing life for the people there. The West was moving ahead. Russia was standing still.

6. In 1904-5, Russia was defeated in war by Japan. The defeat made the Russian people see how backward their rulers were. The Russians demanded a greater voice in their government. For a time the czar allowed a law-making body to be formed. However, it had little real power. The people felt they were helpless.

7. World War I brought about a change in the Russian government. The nation was not prepared for the war when it started in 1914. Nevertheless, Russia joined Great Britain and France to fight against Germany, Austria-Hungary and their allies. The Russian armies were beaten badly. In three years, almost two million Russians lost their lives. The people had had enough. They did not want to continue the war. They wanted peace, food and land of their own. In 1917, Czar Nicholas gave up the throne when a revolt threatened. A republic was formed.

8. The new government wanted to continue the war, but the soldiers and the people at home were tired of fighting. In November, 1917, the Revolution came. It was led by a party called the Bolsheviks, or Communists.

Lenin was their leader. He took Russia out of the war and gave the people peace and food. The Communists gradually ended the private ownership of land, factories, mines, banks and railways. The name of the country was changed to the Union of Soviet Socialist Republics.

9. Joseph Stalin followed Lenin as the leader of the U.S.S.R. until 1953. During his long rule, Stalin directed the building of the great industrial system of the U.S.S.R. He had one aim —to make his nation second to none in power.

10. In 1939, Stalin signed a treaty with Adolf Hitler, the ruler of Germany. They agreed not to attack each other. When Hitler invaded Poland in 1939, Stalin occupied the eastern part of the divided country. He also fought a war against Finland. He brought the Baltic countries (Estonia, Lithuania and Latvia) under Soviet rule.

11. The Soviet-German friendship did not last long. Without warning, Hitler's armies invaded the Soviet Union in 1941. The Germans

Lenin takes control of the Russian government. Note the red flag of the Bolsheviks behind him. What has the artist of this painting tried to convey about Lenin? What has he tried to convey about this moment in history?

were very successful at first. But with the help of the United States, the Soviets stopped the German armies. The Battle of Stalingrad marked the end of the German advance. After that the Russians pushed the Nazis back. In 1945, the Russian army met the Allies crossing Germany from the opposite direction, and the war was won.

12. After World War II, the Communists remained in the Eastern European countries they had occupied during the war. In a short while there were Communist governments in Poland, Rumania, Hungary, East Germany, Bulgaria, Yugoslavia, Czechoslovakia and Albania. Much of what went on in this region was kept secret from the rest of the world. Winston Churchill, Prime Minister of Great Britain, called this secrecy the "Iron Curtain" around Communist lands. In the years that followed, the Soviet Union and the United States drifted further apart. (This later history will be discussed in Chapter 10.)

Lenin and Stalin in 1923. How did each of these men affect the course of Russian history? Of world history?

UNDERSTANDING CHAPTER 4

1. Which questions are answered in this chapter?
   a. How did Russia reach North America?
   b. Why was there a revolution in 1917?
   c. How was Russia ruled by the Mongols?
2. The main idea of *paragraphs 5 through 7* describes:
   a. how the Russians marched eastward in the 16th century.
   b. Russia under the rule of the czars.
   c. Russia's defeat in World War I.
3. Russia was ruled for many years by nomadic herdsmen called:
   a. Mongols.   b. Bedouins.   c. Huns.
4. In 1904-5, Russia was defeated by:
   a. China.   b. Japan.   c. France.
5. Russia left the First World War in 1917 because:
   a. Czar Nicholas wanted peace.
   b. many Russians had been killed.
   c. a new government was formed.
6. Life was hard for many people under the czars because:
   a. the land was owned by a few nobles.
   b. people objected to changes made by the Communists.
   c. people had to work long hours in factories.
7. A *czar* is the same as:
   a. a representative.   b. an explorer.   c. an emperor.

Picture Symbols

These pictures should help you to recall parts of the chapter you have read. What is the main idea of each picture?

SUMMING UP

List these events in your notebook. After each, write *Before the Revolution of 1917* or *After the Revolution of 1917*.

1. Invasion of the Mongols—
2. Russian conquest of Siberia—
3. Rule of Lenin and Stalin—
4. Poland has a Communist government—
5. Russian war with Japan—
6. Battle of Stalingrad—
7. Great Russian industries—
8. Rule of Peter the Great—

FOLLOW UP

Who Am I?   Below are statements about some famous people. Who is described in each statement? Choose your answers from the list of names below.

Bering	Stalin	Lenin
Ivan the Great	Adolph Hitler	Peter the Great
a Mongol	a Viking	Czar Nicholas

1. I was the first czar of Russia. I broke the power of the Mongols. I am ⸺.

2. I led the Russian Revolution in 1917. I took Russia out of World War I. From that time, the Communist Party has been in power. I am ⸺.

3. I liked the ways of the West and tried to bring them to Russia. I defeated Sweden and built a new capital city. I am ⸺.

4. I ruled as a dictator for many years. I helped to build the great industries of the Soviet Union. I am ⸺.

5. I was the last czar of Russia. I was overthrown during World War I. I am ⸺.

6. I was one of many who invaded Russia long ago. My people ruled for hundreds of years. Many of us still live in the Soviet Union. I am ⸺.

7. I discovered a narrow waterway separating Asia from North America. Many Russian traders crossed into North America over this waterway. I am ⸺

5 THE PEOPLE OF THE SOVIET UNION

Reading For A Purpose: Who are the Soviet people?

An open-air market in the Uzbek Republic. In what important ways do the Soviet republics differ from our states?

1. The Soviet Union is made up of fifteen Soviet republics. These Soviet republics are based on racial or national groups. (Our states are simply divisions of land.) Some of the republics are large and others are very small. The largest is the Russian Soviet Federated Socialist Republic, which covers three-fourths of the land area of the Soviet Union. Moscow is the capital of this republic, and of the Soviet Union as a whole. Other important republics are the Ukraine and Byelorussia or White Russia. These republics have votes in the United Nations in addition to that of the Soviet Union.

2. There are about 247 million people living in the Soviet Union today. It is a country of many races in which more than eighty languages are spoken. Most of the people, however, speak Russian or a Slavic language. The rest are descendants of the Mongols and other tribes that came from Central Asia. These different national groups are allowed to speak their own languages and practice their own customs. But all school children must study Russian too. If one desires to advance in Soviet society, it is necessary to know the Russian language well.

3. The population of the U.S.S.R. is not distributed evenly. Some areas, as in Soviet Europe, are thickly settled. In Soviet Asia, however, vast areas are too mountainous, too cold or too dry for many people to live. Most of the people live in a "triangle" of land stretching from the Black Sea to the Baltic Sea to Novokuznetsk (Stalinsk) in Siberia. This is called the Fertile Triangle because it is the region of the best farm land. It is only a small part of the land area, but three-fourths of the Soviet people live in that region. There are more than twenty cities in the Triangle with at least a half-million people. The largest cities are Moscow, Leningrad and Kiev.

4. In 1930, Magnitogorsk in the Ural Mountains was a tiny village. It could scarcely even be called a village then. Today, it is a city of more than 300,000 people. The growth of this village and others like it shows clearly what is happening in the Soviet Union. The population is growing and it is spreading out. In the years since World War II, large cities have sprung up in Soviet Asia near new sources of farm land or minerals. The growth of cities where none had existed is one of the important features of the Soviet Union today. Moreover, this nation in which most people once lived on farms has changed so that half the people now live in cities!

5. While the standard of living of the people is rising, it is still far from the high living standard of the American people. Few Soviet farms have electricity or running water. Farm-

A young Ukrainian couple enjoys an evening of dancing. In what ways do they appear similar to young Americans?

ers are seldom able to spend an evening of recreation in the nearest town. A suit of clothes for a factory worker costs a month's wages. A shirt costs a full day's pay. A worker will labor for a week to buy a pair of shoes. There are only a few million cars in the U.S.S.R., compared with the more than 100 million in the United States. The U.S.S.R. has about 20 million TV sets compared with the 90 million in our country.

6. As more and more people work in factories, another new occupational group is growing in the U.S.S.R. Over the years, the Soviet government has built a great many factories. In order to run these factories, people with special training are needed: engineers, scientists, managers. These people receive much higher pay than factory workers. They can afford to buy homes, automobiles, refrigerators and washing machines. They tend to give strong support to the Soviet system because their jobs and way of life depend upon it. They are the new Soviet middle class.

7. The Communists are against all religion. Despite this policy, there are still many religious people in the Soviet Union. Most of the religious believers of the U.S.S.R. are Christians who belong to the Greek or Russian Orthodox Church. There are also a few Roman Catholics and Protestants. For a long time the Communists closed most of the churches. This practice has not been as strict in recent years. However, church leaders cannot say anything against the Communist government, and a man who practices his religion may find it difficult to advance in the Communist world.

8. The second largest religious group in the

In a corner of a Russian Orthodox cathedral, a woman kneels to pray. What have you read or heard in the news about religious problems in the Soviet Union?

Soviet Union is the Moslems. Most of the Mongol groups are Moslem. They are allowed to have their own schools and houses of worship. There is also a large group of Jews. Since 1960, the Soviet Union has not allowed the Jews much freedom to practice their religion. Their temples or houses of worship and their schools have been closed. Jews and other religious groups in the United States have made strong protests to the Soviet leaders about this lack of freedom of worship. Recently, large numbers of Jews have sought permission to move to Israel.

UNDERSTANDING CHAPTER 5

1. Which questions are answered in this chapter?
   a. How do the Soviet farmers live?
   b. How many Soviet republics are there?
   c. What do the Communists think of religion?
2. The main idea of *paragraph 7* is that:
   a. there is now complete freedom of religion in the Soviet Union.
   b. there are risks in practicing religion openly.
   c. most Russians are Greek or Russian Orthodox Christians.

308

3. The capital of the Soviet Union is:
   a. Kiev.   b. Leningrad.   c. Moscow.
4. Most people in the Soviet Union live:
   a. in the Fertile Triangle.
   b. in the northern regions.
   c. along the Pacific coast.
5. People of the Soviet Union are moving to new areas because they:
   a. feel they are pioneers.
   b. are using new resources.
   c. want to gain riches from using better farm lands.
6. Why is there a growing middle class in the Soviet Union?
   a. Industries need people with special skills.
   b. New political parties are being formed.
   c. There is an increase in farm production.
7. New large cities of the Soviet Union are appearing in:
   a. the Crimea.   b. the Ukraine.   c. Soviet Asia.

DEVELOPING IDEAS AND SKILLS

Pictograph #11—Population, Area and Standard of Living of the Soviet Union

Study the pictograph. Then answer the questions at the top of page 310.

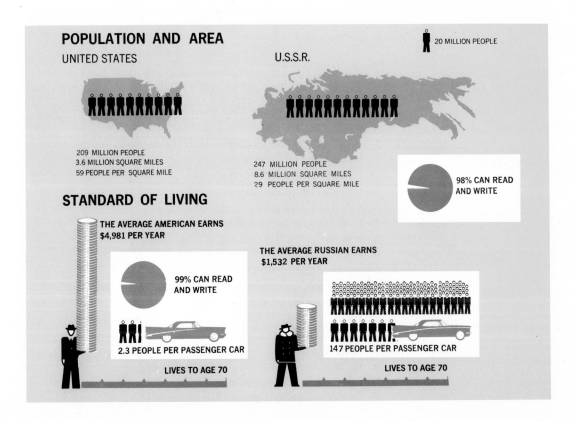

POPULATION AND AREA

20 MILLION PEOPLE

UNITED STATES

U.S.S.R.

209 MILLION PEOPLE
3.6 MILLION SQUARE MILES
59 PEOPLE PER SQUARE MILE

247 MILLION PEOPLE
8.6 MILLION SQUARE MILES
29 PEOPLE PER SQUARE MILE

98% CAN READ AND WRITE

STANDARD OF LIVING

THE AVERAGE AMERICAN EARNS $4,981 PER YEAR

99% CAN READ AND WRITE

2.3 PEOPLE PER PASSENGER CAR

LIVES TO AGE 70

THE AVERAGE RUSSIAN EARNS $1,532 PER YEAR

147 PEOPLE PER PASSENGER CAR

LIVES TO AGE 70

1. Is the standard of living of this region high or low compared with that of the United States?
2. Is the region more or less crowded than the United States?
3. Are the people of this region literate compared with the people of the United States?
4. How long may the average person in this region expect to live?
5. What facts tell you the standard of living of the people of the region?
6. How does this region compare with the United States in size?

SUMMING UP *Agree or Disagree* Decide whether or not each of the following statements agrees with what you have read. If the answer is *disagree*, explain why.

1. The largest cities of the Soviet Union are in the European part of the country.
2. Most of the Soviet leaders are very religious people.
3. More and more of the Soviet people are living in cities.
4. The population of the Soviet Union is rising.
5. Most of the Soviet people are crowded into a small region of fertile land.
6. Most of the Soviet people are able to read and write.
7. Most of the people speak one language and are of the same race.
8. A drive in the country on Sunday is a common recreation of the Soviet people.
9. Moscow is probably one of the fashion centers of the world.
10. The factories in the Soviet Union are owned by the government.

FOLLOW UP Select the item that *does not belong* with the others in each group.

1. We should know more about the Soviet Union because:
   a. it has a huge area.
   b. it has a favorable climate.
   c. it has many resources.
   d. it has strong armed forces.
2. Soviet land forms include:
   a. a vast lowland plain.
   b. a far eastern frontier of mountains.
   c. few rivers.
   d. low mountains.
3. Climates of the Soviet Union include:
   a. rain forest.   b. tundra.   c. steppe.   d. desert.
4. Czars who have ruled Russia are:
   a. Peter.   b. Nicholas.   c. Lenin.   d. Ivan.
5. Among the people of the Soviet Union:
   a. there is a rising standard of living.
   b. the number of farm workers is increasing.
   c. a growing middle class has developed.
   d. new occupational groups are growing.

6 THE COMMUNIST DICTATORSHIP

Reading For A Purpose: How is a small group able to control the people?

A meeting of the Supreme Soviet. How is this council similar to our Congress? How is it different?

1. Communist rulers like to call their governments "democracies." This idea is used over and over again. In China the government is called the "People's Republic." East Germany is called the "Democratic Republic." Actually, the people have little to do with running the governments in Communist countries. In all Communist countries there is an "acting" government and a "real" one. The Soviet Union is ruled by a few highly placed members of the all-powerful Communist Party.

2. Like the United States, the Soviet Union has a written constitution. It was drawn up in 1936. It sets up a union of fifteen republics. The constitution promises certain rights to all citizens. Many of these promises have not been kept. There is little freedom of speech, press, assembly or religion. Although it is a federal government of fifteen republics, the national government has most of the powers. The republics have less power than our fifty states.

3. The Supreme Soviet is the lawmaking body. Like our Congress, it has two "houses." One is elected on the basis of population, like our House of Representatives. The other has representatives from each republic, as our Senate has separate representatives from each state. The members of the Supreme Soviet are elected every four years by all citizens over eighteen years of age. It meets twice a year for only a few days at a time. Only members of the Communist Party or people approved by the Communist Party may hold office in the Supreme Soviet.

4. Since the Supreme Soviet doesn't meet often, the real work of the government is carried on by two small committees or groups. One is called the Presidium; the other is the Council of Ministers. The Presidium makes the laws and the Council of Ministers carries out the laws and directs the government. There is no separation of powers in the Soviet government.

5. There is a Supreme Court. The judges of this court and the lower courts ("people's courts") are chosen mainly by the Supreme Soviet. There is no jury system. The judges decide all cases. They deal harshly with persons who talk or act against the government.

6. You have read about the Soviet officials that are "elected." The "real" government, however, is the Communist Party. Unlike the United States, the Soviet Union has only one political party—the Communist Party. In our country you may join any of several political parties, or change from one party to another as you wish.

7. In the Soviet Union you are *asked* to be a member of the Party. You must have a period of training before you can be accepted. Only the most able people are chosen. As a result,

311

A young man about to become a member of the Communist Party. What are the requirements for joining the Communist Party in the Soviet Union? How do they differ from requirements for joining a political party in this country?

there are only about nine million members of the Communist Party in a total population of 247 million. If you become a member of the Party and do not follow the rules, you may lose your membership.

8. Despite its small size, the Communist Party is able to rule the Soviet Union. There are several reasons why this is so. First, once a decision has been reached by the Soviet rulers, all Party members must carry it out. This is called "following the Party line." Second, Party members are placed everywhere. Every important organization, every state farm, every factory has some members. In the third place, the Communist Party is the only political party. No one can gain high office unless he is a member or is approved by the Party. Fourth, the Party controls what is taught in schools and what is said in the newspapers, on radio and on television. The Party also controls the army. Finally, the Communists have secret police that watch everyone. A person whose behavior is not approved may suddenly "disappear." A country such as this, where everything is controlled by the government, is known as a *totalitarian* state.

UNDERSTANDING
CHAPTER 6

1. Which questions are answered in this chapter?
   a. How is law made in the Soviet Union?
   b. Why are there so few members of the Communist Party?
   c. Why are there secret police?
2. The main idea of this chapter describes:
   a. how the Supreme Soviet works.
   b. how one becomes a Communist.
   c. how the Soviet people are governed.
3. What is the lawmaking body of the Soviet Union?
   a. Congress.   b. Parliament.   c. Supreme Soviet.
4. Who holds the "real" power in the Soviet government?
   a. Scientists.   b. Army officers.   c. The Communist Party.
5. There are only a few members in the Communist Party because:
   a. there are few privileges.
   b. most people want to join many of the other parties.
   c. only the most reliable people are chosen.
6. Citizens of the U.S.S.R. are careful in what they say about their government because:
   a. they fear the secret police.
   b. everyone may be a member of the Communist Party.
   c. they are eager to have friendship with other nations.
7. A *totalitarian* government is the opposite of a:
   a. dictatorship.   b. democracy.   c. monarchy.

Pictograph #12a and b—The Government of the Soviet Union

Study the pictographs. Then tell whether these statements are true or false.

1. The Soviet Union has no written plan of government.
2. The Council of Ministers is elected by the people.
3. The chief lawmaking body of the Soviet Union is the Supreme Soviet.
4. Only Communist Party members are allowed to hold high office in the Soviet Union.
5. Different nationalities can elect their own representatives.
6. The Supreme Soviet is elected by all the people.
7. Women are not allowed to vote in the Soviet Union.
8. There are two houses in the Supreme Soviet.
9. This pictograph tells us how a law is made in the Soviet Union.
10. The Secretary of the Communist Party may be the most powerful person in the Soviet Union.

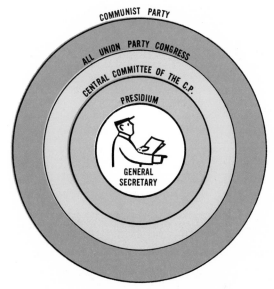

Pictograph # 12a and b—The Government of the Soviet Union

Complete the following chart in your notebook.

Comparing Governments

	UNITED STATES	SOVIET UNION
1. Plan of government:		
2. Branches of government:		
3. How laws are made:		
4. Freedoms allowed:		
5. Political parties:		

Tell whether each of these statements applies to a *democratic* or a *totalitarian* state.

1. We believe in a strong government controlled by a few people.
2. We believe that the law should treat all men equally.
3. We believe that people should be educated to believe only what their rulers want them to believe.
4. We believe that everyone must work for the state.
5. We believe that each person has certain rights that no one can take from him.
6. We believe in the use of secret police.
7. We believe that no one should criticize the government.
8. We believe that newspapers should print the truth.

7 THE SOVIET FARMLAND

Reading For A Purpose: How is Soviet farm life organized?

1. In the Soviet Union, the government owns all the land. It may not be bought or sold by an individual farmer. Like everyone else in the country, the Soviet farmer is dependent upon and is controlled by the Communist Party. This is the complete opposite of the farmer's position in the United States. The American farmer can own his own land. He can decide what he wants to grow on his land. He can hire others to work for him. He can sell his land if he chooses.

2. There are two kinds of farms in the Soviet Union—the state farm and the collective farm. A state farm is very large. It is called a *sovkhoz*. The state farm is used by the government to find better methods of raising crops and animals. It is very much like a factory. Each worker does a certain job on the farm and is paid for his work.

3. The collective farm or *kolkhoz* is also large, but not as large as a state farm. On an average collective farm, there may be one hundred farm families. The farmers work together, tilling the soil and harvesting the crops. Because the farms are large and the land is generally flat, machinery can be used. The harvest is sold to the government. Expenses for machinery and seed are paid. After that, each farmer gets a share of the remaining profits from the harvest. The size of each farmer's share depends upon the amount of work he has done. If the harvest is large, he receives a good reward.

4. Soviet farmers live in villages near their fields. Each farmer owns his own house and tools. He may also own a small garden plot on which he grows vegetables and fruits. He may keep a cow, goats and some chickens. He is allowed to sell whatever he does not need from his garden and keep the profits. The farmer's diet generally consists of black rye bread, beet soup (called *borscht*), cabbage, potatoes, salt pork, buckwheat and tea. He does not get as much meat, milk and eggs as we do because there are fewer farm animals in the U.S.S.R. than in the United States. The collective may have radio and television, but the individual farmer will not. A member of the Communist Party lives among the farmers. He plans the work of the collective with them.

5. The greatest farming area in the Soviet Union is the "Fertile Triangle." This belt of farm land begins near the Black Sea. It

Harvest time on a collective farm near Rostov. What similarities, if any, are there between this farm and a large American farm?

A shepherd in the Georgian Soviet republic. A few herds such as this one are privately owned. Why do you think this is so?

stretches across the Ukraine eastward to the southern Ural Mountains and beyond. This is the heartland of Soviet farming. The soils are rich and black. The area is flat and suitable for the use of machinery. The major crop of this black earth belt is wheat. The Soviet Union is the world leader in the production of wheat.

6. Besides wheat, the chief farm products are rye, barley, potatoes, cotton and wool. Rye is second only to wheat as the important grain product of the U.S.S.R. It can be grown farther north where the climate is cooler. It is used in the black bread that is eaten by Soviet farmers. White potatoes, important in the Soviet diet, are also grown in the cooler areas. This is another food product in which the Soviet Union leads the world.

7. Very fine cotton is grown in scattered oases (fertile areas) in the dry lands east of the Caspian Sea. The Soviet Union has become a world leader in production of cotton, and nearly all of it is produced in the dry regions of Asia. Textile mills are fed with the wool from thousands of sheep. The main grazing lands are found along the border of the steppes and the southern Caucasus Mountains. These are the old grazing grounds of the Mongol tribes. Only Australia produces more wool than the Soviet Union.

8. Soviet leaders and planners once thought that the collective farm would bring huge crops because tractors and other farm machinery could be used. But it has not worked out this way. There are often food shortages in the U.S.S.R. There are several reasons for this. First, the Soviet farmer has little desire to grow a large amount of crops or try new methods because he does not own the land. Second, despite the size of the Soviet Union, there is less fertile farm land than in the United States. Too much of the country is too cold or too dry for crops. To increase farm production, the Soviet government is now giving the farmer more freedom to sell for a profit the foods he grows in his garden. Also, more lands in Soviet Asia are being opened for farming than ever before.

A party committee discusses ways of increasing farm production on a Soviet collective. What are advantages of planned collective farming? Disadvantages?

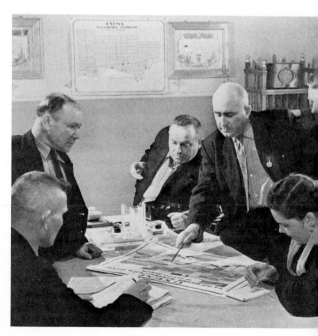

1. Which questions are answered in this chapter?
    a. Why did the government "collectivize" the farms?
    b. Why is most of the Soviet land not good for farming?
    c. Where is cotton grown?
2. The main idea of *paragraphs 1 through 4* describes:
    a. what is grown on Soviet farms.
    b. how Soviet farms are organized.
    c. the use of machinery on Soviet farms.
3. What is the most important crop of the Fertile Triangle?
    a. Potatoes.   b. Rice.   c. Wheat.
4. On a state farm the farmers work for:
    a. a share of the crops.
    b. wages.
    c. the profits from their own gardens.
5. Part of the food problem in the Soviet Union is caused by a lack of:
    a. machinery.   b. seed.   c. fertile land.
6. In the Soviet Union, as in many parts of the world, cotton is grown in dry areas because:
    a. cotton needs little water during the growing season.
    b. water is supplied through irrigation.
    c. cotton needs only a small amount of labor at picking time.
7. On a *collective* farm, people:
    a. own the lands together.
    b. sell the crops to the government and share the profits.
    c. gather the crops from nearby farms for sale.
8. On a *sovkhoz* and *kolkhoz*, people make a living through:
    a. farming.   b. mining.   c. factory work.

Photograph Study

The photograph below should help you to recall parts of the chapter you have read. What is the main idea of the photograph?

Complete the following chart in your notebook.

Comparing Farmers		
	AMERICAN	**SOVIET**
1. Ownership of land:		
2. Kinds of farms:		
3. Farming methods:		
4. Crops:		
5. Animals:		
6. Standard of living:		

Tell whether these statements are true or false. The underlined words make the statements true or false. If a statement is false, what word or words would you place in it to make it true?

1. The farms of the Soviet Union are owned by <u>individual farmers</u>.
2. The greatest farming area is called the <u>Vital Triangle</u>.
3. The chief grain crops of the U.S.S.R. are <u>wheat and rye</u>.
4. The <u>Ukraine</u> is the center of the Soviet wheat belt.
5. A large Soviet farm on which many families live is called a <u>collective farm</u>.
6. Work on a collective farm is divided among the workers by a <u>committee of farmers</u>.
7. The Soviet Union leads the world in the production of <u>wheat</u>.
8. A Soviet farmer will most likely have <u>coffee</u> with his meal.

8 THE SOVIET FACTORIES

A power station in the Irkutsk region of Soviet Asia. Check the resource map on page 322. For what industries may this power be used?

Reading For A Purpose: How did the Soviet Union become a leading industrial nation?

1. Before the Revolution of 1917, Russia was largely a farming nation. While countries of Western Europe were building large factories, Russia had few. In 1928, the government of the Soviet Union began planning the use of its natural resources. Since then, the Soviet Union has changed from a farming nation to a land of mills and factories second only to the United States.

2. There are several reasons for this change. First, the Soviet Union has a greater variety of mineral resources than any other nation in the world, including the United States. There are large deposits of coal, iron ore, copper, manganese, platinum, bauxite and other mineral ores. Second, there are many sources of power: coal, oil and peat—a soft, cheap, coal-like material dug near the surface of the ground. Water-power resources are being developed. In the U.S.S.R. are four of the five largest hydroelectric plants (producing electricity by the power of falling water) in the world, and more projects are now being built. There is also uranium, from which atomic power is developed.

3. Third, the Soviet government owns most of the natural resources and factories in the nation. As a result, the use of these resources is planned by the government. Planners can decide how many houses, dams or factories are to be built. Wherever possible, factories and cities are located near the source of the raw materials. These areas are called "industrial regions." Factories are built and run by the government, and the Soviet leaders decide how and where the goods are to be sold.

4. As a result of this system, there is almost no unemployment in the Soviet Union. Everybody works for the government because all the property is owned by the government. All factory workers do not receive the same pay, but are paid according to their skills and the amount of work they do. It is often very difficult to leave a job without the permission of the government. There are labor unions, but they cannot strike. The unions can only discuss working conditions with the Communist "boss." Each worker receives a pension when he retires. Besides the regular working force, the Communists have often used forced or prison labor. These workers are people who have been arrested by the secret police and kept in camps. Many of the workers used to build roads and railroads in distant and rugged parts of the country have been prison laborers.

5. There are four important industrial regions in the Soviet Union: the Donets Basin in

southeast Ukraine; the Kuznetsk Basin in southcentral Siberia; the Ural region just east of the Ural Mountains and the Moscow-Leningrad region in Soviet Europe. The development of these regions has been greatly encouraged by Soviet planners.

6. The most important industrial region in the U.S.S.R. is the Donets Basin or Donbas, located in the Ukraine. This basin is one of the richest parts of the Soviet Union. Coal, iron ore and manganese are found here. The Donets coal field supplies fuel for the steel mills. Dams on the Dnieper River provide electric power. All these things together make this region very much like the Vital Triangle in Western Europe and our steel centers in the Northeastern United States. Kiev is the capital and chief city of the Ukraine.

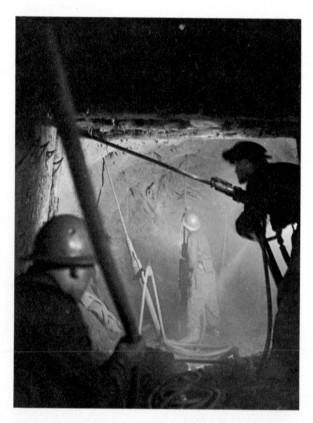

An iron mine in the Ukraine, the most important industrial region in the Soviet Union. What are the major industrial regions in the United States?

7. The Soviets began to develop the Urals as an industrial region before World War II, partly for military reasons. This was a blessing for the Soviets. When the German armies overran the Ukraine, they hardly touched the iron and steel production of the Urals. The mountains are rich in iron, copper, manganese, bauxite and platinum. Oil and natural gas are found on the western side of the mountains. (Oil fields are also located near the Caspian Sea. Pipelines carry the oil directly to ports on the Black Sea.) Coal is brought by rail from newly found deposits in Karaganda, about six hundred miles to the east. Magnitogorsk is the leading iron and steel city in this region.

8. The Kuznetsk Basin or Kuzbas is about 1200 miles east of the Ural Mountains. It is also very rich in coal. At first, Kuzbas coal was taken by rail to the Urals and iron ore was brought from the Urals. This two-way shipment of coal and iron between the two regions made both of them leading iron and steel centers. However, the steel was very expensive because of the long shipping distances involved. Luckily, iron ore has since been discovered near Kuzbas and coal discovered at Karaganda, a city much closer to the Urals. Novosibirsk is the great steel city of the Kuznetsk.

9. The Moscow-Leningrad area is one of the oldest industrial regions. It got its start because it had many people and was a transportation center. It is connected by railroad, river and canal to the needed sources of raw materials. The Black, Caspian and Baltic Seas all have water routes leading to the Moscow region. As a result, goods flow steadily in and out of the Moscow-Leningrad area. The region is known for both *heavy* (automobiles, machinery, etc.) and *light* (textiles, shoes, etc.) industries.

10. There have been handicaps in the development of Soviet industry also. In general, too much government planning and control has hurt the output of the factory as it has the farm. The manager of a factory often has little desire to try new methods. Lately, the Soviet

government has been trying a new policy. It is giving the manager more freedom in deciding what goods to make and how to make them in order to bring about more profits for the factory. Second, the Soviet transportation system is weak. While the country has the second largest railroad system in the world, the nation is vast and many places are far from railroad lines. There are few highways and only a few trucks carrying goods over these highways. Many of the rivers and canals are frozen over much of the year. Finally, coal and iron deposits are not always found near each other. Transporting these heavy materials by rail is expensive. Because of the high cost of transportation the government would like to make each industrial region as self-supporting as possible. This means that each region is encouraged to produce as much of the things it needs as it can.

UNDERSTANDING CHAPTER 8

1. Which questions are answered in this chapter?
   a. Why are steel goods expensive?
   b. What are the Five-Year Plans?
   c. How rich is the Soviet Union in natural resources?
2. The main idea of *paragraph 4* is that:
   a. Soviet workers have little say in choosing jobs or in improving conditions of work.
   b. unions have helped to build highways and railroads in the Soviet Union.
   c. factories have poor working conditions.
3. The chief source of power in the Soviet Union is:
   a. coal. b. water. c. atomic energy.
4. The Soviet Union is one of the leading producers of:
   a. tin and rubber. b. manganese and platinum. c. nitrates.
5. Many steel goods are expensive because:
   a. high wages are paid to workers.
   b. there is a lack of machinery in the factories.
   c. iron ore and coal are often far from each other.
6. The Soviet Union is a leading industrial nation because:
   a. it has many useful resources.
   b. factories are owned by individuals who make a profit.
   c. there has been great use of water power in Soviet Asia.
7. In an *industrial* region there are:
   a. farms. b. mines and factories. c. fisheries.
8. In paragraph 10, the term "self-supporting" means:
   a. "increasing production."
   b. "not depending on others."
   c. "following the state plan."

Map Study

Map #35—Industrial Resources of the Soviet Union

Here is a list of statements about the map below. In your notebook, write the numerals 1—10. Beside each, write T if the statement bearing that numeral is true. Write F if it is false. Write N if no information is given for that statement.

1. The Ural Mountains have a large variety of important minerals.
2. Oil fields are found near the Caspian Sea.
3. All the important iron and coal fields are located in the European part of the Soviet Union.
4. Few of the Soviet minerals are exported.
5. All the Soviet industrial centers are found in the warmer climates.
6. We would find steel mills in both the Urals and the region near Kiev.
7. In order to make steel, coal must be brought to the Karaganda district.
8. Railroad lines lead from Novosibirsk in all directions.
9. Minerals are found in the northern part of Siberia.
10. Uranium is mined west of the Ural Mountains.

The problem of pollution is worldwide. This news article tells of problems on Lake Baikal, in the Soviet Union. (Lake Baikal may be located on the map on this page. It is the large body of water near the city of Irkutsk in Soviet Asia.) As you read, think about what steps should be taken to halt water pollution.

Water Pollution in the Soviet Union

According to most Russians, Lake Baikal is the most beautiful lake in the world. It is certainly the largest body of fresh water on earth and the deepest (one mile down). It is probably among the clearest and purest, and it contains some fish not found elsewhere. Siberians will tell you their fish is tastier than any other fish in the world. Unfortunately, Lake Baikal is dying. It is being killed by pollution from industry. And it is not alone. The Volga River is dying too. So is the Caspian Sea into which the Volga empties. How did this happen?

When a huge cellulose plant was built at Lake Baikal, engineers said there would be little pollution of the waters. Until recently, people were told that the waste from the factory would not disturb the purity of the water. Engineers were heard to say, "I'd drink it myself." An investigation found that fish placed in the factory waste died within a few hours.

The Volga is being hurt in the same way. According to some sources, there has already been a great loss of fish in the river. The battle is being lost to oil, factory and home sewage. Salmon and sturgeon are among the fish being eliminated. Some scientists say it may be too late to halt the loss of fish.

Adapted, by permission, from "Pollution Is Killing Most Beautiful Lake," *San Francisco Examiner*, October 4, 1970.

1. What are the chief sources of pollution mentioned in the selection?
2. What are the sources for the writer's statements that: (a.) "it may be too late to halt the loss of fish" and (b.) "there has been a great loss of fish in the river." Would you question his sources? Why or why not?
3. Look in your local newspaper or in magazines for news about pollution or laws to fight pollution. What action is being taken by governments against those who pollute the water and air?

9 NATION IN A HURRY

Reading For A Purpose: How do the city people live?

1. The Soviet Union has shown its great power to the world in recent years. The nation has a standing army of over two million men. It has exploded some of the most powerful bombs known to man. Its Sputnik, launched in 1957, was the first satellite to orbit the earth. It has also sent rockets to the moon. It placed the first woman in space and sent three men around the earth together in the same space ship in 1964. Yet it has a standard of living lower than that of the United States, Canada and many countries of Western Europe. Its people have little freedom. Great deeds have been accomplished by the nation, but the people have yet to receive full benefit from them.

2. Since 1928, Communist leaders have been eager to prove to the world that communism can work. They have planned to produce much machinery and iron and steel goods. (Although the Soviet Union has made great progress in industry, it now leads the United States only in the production of cement and raw steel.) In the leaders' drive to produce more industrial goods, the Soviet people were left behind. Few goods were produced for them, and little attention was paid to their wants. Recently the government changed its policy. Today more goods are being manufactured for the people.

3. Living in the growing cities has been hard, because of the housing shortage. Most apartments are crowded. If a worker lives in an old building, he may have one room for himself and his family. He may have to share a kitchen or a bathroom with other families. New apartment buildings are going up at a great rate throughout the country. But still there are not enough apartments for Soviet families.

4. Most people in the U.S.S.R. have enough clothing to keep them warm and healthy. But the usual clothing is drab in color, poorly made

Soviet citizens shopping in a Moscow department store. Would you expect to find the same kinds of goods in a Russian department store as you would find in a department store in this country? Why?

and poorly fitted. The city dweller buys his food in government stores. These stores sell just about everything he needs, if he can afford to buy it. There are more goods available now than there were ten years ago.

5. Medical treatment for Soviet citizens is supplied by the government. There are many trained doctors. Doctors are even sent to the far regions of the Soviet Union. As a result of the efforts to improve medical service, the Soviet death rate is now below that of the United States. Health resorts are located near the Black Sea. A citizen may make use of these resorts at little or no cost.

6. All children are expected to go to school. Boys and girls at the age of seven years attend classes six hours a day, six days a week. The homework is heavy, for the government wants an educated population. Most children attend school for eight years. After that, only qualified pupils continue their studies. Those who go on to college study for three more years; science and mathematics are the important subjects.

7. All schools are free for the students who qualify for them. Examinations are required before a student can enter college. Students who are members of working families or members of the Communist Party are most often picked first. The U.S.S.R. invites students from foreign countries, chiefly the new countries of Africa and Asia. The aim of the colleges is to graduate scientists and engineers—to help the Soviet Union become stronger.

8. The Soviet Union has also placed a great emphasis on making women equal with men in job opportunities. Women have the same chance for education as men and are admitted to any job on the same basis. It is not unusual to see women building roads, driving buses and trucks, and working in factories.

9. Most forms of communication are considered by the Soviet government to be ways of "educating" the people. Plays in the theater, operas, dances and musical shows are controlled by the state. Teachers are trained by the Communist Party. Writers of popular books must be careful that they do not offend

An English class in Leningrad. Why do you think Russian students are taught English? Do you think it is a good idea for American students to learn the Russian language? Why?

the Communist leaders. The press is not free. Children are taught from their earliest years that communism is the best system of government. They are told that the people of the Soviet Union are the happiest people in the world—that they enjoy the greatest freedoms and have the most advanced scientists. They are always reminded of the contributions of the Communist Party to their well-being.

10. There is no doubt that the Soviet Union has made progress. The leaders have placed great importance on the education of the people. They want the best engineers and mechanics. Their achievements in exploring space continue to be outstanding. The standard of living of the people is rising slowly but steadily. It is hoped that this progress will lead to better understanding between the people of our countries.

A woman construction worker helps in the building of a new subway in Tashkent, in Soviet Asia. Do you think equal rights for women should include the chance to work at jobs such as this? Why?

1. Which questions are answered in this chapter?
   a. How are women treated in the Soviet Union?
   b. How important is education to the Soviet government?
   c. What is propaganda?
2. The main idea of *paragraph 9* describes:
   a. Soviet control over means of communication.
   b. the problems of writers in the Soviet Union.
   c. Communist education.
3. The Soviets were the first to:
   a. develop atomic energy.
   b. start a system of free education for all.
   c. send a satellite into space.
4. Soviet citizens receive free:
   a. housing.   b. medical care.   c. clothing.
5. As the Soviet Union planned for progress in industry:
   a. farm machinery was not produced.
   b. there was little interest in space exploration.
   c. comforts for the people were not thought to be important.
6. In which way has the Soviet Union become a world leader?
   a. It has made many achievements in science.
   b. The people have many freedoms.
   c. Their houses are models for the rest of the world.
7. In paragraph 8, the words "placed a great emphasis on" mean:
   a. "continued to."   b. "made progress."   c. "considered to be important."
8. The title of the chapter, "Nation in a Hurry," refers to:
   a. the desire of the U.S.S.R. to equal the United States as soon as possible.
   b. the need for free schools for all people.
   c. equal rights for women.

SUMMING UP

For many years after World War II, the world knew little of what was going on inside the Soviet Union. Today, however, the Soviet Union seems to want visitors to see the progress it has made in industry and technology. The following is one visitor's report of what he saw on his visit to the Soviet Union.

A Real Look Inside Russia
Reprinted from *U.S. News & World Report*.

The questions were asked of Mr. Dallas W. Dort, a lawyer and economist who quit government service in Washington, D.C. to become a successful businessman and rancher in Florida. In this interview, Mr. Dort gave his observations from a three-month trip across the Soviet Union, which he first visited 41 years ago.
Some of the questions and Mr. Dort's answers follow.
Question: Would you say the Russian people are relatively happy with their living standards?

Answer: On the whole, yes. They have no way of comparing what they have with what the U.S., or other Western countries have.

They do compare things with what was there before, however. In those terms, there is tremendous improvement. They have more housing than a few years ago, more goods in the stores, more money to spend on what they can buy.

It's hard to compare these standards with ours. The people we met, many of them, were interested in comparing our income and living standards with their own.

In dollar terms, their incomes are small—$120 a month is a pretty high wage. One school principal we met had a salary of about $150 a month and he was quite proud of it.

When you look into what he pays for essentials, you find the gap narrowing. He rented his apartment in that case for about $10 a month, and he said it was a pleasant apartment by Soviet standards. His medical services, many other things of that sort were completely free. He had free education for his children—through the university, if they were good enough—completely free.

In the stores some things are quite expensive—much more expensive than they are here in relation to earnings. Television sets, clothing, such things are not cheap. I have a boating business in the Sarasota (Florida) area and was interested in looking over the nearest thing to it in Russia. They had some small sport boats, outboard motors, snorkeling and scuba-diving equipment, tennis and soccer equipment, some fishing equipment—a very limited supply for even the smaller sporting-goods stores in America. These things were not cheap.

Still, a lot of people were buying. Of course, many of them are on organized teams sponsored by trade unions or other groups which buy the equipment for them.

Question: Did you spot many shortages?

Answer: Yes, quite a few. They varied widely. You would go into a store and there might be lots of certain things on the shelves, but then there would be a long line waiting to buy something else.

We found such a line in one store—to buy soup plates. It turned out that there had been no soup plates for sale in that area for six months. The line of would-be buyers was half a block long. I don't know how long the supply lasted. In a large store, I bought a flashlight but couldn't find any batteries for it anywhere.

Question: Was there much curiosity about the United States?

Answer: A great deal. Some had listened to the British Broadcasting Company or the Voice of America and they weren't sure they were getting the truth. They wanted to check on a person-to-person basis with us.

Students we met were just about like American students of the same age, perhaps more curious about us than our students would be about them—most friendly and anxious to talk, eager to have us join them singing—that sort of thing.

Some of the teachers we met were particularly curious about how teachers in our group could afford to pay for such an expensive trip as the one we were on. They had the idea our teachers were subsidized on such trips. So we told them about our income and how we spent it, how we saved it, what returns we got—all that.

Question: What do the Soviet people do with their leisure time when they haven't the money to splurge?

Answer: They go to the theater a lot, to circuses and movies. There are some beautiful theaters and opera houses way out in what we would call "the sticks." They have resident companies or touring companies that give fine performances, very cheap and very well attended. We were impressed with their high quality.

Also, the people are great for sports. We would see athletes in exercise suits jogging along the streets early in the morning before they went to work—members of sports clubs keeping in condition. They like spectator sports, too—particularly football, the kind we call soccer.

U.S. News & World Report, February 14, 1972. Copyright 1972 U.S. News & World Report, Inc.

Remember that this is one interview with one person. Before you make final judgments about Soviet life, you should read about or listen to others who have traveled to the Soviet Union recently. Perhaps one of your teachers has made such a visit. You can also look through newspapers and magazines to see what other visitors to the Soviet Union have to report. Compare their views with those in this interview.

1. Do you think there might be differences in the way a family in the Soviet Union and a family in the United States takes care of tools and household furnishings? Explain.
2. Why were the Soviet people Mr. Dort met curious about the United States?
3. What should we keep in mind when comparing Russian living standards with our own?
4. According to the interview, what are some important benefits enjoyed by the Russian people?
5. What are some problems of daily life faced by the Russian people?

10 THE GROWING COMMUNIST WORLD

Reading For A Purpose: How has communism spread throughout the world?

1. During World War II, the United States and the Soviet Union were allies. However, when the war ended, real peace did not result. As soon as the war was over, the nations of the West and the Soviet Union moved far apart. The Soviet Union had occupied many countries in Eastern Europe in the march toward the heart of Germany in 1945. After the war, the U.S.S.R. refused to give up control of the countries it occupied—Poland, Hungary, Rumania, Bulgaria and Yugoslavia. These countries' farms and factories were turned over to the state. Those who fought the Communists were killed or sent to labor camps. It was said that an "Iron Curtain" was being placed around Eastern Europe. This was the beginning of the "Cold War." Although there was a kind of peace, there was also a feeling that fighting could start again at any time.

2. The first efforts by the United States to stop the spread of communism came in 1947. The Soviet Union had made moves toward Greece and Turkey in an attempt to gain control of the valuable Dardanelles. President Truman said the United States would give aid to Turkey and Greece in order to stop the Communist threat in these countries. This policy became known as the Truman Doctrine. Later in the year, the United States loaned money to the nations of Europe to help them recover from the damages of World War II. This was called the Marshall Plan. The money was used to restore farm land and to rebuild railroads and factories in Europe. The Marshall Plan played a great part in keeping some of the nations of Europe from turning to communism to solve their problems.

3. Germany has been a "trouble spot" since 1945. After the war, Germany was divided into four parts called zones of occupation. The Soviets occupied eastern Germany; England, France and the United States placed troops in western Germany. Berlin, in the Soviet zone, was occupied by all four nations. In 1948, the three Western nations combined their zones of occupation into one. At once, the Soviet Union cut off shipments of supplies on all roads and railroads leading to the city of Berlin. They hoped this blockade would force the Allies to give up their occupation of the city. The Soviet Union did not want even part of a free city inside Communist territory.

4. Berlin lies about 100 miles inside the Soviet zone. More than three million people live there. They depend upon West Germany for the goods they need in order to live. They depend upon the Allies for their protection. With the blockade, the people of West Berlin found themselves without food, medicine and other necessary goods. The United States decided to break the blockade. American planes began to bring supplies into Berlin. This "Berlin Airlift" was a success; the Soviet Union gave up the blockade after a year. However, in August, 1961, the U.S.S.R. built the Berlin Wall to stop East Germans from crossing to the West. Now the Communist section of Berlin is locked behind the Iron Curtain by a wall of concrete.

5. Early in 1948, the Communists overthrew the democratic government of Czechoslovakia.

East German soldiers guard the Brandenburg Gate at the Berlin Wall. Why do many people consider this wall a symbol of the "cold war"?

The Berlin Blockade and the spread of communism to Czechoslovakia aroused Western nations. Believing that Western Europe was in danger, twelve nations met in 1949 to sign a treaty. They formed the North Atlantic Treaty Organization or NATO. These nations agreed to help each other in case of attack. NATO members also set up an army to defend their countries. By 1955, NATO numbered fifteen nations. In 1967, however, France withdrew.

6. In Asia there were also great changes after World War II. The British colony of India was divided into two self-governing countries, India and Pakistan. Great Britain also gave up its other colonies in Asia. The Communists gained control of China in 1949. Indonesia was formed into an independent state. The little country of Korea was occupied in the north by the Soviet Union and in the south by the United States. The people of South Korea then held elections and established their own government. In North Korea, the Soviets set up a Communist state.

7. In June, 1950, the North Koreans invaded South Korea. President Truman ordered American troops to fight. The United Nations sent other forces to help South Korea. The Soviet Union did not support the United Nations in stopping the invasion. When the United Nations army drove the North Koreans back almost to the border of Manchuria, the troops of Red China entered the battle. This "seesaw" war lasted three years. The end of the fighting did not bring victory for either side. Korea is still divided, but the action of the United States and other members of the United Nations saved the independence of South Korea.

8. French Indochina was also affected by the spread of communism. Local Communists supported a revolt against French rule. The French then divided the country into three separate states—Cambodia, Laos and Vietnam—and gave the people more self-rule. But this did not end the fighting. Despite American aid, the French could not stop the northern part of Vietnam from becoming Communist. Vietnam was divided into two parts, North and South. The peace of the world was seriously threatened by the war waged in Vietnam.

9. Because of the advance of communism in

United States soldiers inspect a collection of Soviet-made weapons captured during the fighting in Vietnam. Who was aided in the war by the Soviet Union?

Asia, the United States has entered into many military agreements with countries in that region. A peace treaty was made with Japan in 1951. In 1952, the Senate of the United States approved treaties with the Philippines, Australia and New Zealand. In 1954, the United States joined six other nations in the Southeast Asia Treaty Organization or SEATO. The purpose of this treaty was to help the nations of Southeast Asia resist communism.

10. Communism has spread all over the world in the years since World War II. In the Middle East, the Soviets have given large numbers of weapons to the Arab nations, particularly Egypt. On the Indian subcontinent, the Soviet Union helped India overthrow Pakistani rule in East Pakistan. There are now large Soviet fleets in the Mediterranean Sea and Indian Ocean.

11. In Latin America, the leader of Cuba is Fidel Castro. He has been very friendly with the Soviet Union. The U.S.S.R. has supplied Cuba not only with food but also with arms. In 1962, it was reported that there were Soviet missile bases in Cuba. They remained there until President Kennedy demanded that the missiles be sent back to the Soviet Union. He set up a naval blockade around Cuba to see that this was done. In all, the struggle between the Communist world and the West has caused much trouble. The United States in the '70's still faces the problem of dealing with communism.

UNDERSTANDING CHAPTER 10

1. Which questions are answered in this chapter?
   a. What is the Marshall Plan?
   b. How did the Communists win control of China?
   c. Why were United States troops sent to Korea?
2. The main idea of this chapter describes how:
   a. Germany was divided after World War II.
   b. the Korean War ended.
   c. communism has spread throughout the world.
3. The main purpose of the Marshall Plan was to:
   a. sell our coal and steel at lower prices.
   b. help European countries after World War II.
   c. build air bases in Asia.
4. NATO was formed to:
   a. develop new weapons of war.
   b. unite North and South America against enemy attacks.
   c. unite Western nations in case of attack.
5. The Berlin Airlift was necessary because:
   a. tourists could not enter the city.
   b. Britain's railroads had been damaged.
   c. goods could not be brought into Berlin by land.
6. One reason we are interested in Asian affairs is:
   a. we want to keep communism from spreading.
   b. much of the continent is still unexplored.
   c. large parts of our navy are stationed there.

7. "The navy moved to *blockade* the island." "Blockade" means:
   a. "bombard."
   b. "bring food."
   c. "keep ships from going in and out."
8. The "Iron Curtain" separated:
   a. European nations from Africa.
   b. African nations from Asia.
   c. Communist nations from the rest of the world.

DEVELOPING IDEAS AND SKILLS

Look at the cartoon. Then answer the questions below.

1. Who is the man in the cartoon?
2. What is he trying to build?
3. Are there other blocks you could place in the wall?
4. Why are blocks of ice used in this cartoon?
5. What would be a good title for the cartoon?

SUMMING UP

The World Since 1945 Below are three headings for an *outline*. Following them are some topics to be placed under these headings. In your notebook, write your outline using the headings and topics listed.

   Headings:
   A. Events in Europe
   B. Events in Asia and Africa
   C. Events in Latin America

Topics:
1. The Korean War
2. United States aid to Greece and Turkey
3. Congo independence
4. The Berlin Wall
5. Division of Vietnam
6. NATO
7. Soviet satellite nations
8. Freedom for India and Pakistan
9. The Marshall Plan
10. Soviet missiles in Cuba

FOLLOW UP

Tell whether these statements are true or false. The underlined words make the statements true or false. If a statement is false, what word or words would you place in it to make it true?
1. Cambodia, Laos and Vietnam were once colonies of Spain.
2. The dictator of Cuba is Marshal Tito.
3. NATO is a group of nations united to defend themselves against communism.
4. One of the important members of SEATO is the United States.
5. Two divided countries today are Germany and Korea.
6. The United States broke the Berlin Blockade by sending supplies into the city by train.
7. Through the Marshall Plan, the United States loaned money to European nations after World War II.
8. India was once a British colony.
9. Berlin is located in the eastern part of Germany.
10. SEATO is the name of a treaty organization.

11 BALANCE SHEET

Reading For A Purpose: How strong is the Soviet Union?

1. It is not often easy to tell what is going on inside the Soviet Union. For many years the "Iron Curtain" of secrecy has made it hard for the world to know the truth about the Soviet Union. Much of the news the world receives is what the Soviet government wants the world to know. Unlike what happens in the free world, failures are seldom reported. Visitors to the U.S.S.R. generally see what the leaders want them to see. However, times are changing somewhat. More people are being encouraged to visit the Soviet Union and even to talk with the Soviet people.

2. As a result, we are better able to learn some facts about the Soviet Union than before. A summary of what we have learned about the U.S.S.R. will help us to get a better picture of this vast Communist country and its standing in the world:

a. The U.S.S.R. is the second leading industrial nation in the world. It has made a great effort to raise its production of iron and steel goods, oil, water power, machinery and machine tools—everything that makes a nation strong.

b. The Soviet Union has powerful armed forces. The army is large and well trained. Soviet jet planes are respected by military experts everywhere. The Soviet Union possesses the largest and most destructive types of bombs and has tested them so that the world would know this fact. Its missiles are also among the best.

c. To many of the new nations in Asia and Africa, the Soviet Union seems to be a suc-

cess. The Communist government has changed it from a backward farming country to a highly industrialized nation. These new nations are chiefly farming nations. They would like to change their countries into nations of mills and factories as soon as possible. In some cases, the Soviet Union has offered to help them. Soviet help often means Soviet control.

d. The countries of Eastern Europe are under Communist control and supply raw materials to help the industries of the U.S.S.R. China, in Asia, is also a Communist country. This nation of 850 million people may not agree with the Soviet Union on a number of policies, but it is under a Communist government. It remains to be seen whether the split between the two giant Communist nations will be healed.

3. There are weaknesses as well as strengths in the Soviet Union. Let us look at some of the problems that exist:

a. The cold climate and great amount of frozen and desert land mean that large areas of the Soviet Union have few people and are little used. The rivers flow into the frozen Arctic or into lakes that have no other outlet. (Compare this with the great river system of the United States and its mild climatic region.) The U.S.S.R. has the same problems with its cold climate as Brazil in South America has with its hot climate.

b. The trade of the Soviet Union is largely within its own borders or with its "satellite" nations. It does not wish to depend upon other nations for its needs. However, in 1972, there was a poor wheat crop in the Soviet Union. A large amount of wheat was bought from the United States. This may be the beginning of a growing Soviet trade with the western countries.

c. The Soviet Union is ruled by a small group of men, the Communist Party. Their rule covers many areas that in our country are left to the individual—jobs, schooling, where to live. Freedom of religion, press and speech as we know it is not allowed in

A suburban Moscow store recently advertised this tea set with napkins for 24 rubles, 50 kopecks. There are 100 kopecks to a ruble, and a ruble is worth about $1.40. How much is this item worth in dollars and cents? Would you be interested in buying it at this price? Why?

use of its resources, many of its people still live poorly compared with the farmers and factory workers in our own country. In the United States a worker can earn in a few days enough money to buy a suit of clothes, a shirt and a pair of shoes. In the Soviet Union a worker must labor about six times as long to buy the same amount of clothing. The Soviet people work chiefly to produce goods for the government. The worker has little reason to work hard and well. The Soviet citizen wants more goods for his own use, not for the state's.

the Soviet Union. While most of the people in the country can read, they have not been able to read books and newspapers of their own choice. The people of the U.S.S.R. cannot learn the complete truth about people in other countries.

d. While the Soviet Union is making greater

e. The Soviet Union has been using much of its resources and the labor of its people in building up its armed forces. Keeping a large army and making war materials such as bombs, tanks, jets and missiles are expensive. As a result, the people have not had many of the comforts we enjoy. However, better housing and clothes, more radios and cars are becoming a part of life in Soviet cities.

f. The Soviet transportation system is weak.

The Soviet Union shows some of its powerful rockets during a parade in Moscow's Red Square. Why do you think weapons are paraded before the public?

The waterways are often icebound. Although the Soviet Union has many railroad lines, most of the country—particularly Siberia—has poor railway transportaton. Large sections are far from any railroads at all. There are not many highways in the Soviet Union, nor are there many cars or trucks to travel them. In most areas, limited air service is the only means of transportation to make up for the lack of railroads and highways.

g. Because it has grown in strength, China threatens the power of the Soviet Union in the Communist world. The rulers of China do not believe that communism and democracy can live together side by side. The Chinese exploded their first atomic bomb late in 1964. Their army is large and well trained. Moreover, China is one of the most heavily populated countries in the world. Just across its northern borders lie the vast uncrowded lands of Siberia. The Chinese may desire some of this land. There are signs of growing differences between China and the Soviet Union.

4. The Soviet Union is one of the most interesting countries in the world. It occupies a vast space on the earth's surface and its people's ideas are very different from those of citizens of the United States. It has great strengths and great weaknesses. The control of this vast nation is in the hands of a few men.

UNDERSTANDING CHAPTER 11

1. Which questions are answered in this chapter?
   a. What does the Soviet Union import?
   b. Why is the Soviet Union a strong nation?
   c. Why do the Soviets help the new nations of Asia and Africa?
2. The main idea of this chapter describes:
   a. the needs of the Soviet people.
   b. relations between Red China and the Soviet Union.
   c. some strengths and weaknesses of the Soviet Union.
3. One of the chief weaknesses of the Soviet Union is lack of:
   a. good transportation.   b. armed forces.   c. natural resources.
4. The largest Communist country in Asia is:
   a. Yugoslavia.   b. China.   c. Indonesia.
5. Why are there differences between the Soviet Union and the Free World?
   a. The Soviets desire to introduce their form of government to other nations.
   b. The Soviet Union does not have enough land.
   c. The United States refuses to trade with the Soviet Union.
6. Why do some people want to leave areas controlled by the Soviet Union?
   a. They lack work.
   b. They have a desire for adventure.
   c. They lack freedom.
7. The emerging nations of Africa and Asia may be favorably impressed by the Soviet Union's:
   a. lack of freedom of speech.
   b. change from a farming nation to an industrialized nation.
   c. rule by a small group of men, the Communist Party.

Look at the cartoon. Then answer the questions below.

Tell whether these statements are true or false.
1. The Soviet Union has many political parties.
2. The Soviet Union is rich in natural resources.
3. The Soviet Union has no problems.
4. The people of the Soviet Union have a high standard of living.
5. From this cartoon it can be seen that the Soviet Union is a powerful nation.
6. A good title for this cartoon is "Strengths and Weaknesses of the Soviet Union."

SUMMING UP

Fact or Opinion Read each statement carefully. If the statement is a fact, write F in your notebook. If it is an opinion, write O.
1. The Soviet Union must change its form of government.
2. The population of the Soviet Union is growing.
3. The Soviet Union should not be allowed to be a member of the United Nations.
4. New nations of Africa will follow the leadership of the Soviet Union.
5. The Ukraine is one of the rich farming regions of the world.
6. In order to help keep peace in the world, the Soviet Union should stop building atomic weapons.
7. The Ural Mountains are a known storehouse of minerals.
8. The control of the government of the Soviet Union is in the hands of a few people.

A. Complete this outline in your notebook. Use the headings shown below. From what you have read, place *three* statements under each of the headings.

The Soviet Union

STRENGTHS	WEAKNESSES
1.	1.
2.	2.
3.	3.

B. *Stereotypes About the Soviet Union*

On page 302 there are several *stereotypes* about the Soviet Union. Look at page 302 now. See whether you agree with the stereotypes. Give good reasons for your judgment.

12 EASTERN EUROPE: THE SATELLITE NATIONS

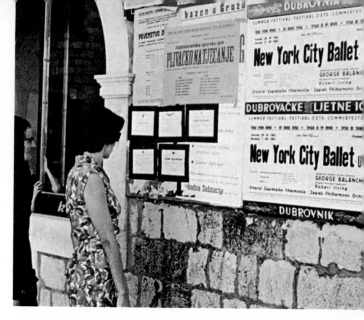

Reading For A Purpose: Why does the Soviet Union keep control of its satellite countries?

Cultural exchanges between western countries and Eastern Europe have become more and more common. What are benefits of such exchanges?

1. Eastern Europe is the belt of land stretching from Poland southward to Czechoslovakia, Hungary, Rumania, Bulgaria, Yugoslavia and Albania. Except for Yugoslavia, these are all Soviet satellite states. After World War II, the U.S.S.R. gradually took over complete control of these countries. (It was also in control of Yugoslavia until 1948. In that year Marshal Tito, the Yugoslav leader, broke away from Soviet rule. Yugoslavia is still a Communist country today, but it is an independent one.) The combined area of these countries is smaller than that of our state of Alaska. Poland is the largest country, about the size of our state of New Mexico.

2. Most of Eastern Europe is made up of hills, mountains and plains. The southern part of the region is hilly and mountainous. The most important plains are in northern and central Poland. They are a continuation of the Great European Plain. The second plains area is found in Hungary. This plain stretches into Czechoslovakia, Yugoslavia and Rumania. The greatest river of Eastern Europe is the Danube. It is the second longest river in Europe. It flows through Czechoslovakia, Hungary, Yugoslavia, Rumania and Bulgaria and is navigable for most of its length. The Danube is much used by the nearby peoples to carry their goods to market.

3. Most of Eastern Europe has a humid-continental climate, like that of our Northeast. Although the winters are cold, the summer growing season is long and warm. There is also plenty of rainfall for the crops. As a result, most people earn their living by farming or herding cattle, sheep and pigs. The main crops are grains such as wheat, rye, barley and oats. Potatoes and sugar beets are also grown. There are also mineral resources—oil (Rumania), iron ore (Czechoslovakia and Poland) and coal (Poland), for example.

4. There are approximately 127 million people living in this area. Most people speak a Slavic language. However, the people of Hungary speak Magyar, a language they learned from Mongolian invaders from Central Asia. The Rumanians speak a Latin language, while Albanians speak Albanian. The people of Poland, Hungary and Czechoslovakia are mainly Roman Catholic in religion. Bulgaria's people belong to the Greek Orthodox Church. Albania is largely Moslem. Many of the people cannot read or write, but this is changing rapidly.

5. Under the influence of the Soviet Union, the ways of living in Eastern Europe are changing. Except in Poland, collective farms have spread throughout the area. There has been a great drive to build industry in these nations. Many workers are leaving the farms to

work in the new factories in the cities. It must be remembered that part of the farm produce is sent to the Soviet Union. Many of the raw materials also go to the Soviet Union to strengthen its industries.

6. Since World War II, Eastern European governments have been modeled after the government of the Soviet Union. The people had little experience in free government before this time, so it was easy for the Communists to establish their form of government. For a long time after, Soviet leaders took strong measures to keep control over their countries. Most signs of revolt were speedily crushed. In 1956, the people of Hungary started a revolt. This uprising was crushed by Soviet tanks and troops. In recent years, Albania, Poland and Rumania have shown a little independence of the Soviet Union. In 1968, the Czechs, like the Hungarians, tried to gain some freedom for themselves. But they failed in their efforts. Today, millions of people in Eastern Europe are ruled by governments not of their own choice.

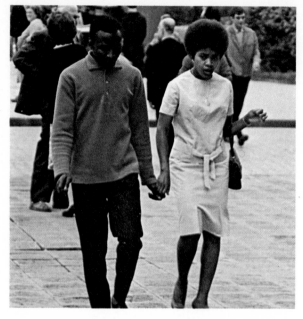

Many foreign students—especially from Africa and Asia—study at East European universities. These students are at the University of Sofia in Bulgaria. Why do many students choose to study in countries other than their own?

UNDERSTANDING CHAPTER 12

1. Which questions are answered in this chapter?
   a. Why is the Danube River important to the people of Eastern Europe?
   b. Why does the Soviet Union need Eastern Europe?
   c. Which countries are landlocked?
2. The main idea of this chapter describes:
   a. trade in Eastern Europe.
   b. the lands and people of Eastern Europe.
   c. how the satellite countries are ruled.
3. Which country is *not now* a satellite of the Soviet Union?
   a. Czechoslovakia.   b. Bulgaria.   c. Yugoslavia.
4. Most of the people of Eastern Europe make a living through:
   a. lumbering.   b. fishing.   c. farming and herding.
5. Why does the Soviet Union need Eastern Europe?
   a. It is a source of food and raw materials.
   b. The workers are highly skilled.
   c. These nations are the chief source of oil for the Soviet Union.
6. Why is there unrest in Eastern Europe?
   a. The people may want to be free from foreign control.
   b. These nations are becoming poorer.
   c. These countries are not members of the United Nations.

7. Most of Eastern Europe's trade is with:
   a. European nations along the Mediterranean Sea.
   b. nations of Western Europe.
   c. the Soviet Union.

Map Study

Map #36a and b—Eastern Europe

Study the maps. Then answer these questions.
1. How many countries do we include in Eastern Europe?
2. Which of these countries border the Soviet Union?
3. Which of these countries are landlocked, without outlets to the sea?
4. Locate the capital cities of each country. Which ones are sea or ocean ports?
5. Locate the Danube River. Through which countries does it flow?
6. The Danube forms the boundary or part of the boundary between which countries?
7. In which direction does the Vistula River in Poland flow?
8. The United States is how many times as large as the entire region of Eastern Europe?
9. How does Eastern Europe compare with the United States in the density of population?
10. Which countries share outlets on the Black Sea with the Soviet Union?

Map #36a—Eastern Europe

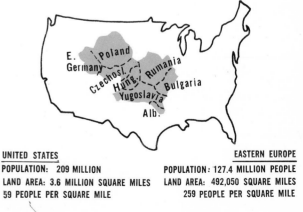

UNITED STATES	EASTERN EUROPE
POPULATION: 209 MILLION	POPULATION: 127.4 MILLION PEOPLE
LAND AREA: 3.6 MILLION SQUARE MILES	LAND AREA: 492,050 SQUARE MILES
59 PEOPLE PER SQUARE MILE	259 PEOPLE PER SQUARE MILE

Map #36b—Eastern Europe and the United States

SUMMING UP   *Agree or Disagree*   Decide whether or not each of the following statements agrees with what you have read. If the answer is *disagree*, explain why.

1. The countries of Eastern Europe are largely farming countries.
2. The Danube River is an important "highway" of trade in Eastern Europe.
3. This region has few mineral resources that modern nations can use.
4. Most of the people of this region are followers of the Moslem religion.
5. The people of Eastern Europe speak a variety of languages.
6. The Eastern European farms and factories are established, in part, to serve the needs of the Soviet government.
7. These countries have more freedom than other countries under the control of the Soviet Union.
8. The people of Eastern Europe have had a long history of democratic government.
9. A visitor from Seattle, Washington, would find the climate of Eastern Europe much like that of his home city.
10. None of the satellite nations have made an effort to break away from Soviet control.

BOOKS FOR UNIT 6

Author	Title, Publisher	Description
1. Abramov, Fyodor	ONE DAY IN THE NEW LIFE, Praeger	A clear picture of life on a collective farm.
2. Bartos-Hoppner, B.	THE COSSACKS, Walck	A description of the war against the Tartars.
3. Baker, Nina Brown	LENIN, Vanguard	The story of the leader of the Russian Revolution of 1917.
4. Crane, Joan S. and John B.	THE STORY OF THE SOVIET UNION, McCormack-Mathers	A good account of Russian history and a look at the way of life of the Soviet people.
5. Francek, Thomas, editor	ARTS OF RUSSIA, American Heritage	Russia's literature, architecture, painting and sculpture in pictures.
6. Franchere, Ruth	TITO OF YUGOSLAVIA, Macmillan	The farmer's son who became a leader of the first satellite state in Eastern Europe to break free of Soviet control.
7. Hall, Elvajean	THE VOLGA, LIFELINE OF RUSSIA, Rand McNally	About the river that was a highway for invaders, explorers and traders and is now a storehouse of energy.
8. Heaps, Willard A.	WALL OF SHAME, Meredith	About the attempts of East Germans to escape from Communist rule.

9.	Liversidge, Douglas	PETER THE GREAT, Franklin Watts	The story of the czar who brought the ways of the West to Russia.
10.	Petrovich, Michael	THE SOVIET UNION, Ginn	Short, readable account of life in the Soviet Union fifty years after the Revolution.
11.	Scherman, Katherine	CATHERINE THE GREAT, Random House	The empress who extended the power of Russia.
12.	Vandivert, Rita	YOUNG RUSSIA, Dodd, Mead	A picture of what it is like to grow up in the Soviet Union.
13.	Westbrook, Robert	JOURNEY BEHIND THE IRON CURTAIN, Putnam	An American teen-ager describes his trip to the Soviet Union.

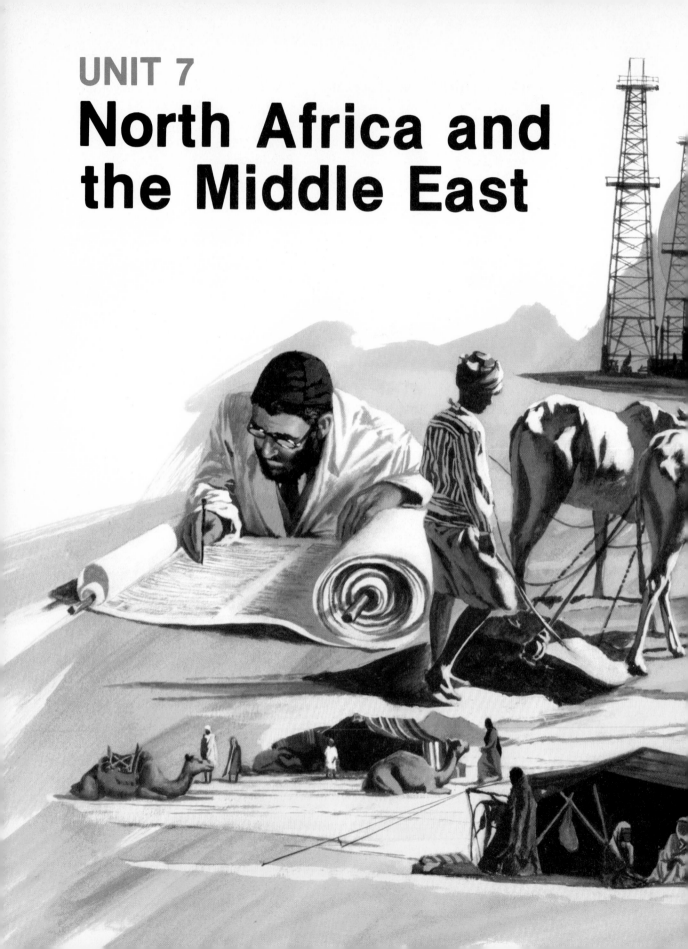

UNIT 7
North Africa and the Middle East

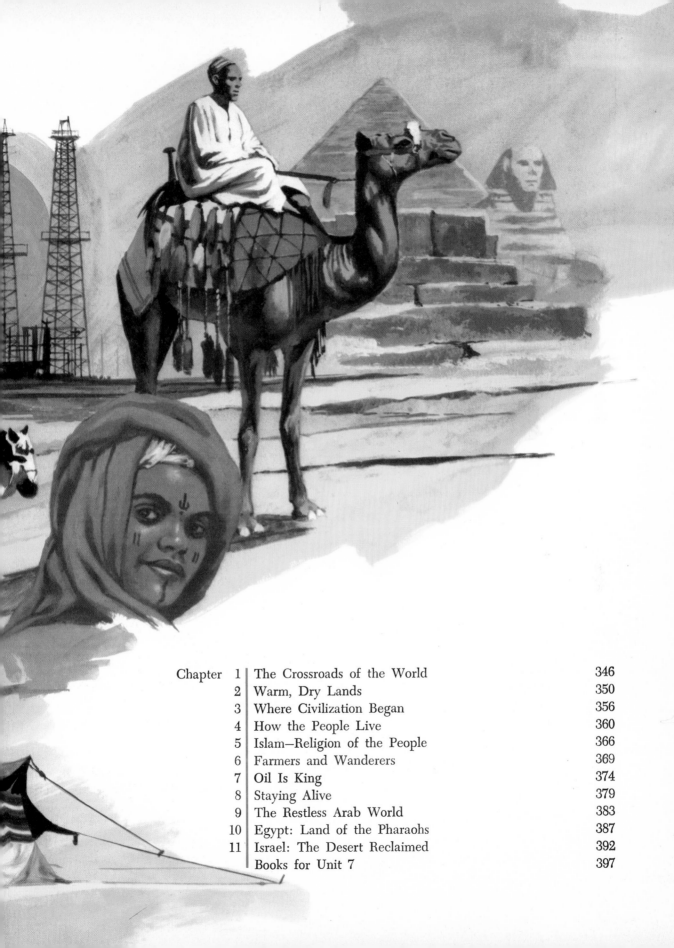

1 THE CROSSROADS OF THE WORLD

Reading For A Purpose: Why are the Middle East and North Africa important to us?

1. Many books have been written and movies have been made about the Middle East and North Africa. These usually show the region to be a land of mystery, adventure and romance. There is another picture, though, and it is far different. In the lands of North Africa and the Middle East, water is in short supply. This is a region of great poverty, hunger and illiteracy. The incomes of most people here are among the lowest in the world.

2. The region known as North Africa and the Middle East begins on the west coast of northern Africa. It stretches across North Africa and southwestern Asia to the mountains of Central Asia. It may be divided into two parts, the "Middle East" and "North Africa." The Middle East includes the Asian countries as far north as Turkey (which is partly in Europe too), as far east as Afghanistan and as far south as the Indian Ocean. It includes Egypt, which is located mostly in Africa. North Africa includes the countries west of Egypt—Libya, Tunisia, Algeria and Morocco.

3. These lands are studied as one region because they are alike in several ways. The climate of the region is generally hot and dry. In fact, much of the land is barren desert. Getting enough water just for everyday needs is a problem. Most of the people are poor farmers, town dwellers or nomads. Most of them speak the Arabic language and follow the Moslem religion.

4. The United States has a great interest in North Africa and the Middle East. First, the Middle East is rich in oil. Most of the oil is used by the people of Europe for their homes and factories. We want to make sure that they will always be able to get this oil. American oil companies have long taken part in exploring and drilling for oil in the Middle East. We also want to make sure that we are able to use the oil of the Middle East.

5. Second, this region is sometimes called the "crossroads of the world." The countries of North Africa and many of those in the Middle East border the Mediterranean Sea. This is one of the busiest trading routes in the world. The Suez Canal is found here. It connects the Mediterranean Sea and the Red Sea. The Suez shortens the distance from Western Europe to India by almost 5,000 miles. More ships pass through this canal than any other canal in the world. The countries of Western Europe and the United States send their products to Asia and Africa through the Suez. In turn, oil, rubber, tin and other raw materials from far-off lands are shipped through the canal to our factories. The countries of the Middle East control the land and sea routes at the eastern end of the Mediterranean Sea. We want to make sure that these routes are always open.

6. Third, three of the world's great religions —Judaism, Christianity and Islam—began in this part of the world. The religious beliefs and customs of millions of Americans began in this area on the eastern side of the Mediterranean Sea. Jesus, the founder of Christianity, lived, taught and died in the lands around Jerusalem. So did the Moslem leader Mohammed and the great Hebrew prophets. This is why much of

the area is thought of as the Holy Land by people of many different faiths.

7. Fourth, the Soviet Union has always been interested in the Middle East. The countries of the Middle East lie south of the Soviet Union. It is no secret that the Soviet would like to be able to control the rich oil fields of the Middle East. The U.S.S.R. is interested, too, in reaching the busy trade routes of the Mediterranean Sea. But to get from the Black Sea to the Mediterranean Sea, Soviet ships must pass through the Dardanelles, the narrow straits controlled by Turkey.

8. Finally, the Jewish state of Israel stands in the middle of the Arab countries of this region. Israel was formed in 1948, largely through the help of the United Nations. Israel is a democracy in a region where most people have little voice in their governments. Since the little country was formed, Arab nations have wanted to destroy the state of Israel. A war was fought between them in 1948. From time to time since then, border fights have broken out. Again in 1967 and in 1973, Israel and its Arab neighbors went to war. The world fears the Arab-Israeli conflict could lead to other costly wars in the future.

A street scene in Nazareth, Israel. Jesus lived and taught in this ancient land. Why is Israel considered a religious "crossroads of the world"?

UNDERSTANDING
CHAPTER 1

1. Which questions are answered in this chapter?
   a. Why is this region important to the United States?
   b. Why is the Suez Canal important?
   c. Who owns the city of Jerusalem?
2. The main idea of this chapter describes the:
   a. resources of the Middle East.
   b. reasons why we should study this region.
   c. importance of religion in the lives of the people.
3. Most of the people in North Africa and the Middle East are:
   a. Christians.   b. Jews.   c. Moslems.
4. The greatest need of people living in this region is:
   a. water   b. wood.   c. a home.
5. A reason why North Africa and the Middle East are important to the United States is that:
   a. their coal and iron are needed for our factories.
   b. the United States has agreed to protect the Arab nations.
   c. this region is the birthplace of three great religions.
6. The Suez Canal is an important waterway because it:
   a. gives the Soviet Union an outlet to the Mediterranean Sea.
   b. connects two great oceans.
   c. carries a great amount of trade between Europe and the Far East.

7. The *Middle East* is a region in:
   a. southwestern Asia.   b. central Africa.   c. northwestern Africa.
8. The *Dardanelles* is a narrow strait connecting the Mediterranean Sea and the:
   a. Atlantic Ocean.   b. Red Sea.   c. Black Sea.

DEVELOPING IDEAS AND SKILLS

Map Study

Map #37—North Africa and the Middle East

Study the map. Then answer these questions.
1. Is the region north or south of the equator?
2. Is the region east or west of the Prime Meridian?
3. How many miles north and south does the region extend?
4. Does the region extend farther from east to west or from north to south?
5. What region or regions are near it?
6. What is the largest country? The smallest?
7. What are the chief bodies of water that border the region?
8. Which countries have no outlets to the sea?
9. What are some of the important rivers in the region?
10. Are there large rivers that form the boundary lines between countries?
11. What are the capital cities of these countries?
12. Which countries are located on peninsulas?

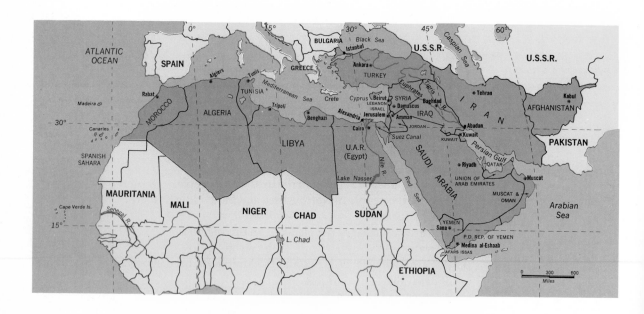

Comparing North Africa and the Middle East with Western Europe
In your notebook make the following chart. Check the column that shows the region to which each statement applies. Check both columns if the statement applies both to North Africa and the Middle East and to Western Europe.

	NORTH AFRICA AND MIDDLE EAST	WESTERN EUROPE
1. There are large deposits of oil.		
2. Factories are most important.		
3. There are rich stores of coal and iron.		
4. Great religions had their beginnings here.		
5. A large population is found in nearly the entire region.		
6. Important waterways provide trade.		
7. The Mediterranean Sea makes trade and travel easy.		
8. Most of the land has a mild, wet climate.		
9. A great desert covers most of the land.		
10. A high standard of living is found in nearly all countries.		

FOLLOW UP   The region of North Africa and the Middle East is in the newspapers daily. You should note news items that apply to this region and bring them with you to class. Start a bulletin-board display or scrapbook that shows the important events taking place in North Africa and the Middle East. You should find clippings that show *why we are interested in this region; areas where there is trouble; statements by our leaders concerning this region.*

2 WARM, DRY LANDS

Reading For A Purpose: How does the geography of the region affect the life of the people?

1. Most of North Africa and the Middle East is desert land. There are mountains and plateaus as well, but the desert most affects the life of the people. The largest desert area is the Sahara in North Africa. The Sahara is almost as large as the United States, without Alaska. It reaches from the Atlantic Ocean eastward to the Red Sea. Beyond the Red Sea there is desert again! The Arabian peninsula, large parts of Iran, Jordan and southern Israel are all desert. Thus, a dry region extends for 5,000 miles from the Atlantic to the Indian Ocean! Except for the coastal areas and the area around a few rivers, fertile land is scarce.

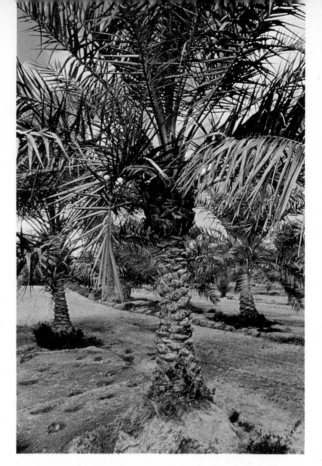

An oasis in the desert of Saudi Arabia. These palm trees are part of a project to hold back moving sand that had threatened to cut the oasis in two. Why are oases welcome relief for nomads on the desert?

The Negev Desert in southern Israel. Why is life on the desert so difficult? What can be done to make desert land liveable?

2. Some people have mistaken ideas about deserts. For example, some believe that the desert is all sand. This is not true. While there are large "hills" of sand (called sand dunes), most of the desert is either bare rock or is covered with small pebbles and sandstones. Some also believe that the desert is flat. In some places the desert *is* a large, flat plain. However, in other areas there are mountains and high peaks. Some people believe that the desert is always hot. This is partly true. During the day, the sun bakes the sand and bare rock until they are very hot. At night, however, the earth cools quickly and may become very cold. Thus, temperatures may range from 100° or hotter during the day to 40° at night—a change of sixty degrees in a single day!

3. Life on the desert is very difficult. The hot sun bakes the earth and the winds blow continually. There is almost no rain. Except for small animals like lizards and snakes, there is very little life. There is not enough grass to support life, not even the herding of animals. Humans living on the desert move from one oasis to another. (An oasis is a fertile spot in the desert where water can be found. Some of the oases are quite large and support many crops.)

4. Parts of the Middle East and North Africa are hilly or mountainous. The highest mountains are found in northern Turkey and Iran. These are the Taurus, Elburz and Zagros Mountains. In northwestern Africa are the Atlas Mountains of Morocco and Algeria. They lie between the desert and the Mediterranean Sea.

5. The mountains are very important to the people of this region. What little rain there is falls in the mountains. Water which is trapped by the mountain peaks travels for hundreds of miles underground. In some places it comes to the top of the earth in springs. In other places, it is reached by digging wells at the base of the mountains.

6. Because of the water from the mountains, there are two great river systems: the Tigris and Euphrates Rivers in Iraq and the Nile River in Egypt. The Tigris and Euphrates Rivers rise in the northern mountains of Iraq. The Euphrates is west of the Tigris River. The two rivers flow almost parallel or next to each other as they wind through Iraq. They finally join together and empty into the Persian Gulf. Where the rivers almost meet on their flow southward, the ancient city of Baghdad is located. For thousands of years the people living along these rivers have used the waters to irrigate their lands.

7. The Nile is the longest river in the world.

Gathering dates from a date palm. Judging from this picture, what kind of climate is suited for date growing?

It begins south of Egypt in the highlands of Central Africa. The Nile River is joined by other streams that rise in Ethiopia and East Africa. This giant river flows northward through Egypt until it reaches the Mediterranean Sea, over 4,000 miles from its source! The river brings both water and rich soils to the people of the Nile Valley. Without the Nile, few people could live in Egypt. Beyond the waters of the Nile there is desert. Thus you can see that Egypt is truly the "Gift of the Nile."

8. While most of the Middle East and North Africa is hot and dry, the lands along the Mediterranean Sea have a more pleasant climate. This is the Mediterranean climate that we found in California and southern Europe. The summers are long, hot and dry; the winters are mild and moist. Because there is more rainfall, more crops can be grown. Olives, fruits and grapes are raised on the hillsides of the coastal lands. This area has a mild climate because of the surrounding mountains, the warm Mediterranean waters and the hot winds that blow in from the desert.

UNDERSTANDING CHAPTER 2

1. Which questions are answered in this chapter?
   a. Why are the rivers of the region important?
   b. Why is the region largely a desert?
   c. How do people live in the desert?
2. A good title for *paragraph 2* would be:
   a. Hot and Cold Regions.
   b. Clearing Up Some Ideas About Deserts.
   c. Traveling in the Sand.
3. The largest desert in the world is the:
   a. Atacama.   b. Gobi.   c. Sahara.
4. The Nile River flows in which direction?
   a. South.   b. North.   c. East.
5. Mountains are important in the Middle East because they:
   a. are the source of rivers.
   b. are rich in minerals.
   c. block the cold winds.
6. More crops can be grown along the coast of the Mediterranean Sea because:
   a. there is greater rainfall.
   b. the dry winds from the desert pick up moisture over the Mediterranean Sea.
   c. some of the world's richest soils are found there.
7. An *oasis* is a:
   a. mountain spot where water is collected.
   b. place where rivers flow into the sea.
   c. place in the desert where water can be found.
8. "Rivers *parallel* each other." This statement means that the rivers:
   a. touch each other.
   b. flow next to each other for a long distance.
   c. rise in the same mountains.

Map Study

Map #38—Land Forms of the Middle East and North Africa

Study this map and the map on page 348. Then tell whether these statements are *true* or *false*. Be able to explain your answers.

1. Much of the desert of North Africa may be called plains.
2. Bordering the Mediterranean Sea throughout the region is a low coastal plain.
3. Mountains guard the western end of the Mediterranean Sea.
4. The Red Sea lies in the area of a plateau.
5. Highlands are found even in desert areas.
6. There is little lowland in the area known as the Middle East.

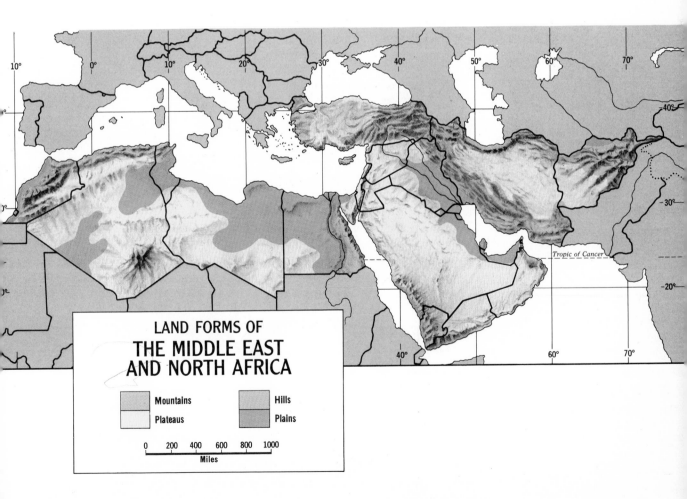

**LAND FORMS OF
THE MIDDLE EAST
AND NORTH AFRICA**

Mountains	Hills
Plateaus	Plains

0   200   400   600   800   1000
Miles

Map #39—Climates of the Middle East and North Africa

Agree or Disagree   Study this map and the map on page 348. Then decide whether or not each of the statements below agrees with the information on the map. If the answer is *disagree*, explain why.

1. The small number of climatic regions here is caused partly by a very narrow range of latitude.
2. Only North Africa has a Mediterranean climate.
3. The desert is the largest climatic region in the Middle East and North Africa.
4. All three climatic regions are found in both the Middle East and North Africa.
5. All of the climates of the region are climates of the low latitudes.
6. No part of this region receives heavy rainfall.
7. If it were not for the Red Sea, the desert would continue unbroken from Africa to Asia.
8. The desert borders the Nile River only on the western side.

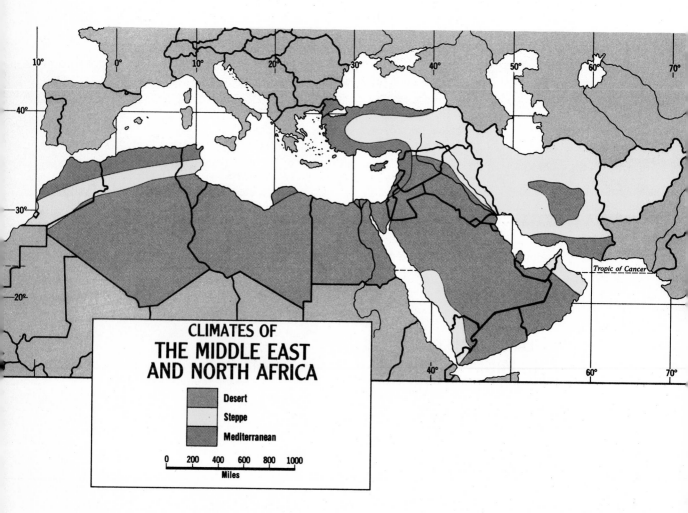

CLIMATES OF
**THE MIDDLE EAST
AND NORTH AFRICA**

Desert
Steppe
Mediterranean

0   200   400   600   800   1000
Miles

SUMMING UP   Tell whether these statements are true or false. The underlined words make the statements true or false. If a statement is false, what word or words would you place in it to make it true?

1. The Sahara is located in <u>northern</u> Africa.
2. The Tigris and Euphrates Rivers flow through <u>Iraq</u>.
3. <u>Potatoes</u> are a major crop near the Mediterranean Sea.
4. Egypt has fertile soil because of the <u>Nile River</u>.
5. There are <u>two</u> great river systems in <u>this</u> region.
6. On the desert, groups of people have gathered to live near the <u>tin mines</u>.
7. The Nile River flows into the <u>Persian Gulf</u>.
8. Some of the highest mountains in <u>this</u> region are found in <u>Egypt</u>.

FOLLOW UP   *Making Inferences*   In our reading, many facts are given to us. From these facts we can draw conclusions. The following are some conclusions or inferences that you might make after reading Chapters 1 and 2. Tell whether these conclusions are correct or incorrect. Give reasons for your answers.

1. In the United States, farmers can grow many kinds of crops that farmers of North Africa and the Middle East cannot grow.
2. Because water is so scarce, much of the available water will be used to supply power for factories.
3. The largest number of people live near rivers.
4. In order to develop its resources, this region will need the help of other countries.
5. European nations have little interest in the problems of the people of the Middle East.
6. Corn, potatoes and pineapples would be an important part of the diet of the people of this region.
7. Irrigation is necessary if the farmers of the Middle East are to grow enough food to supply the needs of the people.
8. Lumbering must be an important industry in North Africa.

3 WHERE CIVILIZATION BEGAN

Reading For A Purpose: How has this region contributed to a changing world?

1. This is a region with a very long history. Many of the farm animals we now use—oxen, sheep, goats, pigs and dogs—were first tamed by the early hunters and farmers of the Middle East. They also tamed wild horses and camels and used these animals to cross the desert. They knew where to find water in the desert and how to grow crops on the oases. Some of the crops that first came from this part of the world are rye, wheat, barley and beans. The region also gave us figs and dates.

2. Farmers settled early in the great river valleys of North Africa and the Middle East. They noticed that the rivers flooded the land every year at a certain time. They learned how to dam the water when it flooded and how to let it out when they needed it. They made up rules for the use of the water. Before long, they had the first government in which laws were being enforced. The first civilizations we know of began in the river valleys of the Nile and the Tigris and Euphrates.

3. Babylonia was one of the great civilizations along the Tigris-Euphrates valley. The people of Babylonia and Egypt learned how to grow crops and irrigate their farm lands. They lived in cities. Both had a form of picture writing. The Egyptians wrote on the treated leaves of the *papyrus* plant. (We get our word *paper* from *papyrus*.) The Egyptian writing was called *hieroglyphics*. The Babylonians used a chisel to "write" on clay tablets. The Egyptians built huge tombs, burial places for their rulers. These were called *pyramids*. The Babylonians built great temples. The Egyptians used a calendar of 365 days. The people around the Ti-

gris and Euphrates Rivers were the first to count in units of sixty. From them comes our method of counting sixty seconds in one minute and sixty minutes in one hour.

4. The Jews also contributed to the civilizations of the Middle East. The Jewish people lived in Palestine, much of which is now called Israel. Their religion taught for the first time the belief in one God. This is called *monotheism.* The history of the Jewish people and their religious beliefs are written in the world's most famous book, the Bible.

5. The Middle East was ruled at different

The Rosetta Stone. This slab has enabled people to figure out early Egyptian writing (hieroglyphics). The message on the stone is written in three different languages. The writing at the top is hieroglyphics.

Many visitors to Egypt travel by camel to see the great pyramids at nearby Giza. Camels are used for transportation in many desert countries. What makes these animals particularly well suited to desert travel?

times by the Persians, the Greeks and the Romans. While the little land of Palestine was under Roman rule, a new religion, Christianity, began. Its founder, Jesus, lived and taught in this land. He taught that men should be brothers. His followers spread his teachings, Christianity, to all parts of the world.

6. About 570 years after Jesus, a man named Mohammed was born at Mecca in Arabia. As a young man, he was a trader or merchant. Later he came to believe that he was a prophet or messenger of God. He taught a new religion that he called Islam. Mohammed gradually *converted* the tribesmen of Arabia and united them. Inspired by their new faith, the Moslems (followers of Islam) began to spread eastward and westward, overrunning many lands.

7. Within 200 years, the Moslems controlled a vast area extending from Spain across North Africa to India. The Arab lands became centers of a great civilization. In time, most of the people of these lands became followers of Mohammed and used the language of the Arabs. Arab traders carried the goods and ideas of the Far East throughout their lands into Europe. They became the "middle men" between the civilization of the Far East and the civilization of Europe. Arabic words such as *soda, alcohol, coffee, algebra* and *magazine* became part of our language. Near the end of the 8th century, the Arab empire began to weaken. First it was conquered by the Turks (who became Moslems themselves). About 500 years later, Mon-

gol tribes from Central Asia invaded Arab lands and destroyed many cities. By 1500, the people of Europe had found an all-water route to the riches of the Far East and could bypass the overland routes controlled by the Arabs. Therefore, the Arab traders were no longer so important as they once were.

8. Europe became very much interested in North Africa and the Middle East in the middle of the 19th century. A French engineer, Ferdinand de Lesseps, came to the East with the dream of building a waterway through the desert. His Suez Canal greatly shortened the distance between Europe and the Far East. The British soon gained control of the canal. Other European nations began to take parts of the empire that had conquered the Arabs. France took Algeria in 1830 and Tunis in 1881. Italy obtained Libya after a war with Turkey in 1912.

9. During World War I, the Arabs helped Great Britain and the Allies. When the Allies won, the Arabs hoped that their lands would be made free. However, after the war the League of Nations was formed. The League gave some of the Arab lands to the Allies, who were to govern them until the Arabs were ready for self-government. These Arab territories were called *mandates.* Among the governing nations, France was given Syria and Lebanon. Great Britain became the protector of Iraq, Palestine and Jordan. Egypt did become free in 1923.

10. The fact that some of their lands were held by nations of Europe made the Arabs want their freedom even more. This dislike of foreign nations has carried over to the present day. It is true that France and Great Britain built dams and railroads, schools and hospitals in the lands they held. It is also true that they probably knew more about good government than the Arabs. But this did not change the desire of Arab people to govern themselves. During World War II, Syria and Lebanon gained their independence. Since that war, independence has been granted to Jordan, Libya, Morocco, Tunisia, Algeria and Israel.

UNDERSTANDING CHAPTER 3

1. Which questions are answered in this chapter?
   a. How did Islam begin?
   b. How did world wars change this region?
   c. How was the Suez Canal built?
2. The main idea of *paragraph 3* is that:
   a. Egyptians and Babylonians built great temples.
   b. ancient Egyptians lived in cities.
   c. ancient people of the Middle East were highly civilized.
3. *Both* of the old civilizations along the Nile and Tigris-Euphrates Rivers had:
   a. a system of writing.
   b. the Christian religion.
   c. great trade with the countries of Western Europe.
4. The Arab civilizations have been important in world history because:
   a. they started the belief in one God.
   b. Arab traders brought goods and ideas from East to West.
   c. they first developed a system of reading and writing.
5. The contributions of the old civilizations of the Middle East include all of these EXCEPT the:
   a. use of gunpowder and printing thousands of years ago.
   b. beginning of cities and governments.
   c. discovery of methods to irrigate land.
6. A *monotheist* believes in:
   a. one God.   b. no gods.   c. many gods.
7. "Many Arabs were *converted* to Islam." The best meaning for *converted* is:
   a. "changed their beliefs."
   b. "opposed something new."
   c. "spoke roughly about."
8. The best meaning for *mandate* in paragraph 9 is:
   a. "order given by a ruler."
   b. "backward territory."
   c. "lands taken care of by other nations."

DEVELOPING IDEAS AND SKILLS

Picture Symbols
These pictures should help you to recall parts of the chapter you have read. What is the main idea of each picture?

In each group are three events in the history of the Middle East and North Africa. Arrange the events in each group *in the order in which they took place.*

1. Beginning Judaism.
   Founding of Islam.
   Beginning of Christianity.
2. Building the Suez Canal.
   Freedom for Egypt.
   End of World War I.
3. Algeria wins freedom.
   End of World War II.
   Some Arab countries were made mandates.
4. Mohammed born in Mecca.
   Arab trade with Europe important.
   Islam spread over parts of Africa and Asia.

The history of North Africa and the Middle East is filled with so many interesting events and people that you will want to know more about it. Special reports may be made on any of the following:

1. How have ancient ruins given us a knowledge of life in: Egypt, Babylonia, Israel?
2. The contributions of these civilizations include great buildings and statues. Find out about the: pyramids, sphinx, Hanging Gardens of Babylon.
3. The building of the Suez Canal and the traffic through the canal make a great story. Find out what you can about this great waterway and report to the class.
4. The religious leaders of this region have been very important in its history. Report to the class on one of them. You will also be interested in such political leaders as: Lawrence of Arabia, David Ben-Gurion, Kemal Ataturk, Gamal Abdel Nasser.

4 HOW THE PEOPLE LIVE

Reading For A Purpose: Who are the people of the dry lands?

1. About 202 million people live in the Middle East and North Africa. Except for those in Israel and Lebanon, most are Moslems. However, they do not all speak the same language. In Arabia, Syria, Lebanon, Jordan, Iraq, parts of Egypt and most of North Africa the people speak Arabic. In Turkey and Iran, other languages are spoken. In parts of North Africa, there are people who have come from Europe. As a result, European languages and customs may be found in this area. (Remember, the nations of North Africa were once European colonies.)

2. The people are scattered unevenly throughout the Middle East and North Africa because of the lack of water. Where there is water, there are people. Many live along the shores of the great rivers, the Nile and the Tigris-Euphrates. (For example, nearly all of Egypt's 35 million people are crowded around the Nile River.) Others live near the borders of the seas or at the foot of mountains where there is more rainfall. The farmers in these mountain areas dig tunnels to catch the streams. These tunnels carry water into the desert. Along the tunnels are farm villages that depend on this method of getting water.

3. Finally, other farmers live near a well or spring that will give them the water they need for growing crops. Such a green place in the middle of the desert is called an oasis. In the oasis is a farm village. The fields are planted for grains. Date palms also grow. There is even grass for sheep and goats.

Fresh water from drilled wells pours into an irrigation project in Saudi Arabia. Why is irrigation necessary for farming in desert areas?

4. About seventy-five per cent of the people in the Middle East are peasants who till the soil. About twenty per cent are city dwellers, and the rest are nomads who wander about the desert. The farmer, the townsman and the nomad live very different lives. Few farmers own their own land. The landowner supplies them with water, farm tools and work animals. In return for his work on the land, the farmer keeps a small part of the crop. Many farmers are in poor health and cannot read or write.

5. The second largest group of people live in towns and cities. These cities are different from the small villages of the farmer. Arab cities are a fascinating mixture of the old and the new. There are new buildings and "old quarters" with narrow streets and crowded, dingy houses. Automobiles and camels fill the streets. Modern Western dress is seen along with the long, flowing cotton robes that Middle Easterners have worn for thousands of years. There are modern schools and hospitals, but many of the women still wear veils to cover their faces. There are television antennas, radio stations and newspapers. Some of the largest and most important cities are: Cairo and Alexandria, Egypt; Tehran, Iran; Istanbul, Turkey; Tel Aviv and Haifa, Israel; Damascus, Syria and Baghdad, Iraq.

6. The towns and cities are the homes of factory workers, government officials, doctors, merchants and craftsmen. The factory workers are often farmers who have moved to the cities in search of a better life. The craftsmen are the people with special skills who make all kinds of beautiful and useful things. They turn cotton into cloth, wool into rugs, skins into leather and silver into jewelry. Their articles are sold by merchants in the market place, called the *bazaar*. The bazaar is the meeting place where the goods are sold or exchanged with the oasis farmer and other workers. It is also the place where ideas from the outside world reach the Moslem world.

7. Although many people think of Arabs only as nomads who live in the desert, they are the smallest group of people in the region. The

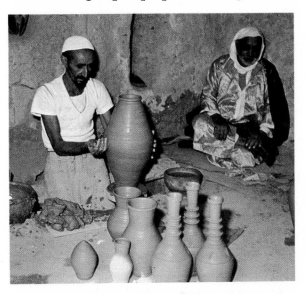

An Arab pottery maker. Why may a skilled craftsman take greater pride in his work than a factory worker may take in the goods which he helps produce?

Tel Aviv means "Hill of Spring." This bustling city was built on sand dunes along the sea. As can be seen by this aerial shot, Tel Aviv appears much like a modern western city.

nomad tribes are always traveling over deserts and dry grass lands in search of food for their sheep, goats and camels. They live in tents of tanned skins or cloth. They carry all their belongings with them. The camel is their chief means of transportation and provides many other things as well. Milk from goats, sheep and camels is the most important food of the nomads. They weave the hair of camels into robes and make their hides into sandals. The nomads exchange their wool and camel's hair for grain, rice, tea and other crops raised by the farmers.

1. Which questions are answered in this chapter?
   a. How do the Arab people make a living?
   b. How do the nomads use their animals?
   c. Who are the rulers of the Arab countries?
2. A good title for *paragraphs 5 and 6* would be:
   a. The Bazaar—Meeting Place of the World.
   b. Booming Factories of the Middle East.
   c. The Cities—Where the Old Meets the New.
3. Most of the people of this region are:
   a. farmers.   b. city dwellers.   c. nomads.
4. The people get most of their water from:
   a. rainfall.   b. the ocean.   c. springs and wells.
5. Some people have moved to the cities to:
   a. learn about the modern world.
   b. find work in factories and mills.
   c. be near the oil fields.
6. Nomads are always moving because they are:
   a. looking for minerals.
   b. warlike people.
   c. looking for water and pasture.
7. *Craftsmen* earn a living through:
   a. making goods by hand.
   b. working in the oil fields.
   c. building irrigation ditches.
8. "The lady purchased some pots at the *bazaar*." A *bazaar* is a place where:
   a. clothes are washed.
   b. goods are bought and sold.
   c. movies are shown.

DEVELOPING IDEAS AND SKILLS

Pictograph #13—Population, Area and Standard of Living of the Middle East and North Africa

Study the pictograph on page 363. Then answer these questions.
1. Is the standard of living of this region high or low compared with that of the United States?
2. Is the region more or less crowded than the United States?
3. Are the people of this region literate compared with the people of the United States?
4. What is the average life expectancy of people in this region?
5. What facts tell you the standard of living of the people of the region?
6. How does this region compare with the United States in size?

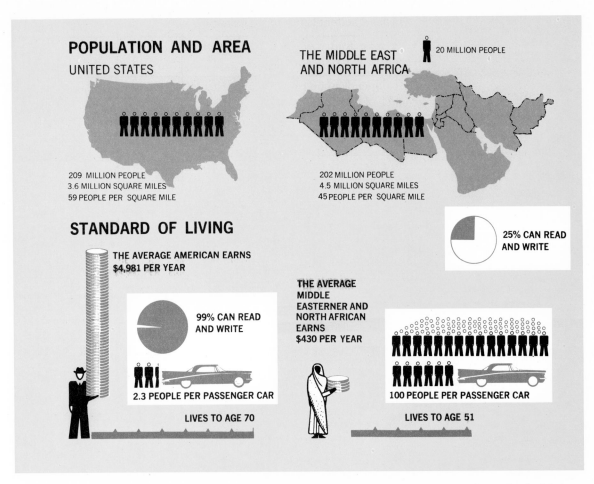

POPULATION AND AREA

UNITED STATES

209 MILLION PEOPLE
3.6 MILLION SQUARE MILES
59 PEOPLE PER SQUARE MILE

THE MIDDLE EAST AND NORTH AFRICA

20 MILLION PEOPLE

202 MILLION PEOPLE
4.5 MILLION SQUARE MILES
45 PEOPLE PER SQUARE MILE

STANDARD OF LIVING

THE AVERAGE AMERICAN EARNS $4,981 PER YEAR

99% CAN READ AND WRITE

2.3 PEOPLE PER PASSENGER CAR

LIVES TO AGE 70

25% CAN READ AND WRITE

THE AVERAGE MIDDLE EASTERNER AND NORTH AFRICAN EARNS $430 PER YEAR

100 PEOPLE PER PASSENGER CAR

LIVES TO AGE 51

Pictograph #13—Population, Area and Standard of Living of the Middle East and North Africa

SUMMING UP

Complete this chart in your notebook. Place a check (√) in the column to which each statement applies. (A statement may apply to more than one column.)

	FARMER	NOMAD	CITY DWELLER
1. His home is a tent.			
2. He lives in the oasis.			
3. He visits the bazaar.			
4. People are organized into tribes.			
5. Herding is his chief occupation.			
6. Land and water are his wealth.			

7. He has a better chance for schooling.			
8. He may trade, work for the government or weave beautiful rugs.			
9. He depends upon camels and horses for much of what he needs.			
10. He may wear the Western style of dress.			
11. His chief work is raising crops.			
12. The greatest number cannot read or write.			
13. He is probably a Moslem.			
14. He may speak a European language.			

FOLLOW UP

Cairo is the largest city in Africa and one of the oldest cities in the world. In the following selection, you will read how one writer views Cairo as being three cities in one.

Three Cities In One

[The old Cairo of 1,000 years ago] is not the industrial part of the city. It is simply an exciting place of unorganized manufacture. But nothing can hide the fact that it is a large slum. You sometimes have to tear your eyes away from the exciting streets to look up at the awful old houses. Sometimes five people live in one tiny room in these tenements. Some people sleep and eat under stairways or in tin shacks on the roofs. Or they bed down on a balcony among the chickens and the goats.

Hygiene just cannot be found. Almost every man, woman and child living here suffers from some sort of unpleasant disease which they pass on to each other. Not many here have enough to eat. Few have more than one change of clothing. Not many adults can read or write.

In building the New Cairo, the overcrowding of living space is not the only problem. Getting people in and out of the city may cause greater trouble. Already, at noon every day, Cairo's buses are jammed with people going home for lunch and to their siestas (rest), hanging on to the open doors like bees on a hive. I have seen men riding by simply hanging on the shoulders of others. A young woman typist hoping to get on one of these buses, simply takes a look at the mess and gives up. An older woman doesn't even look at it. . . . On the whole, the public crush of Cairo at noon is probably not much worse than it is in most cities at peak hours these days. But there is much more noise, more sport, more contest, more laughter, and a lot more death.

Most of Cairo's other problems are copies of those facing most world capitals. Sometimes standing in the street and looking at the sunburned skyscrapers, one longs for a sign that will make it clear that this is Cairo, not Rome or Paris or Dallas. There is, in fact, one special thing about Cairo that does make it different. But, you can't see it from ground level.

On the roofs of Cairo there is a third city—a town of modern roof dwellers. Tens of thousands of people live on Cairo's rooftops. In the days when you could fly a small plane over Cairo, you could clearly see its two levels of life. One is on the ground, and one is in the air ... I have seen on a roof opposite the Continental Hotel, someone cooking under a bamboo shelter, village women washing clothes, naked children, a goat or two and a mangy dog. These rooftop slums are mostly servants' quarters but in the old city, they are the result of overcrowding.

Twenty years ago, Cairo was a very personal city. Everyone living in it seemed to really belong there. But, now it has grown so big that people do not make one feel that this Cairo is theirs. It is still a children's city. One sees them on the street and they are among Cairo's busiest and most responsible working citizens. Very few of them beg anymore and now they must all go to school (although many do not). There are laws against children working, but they do work. You can see them in laundries almost sitting on the hot irons they are pressing shirts with. You might also see a boy of ten carrying a tin tray of coffees from a sidewalk cafe to a nearby shop. Or there may be a twelve-year-old mechanic lying along the fender of a car, working on it with a handful of tools. Not all these child occupations are dying out as labor laws are more strictly enforced.

Adapted from *Cairo: Biography of a City* by James Aldridge, by permission of Little, Brown and Co. Copyright © 1969 by James Aldridge.

1. What are the three cities of Cairo described by the writer?
2. From this article, what do you know about the standard of living in the old city? The new city?
3. In what ways is Cairo similar to cities you know in Anglo-America? How is it different?
4. Why do you think the laws against children working are not strictly enforced?

5 ISLAM–RELIGION OF THE PEOPLE

Reading For A Purpose: How does the Moslem religion unite the people of the Middle East?

1. In the Middle East and North Africa, the Moslem religion is an important part of the life of the people. Except in Israel, Turkey and Lebanon, most people in this region are Moslems—followers of Mohammed—and speak Arabic. (It is a mistake to believe that all Arabs are Moslems. Lebanon is an Arab-speaking country, but half its people are Christians. In Turkey, the people do not speak Arabic, but most of them are Moslems). Since the Moslem religion affects almost everything the people do, we should know something about it.

2. The Moslem religion was founded by Mohammed early in the 7th century. Mohammed lived in Mecca, Arabia, a city that is holy for Moslems all over the world. Mohammed called his religion Islam. Islam means "surrender to the will of God." Those who follow Mo-

hammed's religion are called Moslems, or "surrendered ones." It is not correct to call them Mohammedans, for Mohammed did not put himself before his people as God. He said that he was the prophet or messenger from God.

3. Mohammed taught that there was only one God. He called that God "Allah." There could be no images or idols of Allah. Mohammed set up some rules that all Moslems had to follow, and that they still follow today. First, all Moslems believe in one God, Allah. Second, each Moslem must pray five times a day. (When Moslems pray, they turn toward Mecca, the holy city.) Third, Moslems are expected to fast (go without food) from sunrise to sunset during the holy month of Ramadan. Fourth, they are required to give help to the needy and poor of the community.

4. Finally, each member of the Moslem faith must make a trip to the sacred mosque, or temple of worship, at Mecca. This religious trip is called a pilgrimage. This pilgrimage should be made once during the life of each Moslem. Every year, thousands of Moslems from different parts of the world travel to Mecca to fulfill this duty.

5. After his death, Mohammed's followers put his words and beliefs into a book called the Koran. This holy book is considered by Moslems to be the word of God. It is the book used by most Moslem children in learning to read.

6. Moslems believe that theirs is the only true religion. Each Moslem city has a mosque or temple of worship. Every morning the Moslem is awakened by a call to prayer from the mosque. Every Friday, the faithful Moslem goes to the mosque and listens to a reading from the Koran. There are no idols or images in the mosque, and no one may enter who is not a Moslem. The religious beliefs that Moslems share have brought them close together. These beliefs have been carried over into their day-to-day living and into their forms of government. For example, shopkeepers must close down during prayer time.

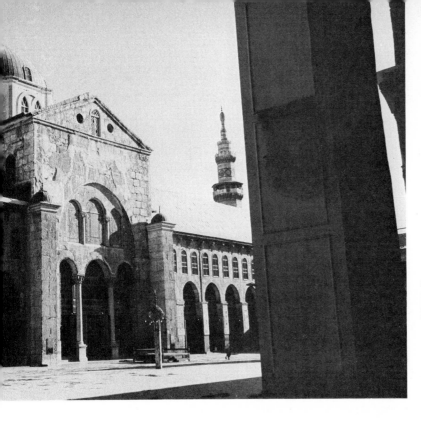

A mosque in Damascus, Syria. University students study here between hours of prayer.

UNDERSTANDING CHAPTER 5

1. Which questions are answered in this chapter?
   a. How does Islam differ from other religions?
   b. What is a mosque?
   c. What is the meaning of "Islam"?
2. The main idea of this chapter describes the:
   a. Moslem religion.   b. duties of Moslems.   c. life of Mohammed.
3. The holy city of the Moslems is:
   a. Rome.   b. Jerusalem.   c. Mecca.
4. Mohammed lived in:
   a. Egypt.   b. Arabia.   c. Turkey
5. The Moslem religion is important in the Middle East because it:
   a. affects the actions of the people in all walks of life.
   b. forces members to travel great distances.
   c. is the religion of all Arabs.
6. Islam, Judaism and Christianity are alike in that they:
   a. have many statues and holy pictures.
   b. teach belief in one God.
   c. require their members to make a pilgrimage to a holy city.
7. "The people visited a *mosque* to pray." A *mosque* is like:
   a. a church.   b. a school.   c. an office.
8. "The old man went on a *pilgrimage* to see the Holy Land." A *pilgrimage* is a trip taken for:
   a. health.   b. study.   c. religious reasons.

Picture Symbols

These pictures should help you to recall parts of the chapter you have read. What is the main idea of each picture?

SUMMING UP   Complete the following chart in your notebook.

	JUDAISM	ISLAM	CHRISTIANITY
1. Founder			
2. Holy Book			
3. Name of Place of Worship			
4. Idea of God			
5. Day of the Week for Special Worship			

6 FARMERS AND WANDERERS

Reading For A Purpose: How do the village farmer and desert nomad meet their needs?

Farmers in the Middle East. Why are many Arab farmers barely able to raise enough to feed their families?

1. Three out of four people in the Middle East and North Africa are small farmers. They are often called *fellahin*, an Arabic word that means "peasants." Most of the farmers live in villages. Where there is plenty of water (as in the Nile Valley), the villages are close together. Most villages are small—about ten to fifty families. The fields lie outside the villages.

2. The Middle Eastern peasant is a subsistence farmer. He turns his soil with a wooden plow drawn by a buffalo or an ox. He harvests his crops with a hand sickle. He also threshes his grain by hand or uses his animals to trample it. Because of poor soil and crude tools, the farmer raises barely enough food to feed his family. He owns little clothing and has few comforts. Because wood is scarce, his house has wood only for door frames or windows, if at all. The house has little furniture. The family usually eats and sleeps on mats and rugs on a hard dirt floor.

3. Most fellahin are in debt. Nearly all the land in an Arab village belongs to a rich landowner, who usually lives in the city. The landowner also owns the water the villagers use. In return for the use of the land, water, seed and sometimes fertilizer, the village farmer must turn over a sizeable part of his crops to the landlord. There have been promises of land reform in some countries, but changes are slow in coming.

4. Where crops are raised for cash, the most important one is cotton, which is grown in the irrigated fields of the Nile Valley. The waters of the Nile River and the warm climate have made Egypt a leading cotton producer.

5. Poverty causes many problems in the villages. Only a few boys and girls learn to read and write. There are not enough teachers or schools. Only a few villages can afford pure drinking water. The few sources of water are used by the women of the village not only for cooking and drinking, but also for bathing and washing clothes. Farmers throw their garbage into the irrigation ditches. As a result, villagers are often sick. Many are maimed for life by serious diseases.

6. In Israel, farming is different. Most Israeli farmers use modern machines and up-to-date farming methods. As in the rest of the Middle East, many Israeli farmers live in villages. But

Irrigated farmland in the Galilee region of Israel. How is the system of farming in Israel different from that in the rest of the Middle East?

the land is owned by the villagers rather than by wealthy landowners. The people work together and share in the goods and services of the community. The community is called a *kibbutz* or cooperative farm.

7. Beyond the village fields and the oasis farms of North Africa and the Middle East are the dry, lonely lands of the desert. The people of the desert are nomads, or wanderers. They live in tribes that roam over the dry lands in search of water and pasture for their herds of sheep, goats and camels. Nomads are expert at finding water. The nomad tribesmen make up about 5 per cent of the population of this dry region.

8. One kind of nomadic tribe lives in and around the mountains. In the winter, their herds graze in the valleys. In the summer, they are moved to pastures in the mountains. A second group of nomads lives in the desert. They move every few days or weeks in search of grass and water. These desert nomads are called *Bedouins*. The Bedouin tribes often split into smaller groups because desert pastures are often too small to feed all their animals. When water is found, the group settles down for a short time to enjoy its new-found riches.

9. Because he is always on the move, the nomad has few goods besides his cooking pots, his loose, flowing clothes, his rugs and blan-

Bedouin tribesmen and their animals camp near a well in the desert. What is life like for the desert nomads?

kets. He lives in a tent. He sleeps and eats on rugs. When the tribe is ready to move, the tents are folded up and packed on the camels along with other belongings.

10. The animals—sheep, goats and camels—provide the nomad with all he needs. Goat's milk and cheese are his main foods. His blankets, his tent and most of his clothes are woven from goat or camel hair. Leather from the hides of the animals is used to make baskets and sandals. Whatever the animals do not supply, the nomad buys when he reaches an oasis. He may also have horses, which are useful for faster travel. His wealth is judged by the number of camels and horses he owns.

11. During the hot summer months, when his desert wells are dry, the Bedouin goes to an oasis. Here he exchanges his camels, wool and rugs for dates or flour raised by the farmer. He buys other goods he needs—knives, tea, clothing, sugar and coffee.

12. The herders of the desert were once the rulers of the Middle East. They crossed and recrossed borders as they pleased. They were able to conquer oasis farmers because they could attack swiftly on their horses and camels. The farmers were forced to give their crops to the desert nomads. Today, only a few tribes remain in the desert. Many of the tribal rulers (*sheiks*) are now large landowners.

UNDERSTANDING CHAPTER 6

1. Which questions are answered in this chapter?
   a. Why is the Arab farmer poor?
   b. Why does the nomad live in a tent?
   c. Why is the camel important to the nomad?
2. The main idea of *paragraph 9* is that:
   a. the tent is the home of the Bedouin.
   b. camels are the most important possessions of Bedouins.
   c. the need for moving from place to place decides how the nomad lives.
3. Most of the farmers in North Africa and the Middle East:
   a. own their farms.
   b. rent their farms.
   c. work on government-owned farms.
4. Cotton is grown in the Nile Valley because:
   a. the climate of Egypt is different from the rest of the Middle East.
   b. a warm climate and irrigated land are best for growing cotton.
   c. farmers in Egypt are richer than farmers in the rest of the region.
5. Farmers are poor in the Arab world for all of these reasons EXCEPT:
   a. farmlands are too small for much use of machinery.
   b. there is little demand for fine cotton.
   c. few farmers own their land.
6. A rich Bedouin owns:
   a. camels and horses.
   b. oil fields.
   c. water rights and land.

Photograph Study
This photograph should help you to recall parts of the chapter you have just read. What is the main idea of the photograph?

SUMMING UP

A. *Which Does Not Belong?*
Choose the item that does not belong with the others in each group.
1. *Crops grown on an oasis*—dates, olives, sugar cane.
2. *Animals of the nomad*—goats, horses, chickens.
3. *Farm tools*—sickle, thresher, wooden plow.
4. *Items traded*—camels, tractors, wool.
5. *Work*—farming, herding, lumbering.
6. *Farming in Israel*—large landowners, cooperative farms, use of machines.
7. *Belongings of the nomad*—camels, land, skins.

B. *Making Comparisons*   Make a chart in your notebook. Compare the Arab village farmer with the American corn-belt or wheat farmer. Consider land ownership, tools used, use of crops, farm animals, size of farm, climate and home life.

FOLLOW UP

The following is a description of village life in the Middle East.

Village Life In Iran

The countless farming villages of Iran are found wherever there is water for drinking purposes and irrigation ... and where the soil is suitable for growing crops. The traveler along the main roads will see many such villages, but the largest number are hidden away in mountain valleys. He will also see the ruins of villages that farmers deserted.

Most farmers live in crowded settlements and work in fields at a distance from the village. Within each village is a network of narrow lanes and one straight main street along a water channel. Without this water, there can be no village life. At one end of the village is the village threshing floor.

The narrow lanes are bordered by high mud walls, in which double doors lead into the courtyard of each house. The houses face the south so that the winter sun warms the main rooms directly. A porch across the front of the house gives shade all day during the hot months.

Rugs cover the floor. Quilts, mattresses and pillows are neatly piled near the wall. An oil lamp stands close by. There is a mirror on the wall, and usually a few religious pictures from magazines.

Many villages have a bath. The building has a series of rooms, mostly underground. One man is put in charge. He must keep the bath clean and see that the steaming water is ready for use a number of hours each week. The villagers can bathe as often as they want, and everyone helps to support the bath attendant by giving him wheat, straw, fuel and fruit.

Stores and schools are much less common than baths and mills. There may be one very small shop in every seven or eight villages. A few things are for sale, chiefly sugar, tea, tobacco, rice, spices, threads, needles, nails, salt, dyes, cotton goods, matches, kerosene, lamp chimneys. There are few public schools in the villages and for good reasons. First, the average family is small. Children must help in the fields. The work cannot be done without them. Second, what is taught in the schools has little meaning in everyday life.

The villagers keep their own sheep and goats. The animals give milk, mutton, cheese and some butter. However, bread or rice are the chief foods. Eggs, chickens, onions, melons, fruits, nuts and tea round out the simple diet.

The villagers have little contact with the outside world. The men may travel to larger towns with donkey-loads of straw, fuel, fruit and vegetables. Sometimes families go to town to shop in the markets, but not often. In village life, there is little leisure except in the winter months. Talk is the chief form of relaxation.

Adapted from *Iran Past and Present* by Donald L. Wilber, 6th revised edition. (Copyright © 1967 by Princeton University Press.) Reprinted by permission of Princeton University Press.

1. Why are many villages found in mountain valleys?
2. In what ways do villagers cooperate with one another?
3. What can we figure out about Iran's climate?
4. In what ways is the diet of the village farmer similar to that of the desert nomad? How is it different?
5. Few villagers read newspapers. Why do you think this is so?

7 OIL IS KING

Reading For A Purpose: Why is oil so important in North Africa and the Middle East?

Oil field in Libya. The Middle East and North Africa are rich in oil. Why is oil from these areas important to nations like the United States and the Soviet Union?

1. At one time it was thought that the deserts of the Middle East were almost worthless. But with the discovery of oil under the desert sands, this region has become one of the most important in the world. In the Middle East are almost two-thirds of the world's entire oil reserves! Most of the oil comes from the countries around the Persian Gulf. Some oil is also found in Egypt, Israel, Turkey and in the Sahara region of Algeria and Libya. There are those who believe that the Sahara may hide one of the world's largest areas of oil.

2. Most of the oil wells in the Middle East are owned by oil companies from Europe or the United States. In return for working the oil fields, these companies share their profits with the governments of the Middle East. The governments of these Middle Eastern countries, then, control much of the world's supply of oil. Four countries—Saudi Arabia, Iran, Iraq and Kuwait—produce 95 per cent of the oil from the Middle East. Kuwait, on the Arabian peninsula, is no larger than the state of Connecticut. It has about the same population as Richmond, Virginia, or Des Moines, Iowa. Yet this tiny state has about one-sixth of all the oil reserves in the world!

3. Oil must be *refined* before it can be used. Seven hundred gallons of water are needed to refine one barrel of oil. Since water is lacking in the Middle East, little of the oil is refined there, or used there. The oil is carried by pipelines to seaports along the Mediterranean Sea and the Persian Gulf. Every few miles along the lines there are pumps to keep the oil moving to the sea. Ocean-going ships called tank-

ers carry the oil from the Middle East to ports all over the world. Much of the oil goes to the nations of Western Europe and to the United States. It is used in many forms in homes, automobiles and factories.

4. Oil has brought about great changes in the Middle East. Oil profits have made some of the Middle Eastern rulers very rich. In some cases, the money has been used to build schools, hospitals and railroads and to increase the water supply. In other cases, the rulers have spent the money on themselves. The peasant who works his poor lands has gained little from the wealth brought by oil.

5. The oil companies have provided a large number of new jobs for the people of the Middle East. Men whose fathers were poor farmers or nomads now work in the oil fields. They live better lives. They have concrete houses instead of tents or mud huts. They make more money. Their children go to school and receive medical care. They can buy goods in supermarkets. There are electric power plants in the oil settlements. There are good roads across the desert. The ways of life in Europe and America

have come with the oil companies and have changed the lives of many people in the Middle East.

6. Except for oil, there are few mineral resources in this region. There is very little iron ore. Turkey alone has a useful supply of coal. Turkey also has some iron ore, copper and chromium. In the western part of North Africa there are rich deposits of phosphates, used in manufacturing fertilizer. Fuels and power resources are very small indeed. Because there are few trees, there is little wood.

7. There are some factories in North Africa and the Middle East. These make such items as clothing, flour and cement for new homes. Israel has a larger percentage of its people working in factories than any of the other nations. There are not enough factories in the rest of the region to meet the needs of the people. (Many of the goods of this region—leather products and rugs, for example—are made at home or in small shops. They are called *handicrafts*.) Most of these nations' leaders would like to have more factories. However, the change from workshops to factories is taking place slowly for several reasons. First, the countries of North Africa and the Middle East lack coal and iron. Second, most of the people

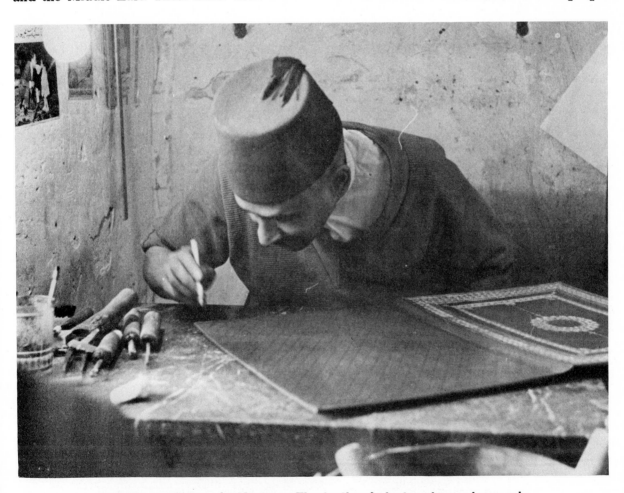

A leather craftsman in Morocco. The leather industry plays a large role in the Moroccan economy. The government has been trying to introduce modern methods to build this craft into an industry. Why are such efforts being made?

cannot read or write; they have not been trained to work with machines. Third, in the past, there was little money within the region to build factories. However, this situation is now changing. Fourth, many of the people are too poor to buy manufactured goods. Therefore, many products of the factories must be shipped to other parts of the world.

UNDERSTANDING CHAPTER 7

1. Which questions are answered in this chapter?
   a. Why is oil important in the Middle East?
   b. How are oil wells drilled?
   c. Why are there few factories in this region?
2. The main idea of *paragraphs 4 and 5* describes:
   a. the oil pipelines of North Africa and the Middle East.
   b. the little benefit that the common people have received from the riches in oil.
   c. how oil changed ways of life in this region.
3. Most of the oil fields have been developed by:
   a. foreign companies.   b. national governments.   c. fellahin.
4. Factories have become important in which nation?
   a. Israel.   b. Libya.   c. Saudi Arabia.
5. This region has been slow to develop industries because:
   a. the oil fields keep so many people busy.
   b. there are few educated people.
   c. trading with other nations is more important.
6. Little oil is refined in the Middle East because:
   a. there are few electric plants.
   b. the leaders of the governments are against it.
   c. refining oil requires a large amount of water.
7. *Tankers* used to carry oil from the Middle East travel by:
   a. land.   b. air.   c. sea.
8. *Phosphates* may be described as:
   a. minerals used in refining oil.
   b. minerals from which hard steel is made.
   c. salts used in making fertilizer.

DEVELOPING IDEAS AND SKILLS

Map Study

Map #40—Oil Fields and Oil Pipelines

Study the map on page 377. Then tell whether these statements are true or false.
1. The United States produces more oil than any other region in the world.
2. The Persian Gulf lies almost in the center of oil fields.
3. Most Middle Eastern oil is piped to the Red Sea for export.
4. Venezuela is one of the world leaders in oil production.
5. Among the other nations that produce oil, Egypt ranks high on the list.
6. Important pipelines run through Lebanon and Syria.
7. All Middle Eastern countries have rich oil reserves.
8. Most pipelines leading from the Persian Gulf area connect on their way to seaports.

9. Almost no oil is produced by countries bordering the Mediterranean Sea.
10. Iran, Iraq and Saudi Arabia are three of the biggest producers of oil in the Middle East.

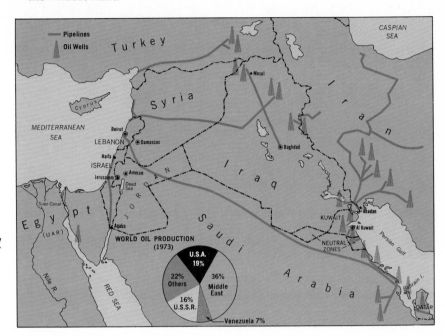

Map #40—Oil Fields and Oil Pipelines

SUMMING UP

Tell whether the following items refer to the United States, the Middle East, or both regions. If an item refers to the United States only, use the letters US; if the item refers to the Middle East only, use the letters ME; if the item refers to both regions, use the letter B.

1. Large amounts of oil are used within the region.
2. Much oil is exported.
3. Much oil is produced.
4. There are many large oil-refining plants.
5. Great pipelines carry oil to ports.
6. Tankers are used in shipping oil.
7. Many engineers from foreign countries help in the oil fields.
8. There is a large supply of coal along with oil.
9. Profits from oil make government leaders rich.
10. Much water is used in refining oil.

FOLLOW UP

Choose one or more of the following activities.
1. Report to the class on this subject: "How Oil Is Changing the Lives of People in North Africa and the Middle East."

2. Prepare a classroom debate on one of these topics:

RESOLVED: That Arab nations have too few resources ever to become leading nations of the world.

RESOLVED: That without foreign help, the Middle East would never produce much oil.

8 STAYING ALIVE

Reading For A Purpose: How are the people of this region facing their problems?

This Iranian farmer tills the soil in the way of his forefathers. Economic development plans aim to replace the old wooden plough and the two tired donkeys with modern agricultural equipment. In what ways can farmers such as this one benefit from such change?

1. Except for Israel, Turkey and Lebanon, the great majority of farmers in the Middle East are poor and are likely to remain that way. There are reasons why this is so. Egypt and Iran have made some attempts at land reform. But most farmers still do not own their own land. They must still give part of their crops to the large landowner for the use of his land and seed. Although the farmers work very hard, their crop yields are low. This is because the same crops are raised year after year. The soil wears out, since there is little money to buy fertilizer. Thus, the lack of land, small plots, poor soil and high rents keep most of the farmers in extreme poverty.

2. Besides these problems, the farmer of this region must always worry about his water supply. Important as oil is in the Middle East, water is still more important. Water is the most needed natural resource of the region. The future of the Middle East and North Africa depends upon the full use of the scarce water resources of the area.

3. The Aswan Dam on Egypt's Nile River was an early effort to make use of water in a desert land. This dam "saves" or holds back a part of the Nile's yearly flood. The water is then used for irrigation. The first Aswan Dam was built in 1902. The government of Egypt, with Russian aid, has since built a higher dam at Aswan. This dam holds back an even larger supply of water and creates new farmlands through irrigation. The water spilling over the huge dam also provides electric power for areas that never had it before. Using a different method to solve its problems, Kuwait has one of the world's largest plants for making fresh water by removing salt from sea water. A little more than three gallons of salt water can be converted into a gallon of fresh water. The Kuwait plant produces millions of gallons of fresh water daily.

4. Israel would also like to increase its water supply. Most of southern Israel is a desert. The Jordan River forms part of the boundary between Israel and Jordan. Under the Jordan River Plan, the Israelis hope to build dams and canals that will bring more water to their desert region. They wish to share this development with the Arab country of Jordan, but so far Jordan has refused to join them, or to agree to Israel's going ahead alone. The Israeli government has taken control of all water resources that are within the country. As a result of careful planning of wells and pipelines and strict control of all water resources, only a

small percentage of Israel's population does not have pure running water for at least part of each day.

5. Many of the people of North Africa and the Middle East are in poor health. Because the rivers and irrigation ditches are used for bathing and washing, pure drinking water is scarce. In the waters of irrigation canals are snails that carry tiny worms. These worms enter the skin of barefoot farmers and weaken their bodies. Such diseases as snail fever, trachoma, malaria, typhoid fever and hookworm are common in the farming villages. Most Arab countries are trying to solve the problem of poor health among their people. However, it is difficult to get the villagers to follow such simple health measures as wearing shoes, washing their hands before eating or boiling drinking water. Villagers feel that they have no money to buy shoes and that water is too scarce to be used only for washing.

6. Until the rising oil prices of recent years made some Arab governments very rich, lack of money presented many problems for these governments. Without money, the nations of

Laying pipes to bring the waters of the River Yarkon to the dry Negev Desert in Israel. Why is cooperation among nations in planning the use of water resources desirable?

Women from a Moroccan village do their laundry. What does this scene tell you about life in Morocco?

North Africa and the Middle East had to depend on the money of people of other countries to develop their resources. (The Soviet Union helped Egypt build the great Aswan Dam. Foreign money developed the oil fields at first.) Money is needed in order for people to be able to buy goods made in their factories. Although many Arab governments have made huge profits from oil sales, the leaders often spend much of this money in countries other than their own.

7. Not only are so many of the people poor and hungry, but they also cannot choose their own leaders or make their own laws. Most of the countries in this region are ruled by kings or military men. Only in Turkey, Israel and Lebanon are elections held and people able to vote for their leaders. This is another reason why there is often unrest in the Middle East.

UNDERSTANDING
CHAPTER 8

1. Which of the following questions are answered in this chapter?
   a. Who are the rulers of the Middle Eastern countries?
   b. Why are dams important in North Africa?
   c. Why is there often unrest in the Middle East?
2. The main idea of this chapter describes:
   a. the problems of people in North Africa and the Middle East.
   b. the need for more electricity.
   c. how land can be divided among the peasants.
3. Of these, the country with the highest standard of living is:
   a. Israel.   b. Egypt.   c. Algeria.
4. The new Aswan Dam brings water and power to the people of:
   a. Saudi Arabia.   b. Lebanon.   c. Egypt.
5. A big problem in government in this region is that:
   a. only men are allowed to vote.
   b. few leaders are elected by the people.
   c. Arab nations believe in communism.
6. Water is called the most important resource of this region because:
   a. so much water is needed for refining oil.
   b. it is needed merely to stay alive and in good health.
   c. without water power, the people could not improve their standard of living.
7. In paragraph 1, "crop yields" means:
   a. profit gained.   b. amount produced.   c. time saved.

DEVELOPING
IDEAS AND
SKILLS

Look at the cartoon on page 382. Then answer the questions below.

1. What do the plants represent?
2. What is the man pouring on the plants?
3. What does the man represent?
4. Why does it seem that the plants may not grow?
5. What is the artist trying to tell us in the cartoon?

FOLLOW UP   *Comparing*   Many events and ideas of North Africa and the Middle East may remind you of something similar in another region you have studied. See if you can choose the correct answer from each of these, based upon what you have already studied in other regions.

1. The *problem of land ownership* in the Middle East and North Africa is much like the problem of the people of: a. Western Europe. b. Latin America. c. Anglo-America.

2. The *low income* of many people of North Africa and the Middle East is also a problem faced by a large number of people in: a. Western Europe. b. Latin America. c. Anglo-America.

3. *Dams* built for irrigation and electric power are found also in: a. the Netherlands. b. the United States. c. Argentina.

4. The Jordan-Israel *border problem* over the Jordan River is much like a problem solved by: a. the United States and Canada. b. Norway and Sweden. c. the Soviet Union and Red China.

5. Foreign businessmen *investing money* in Middle Eastern oil fields is like foreign businessmen investing in the: a. tin mines of Bolivia. b. oil fields of the United States. c. coal fields of Belgium.

6. Much of North Africa and the Middle East is wasteland, in the form of desert. This *problem of wasteland* is also faced by: a. France. b. Great Britain. c. Canada.

9 THE RESTLESS ARAB WORLD

Reading For A Purpose: Why are the problems of North Africa and the Middle East so important to the peace of the world?

1. The presence of the Suez Canal alone would make the Middle East and North Africa one of the most important regions of the world. The canal is one of the busiest of all water routes. For years, Great Britain controlled the canal. In 1956, Egypt seized it. Now the Suez Canal brings money to Egypt. It also enables Egypt to control a great part of the world's shipping, for Egypt could refuse to allow ships to go through the canal. Most countries want to make sure that the canal is always open for their ships.

2. Nationalism—the pride that a person has in his country—is growing stronger within the Arab nations. For years, this region was under the control of foreign nations, chiefly Great Britain and France. Syria, Lebanon, Jordan and Libya have all become independent since World War II. Morocco became free in 1956, Tunisia in 1957 and Algeria in 1962. Many of the people now feel that they can make a better life for themselves. But they are bitter about the years spent under foreign rule. Western nations are often blamed for the troubles of the Arab people.

3. There has been a strong feeling among some Arab leaders that there should be a single Arab nation. The "Arab League" was formed in 1945 in order to bring the Arab states closer together. But the League has not grown into a single nation of Arab peoples. Leaders of the Arab nations are not eager to give up their newly won power to a larger central government. In 1958, President Nasser

of Egypt led his nation into a union with Syria that was called the United Arab Republic. This union lasted only three years.

4. Probably no other single problem in North Africa and the Middle East causes as much

Two former Arab leaders—King Saud of Saudi Arabia, left, and President Nasser of Egypt. How can cooperation among the nations of the Middle East benefit the people?

383

trouble as the dispute over the state of Israel. Israel was formed in 1948 as a homeland for the Jews. The Arab nations invaded Israel soon after but were thrown back. The two sides agreed to a truce arranged by Ralph Bunche of the United Nations. Fighting broke out again in 1967. Again, the United Nations tried to stop the war. In six days, Israel defeated the Arab forces. But no treaty between Israel and Arab states has yet been made. From time to time, fighting still breaks out.

5. Another problem resulted from the Arab-Israeli wars. This is the problem of the refugees. Starting in 1948, thousands of Arabs fled or were forced to leave Israel. Today more than two million of these people are still without a homeland. They are called refugees. The Arab nations have refused to find homes and jobs for them within their borders. They say the refugees belong to Israel and should return to that country. Israel says these people cannot return because they are unfriendly. The United Nations has been supporting camps for them until the issue is decided.

6. The Soviet Union also has a deep interest in the Middle East. The history of Russia is filled with efforts made by that nation to extend its power toward the Persian Gulf and Mediterranean Sea. Soviet troops were in Iran during most of World War II. In 1946, the U.N. had to step in before the U.S.S.R. would remove its troops. Egypt received great help from the Soviet Union in building the second Aswan Dam. About one-half the aid that the U.S.S.R. has given to poorer countries has gone to this region, chiefly Egypt and Syria. Much of this aid has been arms, planes and missiles.

7. In order to prevent the Soviet Union from gaining control over the oil resources and trade routes of this region, the United States has taken action. In 1947, when the U.S.S.R. began to threaten the Dardanelles, President Truman announced that aid would be sent to Greece and Turkey to help them fight the spread of communism. In 1955, Iran, Iraq, Turkey and Pakistan joined with Great Britain in an alliance for their protection. The United States supported this organization, although we did not join it. (Iraq has since withdrawn.) The name of this group of nations is CENTO, or Central Treaty Organization.

8. It is hoped that cooperation between the United States and this poor and troubled region will increase. The United States wants the Arab nations to know that we have no desire to control them as they have been controlled before. The North African and Middle Eastern nations need help in many ways. They are

A refugee camp in the northern part of the Gaza Strip in Israel. Why are these people without homes? What do you think should be done to help them?

384

trying to find the respect among the nations of the world that they have not had for so long. They face great problems caused by the nature of their land and climate. People of the United States must know the deep problems of this region in order to help its people.

UNDERSTANDING CHAPTER 9

1. Which questions are answered in this chapter?
   a. How is the Suez Canal operated?
   b. Why have Arab nations worked together in world affairs?
   c. Why is the United States interested in this part of the world?
2. The main idea of this chapter describes:
   a. why the Suez Canal is important to the whole world.
   b. the freedom of the Arab nations.
   c. how affairs of the Middle East affect the rest of the world.
3. In 1956, the Suez Canal was seized by:
   a. Egypt.   b. Great Britain.   c. Israel.
4. The last country in this region to gain freedom was:
   a. Egypt.   b. Israel.   c. Algeria.
5. Arabs left Israel in 1948 because:
   a. war broke out between Israel and the Arab states.
   b. new farm land was opened near the Red Sea.
   c. freedom came to the people of Arabia.
6. A person's pride in his country is called:
   a. nationalism.   b. militarism.   c. imperialism.
7. When nations agree to help each other, they form:
   a. a government.   b. an alliance.   c. a political party.
8. Persons who leave their homes to escape danger are called:
   a. pioneers.   b. traitors.   c. refugees.

DEVELOPING IDEAS AND SKILLS

Look at the cartoon. Then answer the questions at the top of page 386.

SINAI PENINSULA

385

1. What problem is raised by the people in the lower left corner?
2. What problem is raised by the people in the lower right corner?
3. Where are these problems taking place?
4. How do these problems affect us in the United States?
5. What is a good title for this cartoon?

SUMMING UP *Fact or Opinion* Read each statement carefully. If the statement is a fact, write F in your notebook. If it is an opinion, write O.

1. The Soviet Union has the same right as the United States to be interested in the Middle East.
2. The United States should not send arms either to Israel or to the Arab nations.
3. The Suez Canal is one of the most important waterways in the world.
4. Many Arab refugees live on the borders of Israel and Jordan.
5. The independence of the nations of North Africa and the Middle East will bring the needed improvements to the region.
6. The United States helped Greece and Turkey in 1947 because of the threat of the spread of communism.
7. Arab states wish to destroy the state of Israel.
8. A single Arab nation may solve most of the problems of the region.

FOLLOW UP In each group below, match each item in Column A with one of the descriptions in Column B.

COLUMN A	COLUMN B
1. Turkey	a. tiny, oil-rich country.
2. Kuwait	b. some minerals besides oil.
3. Islam	c. has great influence throughout the region.
4. Egypt	d. mountains of North Africa.
5. Aswan	e. important dam on the Nile River.
	f. ruled at one time by President Nasser.

1. wheat	a. chief product of Iran.
2. cotton	b. valuable produce of the Nile Valley.
3. dates	c. big import from Western Europe.
4. oil	d. found on the oases of the desert.
5. coal	e. very little supply in the Middle East.
	f. chief food of the small farmer.

10 EGYPT: LAND OF THE PHARAOHS

Reading For A Purpose: Why is Egypt called the "Gift of the Nile"?

1. It has been said that Egypt is the Nile, and the Nile is Egypt. Without the Nile, this North African country would be a vast desert. Except for a few scattered nomads, nearly all of Egypt's 35 million people live and work in the Nile Valley. It has always been so in Egypt. The Nile has been the center of Egyptian life for thousands of years. One of the earliest civilizations in the history of the world grew up around this great river.

2. More than 5,000 years ago, the Egyptians had learned to irrigate the land in the Nile Valley and raise crops. They built large stone temples to their gods. The great pyramids, one of the wonders of the ancient world, were huge stone burial places for their rulers, the *pharaohs.* The pyramids have lasted to this day. In the 8th century, the Egyptians were conquered by the Arabs. They became Moslems then and were ruled by Moslem kings or sultans for more than a thousand years.

3. In 1869, the Suez Canal was built on Egyptian land. In time, Great Britain gained control of the canal. The government of Egypt grew weaker and, in 1952, it was overthrown. A new government was formed by Gamal Nasser. When Great Britain withdrew her soldiers from guarding the canal in 1956, Nasser seized it. The armies of France, Britain and Israel attacked Egypt after this act. The United Nations forced these nations to remove their troops and Nasser kept control of the canal. As a result of this action regarding Suez, Egypt remained angry with the West.

4. Egyptians today, like Egyptians long ago, depend upon the Nile. It is the longest river in the world, flowing from central Africa through the Sudan and Egypt into the Mediterranean Sea. Each year there are heavy summer rains in the mountains to the south. As a result, the Nile floods its banks each fall, bringing rich soil to the lands near it.

5. The Egyptian farmers no longer depend upon the yearly flood alone to water their land. In 1902, the first Aswan Dam was built. This dam holds back the water of the Nile until it is needed. When the water is released, it is carried by a system of canals to the fields. In this way, water is available for irrigation throughout the year and can cover more distant farms. With enough water and a warm climate the Egyptian farmer can grow two or three crops a year. Egypt's chief crops are cotton and wheat. Growing two or three crops a year, however, "wears out" the soil. And the poor farmer has little money to buy fertilizer.

6. The Egyptian farmer or *fellah* lives in one of the many small villages that lie in the Nile Valley. If he is lucky, he owns his own farm. Otherwise he rents land from a large landowner or works for others. He uses simple tools and yet he produces a great deal on his small plot. Still, he does not make enough to feed his family. He earns about $100 a year from the sale of cotton or wheat. An Egyptian farmer's chief foods are corn and vegetables. His animals provide a little milk and cheese. He rarely

These ancient Egyptian temples are 32 centuries old. They were moved atop a cliff to escape the lake created by the Aswan Dam on the Nile. Do you think the preservation of ancient structures such as this is worth the expense and effort involved? Why?

eats meat. Because of the small amount of food and poor sanitary conditions, most farm families are often sick. Many of the farmers and their children cannot read or write.

7. Though Egypt is mainly a farming country, it has some large and well-known cities. Cairo, its capital, is the largest city in all of Africa! The city of Cairo marks the beginning of the delta of the Nile. Northwest of Cairo is Alexandria, second largest city in Africa. It is Egypt's chief seaport.

8. The cities of Egypt contain both the old and the new. There are new shops, offices and apartment buildings, large hotels and department stores. There are both factories and smaller workshops. There are schools and several universities. But the older sections have dark, narrow streets, dried brick houses and small shops. These sections are crowded with fellahin who can neither find jobs in the city nor obtain land in the country.

9. Like other nations in North Africa and the

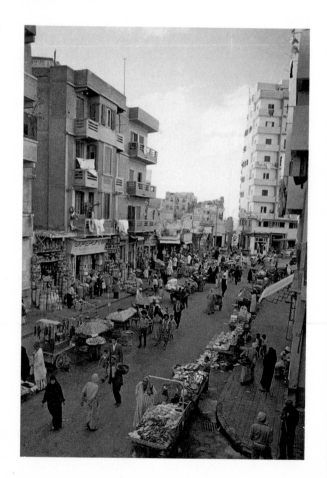

A Cairo street scene. What mixture of traditional life and modern life can you see in this photo?

Middle East, Egypt is a poor country. There is not enough fertile land for all its people. Secondly, many of the people suffer from sicknesses and have little education. However, this is changing. The new dam at Aswan makes it possible for more land to be irrigated. More electricity is being provided for the villages. Pure water is becoming available. Although there is a shortage of mineral resources, new industries are being started. More children are going to school than could in the past. Under the present government, the amount of land that a person may own is being limited so that more peasants can own land.

10. Egypt's chief imports are cloth, machinery and iron and steel goods. These must always be imported by a farming country without large industries. Egypt pays for the goods by the sale of cotton. As in Latin America, this dependence upon one export crop can cause trouble. A drop in the price of cotton throughout the world will seriously hurt the Egyptian farmer and the income of the nation.

11. With all its problems, Egypt is still important to the world. First, though Gamal Nasser is dead, Egypt is still a leader of the Arab nations. Its policies can decide if war or peace will prevail in the Middle East. Second, it owns the Suez Canal. A great part of the world's trade passes through the canal. Not only does Egypt get income from the canal; it also gets control of ship traffic from Europe to the Far East. This is a powerful position for a nation to be in.

UNDERSTANDING CHAPTER 10

1. Which questions are answered in this chapter?
   a. How long is the Nile River?
   b. Where is the source of the Nile?
   c. Why does the Nile River flood?
2. The main idea of *paragraphs 4 through 7* describes:
   a. how the Suez Canal has changed the government of Egypt.
   b. improvements in irrigation along the Nile.
   c. how people live along the Nile.
3. The Nile River begins in the:
   a. Mediterranean Sea.
   b. highlands of east and central Africa.
   c. Sahara Desert.
4. Most people of Egypt live:
   a. along the route of the Suez Canal.
   b. in the valley of the Nile River.
   c. in the cool southern mountains.
5. Dams are of great importance to the people of Egypt because:
   a. electric power is provided in this way.
   b. farmers will be able to use the water in the fall.
   c. a larger amount of land can be used for grazing cattle.
6. Egypt's income from selling goods is never certain because:
   a. her machinery often breaks down.
   b. the Suez Canal can easily be closed to ships.
   c. she depends largely upon the sale of cotton.
7. A *pharaoh* is the same as a:
   a. king.   b. soldier.   c. engineer.
8. A *fellah* is the same as a:
   a. fisherman.   b. teacher.   c. farmer.

Map #41a—Egypt

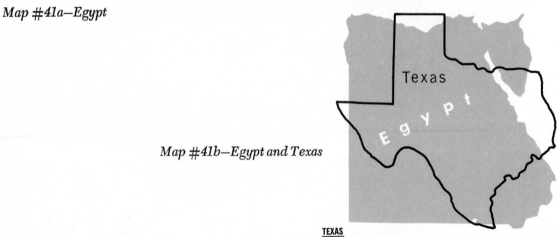

Map #41b—Egypt and Texas

TEXAS
POPULATION: 11.6 MILLION
LAND AREA: 262,134 SQUARE MILES
44 PEOPLE PER SQUARE MILE

EGYPT
POPULATION: 34.8 MILLION
LAND AREA: 386,662 SQUARE MILES
86 PEOPLE PER SQUARE MILE

Map Study

Map #41a and b — Egypt

Study the maps on page 390. Then answer these questions.

1. What is the distance from the Mediterranean Sea to the southern border of Egypt?
2. What bodies of water are connected by the Suez Canal?
3. What direction is *downstream* on the Nile River?
4. To what continent is the Sinai Peninsula connected?
5. What continent lies north of the Mediterranean Sea?
6. How would you describe the topography of Egypt?
7. Where do you think most of Egypt's 35 million people live?
8. How would you compare Egypt with Texas in size and population?
9. What city is located at 31° N. Lat. and 30° E. Long.?
10. What countries border Egypt?

Tell whether these statements are true or false. The underlined words make the statements true or false. If a statement is false, what word or words would you place in it to make it true?

1. Egypt is located on the continent of <u>Africa</u>.
2. Until 1956, the Suez Canal had been controlled by <u>Great Britain</u>.
3. Egypt looks upon its neighbor <u>Libya</u> as an enemy to be destroyed.
4. The Nile River flows <u>north</u> through Egypt.
5. An Egyptian farmer and his family usually have a meal of <u>meat</u> and vegetables.
6. The largest city in Africa is <u>Alexandria</u>, the capital of Egypt.
7. Egypt's chief export crop is <u>wheat</u>.
8. Most of Egypt's land is <u>desert</u>.

Fact or Opinion Read each statement carefully. If the statement is a fact, write F in your notebook. If it is an opinion, write O.

1. The new Aswan Dam has made Egypt one of the most powerful nations in the world.
2. Egypt's people are poor because there is not enough farm land to feed all the people.
3. Dams along the Nile will provide more water for irrigation.
4. Most of Egypt's land is too dry to grow crops.
5. It is said that Egypt will soon lead a union of Arab states.
6. The Nile River will always be important in the life of the people of Egypt.
7. President Nasser's leadership made Egypt the leading state in the Middle East.
8. Great Britain waits for a chance to regain control of the Suez Canal.

11 ISRAEL: THE DESERT RECLAIMED

Reading For A Purpose: Can Israel continue to grow in the Arab world?

1. Israel is a tiny land (about 8,000 square miles in area) at the eastern end of the Mediterranean Sea. It has the same desert climate as the other nations in the Middle East. Nevertheless, Israel is different from them in several ways. First, its people are Jews rather than Moslems. Second, most Israelis live in towns and cities rather than in farm villages. Many work in factories. Third, Israel has one of the few democratic governments in this region. Fourth, most of its people can read and write. It is a land of newspapers, books, schools and modern hospitals.

2. This tiny nation is bordered by four countries: Lebanon on the north, Syria on the northeast, Jordan on the east and Egypt on the south. To the west lies the Mediterranean Sea. At its southernmost end, Israel comes to a sharp point at the Red Sea. Despite its small size, this country is important to the United States. It lies close to the Suez Canal. An important pipeline runs through it. And it is a bridge for three continents: Europe, Asia and Africa.

3. Israel has a fertile plain along the Mediterranean Sea. East of the plain, the land rises and then drops sharply to the valley of the Jordan River. Much of this valley is below sea level. Part of the river valley lies outside Israel and belongs to Jordan. The Jordan River flows south and empties into the Dead Sea, the lowest spot on earth. The waters of the Dead Sea are very salty because they do not flow out of the sea. South of the sea is the Negev Desert. It is by far the largest part of Israel.

4. Along the coast, the climate is Mediterranean, very much like that of southern California. In the summer it is hot and dry; in the winter it is milder. The winter season is the season of rain. However, much of Israel is desert—the Jordan Valley and the Negev.

5. Israel was once called Palestine. It was the home of the Jewish people for centuries until the Romans destroyed it in 70 A.D. Then most of the Jews left and were scattered throughout the world. As one nation or another conquered Palestine, the Jewish people became a people "without a country." In many countries they were forced to live apart in sections of cities called *ghettos*. They dreamed of returning to their homeland. In the 19th century, a Hungarian Jew named Theodor Herzl urged the Jews to return to Palestine. His followers were called Zionists.

6. Palestine became a mandate of Great Britain after World War I. With the permission of Britain's government, Jews began to settle in Palestine alongside the Arabs. (The Arabs also had been living there for many centuries with their own religion and customs.) The number of Jews in Palestine grew yearly. The largest number came from 1933 to 1945, when the Nazi government of Germany carried out Hitler's program to destroy the Jewish people. During this time, more than six million Jews were killed by the Nazis in Europe. Many of

those who escaped fled to Palestine. The Arab leaders wanted this movement of Jews to the Middle East stopped.

7. When Great Britain gave up its control of Palestine after World War II, the United Nations wanted to settle the problem growing in Palestine. It was suggested that Palestine be divided into two states, one Jewish and one Arab. In 1948, the nation of Israel was formed. This started a war. The Arab nations invaded Israel, but they were defeated by the small nation. In 1956, Israel, Britain and France invaded Egypt after Egypt seized the Suez Canal. However, they had to withdraw. In 1967, a new war broke out after Egypt closed the Gulf of Aqaba, Israel's only way to the Red Sea. After a few days of fighting, Israel defeated the Arab states. There is still no real peace between the Arabs and the Jews.

8. The Israelis have set up a government like that of Great Britain. The lawmaking body is called the Knesset and is elected by the people. The Knesset chooses a president who has little power. The chief officers are the prime minister and the members of his cabinet. The new government has made great progress in building a modern nation in a short time.

9. The people of Israel have come from all over the world—Europe, Asia, North Africa, America. They speak different languages and have different customs. Some are highly skilled; others cannot even read or write. Some are from poor lands; some come from rich, industrial nations. Some were farmers before they came to Israel; others were factory workers. The only thing they have in common is that they are Jews. (But while Israel is a Jewish state, about 300,000 Moslems and some Christians live in the country.)

10. Like other places in the Middle East, Israel is short of water and fertile land. Despite these difficulties, more and more land is being reclaimed through irrigation. However, Israel cannot make greater use of the waters of the Jordan River because part of this important river is located in Jordan.

11. Most Israeli farms are found along the fertile coast and on the "reclaimed" land—land made useful again—of the desert. The chief crops are olives, grapes and citrus fruits (lemons and oranges). The farms do not produce enough food for all the people, however, so much must be imported. In the more distant parts of Israel, the people live in small villages or *kibbutzim*. (In a kibbutz the land is shared by all the people who live there. They not only farm, but they also have the job of patrolling the border between Israel and her hostile neighbors.)

12. There are many small factories in Israel, despite the fact that it lacks coal and iron. These factories depend upon the skills of the people, such as watchmaking, metal work or diamond cutting. By bringing water to the Negev, Israel is now able to mine there. Near the southern tip are the copper mines first worked by King Solomon more than 3,000 years ago. The Dead Sea is also rich in minerals used for fertilizer.

13. Israel's cities have grown in size with the increase in factories. The cities are different from the border settlements. The largest city, Tel Aviv, is only fifty years old, yet it has over 400,000 people. Northward along the Mediterranean Sea is Haifa, the main seaport. Haifa is at the western end of an oil pipeline. The capital of Israel is Jerusalem. This very old city contains the holy places of three religions—Judaism, Christianity and Islam. Jerusalem was at one time divided between Israel and Jordan.

Haifa is a modern port. Its gleaming white buildings lie on Mount Carmel, overlooking the Mediterranean Sea.

A view of Jerusalem, capital of Israel. Why is Jerusalem an important city for Moslems, Jews and Christians alike?

In the 1967 war, the Jews captured Jordan's half of the city and still control it.

14. One of Israel's most serious problems is the hatred felt by its Arab neighbors. The Arab states feel that Israel belongs to them because they have lived there for so long a time. They refuse to trade with Israel. Egypt won't let Israel use the Suez Canal. The Arab leaders have said that they will destroy this new and tiny nation. As a result, Israel keeps a large army. This is a great expense for the small country.

15. The citizens of Israel are showing the world how people from many lands can live together. They are also proving that a skilled and hard-working people can develop even the poorest land. This has brought respect for Israel from other new nations in Asia and Africa. And in Israel there is a democratic way of life, unlike other nations in North Africa and the Middle East.

UNDERSTANDING CHAPTER 11

1. Which questions are answered in this chapter?
   a. Why is there trouble between the Arabs and the Jews?
   b. What are Israel's problems?
   c. How large is Israel?
2. The main idea of this chapter describes:
   a. how Israel began.　　b. Israel's growth.　　c. Israel's farms.
3. The name of the lawmaking body of Israel is the:
   a. Congress.　　b. Knesset.　　c. Senate.
4. The founder of Zionism was:
   a. Meir.　　b. Einstein.　　c. Herzl.
5. Israel is important in this region because it:
   a. has the highest standard of living in the region.
   b. is located near the oil fields.
   c. has the only river near the Mediterranean.
6. The Arab states of the Middle East dislike Israel because:
   a. in Israel are the only iron and coal resources of the region.
   b. Israel has a large and modern army.
   c. they feel Israel is a state on land that belongs to the Arabs.
7. If a farmer *reclaims* a swamp, he has:
   a. made it into useful land.　　b. watered it.　　c. sold it.
8. A section of a city in which people of a particular race or religion live apart from others is often called a:
   a. ghetto.　　b. slum.　　c. province.

Map Study

Map #42a and b—Israel

Study the maps. Then answer these questions.
1. How long is Israel in a north-south direction?
2. What river is important to the people of Israel?
3. Is Israel in the high, middle or low latitudes?
4. How does Israel compare with New Jersey in density of population?
5. What countries border Israel?
6. Where are the large cities of Israel located? Why?

Map #42a—Israel

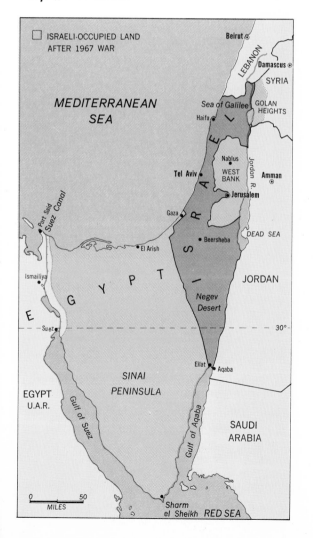

Map #42b—Israel and New Jersey

NEW JERSEY
POPULATION: 7.3 MILLION
LAND AREA: 7,521 SQUARE MILES
980 PEOPLE PER SQUARE MILE

ISRAEL
POPULATION: 3.1 MILLION
LAND AREA: 7,992 SQUARE MILES
362 PEOPLE PER SQUARE MILE

Agree or Disagree   Decide whether or not each of the following statements agrees with what you have read. If the answer is *disagree*, explain why.

1. People of many different religions are visitors to Jerusalem.
2. To support a growing population, Israel must irrigate more land.
3. Arab nations will cooperate with Israel to make use of the waters of the Jordan River.
4. The land along the Mediterranean coast provides much of Israel's food.
5. The people of Israel have little use for the Suez Canal.
6. Israel is a fairly new state in the Middle East.
7. The Dead Sea is a source of water for future irrigation.
8. The people of Israel have in common religion, customs and skills.

FOLLOW UP   Tell whether the following items refer to Israel, Egypt or to both countries. If the item applies to Israel only, write the letter I; if the item applies to Egypt only, write the letter E; if the item applies to both Israel and Egypt, write the letter B.

1. Oil pipelines.
2. Suez Canal.
3. Export of cotton.
4. Most people live in cities.
5. Coastline on the Mediterranean Sea.
6. Many skilled workers.
7. Much of the land is desert.
8. People have come from many countries.
9. Larger than the state of Texas.
10. Fertile river valley.
11. Most people of the Moslem religion.
12. Dependence on one export crop.

BOOKS FOR UNIT 7

Author	Title, Publisher	Description
1. Cottrell, Leonard	LAND OF THE PHAROAHS, World	The story of the early civilization of Egypt.
2. Cottrell, Leonard	LAND OF THE TWO RIVERS, World	The story of the early civilization of Mesopotamia.
3. Editors of Sterling Publishing Co.	WORLD GEOGRAPHY SERIES: IRAN, IRAQ, ISRAEL, KUWAIT, LEBANON, TURKEY, Sterling	Interesting accounts of the life and culture of people in each country.
4. Ekrem, Selma	TURKEY, OLD AND NEW, Scribner	The story of a young woman who grows up in Turkey.
5. Ellis, Harry B.	THE ARABS, World	Describes Arabian history and ways of living.
6. Gidal, S. and T.	MY VILLAGE IN ISRAEL, Pantheon	Life in Israel today.
7. Glubok, Shirley	THE ART OF ANCIENT EGYPT, Atheneum	Examples of striking works of art, old and new, that reflect the culture of the land.
8. Kaufmann, Herbert	ADVENTURE IN THE DESERT, Obolensky	A story of danger in the Sahara.
9. Lengyel, Emil	THEY CALL HIM ATATURK, Day	The story of the man who founded modern Turkey.
10. Najafi, N. and Helen Hinckley	PERSIA IS IN MY HEART, Harper	The home life of a Moslem girl.
11. Nurenberg, Thelma	MY COUSIN, THE ARAB, Abelard-Schuman	A young girl and her brother move to Israel and get caught up in war with Arabs, some of whom are friends.
12. Russcol, Margalit	ACHMED, BOY OF THE NEGEV, Putnam	A young Bedouin faces the hardships of life on the desert.
13. Thomas, John	THE TRUE STORY OF LAWRENCE OF ARABIA, Children's Press	The story of the Englishman who led the Arabs against the Turks in World War I.
14. Zahn, Muriel	JEMAL OF THE HILL COUNTRY, McGraw-Hill	A story of two courageous boys, one Roman, the other Jewish, in the days when Rome ruled the Holy Land.

UNIT 8
Africa, South of the Sahara

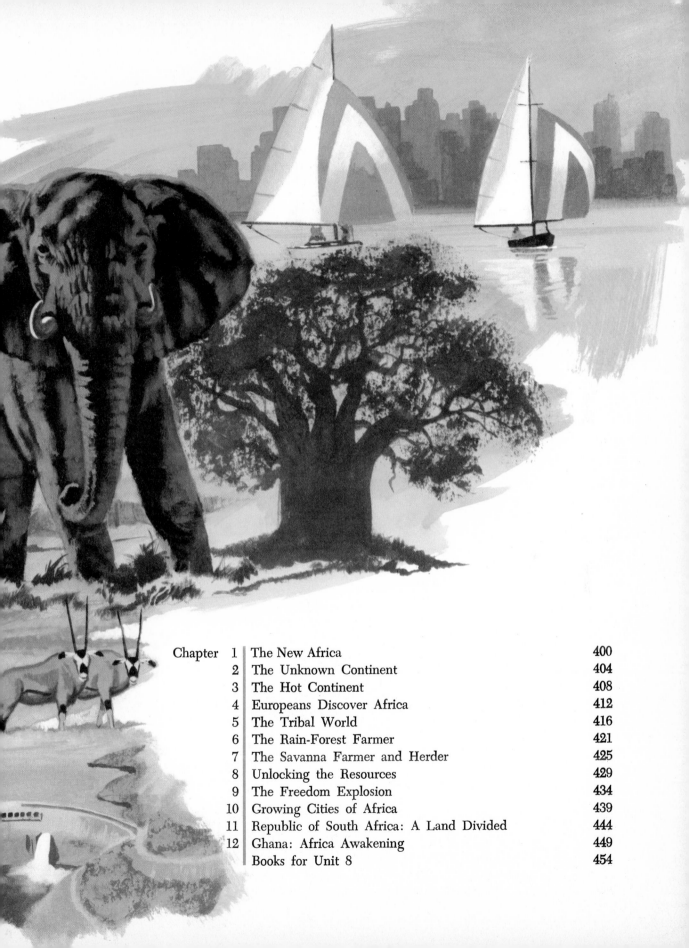

1 THE NEW AFRICA

Reading For A Purpose: Why are we interested in Africa?

1. Nigeria, Kenya, Ghana, Mali, Tanzania! A few years ago, these names were unknown to most Americans. Now they appear almost daily in our newspapers. These are only a few of the new nations in Africa. In our changing world, no other region is changing as much as Africa —the giant continent. Africa is over 9 million square miles in area, larger than either North or South America. It is more than three times the size of the United States!

2. Africa's geography really makes it two regions. In the north is the vast Sahara Desert. Stretching eastward from the Atlantic Ocean to the Red Sea, it divides Africa in two. North of the Sahara, the people have a way of life much the same as that of Middle Eastern peoples. South of the Sahara, the people are largely blacks whose ways of living are different from their northern Arab neighbors. Africa, South of the Sahara—or Sub-Sahara Africa —is the region we are going to learn about in this unit.

3. There are several reasons why the United States is interested in Africa, South of the Sahara. First, since World War II, many nations have won their freedom in this part of Africa. In some nations, the struggle for independence was as hard as was our fight for independence from Great Britain. These new nations want to

Maintenance of railroad tracks in Dahomey. How may new railroads, highways, schools and factories help the people of Dahomey and other African nations?

take their place among the older nations of the world. They want to do in a few years many things that took us 200 years. They want to set up stable governments, develop their natural resources and give their people a better way of life. They want new roads, factories and schools. In these tasks, they need help. The United States gives aid to the nations of Africa. Also, through such projects as the Peace Corps and "Operation Crossroads Africa," young

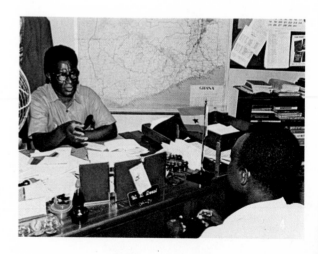

The man behind the desk is a government administrator in Accra, Ghana's capital and largest city. Ghana is a republic in western Africa. What does this picture suggest to you about Africa today?

Americans have gone to Africa to help these new nations reach their goals.

4. Second, Africa, South of the Sahara is rich in mineral resources. No one knows just how great these resources are, for it has been difficult to explore and develop the region up to now. We do know that gold, diamonds, uranium, copper, bauxite and manganese can be found in this part of Africa. All of these minerals are important to the modern world. Many of them are part of our daily lives.

5. Third, U.S. businessmen have invested large amounts of money in the development of Africa's resources. Although we do not trade as much with this region as with some others, still our trade with the nations south of the Sahara amounts to more than one billion dollars a year. The Firestone Rubber Company owns millions of rubber trees in Liberia. Plans for aluminum plants in Ghana have been formed by several American companies. One of our large chemical firms has a plant in Nigeria. The United States Steel Corporation has invested millions of dollars in producing manganese in Gabon.

6. Fourth, the forming of so many new nations in Sub-Sahara Africa has made that region important in the affairs of the world. The African nations now have the largest vote of any group in the United Nations General Assembly. This large vote is one reason why the United States and the Soviet Union want to hold their friendship.

7. Fifth, there is still unrest in the African world. A few nations, such as the Congo, have had trouble in setting up stable governments. In some cases, larger tribes have made war on smaller tribes. The world is worried that a small war in Sub-Sahara Africa could easily grow into a world war.

8. Finally, the rise of new independent nations in Africa is a source of pride and interest to black Americans, who make up ten per cent of our population. What's more, Africans are interested in how black people in the United States are treated. We cannot talk equality to the peoples of Africa and practice inequality in the United States. It is important that the new African nations look upon our democracy as a real one.

UNDERSTANDING
CHAPTER 1

1. Which questions are answered in this chapter?
   a. How many people live in Africa, South of the Sahara?
   b. What is the greatest change taking place in Africa?
   c. Why should we know more about Africa?
2. The main idea of this chapter describes:
   a. Africa's needs.
   b. Africa's resources.
   c. why Africa is important to us.
3. The continent of Africa is divided into two parts by the:
   a. Sahara Desert.   b. Atlas Mountains.   c. Congo River.
4. Most of the people living in Sub-Sahara Africa are members of the:
   a. white race.   b. black race.   c. yellow race.
5. Africa, South of the Sahara is important to us because:
   a. it is rich in mineral resources.
   b. it is our biggest source of trade.
   c. there are many highly skilled workers.
6. New nations of Africa need our help because they:
   a. lack natural resources.
   b. want to be admitted to the United Nations.
   c. need help in developing their resources.

7. In *paragraph 7*, the term "stable government" means a government that is:
   a. new.   b. lasting.   c. changing.

Map #43—Africa, South of the Sahara

Map Study

Map #43—Africa, South of the Sahara

Study the map on page 402. Then answer these questions.

1. Is the region north or south of the equator?
2. Is the region east or west of the Prime Meridian?
3. How far north and south does the region extend?
4. What region or regions are near it?
5. What are the chief bodies of water that border the region?
6. Which countries have no outlets to the sea?
7. What are some of the important rivers in the region?
8. Which large rivers form boundary lines between countries?
9. Which capital cities are sea or river ports?
10. Which country is an island nation?

Agree or Disagree   Decide whether or not each of the following statements agrees with what you have read. If the answer is *disagree*, explain why.

1. In North Africa and Sub-Sahara Africa we find different ways of living.
2. Equal treatment for all people in our country is important to the people of Sub-Sahara Africa.
3. Africa has mineral resources the United States can use.
4. African nations have a long history of governing themselves.
5. New African nations cannot become world leaders without the help and understanding of older nations in the world.
6. Many of Africa's resources could be more greatly developed.
7. The people of Africa, South of the Sahara have little interest in events taking place in the United States.
8. African nations are an important voice in the United Nations.

Recognizing Stereotypes   On page 302 you learned of the danger of making generalizations without facts. These sweeping generalizations are called *stereotypes*. Following are common stereotypes about Africa. South of the Sahara. Note them. As you learn more about the real Africa, see if these statements are accurate.

1. Africa is a land of thick jungles.
2. Africa is filled with wild animals.
3. All of Africa is hot and wet.
4. Africans wear few clothes and are drum-beating savages.
5. Africans live in small tribes.
6. Africans live in villages of grass huts.
7. There have been no great civilizations in Africa.
8. There are no factories in Africa.

2 THE UNKNOWN CONTINENT

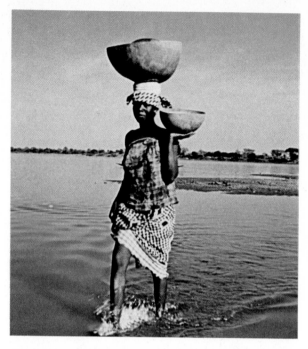

A Mali woman walks across the Niger River, which is very low during the hot season. But when the rainy season comes in June, the river may rise forty to fifty feet. In what ways can rivers be a threat as well as a friend to man?

Reading For A Purpose: Why was it difficult for outsiders to reach inner Africa?

1. Africa was once called the "Unknown Continent." While today it is no longer unknown to us, there are still parts of Africa about which the world knows little. The mystery of Africa is caused partly by the geography of the continent. In this chapter, we are going to learn some of the reasons why Africa was not well known by the rest of the world for so long.

2. Most of Africa is a plateau. There is very little coastal plain or lowland. The land rises sharply near the coast. The plateaus vary from 1,000 to 5,000 feet above sea level. The surface of the continent is very much like a saucer. Near the coasts, the land rises and then dips toward the center.

3. The plateaus of Africa below the Sahara are drained or hollowed by three large rivers: the Congo, the Zambezi and the Niger. Because the rivers begin on high ground, they

Mount Kilimanjaro in Kenya can be seen in the distance. What are the differences between the two climate areas shown here?

flow rapidly "downhill" toward the narrow coastal plains. In this drop there are many rapids and falls. Travel on the rivers is possible, but boats must stop at the rapids. Travelers must then go by land to the next place where they can board a boat. The Congo is more widely used for transportation than the other large rivers. Some of the rivers also form muddy deltas or sand bars at their mouths.

4. On the eastern coast, there is a range of mountains that extends from South Africa northward to Ethiopia. In this range there are many high peaks. Mount Kilimanjaro is over 19,000 feet high. Mount Kenya is over 17,000 feet above sea level. Both of these mountains are located almost on the equator. Yet they are so high that they are covered with ice and snow. In the mountains the largest number of Europeans are found. They prefer to live where it is cooler. The largest cities are also located in these eastern highlands.

5. Some huge lakes have been formed in the deep valleys of the African highlands. The snow from the high mountains has provided the water for these lakes. Lake Victoria is the largest lake. It is almost the size of Lake Superior, the largest of the North American Great Lakes. Lake Tanganyika and Lake Nyassa are other important lakes in the highlands. These lakes also can be compared in size to our Great Lakes. But the Great Lakes of North America are busy water routes. The lakes of Africa are hardly used for trade at all.

6. Why was Africa, South of the Sahara so hard to explore? First, the Sahara made it nearly impossible to reach central Africa by land from the north. Second, the African coastline is regular so that there are few harbors. (Africa has fewer miles of coastline than Europe, which is one-third its size.) Third, many of Africa's river mouths are difficult to enter because of the deltas and sand bars. Transportation up the rivers is not easy because of the falls and rapids. Fourth, in the 17th and 18th

A man takes a refreshing swim in a peaceful spot of one of Africa's many rivers. Although some of these rivers do not provide good transportation, they are still useful. In what ways?

centuries, many Africans were taken as slaves. As a result, African tribes were often unfriendly because they were afraid the Europeans were looking for slaves. This made exploration even more dangerous.

UNDERSTANDING CHAPTER 2

1. Which questions are answered in this chapter?
   a. What is the Great Rift?
   b. Why was Africa unknown for so long?
   c. Where do most Africans live?
2. The main idea of this chapter describes:
   a. the rivers of Sub-Sahara Africa.
   b. African land forms.
   c. the mountains of Sub-Sahara Africa.
3. Most of Africa is a:
   a. lowland.   b. plateau.   c. rain forest.
4. Most of Africa's highlands are located in the:
   a. east.   b. north.   c. west.
5. Africa's rivers are often of little help in transporting goods because:
   a. there is a lack of boats.
   b. most of the rivers flow inland.
   c. many of the rivers have falls and rapids.
6. Most Europeans live in the highlands because:
   a. the best farm land is found there.
   b. the mountains are rich in minerals.
   c. the climate is cooler.

Map Study

Map #44—Land Forms of Africa, South of the Sahara

Study the map. Then tell whether the statements at the top of page 407 are true or false. Be able to explain your answers.

LAND FORMS OF
AFRICA
SOUTH OF THE SAHARA

	Mountains
	Plateaus
	Hills
	Plains

0 200 400 600 800 1000
Miles

Mt. Kilimanjaro

Tropic of Cancer

Equator

Tropic of Capricorn

Equator

1. A vast plain stretches completely across the continent of Africa at the equator.
2. Plateaus are an important land form in southern Africa.
3. Chains of mountains stretching more than a thousand miles are located in this region.
4. The western part of this region north of the equator has more lowland area than the part south of the equator.
5. The lowlands along the southeastern coast extend inland for 500 miles.
6. Most of the land in Africa, South of the Sahara is highland.

SUMMING UP   In your notebook, write the numbers of the statements that explain why Africa was unknown to the people of Europe for so long.
1. a vast desert in the north
2. thick forests and heavy rains
3. southern tip near the cold southern ocean
4. few openings into the land for harbors
5. lack of natural resources
6. unfriendly people
7. not near other continents
8. large inland lakes
9. disease-carrying insects
10. cliffs and mountains near the coasts

FOLLOW UP   *True or False*   Tell whether these statements are true or false. The underlined words make the statements true or false. If a statement is false, what word or words would you place in it to make it true?
1. The Sahara Desert crosses the <u>middle</u> of Africa.
2. Most of Sub-Sahara Africa is a <u>plateau</u>.
3. One of the large rivers of Sub-Sahara Africa is the <u>Congo</u>.
4. <u>Rapids and falls</u> cause troubles in water transportation.
5. <u>Mud piled up</u> at the mouth of a river is called its <u>source</u>.
6. <u>Lake Victoria</u> is the largest lake of Africa.
7. <u>The large cities</u> of Sub-Sahara Africa are found in the <u>highlands</u>.
8. Early Europeans came to Africa in search of <u>slaves</u>.

3 THE HOT CONTINENT

Reading For A Purpose: What are the climates of Africa?

The savanna of Kenya. When do you think this photo was taken—during the rainy season or the dry season?

1. The equator runs through the middle of Africa. This means that most of the continent lies in the low latitudes. (Even in the tropics, however, it is not always hot. Where there are highlands it is always cooler than it is at sea level.) No part of Africa is as far from the equator as New York or Chicago. Thus, it is easy to remember the climate of Africa, South of the Sahara with the simple statement, "Africa is warm, but some places are warmer than others."

2. Near the equator in Africa is a large rain forest. It extends from the Gulf of Guinea on the west to the highlands of East Africa. The rain forest of the Congo is very much like the rain forest of the Amazon River in South America. It is always hot and rainy. Winds of more than ten miles an hour are almost unknown. The growth of the jungle is thick. It is crowded with birds, snakes, monkeys, fish and apes. The rain forest is full of mosquitoes that carry malaria and yellow fever. Sleeping sickness is carried by the tsetse fly. This is one of the most deadly diseases of Africa.

3. Most of tropical Africa is not a rain forest, but a dry grassland called a *savanna*. The savannas lie north and south of the rain forest. Here summer is the rainy season and the winters are dry and dusty. It is always hot. During the dry season the grasses turn brown. Cattle and people grow thin as food becomes scarce. During the rainy season the earth is green again and grain grows. Cattle and people become healthier as more food can be found. Most of Africa's large animals—the antelope, lion, elephant, giraffe and zebra—live on the savannas.

4. North and south of the savannas are the deserts. The great Sahara Desert occupies nearly all the northern part of the continent. In southern Africa is the smaller Kalahari Desert. (This desert is only as large as the whole of Western Europe!) The edges of the desert may receive as much as ten inches of rain a year, but most of this area rarely has rainfall.

5. You will remember from your study of North Africa that the lands of the northern coasts border the Mediterranean Sea. They have the sunny climate of the Mediterranean. The same climate is found in southwestern Africa near Capetown. The summers are almost rainless. Whatever rain there is comes during the winter months.

A scene in Senegal. Locate Senegal on the map on page 402. Then look at a map of climate areas in Africa on page 410. Which climate regions are found in Senegal? Which climate region is shown here?

6. On the southeastern coast is the region of the humid-subtropical climate. Can you remember the sections of North and South America that have the same climate? Southeastern Africa is about 35 degrees from the equator and is on the east coast of a large continent. This is the climate we find in other regions with the same conditions—Argentina and Uruguay in South America, and our own southeastern states.

7. Rainfall is a problem in most of Africa. Some parts get too much, while others get too little. The savannas and the Mediterranean regions both have very dry seasons. One year the rains may come early and soak the earth. In other years they may be too late and too scarce. There are few ways of storing water for the dry season. What is worse, the heavy rains wash important minerals out of the soil.

8. As you study the geography of Africa, you are probably thinking that Africa is like South America in many ways. This is true. The shapes of the two continents are very much the same. Both have a large mass of land in the north and a narrower section of land in the south. Both have large rain forests. (The one in South America is much larger, however.) Both have deserts, although the Sahara in Africa is much larger than any in South America. On both continents it is hard to travel because of the thick forests, deserts and mountains. In both areas, most of the people are farmers and raise food chiefly for themselves only. (South America has one great farming region, however—the pampas. There is no section like it in Africa.) Only now are the people of both regions beginning to manufacture goods for themselves.

UNDERSTANDING
CHAPTER 3

1. Which questions are answered in this chapter?
   a. Why isn't it always hot in the tropics?
   b. Where is the Kalahari Desert?
   c. Why is life difficult in Sub-Sahara Africa?
2. The main idea of *paragraph 8* is that:
   a. the geography of Africa and South America is alike in several ways.
   b. large farming regions are found in both Africa and South America.
   c. jungles are thicker and mountains are higher in Africa than in South America.
3. Most of Africa has the climate of the:
   a. rain forest.   b. savanna.   c. desert.
4. The tsetse fly causes:
   a. malaria.   b. sleeping sickness.   c. smallpox.
5. One reason why life is hard in parts of Sub-Sahara Africa is that:
   a. it is too cold in the mountains.
   b. there are many sandstorms.
   c. diseases are common.
6. Water is a problem to many Africans because:
   a. the people can't store it during dry seasons.
   b. rains cause frequent floods.
   c. too much water is used to provide electricity.

Map Study

Map #45—Climates of Africa, South of the Sahara

Agree or Disagree   Study the map. Then decide whether or not each of the statements at the top of page 411 agrees with the information on the map. If the answer is *disagree*, explain why.

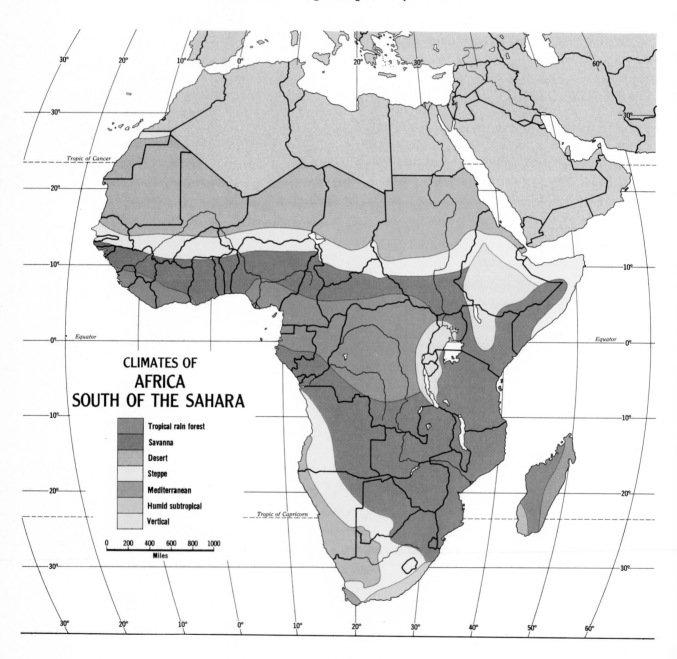

CLIMATES OF
AFRICA
SOUTH OF THE SAHARA

Tropical rain forest
Savanna
Desert
Steppe
Mediterranean
Humid subtropical
Vertical

0   200   400   600   800   1000
Miles

1. Mountains have a great effect on the climate of all Sub-Sahara Africa.
2. The savannas are located both north and south of the equator.
3. The African rain forest extends from one coast to the other.
4. No part of the southern tip of Africa receives enough rainfall for good farming.
5. Great differences in latitude are one reason for the different climates of the region.
6. At the equator the climate is the same across the continent.
7. Most of Africa, South of the Sahara is rain forest.
8. Considering the entire continent of Africa, many of the same climatic regions are found north and south of the equator.
9. High mountains are located in eastern Africa.
10. The rain forest is found within ten degrees' latitude north and south of the equator.

SUMMING UP

I. Complete the following outline in your notebook.

AFRICA AND SOUTH AMERICA

A. Ways in which these two continents are *alike*.
   1.   3.
   2.   4.
B. Ways in which these two continents are *not alike*.
   1.   3.
   2.   4.

II. *Fact or Opinion*   Using the information you have gained in Chapters 1, 2 and 3, tell whether each of the following statements is a fact or an opinion. If the statement is a fact, write F in your notebook. If it is an opinion, write O.
1. The Peace Corps should be extended so that all Africans receive proper medical care.
2. Africa today is not the same as it was 100 years ago.
3. The lakes of Africa have not been very useful in providing transportation.
4. Africa is similar to South America in a number of ways.
5. There are few good harbors in Africa because of the regular coastline.
6. The largest animals of Africa do not live in the rain forest.
7. Some climates of Africa are like those in the United States.
8. Africa, South of the Sahara cannot be as highly developed as North Africa.

4 EUROPEANS DISCOVER AFRICA

Reading For A Purpose: How did Europeans gain control of Africa?

1. Africa, South of the Sahara was almost completely unknown to the people of Europe until the late 1400's. Then the rulers of Portugal began a search for an all-water route from Europe to India. They were interested in trade. The Portuguese sea captains sailed along the west coast of Africa, each time going farther and farther south. They traded with the African tribes and returned with shiploads of gold and ivory. Finally, in 1498, Vasco da Gama rounded the southern tip of the continent, turned north and sailed on to India.

2. Before this time, Europeans had not been able to learn much about the African continent. It was believed that the Sahara could not be crossed. However, Arabs of the north had opened trade routes across the desert. They had met and traded with African tribes and kingdoms south of the Sahara. In West Africa, from 700 to 1500, there were strong kingdoms —Ghana, Mali and Songhay. These had courts, cities and governments such as were found in Europe at that time. The Arab traders brought their customs and religion with them. Many Africans became Moslems.

3. After Vasco da Gama found the all-water route to India, Portugal established trading posts or stations along the eastern and western coasts of Africa. Africans brought goods that the Portuguese wanted to these trading stations. Other peoples besides the Portuguese soon set up African trading posts. The land along the coasts was divided up by several European countries. In 1652, the Dutch settled at the southern tip of the continent in what is today called Capetown. This southern settlement supplied Dutch sailors with food and water.

4. In the 1500's, the European nations wanted slaves for their colonies in the New World. In 1619, Dutch ships brought the first blacks to the English colonies. The Europeans did not go into Africa's interior for their slaves. The slaves were captured and brought to the coastal stations by strong black tribes who raided other villages. While they were waiting, the Europeans kept themselves supplied with food by planting New World crops such as maize, peanuts, potatoes and tomatoes. They also grew tobacco. These crops were later adopted by African farmers.

5. The great inland explorations did not begin until the 1800's. Mungo Park, an explorer from Scotland, traveled the route of the Niger River in western Africa. John Speke and Samuel Baker discovered Lake Tanganyika in East Africa. But the two most famous explorers were David Livingstone and Henry Stanley.

6. Livingstone first came to Central Africa as a missionary in 1840. For 26 years, he explored the regions of East Africa. He discovered the Zambezi River and Victoria Falls, the source of the Nile River. He fought the slave trade and won the friendship of many African people. In 1866, Livingstone disappeared. In 1869, a New York newspaper sent Henry Stanley to find the missing missionary. Stanley found Livingstone two years later near Lake Tanganyika. He was

the world information about the riches of Africa: gold, ivory, animal skins and fine tropical woods. The news reached Europe at a time when European nations were looking for raw materials for their factories. They also wanted places to sell their manufactured goods. Great Britain, France, Belgium, Germany and Italy soon divided most of Africa into colonies.

8. For a time, Ethiopia and Liberia were the only independent countries on the entire continent. Liberia, on the west coast, had been started by the United States as a home for its former slaves. In 1910, the Union of South Africa gained self-government. For most purposes, Egypt gained freedom in 1922, but it was under the protection of Great Britain until after World War II. This situation remained unchanged in Africa until after World War II. Since that time, the world has seen the great movement of African peoples to free themselves of their European rulers and establish their own governments.

very sick. When he recovered, the two men continued exploring in East Africa. Livingstone died in Africa in 1873. Stanley remained and explored along the Congo River.

7. Stanley and Livingstone opened Africa for other missionaries. These men came to Africa to help the natives and to teach them the Christian religion. They opened schools, hospitals and churches for the African people. The reports of Stanley and Livingstone also gave

Slave traders separate the members of an African family.
What was the fate of Africans upon their capture?

1. Which questions are answered in this chapter?
   a. Who explored Africa?
   b. Who was Cecil Rhodes?
   c. Why were Europeans interested in Africa in the 1600's?
2. The main idea of this chapter describes:
   a. the exchange of goods between Europe and Africa.
   b. how missionaries went into Africa.
   c. the exploration of Africa, South of the Sahara.
3. A great explorer of Sub-Sahara Africa was:
   a. David Livingstone.   b. James Cook.   c. John Cabot.
4. The search for a route around Africa to India was begun by:
   a. Portugal.   b. Great Britain.   c. Italy.
5. Europeans became interested in Africa in the 1600's because they:
   a. needed raw materials for factories.
   b. wanted slaves and ivory.
   c. wished to make the land safe for missionaries.
6. Europeans had a great interest in Africa in the 1800's because they:
   a. were looking for a new route to India.
   b. wanted more fertile farm land.
   c. wanted raw materials for factories.
7. People who went to Africa to teach the Christian religion were:
   a. sea captains.   b. traders.   c. missionaries.

Picture Symbols
These pictures should help you to recall parts of the chapter you have read. What is the main idea of each picture?

Steps in the Exploration of Africa
In your notebook, place the following explorations in the order in which they happened. The first event is No. 1. The next event is No. 2, etc.

Europeans sailed along the western coast and set up trading posts.
Livingstone explored East Africa.
Arabs crossed the Sahara.
Europeans divided Africa into colonies.
Stanley explored the Congo.
Mungo Park explored the Niger River.

Complete the following sentences, using the names listed below.

Arabs	Dutch sailors	Vasco da Gama
European nations	Missionaries	David Livingstone
Slave traders	Portuguese sailors	Henry Stanley
Egypt		

1. ———— crossed the Sahara to trade with Negro tribes.
2. ———— began searching for an all-water route around Africa to India.
3. ———— went as a missionary to central Africa.
4. ———— reached India by rounding the southern tip of Africa and then sailing northward.
5. ———— divided Africa into many colonies.
6. ———— was sent to Africa to find a missing missionary.
7. ———— brought the first Negroes to the English colonies.
8. ———— did much good by building schools and hospitals in Sub-Sahara Africa.

5 THE TRIBAL WORLD

In many African villages, each family lives in a group of buildings called a compound. In this compound, the kitchen is on the left, beside it are rooms for the men, and farther to the right are rooms for the women. What are some advantages of this kind of housing arrangement?

Reading For A Purpose: Who are the peoples of Africa?

1. Africa is not a crowded continent; about 270 million people live in Africa, South of the Sahara. As you have learned, much of tropical Africa is either too wet or too dry. Africa below the Sahara is black Africa—the home of people with brown or black skin. Most of the black peoples are Bantus or Sudanese (which mean black). The Bantu-speaking peoples live south of the equator. The Sudanese live in the grasslands between the Sahara and the tropical rain forest. Both of these peoples are divided into hundreds of tribes.

2. There are three important smaller black groups in Sub-Sahara Africa. The Pygmies, averaging about 4½ feet tall, are found mainly in

This family lives near the border of Upper Volta and Togo. They are members of the Moab tribe. What helps to keep the members of a tribe united?

the rain forest of the Congo Basin. They live by hunting wild game. The Bushmen live in the Kalahari Desert in southwest Africa. They hunt and gather food for a living. The Hottentots live on reservations in southwest Africa. These people are herdsmen who raise sheep, goats and long-horned cattle.

3. Besides the black peoples, there are smaller groups of Asians and whites or Europeans living in this region. The Europeans number only about four million of the total population. Most of them live in the Republic of South Africa, Rhodesia and Kenya. (The eastern highlands and southern plateaus of these countries appeal to them because the climate is cooler and free of tropical diseases.) Despite their small numbers, the Europeans have been the rulers of the continent since colonial times. They have controlled the governments. They have been the professional people, the traders, the owners of farms and mines. The hard work has been done by the native Africans.

4. Many Africans live in the world of the *tribe*. A tribe is a group of people who live together in a single place, united by their own

This young African doesn't go to school, for there is no school in his village. Instead he usually helps his father, a cattle herder. Here he uses a slingshot to frighten the birds so they won't eat the fruit on the trees. Do you think he is likely to become a cattle herder also? Why?

customs and their own language. (Many of the tribal languages have not been written down. Tribes often do not understand the languages of other tribes.) Each tribe has its own chief. While the chief has great power, he usually rules by the customs of his people. The land that a family farms and uses for cattle does not belong to the family. It belongs to the tribe. Many of the tribes are so large that they include a million or more members. The tribes differ from each other in many ways.

5. It is up to the parents to teach their children the laws and customs of the tribe. The boys learn to hunt, fish, tend cattle, make weapons and be brave in battle. The girls are taught to cook, farm and keep house. Much is learned through songs, stories and dances. Some children live and work with the craftsmen of the tribe. They are taught to make tools, masks and jewelry. The tribe cares for its members throughout their lives.

6. While many Africans are Christians, Moslems or Hindus, most follow the religion of the tribe. Many tribal people believe that each thing or object has a spirit. These spirits are ei-

ther good or evil. The African tries to please these spirits so they will help him. Each tribe has medicine men or witch doctors who try to make the spirits bring good fortune to the tribe.

7. In general, tribal Africans are always "on the go." If they are hunters they move about in search of game. If they are herdsmen they are always looking for better pasture lands. If they are farmers they want better land. The soils of Africa are not good. The heavy rains of the rain forest wash away the valuable minerals. After two or three years the farmer must move on to find a new plot of ground. The farmer grows only what he needs for food or to trade for the things he cannot grow.

8. The tribal African has lived most of his life in a world of sickness. From the time he was born, he has probably had many diseases. The insects of the wet regions bring yellow fever, malaria and sleeping sickness. People who live where the tsetse fly breeds cannot raise cattle, for this insect lives in the blood of the cattle. As a result, the tribesman's diet is poor, because he cannot drink milk or eat meat. A diet of starches causes his bones to be poorly formed. Pure drinking water is seldom found. People of the tribe have long depended on the tribal medicine men to cure their diseases with strange mixtures or with "magic."

This child's swollen belly comes from a poor diet. Because they don't get some of the foods they need, many African children become ill and die. Do you think the United States should try to help these people? Why?

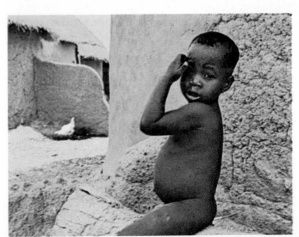

9. In many places the tribes still carry on their old ways of living. In other places Africans have welcomed the changes brought by Europeans. Missionaries have done a great deal for the people as teachers, doctors, nurses and ministers. They have worked to build schools and hospitals. One of the most famous of modern missionaries was Dr. Albert Schweitzer. He came to Africa because he felt that the African people needed doctors more than the people of Europe did. He built a hospital in the jungles of Gabon near the equator. In 1952, he was awarded the Nobel Peace Prize for his work in helping others. He died in 1965 after fifty years of service to the people of the continent of Africa.

10. The life of the African is changing rapidly. A short time ago, many Africans lived in tribal villages and used only simple tools. Now more and more own their own farms or work in the city, using modern machinery and earning wages. The cities are places where Africans of many different tribal backgrounds meet and exchange ideas. There is a growing number of schools for those who want to learn. There are modern hospitals and other signs of a new Africa. More and more, Africans are preparing themselves to take part in their new nations.

UNDERSTANDING CHAPTER 5

1. Which questions are answered in this chapter?
   a. How do Africans live?
   b. How do African children learn tribal ways?
   c. How do Africans communicate with each other?
2. The main idea of this chapter describes:
   a. how the African uses his land.
   b. the religions of African people.
   c. the importance of the tribe in African life.
3. Most Africans are:
   a. miners.　　　　b. herders and farmers.　　　　c. factory workers.
4. Most Africans still live:
   a. in cities.　　　　b. on tribal lands.　　　　c. on their own farms.
5. Tribal Africans seem to be always "on the go" because they:
   a. search for better farm lands.
   b. move from one kind of factory work to another.
   c. are driven from their land by wild animals.
6. New African nations may have some trouble in uniting all their people because:
   a. there is a big health problem.
   b. much of Africa is too dry for a large population.
   c. many people are loyal to many different tribes.
7. A *tribe* is:
   a. one family.
   b. a large number of families.
   c. all the people of a certain race.

Pictograph #14—Population, Area and Standard of Living of Africa, South of the Sahara

Study the pictograph. Then answer the questions below.

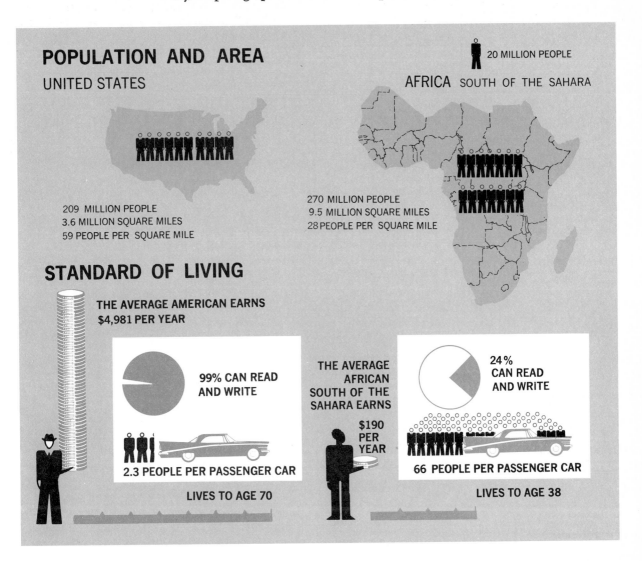

POPULATION AND AREA

UNITED STATES

20 MILLION PEOPLE

AFRICA SOUTH OF THE SAHARA

209 MILLION PEOPLE
3.6 MILLION SQUARE MILES
59 PEOPLE PER SQUARE MILE

270 MILLION PEOPLE
9.5 MILLION SQUARE MILES
28 PEOPLE PER SQUARE MILE

STANDARD OF LIVING

THE AVERAGE AMERICAN EARNS
$4,981 PER YEAR

99% CAN READ AND WRITE

THE AVERAGE AFRICAN SOUTH OF THE SAHARA EARNS $190 PER YEAR

24% CAN READ AND WRITE

2.3 PEOPLE PER PASSENGER CAR

66 PEOPLE PER PASSENGER CAR

LIVES TO AGE 70

LIVES TO AGE 38

1. Is the standard of living of this region high or low compared with that of the United States?
2. Is the region more or less crowded than the United States?
3. Are the people of this region literate compared with the people of the United States?
4. How long may the average person in this region expect to live?
5. What facts tell you the standard of living of the people of the region?
6. How does this region compare with the United States in size?

SUMMING UP Compare the standard of living of a tribal family with that of your own family.

YOUR FAMILY		AFRICAN TRIBAL FAMILY
	Education	
	Health Care	
	Occupations	
	Religion	
	Kind of Community	

FOLLOW UP In your notebook, write the word that makes each statement correct: *Most, Some, Few.*

1. _____ Europeans in Sub-Sahara Africa live in the highlands.
2. _____ Africans are members of a Christian religion.
3. _____ Africans are members of the Pygmy group.
4. _____ Africans are members of the Negro race.
5. _____ tribes speak the same language.
6. _____ Negro people in Sub-Sahara Africa are owners of farms and mines.
7. _____ small farmers grow just enough to feed their families.
8. _____ Africans now work in the cities.
9. _____ doctors and nurses have come from outside Africa.
10. _____ African tribes are very large.

6 THE RAIN-FOREST FARMER

Reading For A Purpose: How does the African farmer meet his needs?

Women clear a field for planting in Cameroon. What tools are they using?

1. As you have learned, much of the climate in Sub-Sahara Africa is either rain forest or savanna. These climates are not good for farming. Despite this fact, most people in Africa, South of the Sahara are either farmers or herders of cattle. Most of these people use whatever they raise for their own needs. Starting with the rain forest, let us see what kind of farming is carried on by the people who live there.

2. The rain-forest people live in small villages near a stream or river. The village huts are small and dark. They have cone-shaped roofs made of grass and leaves. The shape of the roof allows the rain to run off quickly.

Manioc is grown at the edge of the forest in a section called a "bush farm." Why is farming in the rain forest so difficult?

Around the village are the clearings for the main food crops, such as bananas, yams, rice and manioc. (Manioc is a plant with a root like a potato. It is the source of the bread of all rain-forest peoples.) Besides these crops, the natives also grow fruits and vegetables in small garden plots.

3. The women farm the clearing with simple tools like the hoe and digging stick. The yields from their fields are very low. The men fish and hunt, but meat is hard to get. There are few cows in the rain forest because they die of the tropical diseases. When the crop or the hunt is good, there is plenty to eat. However, the food cannot be kept long because it spoils in the heat. When the crops are poor, the problem of having enough food is serious. Some men earn money by gathering palm-oil nuts or rubber to sell to traders. Others work on plantations.

4. Rain-forest people are always moving because the soil is so poor. They do not have modern methods of farming. It is easier to change a clearing and start over in a new field. The trees are cut down, but the stumps remain. The thick undergrowth is cut and burned. The ashes enrich the soil. Crops are planted among the tree stumps. These crops

421

grow well for about two or three years, but after that time, the thick brush returns. Rather than fight it, the tribe moves out and looks for a new place to clear. This kind of farming is called *migratory* farming because it involves moving from place to place. The same kind of farming is also found in the Amazon rain forest.

5. Most rain-forest people are subsistence farmers. However, plantation farming is also found in the rain forest. Many of the plantations are owned by foreigners but are worked by Africans. Two of the leading plantation crops in the rain forest are palm-oil nuts and cacao beans. Lately, there has been a growing number of farms and plantations owned by Africans.

6. The palm nut, from which oil is made, is one of Africa's leading products. The soap you use today may be made from Africa's palm oil. This same oil is important in the manufacture of cosmetics. The oil palm grows wild in the Congo rain forest. Plantations are also located along the river valleys. Africa produces ninety per cent of the world's supply of palm nuts. The nuts are shipped to Europe for processing —that is, changing into oil products. The leading producer of palm nuts is Nigeria.

7. Americans love chocolate. Most likely the chocolate you eat comes from the cacao trees

This man earns money by cutting down branches at the top of palm oil trees. His only tools are a knife and a tree belt made of vine. After fastening the belt around the tree trunk, he uses the belt to help him "walk" up the tree. Which products that you use may have been made from the oil which comes from this tree?

of Africa. Ghana and Nigeria produce about *half* the world's total supply of cacao beans. The cacao trees grow best in the tropical climate. Natives gather the pods from the trees and remove the beans. Then the beans are carried to the trading stations which are located along the rivers. They are shipped to the United States and Europe where they are made into chocolate.

UNDERSTANDING CHAPTER 6

1. Which questions are answered in this chapter?
   a. Why is the oil palm important?
   b. How do the native people work with iron?
   c. What crops are raised on plantations?
2. The main idea of *paragraph 4* is that:
   a. the thick undergrowth is cut, but it grows back in a short time.
   b. migratory farmers farm wherever they can find land.
   c. rain-forest soils produce good crops.
3. The chief plantation crops of the African rain forest are:
   a. palm nuts and cacao beans.
   b. olives and oranges.
   c. corn and millet.

4. The chief foods of the rain-forest people are:
   a. proteins, like meat and beans.
   b. starches, like manioc and yams.
   c. sugars, like chocolate and oranges.
5. Farming is difficult in the rain forest because:
   a. the land is hilly.   b. weeds grow rapidly.   c. soils are poor.
6. The oil of the palm nut is important because:
   a. Africans use it for heating their homes.
   b. it is used to make machinery run more smoothly.
   c. it is an important export crop.
7. *Migratory* farmers:
   a. use irrigation canals.
   b. move from place to place.
   c. build terraces on hillsides.
8. "The factory *processes* wool and turns out beautiful cloth." *Processes* means:
   a. "buys directly from herders."
   b. "imports from distant lands."
   c. "changes raw material into finished goods."

DEVELOPING
IDEAS AND
SKILLS

Photograph Study

This photograph should help you to recall parts of the chapter you have just read. What is the main idea of the photograph?

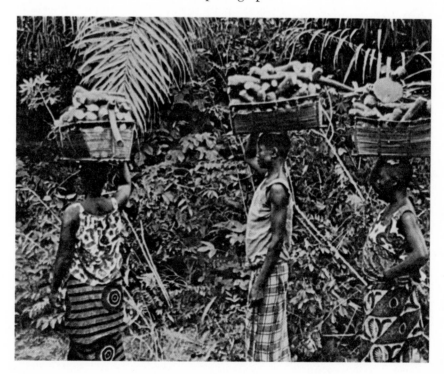

Compare the life of the people in the Congo and Amazon regions.

AMAZON	*How People Live*	CONGO
	Location and Climate	
	Main Foods	
	Main Occupations	
	Transportation	
	Important Crops	
	Problems	

FOLLOW UP   *Making Inferences*   In our reading, many facts are given to us. From these facts we can draw conclusions. The following are some conclusions or inferences that you might make after reading this chapter. Tell whether these conclusions are correct or incorrect. Give reasons for your answers.

1. Farmers of the rain forest use little fertilizer on their land.
2. Wheat bread is little known to rain-forest families.
3. At night, after a hard day's work, rain-forest families probably spend some time reading.
4. When an African goes to the city, he will probably look for other people from his own tribe.
5. Cotton plantations are probably found in the rain forest.
6. Some customs of American women might change if we did not trade with Ghana and Nigeria.
7. The African jungle grows back almost as fast as the natives can clear it away.
8. Drier areas of Africa usually have the greatest number of insects.
9. Most people in the rain forest have plenty to eat.
10. Most rain-forest people live near rivers.

7 THE SAVANNA FARMER AND HERDER

Reading For A Purpose: How does the African adapt himself to the wet and dry lands?

Working in a dry field. What must this farmer wait for before his planting season can begin?

1. Africans of the savannas are usually farmers or herders. In the northern grasslands of western Africa live the Hausa tribe. They are farmers who live in huts of dried mud thatched with grass. Like most African farmers, the Hausa use only a hoe or digging stick. They build ridges on their farm land to catch the water during the rainy season and hold it for the dry season. Their chief crop is corn. They use the grain for food and the stalks for roofs and fences. They also grow wheat, millet and yams. The Hausa grow crops to feed themselves and their families. However, they may grow a cash crop such as peanuts to get money for other goods.

2. Some of the farming peoples of western Africa are also herders. However, raising cattle is difficult in this area. Good cattle cannot be grazed on the western savannas because of the disease-carrying tsetse fly. The cattle are thin, particularly in the dry season. The little milk they give is used to make butter and cheese. When the animals die, their hides are sold and tanned to make clothing.

3. In the highlands of eastern Africa, safe from the tsetse fly, herding is the chief occupation. Two typical herding tribes are the Masai of Tanganyika and the Karamojong of northeast Uganda. The Masai wander with their herds. They are nomads like the Bedouins of the Middle East. The Masai measure their wealth in cattle. They rarely kill their animals for food or use them to provide fertilizer. Their chief use for cattle is their milk. The Masai often drink the blood of the cow with the milk. They believe it gives them strength.

4. During the rainy season, the Masai herder keeps his cattle in the valley. During the dry season, he moves to the highlands where there is more rain and more grass. The cattle have a hump of fat on their backs. When there isn't enough food to eat during the dry season, the cattle "use" the fat they have stored. In this,

A Masai herder guards his cattle. What special beliefs do the Masai have about their cattle?

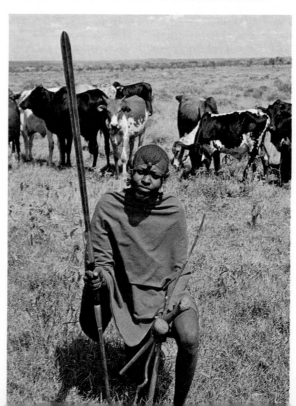

they are like the camels of North Africa. The Masai have so many cows on the grazing lands that the grass is soon killed and the soil is washed away when the rains come. While the men are away, the women care for any crops that are planted.

5. The Masai live in a village called a *kraal*. They live in round thatched huts. The thatched huts form a large circle with only one entrance. Inside the circle are many cattle pens. There is a special pen for the chief's herd. Each morning, the men of the tribe drive the cattle out onto the grazing land. They are watched carefully during the day and returned to the kraal at night. Whenever there is need for a new pasture, the village is given up by the herders. The village is surrounded by a fence of thorny brush to protect it against wild animals and enemy tribes.

6. The Masai believe that God gave cattle only to the Masai. This seems to give them the right to raid other tribes and steal their cattle. When the Masai marry, they pay a "bride price." This means that a man pays to the girl's father a certain number of cattle. This payment is to make up for the father's loss—the work done by the girl around the home.

7. The Karamojong live on a plateau. They also live in thatched villages near wells or a river bank where they can raise crops as well as tend herds of cattle, goats and sheep. The men and boys take care of the herds. The women and girls tend the fields, grind the grain, fetch the water and collect the firewood. The chief food is a grain called *sorghum*. It is

A Zulu kraal, or village, in South Africa. In what formation are the thatched huts arranged? What is the area in the center used for?

planted in the dry season and ripens in the rainy season. It is eaten with sour milk or vegetables. During the dry season the men move the cattle far from the village in search of grass and water. As with the Masai, guarding cattle is the Karamojong way of life. The animals make it possible for the tribesmen to marry and support their families. When they are away with their herds, they also live on blood and milk.

8. As you have learned, most of Africa's people are herders or subsistence farmers. As such, their income is low and they cannot buy many goods. (Ghana has the highest average income of the new nations of Sub-Sahara Africa—about $260 per year per person.) In recent years, however, there has been an increase in the number of "cash crops" such as cacao, coffee, sisal, palm oil, peanuts and cotton. These crops are grown on both small farms and plantations.

UNDERSTANDING CHAPTER 7

1. Which questions are answered in this chapter?
   a. What is a kraal?
   b. How do peanuts grow?
   c. Why do herding tribes move?
2. The main idea of this chapter describes:
   a. how the African uses the dry grasslands.
   b. the customs of the Masai.
   c. life in African villages.

3. The chief form of wealth of the Masai is their:
   a. water rights.　　　　b. camels.　　　　c. cattle.
4. An important food crop of the grasslands is:
   a. palm oil.　　　　b. peanuts.　　　　c. corn.
5. Masai tribes are always on the move because they:
   a. fear attacks by other tribes.
   b. need to find new pastures.
   c. are looking for fertile farm land.
6. Few cattle are grazed in certain parts of the grasslands because:
   a. there is no grass.
   b. Africans have little use for cattle.
   c. the tsetse fly kills many of the cattle.
7. A *kraal* is a native:
   a. village.　　　　b. drum.　　　　c. boat.
8. All of these are food *grains* grown in the grasslands EXCEPT:
   a. yams.　　　　b. sorghum.　　　　c. millet.

DEVELOPING
IDEAS AND
SKILLS

Young Africans who move to the cities often find it difficult to continue to follow the customs of their native tribes. The thinking and customs of the modern world often come into conflict with tribal ways. The problem of leading "two lives" is described by an African student in the selection which follows.

An African Student Speaks

. . . My life is between two worlds, each of which has a hold on me. The first world is the world of civilization (embodied by the school and college environment), and the other is the primitive world of the past represented by my home life amidst the proud and conservative Masai who have not yet taken to Western ways. . . .

. . . When I go home on leave now I find it difficult to associate with youths of my age. They don't understand my putting on Western clothes. They cannot tolerate a half-Masai. All the same I understand their pride and stick to them through thick and thin. When I go home I try to adjust to their way of thinking. It is also true that when I leave home and go back to school, I have again to adjust my way of thinking. And so it ends that I am destined to be between two worlds, each of which has a hold on me. Will it always be so? I think it will be.

From Katharine T. Kinkead, "Something to Take Back Home," *The New Yorker*, May 23, 1964.

1. Why is progress a burden for people like this young African?
2. Why will progress be hard to achieve for the new governments of Africa, South of the Sahara?
3. Do you think the problem will "always be so" as the young half-Masai says?

Complete the following chart in your notebook.

MASAI HERDSMEN   BEDOUIN TRIBESMEN

	Wealth	
	Use of Land	
	Foods	
	Clothing	
	Shelter	
	Goods for Trade	

FOLLOW UP   Below are some headings for an *outline*. Following them are some topics. In your notebook, place the topics under the correct headings.

HEADINGS

A. Farmers and Herders of Western Africa
B. The Herders of East Africa
C. Problems of African Farming

TOPICS

Use ridges to hold water.
Raise corn and wheat.
Believe cattle are a gift from God.
Sorghum and milk are products.
Low income per person.
Measures his wealth in cattle.
Problem of the tsetse fly.
Storage of water during the dry season.
Live in a kraal.
Few "cash crops" for sale.

8 UNLOCKING THE RESOURCES

Reading For A Purpose: Why has Africa gone so long without making full use of its resources?

Elephants roam the savanna of Uganda. In what ways are elephants valuable to the people of Africa?

1. Africa, South of the Sahara has many resources: animals, forests, minerals and falling water. There are more different kinds of wild animals in Africa than in any other region. The animals have both helped and harmed the African. Many tribes of the forest still depend upon hunting for their meat supply. However, some of the animals, such as leopards and lions, wander near the villages and destroy property and human life. The wild animals are becoming fewer in number, though, as place after place is cleared for settlement.

2. Of equal importance to the people of Africa are the trees and plants. Great forests still cover more than one-third of Sub-Sahara Africa. From certain trees come the raw materials for many waxes and medicines. In the rain forests are valuable hardwood trees: mahogany, ebony and many others. Yet, few of the trees are cut down because of the difficulty in getting the wood to the seaports. Before the forests can be used fully, more railroads and highways will have to be built.

3. The land contains great mineral riches. The most important industry in Africa is mining. Many of the mineral deposits are found in the highland areas. One of the world's richest mining areas is the southeastern part of Zaire and Zambia. Zaire leads all regions of the world in the mining of industrial diamonds. (Because diamonds are so hard, they are used in high-speed drills in factories.) Zaire and Zambia are also leading copper producers.

More copper is mined here than in any other area of the world except the United States. Cobalt, used in the manufacture of special steel, is also mined.

4. Important mining areas also extend south into Rhodesia and the Republic of South Africa as well. South Africa has long been famous for its gold and diamonds. These diamonds are large and very beautiful. They are made into jewelry. Gold mines are located near the city of Johannesburg. For this reason it is sometimes called the "City Built on Gold." Uranium, now one of the world's most important minerals, is also mined in South Africa. Uranium is used in producing atomic power.

5. In West Africa, Ghana has large deposits of manganese, gold, diamonds and bauxite. The small nation of Guinea may have the world's largest supply of bauxite, from which aluminum is made. Nigeria has rich supplies of tin. Iron ore deposits are found in Guinea, Liberia and Sierra Leone.

6. Mining is big business in Africa. Thousands of workers are needed in the mines. Mining companies bring Africans from a wide area

to live in the villages built by the mining companies. The Africans come because more money can be earned in the mines than on the farms. The movement of people from the farms to the mines has done much to change the life of the African. More and more, he works for wages and has new needs.

7. Most of Africa's riches have not been fully used. There are several reasons for this. First, until recently, most mines were directed by foreigners, and most of the profits went back to owners in Europe and America. While Africa's new leaders still allow foreigners to develop their resources, Africans keep a bigger share of the profits. In this way they are raising money for the needs of their people.

8. Second, fuels used to supply power are scarce. Except in the Republic of South Africa, there is little coal for fuel. There is almost no oil in the entire region. In many places water power could be used, for Africa has the greatest water-power resources in the world. However, this source has hardly been touched because of the difficulty in reaching streams and waterfalls.

Unlike their parents, many young Africans today are going to school. These women are learning how to operate business machines. What other kind of training might be helpful to the Africans of today?

9. Third, factories need skilled workers. However, a great number of Africans have not had the opportunity to go to school. African leaders today recognize the need for educated people and are trying to provide schools for their citizens.

10. Fourth, there are a few good highways and railroads in Sub-Sahara Africa. What railroads there are do not connect with other roads to form a large transportation system. Early in the twentieth century, Cecil Rhodes, the great developer of South Africa, announced a plan for a railroad from Capetown, South Africa, to Cairo, Egypt. It is still a dream. Then too, Africa's rivers have many falls and rapids that make them difficult to navigate. The coastline has few good harbors. Transportation improvement is a goal for modern Africa.

11. Fifth, the local market for African products has been small. Most of the people do not have the income to buy the products of the farms and mines. Foods and minerals have been shipped to Europe or America, where they were sold. Now, however, there is a growing number of factories to make use of the products of the continent. Processing plants will use the oils of the palm and coconut. Refineries will use the raw tin, copper, bauxite

An early morning donkey caravan heading into the city of Fort Lamy, Chad. The donkeys are carrying kerosene to people in the city. How will the kerosene be used?

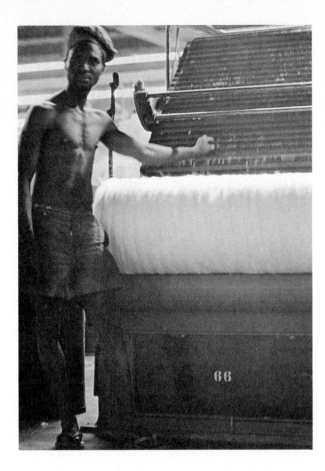

and manganese. Textile mills will produce goods from cotton.

12. The new nations of Africa are getting help from other countries to develop their resources. Many American companies have started new plants and power projects. Members of America's Peace Corps have helped people in several African nations. American and British companies are exploring for oil in Nigeria. The United States and France provided money to improve education and transportation in Upper Volta. Britain is spending $5 billion in five years to develop water power in Gambia. The Soviet Union and China are also giving aid to the African people. Along with the United States and Britain, they have helped the Sudan with money for highways and hospitals. Chinese money and workers are building a 1,000-mile railroad through Tanzania. Besides aid from individual nations, Africa also gets help from the United Nations. In time, Africa's resources may be "unlocked."

A textile mill in Lagos, the capital of Nigeria.

UNDERSTANDING CHAPTER 8

1. Which questions are answered in this chapter?
   a. How has mining changed the life of the African?
   b. Why are Africa's riches not fully used?
   c. How are the minerals brought to the coast?
2. The main idea of this chapter describes:
   a. how Africa trades with the world.
   b. how Africans work in the mines.
   c. mineral resources of Africa.
3. Zaire leads in the production of:
   a. nickel. b. gold. c. industrial diamonds.
4. Most of Africa, South of the Sahara has little:
   a. coal and oil. b. gold and diamonds. c. copper and tin.
5. Zaire has been an important section of Africa because:
   a. it lies along the trade routes from north to south.
   b. its mines have copper and diamonds.
   c. it has the only oil processing plants in Africa.
6. Africa's forests are useful because:
   a. soils are fertile.
   b. they contain good grazing lands.
   c. they provide raw materials for furniture, waxes and medicine.

431

Map Study

Map #46—Africa's Imports and Exports

Study the map. Then tell whether these statements are true or false.

1. Africa sends most of its goods to the United States.
2. Africa exports chiefly raw materials and imports mostly finished goods.
3. Two of the leading copper-producing nations are the Republic of Zaire and Zambia.
4. Much mineral wealth is found along the western coast.
5. Palm-oil nuts are exported by Nigeria.
6. Africa has little oil and iron ore.
7. Several countries grow coffee for export.
8. We get much of our chocolate from Africa's rain forest.
9. South Africa is rich in gold and diamonds.

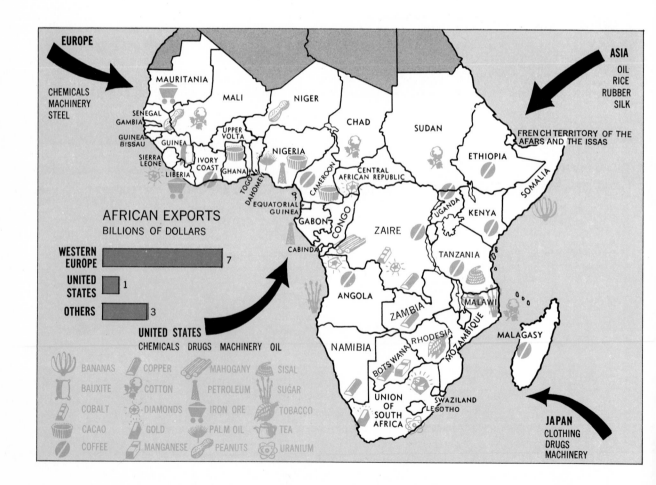

Making an Outline of Chapter 8

1. Review the steps in making a good outline in Chapter 6 of Unit 2.
2. Then, choose the main ideas or headings for your outline as follows:
    a. The main idea of paragraphs 1 through 6.
    b. The main idea of paragraphs 7 through 11.
    c. The main idea of paragraph 12.
3. Choose a title for the outline that includes all the main ideas you have chosen.
4. See what information (details) there is in each of these paragraphs that you want to include under each main idea.
5. List three or four of these details under each main idea in the outline.

Which way do these products go—to or from Africa? In your notebook, write *EX* for each item that is exported from Africa, and *IM* for items imported by Africa.

1. palm oil	6. machinery	11. copper
2. automobiles	7. oil	12. candy
3. peanuts	8. gold	13. radios
4. cacao	9. diamonds	14. cotton cloth
5. tin	10. medicines	15. building materials

9 THE FREEDOM EXPLOSION

Reading For A Purpose: Can the new nations survive?

1. In 1950, only four nations in Africa were free. Today, more than 42 nations are independent. A true "freedom explosion" has taken place, ending the colonial empires of Africa. The European nations themselves have been partly responsible for this change on the African continent. It is important to understand how this came about.

2. As you remember, Europeans became very interested in Africa in the 1870's. Explorers had found great riches there. The leading countries in Western Europe needed raw materials. Because of this, almost all of Africa was divided into colonies. Three nations—Britain, France and Germany—had the most colonies. Belgium, however, gained possession of the valuable Congo.

3. When the Europeans first came to Africa, they found they had to teach the Africans their way of doing things in order to bring out the riches of the mines and forests. They built roads and railroads to bring the ore and other products to the sea. They brought schools and better health to many Africans. They trained Africans to run the railroads and to work in the offices. They educated Africans for a certain amount of leadership. This system is sometimes described as *imperialism* or *colonialism*.

4. Great Britain and France did the most to prepare the African people for their freedom. As more and more Africans became educated, they realized that it was possible for them to govern themselves. During World War II, many Africans served in the armies of the Allies. After the war they saw that other people were gaining their freedom—India, Indonesia and the Philippines. Africans wanted a share of freedom to make a better life for themselves.

5. The year 1957 was the beginning of the great freedom movement south of the Sahara. Ghana was the first African colony to gain independence, and native-born Kwame Nkrumah became the first prime minister of the new government. After Ghana, freedom came rapidly to many other nations. Guinea was given its freedom in 1958. In 1960, seventeen new nations were formed. In this group were Cameroon, Nigeria, Republic of Zaire, Malagasy (the island of Madagascar), Niger, Congo, Chad and Gabon. Tanzania and Kenya won independence in 1961, Zambia in 1964. In 1965, Rhodesia declared itself independent

The lawmakers of Somalia meet in this modern assembly hall. What important problems must African governments deal with today?

434

from Great Britain. Gambia became free in 1965, Lesotho and Botswana in 1966, Swaziland in 1968. You will have to examine the map of Africa on page 402 very carefully to find all the changes since 1950.

6. The new nations of Africa face many problems. First, some countries have not been so well prepared as others for self-government. In the Congo (now Zaire), the Belgians left few Africans who were trained to run a government. Fighting broke out when the country became free. That fighting has continued from time to time ever since. Though a government was quickly formed in Nigeria, that country has been troubled by civil war.

7. Second, the new national governments of Africa are troubled by the fact that many people are still loyal to their tribes. Within any one country there may be many tribes, each with its different customs and languages. These tribes may have many members. The tribal chiefs do not want to give up any of their power to the head of a new national government.

8. Another problem is that boundaries separate people of the same tribe. When the European nations divided Africa in the nineteenth century, they took what they could get without war. Boundary lines were placed almost anywhere. As a result, a tribe may have members in two different nations. The Somali people of East Africa are divided in this way. Some tribes have tried to break the national boundaries that now exist to form new countries along tribal lines. There have been bloody wars as a result.

9. There is also the problem that a dictator may gain control of a new government. The new African nations would like to set up democratic governments. This is not done overnight. At the same time, they must fill the growing desire of their people for more comforts. Millions of Africans know of and want Western clothes, cars, radios and television sets. If the needs of the people cannot be met quickly, there is always the danger that a popular leader will be able to seize power and rule as a dictator. The new nations need help from the "richer" nations of the world in order to meet the problems of their early years of being free.

10. One of the most important problems is

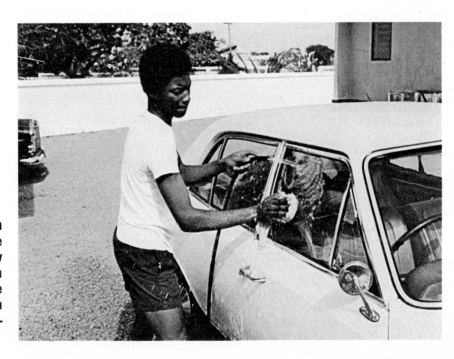

In Africa today, western comforts are part of the daily life of many. How may problems result when people try to combine their traditional ways with the ways of western countries?

how to build greater cooperation between Africans and Europeans. For a long time, Africans worked in mines or on farms owned by Europeans. They worked for the Europeans to develop the natural resources of Africa. Today, however, Africans control most of the governments of Sub-Sahara Africa—and the resources of these nations. What kind of governments will develop? Will there be a place in Africa for the smaller white groups?

UNDERSTANDING CHAPTER 9

1. Which questions are answered in this chapter?
   a. What did European countries do for their colonies?
   b. What happened when Zaire became free?
   c. What are the leading tribes of Africa?
2. The main idea of this chapter describes:
   a. the religions of new African nations.
   b. how Africa changed from colonies to independence.
   c. why European countries were interested in Africa.
3. Much of Africa in 1920 was controlled by:
   a. Great Britain and France.
   b. Spain and Portugal.
   c. the United States and the Soviet Union.
4. Today, most African territory is:
   a. colonized by European nations.
   b. controlled by European nations.
   c. free and independent.
5. Some leaders of new nations have had difficulties in organizing their new governments because:
   a. the United Nations will not admit them as members.
   b. the tribal chiefs still have much power.
   c. the people want their old governments.
6. A big problem facing new nations of Africa is that:
   a. the new governments are ruled by Europeans.
   b. tribes have given up their old customs.
   c. few people have had the opportunity for an education.
7. An *imperialist* believes in:
   a. obtaining colonies.
   b. self-government.
   c. keeping tribes together.

DEVELOPING IDEAS AND SKILLS

Map Study

Map #47—Africa in 1914

Study the map on page 437. Then tell whether these statements are true or false.
1. Most of Africa was free in 1914.
2. Most of the continent was made up of colonies of Great Britain and France.
3. The United States had colonies in Africa.

4. All the African colonies were ruled by European countries.
5. There were four independent African nations in 1914.
6. English colonies stretched in an unbroken line from north to south.
7. Much of the French territory was desert.
8. Germany had colonies in some of the hottest parts of Africa.

ALGERIA

LIBYA

EGYPT

ANGLO-
EGYPTIAN
SUDAN

FRENCH WEST AFRICA

ETHIOPIA

LIBERIA

BELGIAN
CONGO

■ FREE COUNTRIES
□ ITALIAN COLONIES
□ FRENCH COLONIES
□ ENGLISH COLONIES
□ GERMAN COLONIES
□ PORTUGUESE COLONIES
□ SPANISH COLONIES
□ BELGIAN COLONIES

S. W. AFRICA

SOUTH
AFRICA
(Dominion)

Map #47—Africa in 1914

437

A. *Who Am I?*   What person is speaking in each of the following paragraphs? Choose your answer from the list of people below.

Leader of a new African nation	Tribal chief
Rain-forest farmer	African miner
Masai herder	European plantation owner
	Missionary

1. "I have had power over thousands of people for a long time. I don't intend to give up this power. I want to have some say in the new government, too. My people will stick together." ▄▄▄▄▄

2. "The new government doesn't interest me very much. I am too busy watching my animals and trying to make a living. How can the new government bring water to my land?" ▄▄▄▄▄

3. "I work hard for the minerals everyone wants. I'd like to have a share in the profit my work brings. I'd like our resources to be used for my benefit, too." ▄▄▄▄▄

4. "I want this nation to be for the African people. I want all Africans to act like free men. We must all unite to make our government work." ▄▄▄▄▄

5. "I still have work to do in the new Africa. There is still a need for more schools and hospitals." ▄▄▄▄▄   .

B. On page 403, some common stereotypes of Africa are listed. Look at them now and see if you agree with them. Whether you agree or disagree, give good reasons for your judgment.

10 GROWING CITIES OF AFRICA

This city resident relaxes at home in native African clothes while he listens to a modern record player. What other items of modern living do you see in this picture?

Reading For A Purpose: Why are Africa's cities growing in size?

1. A look at the chart on page 440 shows what is happening in the cities of modern Africa. The chart lists the twelve largest cities in Africa, South of the Sahara. All cities outside the Republic of South Africa have grown at a fast rate since 1960. Two cities, Lagos and Kinshasa, are nearing the one million mark. They have more than doubled in size in just ten years. In Dakar, Nairobi and Abidjan, the growth has been just as rapid. Yet in spite of the great growth in the population of cities, only about one African in five lives in an urban (city) area.

2. Why is this movement to the cities taking place? The chief reason is that farmers and villagers hope for jobs and a better life in cities. Life is hard in rural (country) areas. The city has become the place of opportunity. As new nations in Africa develop their industries, more skilled workers are needed. A large number of

Workers wrapping packages in the back of a city store. What other kinds of jobs do you think might be available in African cities that would not be found in rural areas?

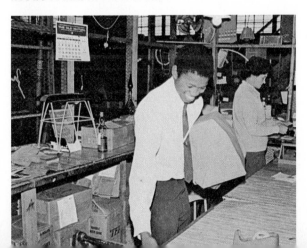

people must be trained in the skills that industries can use. The city gives a chance for this training that the farm and village cannot give. Universities, usually located in the large cities, are turning out growing numbers of engineers, electricians and laboratory workers. But not everyone who comes to the city looking for a better life finds it. There are not enough good-paying jobs for everyone who wants one. Many who come to the city find the same poverty they thought they were leaving behind.

3. The large African cities are a mixture of the old and the new. In some, visitors can live in the finest modern hotels. They can eat good foods in air-conditioned comfort in the finest restaurants. Taxis take them to theaters and other entertainments. There are wide boulevards and beautiful new buildings. Nairobi, Kenya, has a main drive bordered by flowers. Some say it has the most beautiful entrance to any city in the world.

4. But behind the bright, shiny face of the new city, a few blocks from the new buildings and wide streets, there are narrow alleys, tin shacks and open sewers. Crowding is as bad as in the large cities of America. Housing is being built as fast as possible, but people keep coming and cities cannot keep up with the demand. Crude wooden boxes are the only homes

As one passes through modern African cities, it is not uncommon to see people in carts moving alongside buses and trucks. In what other ways are African cities a mixture of the old and the new?

Peru, or Calcutta, India. Life is worse elsewhere. And, to the African, there is a freedom in the city that he has not known before. The government is his. The old rulers from European countries have gone. He has few fears that he will not be able to do what he wants.

6. The first Africans who came to the cities in large number may have felt very much alone. They had left their tribes and their families upon whom they depended for so much. Now, however, the newcomer to the city will find others of his tribe who have gone before him. If they are in the city, he will find them. The custom of the tribe demands that his friends and relatives invite him to stay with them. If he finds a job, he may find that city life offers him more comforts than he has ever known. He will then bring his wife and family to the city, and he stays. This is what is happening in Africa today. It is not likely to slow down so long as there is poverty on farms and villages and hope for the comforts that the city can offer.

for some families. Markets are jammed with buyers and sellers. Small cars can hardly make their way through jammed streets.

5. If life is hard for some who have come to the cities, why do they stay? For many, bad as the city may be, it is better than the farm or small village. People stay for the same reasons they continue to crowd the slums of Lima,

People in Cities Throughout the World	
North America	74%
Europe	64%
Soviet Union	57%
Latin America	56%
Asia	25%
Africa	22%

City	Country	Population 1960	Population 1970
Johannesburg	Rep. of South Africa	1,100,000	1,152,500
Kinshasa	Zaire	390,000	901,520
Lagos	Nigeria	379,000	841,000
Ibadan	Nigeria	600,000	727,500
Addis Ababa	Ethiopia	500,000	644,120
Accra	Ghana	388,000	615,800
Dakar	Senegal	234,000	581,000
Durban	Rep. of South Africa	655,000	560,000
Capetown	Rep. of South Africa	731,000	508,000
Nairobi	Kenya	186,000	478,000
Salisbury	Rhodesia	260,000	435,000
Abidjan	Ivory Coast	125,000	282,000

1. Which of the following questions are answered in this chapter?
   a. Why are Africans moving to cities?
   b. What are some of the needs of African cities?
   c. Why have cities in South Africa not grown as fast as cities in western Africa?
2. The main idea of *paragraph 2* is that:
   a. universities are the center of city life.
   b. the city means opportunities for a job.
   c. engineers are needed in new African nations.
3. The largest city of Africa, South of the Sahara, is:
   a. Johannesburg, Republic of South Africa.
   b. Addis Ababa, Ethiopia.
   c. Accra, Ghana.
4. The lower chart on page 440 tells us that:
   a. Nigeria has the largest population of all African countries.
   b. all cities of Africa have grown in population.
   c. Kinshasa has more than doubled its population in ten years.
5. According to Chapter 10:
   a. the movement to the cities is slowing down.
   b. Africans have a feeling of freedom in the city.
   c. Africa's large cities were started by Europeans.
6. In modern African cities:
   a. air conditioning is not known.
   b. there is a desperate need for housing.
   c. crowding is not so bad as in American cities.

**DEVELOPING
IDEAS AND
SKILLS**

Problems of large cities seem to be much the same all over the world. The following selections describe some features of life in African cities. How are these cities similar to American cities?

Transportation Headaches in Urban Africa

Modern living has made commuting (traveling to the city and back for work each day) important to the African. But most commuter transportation is not comfortable, reliable or safe.

Few African cities have regular bus service and nearly all buses are jammed with people. The buses are generally old vehicles. Often they do not reach their destination without time out for repairs.

Drivers with their own cars are more comfortable, but they have problems, too. For example, in Lagos, Nigeria, when traffic slows in one direction, drivers form new lanes on all available ground space to either side of the stalled lane. Since cars coming from the other directions do the same, cars traveling in opposite directions find themselves in the same lane. Soon all lanes are blocked and no one can go anywhere.

Moving from city to city can be just as difficult. African roads are pot-holed if they are paved. And they are full of ruts if they are not. All but the rich travel the roads in open-backed trucks or hard-benched, windowless buses. Sometimes smaller, closed buses cover the routes, but usually chickens and baskets take up space the passengers leave.

Railroad tracks have been laid to carry freight, not passengers. Railroad routes do not always follow the large cities. Passenger cars are often without windows and short of seats. Accidents are common. For those with money, air travel from city to city is speedier.

The New York Times, November 29, 1970. Adapted by permission of The Associated Press.

1. According to the selection:
   a. most people travel to work in their own cars.
   b. all African cities have regular bus service.
   c. bus service in most cities is not reliable.
2. Travel from city to city is:
   a. carried on chiefly by bus.
   b. largely over new concrete highways.
   c. as bad as travel within the city.
3. A problem with train service between cities is that:
   a. freight seems to be more important than passengers.
   b. a city like Lagos has no train service.
   c. bus service is more comfortable.
4. One way in which African and American cities are alike is that in both:
   a. there are problems getting from one city to another.
   b. there are rush-hour traffic jams.
   c. people with money usually travel by bus.

Nairobi: Problems and Progress

In the street cafe next to the new Stanley Hotel, I can see in an hour citizens of half the world's nations and more than half its races. Tourists from Germany pour in. Japanese traders brush shoulders with Brazilian coffee planters. Planners of industry from Yugoslavia mix with teachers from Indonesia.

Nairobi, Kenya, used to be one of the nastiest places in the world. It was dirty, dusty and poor. It was a frontier town filled with rich visitors preparing to go on safari (game hunts). Now it is one of the most attractive of capitals. Flowers greet you on every corner. Most of the old, little wooden buildings have been replaced with modern concrete towers. The streets are lined with parked cars, and at rush hours choked with traffic. Every empty lot is a parking lot crammed with vehicles.

Of course, there is still plenty of poverty. Just off the center of the city are narrow, winding streets with Asian shops, smelling of spices. On the edge of town there's still a vast, ever-growing, poor African population packed into ugly little boxes, on a hot, treeless wasteland. The city government keeps rehousing people as fast as it can. But Nairobi is a magnet, drawing people from all over Africa. It is like a man racing for the morning train and never quite catching it.

Apartments and houses for white-collar workers are in Western style. They are neat little houses, with a small garden in front and a larger one behind. There's a living room, a dining room and a kitchen, where a charcoal fire burns. Families seem to like the city and their neighbors. Most of all, they like to have water running from a tap. All the new apartments and houses have electricity. Sales of electric kettles, irons and hot plates rise year by year. The dryer and dishwasher are on their way.

Adapted by permission of William Morrow & Company, Inc. and of Chatto and Windus, Ltd. From *With Forks and Hope* by Elspeth Huxley. Copyright © 1964 by Elspeth Huxley. Adaptation from the chapter, "Nairobi," pages 146-151 of the American edition and pages 102-105 of the British edition.

1. Why does the writer tell us about the people he can see from his hotel?
2. What is meant by a "white-collar worker"?
3. Why does water from a tap delight a family of Nairobi?
4. If cities are like magnets, as the writer says, what are their problems likely to be?

FOLLOW UP   *Who's Who?* See if you can identify the following people connected with the history of Africa. Use an encyclopedia or biographical dictionary to find out about names you don't already know.

David Bruce   Haile Selassie
David Livingstone   Moise Tshombe
Albert Schweitzer   Jan Smuts
Cecil Rhodes   Alan Paton
Patrice Lumumba   Lobengula
Kwame Nkrumah   Albert Luthuli
Jomo Kenyatta   Ian Smith

11 REPUBLIC OF SOUTH AFRICA: A LAND DIVIDED

Reading For A Purpose: Why is this richest of southern African lands troubled?

1. The Republic of South Africa is one country that has not taken part in the "freedom explosion" in Africa. This nation became independent in 1910. The white people in the republic make up only one-fifth of the population. More than two-thirds of the people are black. Yet South Africa's black people have no share in the government of their country. In spite of the freedom movement among its African neighbors, the Republic of South Africa has not changed its traditional policy of keeping Africans down.

2. The Republic of South Africa is located at the southern end of the African continent. It is made up of four provinces and a "trust territory" to the west called South-West Africa. It is the only country on the continent that is almost entirely in the middle latitudes. Except for a narrow belt of lowland along the coast, the country is a great plateau. The western and northern parts of the plateau are desert. The rest is a grassy prairie land known as the *veld*. The winds from the Indian Ocean provide this area with enough rain for farming and grazing.

3. The Dutch were the first European settlers in South Africa. In 1652, they set up a small trading post at Capetown. In the early 1800's, the British occupied Capetown and the Dutch moved north, away from British rule. The Dutch settled on the veld and called their new homelands the Orange Free State and Transvaal. While they were moving north, they defeated Bantu tribes who were then moving south.

4. The Dutch farmers and herders on the veld were known as *Boers* (Dutch for "farmer"). When gold and diamonds were discovered in the lands of the Boers (1886), the British moved into their land. Before long, a war broke out between the Dutch descendants and the British. After several years of fighting, the Boers were defeated. All the provinces were united into a new self-governing part of the British Commonwealth. Today the Republic of South Africa is completely independent. In 1961, South Africa left the British "family" of nations because the British opposed its policy toward Africans.

5. Because of its natural resources, South Africa has become the richest country in Africa. Gold and diamonds are mined, and these industries are very important. The gold fields near Johannesburg are the richest in Africa. South Africa also has iron and coal. There are many factories that produce textiles, chemicals and automobiles. There is a modern transportation system. This republic has the highest standard of living on the continent—for its white people. It has the largest cities in Sub-Sahara Africa. Johannesburg has a population of more than a million. Other large cities are Capetown, Durban and Pretoria, the capital.

6. Despite the fact that it is the richest nation on the continent, the Republic of South Africa has a serious problem. The policy of the government is *apartheid*, or separation of races. The government does not want equality between black and white. As a result, the Bantu natives of South Africa live on *reserves*

A white South African store owner waits on a Bantu customer. In South Africa, black people deal with white people only when they shop or work. Otherwise, they stay in the areas set aside for them by the government. How do you feel about such a system of separation? Why?

that have been set aside for them. The soil and pasture land in the reserves are poor and it is hard for the native people to make a living. Many leave the reserves in search of a better living. Some move to the large cities, others to farms and mines owned by Europeans. When the Bantus move to the cities, they must live apart from the white people. Many of their homes are in slum areas. Now there are about six million Bantus living in the cities. Many are forgetting their old tribal ways of living.

7. What does apartheid mean to the Bantus of South Africa? It means that they live in two worlds. During the day, they work in the white world of skyscraper offices, department stores, factories and warehouses. When night comes, they must return to the all-black world of the Bantu reserve or section of the city. It means that they receive lower wages than white workers. Many are probably unable to read and write, for little schooling is provided for them. They are not able to vote and cannot take an active part in the government. When they move from one part of the city to the other, they are forced to have a special pass.

8. To Americans, and to most other people all over the world, apartheid is wrong and should be ended. But the white people of South Africa think differently. They believe that South Africa is theirs because they have worked and lived in it for many years. They feel they have the right to control the land and its resources. They feel that if Africans vote, they will lose their rights because there are more Africans than whites.

9. Africans feel apartheid is close to slavery. There have been many protests. Some of the demonstrations have led to bloodshed. The policy of the government toward Africans has brought criticism from other parts of the world. The United Nations has asked South Africa to end apartheid and to give up its colony of South-West Africa (Namibia).

UNDERSTANDING
CHAPTER 11

1. Which questions are answered in this chapter?
   a. Why do we say that the Republic of South Africa is rich?
   b. Where do many native people live?
   c. How are the people governed?
2. The main idea of *paragraph 6* is that:
   a. the Republic of South Africa has unequal laws for whites and blacks.
   b. large numbers of Bantus are moving to cities.
   c. reserves have been set aside for Bantus.
3. Most of the people of South Africa are:
   a. Africans.   b. Europeans.   c. Asians.
4. The largest city in Sub-Sahara Africa is:
   a. Nairobi.   b. Leopoldville.   c. Johannesburg.

5. We call the Republic of South Africa a rich country because:
   a. it has many natural resources.
   b. there is a great deal of fertile farm land.
   c. it has a democratic form of government.
6. There is unrest in the Republic of South Africa because:
   a. the government has changed often.
   b. the policy of apartheid separates people.
   c. there is no religious freedom.
7. A policy of *apartheid* means:
   a. equal rights.   b. separation of races.   c. religious persecution.
8. The Bantu tribes live on *reserves.* "Reserves" are:
   a. crowded sections of cities.
   b. river boats.
   c. lands set aside for farming and herding.

Map Study

Map #48a and b—Republic of South Africa

Map #48a—Republic of South Africa

Map #48b—Republic of South Africa and the United States

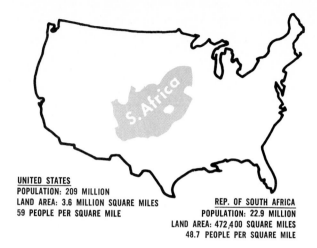

UNITED STATES
POPULATION: 209 MILLION
LAND AREA: 3.6 MILLION SQUARE MILES
59 PEOPLE PER SQUARE MILE

REP. OF SOUTH AFRICA
POPULATION: 22.9 MILLION
LAND AREA: 472,400 SQUARE MILES
48.7 PEOPLE PER SQUARE MILE

Study the maps on page 446 and this page. Then answer these questions.

1. In which direction is the equator from the Republic of South Africa?
2. Is the Republic of South Africa in the high, middle or low latitudes?
3. The Orange River flows into which body of water?
4. Which independent countries border the Republic of South Africa?
5. What is the latitude and longitude of the city of Durban?
6. Why do you think there are only a few large seaports in the Republic?
7. How does the map show you why early settlers remained near the coast?
8. The United States is how many times as large as the Republic of South Africa?
9. If you flew from your community to Capetown, in which direction would you be traveling? (See the map on page 584.)
10. Why has a large city grown inland at Johannesburg?

SUMMING UP   Complete the following chart in your notebook.

REPUBLIC OF SOUTH AFRICA

1. Location	
2. Size	
3. People	
4. Resources	
5. Problems	

Tell whether these statements are true or false. The underlined words make the statements true or false. If a statement is false, what word or words would you place in the statement to make it true?

1. The largest city in South Africa is <u>Capetown</u>.
2. The first white settlers of South Africa were <u>French</u>.
3. The <u>veld</u> is the farming and grazing land of <u>South Africa</u>.
4. The <u>separation</u> of races is known as <u>apartheid</u>.
5. The greatest number of people in the Republic of South Africa are the <u>Dutch</u>.
6. South Africa is bordered on the east by the <u>Indian Ocean</u>.
7. Most of the Republic of South Africa is located in the <u>middle</u> latitudes.
8. Before it became free, South Africa was ruled by <u>Great Britain</u>.
9. One of South Africa's great riches is <u>oil</u>.
10. The <u>Boers</u> were Dutch farmers in <u>South</u> Africa.

12 GHANA: AFRICA AWAKENING!

Reading For A Purpose: Can Ghana become one of Africa's leading nations?

1. Ghana was the first African nation on the continent to win its freedom from its European rulers. Ghana's people today are working hard to develop their land. There are many schools, fine roads, new hospitals and airfields, radios, telephones and modern buildings in its cities. The people are greatly interested in making their new government work. How have these changes come about?

2. The nation of Ghana is not far north of the equator. It lies almost in the center of the countries along the Gulf of Guinea. It is not a crowded country. Its population of about ten million lives in an area about the size of our state of Wyoming. Except for the sandy coast in the south and plateau in the north, most of Ghana is low forest-covered hills. Many rivers and streams crisscross the plateau. The chief river is the Volta. It rises in the country of Upper Volta to the north and flows southeastward to the sea.

3. There are heavy rains in the southwest of Ghana—as much as 100 inches a year. This is the rain forest. Most of Ghana, however, has a savanna climate. The savanna woodlands lie north of the rain forest. There are two seasons, wet and dry. During the wet season—the summer—the woodlands turn green and the rivers overflow their banks.

4. Portuguese sailors reached this part of Africa at the end of the 15th century. They were looking for gold, ivory, spices and slaves. So much gold was found and taken out that this country was called the Gold Coast. The Portuguese traders became so rich that the English, French, Dutch and Germans followed. In 1886, the coastal area became a British colony. The British gradually extended their power and territory northward.

5. When the British first came to the Gold Coast, they found they had to do certain things to get the raw materials out of the forests. They needed men to work in offices. They had to build schools and train people for jobs. They educated many Africans for leadership. These educated Africans gradually became unhappy with the rule of the British. During World War II, they fought on the side of the British, but they came back after the war filled with new ideas. They had fought for freedom; now they wanted it for their own land. In March, 1957, the Gold Coast became independent of Great Britain. The name of the country was changed to Ghana, the name of an ancient and powerful African kingdom. Ghana's "father of independence" was Kwame Nkrumah. Ghana is a member of the British Commonwealth of Nations.

6. Native-born Kwame Nkrumah governed for nine years. During these years, he did many things for the people. However, they began to fear his ways and his strong drive for power. Under his rule, the tribal chiefs lost much of their power. The National Assembly or parliament, the chief lawmaking body, became weak. Many people who did not agree

449

A chief of Ghana with members of his tribe. Today among the independent African nations there are at least 700 different tribes. Most tribes have a language of their own. Why is this a problem for Africa's new governments?

with him were put in jail. The newspapers, the courts and the schools had little freedom. Although he said that Ghana would not take sides in the Cold War, he became very friendly with the Communists. In 1966, the army removed him from office. He died in 1972.

7. The most powerful of the country's many tribes is the Ashanti. While English is the official language, many of the tribes speak their own languages. The religion of most Ghanaians is the religion of their tribe, although there are many Christians and Moslems. Ghanaians wear the most colorful dress in Africa. Their native dress is a many-colored robe called the "kenti." Modern dress is worn in the cities, but visitors will see many people in the gay colors of the kenti. The chief city and capital is Accra.

8. Most of Ghana's people are small farmers who own their own lands. The chief crop is cacao. It makes up seventy per cent of Ghana's exports. Palm oil, nuts, coconuts (copra) and cotton are also exported. For food, the people grow cassava, maize, yams and plantains (a fruit like a banana). Most villagers raise sheep,

goats and chickens as a source of meat. Fishing and cattle-raising are growing in importance. The government is also setting up a number of state farms. The average income of a Ghanaian worker is about $260 per year.

9. Before Ghana became free, most of its wealth came from its farms, chiefly from the growing of cacao. Today, the government is trying to develop other resources. Timber is being cut from the forest lands. Minerals such as gold, industrial diamonds, bauxite and manganese are being mined and exported. With the help of money from the United States, Ghana has built a dam on the Volta River. Opened in 1965, it provides water for irrigation and electric power. The electric power will be used to change bauxite into aluminum. New plants have been opened for the production of such items as matches, paper, tobacco products and insecticides (insect killers).

10. Independence has done much for the people of Ghana. Although schools had been started by the British government and missionaries, it is the new nation that is ending illiteracy through education for all. There are two fine universities, and a third one is planned. With the help of the Peace Corps, leaders have been trained for the government. Hospitals and clinics are being built to improve health conditions. Doctors are fighting sleeping sickness, malaria and tuberculosis, which are the three chief killers.

11. In Ghana, as in many nations of Africa, most new industries have been started by the government. Leaders no longer want their resources to be controlled by outsiders. Despite this development, however, much of Ghana is still influenced by Great Britain and the United States. Many of the government officers were educated in Britain. English books and magazines and American films, foods and clothing are plentiful. English is the language of business, government and the schools. Ghana still has strong ties with the Western world.

A government health worker in Ghana sprays a village to destroy mosquitoes. What other measures are needed to help prevent the spread of disease in Africa?

UNDERSTANDING CHAPTER 12

1. Which questions are answered in this chapter?
   a. Which Negro kingdoms once ruled Ghana?
   b. What are the chief minerals of Ghana?
   c. Who is Kwame Nkrumah?
2. The main idea of *paragraph 6* describes the:
   a. rule of Kwame Nkrumah.
   b. nation's system of government.
   c. place of Ghana in the "Cold War."
3. The main idea of *paragraph 9* describes:
   a. the Volta River dam.
   b. the importance of the sale of cacao.
   c. other resources of Ghana.
4. The old name for Ghana was:
   a. Gold Coast.   b. Mali.   c. Upper Volta.
5. One of Ghana's farm problems is that:
   a. the land is not owned by the people.
   b. the rain forest is of little use.
   c. there is too much dependence on cacao.
6. Ghana's freedom was important in the history of Africa because:
   a. No other African country has become free since.
   b. Ghana was the first African colony to become free.
   c. Ghana's freedom ended British rule in Africa.
7. The government of Ghana has built the Volta River dam to:
   a. provide more electric power.
   b. increase the importance of ocean fishing.
   c. change the course of the river.

Map Study

Map #49a and b—Ghana

Study the maps on this page and page 453. Then answer these questions.
1. Is Ghana north or south of the equator?
2. Is Ghana located in the high, middle or low latitudes?
3. What does the location of Ghana tell you about its climate?
4. What is the important river of Ghana? In what direction does it flow?
5. What is the distance from the northern border to the southern border?
6. What is the capital city of Ghana?
7. Which is more thickly populated, Ghana or our state of Wyoming?
8. How would you describe the topography of Ghana?

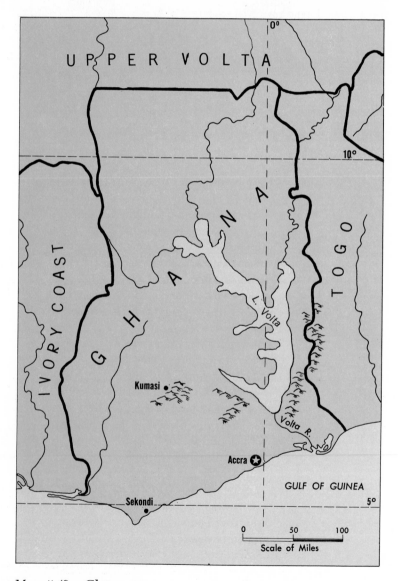

Map #49a—Ghana

Map #49b—Ghana and Wyoming

WYOMING
POPULATION: 332,400
LAND AREA: 97,914 SQUARE MILES
3.4 PEOPLE PER SQUARE MILE

GHANA
POPULATION: 9.6 MILLION
LAND AREA: 92,099 SQUARE MILES
96 PEOPLE PER SQUARE MILE

SUMMING UP   Complete the following chart in your notebook. Head it, "Some New Nations of Africa." Use an almanac, an encyclopedia or an atlas to get additional facts.

NEW NATION	CLIMATE	LAND	PEOPLE AND GOVERNMENT	RESOURCES
Ghana				
Ivory Coast				
Nigeria				
Kenya				
Zambia				

FOLLOW UP   I. *True or False*   The following statements are true or false. The underlined words make the statements true or false. If a statement is false, what word or words would you place in it to make it true?
1. Most of Ghana has a <u>desert</u> climate.
2. The first Europeans to be interested in Ghana were from <u>France</u>.
3. Ghana's "father of independence" was <u>Kwame Nkrumah</u>.
4. The chief export crop of Ghana is <u>copra</u>.
5. The capital of Ghana is <u>Accra</u>.
6. The official language of Ghana is <u>French</u>.
7. Ghana is a member of the <u>British Commonwealth of Nations</u>.
8. Most Ghanaians are <u>small farmers</u>.

II. *Fact or Opinion* Read each statement carefully. If the statement is a fact, write F in your notebook. If it is an opinion, write O.
1. Kwame Nkrumah did more for Ghana than the British did.
2. Some of the tribes would like to have more power in the government.
3. The education of the people is improving year by year.
4. The new Volta Dam will make Ghana the richest nation in western Africa.
5. Ghana is a member of the United Nations.
6. Ghana would become richer if the cotton industry were developed.
7. Only a small part of Ghana borders the sea.
8. Ghana cannot stay neutral in world affairs for very long.

BOOKS FOR UNIT 8

Author	Title, Publisher	Description
1. Ames, Sophia	NKRUMAH OF GHANA, Rand McNally	A biography of the leader of Ghanaian independence.
2. Arnold, Richard	THE TRUE STORY OF DAVID LIVINGSTONE, EXPLORER, Children's Press	The story of the missionary doctor who mapped the unknown regions of central Africa.
3. Archer, Jules	AFRICAN FIREBRAND: KENYATTA OF KENYA, Jules Messner	A biography that helps us understand the problems of new nations in Africa.
4. Archer, Jules	CONGO: THE BIRTH OF A NEW NATION, Messner	How a new nation began amid war, mutiny and murder.
5. Brown, Leslie	AFRICA, A NATURAL HISTORY, Random House	Illustrated text on animal and plant life of the continent.
6. Chu, Daniel and Elliott Skinner	A GLORIOUS AGE IN AFRICA, Doubleday	The story of the three great empires of Western Africa.
7. Davidson, Basil	A GUIDE TO AFRICAN HISTORY, Doubleday	Bright, general survey of the African past.
8. Dobler, Lavinia and William A. Brown	GREAT RULERS OF THE AFRICAN PAST, Doubleday	An account of the great African empires as seen through the lives of great rulers.
9. Editors of Sterling Publishing Co.	VISUAL GEOGRAPHY SERIES: GHANA, KENYA, SOUTH AFRICA, Sterling	Interesting accounts of the life and culture of the people of each country.

454

10.	Glubok, Shirley	THE ART OF AFRICA, Macmillan	Illustrations of striking works of art that show the history and culture of the continent.
11.	Guillot, Rene	SAMA, Hale	An elephant prince is humbled by capture and life in a circus.
12.	Mennett, John	ALBERT SCHWEITZER, HUMANITARIAN, Children's Press	The story of the doctor who devoted his life to helping the people of West Africa.
13.	Mirsky, Reba	SEVEN GRANDMOTHERS, Follett	Life among the Zulu people.
14.	Spencer, Cornelia	CLAIM TO FREEDOM, John Day	The awakening of new nations in Africa.
15.	Turnbull, Colin	THE PEOPLES OF AFRICA, World	Understanding of the life and culture of hunters, herdsmen and farmers.
16.	Waldeck, Theodore	LIONS ON THE HUNT, Viking	A study of the African veld.

UNIT 9
The Far East

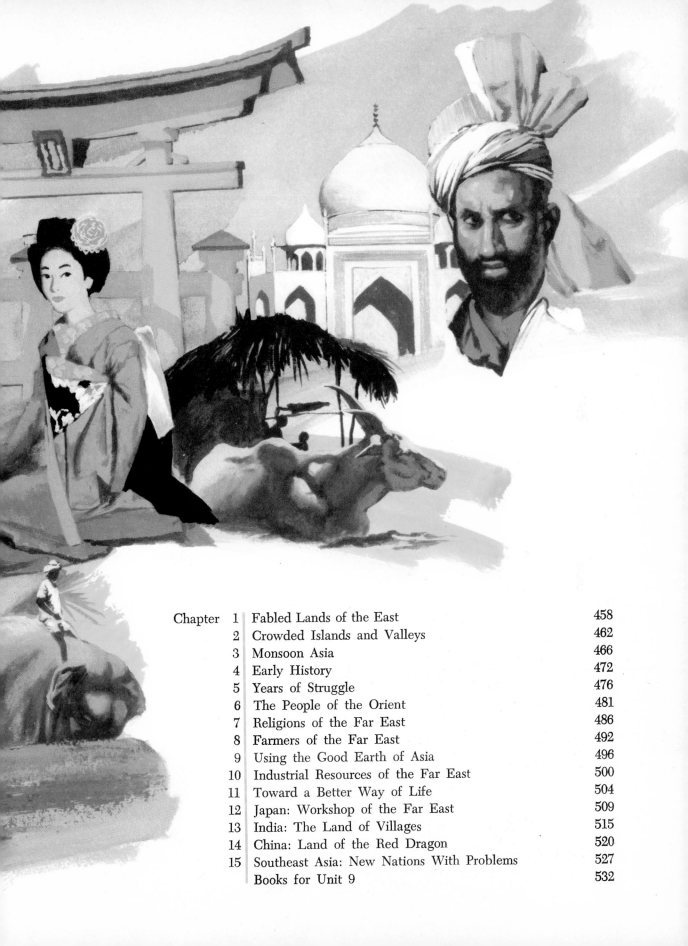

1 FABLED LANDS OF THE EAST

Reading For A Purpose: Why are we interested in the Far East?

1. The Far East is the home of more than half the people of the world. Many of them are poor and hungry. Almost 2 billion people live in a vast region extending over 4,000 miles, from Pakistan on the west to the Philippine Islands on the east. What's more, the Far East is a region of great change. Most of the people live under new governments whose leaders are hopeful of providing them with a better way of life. Millions of people throughout Asia and the rest of the world are watching to see how these new nations will develop.

2. The Far East is often divided into three parts. First, there is the Indian peninsula, which is so big that it is sometimes called a *subcontinent*—that is, almost a continent. This area includes the countries of India, Pakistan, Bangladesh and Sri Lanka, an island nation. Eastward are the smaller nations of Southeast Asia, the second part. This includes the island republics of Indonesia and the Philippines and a Texas-sized peninsula divided among the countries of Burma, Thailand (Siam), Malaysia and the countries of what was Indochina (Cambodia, Laos, Vietnam). Northward in the third part of the Far East are the countries of eastern Asia: China, North and South Korea, and the easternmost islands of Japan and Taiwan (Formosa).

3. The whole region is called the Far East because it lies far to the east of Europe. These lands were visited by Marco Polo in the thirteenth century. When he returned to Europe, he described the riches of these faraway lands. The term "Far East" was used by early mer-

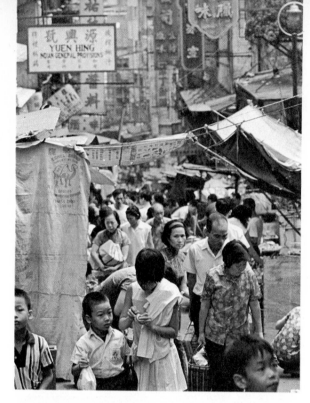

Hong Kong street scene. The tiny British colony of Hong Kong supports a population of more than four million people. What problems can such overcrowding create?

chants who traveled to these lands in search of the goods described by Marco Polo. Part of this region is called the Orient, because the word means "the East."

4. The Far Eastern countries vary in size. The largest country in the region, and the third largest in the world, is China. The second largest country in the Far East is India. The

What differences do you note between the Hong Kong street scene and this scene of village people in southern India? What similarities do you note?

three nations on the Indian subcontinent—India, Pakistan, and Bangladesh—are about half the size of the United States. Indonesia is not much larger than our state of Alaska, but its many islands extend over 3,000 miles from east to west. The Philippines is not much larger than our state of Colorado, but its islands reach about 1,100 miles north and south. Japan, the richest country of the Far East, is about as large as our state of Montana.

5. The United States is interested in the Far East for many reasons. First, we get many valuable raw materials from the people of the Orient—tin, rubber, silk, quinine, spices and jute. In exchange, we send them the manufactured goods of our factories. Our trade with Japan is greater than our trade with either Great Britain or West Germany.

6. Second, the United States is concerned about the growing power of China in the countries of the Far East. The Communists took over China in 1949. The former Nationalist government of Chiang Kai-shek moved to the island of Formosa or Taiwan. Now about 850 million people live under the rule of the Communist Party in China. In 1964, China became the only Asian nation to explode an atom bomb.

7. China is using its growing power throughout the region. In 1950, Chinese soldiers fought United Nations troops in Korea. In

Unloading jute at a mill in Calcutta, India. Jute fibers are removed from the stalk and are taken to the mill for processing into burlap and twine.

1962, they battled Indian soldiers along the Himalayan border. They are giving support to local Communists and to "civil wars" in the smaller countries of Southeast Asia.

8. While China, North Korea, Cambodia and Vietnam have Communist governments, other Asian nations are trying to develop a democratic way of life. These are the nations of India, Japan, the Philippines and some of the nations of Southeast Asia. (The Philippines was given its independence by the United States in 1946.) They need time to develop their resources and to give their people a better way of life. Since the end of World War II, there has been much fighting in Southeast Asia between Communists and those who oppose communism.

UNDERSTANDING CHAPTER 1

1. Which questions are answered in this chapter?
   a. Why are we interested in the Far East?
   b. What were the results of the Korean War?
   c. What government has headquarters on Formosa?
2. The main idea of this chapter describes:
   a. how the new nations of the Far East have won their freedom.
   b. why the Far East is important to us.
   c. the growing power of China.
3. The largest country of the Far East is:
   a. India.   b. Indonesia.   c. China.
4. Most of the countries of the Far East are part of the continent of:
   a. Asia.   b. Australia.   c. Africa.

5. Why are these lands called the Far East?
   a. They lie far to the east of Europe.
   b. The sun rises in the east.
   c. The Pacific Ocean is east of the mainland.
6. Why are India, Japan and the Philippines of unusual interest to us?
   a. All are island groups off eastern Asia.
   b. All have had civil wars in the past few years.
   c. All are trying to make democratic governments work.
7. The *Orient* is the same as the:
   a. West.   b. East.   c. North.
8. A *subcontinent* is:
   a. like an archipelago.
   b. land "below" the equator.
   c. a body of land almost as large as a continent.

Map #50—The Far East

Map Study

Map #50—The Far East

Study the map on page 460. Then answer these questions.
1. Is the region north or south of the equator?
2. Is the region east or west of the Prime Meridian?
3. Does the region extend farther from east to west or from north to south?
4. What region or regions are near it?
5. What are the chief bodies of water that border the region?
6. Which countries have no outlets to the sea?
7. What are some of the important rivers in the region?
8. Are there large rivers that form boundary lines between countries?
9. How do you know which cities are capitals of their countries?
10. Which countries are island nations?
11. Which countries are located on peninsulas?
12. Which lands are colonies of other nations?

Reasons for Our Interest in the Far East   In your notebook, copy the following and place a check (√) next to those items that are reasons for our interest in this region.
1. The power of Communism is spreading in the Far East.
2. Half the people of the world live there.
3. The Suez Canal is an important waterway.
4. Our troops were fighting in the Far East.
5. These people are customers for our manufactured goods.
6. Many Far Eastern nations have won their freedom lately.
7. There are many raw materials there that we need.
8. In this region the Industrial Revolution began.

Match each country in Column A with one of the items in Column B.

COLUMN A	COLUMN B
1. China	a. Government of Nationalist China.
2. Japan	b. Island republic that once belonged to the United States.
3. Taiwan	c. Center of a civil war.
4. India	d. Largest Communist country.
5. Vietnam	e. Carries on greatest trade with the United States.
6. The Philippines	f. Negro republic.
	g. Occupies a subcontinent.

461

2 CROWDED ISLANDS AND VALLEYS

Reading For A Purpose: What is the topography of the Far East?

The Himalayas form a natural barrier on the border of India and China. What influence do you think these mountains have had upon the relationship between the Indians and the Chinese?

1. Much of the Far East is mountainous. The inner highlands of the Far East are the highest in the world. In the south are the Himalaya Mountains. These mountains extend east and west for 1500 miles, separating India from the countries to the north. Mount Everest, in the Himalayas, is the highest mountain peak in the world. In the middle of these great mountains is the lonely Plateau of Tibet. This plateau, about 16,000 feet above sea level, is sometimes called the "roof of the world."

2. Ranges of high mountains continue from Tibet southward across the Malay Peninsula. There they drop below the surface of the seas and appear again above water to form the main islands of Southeast Asia. Another mountain range runs eastward through the center of China, dividing it into two regions. In general, however, the land slopes downward from the inner highlands until it reaches the great Chinese plains in the north and the Pacific Ocean in the south.

3. Many rivers rise in the mountains of the Far East and form plains as they flow toward the oceans. The lowlands formed by these rivers are bordered by hills and low mountains. Millions of people in the Far East are crowded into these river valleys, working the fertile land. The rivers bring the rich soil of the mountains into the valleys and supply water to irrigate the crops.

4. Three major rivers rise in the Himalayas —the Ganges, the Brahmaputra and the Indus. The Ganges flows across northern India, forming a great lowland plain. It flows southeastward and empties into the Indian Ocean near the city of Calcutta. The Brahmaputra flows southwestward from the northern mountains and joins the Ganges in East Pakistan. The Indus flows through the dry lands of West Pakistan and empties into the Arabian Sea.

5. China has three great rivers that rise in the mountains to the west. The Hwang, or Yellow, River begins in the Plateau of Tibet and flows through northern China to the sea. (The region through which it flows is covered with a fine yellow dust called *loess*. As it flows through the loess hills, the river picks up the yellow dirt. Thus, it has been given the name of Yellow River.) The Hwang is not a deep river. When there are heavy rains, the river overflows its banks and floods the land. For this reason it is sometimes called "China's Sorrow."

6. The Yangtze, the fourth longest river in the world, is China's longest and most useful river. It rises in Tibet and flows eastward to the sea near the city of Shanghai. The Yangtze is comparable to our Mississippi. Along this waterway, one-tenth of all the world's people live. The Yangtze is connected to the Hwang by a canal. Farther south is the Hsi River, flowing into the sea near the city of Canton.

7. Several large rivers also flow southward across the vast peninsula of Southeast Asia. The Irrawaddy, Mekong and Red Rivers rise in the Himalayas. They form broad valleys and deltas as they flow toward the sea. These valleys are separated by rugged mountain ranges.

8. Off the mainland of southern and eastern Asia are thousands of islands. These groups of islands are called *archipelagoes*. The main archipelagoes are Japan, the Philippines and Indonesia. A large number of these islands have volcanoes. The lava from the volcanoes has kept the soil of some of these islands in a very fertile condition.

9. Finally, one of the most striking features of this region is that, like Western Europe, there are so many peninsulas. India is almost completely surrounded by water as it reaches out into the ocean. The Malay-Indochina peninsula is very heavily populated. It is near the important trade routes that lead to the great city-state of Singapore. The Korean peninsula has long been a center of dispute between

This photograph taken from a spacecraft shows the subcontinent of India. What bodies of water and land forms can you identify?

Japan, China and the Soviet Union. Many of these peninsulas are near much-traveled bodies of water and are therefore important in world trade.

UNDERSTANDING CHAPTER 2

1. Which questions are answered in this chapter?
   a. Why are the rivers of Asia important?
   b. When was Mount Everest first climbed?
   c. How does the Yellow River cause sorrow?
2. The main idea of this chapter describes:
   a. the topography of the Far East.
   b. the chief rivers of the Far East.
   c. the mountains of the Far East.
3. The highest mountain chain in the world is the:
   a. Rockies.   b. Andes.   c. Himalayas.
4. The city of Calcutta is located near the mouth of which river?
   a. The Ganges.   b. The Yangtze.   c. The Mekong.
5. The rivers are important to the people of the Far East for all these reasons EXCEPT:
   a. they furnish rich soil for farming.
   b. they serve as boundaries between countries.
   c. they provide water for irrigation.

6. Rivers are said to have the opposite effect of mountains because:
   a. rivers are a source of great mineral wealth.
   b. mountains have kept people apart; rivers have brought people together.
   c. the mountains of the Far East have the best soils.
7. The word *loess* would have most meaning to a:
   a. farmer.   b. factory worker.   c. fisherman.
8. A group of islands surrounded by a large body of water is:
   a. a continent.   b. an archipelago.   c. a peninsula.

LAND FORMS OF
THE FAR EAST

Mountains
Plateaus
Hills
Plains

Miles

Map Study

Map #51—Land Forms of the Far East

Study the map on page 464. Then tell whether these statements are true or false. Be able to explain your answers.

1. Three great river systems have formed broad plains in the north of the Indian subcontinent.
2. Mountains are found on all the important islands of the Far East.
3. In Japan, there is more lowland than any other land form.
4. Lowland makes up a small part of the total land area of China.
5. A long, narrow plain stretches from north to south along the eastern coast of Asia.

Comparing Rivers Complete the following chart in your notebook. Refer to the regions you have already studied. If you need more information, use an almanac in the classroom or library.

RIVER	CONTINENT	LENGTH	MOUTH	KIND OF REGION THROUGH WHICH IT FLOWS
1. Yellow				
2. Yangtze				
3. Ganges				
4. Mekong				
5. Mississippi				
6. Amazon				
7. Nile				
8. Congo				
9. Danube				
10. Ob				

Complete the following sentences in your notebook.

1. The _____ are the highest mountains in the world.
2. The Plateau of _____ is sometimes called the "roof of the world."
3. A great number of the island mountains are _____.
4. The great northern plain of India is formed by the _____ River.
5. Most of the people who live in the river valleys make a living by _____.
6. Two large archipelagoes of the Far East are Japan and _____.
7. The great port of _____ is located at the southern end of the Malay Peninsula.
8. The island of _____ is located at the southern end of the Indian peninsula.

3 MONSOON ASIA

Reading For A Purpose: How do the climates of the Far East affect the way people live?

1. As you might guess, a region as large as the Far East has many kinds of climate. The Far East extends from the equator a great distance north. From Indonesia in the south to the Chinese-Soviet border is a distance of more than 60 degrees! This is the same distance as from the tropics of Brazil to Newfoundland, Canada. In the second place, much of the region is mountainous. Also, many of the land areas border or are surrounded by large bodies of water.

2. The equator passes through the southern part of this region. Indonesia, Malaysia, Sri Lanka and much of the Philippines, Southeast Asia and southern India are all within fifteen degrees of the equator. Indonesia, Malaysia and the Philippines are hot and rainy the year round. (Mountains provide some relief from the heat.) There is thick jungle and a year-round growing season. The heavy rains wash minerals from the soil. This is the same kind of climate as is found in the Amazon Basin in South America and the Congo in Africa; it is the rain forest.

3. In many ways, however, the rain forest of Southeast Asia is different from the others we have studied. One of the chief differences is caused by the land itself. The Amazon and Congo forests are within the hearts of their continents. In Southeast Asia, this climate is found largely on islands off the mainland. Again, in the Amazon and Congo, the land is largely lowland plains. The Asian rain-forest lands are mountainous. Around the mountain

"centers" of the islands is a narrow belt of hilly lands, next to which are the coastal plains.

4. The rain forests of Asia support a huge population. Some of the fertile areas of rain forest in Southeast Asia have more people for each square mile of land than any other farming area in the world! These people have cleared more land in the Asian forests than have the people of either the Amazon or the Congo. The example that the people of Southeast Asia have set gives hope that the Amazon and Congo rain forests will some day contain more people and be more productive.

5. North of the rain forest, the tropical savanna climate is found. As in other savanna regions, there is a wet and a dry season. This climate is found in most of India, Sri Lanka, Burma, Thailand and the new countries of Southeast Asia. These lands are affected by winds called *monsoons*. The monsoons are winds that blow steadily either from the water or from the land for several weeks at a time. During the summer, the winds blow from the ocean to the land; they are hot and rainy. During the winter, they blow from the land to the sea; they are dry and cold.

6. The reasons for the monsoon winds are easy to understand. Land heats more quickly than water. During the summer months, the hot rays of the sun beat down on the lands of

The Great Indian Desert in the northwest is hot and dry throughout the year. Which other regions have this same climate?

Southeast Asia. The air is also heated. The warm air then rises because it is lighter. Because the ocean waters are cooler than the land, the ocean air remains cool and heavy. When the warm land air rises, the cool air over the oceans rushes toward the land to take the place of the rising warm air. It brings rain to the land. This rainfall takes place from May to October. During the winter months, the monsoon winds change because the land becomes cooler than the water. The air over the ocean is then warmer than the air over the land. The warm ocean air rises and the cooler land air moves in to take its place, making dry winds. These blow from November to March.

7. The people of Southeast Asia cannot get along without the monsoons. In May, they begin to watch the skies for the coming of the summer monsoons. The summer winds bring rain and the land becomes green again. Without this rain, the crops would fail. The farmers try to save some of the water in small tanks or reservoirs. If there is too little or too much rain, or if it is too late, farmers can be ruined.

8. In southeastern China and in parts of Japan, the climate is humid subtropical. This region is much like our southeastern states. The summers are long, hot and rainy. The winters are mild and there is less rain. This makes for a long, moist growing season. Southern

The southwest monsoon, or seasonal wind, brings needed rain to the northern plains. What causes rain to fall during the summer months?

Farmers in China working in the rice fields. What kind of climate is necessary for a good rice crop?

China is a rice-growing region. (You will remember that rice can also be grown in our southeastern states from South Carolina to Louisiana.)

9. Farther north in China and Japan, the climate is like that of the northeastern United States. Peking, China, is the same distance from the equator as New York City is, while the boundary between North and South Korea is 38° North Latitude. There are long, cold winters, hot summers, and enough rainfall to support crops. Near the sea, the temperatures are milder throughout the year. In the mountains, the cold of winter is very severe. The lower rainfall in the north has made this an area of wheat growing.

10. Most of western China lies in the dry regions of Asia. Almost half of this land is desert; the other part is a region of grassy steppes. (Grass will grow where the rainfall is at least ten inches a year.) The desert areas are almost completely surrounded by mountains, which keep out the rain-bearing winds. The Gobi Desert of northwestern China is one of the loneliest places on earth. Few people live there. In Pakistan there is another vast dry region. The Indus River is important, for it provides water for irrigation.

UNDERSTANDING CHAPTER 3

1. Which questions are answered in this chapter?
   a. When was the Asian rain forest cleared?
   b. What causes the monsoon winds?
   c. Why is the Gobi Desert such a dry place?
2. The main idea of *paragraphs 3 and 4* is that:
   a. the problems of all rain forests are alike.
   b. the rain forest of Southeast Asia is chiefly lowland.
   c. the rain forest of Southeast Asia supports more people than rain forests in America or Africa.
3. The climate of many lands of Southeast Asia is affected by the:
   a. monsoons.   b. Himalayas.   c. winds from Siberia.
4. Southeastern China has a climate like that of:
   a. Oregon and Washington.
   b. Massachusetts and New York.
   c. South Carolina and Georgia.
5. Monsoons are important to the people of the Far East because they:
   a. bring rain for crops.
   b. bring cool weather.
   c. bring fine soil from the interior.
6. The Asian rain forest is more important in our changing world than the Amazon rain forest because it:
   a. is a wonderful place for visitors to spend their vacations.
   b. is drained by a great river.
   c. supports a greater population.
7. People in *monsoon* lands have:
   a. rain throughout the year.
   b. a wet and dry season.
   c. only ten inches of rain a year.

Map Study

Map #52—The Monsoons

Study the maps. Then answer these questions.
1. Where do the winds come from in the summer?
2. Where do the winds come from in the winter?
3. Which monsoons bring rain?
4. Which are the dry monsoons?
5. Why does this change of wind direction take place in India?

Map #53—Climates of the Far East

Agree or Disagree   Study the map. Then decide whether or not each of the statements below agrees with the information on the map. If the answer is *disagree*, explain why.

1. Almost all of the islands of Southeast Asia are located in the region of the rain forest.
2. Japan and the Philippines have climates that are very much alike.
3. Mountains cause some changes in the climate of the islands of Southeast Asia.
4. No Mediterranean climate is found in the Far East.
5. Colder areas are found in central Asia.
6. Most of the climatic regions of the Far East are in the low latitudes.
7. Nearly all of India is rain forest.

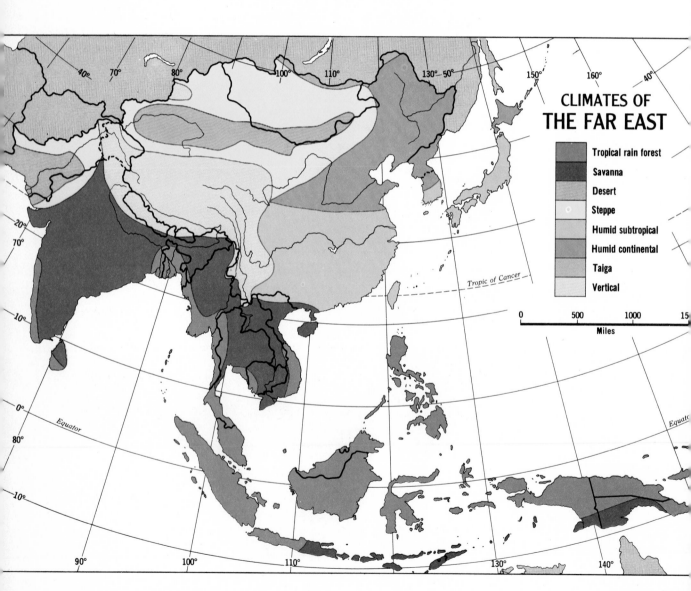

CLIMATES OF THE FAR EAST

Tropical rain forest
Savanna
Desert
Steppe
Humid subtropical
Humid continental
Taiga
Vertical

8. The differences in climate along the eastern coast of China are caused chiefly by changes in latitude.
9. This region is unusual in that deserts are located in the low latitudes.
10. The climate of northeastern China is like that of northern Canada.

SUMMING UP   Complete the following outline in your notebook.

Comparing Rain Forests—Amazon, Congo and Asian

I. How They Are Alike.
  1.
  2.
  3.

II. How the Asian Rain Forest Is Different.
  1.
  2.
  3.

FOLLOW UP   *Making Inferences*   In our reading, many facts are given to us. From these facts we draw conclusions. The following are some conclusions or inferences that you might make after reading Chapter 3. Tell whether these conclusions are correct or incorrect. Give reasons for your answers.

1. The farmers of Indonesia and the Amazon River Valley could grow the same crops.
2. On the Gobi Desert, life would be very different from that on the Sahara in Africa.
3. A large part of the population of Pakistan probably lives near the Indus River.
4. In Indonesia and the Philippines, temperatures throughout the year might vary from 20° to 100°.
5. If the wet monsoon should arrive later than usual, millions of Asian people might starve.
6. The growing season in Indonesia is shorter than the growing season in northeastern China.

4 EARLY HISTORY

Reading For A Purpose: How did people live in the ancient lands of China and India?

1. The ancient Chinese were almost completely shut off from the outside world by natural barriers. To the east lay the great Pacific Ocean. To the south was a dense tropical forest where elephants, tigers and other wild animals lived. The high Himalayas and the highlands of Tibet shut off the ancient people on the west. The only opening into China was through the Gobi Desert to the north. As a result, these ancient people developed their own way of life.

2. Some of the earliest civilizations known to man started in the Far East. It is believed that the art of government first began in the valley of the Yellow River and spread southward to the Yangtze River Valley. (The early Chinese people had to have laws in order to share the work of fighting floods and building canals.) It was near the Yangtze that rice became the main food of the ancient Chinese people. The rice-growers changed the land. They built terraces on the hillsides. They divided the land into hundreds of small, diked fields.

3. For much of its history China was ruled by powerful families. These ruling families were called *dynasties*. The founder of a dynasty would take and hold power over the people by means of a strong army. Over the years, the dynasty would grow weak and a new family would take its place. In time, another man would build up a powerful army and set up a

In the third century B.C., the Great Wall was built to keep out invaders from the north. This 1500-mile wall is a symbol of the isolation which for years China maintained from the outside world. Why is isolation from other countries almost impossible in today's world?

strong government. Then his dynasty would rule for a while. This happened many times.

4. The history of China is also the history of many invasions. On the northern steppes were tribes of nomads who raised goats and sheep. These nomads often moved southward in search of better pastures for their herds. The Chinese built a great wall along their northern border to keep the nomads out. The wall did not succeed. Again and again, Chinese armies had to battle invaders from the north. Finally, a very strong tribe called the Mongols overran large parts of Asia and Russia. Their leader was Genghis Khan. About 1260, his grandson, Kublai Khan, became the ruler of all China.

5. The stories of Marco Polo tell us much of the size and riches of the great empire of the Mongols. Marco Polo went to the Far East with his father and uncle and lived in Cathay, as China was called, from 1275 to 1292. He was amazed to see the beauty and wealth of China. When he returned to Europe, he described what he had seen. Marco Polo told the people of Europe about such Chinese inventions as printed money, gunpowder, the compass and a counting machine. He described how the Chinese made silk and paper and printed by wood blocks and movable type.

6. Chinese civilization did not remain within the borders of that country. It spread to Korea and later to Japan. The Japanese, over a period of years, imitated the Chinese in many ways. They used their system of writing. They adopted their religion and copied their form of government. In time, the Japanese people were taught to obey their emperor because he was supposed to have descended from the gods.

7. There were other early civilizations in the Far East, as we know from certain ruins that still exist. We are just beginning to learn that in India there was a civilization as old as that of China. A dark-skinned people had settled in the river valleys of the northern plain. About 2,000 years before the time of Christ, they were invaded by wandering herders from the northwest. These nomads were a light-skinned

The Taj Mahal was built in the 1600's by an emperor of India. It is constructed entirely of white marble. This magnificent structure symbolizes for many the beauty and mystery of India.

people called Aryans (from the language they spoke). The Aryans pushed the earlier people slowly toward the south. Under the Aryans, the Hindu religion began to develop.

8. India was invaded many times. In 327 B.C., Alexander the Great of Greece reached India. In the tenth century, Moslems from Central Asia invaded India through the Himalayas and overran much of the land. India was ruled during the next few centuries by Moslem dynasties. In the thirteenth century, the Mongols (who were also Moslems) began their invasion of India. The invasions by Mongol tribes continued for several hundred years, during which the Mongol chiefs ruled India.

9. Meanwhile, the ships of Europe were beginning to come to the Far East. Since the time of Marco Polo, the people of Europe wanted the precious jewels, cloth and spices of the Orient. Most of these goods were reaching Europe over land routes. The kings of Europe wanted an all-water route that would be quicker, safer and cheaper. This all-water route was found in 1498 by the Portuguese explorer Vasco da Gama, who sailed around Africa. After the Portuguese established a colony in India, the English, Dutch and French followed the same route and set up their own trading posts in the Orient.

1. Which questions are answered in this chapter?
   a. Why did the Chinese build a great wall?
   b. Why did Europeans want an all-water route to the Far East?
   c. Who built the Taj Mahal?
2. The main idea of *paragraphs 2 through 5* describes the:
   a. early history of China.
   b. importance of Mongol invasions.
   c. journeys of Marco Polo.
3. The Koreans and Japanese can trace their civilizations to the:
   a. Aryans.   b. Chinese.   c. Greeks.
4. An early invader of India was:
   a. Kublai Khan.   b. Vasco da Gama.   c. Alexander the Great.
5. The Chinese built a great wall to:
   a. keep out nomad tribes.
   b. keep their people from moving west.
   c. stop trade with European nations.
6. Europeans wanted an all-water route to the Far East because they:
   a. wanted more knowledge of the oceans.
   b. wanted the spices and jewels of the Orient.
   c. were looking for adventure.
7. A *dynasty* is in many ways like:
   a. a democracy.
   b. the dictatorship of a few men.
   c. a royal family or monarchy.
8. In *paragraph 6*, the phrase "descended from the gods" means:
   a. "following a tribal religion."
   b. "the gods were his ancestors."
   c. "ruled according to the teachings of the Bible."

Picture Symbols

These pictures should help you to recall parts of the chapter you have read.
What is the main idea of each picture?

Which Does Not Belong?   Select the item in each group that does not belong with the others.

1. What the ancient Chinese invented: a. printing,   b. use of gunpowder, c. a calendar of 365 days.
2. How China was shut off from the world: a. Mediterranean Sea,   b. Gobi Desert,   c. Pacific Ocean.
3. People who came to China: a. Mongols,   b. Aryans,   c. Marco Polo.
4. European nations that settled in the Far East after 1498:   a. Portugal,   b. France,   c. Italy.
5. People who came to India: a. da Gama,   b. Alexander the Great,   c. Kublai Khan.
6. How the Japanese imitated the Chinese: a. trade with Europe,   b. followed the religion of the Chinese,   c. used the Chinese system of writing.

FOLLOW UP   Some of the people who are outstanding in the history of the Far East had interesting lives. In your class or school library, find out more about these famous people in the history of the Far East:

Alexander the Great   Marco Polo
Genghis Khan   Asoka
Kublai Khan   Akbar
Baber   Gautama Buddha

5 YEARS OF STRUGGLE

Reading For A Purpose: How did the lands of the Far East win their freedom?

1. After Vasco da Gama's voyage, the European nations rushed to obtain the riches of the Orient. Gradually, they gained control of many lands in the Far East. By 1858, Great Britain had won control of the Indian subcontinent. The Dutch ruled the Netherlands East Indies. The French were powerful in Indochina, the lands of the southeast peninsula. Portugal never became as strong as the others and held only small territories.

2. The nations of Europe and North America knew very little about China and Japan. China was ruled by an all-powerful emperor and a strong army. Japan was divided among powerful landowners called feudal lords. Each lord ruled over the peasants who worked his fields. The most powerful lord, or *shogun*, was stronger than the emperor who ruled the land. The Chinese emperor and the Japanese shogun kept their lands shut off from the rest of the world.

3. The Western nations, however, were beginning to produce great amounts of goods by machine. They became interested in the Far East as a place to sell their goods. They began to force the Chinese nation to allow trade with them. At the same time American sailors, shipwrecked on Japanese shores, reported that they were badly treated. In 1853, Commodore Perry was sent to make a treaty with Japan. The Japanese agreed not to harm American sailors and to let the United States trade in several of their harbors.

4. The Japanese rulers saw that they could no longer keep their country shut off from other nations. The government decided that the people must change their ways of living. Within a short time Japan built up a strong army and navy. It learned to make use of the machines of European nations. Factories were started. Japan became the strongest nation in the Far East. It attacked China and occupied Formosa and Korea.

5. At the same time, China was growing

This painting shows the arrival of Matthew Perry in Japan in 1853. Why did the United States become interested in Japan in the mid-1800's?

weaker. The British, French, Russians, Germans and Japanese soon gained control over parts of the country. In order to help China and to protect American trade with that country, the United States announced the "Open Door Policy" in 1899. By this, we meant that China should be open to all nations that wished to trade or do business there.

6. In 1911, the Chinese people overthrew their weak ruler and formed a new government. The revolution was led by a young doctor named Sun Yat-sen. His government was called the Nationalist government. Sun Yat-sen died in 1925, before he could unite China. He was followed by General Chiang Kai-shek. From the beginning, Chiang fought to rid his government of Communists. He drove them to hideouts in northern China.

7. Japan was becoming warlike. The Japanese wanted to extend their control over the entire Far East. They wanted the rich natural resources of Southeast Asia. In the 1930's Japan again attacked China, took away Manchuria, and occupied much of the east coast. The United States protested these conquests of Japan. On December 7, 1941, Japan made a surprise attack on the American naval base at Pearl Harbor in Hawaii. The United States was now in World War II.

8. For a time, Japan was successful. Japanese armies overran many of the lands of Southeast Asia. They also came close to landing in Australia. In the Pacific, World War II lasted almost four years. The Japanese were finally defeated. Toward the end of the war, the United States used a new weapon, the atomic bomb, to destroy two cities on the Japanese mainland. Japan lost all that it had gained by conquest as a result of the war. Instead of an empire, Japan's rulers brought only hardship and suffering to their people.

9. Following the war, the colonies of European nations demanded their independence. India, Sri Lanka, Pakistan and Burma broke away from Great Britain and became self-gov-

Chiang Kai-shek, for many years head of the Nationalist Chinese government on Taiwan. Do you think two separate Chinese governments—the Communist government of the People's Republic of China and the Nationalist government on Taiwan—each of which claims to represent the Chinese people, can both survive? Why?

erning. Civil war broke out again in China between the Nationalists and the Communists. By 1949, the Communists under Mao Tse-tung had defeated the Nationalists of Chiang Kai-shek and become rulers of China.

10. Chiang moved his Nationalist government to the island of Taiwan. France's possessions in Indochina were broken up to form the new nations of Cambodia, Laos and Vietnam. The Philippines, a possession of the United States, was given its freedom in 1946. Korea,

which was taken from Japan, was divided into North and South Korea. Indonesia became free after a long struggle with the Netherlands.

11. In June, 1950, North Korea invaded South Korea. The United States and other members of the United Nations sent armed forces to help South Korea. The Chinese Communists helped the North Koreans. The end of fighting did not bring victory for either side. Korea is still divided as before, but the action of the United States and the United Nations saved the independence of South Korea.

12. There is still no peace in the Far East. Vietnam has been divided into North and South Vietnam. The north is Communist. It would like to see a Vietnam united under a Communist government. United States forces fought in South Vietnam to try to keep it from falling into Communist hands. The war was the most costly in United States history. More than 45,000 Americans were killed. American soldiers were withdrawn in 1973, with Vietnam still divided.

13. More bloodshed came to this region in 1971, when the eastern and western parts of the Moslem nation of Pakistan went to war. The main government was in West Pakistan, though most people lived in East Pakistan, 1,000 miles away. The people of East Pakistan wanted a stronger voice in the government. The western rulers refused and sent an army to the eastern half to crush the movement toward self-government. A bloody war followed. However, with the help of India's army, the people of East Pakistan fought back and won their freedom. Their new nation is now called Bangladesh.

UNDERSTANDING CHAPTER 5

1. Which questions are answered in this chapter?
   a. Why did Europe become interested in the Far East?
   b. How did India become British?
   c. How did Japan become a modern nation?
2. The main idea of *paragraphs 5 through 13* is that:
   a. new nations were formed in Asia and Africa at the same time.
   b. wars among people of the Far East fill its modern history.
   c. there are two Chinas and two Koreas today.
3. The first nation in the Far East to develop large industries was:
   a. China.   b. Japan.   c. India.
4. India was ruled for a long time by:
   a. the Netherlands.   b. Great Britain.   c. Japan.
5. European nations established colonies in Asia in the nineteenth century because they:
   a. needed lands for their growing populations.
   b. wanted to try out their new ideas of government.
   c. wanted markets for their goods.
6. The United States announced the Open Door Policy because it wanted:
   a. to keep China open to trade.
   b. to obtain land in China.
   c. the friendship of the Japanese.

Picture Symbols

These pictures should help you to recall parts of the chapter you have read. What is the main idea of each picture?

SUMMING UP

Match each item in Column A with one of the time periods listed in Column B.

COLUMN A

1. French obtain colonies in Indochina.
2. Chinese build a great wall.
3. The Philippines obtains independence.
4. War in Korea.
5. Alexander the Great invades India.
6. The Open Door Policy is announced.
7. Mongols invade China.
8. United States begins trade with Japan.
9. Japan invades Manchuria.
10. Chinese Nationalist government moves to Taiwan.
11. The Chinese revolution changes the government.
12. Indochina is divided into many small nations.

COLUMN B

A. Before Vasco da Gama's Voyage.
B. From Vasco da Gama to 1900.
C. From 1900 to World War II.
D. Since World War II.

FOLLOW UP *Who Am I?* Who is described in each of the following statements? Choose your answer from the names below.

a rice farmer	Marco Polo	Sun Yat-sen
Aryans	Chiang Kai-shek	Commodore Perry
Kublai Khan	Vasco da Gama	a Mongol

1. We invaded India from the north. We forced out the darker-skinned peoples. We started the religion of Hinduism. We are ▬▬▬.
2. I visited Japan in 1853. I made a treaty protecting American sailors and opening trade. I am ▬▬▬.
3. I fought the Communists for control of China. I left China in 1949 and moved the Nationalist government to Taiwan. I am ▬▬▬.
4. I terraced the hillsides of the river valleys to get more land. I divided the valley land into small, diked fields. I am ▬▬▬.
5. I found an all-water route to India by sailing around the southern tip of Africa. I am ▬▬▬.
6. I was the ruler of Cathay in the thirteenth century. I was a descendant of the Mongols who invaded that country. I am ▬▬▬.
7. I wrote an account of my travels in Cathay. As a result, the people of Europe were eager to get the goods of the East. I am ▬▬▬.
8. I led the overthrow of the Chinese kingdom in 1911 and started a new government. I did not live to see a united China. I am ▬▬▬.

6 THE PEOPLE OF THE ORIENT

This Indian farmer rides a steel plow pulled by bullocks. In what ways is he mixing the old with the new?

Reading For A Purpose: Who are the people of the Far East?

1. The Far East has about one-half the people of the world. China, with about 850 million people, and India, with about 560 million people, are the most populous countries in the world. Since a great part of the Far East is covered with either mountains or desert, most people are crowded into the fertile river valleys and coastal plains. The fertile island of Java in Indonesia has nearly 1,100 people for each square mile of land. In Japan there are about 725 people for each square mile. Compare these figures with our own country, which has about 59 people for each square mile!

2. The Far East is the home of many racial groups. In China, Korea and Japan live the "yellow" or Mongoloid peoples. Caucasians or "whites" are found mainly in India and Pakistan. It is believed that they came from the northwest a long time ago. Many of these "white" peoples are actually dark-skinned. The Malays or "brown-skinned" peoples make up the majority of the population in Southeast Asia (including Indonesia and the Philippines). However, people from India and China have lived in Southeast Asia for centuries. At one time there were so many Chinese living in Indochina that it was part of the ancient Chinese empire.

3. Most of the people of the Far East are poor farmers. They live in thousands of small villages, not in widely separated houses as in our country. The farmers have a deep love for their fields. Most of the work is done by hand on small, scattered plots. The main crop in the warm areas is rice. Many of these farmers cannot read or write, and they are sick much of the time. Since most families raise barely enough food for themselves, they cannot afford to pay taxes to build schools or hospitals.

4. Even where schools have been built, children are often kept at home. Many parents be-

Thatched huts set among palm trees are common in east coast Indian villages. In what other areas might a similar scene be found?

481

A marriage ceremony in India, where for centuries it has been the custom for Hindu parents to arrange the marriages of their children. Why do you think such a custom developed? Would you like to see this custom become a part of the culture in this country? Why?

lieve that their children can't help growing up to be poor farmers like themselves and therefore do not need an education. In many villages there is no pure water. People use the water of village "ponds" and tanks where animals are brought to drink. Poor diet, overcrowded houses, dirt and disease-carrying insects are a few other reasons why many people of the Far East are sick and die at a young age.

5. In addition to the many villages, there are also large cities in the Far East. In Japan, the majority of the people live in cities. Tokyo, its capital city with eleven million people, may be the largest city in the world. Other large cities in the Far East are Shanghai, Peking and Tientsin, China; Bombay and Calcutta, India; Osaka, Japan; Jakarta, Indonesia and Manila in the Philippines. Each year, more and more people come to live and work in the cities. Not all of them find the better way of life they are looking for. In many cities of India, people must sleep and eat in the streets, for they have no other place to go.

6. Not only are there different racial groups in the Far East, but many languages are spoken as well. As a result, it is difficult for the people of various countries to understand each other. People often speak different languages

In Bombay many people are homeless and end up sleeping on the sidewalks. In which other cities do such conditions exist?

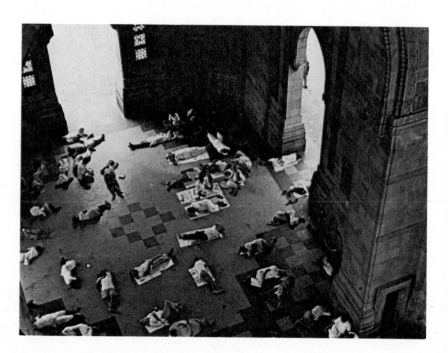

482

within the same country, as in India and Indonesia.

7. Family life is important in the Far East. Boys and girls in thousands of villages are taught to think of their families before themselves. Families are usually large. When a daughter marries, she joins the family of her husband. The father is the head of the family and is respected by all. All members of the household share what the family owns. Each family is expected to look after its own affairs and help each of its members. It is not unusual to find whole villages made up of one or two families, with all the relatives living together.

UNDERSTANDING CHAPTER 6

1. Which questions are answered in this chapter?
   a. How many people live in Japan?
   b. How do people feed themselves in the Far East?
   c. Why do so few children there have schooling?
2. A good title for *paragraphs 3 through 6* would be:
   a. Home of the Yellow Race.
   b. Crowded Cities of the Orient.
   c. Oriental People and Their Problems.
3. The country in the world with the most people is:
   a. India.   b. the Soviet Union.   c. China.
4. Most people in the Far East are:
   a. fishermen.   b. farmers.   c. factory workers.
5. There are few schools in many Far Eastern countries because:
   a newer nations have little interest in schools.
   b. there is little money to support schools.
   c. the villages are too far apart.
6. In Japan and Indonesia:
   a. people are more crowded together than in the United States.
   b. the climates are the same as those of the United States.
   c. there are more people in each country than there are in the United States.
7. Members of the *Caucasian* race have:
   a. yellow skins.   b. black skins.   c. white skins.
8. A *majority* of the people of the Malay peninsula are brown-skinned. *Majority* means:
   a. "all."   b. "more than half."   c. "less than half."

DEVELOPING IDEAS AND SKILLS

Pictograph #15—Population, Area and Standard of Living of the Far East

Study the pictograph on page 484. Then answer these questions.
1. Is the standard of living of this region high or low compared with that of the United States?
2. Is the region more or less crowded than the United States?
3. Are the people of this region literate compared with the people of the United States?
4. How long may the average person in this region expect to live?
5. What facts tell you the standard of living of the people of the region?
6. How does this region compare with the United States in size?

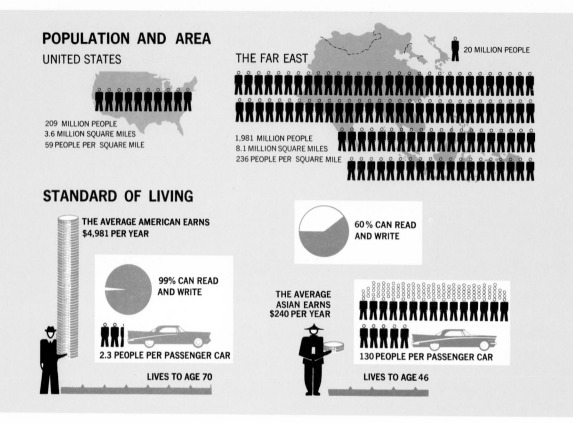

POPULATION AND AREA

UNITED STATES

209 MILLION PEOPLE
3.6 MILLION SQUARE MILES
59 PEOPLE PER SQUARE MILE

THE FAR EAST

20 MILLION PEOPLE

1,981 MILLION PEOPLE
8.1 MILLION SQUARE MILES
236 PEOPLE PER SQUARE MILE

STANDARD OF LIVING

THE AVERAGE AMERICAN EARNS $4,981 PER YEAR

99% CAN READ AND WRITE

2.3 PEOPLE PER PASSENGER CAR

LIVES TO AGE 70

60% CAN READ AND WRITE

THE AVERAGE ASIAN EARNS $240 PER YEAR

130 PEOPLE PER PASSENGER CAR

LIVES TO AGE 46

Pictograph #15—Population, Area and Standard of Living of the Far East

SUMMING UP

Making an Outline of Chapter 6

Review the steps in making a good outline in Chapter 6 of Unit 2. Select three *main ideas* of the chapter as your headings. (If you wish, you may choose more than three headings.) Then select the important facts that should be placed under each heading.

FOLLOW UP

A. *Which Does Not Belong?* Select the item in each group that does not belong with the others.

1. *Our interest in the Far East:* a. source of raw materials, b. spread of communism, c. many canals, d. important trade routes.
2. *Land forms of the Far East:* a. highest mountains in the world, b. few harbors, c. fertile river valleys, d. islands.
3. *Climates of the Far East:* a. rain forest, b. wet and dry seasons, c. tundra, d. steppes and deserts.
4. *History of the Far East:* a. ruling families, b. control by European powers, c. invasions by nomadic tribes, d. exploration of the coast of Africa.
5. *People of the Far East:* a. one language in each country, b. overcrowded lands, c. rice farmers, d. low standard of living.

B. Hong Kong is a city on a small island off the southern coast of China. It is a colony in the British Commonwealth. The selection you are about to read gives you a feeling for the city.

Hong Kong: People to Meet, Places to Go

Any visitor's first impression of Hong Kong is people—thousands of them hurrying along the streets, crowding on buses, running for ferries, jamming into shops and restaurants, squatting in doorways. There are business men in tropical suits, students in sweaters and jeans, women in baggy black pajamas, a stringy rickshaw man hauling a tourist through the crowd. That's Hong Kong—people in incredible numbers, the colony's biggest headache and its biggest asset.

There are more than 4 million of them crowded into less than 400 square miles, most of which is steep mountain slopes and rocky valleys. The city spreads up the slopes and spills into the sea. Thousands of "water people" spend their lives on "floating cities" in the harbor.

A million or so refugees have streamed into Hong Kong over the last 20 years . . . and perhaps housing in high-rise apartments or cottage colonies has been built for that many.

Today, Hong Kong is a major manufacturing center turning out everything from art objects to textiles to ships. At the same time, it has grown into one of the world's great banking and trading cities.

Make no mistake, in spite of the British names on streets and British uniforms, Hong Kong is China. All but 60,000 of the 4 million people are Chinese. Red double-decker buses edge through narrow streets, all of which have signs and banners in Chinese. Junks and sampans weave between ocean freighters and ferries.

Adapted from the *Montreal Gazette*, July 25, 1970.

1. What is your impression of Hong Kong?
2. What are the "floating cities" in Hong Kong?
3. What can you infer about housing in Hong Kong from statements in the selection?
4. Would you like to visit Hong Kong? Why?

7 RELIGIONS OF THE FAR EAST

Reading For A Purpose: What are the chief faiths of the Oriental peoples?

About 80% of India's people are Hindus, who worship in temples such as this one. What other Eastern religions do you know of?

1. In the United States, most people are members of the Christian religion. This is not true of the Far East. The Far East is the home of religions little known to us. Four of these together—Hinduism, Buddhism, Confucianism and Islam—have more followers than Christianity. These religions have played a great part in the history of the Far East and in the lives of the people. To understand the people of the Far East and how they live, we must know something of their religious beliefs.

2. The religion of the great majority of people in India is Hinduism. The Hindus worship many different gods or spirits. They believe that certain pools and rivers, like the Ganges, are sacred. Among their most important beliefs are the ideas of *caste, karma, dharma* and *reincarnation.* The caste system, while no longer legal in India, is still widely followed. It is based on the belief that a person has the same caste or place in society from birth that his father had. He cannot change his caste and is expected to do the same work as his father. (Certain work could be done only by certain castes.)

3. From earliest times there were four main castes. The highest caste was that of the priests or Brahmins. The second caste was made up of the warriors. The third class was that of the craftsmen, traders and farmers. The lowest caste was the unskilled workers. These four main groups were divided into many smaller castes. These were formed as new jobs were needed in the village or town. Each caste had rules by which its members lived. (These rules are called "dharma." Dharma is knowing what to do and what not to do.) Members of one caste did not eat with or marry members of another caste. They did not mix at social affairs. Lower than even the fourth caste were people called "untouchables." They belonged to no caste and did the jobs that no other people would do.

4. Another major belief of Hinduism is "reincarnation." According to this belief, a person's soul never dies. After death, the person can be born again. The kind of life a person can expect after he is reborn depends on how he has lived before. A Hindu believes that a person can be reborn many times until his soul reaches its final resting place. The numbers of times that a person is reborn depends on "karma," the way he lived before. (According to the idea of "karma," every action brings about certain results. In short, if a person acts badly, the results will be bad. If he acts well, the results will be good.) For example, if a person has worked and followed the rules of his caste (dharma), he will be rewarded. If a person has been evil and broken the rules of his caste, he may be reborn into a lower caste. He might become in his next life an untouch-

able or even an animal. (According to Hindu belief, a person has no one to blame but himself for his place in life. Instead of complaining, he should lead a good life so that he can be reborn into a higher caste.)

5. Islam is another religion of the Indian sub-continent. Islam was brought to India by the followers of Mohammed. When this land was ruled by Great Britain, the Hindus and Moslems lived side by side. Now the subcontinent is divided into three countries, India, Pakistan and Bangladesh. Today, India is largely Hindu, while Pakistan and Bangladesh are largely Moslem. However, a large minority of Hindus lives in Pakistan and Bangladesh, and millions of Moslems live in India. Indonesia is another large Moslem country in this part of the world.

Hindus bathe in the Ganges River. They believe this river is sacred. What are some other beliefs of the Hindu religion?

A mosque in Delhi. What are some major differences between the followers of Islam and Hinduism? Why have religious differences so often been the cause of hatred and war?

6. When the followers of Hinduism and Islam lived together in British India, there were many disputes because of their different beliefs. Hindus worship many gods; Moslems believe in one God. Moslems have one sacred book, the Koran; Hindus read many sacred

487

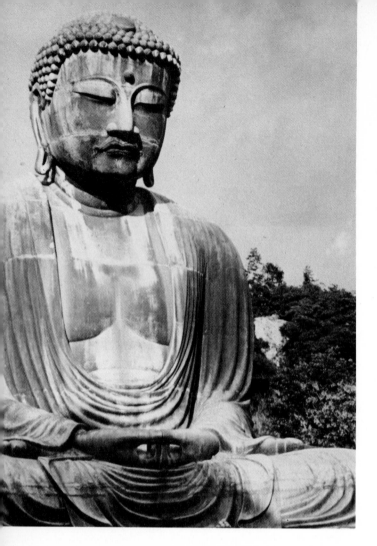

Buddhist temples and statues can be found throughout China. What are some beliefs of Buddhism?

called Gautama. He decided to spend his life helping others. The Buddhists have no God such as is found in Christianity, Islam or Judaism. Buddhism teaches that man has many desires that lead to evil. He must fight himself to drive away these desires and do what is right. The best way to do this is to forget yourself and help others. Buddhism spread throughout Asia. Millions of people in China, Tibet, Japan and Southeast Asia are Buddhists. A Buddhist temple is sometimes called a *pagoda*.

8. While Buddhism and other religions became part of Chinese life, it was really the teachings of a wise man called Confucius that guided the everyday life of the Chinese people. Confucius lived in the 6th century B.C. and began his teachings about the same time as Gautama in India. He did not teach about a life after death but about how to live on earth. He believed that man should be more concerned about his responsibilities than his rights. These responsibilities included respect for learning, love and obedience to parents and family, loyalty to the emperor and understanding of one's "place" in society. As a result of Confucius' teachings, the Chinese form of government developed: power was in the hands of a small, educated group while the majority of the people worked hard, lived simply and loyally supported them. This way of life lasted far into the twentieth century.

9. There are other groups of people who follow different religious beliefs in the Far East. Lao-tse was another famous teacher in China. The book of Tao contains many of his teachings. In time, Taoism became a religion with many gods, priests and colorful ceremonies. There are many Christians in the Far East, too, although they are few in number when compared with the number of people of other religions. The Filipinos are a Christian people.

texts. The Moslems have no images or idols in their mosques; the temples of the Hindus are filled with them. The Moslems eat meat; the Hindus worship the cow and often will not eat other animals either. Islam has only a few rules that all must follow; Hinduism has many rules. The Hindus follow a caste system. The Moslems believe that all are equal if they follow Mohammed. There are many holy places in the Hindu religion; in Islam, there is only one, Mecca. When a Hindu dies, he is burned and his ashes are scattered in a sacred river. When a Moslem dies, he is buried with his face toward Mecca.

7. Buddhism began in India more than 2,500 years ago. It was started by a young prince

Their early Spanish rulers brought Christianity to the islands. Christian missionaries are teaching in many of the Far Eastern countries. About ten million people in India are Christian. In Japan, the religion followed at least in part by many people is Shintoism.

UNDERSTANDING CHAPTER 7

1. Which questions are answered in this chapter?
   a. Why don't Hindus eat meat?
   b. What is Shintoism?
   c. How do Hinduism and Islam differ?
2. The main idea of this chapter describes the:
   a. beliefs of Oriental people.
   b. importance of Buddha.
   c. teachings of Confucius.
3. Most of the people of India are:
   a. Hindus.   b. Buddhists.   c. Moslems.
4. The Christian religion was brought to the Far East by:
   a. nomads.   b. explorers.   c. missionaries.
5. Confucianism is not a religion in our sense of the word because there are:
   a. no beliefs in God or an afterlife.
   b. no ways of worship.
   c. no sacred books.
6. There have been disputes between Hindus and Moslems because they:
   a. are both warlike people.
   b. try to spread their beliefs throughout the world.
   c. have different religious beliefs.
7. Under a *caste system*, people are:
   a. united.   b. divided.   c. enslaved.
8. *Reincarnation* is the belief in:
   a. many lives after death.
   b. one God.
   c. help to needy people.

DEVELOPING IDEAS AND SKILLS

Map Study

Map #54—Religions of the Far East

Study the map on page 490. Then tell whether these statements are true or false.
1. Most of the people of India are Hindus.
2. Most of the people of Indonesia and Pakistan are Moslems.
3. The Philippine people are chiefly followers of Christianity.
4. There are Buddhists in both Japan and China.
5. People in Southeast Asia practice religions that are different from those of their neighbors in China.

Answer these questions.
1. How did the Philippines become Christian?
2. Where did Buddhism begin?
3. How did Islam reach the Far East?
4. How did Confucianism begin?

489

U.S.S.R.

N. KOREA

S. KOREA

JAPAN

CHINA

PAKISTAN

TAIWAN
(Nationalist China)

INDIA

BURMA

BANGLADESH

THAILAND

LAOS

N. VIETNAM

PHILIPPINES

S. VIETNAM

INDONESIA

BUDDHIST
MOSLEM
CHINESE (Buddhist, Confucian, Taoist)
HINDU
CHRISTIAN
JAPANESE (Buddhist, Shintoist)

Map #54—Religions of the Far East

SUMMING UP

Agree or Disagree Decide whether or not each of the following statements agrees with what you have read. If the answer is *disagree*, explain why.

1. Most of the people of the Far East belong to one of three great religions.
2. All religions of Far Eastern peoples have a belief in one God.
3. India is the only Far Eastern country in which cattle are raised for their meat.
4. There are more Christians than non-Christians in the world.
5. The caste system divided the Indian people into various groups.
6. Hindus believe in sacred rivers and pools.
7. In Buddhism the main belief is that a man may be born again several times.
8. Confucius is known as a great teacher rather than as a religious leader.
9. Since the caste system was ended in India, all people are considered equal by their fellow Indians.
10. Because Buddhism was founded by an Indian prince, its followers are found only in India.

490

FOLLOW UP   Choosing either Hinduism, Buddhism or Confucianism as your subject, complete the following outline about a Far Eastern religion.

Title: ▬▬▬

I. How it began.
1.
2.

II. Major beliefs.
1.
2.

III. How it affects the lives of the people.
1.
2.

8 FARMERS OF THE FAR EAST

Reading For A Purpose: How do most Asians meet their daily needs?

1. Good land is like a precious gem in the Orient. This is because so much of the land is not suited for farming. Most of the people in the Far East live in thousands of small villages. Each of these villages is a little world of its own. Its people take care of their own needs. They use nearly everything they raise and rarely have any products left over for sale. As a result, little is brought into the village from other areas. In most villages there is probably no electricity, school or movie. There are few roads to the big cities.

2. The farmer's fields are outside the village. These may be a dozen or more scattered plots, seldom larger than four or five acres. The farmer tends these small plots of land very carefully. He does almost everything by hand: planting the seeds, removing the weeds and harvesting the crops. Since much of the region is hilly, it is not unusual to find the farmer and his family working on terraces carved out of the hillsides. The plots are too small to use machinery. Because of his methods of farming, the Asian farmer's yields per acre are higher than those of the American farmer. This kind of farming is called *intensive* farming. It is much like the farming practiced in Western Europe.

3. Except for a few pigs and chickens, the Far Eastern farmer does not raise animals for food. He must use all of his land to raise food for his family; he cannot afford to graze animals on it. As a result, the people of the Far East eat less meat than we do. (While India has more cattle than any other nation, the people cannot eat them because it is against their religious beliefs.)

4. Despite their hard work, farmers of the Far East have low incomes. Many farmers do not own their own land, but rent it from large landowners. The tenant farmer pays his rent with the crops he raises. If it is a good year, he has enough to pay his debts to the village moneylender or to the government. If he is very lucky, he may have enough left over to buy a water buffalo or some fertilizer.

5. In the monsoon region, water is as precious as land. Every effort is made to save it during the dry season. In some places the fields are irrigated by water brought from the rivers through canals. In other places there are wells. In India there are many ponds or "tanks." For some villages, these tanks are the only source of water. The people wash their clothes in the tanks and bring their cattle to them to drink.

6. Besides the subsistence farmer, there is both primitive and commercial (plantation) farming in the rain forest. The "primitive" farmer goes about his work much the same as the rain-forest farmer in central Africa or South America does. To clear a field, he first burns the thick underbrush. Then he digs holes in the ground with a stick and drops in his seeds. When the crop ripens, he picks it. After two or three years, the farmer leaves his field and goes on to another. This migratory farmer

finds that it is easier to prepare a new field than to continue with one that is no longer producing good crops.

7. There are also many plantations scattered throughout the rain forest. Each plantation raises a cash crop such as rubber, tobacco, coffee, tea or sugar cane. These crops are not grown for use by the people in the home countries. They are exported to other lands throughout the world. Plantations are big businesses with directors and hundreds of workers. Many have stores and shops, a school, a hospital and a water and electric plant on the plantation property. Many of the plantations are owned by people who live in Europe and North America.

8. In China, as in other countries, most people are farmers. However, the Communist Chinese have introduced a new way of farming to the Far East. In 1958, they started to organize their people into large state farms or *communes*. The commune is very much like a factory. The people work in the fields ten hours a day, six days a week. As on a Soviet state farm, they receive wages. The crops belong to the Communist government. The workers live in villages scattered throughout the commune.

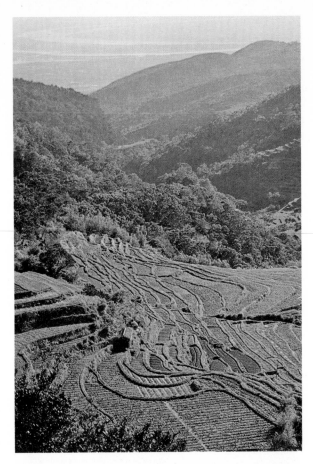

A terraced valley in Taiwan. How does terracing help prevent soil erosion?

India is the world's leading tea exporter. The woman shown here is picking tea leaves in the Himalayan region. What are some other countries in which tea is grown?

493

1. Which questions are answered in this chapter?
   a. Why does the Far Eastern farmer get a high yield from his land?
   b. Why is the Far Eastern farmer poor?
   c. Why don't Oriental peoples eat much meat?
2. The main idea of this chapter describes:
   a. a new kind of farming in China.
   b. how the farmer of the rain forest meets his needs.
   c. different kinds of farming in the Far East.
3. The chief farm animal of the Far East is the:
   a. camel.   b. water buffalo.   c. horse.
4. Most of the work on Far Eastern farms is done by:
   a. hand.   b. machinery.   c. animals.
5. There are few farm animals in the Far East because:
   a. there is a lack of water for them.
   b. religious beliefs forbid owning animals.
   c. farmers use all the land to raise food for their families.
6. In the Far East, farm machinery has not been widely used because:
   a. the religions are against it.
   b. the farms are too small.
   c. climates are not favorable for use of machines.
7. In *intensive* farming, the farmer:
   a. uses machinery and plants his crops a distance apart.
   b. uses hand labor and plants seeds close together.
   c. gets a smaller amount of grain from each acre planted.
8. A *commune* may be best compared with:
   a. a state farm in the Soviet Union.
   b. a coffee plantation in Latin America.
   c. a corn-belt farm in the United States.

SUMMING UP

Comparing Farmers   Complete the following chart in your notebook.

WESTERN UNITED STATES		FAR EASTERN VILLAGE
	Size of farm	
	Crops raised	
	Yield per acre	
	Land ownership	
	Homes of farmers	
	Saving resources	

FOLLOW UP

Farmers in Indian villages have a difficult life. How do they and their families feel about the hardships they face? Do they wish they were somewhere else? Do they wish they could be other people? These questions are answered by an Indian villager in the selection on page 495.

An Indian Farmer Speaks

People in cities have little that we do not already have. They may have better and more schools. They keep their streets cleaner than we do and some of them have cleaner habits. But someday we shall have all that they have besides what we have now: plenty of fresh air, which they lack, and plenty of sunshine, and room for our children to run and play in safety.

We do not have to go to the crowded, dirty market to buy our grain or vegetables or our fruit and milk. In the city, vegetables and fruit are half wilted, the milk is half water. We have our own food, fresh from our fields and groves, or from our animals.

We are not driven the way men in the city seem to be. We take time to enjoy our families before we go to work in our fields. And after work, we sit with our friends. We do not have the movies and loudspeakers that make city life exciting, but we do have our own good times. We enjoy every holiday, and there are plenty of them during the year.

Of course, some city men have easy jobs. But most men in cities work in mills. That is not for us. We want to be free. We have our worries but they are not so bad as those of city people. When we stop to think about it, we have a good deal in our favor.

Adapted from William and Charlotte Wiser, *Behind Mud Walls, 1930-1960*. University of California Press, 1963. Originally published by the University of California Press; reprinted by permission of The Regents of the University of California.

1. Why does the farmer believe that city people are not free? Do you agree?
2. Do you agree with the Indian villager on the advantages of village life? Explain.

9 USING THE GOOD EARTH OF ASIA

Reading For A Purpose: How does the Asian farmer make use of his lands?

A farmer guides his plow through a wet rice field. As soon as one rice crop is harvested, the field is flooded and made ready for another planting. Why is this flooding necessary?

1. Wherever the climate of the Far East is warm and wet, rice is the chief crop. Rice is a way of life for millions of people in this region. There are many reasons why this is so. First, in a region where there are many people and little fertile land, rice provides more food for each acre planted than any other grain. Second, in a hot climate, rice can be stored without spoiling. Third, rice has many uses. It is the Orientals' substitute for bread, potatoes and even milk and cheese. When boiled, it is eaten with meat or fish. It can be used to make wine. Animals can also be fed rice straw.

2. The rice plant is grown in small fields called *paddies*. The paddy is surrounded by dikes or walls made of earth. While the rice seedlings are growing, the paddies are flooded with water. The dikes control the supply of water. On the hillsides, terraces are built for the paddies.

3. The farmer first plants his rice seeds in a small plot of ground. As the plants start to grow, he clears the rest of his land. He uses a wooden plow pulled by a water buffalo or carabao. The fields are flooded by means of the dikes. When the young rice plants are about six inches high, he transplants or moves them to the flooded fields. (In a monsoon area, there may not be enough rainfall. Therefore, the farmer gets water by digging ditches from nearby streams or pumping water from a well.) In four months the rice plants are fully grown. The water is then drained from the paddy and the rice is cut and threshed. (Burma, Thailand and the countries of the Malay peninsula are known as the "rice bowl." The farmers there produce more rice than they need. Much of it is sold to neighboring countries, which cannot raise all the food they need.)

4. The warm, rainy climate of the Far East is good for other crops as well. Scattered throughout the rain forest are many planta-

Cotton field in southern India. Which area of the United States is also an important cotton-growing region?

tions on which are grown special crops such as rubber, tea, coconuts, tobacco, coffee and sugar cane. Southeast Asia is the largest rubber-producing area in the world. The rubber is gathered by hundreds of native workers. The worker first makes a cut in the tree. The sap of the rubber tree, *latex*, drips out of this cut into small pails. The latex is collected and then processed or turned into rubber. It is then shipped to factories all over the world.

5. The rain forest has other valuable products. *Quinine*, a medicine used to treat the disease of malaria, is obtained from the bark of the cinchona tree. *Kapok* is a light waterproof fiber used to fill mattresses and life preservers. Wood from the *teak* tree is used in making furniture. *Rattan* is a palm that is made into baskets, chairs and furniture. *Bamboo* is a tall grass with hard stems. It is used to make poles, furniture and even houses. And then there are spices. Indonesia produces more than half the pepper used by Americans. *Cinnamon* comes from the inner bark of a tree grown in Sri Lanka and India.

6. *Jute* is a wet-season crop grown in India and Bangladesh. It is a fiber that is made into burlap bags and rope. In the Philippines, *abacá*, another rope fiber, is grown. This product is often called Manila hemp and is used in making the strongest kind of rope.

7. China, India and Pakistan are leading growers of cotton. Indian cotton was among the first products to be introduced to the countries of the Western world. The silk products of China and Japan have long been famous. Silk is obtained from a worm that eats the leaves of the mulberry tree. A great amount of labor is needed to care for the mulberry trees. Silk is not as important in world trade as it once was. The creation of nylon, dacron, orlon and other such products has reduced the demand for silk throughout the world.

8. Where it is too cool or dry for rice to grow, such grains as wheat, barley, millet and corn are raised. China ranks third after the United States and the Soviet Union in wheat production. Spring wheat is planted in northern China and Manchuria where the climate is cooler. China is also a world leader in growing corn. Corn is used chiefly as a food for the people. Manchuria, in northern China, is a leading producer of *soy beans*. This vegetable has many uses. It provides flour and breakfast food, and its oil is used in cooking. Soups and

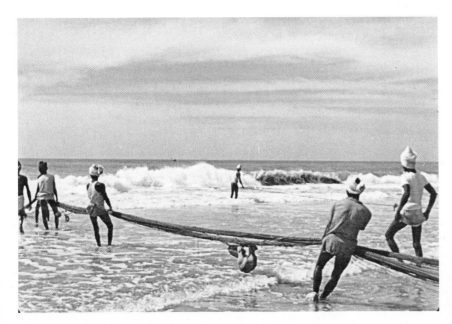

In coastal areas, men earn a living by fishing. Why does the diet of many Far Easterners include more fish than meat?

sauces are also made from it. The plant is valuable, too, for it can be used to feed animals. The soy bean plant enriches the soil where it is grown, restoring minerals to the earth.

9. As you have learned, the Far Eastern farmer eats little meat because he lacks the land to raise large animals. Therefore, the peoples along the coast have turned to the sea for other sources of food. Fish is more important in the diet of many Far Easterners than meat. Thousands of little fishing boats sail along the coasts of China and Japan every day to catch fish. Japan has some of the finest fishing grounds in the world. Not only do small boats go out, but Japan also has very modern fishing boats that can sail far from land. The fish are not only caught aboard these boats, they are also prepared for sale on board ship.

UNDERSTANDING CHAPTER 9

1. Which questions are answered in this chapter?
   a. What is "a paddy"?
   b. What is jute used for?
   c. Why does India import rice?
2. The main idea of this chapter describes:
   a. how the Oriental uses the seas.
   b. the products of the rain forest.
   c. how the Oriental people make use of their land.
3. The warm, rainy climate is suited to the growing of rice and:
   a. millet.   b. tea.   c. olive trees.
4. The Asian rain forest has plantations that grow:
   a. rubber.   b. bananas.   c. corn.
5. How does the Asian farmer provide water in the dry season?
   a. He depends upon dams.
   b. He draws water through canals.
   c. He plants only in the highlands.
6. Wheat and corn are grown instead of rice where:
   a. the growing season is longer.
   b. the growing season is shorter.
   c. rainfall is steady throughout the year.
7. A *paddy* is important to the:
   a. rice farmer.   b. fisherman.   c. rubber planter.
8. Many of our modern paints for the home are "rubber-based" paints. These are called:
   a. enamels.   b. flat paints.   c. latex paints.

DEVELOPING IDEAS AND SKILLS

Photograph Study
The photograph on page 499 should help you to recall parts of the chapter you have just read. What is the main idea of the photograph?

498

SUMMING UP

A. In your notebook place each item listed below in the proper column.

A rice paddy
A smoking volcano
A tea plantation
A Pygmy village
A farmer with a water buffalo
A man cutting bamboo and teak
A man picking bananas

A cow dead of sleeping sickness
A woman making palm oil
An Indian eating manioc
A Bantu growing sorghum
A native collecting cacao pods
A worker picking spices

I	II	III
AMAZON RAIN FOREST	CONGO RAIN FOREST	ASIAN RAIN FOREST

B. Match each statement in Column B with one of the Far Eastern products listed in Column A.

COLUMN A

1. wheat
2. tea
3. cotton
4. jute
5. rubber
6. soy beans
7. pepper
8. rice
9. silk

COLUMN B

a. Indonesia has more than half the world's supply.
b. Plantation crop of Sri Lanka.
c. From trees grown on plantations of Southeast Asia.
d. Chinese crop of many uses.
e. Grain grown in northern China.
f. Chief farm crop of the Malay peninsula.
g. Special fiber found in Japan.
h. India has been a leader in exporting this fiber.
i. Produced in Bangladesh and used in making rope.

10 INDUSTRIAL RESOURCES OF THE FAR EAST

Reading For A Purpose: How are the people of the Far East becoming industrialized?

Men quarry stone in India. What other natural resources does India have in good supply? What, in addition to natural resources, is necessary for a nation to develop industries?

1. The population of the nations of the Far East is continuing to grow rapidly. Since much of the land is not farmed, the problem of feeding this growing population becomes more and more serious. In most cases, food must be imported. In order to buy food from abroad, a country must have goods to sell. These are products of the nation's mines, fields or factories. The island of Japan was the first nation in the Far East to realize it could not depend on its land alone to feed its large population. As a result, it changed its ways of living.

2. The change in Japan came rapidly. The Japanese bought machines from the West and built factories. They imported raw materials from other nations. They used their small amount of coal and their swift-flowing mountain streams as sources of power for their factories. The country's large population provided plenty of workers for the factories. They were sent to schools and trained for their new jobs.

3. In time, Japan became the leading industrial nation in the Far East. Its goods are now sold throughout the world. Our shops and stores are filled with products "made in Japan." The Japanese exchange their finished goods for rice and other foods they need. Japan has the second largest merchant fleet in the world. This fleet brings to the islands food and raw materials from all over the world.

4. Other countries in the Far East must now face the problem of how to industrialize. They would like to increase the production of their mines and factories. As far as we know, the Far East has the power resources and raw materials needed to do this. India has good supplies of iron and coal. In addition, it has reserves of manganese, bauxite, gold, chromite and other minerals. While lacking oil for power, the Himalaya Mountains are a good source of water power to produce electricity. Some dams are now being built there. India also has the raw materials of its farms and plantations—cotton, tea, jute and sugar cane. And there are millions of people to do the work needed.

5. China is also rich in natural resources. Only two nations in the world produce more coal than China. It also has iron ore, manganese, tungsten, antimony and other minerals. These are all useful in the manufacture of fine steel products. China's huge population can supply all the workers needed in factories and mines. Under Communist rule, China has made tremendous gains in the production from her mines and factories.

6. Southeast Asia has other riches. Malaysia, Thailand and Indonesia mine great amounts of

tin. Almost two-thirds of the world's supply of tin comes from this region. Indonesia has oil, but it is not enough to supply the needs of the Orient. Many of these mine and oil fields are still managed by foreign companies. Many governments are training their own people to take over. In this way, they will be using their resources for their own benefit rather than for the benefit of companies in Europe and North America.

7. In spite of their resources, there are several reasons why these nations did not develop industries as Japan did. Some training and education are necessary to run machines, but most people cannot read or write. Many people do not want to work in factories. They prefer to work at home, making things by hand for people they know. Most of the people are poor. They cannot afford to buy the goods made in factories. Since there are few "markets"—little demand for machine-made goods —factories are not built. There is not much money to start costly modern factories and businesses.

8. Transportation throughout much of the Far East is poor. Japan has a fine network of railroads. India has a large railway system too. When the British ruled India, they built railroads in what are now India, Pakistan and Bangladesh. Throughout much of the Far East, however, there are few good highways. The mountains, jungle and desert make roads very difficult to build and maintain. In China, most people use the rivers for travel. (We know that the Communist government is now improving the transportation system inside China.) Good transportation is needed if raw materials and manufactured goods are to flow back and forth between buyers and sellers in the Far East. Without good transportation, the cost of moving goods is very high.

9. Most Far Eastern nations trade with each other. Japan alone carries on a heavy trade with the United States. Indonesia sells oil to Japan and Indian cotton supplies Japanese mills. Rice from Burma and Thailand is sent to China. Most nations trade more with Western Europe than they do with the United States. But the United States is a good customer for the tin, rubber and spices of the Far East.

10. Two of the greatest seaports in the world are centers of trade in the Far East. Both are islands. The island of Singapore is located off the coast of the Malay peninsula. Trade from the Indian Ocean to the Pacific Ocean passes

For centuries, most manufacturing in India has been carried on by small family businesses. Today, however, India is modernizing and expanding its industries. What changes do you suppose are being introduced?

through the straits near Singapore. Hong Kong lies off the coast of southern China. This island is still owned by Great Britain. Visitors from all over the world travel to Hong Kong (see page 485). It is a meeting place of East and West.

Women workers at a textile mill in China. In what way is China's huge population of 850 million a valuable resource in industrial development?

UNDERSTANDING CHAPTER 10

1. Which questions are answered in this chapter?
   a. What is Japan's chief source of power?
   b. What are the resources of Southeast Asia?
   c. Why did Japan go to war in 1941?
2. The main idea of *paragraph 7* is that:
   a. people prefer to work at home.
   b. the United States is a good customer for Far Eastern goods.
   c. dislike of factory work and the general poverty have hindered the development of industry in the Far East.
3. China has a large supply of:
   a. oil.   b. coal.   c. copper.
4. The most industrialized country in the Far East is:
   a. Japan.   b. China.   c. India.
5. In spite of the great population of this region, there is no great market for factory goods because:
   a. too many people work in the mines.
   b. people have little money to buy goods.
   c. schools train people for office work rather than factory work.

Developing Industry in the Far East Copy this list in your notebook and place a check before each item that is *true* about the Far East.

1. Good water power resources.
2. Coal reserves in every country.
3. Enough oil for the entire region.
4. Few trained workers for factories.
5. Many raw materials to sell.
6. Money to invest in new industries.
7. Good seaports.
8. Large population.
9. Iron ore deposits in India.
10. Large, modern highway system.
11. Minerals that other nations need.
12. More trade with the United States than with any other region.

Look at the chart. Then answer the questions that follow.

WORLD PRODUCTION OF MOTOR CARS, 1971

Country	Cars Produced
United States	10,644,452
Japan	5,810,774
West Germany	3,982,722
France	2,198,128
Italy	1,817,029

Company	Country	Cars Produced
General Motors	United States	5,760,000
Ford	United States	2,819,000
Volkswagen	West Germany	1,998,000
Toyota	Japan	1,955,000
Nissan	Japan	1,591,000
Chrysler	United States	1,518,000
Fiat	Italy	1,461,000
Renault	France	1,174,000
Leyland	Great Britain	1,062,000
Adam Opel	West Germany	838,000

1. How many Japanese companies are among the "top 10" producers?
2. Are any other Far Eastern countries among the leaders in auto production? If there are none, explain why not.
3. In which regions do we find the largest producers of cars?
4. From the chart, what might you infer about the region with the greatest number of cars produced?

11 TOWARD A BETTER WAY OF LIFE

Reading For A Purpose: What are some of the needs of the Far East?

1. Despite the fact that they are hard-working, many of the people of the Far East are poor and hungry. The farms are too small, and many peasants do not own their own land. They cannot grow enough food. The farmer is often in debt to the village moneylender or large landowner. They have few of the comforts of life that we enjoy. A way must be found for farmers to own more land and to learn how to use it wisely.

2. In Japan, most people can read and write. China claims that more than ninety per cent of its children are now going to school. India, Indonesia and the Philippines are all building more schools. However, in much of the Far East, many people cannot read or write. They know little about the rest of the world. In the villages far from the cities, most farmers do not have radios or TV sets. They have probably never been on a train, or in an automobile or to a motion picture.

3. Many of the people are in poor health, and death at an early age is common. Many of the countries are trying to improve health through better water supplies, vaccination and the use of insect-killers. United Nations teams have visited many of the small villages to give

medical help and advice. As health improves, however, the population grows at an even faster rate. This raises a new problem—namely, will the growing of food keep pace with the growing population?

4. There is a need to improve the water supply in the monsoon lands. In many of the countries affected by the monsoon, there is either too little or too much water. More reservoirs and tanks must be built so that rain water can be stored during the wet season for use during the dry season. There is a need for more dams

As in the United States, cities in the Far East are growing rapidly. What are some problems that are found in both U.S. and the cities of the Far East?

to hold back water and provide irrigation for the dry lands. If more water is available, more food can be raised for the fast-growing populations of Far Eastern countries.

5. Because fertile land is scarce and the population is growing, many people are leaving their villages to go to the cities in search of work. Cities are growing at a faster rate than farm lands. Yet while some people find work in the cities, millions of others are jobless. The movement of the people to the cities increases the need for more homes and better health care. It is not unusual to find people living and sleeping in the streets in many Far Eastern cities. Calcutta, India, has some of the worst slums in the world.

6. Many of the nations—India, Pakistan, Burma, Malaysia, the Philippines, Indonesia, Sri Lanka and others—have gained independence since 1945. Bangladesh (formerly East Pakistan) is the newest of them all. This country revolted and gained freedom from Pakistan in 1971. Many of these peoples have lived under foreign rule for centuries. Their leaders must solve many problems soon. They must set up stable governments, and feed and educate millions of people.

UNDERSTANDING CHAPTER 11

1. Which questions are answered in this chapter?
    a. Why are people moving to Far Eastern cities?
    b. Why are all nations in the Far East overcrowded?
    c. What are the problems that face new nations?
2. The main idea of this chapter describes:
    a. the greatest needs of the Far Eastern peoples.
    b. conditions in the crowded cities.
    c. the plans of India and China to improve the life of the people.
3. The greatest problem of nations in the Far East is the:
    a. need for food for a growing population.
    b. lack of foreign aid.
    c. the use of the sea for transportation.
4. A "problem" caused by improved health care in the Far East is:
    a. cholera.   b. larger population.   c. lack of education.
5. Land ownership is a problem in the Orient because:
    a. the government owns the farms in all countries except China.
    b. most of the land is owned by foreign businessmen.
    c. many farm lands are rented from large landowners.

Look at the cartoon. Then answer the questions below.

1. Who is the main figure in this cartoon?
2. How does the cartoonist show that the region interests both East and West?
3. Where did wars take place in this region?
4. What is a good title for this cartoon?

Making Comparisons Choose the best answer or answers.
1. Which country has the largest population? a. China. b. the Soviet Union. c. the United States.
2. Which country of Europe is most like Japan in its dependence upon foreign trade? a. France. b. Great Britain. c. Spain.
3. Germany is divided into a Communist and a Western section; which of the following countries are also divided? a. Vietnam. b. Korea. c. Burma.
4. The equator crosses the Congo Republic, Brazil and which of these Far Eastern nations? a. Indonesia. b. India. c. Japan.
5. Which part of the Far East has a climate like that of our southeastern states? a. Indonesia. b. Malaysia. c. Southeast China.

There are more cities of one million people or more in the Far East than in any other region. Although people move to cities to find relief from some of their problems, they often find other problems instead. The following news reports tell about problems faced by the people in two Far Eastern cities.

Sewage Pipes, Shacks and Caves
Are the Poor's Homes in Jakarta

Jakarta, Indonesia, Sept. 10—In Merak Park they sleep in large sewage pipes imported from France long ago and never used; in the fashionable Menteng district they live in caves dug into the sides of a canal the Dutch built or on a platform under a bridge. In the district called Planet, their homes are shacks erected beside the tracks in railroad freight yards and between the yards and the canal.

No one seems to know how many of the 4 million people of this capital live in conditions that would not be tolerated in the West. Some say about half, others say most.

Since there are no figures, it can be said that on a tour of the city one sees little other than the villas of the wealthy and the shacks and worse. Neither the Dutch who founded the city, nor Indonesia built public housing.

In the center of Jakarta, one can find low rows of wood and cardboard shanties between the tracks and the canal. The roofs are of palm leaves and straw. To reach the houses, one crosses the rails, climbing through trains standing in the yard. Now and again a train with passengers hanging from the sides plows through the crowds of children whose playground this is. Few of the children go to school which is on the other side of the tracks, because it costs a little more than a dollar a month. Some learn to read in an open space between the shacks. They are taught by members of their community. . . .

In the Dutch days, before people from the villages left their better houses and regular meals in search of money, the grassy banks of the canals matched the well-kept villas. Now, they are filled with squatters. Sometimes the police tear down the shacks, but they are easily put up again.

Many people have dug caves into the banks, and others have planted vegetables where the grass used to grow. The wealthy have put up barbed wire to keep the others out.

Asia's Mr. Clean

With more than 2.1 million people crammed into its 73-square mile residential areas, Singapore is one of the world's most tightly compacted cities. Singapore Harbor, the world's fourth busiest, is jammed with freighters and oil tankers. Jurong Industrial Estate contains 275 plants that turn out everything from ships to toothbrushes. Another 112 factories are planned or under construction.

But despite such dire pollution indicators, Singapore is a breath of fresh air in the miasma [harmful and foul-smelling atmosphere] of Asian cities, some of which are among the dirtiest on earth.

Cleanliness works in Singapore where it fails elsewhere because the government, and especially ... Prime Minister Lee Kuan Yew, cracks down on polluters with a vengeance. Strict laws are well understood in a compact city-state where the citizenry has a high literacy rate. But it is the sting of the law—hitting Singaporeans in the pocketbook—that has been the most effective antipollution measure.

Smoke-belching vehicles are stopped by policemen who slap drivers with a court summons on the spot. Drivers with noisy exhausts or "musical" horns can be fined up to $333—the equivalent of a year's wages for many laborers—or sentenced to three months in jail. Just tossing a cigarette butt on the street can bring a $166 fine. Now Prime Minister Lee has permanently closed Raffles Place, Singapore's Fifth Avenue, to most vehicular traffic. . . .

Lee has balanced his tough laws and policies with urban-renewal projects and occasional charming touches. Long a city of parks, Singapore now has more greenery than ever. . . . Most of the city's slums and shanty towns have been razed, and a third of Singapore's residents have been moved into low-rent, high-rise apartments. By 1975, half the population will live in new buildings. . . .

Time, January 25, 1971. Reprinted by permission from TIME, The Weekly Newsmagazine; Copyright Time Inc.

1. From where have Jakarta's poor people come? Why have they come?
2. How do the conditions of the poor in Jakarta compare with the conditions of the poor in Anglo-America?
3. What has Singapore done for its citizens that Jakarta has not done?
4. Do you agree with the methods used to keep Singapore clean and quiet? Why?

12 JAPAN: WORKSHOP OF THE FAR EAST

Reading For A Purpose: How has this small land become one of the leading nations in the world?

1. Off the eastern coast of Asia is the archipelago of Japan. Japan has four main islands, all of which are very mountainous. While only a very small part of the land is good for farming, the Japanese have used their resources wisely and have the highest standard of living in the Orient. Japan's more than 105 million people live in a country smaller than our state of Montana.

2. While Japan is narrow, it extends for a long distance north and south—as far as the distance from Vermont to Alabama! In the northern islands the climate is humid continental, like that of our northeast. In the winter, cold air from Asia blows over these islands and brings heavy snows. In the southern islands the climate is milder or humid subtropical. Rainy winds from the Pacific Ocean blow across Japan. Like Great Britain, Japan is surrounded by water and is affected by a warm ocean stream, the Japanese Current. This current comes from east of the Philippines and warms the southern coast of Japan. Therefore, Japan's year-round temperatures are milder than those of lands in the same latitude on the Asiatic mainland.

3. The modern history of Japan began a little more than a hundred years ago. In 1853, an American fleet under the command of Matthew Perry came to Japan. The Japanese were forced to trade with Europe and the United States. After seeing the inventions of the Western world, Japan decided it had to copy Western ways in order to grow strong and remain free. Before long, the Japanese built factories and made machines, ships and guns. By 1900, Japan had become one of the strong nations of the world.

4. As the nation's strength grew, Japan set out to build a large empire. It took Formosa from China in 1895. In 1904-5, it defeated Russia and gained Korea. In 1931, Japan invaded China and took Manchuria. Fighting against us during World War II, the Japanese held much of Southeast Asia. However, Japan was defeated by the Allies and lost all its colonies. Atomic bombs had been dropped on its cities of Hiroshima and Nagasaki. When the war was over, a new government was started with the help of the United States. In time, Japan recovered from the war. Its goods are again being sold throughout the world.

5. Japan's chief lawmaking body is called the Diet. It is made up of two houses. Members of these houses are elected by all persons over twenty-one years of age. The chief officer is the prime minister, who is chosen by the Diet. The Japanese still have an emperor, or king, but he has no real power. Tokyo is the capital city of this country.

6. Japan is one of the most thickly populated countries in the world, having 725 people for each square mile of land. One out of five working people is a farmer or fisherman. Some are

A view of modern Tokyo, a leading seaport and Japan's capital city. Why is trade with other nations so important to the Japanese?

7. The Japanese people have the highest standard of living in the Far East. Most people can read and write. Japanese students study much the same things American students do. English is also taught. The Japanese people even enjoy many of the same sports Americans do, such as baseball, tennis and swimming. Most Japanese are both Buddhists and Shintoists. Some have no strong religious beliefs, though they make use of Shinto and Buddhist ceremonies. The Christian religion was brought to Japan about 400 years ago and today has many followers. The temples, shrines and churches of these religions can be seen throughout the islands.

8. The Japanese are very good farmers. Because there is so little farmland, each acre must produce enough to feed seven people. The farmers live in small villages on the coastal lowlands. These villages have radios, TV, electric lights, sewing machines, newspapers and schools. Many of the farmers have second jobs as fishermen or factory workers in order to support their families better.

9. Most Japanese farmers own their land. Since the 1950's, most farm work has been done by machinery. Hillsides are terraced to provide more farmland. In the warm southeast, the chief crop is rice. On the hillsides, the farmer may also have tea bushes and mulberry trees. (Silkworms, you remember, feed on the leaves of the mulberry tree.) In the cooler north, wheat, barley and beans are grown. Despite their hard work, Japanese farmers cannot produce all the food the people need. Much food must be imported.

service or professional workers. Nearly all the rest work in factories. There are many large cities: Tokyo, Osaka, Kyoto, Kobe, Nagoya and Yokohama. All except Kyoto are seaports. All are on the main island of Honshu. The large cities have crowds of busy people, traffic problems, neon lights, mostly Western-style dress, modern buses, subways and tall buildings.

Most people in Japan can read and write. Here a student writes Japanese characters, the symbols which make up the Japanese language. Each character represents either a word or an idea. How does this differ from our written language?

510

10. Next to rice, fish is the most important food. There are many inlets along the coast, so it is easy for village fishermen to put out to sea and return. Giant ship canneries roam all over the Pacific. Fish are processed on board as soon as they are caught. Since World War II, meat and dairy foods have also become important in the diet. The Japanese are the best-fed people in the Orient.

11. Compared with India and China, Japan is not rich in natural resources. The chief minerals are coal, gold, copper and sulphur. To keep its factories going, Japan imports such raw materials as oil, cotton, rubber, iron ore and manganese. Large forests cover the mountainsides. The wood is used for fuel and papermaking. However, so much wood has already been used that it must now be imported as well. Besides oil, a chief source of power is falling water, from the many streams that flow down the mountainsides. (These are fed by Japan's heavy rains and snows.)

12. Despite its need for food, raw materials and minerals, Japan is the most highly industrialized country in Asia. It was the first Far Eastern nation to build factories to supply its people with jobs and food. Japanese workers are known for their skill. There are great modern factories employing thousands of workers, as well as many small businesses made up of families working in their homes. Japan also leads the world in shipbuilding. It is the world's leading producer of silk goods. It ranks third behind the United States and Soviet Union in steel manufacturing. Japanese cameras and instruments are also known throughout the world.

13. Japan can be compared with Great Britain. Both are island nations. Britain's great power resource is coal; Japan's is water power. Both nations have developed a factory system that produces goods to trade for food and raw materials. Both have large merchant fleets. Both once ruled overseas empires to provide themselves with raw materials and markets. Now both must provide for their large popula-

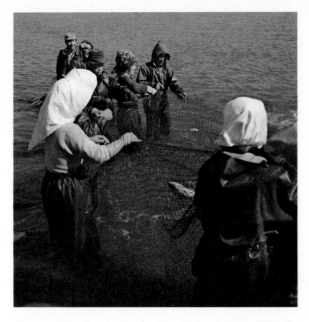

Salmon fishing off the Japanese coast. Why is the fishing industry important to Japan?

tions through world trade. Japan's best customer is the United States. Its chief exports are tools, machines, metal and chemical products, textiles and fish. Japan's imports are chiefly the foods and raw materials that it does not have —oil, wheat, raw cotton, rubber, iron, wool and tin.

14. Although it is the most modern nation of the Orient, Japan is not without problems. You have learned that its population is large and is growing larger. Japan must be able to provide more and more food for its people. The nation must also continue to carry on world-wide trade. It must sell goods to pay for its imports. Many of the markets for the goods Japan sells are in Southeast Asia. Its supply of oil, rubber and tin comes from this area too. Unrest in Southeast Asia threatens this source of trade and raw materials. Finally, the Japanese are trying to build democracy within their homeland. They must have peace if their government is to grow in strength. The United States has promised to defend Japan against attack. It is important to us, too, that the Japanese people prosper in peace.

1. Which questions are answered in this chapter?
   a. How is Japan governed?
   b. How did the United States help Japan after World War II?
   c. How do the Japanese make use of the waters around their islands?
2. The main idea of *paragraphs 6 through 9* describes:
   a. how a small nation supports its people.
   b. the farm life in a Japanese village.
   c. the Japanese people and their work.
3. The population of Japan is about:
   b. 75 million.
   a. 50 million.
   c. 100 million.
4. There is intensive farming on the islands of Japan because:
   a. the Japanese know little of scientific farming.
   b. farmers do not have machinery.
   c. there is very little farmland.
5. The Japanese depend a great deal upon manufacturing because they:
   a. must import raw materials.
   b. must use finished goods to pay for imports.
   c. need clothing for their armed forces.
6. A *dense population* means that:
   a. the population is large.
   b. people are crowded close together.
   c. people live mostly near the seacoast.
7. *Canneries* are places in which:
   a. foods are prepared for packaging.
   b. fishermen prepare to catch fish.
   c. tin goods are made.

Map Study

Map #55a and b—Japan

Study the maps on page 513. Then answer these questions.

1. Is Japan located in the high, middle or low latitudes?
2. What is the distance of the Japanese islands, from north to south?
3. On which of the islands are the largest cities located?
4. Osaka, Kobe, Yokohama and Nagoya are all large cities and have the same kind of location. What do they have in common?
5. How would you describe the topography of Japan?
6. What is the name given to a large number of islands surrounded by a large body of water?
7. Which is the more crowded area, Montana or Japan?
8. Why do you think there are few rivers of great size on the Japanese islands?
9. If you traveled from Osaka to Tokyo, in which direction would you be traveling?
10. In which direction is the equator from Japan?

Map #55a—Japan

HOKKAIDO

Sea of
Japan

H O N S H U

Tokyo
Yokohama

Nagoya
Kyoto
Kobe
Osaka

PACIFIC
OCEAN

SHIKOKU

KYUSHU

40°

30°

| 0 | 100 | 200 | 300 |

Scale of Miles

MONTANA

MONTANA
POPULATION: 694,409
LAND AREA: 145,587 SQUARE MILES
4.8 PEOPLE PER SQUARE MILE

JAPAN
POPULATION: 105.8 MILLION
LAND AREA: 142,812 SQUARE MILES
725 PEOPLE PER SQUARE MILE

Map #55b—Japan and Montana

513

Agree or Disagree   Decide whether or not each of the following statements agrees with what you have read. If the answer is *disagree*, explain why.
  1. The Japanese eat much the same foods we do.
  2. Japan's islands are very mountainous; there is little lowland for farming.
  3. Japan's huge population is crowded into narrow lowlands.
  4. Most Japanese are farmers or fishermen.
  5. The Japanese depend on manufacturing and trade to pay for the food and goods they import.
  6. Japan has built a modern nation with few natural resources.
  7. Japan sells many of her goods to other Asian nations.
  8. After World War II, Japan was rebuilt with the help of the United States.
  9. Most Japanese cannot read or write.
  10. Japan has more factories than any other nation in the Far East.

Complete the following sentences in your notebook.
  1. The capital of Japan is ———— .
  2. The chief food crop of the Japanese people is ———— .
  3. ———— visited Japan in 1853 and began Japanese-American trade.
  4. There are ———— main islands in Japan.
  5. The ———— is the lawmaking body of Japan's government.
  6. The Japanese substitute ———— for meat in their diet.
  7. ———— buys more goods from Japan than any other nation.
  8. Because of the lack of farm land, the Japanese farmer practices ———— farming.

13 INDIA: THE LAND OF VILLAGES

Reading For A Purpose: Why are so many Indians poor when their country has many advantages?

Mahatma Gandhi was one of the leaders of Indian independence from British rule. He urged the people not to use violence in their struggle. Which of our great leaders in recent years have urged their followers to use nonviolence in seeking change?

1. South of the Himalaya Mountains of Asia is a large triangle-shaped peninsula. This large area, about half the size of the United States, is sometimes called a subcontinent. While it is occupied by three countries, India, Pakistan and Bangladesh, the nation of India covers most of it. India is the seventh largest nation in the world, taking up about 1,300,000 square miles. With about 563 million people, it is the second most populous country in the world.

2. The Himalaya Mountains form the northern border of India. South of the mountains, a great plain stretches east and west across the subcontinent. The western part of the plain is drained by the Indus River. The eastern part is the valley of the Ganges and Brahmaputra Rivers. Many people live in this valley because the land is so fertile and well watered. South of the plains is the Deccan Plateau. On both sides of the plateau are long, narrow coastal lowlands or plains.

3. India lies mainly in the low latitudes. (Its latitude is about the same as that of Mexico and Central America.) Except in the highlands and mountains, the climate is generally hot and humid. (Because of the Himalayas in the north, the cold winds of central Asia do not reach India.) The rainfall varies throughout the country from the heaviest in the world to very small amounts. The rainfall is controlled by the seasonal winds called monsoons. In the summer (from June to September) the southwest winds bring rain to the land. In the winter the northeast monsoon takes over and blows from the land to the sea. Since it blows from the land, it brings little rain.

4. India had a long history before the Europeans came to its shores looking for tea, spices and jewels. When, in 1601, the British came, they built trading posts and in time ruled all of India. As they educated more people, a strong desire for freedom grew. One of the great leaders for Indian independence was a man called Mahatma Gandhi. He urged the people to fight against British rule, but not to use violence. He asked the people to refuse to buy British goods and to disobey British laws. He was put in jail many times, but this made him a greater hero to his people. It was largely because of Gandhi that the people of India gained their freedom from Great Britain in 1947.

5. The government of India is partly like that of Great Britain and partly like that of the United States. There is a written constitution. The chief lawmaking body is the Parliament,

515

which has two houses. There is a president, but he has little power. The chief officer is the prime minister. He has the power to suggest laws and to carry them out when they are approved by Parliament. Like the United States, India has a federal government. The powers of the government are divided between the national government and the fifteen states. The capital city is New Delhi. The first prime minister and the leader of India through the first seventeen years of its independence was Jawaharlal Nehru.

6. India is one of the most crowded nations in the world, with over 400 people for each square mile of land. Its people speak many different languages, wear different clothing, eat different foods and have different colored skins from one part of the country to another. Most of the people are poor farmers who live in thousands of small villages. The farms are owned mostly by large landholders; the farmer gives a share of his crops as payment to the owners. Farmers barely make a living and know little of the great modern world. Most work is done with a wooden plow and simple hand tools. The water buffalo often pulls the plow and the heavy carts. Cattle manure is used for fuel instead of fertilizer for the soil. When the cattle die, their hides are sold. In

each village, there is a Hindu temple where the people worship.

7. The chief food crop of the Indian farmer is rice. The big rice-growing areas are the rainy river valleys of the north. On the Deccan Plateau, wheat and millet are grown. These grains can withstand the drier climate. For years, Indian farmers could not raise enough grain to feed the huge population. But in 1971, for the first time India produced enough wheat and rice to feed its millions of people. Indians have learned to grow wheat during the summer dry season, when the rice paddies are low. Underground water from the Ganges River means farmers do not have to depend on monsoon rains. The chief cash crop of India is cotton. Much of it is grown near the city of Bombay. Indian farmers also raise jute, tea and rubber for export to other lands.

8. Although the nation is largely one of farmers, the number of people who live and work in the cities is growing. Bombay, the largest city of the country, is a seaport on the western coast. Calcutta, at the delta of the Ganges River, is the gateway to the fertile farming lands of the north and east. In the cities, old India and new India live side by side. The new India can be seen in the many cars and trucks, the Western style of dress, the modern office buildings and shops. Old India is seen in the buffalo carts, the sacred cows, the old bazaars and the many poor that crowd the streets.

9. For hundreds of years, the Indian people turned out wonderful handmade goods in their villages. Now factory production is growing in importance. The largest industry is textiles, made mostly from the native cotton. However, iron- and steel-making is growing steadily, for India has many mineral resources. There are large deposits of iron in the Deccan Plateau. India also has coal, manganese and chromium. The Tata steel works near Calcutta are the largest mills in India. The rising industries—

There is never enough water in India, and irrigation methods are often crude.

516

textiles, burlap bags (from jute), iron and steel goods—will gradually change the ways of living of millions of Indians.

10. India is trying very hard to make its government work. There are many problems, however. First, there is a huge population. One out of every seven persons in the world lives in India. Most Indians are underfed. Enough food is grown, yet most people are too poor to buy all the food they need. India has too many cattle, and these animals use valuable land. Second, much of India is dry for part of the year. Irrigation projects are needed to water land so that more food can be produced.

11. In the third place, many village people are sick and cannot read or write. So many different languages are spoken that Indians have a difficult time communicating with one another. Many are terribly poor. The caste system still divides the people, though it has been outlawed by the new government. Finally, India needs help and money to make better use of its resources.

Bombay is a center of commerce. Modern apartment buildings overlook its fine harbor. In contrast are Bombay's "chawls," among the worst slums in the world. Why is it that luxury and comfort often exist side by side with poverty?

UNDERSTANDING CHAPTER 13

1. Which questions are answered in this chapter?
   a. Where are Kashmir and Goa?
   b. What is the chief food crop of India?
   c. What are India's farm problems?
2. A good title for *paragraph 9* is:
   a. "Mining Giant of the East."
   b. "Too Much From Too Little."
   c. "India's Growing Industries."
3. India gained its freedom largely through the efforts of:
   a. Clive. b. Churchill. c. Gandhi.
4. The winds that bring rain to India's farmers are the:
   a. monsoons. b. easterlies. c. hurricanes.
5. Wheat is grown on the Deccan Plateau because:
   a. water is more plentiful.
   b. it can grow better than rice in a drier climate.
   c. machinery can be used.

6. Cattle in India are a problem because:
   a. Moslems consider them to be sacred animals.
   b. they graze on valuable land.
   c. their meat is of a very poor grade.

DEVELOPING IDEAS AND SKILLS

Map Study

Map #56a and b—India

Study the maps. Then answer these questions.
1. Is India located in the high, middle or low latitudes?
2. How does India compare in size with the United States?
3. In which direction is the equator from India?
4. What are two important port cities of India?
5. How is India separated from China?
6. The rivers of India flow in many directions. Why is this so?
7. What is the great river of northern India?
8. What nations border India?
9. How does the topography of northern India differ from that of the southern half of the country?
10. What is the approximate latitude and longitude of Bombay?
11. Which country is more crowded, India or the United States?
12. What word would you use to describe the land formation of India?

Map #56a—India

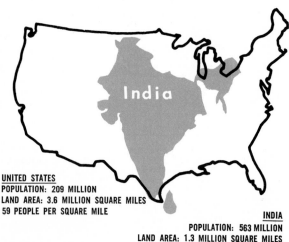

UNITED STATES
POPULATION: 209 MILLION
LAND AREA: 3.6 MILLION SQUARE MILES
59 PEOPLE PER SQUARE MILE

INDIA
POPULATION: 563 MILLION
LAND AREA: 1.3 MILLION SQUARE MILES
446 PEOPLE PER SQUARE MILE

Map #56b—India and the United States

SUMMING UP

In the following, place before each statement the word that makes the statement correct: *Most, Some, Few.*

1. ———— Indians live in river valleys.
2. ———— of India's people live in small villages.

518

3. _____ people are able to read and write.
4. _____ cattle in India are used for their meat.
5. _____ people of India are poor.
6. _____ people of India work in steel mills.
7. _____ people speak the same language.
8. _____ large cities are seaports.
9. _____ powers of the government are in the hands of the president.
10. _____ parts of India lie in the low latitudes.

FOLLOW UP

I. *True or false* Tell whether these statements are true or false. The underlined words make the statements true or false. If a statement is false, what word or words would you place in it to make it true?

1. India was once a colony of Great Britain.
2. The chief cash crop of India is rice.
3. India's farmers grow jute, a fiber used in making sacks.
4. Most people of India are members of the Moslem religion.
5. The first prime minister of India was Mahatma Gandhi.
6. India's capital is located at New Delhi.
7. India is thought to have great deposits of iron ore.
8. Bombay is India's great city near the delta of the Ganges River.

II. *Thinking It Through*
Why are many millions of Indians living in poverty and poorly fed when the nation has so many advantages: large size, many people, fertile land, great numbers of cattle, reserves of iron and coal, much trade?

III. *For Further Involvement*
Prepare a model of a typical village in India, showing these items:
   a. the water wells.
   b. kinds of roads and buildings.
   c. kinds of homes.
   d. work the people are doing.

14 CHINA: LAND OF THE RED DRAGON

Reading For A Purpose: Can China become a leading industrial nation?

1. China is the largest country in the Far East—slightly larger than the United States. When we speak of China and its people, we are really speaking about the land along the eastern coast. This is where most of China's 850 million people live. There are high mountains in the south and west. In these mountains is the cold, empty plateau of Tibet. On the west and northwest are dry lands, including the Gobi Desert. On the north is the Soviet Union and on the east, the Pacific Ocean.

2. Unlike the high, dry areas of the west, southeastern China is lined with fertile river valleys and plains. This is the busy center of rice farming and trade. Canals by the thousands connect streams and have been the chief avenues of travel for hundreds of years. The major lowlands are the plains formed by the Hsi and Yangtze Rivers. The winds bring plenty of rain to the rice fields here. The climate of this part of China is the same as in our southeastern states. The largest cities are Shanghai and Canton.

3. The lands farther north are sometimes called North China. They include the valley of the Hwang Ho (Yellow River) and the fertile North China Plain. There is not as much rain-

fall here. The climate is cold, and there is a shorter growing season. For these reasons, this is the wheat-growing region of China. Most of the land is covered by a fine yellowish-brown dust that is called *loess.* The Hwang Ho, or Yellow River, gets its name from the yellow loess it picks up. The Hwang Ho frequently overflows its banks, causing great damage to the nearby farmlands. The largest cities of North China are Peking and Tientsin. Peking is the capital of China.

4. In the northernmost part of China is the province of Manchuria. The climate is humid continental, like that of our northeastern states. Mukden, the iron and steel center, is about the same distance from the equator as

A group of students and soldiers wave copies of a book containing quotations from Mao Tse-tung. Mao was leader of the People's Republic of China until his death in 1976. In what ways do rallies such as this help strengthen loyalty to the Communist Party?

New York City. Here iron ore and coal are found near each other. This area has long been wanted by both Japan and the Soviet Union. Manchuria also has fertile farmland where wheat and millet take the place of rice as the chief food. Fewer people live here than in the warm southeast.

5. The government and life of the Chinese people have changed greatly in the last sixty years. You will recall from Chapter 5 that the republic in China never had a good chance to work. From 1920 to 1949, the Chinese people were invaded by Japan and also fought wars among themselves. In 1949, the Communist forces under Mao Tse-tung forced the Nationalist followers of Chiang Kai-shek to retreat to Formosa. The Communists have ruled in China since that time.

6. The government of China is much like that of the Soviet Union. This means that there are two governments, the "acting" government and the "real" government. Under the "acting" government, the chief lawmaking body is the National People's Congress. It meets yearly and has little power. The executive branch is the State Council or Cabinet, headed by a premier. The real rulers are the leaders of the Communist Party. There are about 13 million Party members, forming the largest Communist Party in the world. Party members hold the most important jobs and carry out government plans throughout the nation. Party-controlled newspapers and radio continually explain the plans of the Party to the people. The Party controls the army, the labor unions and the new youth groups. It decides what is to be taught in school. It controls most of the resources of the nation.

Political posters can be found everywhere in China. Many picture Mao Tsetung. Others contain slogans of the Chinese Communist Party, and still others show people hard at work on farms and in factories. What is the pupose of such posters?

These "militia women" are members of a commune in southern China. Young women as well as young men receive military training. They will be called upon if China is attacked. Do servicewomen in this country receive this kind of training? Why?

7. The Communists are changing the ways of living in China. For hundreds of years, the custom was for all members of a Chinese family to live together in the same house. The oldest male was the head of the home and the family worked for him. Most people could not read or write, so the village scholar was a respected person. Furthermore, most of the people practiced Buddhism, Confucianism, Taoism or Christianity. This way of life has been changed by the Communist rulers. Most children are now sent to school. Instead of loyalty to family and friends, loyalty to the Party is now taught. Religion is frowned upon. Instead of working for the family, people now work for the state. Women have been encouraged to work alongside men.

8. Farm life is also being changed by the Communist government. In China, as in other Asian lands, most people are farmers. More and more of their farmlands have been turned into "communes" or state farms. These communes are like factories in the fields; some are

as large as 10,000 acres. The communes are different from the Soviet collective farms. On the Soviet collective farm, each member of the collective shares in the crop that is raised. In the commune, the workers are paid for the jobs they do, as on a Soviet state farm. Communes are directed by members of the Communist Party. On a rice commune, hand labor is still used. On a wheat commune, there may be tractors and a mill to grind the grain. Most villages in the commune have electricity and schools. There is now plenty of food for all, though some of it must still be imported.

9. The government of China owns the factories and mines as well as the farms. The Communist goal is to make China an industrial power. China has coal and iron, manganese and tungsten. Only oil is lacking. The Chinese people are being pressed to build new factories and open new mines. Dams are being built to control floods and provide water for irrigation. Miles of railroad track are being laid. Trade with other Asian nations is rapidly expanding.

10. In the Far East, the improvement in the standard of living of the millions of poor farmers is a goal of most governments. India and Japan are trying to follow the democratic way toward improvement. China is trying the Communist way. Millions in Asia are watching the work of communism very closely. The United States is watching as well, for it has a great interest in the outcome.

11. The United States is also worried about the growing military strength of China. China used its armies to support North Korea in the war with South Korea, 1950-1953. In 1962, Chinese soldiers invaded northern India; there were further misunderstandings between the two nations in 1965. Also, China has supported the forces of North Vietnam. In 1964, China exploded an atomic bomb. China's growing power must have an effect on the newer nations of Asia and Africa. But this power has made enemies, too. India does not look upon China as a friend. What's more, the Soviet Union and China have "split" in their views of the goals of communism. In 1972, President Nixon visited China. Leaders of both countries said they wanted good relations.

12. The Nationalist government of China still occupies the island of Taiwan, about 100 miles east of the Chinese mainland. Taiwan is a crowded island of some ten million people. As in most of the Far East, the island is mountainous and the people live in the plains. Rice is the important product, though tea is grown for export.

Harvesting rice on a commune near Peking. How is a commune in China different from a collective farm in the Soviet Union?

UNDERSTANDING
CHAPTER 14

1. Which questions are answered in this chapter?
   a. How did the Communists come into power?
   b. Where do most of the people of China live?
   c. Where is Hong Kong?
2. The main idea of *paragraphs 5 through 9* describes:
   a. how the Communists are changing China.
   b. how China differs from the Soviet Union.
   c. the strength of China today.
3. The capital of China is:
   a. Nanking.   b. Shanghai.   c. Peking.
4. The chief area of fertile farmland in China is located in the:
   a. northwest.   b. northeast.   c. southeast.
5. The Communists have changed the farm life of the people in that:
   a. large farms called "communes" have sprung up.

b. much farm machinery is seen everywhere on Chinese farms.

c. more people own their own land.

6. China is causing concern to the United States because:

a. the Chinese now produce enough food to feed all their people.

b. China produces enough steel for all its uses.

c. Chinese military strength is growing.

Map Study

Map #57a and b—China

Study the maps. Then answer these questions.

1. Is China in the high, middle or low latitudes?
2. Which is larger in size, the United States or China?
3. According to the map, where do most of China's millions of people live?
4. How would you describe the topography of China?
5. What countries border China?
6. Where do both the Yellow and Yangtze Rivers begin?
7. Haw far is Taiwan (Nationalist China) from the mainland of China?
8. What is the approximate latitude and longitude of Nanking?
9. If you traveled by air to Peking from California, would it be quicker to travel east, or west?
10. What is the British-held city off the coast of southern China?

Map #57a—China

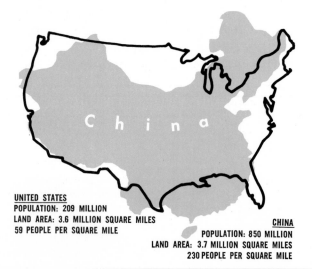

UNITED STATES
POPULATION: 209 MILLION
LAND AREA: 3.6 MILLION SQUARE MILES
59 PEOPLE PER SQUARE MILE

CHINA
POPULATION: 850 MILLION
LAND AREA: 3.7 MILLION SQUARE MILES
230 PEOPLE PER SQUARE MILE

Map #57b—China and the United States

SUMMING UP

I. Tell whether the following items refer to China, India or to both countries. If an item applies to China only, write C in your notebook; it it applies to India only, write I; if it applies to both countries, write B.

1. Not enough food is grown to feed all the people of the country.
2. More than half the people cannot read or write.

3. Rice is the chief food crop.
4. There is a population of more than 700 million people.
5. This nation is trying to have friendly relations with the United States.
6. This nation is larger in area than the United States.
7. There are fertile river valleys.
8. Farms are organized into communes.
9. Most people are farmers.
10. The government is similar to Great Britain's.

II. In many ways, China and the United States are similar in geography. For example, the shape of China is very much like that of the U.S. Both are located about the same distance between the equator and the North Pole. Can you think of other geographic similarities between the two countries?

FOLLOW UP

China Revisited

Reprinted from *U.S. News & World Report.*

Robert P. Martin, Directing Editor of the International Staff of "U.S. News & World Report," returned from Communist China on February 28, one of the American newsmen who covered President Nixon's mission from start to finish.

Mr. Martin's eight days on the mainland marked a return to a scene where he had been a reporter for a decade, until after the Communist take-over in 1949....

What follows is a personal report based on a journey back to a once-familiar land, now greatly changed.

• • • • •

This is a report about a China that really exists, not a China of the imagination or one created by propaganda. That part of the country I have just seen is healthier, more prosperous, and far more orderly than the China I left in 1949 after the Communists had seized the mainland.

The people I saw and talked with are better fed, better dressed, bigger and huskier than the generation that had fought —or sat out—eight years of Japanese occupation and four years of brutal civil war.

Medical services are incomparably improved and reach far more families than ever before. In the countryside and in the cities, housing is better, though far below U.S. standards. Food supplies seem to be satisfactory, at least in the cities I visited, and consumer goods—most of them utilitarian, although you do see toys and decorative items for the home—are available. A Chinese cannot buy an automobile or a TV set for his personal use, and most of the sewing machines I saw offered for sale at the equivalent of $75 were operated by a foot pedal, not by electricity....

The stores I visited in Peking, Hangchow and Shanghai during President Nixon's trip to mainland China are amply supplied with consumer goods, and people seem to have some money to spend.

I was told that a working family—mother and father—can save from $12 to $14 a month.

The products are almost all made in Chinese factories. Foreign-made goods, aside from what is needed in industry and agriculture, are almost nonexistent.

The Chinese, as an individual, seems to me to have paid a rather heavy price for these economic gains. His life is regimented.

The Government tells him where he can work, and he can be—and often is—sent to work in factories or on communes far from his home and family.

The newspaper he reads or the news programs he hears on the radio are not controversial, not even very informative. He has access only to what the Government wants him to know. . . .

Young people, I was told, are permitted to enroll in schools of higher education, only if they are the children of peasants, workers or soldiers, and they must be "recommended" by the all-powerful "revolutionary committee" of their communes or factories. . . .

The Communists also introduced thought control. The effect may not be total; the Chinese are not automatons. But a continuing and pervasive propaganda campaign that relentlessly strikes at everyone, day after day, has turned a normally turbulent people into an obedient, well-disciplined mass quite unlike Chinese of the past.

You see the effects of all this everywhere. In cities I visited the Chinese were far more courteous to each other than in pre-Communist days.

I saw no shoving or pushing to gain a position of advantage in a store, or in line waiting for a bus or entry to a "cultural palace." . . .

There is a cleanliness in the cities and in the agricultural communes that might not impress one who had never lived in China before. But it is striking to one who can remember the small carts that were pulled through Shanghai's streets every morning to collect the bodies of men, women and children who had frozen to death during the night. Back alleys and side streets that had once been ankle deep in filth are all clean.

The streets are swept daily, even the alleys or hutungs—side streets—far from the main thoroughfares. Block wardens assign the task to individual households, and managers of each store are responsible for keeping their frontage clean. . . .

U.S. News & World Report, March 13, 1972.
Copyright 1972 U.S. News & World Report, Inc.

1. Which statements are opinions of the writer?
2. Make a balance sheet of a) items that you believe are desirable and b) items you believe are undesirable about life in China today. What conclusions have you reached about life in China today?

15 SOUTHEAST ASIA: NEW NATIONS WITH PROBLEMS

Reading For A Purpose: Why are the lands of Southeast Asia important to us?

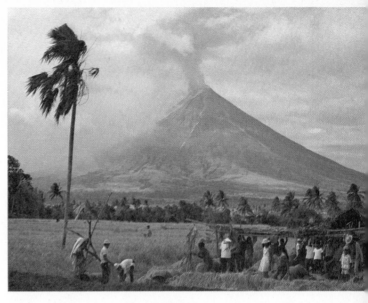

Mount Mayon, in the Philippines, has erupted in the past and is still considered an active volcano. Why do you think people are willing to live near volcanoes when they know of the danger?

1. The world has long been interested in the lands of Southeast Asia. Early explorers sought a water route to the "Spice Islands," as part of Southeast Asia was once called. European nations were so eager for the resources of these lands that almost the entire region became colonies of nations of Europe. High as the interest of the world may have been in this area in past centuries, it was never greater than it is at this moment. Since independence came to most of the small countries of Southeast Asia, wars have made the most news from this part of the world.

2. Southeast Asia includes the lands east of India and Bangladesh and south of China and Japan. Part of this region lies on the continent of Asia, ending in the Malay Peninsula that extends southeast from the continent (see map, page 460). On the mainland of Asia are the nations of Burma, Thailand, Malaysia, Cambodia, Laos, Vietnam and the city-state of Singapore. To the south and east are the archipelagoes of Indonesia and the Philippines and thousands of smaller islands. The total land area of Southeast Asia is about one-half as large as the land area of the United States, although it stretches across a greater distance from east to west.

3. In the entire region there are more than 280 million people, twice the number for each square mile of land as in the United States. The island of Java, part of Indonesia, has more than 1,000 people per square mile of land. This island alone has more than half of Indonesia's total population of 124 million.

4. Because so much of the region is water, and because it lies near the busy mainland of Asia, it contains many important waterways. The Strait of Malacca, which separates the Malay Peninsula and the island of Sumatra, is one of the most important water passages in the world. The city of Singapore, located on the strait, is one of the world's leading ports. A huge amount of trade passes through the waters of Southeast Asia to and from the Far East and the ports of Europe and America.

5. After the early explorers found the Spice Islands, European nations divided up almost the entire region among themselves. The Dutch held control over many of the islands, chiefly the ones that today make up Indonesia. Great Britain held Burma, the Malay Peninsula and Singapore. (That nation still has close ties with its former colonies.) The French colonized Indochina. This region is now the countries of Cambodia, Laos and Vietnam. Because of Magellan's voyage, the Spanish claimed the Philippines and ruled them until

A mother and her children in a Southeast Asian village.

may be little or no rain during the winter months, but from sixty to eighty inches of rain may fall from June to September. The archipelagoes of Indonesia and the Philippines were partly formed by volcanoes. On the Indonesian island of Java, the volcanic soils are fertile. Because much food can be grown, there is a huge population on the island.

7. Most of the people of Southeast Asia are "brown-skinned" Malays. However, in most countries there is a mixture of nationalities and religions. Chinese influence on these nations has been very strong. The Chinese are the largest minority group in Southeast Asia. In Malaysia, Chinese and Indians make up more than half the population. In the countries that border China, Buddhism is the largest religion. The Moslem religion has spread throughout the Malay Peninsula and Indonesia. In the Philippines, because of its Spanish settlement, more than ninety per cent of the people are Christians.

8. As you might expect, most of the people of Southeast Asia are farmers. They live in villages near their fields. This village life, in which people of different cultures live close together in peace, is a striking feature of life in this part of the world. One of the problems now in the region is the movement of people from the villages to the cities. The old family and village ties are breaking up. Cities are growing in size: Jakarta, Indonesia; Bangkok, Thailand; Saigon, Vietnam; Rangoon, Burma; Manila, the Philippines; and Singapore. The outside world comes to Southeast Asia through the cities. Many are modern with wide, paved streets, tall buildings, electricity and air conditioning. Behind the main streets, however, are the slums that are a part of all Far Eastern cities.

9. The largest number of people make their

war with the United States in 1898. After that, the U.S. owned the Philippines until 1946, when freedom was granted. Only Thailand was ruled by its own kings for hundreds of years. Since 1946, all the nations here that were once colonies have gained their freedom.

6. This is a tropical region. Only the northern part of Burma lies outside the low latitudes. Yet because the lands are mountainous, almost any kind of climate may be found. The hardships are greatest in the lowlands where most of the people live. There are heavy rains, thick forests, poor soils in many places and the ever-present tropical diseases. Burma, Thailand, Vietnam and parts of the Philippines have the monsoon climate as in India. There

living growing rice. The best rice-growing areas are the river valleys; the Irrawaddy in Burma, the Chao Phraya in Thailand and the Mekong in Vietnam. The river valleys make these three nations the leading rice-exporting nations in the world. Most is exported to neighboring countries where it is badly needed. In areas of less rainfall, corn, millet, beans and sweet potatoes are grown.

10. Plantation farming is important in Southeast Asia. Plantation products are sold mainly to foreign countries. This kind of farming was begun by European and American businessmen. Each of the large farms specializes in one crop. The rubber plantations supply ninety per cent of the world's supply of natural rubber. Malaysia and Indonesia are the leading producers. Indonesia is also a large exporter of tea. More than half the world's coconut oil is produced in Malaysia and the Philippines. Palm oil, sugar, coffee and pepper are other plantation crops. Teakwood and quinine (used as a medicine in treating malaria) are products of the forests.

11. There are rich mineral resources, too. Southeast Asia produces half the world's supply of tin. Malaysia and the Philippines mine iron ore and manganese, a metal used in making fine steel. From Thailand we get tungsten, the long-burning metal in light bulbs. Oil is found in Indonesia, although it is a small part of the world's supply. These minerals are mined for export. Because there is such mineral wealth in Southeast Asia, we can expect future development of industries in these countries.

12. The problems of the Southeast Asian nations are similar to problems of other underdeveloped regions around the world. Most of the people are poor, hungry, sick and illiterate. Indonesia, however, has made great gains in increasing the education of her people. The wealth of Southeast Asia is produced largely for the rest of the world. Very little of it is shared with the people who produce it. Fur-

thermore, the people have had little experience in democratic government. They have lived far removed from the large cities, away from the ports and contact with the world. Skilled workers and money are needed to start local industries. This will help to develop local buyers for the goods produced in Southeast Asia.

13. The long war in Vietnam was a serious problem. North Vietnam became free from France in 1954 and formed a Communist government. In the south, the Republic of Vietnam was formed one year later. Almost at once, small groups of Communists began a civil war in South Vietnam. At first, the United States sent military advisers and supplies to help the government of South Vietnam. When this did not work, our troops began pouring in —over 400,000 from 1965 to 1968. Representa-

Floating goods to market in Bangkok, Thailand. Do you think this is a good way to bring goods to market? Why?

529

A rural scene in the Mekong Valley of Cambodia. How do you think the lives of farmers in this region have been changed by years of bombing and fighting between communist and anti-communist forces?

tives of all sides in the conflict went to Paris for peace talks. Yet the war went on, killing and wounding hundreds of thousands. Finally in 1973, a peace agreement was made. Fighting continued, however. In 1975, the Communists won. North and South became one Vietnam.

UNDERSTANDING
CHAPTER 15

1. Which questions are answered in this chapter?
   a. Why is the city of Singapore important?
   b. How do people farm in Southeast Asia?
   c. What countries are located on the mainland of Asia?
2. The main idea of *paragraphs 9 through 11* describes:
   a. the chief products of Southeast Asia.
   b. reasons for our interest in this region.
   c. kinds of rice farming in Southeast Asia.
3. Most of the people of Southeast Asia live in:
   a. large cities.   b. fertile lowlands.   c. hilly woodlands.

4. All of these are countries of Southeast Asia EXCEPT:
   a. Malaysia.   b. Laos.   c. Iran.
5. All of these are important minerals of Southeast Asia EXCEPT:
   a. mercury.   b. manganese.   c. tin.
6. All of these are large exports of Southeast Asia EXCEPT:
   a. wheat.   b. rubber.   c. tea.
7. A reason why Southeast Asia is important in world affairs is that:
   a. it has large deposits of coal.
   b. its people have a high standard of living.
   c. a great amount of trade passes in and around these lands.
8. A reason for poor transportation in Southeast Asia is that:
   a. the lands are largely unexplored.
   b. much of the land is forest.
   c. narrow straits keep ocean-going ships from passing near the large land area.

SUMMING UP *Agree or Disagree* Decide whether or not each of the following statements agrees with what you have read. If the answer is *disagree*, explain why.
1. The lands of Southeast Asia were ruled by one nation until 1946.
2. It would be unusual to find a Hindu temple or Moslem mosque in the villages of Southeast Asia.
3. Some of these lands were once known as the "Spice Islands."
4. Only since 1950 has the world become interested in Southeast Asia.
5. In some countries of this region, there is more than enough rice to feed the nation's people.
6. Mountains and large bodies of water have kept the people of Southeast Asia free from the influence of China.
7. The tiny country of Vietnam is of great interest to the people of the United States.

FOLLOW UP Make a report on one of the countries of Southeast Asia. You may prepare your report using these headings:

a. Land and Climate
b. The People
c. Progress in Farming and Industry
d. Leading Figures of the Country's History
e. Population Centers and Cities
f. Problems Faced by the Country
g. Plans for the Future

Groups in the class may study individual countries. Assemble pictures or bulletin-board displays of the nation you are studying. Current magazines, travel folders, government information agencies or magazines that deal with geography will provide you with information. Use the same headings for your display as for the written report.

Author	Title, Publisher	Description
1. Archer, Jules	HO CHI MINH, LEGEND OF HANOI, Crowell-Collier	Story of the North Vietnamese leader, his loyalty to his land and the Vietnam War.
2. Brandman, Gwenn R.	INDIA, LAND OF THE RIVERS, Nelson	The story of the thousand years of India's history.
3. Bryce, Winifred	LIVING IN TOKYO, Nelson	Tokyo's history, customs and "many sides" today.
4. Buck, Pearl	THE MAN WHO CHANGED CHINA, Random House	Biography of Sun Yat-sen. Covers events leading to the beginning of the Republic of China.
5. Buell, Hal	FESTIVALS OF JAPAN, Dodd, Mead	Illustrations and stories of Japanese celebrations.
6. Cartier-Bresson, Henri	THE FACE OF ASIA, Viking	A striking picture account of life in the chief countries of Asia.
7. Chinnock, Frank	KIM, A GIFT FROM VIETNAM, Paperback Library	A father's search for a lost child in a land where thousands are lost.
8. DeJong, Meindert	HOUSE OF SIXTY FATHERS, Harper	The story of a Chinese boy during the Japanese occupation of China in World War II.
9. Editors of Sterling Publishing Co.	VISUAL GEOGRAPHY SERIES: CEYLON, HONG KONG, INDIA, INDONESIA, PAKISTAN, PHILIPPINES, THAILAND, KOREA, Sterling	Interesting accounts of the life and cultures of the people of each country.
10. Fairservis, Walter	HORSEMEN OF THE STEPPES, World	Exciting tale of the nomadic horsemen who overran parts of Europe and Asia.
11. Garnett, Emeline	MADAME PRIME MINISTER, INDIRA GANDHI, Farrar	A widow and mother of two who became Prime Minister of over a half billion people; her role in making modern India.
12. Glubok, Shirley	THE ART OF INDIA, Macmillan	Striking illustrations of art, old and new, reflecting the history and culture of India.

13.	Glubok, Shirley	THE ART OF JAPAN, Macmillan	Art, old and new, reflecting the history and culture of Japan.
14.	Hersey, John	HIROSHIMA, Knopf	Prize-winning account of the dropping of the atomic bomb on Hiroshima, its effects upon people and property.
15.	Lamb, Beatrice	INDIA, Macmillan	A brief account of India, its history, religion and plans for the future.
16.	MacGregor-Hastie, Roy	THE RED BARBARIANS, Chilton	The life and times of Mao Tse-tung.
17.	Sommerfelt, Aimee	THE WHITE BUNGALOW, Criterion	The story of life in a small Indian village.
18.	Spencer, Cornelia	THE LAND OF THE CHINESE PEOPLE, Lippincott	This history has a large section about life in China shortly after World War I.
19.	Tooze, Ruth	CAMBODIA, LAND OF CONTRASTS, Viking	About the people of Cambodia, their work and problems, with fine illustrations.
20.	Warren, William	BANGKOK, Weatherhill	Text with pictures of the city and people that tourists see and don't see.

UNIT 10
The Pacific World

1 THE WORLD OF WATER

Reading For A Purpose: How were the lands of the Pacific settled?

1. The Pacific World is the "world of water." In this region we find Australia, New Zealand and the thousands of islands of the Pacific Ocean. The Pacific World covers an area of 69 million square miles, more than all the land areas on the earth put together! The Pacific Ocean is the most important influence in the life of the people here. Australia, the island continent, is the largest mass of land in this large region.

2. The entire region of the Pacific World is made up of islands. These range in size from the large continent of Australia to the tiny coral reefs or *atolls*. Except for Australia and New Zealand (and the islands of Indonesia that we studied with the Far East), these lands are governed by other nations. Their people have different ways of making a living, from simple hunting, fishing and farming to the most modern kinds of manufacturing. Some of the people live very poorly, while others have a high standard of living.

3. It is thought that Australia was once connected to the mainland of Asia. Long ago, part of the land between them sank and the ocean waters covered it. All that remained above water were the islands of Indonesia and New Guinea. Over these island "bridges" from Asia came many of the animals and people who now live in the Pacific World. These early people were called *aborigines*. They lived by hunting, fishing and gathering fruits. They roamed freely until the Europeans came in the eighteenth century.

4. In 1770, long after our own New World had been found, Europeans discovered Australia. In that year an Englishman named Captain James Cook sailed along the eastern coast of Australia and claimed the land for Great Britain. The first English colony in Australia was started in 1788—twelve years after our Declaration of Independence from Great Britain! This colony was made up of convicts or prisoners. New Zealand was not settled until more than fifty years after that. Settlements did not grow quickly in the region because it was felt that the lands had few resources.

This painting shows people of a Pacific island rushing to the harbor to greet trading ships. Why do you think they were so glad to see traders from Europe and America?

5. In the middle of the nineteenth century, whaling ships began to sail throughout the Pacific World in search of whales for oil. They stopped at the islands to get fresh water and food. In exchange for these items, they gave the natives such goods as cloth, tobacco and glass beads. At the same time, missionaries began to go to the islands. The ways of life of the natives began to change as contact with Westerners increased.

6. In 1851, gold was discovered in Australia. This was two years after our own gold rush in California. People hurried in great numbers to the southern continent. In less than seven years, Australia's population doubled. The Europeans pushed the native people farther inland as they settled.

7. Later in the nineteenth century, European nations took a new interest in the Pacific World. They wanted some of the raw materials of this area. They also wanted places of supply for ships sailing across the Pacific Ocean. When the west coast of the United States was settled after 1850, our nation also increased trade with the Far East. In 1898, the United States gained Hawaii. After the Spanish-American War we also acquired the Philippines and Guam. Our interest in the other Pacific islands and Australia grew as well.

8. After World War I, Japan was given many islands in the Pacific as "mandates" by the League of Nations. The Japanese fortified these islands with guns. After attacking Pearl Harbor in 1941, Japan overran other Pacific islands and lands in Southeast Asia. Battles were fought throughout the Pacific before the war ended in August, 1945. The islands of Tarawa, Guadalcanal and Iwo Jima are familiar to Americans as battlegrounds in the Pacific dur-

Australia drew many people to her shores during the gold rush days of the 1850's. How had people reacted to the discovery of gold in California in 1848?

ing the war with Japan. After World War II, many of the islands were made a United Nations trust territory under the care of the United States. Some other trust territories in the Pacific were assigned to some European nations at that time.

UNDERSTANDING
CHAPTER 1

1. Which questions are answered in this chapter?
   a. Who were Tasman and Bougainville?
   b. What event in the nineteenth century caused an increase in the population of Australia?
   c. Why were Europeans slow to settle in Australia?
2. The main idea of this chapter describes:
   a. early settlements in New Zealand.
   b. Australia's part in World War II.
   c. important events in the history of the Pacific World.
3. Australia was claimed by Great Britain because of the voyages of:
   a. Cook.   b. Magellan.   c. da Gama.
4. The first settlers in Australia were:
   a. traders.   b. farmers.   c. convicts.
5. Europeans were slow to explore Australia because:
   a. the natives were unfriendly.
   b. Europeans thought it had no riches.
   c. there were no good harbors.
6. The Europeans first came to this region in search of:
   a. colonies.   b. whales.   c. slaves.
7. The *aborigines* of Australia are like which people in the history of the United States?
   a. Indians.   b. Spanish.   c. Negroes.
8. *Atolls* are:
   a. early people of New Zealand.
   b. small coral islands of the Pacific.
   c. early whaling ships.

DEVELOPING
IDEAS AND
SKILLS

Map Study

Map #58—The Pacific World

Study the map on page 539. Then tell whether these statements are true or false.
1. The continent of Australia is occupied by many countries.
2. Micronesia and Polynesia are in the Atlantic Ocean.
3. New Zealand is northeast of Australia.
4. Australia is south of the equator.
5. The islands of Micronesia lie both north and south of the equator.
6. The Hawaiian Islands are the largest group in Polynesia.
7. Most islands in the Pacific belong to other nations.
8. The United States has a "trust territory" in the Pacific.
9. Most of Australia's people live on the western coast.

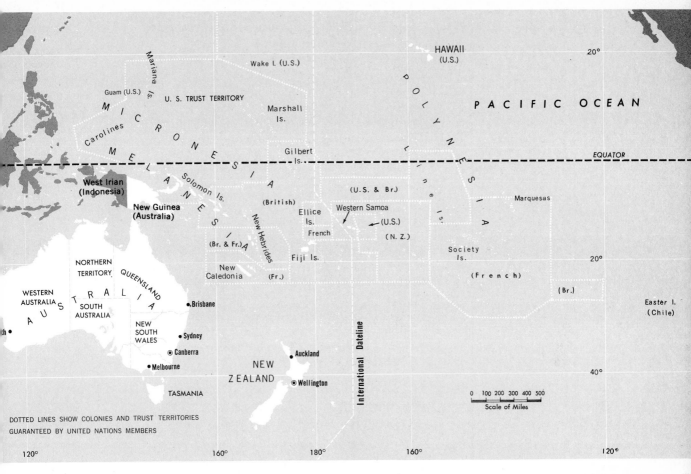

Map #58—The Pacific World

Agree or Disagree   Decide whether or not each of the following statements agrees with what you have read. If the answer is *disagree*, explain why.

1. Australia was settled long after our New World was found.
2. Nearly all people in the Pacific World do the same kind of work.
3. Most of the people of the Pacific islands govern themselves.
4. As a result of several wars, the United States now has a real interest in the Pacific World.
5. Before World War II, the most powerful nation in the Pacific World was Japan.
6. Between Australia and Asia there are many islands.
7. In the last few years, whaling ships have begun to visit the Pacific lands.
8. The United States has island possessions in the Pacific Ocean.

Arrange these events *in the order in which they took place.*
1. Whaling ships and traders appear.
2. Aborigines come to Australia.
3. World War II ends.
4. The Spanish-American War is fought.
5. Voyages of exploration take place.
6. Gold rush to Australia brings settlers.
7. First colony in Australia is established.

2 THE LANDS DOWN UNDER

Reading For A Purpose: What are the topography and climate of Australia and New Zealand?

1. Australia is called the island continent. It is the only country to occupy an entire continent by itself. You could call Australia the smallest continent or the largest island on earth. With approximately three million square miles, it is the sixth largest country in the world. Australia is also called a "land down under," for it is entirely south of the equator. Therefore, its seasons are the opposite of ours. Australia's summer lasts from November to April; winter is from May to October.

2. Australia is located partly in the low latitudes and partly in the middle latitudes. Its location can be compared with that of Mexico and Central America, except that it is south of the equator instead of north. The large city of Melbourne, on the southeast tip of the continent, is 37° south—not as far south of the equator as Cincinnati, Ohio, is north. Australia is farther from the United States than any other major country. The airline distance from San Francisco to Sydney, Australia, is 7,500 miles!

3. Along Australia's east coast is a narrow coastal plain. A few miles inland, the land rises to become the eastern highlands or Great Dividing Range. These are the only mountains in Australia. They are not as high as some of the peaks in our Rocky Mountains. West of the mountains is a great central plain. This is called the "outback." Farther west, the land rises to form a vast, dry plateau. This plateau extends all the way to the western coast. Off the northeastern coast is a long coral reef called the Great Barrier Reef. It has been built

Kangaroos are found in Australia and the nearby islands. Their tails help them to keep their balance as they jump along rapidly on their strong hind legs.

A highway through the outback of Australia. Which areas of the United States are similar to Australia's outback?

up over the ages by millions of tiny sea animals.

4. Lack of water is a serious problem in most of Australia. There are no great rivers like the Congo, Mississippi or Amazon leading into the continent. The largest river is the Murray-Darling, which rises in the eastern highlands and flows southwest into the Indian Ocean.

5. Australia has a varied climate. The north and northeast have a savanna climate. In these areas there is a rainy season and a dry season. During the summer, the monsoons bring rain. During the winter, the wind shifts and the area is dry. It is always hot. The soil is poor because of the heavy rains. As you might guess, few people live in this part of the continent.

6. Most Australians live along the eastern coast. In general, this part of the country has a mild, damp climate. There is plenty of rainfall for farming. The largest cities are also located here. North of the city of Sydney, the climate is humid subtropical. South of Sydney, it is a marine climate as in our northwestern states.

7. Beyond the mountains to the west there is less rainfall. The winds that blow over the mountains have lost much of their moisture by the time they reach this area. This is a region of dry grasslands where the rainfall is from ten to twenty inches a year. It is a steppe climate. The region is almost too dry for farming, but it is good for sheep grazing.

8. As you travel farther west, the land be-

comes drier and drier. The western half of Australia is a vast desert of sand and rock. (In fact, forty per cent of the country is desert!) Because of the mountains, no rain-bearing winds can reach this part of the continent. There are no regular winds blowing from the Indian Ocean to the east. South of the desert, the coastal areas have a Mediterranean climate —warm, dry summers and mild winters with some rain.

9. New Zealand lies about 1,200 miles southeast of Australia. It is located entirely in the middle latitudes. This country is made up of two main islands, North Island and South Island. Although they are each nearly 1,000 miles long, the islands are narrow, scarcely more than 200 miles wide. This means that the climate of the islands is affected by the ocean around them. These are mountainous islands; there are no deserts as in Australia. The winds blow from the west, so the west coast has more rain than the east coast. New Zealanders enjoy a marine climate, with mild and rainy summers and winters. The climate of New Zealand may be compared with that of its "mother country," Great Britain.

UNDERSTANDING CHAPTER 2

1. Which questions are answered in this chapter?
   a. How do the people live in the northeast of Australia?
   b. Why is it warm in Australia at Christmas time?
   c. How do the mountains of Australia affect its climate?
2. The main idea of this chapter describes:
   a. New Zealand's climate.
   b. the desert area of Australia.
   c. the land and climate of both countries.
3. New Zealand's climate is chiefly:
   a. marine.   b. desert.   c. rain forest.
4. A great part of Australia cannot be used because it is:
   a. too wet.   b. too dry.   c. too cold.
5. Seasons in Australia and New Zealand are the opposite of ours because these countries are in the:
   a. northern hemisphere.   b. southern hemisphere.   c. high latitudes.
6. The heart of Australia is dry because:
   a. rain-bearing winds are blocked by eastern mountains.
   b. there are few rivers.
   c. the country is too near the equator.
7. The "outback" refers to:
   a. the coral reefs along the Australian coast.
   b. the dry central plain.
   c. reservations where the aborigines live.

Map Study

Map #59—Land Forms of Australia and New Zealand

Study the map. Then tell whether these statements are true or false. Be able to explain your answers.

1. The striking feature of New Zealand is that it is chiefly a plateau.
2. There is a mountain range in Australia located along the southeastern coast.
3. Comparing the climate of Australia with its land forms, it is clear that most of Australia's desert is lowland.
4. Plains line the Australian coast on the south.
5. Most of the warm part of Australia is highland.
6. The eastern and western coasts of Australia have the same kinds of land forms.

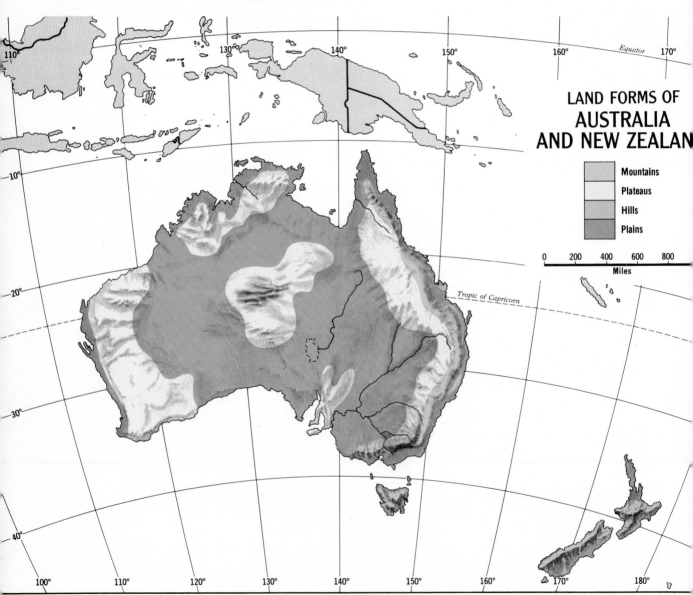

LAND FORMS OF
**AUSTRALIA
AND NEW ZEALAN**

Mountains
Plateaus
Hills
Plains

0   200   400   600   800
Miles

Map #60—Climates of Australia and New Zealand

Agree or Disagree Study the map. Then decide whether or not each of the statements below agrees with the information on the map. If the answer is *disagree*, explain why.

1. Both Australia and New Zealand have a great variety of climates.
2. The largest climatic region in Australia is desert.
3. Part of southern Australia is like southern California.
4. New Zealand has the same kind of climate as our northeastern states.
5. Only a small part of Australia has a climate like that of New Zealand.
6. As you travel northward along the eastern coast of Australia, temperatures become higher.
7. The heaviest rainfall in Australia is along the southwestern coast.
8. New Zealand's climate is strange for a country that lies largely in the middle latitudes.

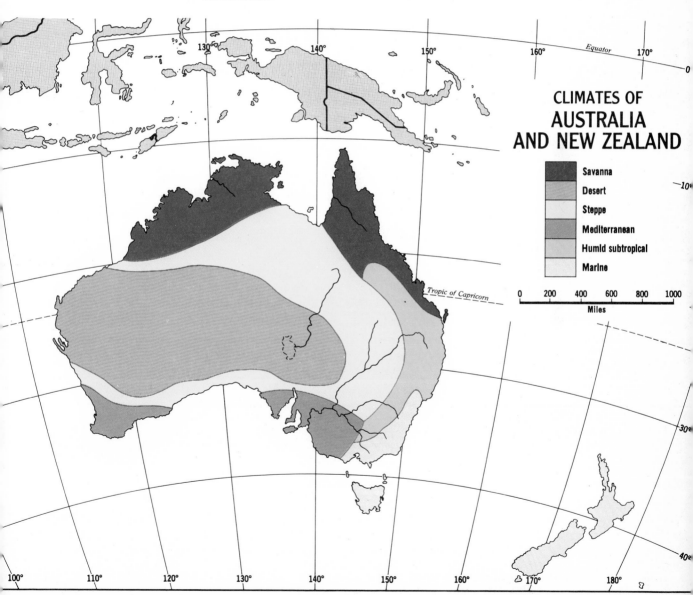

CLIMATES OF
**AUSTRALIA
AND NEW ZEALAND**

Savanna
Desert
Steppe
Mediterranean
Humid subtropical
Marine

0   200   400   600   800   1000
Miles

Tell whether these statements are true or false. The underlined words make the statements true or false. If a statement is false, what word or words would you place in it to make it true?

1. As you travel <u>north</u> in Australia, the climate becomes warmer.
2. August is one of Australia's <u>summer</u> months.
3. <u>Australia</u> is the smallest of the continents.
4. Most of New Zealand is a <u>great lowland plain</u>.
5. New Zealand is located in the <u>middle</u> latitudes.
6. Most Australians live in the <u>eastern</u> part of the continent.
7. The largest single climate of Australia is the <u>rain forest</u>.
8. West of Australia is the <u>Indian</u> Ocean.
9. New Zealanders enjoy largely a <u>marine</u> climate.
10. Australia has a <u>regular</u> coastline.

Plan a trip to Australia.
1. How would you travel?
2. What time of year would you plan to go?
3. Which part of Australia would you like to visit?
4. What clothes would you take with you?
5. What languages would you study to prepare yourself?
6. What kind of people would you expect to find?

3 THE MODERN PEOPLE

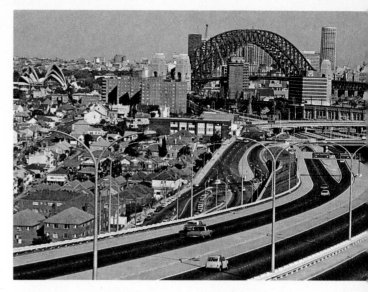

Reading For A Purpose: Who are the people of the "lands down under"?

A view of Sydney, Australia's largest city. Australia attracts thousands of immigrants each year. Why do you think so many immigrants decide to make Sydney their home?

1. The populations of Australia and New Zealand are both small. Australia has about thirteen million people (fewer than the state of New York or California) and New Zealand has about three million. These are mostly white people whose language, customs and ways of living are like those of Great Britain, Canada and the United States.

2. Australia is one of the most lightly populated countries in the world, with an average of only four people for each square mile of land. Because so much of the country is dry, most of the people live around the "rim" of the continent. In this respect, Australia is much like South America. The population is growing slowly. The Australians want people to come to their country, but they do not allow "nonwhites" from Africa and Asia to settle there. This lack of a rapidly growing population holds back the full development of the nation.

3. The first people of both Australia and New Zealand were the nonwhite aborigines. In Australia, these people are called Bushmen. They lived by hunting and gathering wild fruits. The Bushmen of Australia were pushed off their land by the white settlers in much the same way as the Indians were in North America. Today the aborigines make up less than one per cent of the people of Australia. Some are nomads on the "outback"; others live on government reservations or near the large cities.

4. In New Zealand the aborigines are Maoris. The Maoris are brown-skinned people. They fought against white men's settlement of the islands. After a while they accepted the newcomers and their ways of life. Today, there are about 300,000 Maoris in New Zealand; they enjoy the same rights as all other people in the country. They are educated, and many are lawyers, doctors and teachers.

5. While most of the land is used for raising sheep and cattle, most Australians live in cities where they work in factories, offices and shops. Most of the large cities are located in the southeast. (The port city of Perth on the west coast is the only large city outside the east.) The largest city is Sydney, which has more than two million people. Melbourne, in the mild marine climate of the southeast, is a seaport with more than one million people. Other large cities are Brisbane, Adelaide and Canberra, the capital.

6. The cities of Australia are modern. They are remarkably clean and have very few areas that could be called slums. The people enjoy the comforts of modern living. Washing machines, refrigerators, radios and television sets are part of most city homes. The streets are wide and automobiles are everywhere. The

547

Australians love to travel. If one considers the small population, Australia has more miles of highway and railroad track for its people than any other nation in the world. (However, the roads and railroads are found mostly in the populated areas.) Most of the major airlines also have routes to Australia. World travelers find Australia a wonderful place to visit.

7. Much of the success of the people of Australia and New Zealand can be traced to their governments. Both countries have a democratic form of government modeled after that of Great Britain. The chief lawmaking body in each is a parliament, elected by the people. The head of each government is the prime minister. They and the members of their cabinets lead their countries with the help of the parliaments. The governments of Australia and New Zealand were the first to pass many laws that have since been adopted by our own country: the secret ballot, the right of women to vote and pensions for workers. Both countries are members of the British Commonwealth of Nations.

8. The people of these two nations are among the most highly educated in the world. Children must attend school to the age of fifteen. It would be difficult to find an adult in either country who is not able to read and write. These nations wish to keep their high standards. As a result, their laws allow only people of a certain income or training to become citizens of these countries.

A meeting of the Australian Parliament in Canberra. Why do you think Australia's form of government is modeled after that of Great Britain?

9. Both Australians and New Zealanders are great sports-loving people. In Australia, tennis is a favorite sport. Great tennis players have represented Australia in tournaments around the world. In track meets and swimming contests among nations, runners and swimmers from Australia have also become world-famous. Horse racing and cricket draw large crowds everywhere in the country.

10. In many ways, Australia is much like Canada. Both countries are very large but have small populations. Most of the people live along the "rim" of each country. In one case, the interior is largely a cold, watery wilderness; in the other, it is a dry, sandy desert. Both peoples have a high standard of living. Most of them live in cities and work in offices, shops or factories. Despite their small populations, they are able to export foodstuffs and raw materials. Much of their trade is with either the United States or Great Britain.

UNDERSTANDING CHAPTER 3

1. Which questions are answered in this chapter?
   a. What are the large cities of New Zealand?
   b. How are the Maoris treated in New Zealand?
   c. How are the people of Australia governed?
2. The main idea of this chapter describes:
   a. the cities of the Pacific World.
   b. the ways of living of people "down under."
   c. the life of the aborigines.
3. Most people in Australia work:
   a. on farms and plantations.
   b. on ranches.
   c. in factories and offices.

4. Both Australia and New Zealand have ways of life that have come from the:

    a. Spanish.   b. British.   c. aborigines.

5. The population of Australia is growing slowly because:

    a. nonwhite immigrants are not welcome in the country.

    b. only a small part of the land can be used.

    c. the standard of living of the people is very low.

6. Australia may be called a "hollow continent" because:

    a. most people live along the coasts.

    b. it is shaped like a saucer.

    c. there are no rivers in the interior.

7. *Aborigines* refer to the:

    a. earliest people in a region.

    b. original plants and trees of a region.

    c. earliest European settlers.

DEVELOPING IDEAS AND SKILLS

Pictograph #16—Population, Area and Standard of Living of the Pacific World

Study the pictograph. Then answer the questions at the top of page 550.

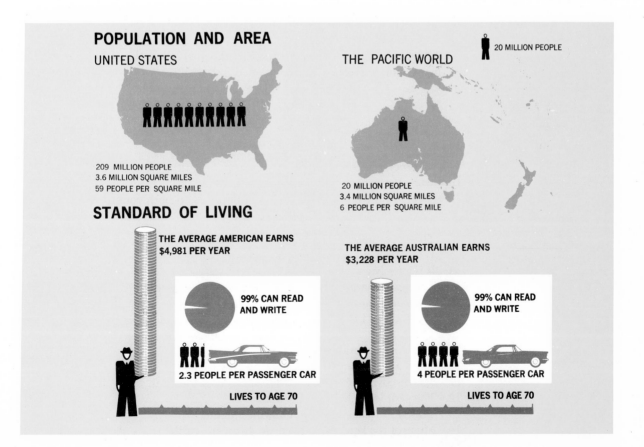

POPULATION AND AREA

UNITED STATES

20 MILLION PEOPLE

THE PACIFIC WORLD

209 MILLION PEOPLE
3.6 MILLION SQUARE MILES
59 PEOPLE PER SQUARE MILE

20 MILLION PEOPLE
3.4 MILLION SQUARE MILES
6 PEOPLE PER SQUARE MILE

STANDARD OF LIVING

THE AVERAGE AMERICAN EARNS $4,981 PER YEAR

99% CAN READ AND WRITE

2.3 PEOPLE PER PASSENGER CAR

LIVES TO AGE 70

THE AVERAGE AUSTRALIAN EARNS $3,228 PER YEAR

99% CAN READ AND WRITE

4 PEOPLE PER PASSENGER CAR

LIVES TO AGE 70

1. Is the standard of living of this region high or low compared with that of the United States?
2. Is the region more or less crowded than the United States?
3. Are the people of this region literate compared with the people of the United States?
4. How long may the average person in this region expect to live?
5. What facts tell you the standard of living of the people of the region?
6. How does this region compare with the United States in size?

SUMMING UP

Making Inferences In our reading, many facts are given to us. From these facts we can draw conclusions. The following are some conclusions or inferences that you might make after reading Chapters 1, 2 and 3. Tell whether these conclusions are correct or incorrect. Give reasons for your answers.

1. The aborigines of Australia were never a farming people.
2. The early settlers of Australia did not travel far inland.
3. There are few highways on the "outback."
4. A visitor from a large city in the United States would find few things in an Australian city that would be familiar to him.
5. Automobiles would not be as important in New Zealand as in Australia.
6. Many railroad lines cross Australia from one coast to another.
7. The mountains of New Zealand give it a climate like that of Norway.
8. Athletes from the United States have been rivals of Australian athletes in many sports.

FOLLOW UP

Tell whether the following items refer to Australia, New Zealand or to both countries. If the item applies to Australia only, write A; if the item applies to New Zealand only, write N; if the item applies to both countries, write B.

1. Maoris fought against the white settlers.
2. The government is like that of Great Britain.
3. Women are allowed to vote.
4. It is largely a mountainous country.
5. There are a large number of English-speaking people.
6. It is sometimes called "land down under."
7. The country is only a little smaller than the United States.
8. The country lies partly in the low latitudes.
9. Much of the nation is desert.
10. The country is made up of long, narrow islands.
11. The discovery of gold helped to speed its settlement.
12. The people are highly educated.
13. The country has a pleasant marine climate.
14. Much of the land is used to raise sheep and cattle.

4 WEALTH IN A DRY LAND

Reading For A Purpose: How do the people of Australia make use of their resources?

1. Much of Australia's land is too dry for farming. What's more, there are not enough people to work the land. Nevertheless, Australia produces more food than its population needs. It is one of the world's great food exporters and sends shiploads of meat and dairy products to Europe every year. Let us find out why.

2. Northern Australia is hot and rainy. It contains many plantations on which sugar cane and tropical fruits—pineapples, bananas and coconuts—are raised. Large amounts of these fruits are exported. The sugar cane lands reach almost to Brisbane, about halfway between northern and southern Australia. Sugar is another food export.

3. South of Brisbane, fruit and dairy farming takes place along the narrow coastal plains. The summers are cool and there is plenty of rain from the winds of the Pacific Ocean. As a result, there is good pasture land. The dairy farmers have good cattle and modern equipment and barns. They supply the people of nearby cities with many dairy products.

4. On the western side of the mountains are the wheat lands of Australia. Here the fields are large and the land is level. Therefore, machinery can be used. In this way, a few farmers can grow a great deal of wheat. Wheat is the chief farm crop of Australia. Next to wool, it is the most important export crop. Many wheat farmers also raise sheep.

5. Farther west it is too dry to grow wheat, but there is enough grass for sheep grazing.

This is the area of the huge sheep ranches called *stations*. These stations are very large, because sheep have to roam far and wide to get enough to eat. The poorer the land, the larger the station. The few ranchers who live here are far apart. The nearest neighbor might be 100 miles away. Travel is difficult and water is scarce. It is not unusual for the sheep rancher to travel by jeep or airplane to look over his vast station. Most sheep are raised for their wool rather than their meat. Wool is Australia's chief export.

6. The sheep rancher has many problems. First, there is not enough water for the people and animals. This problem has been partly solved by digging deep wells called *artesian* wells. These wells are dug through a layer of rock. The water shoots to the surface. If it were not for the artesian water, many stretches of desert and "bush land" would have no drinking water at all for man or sheep.

7. Second, the sheep herder must fight all kinds of animal pests. There are wild dogs, rabbits, cattle ticks and kangaroos. The wild dogs or *dingos* were first brought to Australia as pets. They are hated because they kill the sheep—even more than they need for food. Rabbits are the worst enemies of the sheep herders, however. They eat the precious grass and the bark of the bushes. Rabbits limit the number of sheep that the pastures can feed. Another great pest is that unusual creature, the kangaroo. It was one of the first animals to come to Australia. Kangaroos like to eat the

A sheep flock in Queenstown, New Zealand. Why is some of this land better suited to sheep raising than to the growing of wheat?

grass and brush too. The Australian is doing his best to fight the problems caused by these animals.

8. In the northern plains, cattle are raised. The cattle feed on the coarse grass that grows during the rainy summers. From these cattle Australians get large amounts of hides and beef. The cattle ranches are far from railroads and seaports. Therefore, the animals must be driven to market across the country just as our cattle are herded great distances by cowboys.

9. Unlike Australia, New Zealand is a rainy country that is always green. The hills and lowlands of New Zealand are good for raising dairy cattle and sheep. The dairy farms are among the best in the world. New Zealand ranks high in the export of cheese, lamb, butter, wool and beef. Because of their exports, the people of New Zealand have a very high standard of living.

10. While sheep-herding and cattle-raising produce most of its exports, Australia is also a leading industrial nation. There are several reasons for this. First, because many machines are used on the farms and ranches, fewer people are needed there and they can go to work in the mills and factories.

11. Second, Australia is rich in mineral resources. Broken Hill, in southeast Australia, is one of the richest mining areas in the world. Lead, zinc and copper are mined here. Nearby are large deposits of coal and iron. Australia's mills turn out steel for making automobiles, ships, airplanes and locomotives.

12. Third, Australia has two sources of power; coal and falling water. Despite the fact that there is a water shortage in much of Australia, water power is available in the eastern part of the country. The snow and rain from the Great Dividing Range cause many small streams to flow down the mountainsides toward the ocean. Australians have made good use of this power supply. Finally, good roads and railroads have been built so that raw materials from the mines and farms can easily be sent to the factories and seaport cities.

13. New Zealand does not have as many mineral resources as Australia. Therefore, it does not have as many large factories. Because much of New Zealand is mountainous, power from falling water is used. Most of the factories make use of the products of New Zealand's farms. There are woolen and flour mills, meat-packing plants and dairies.

A steel mill in New South Wales, Australia. Why has Australia become a leading industrial nation?

1. Which questions are answered in this chapter?
    a. How is water obtained in the "outback"?
    b. Why can Australia grow large amounts of wheat?
    c. What animals bother the sheep rancher?
2. The main idea of *paragraphs 5 through 7* describes:
    a. how the people of Australia use their resources.
    b. the sheep country of Australia.
    c. wheat-growing on the plains.
3. Water is obtained in the "outback" through:
    a. artesian wells.   b. irrigation canals.   c. dams.
4. Australians are able to grow large amounts of wheat because:
    a. the fields are large, flat and suited to the use of machinery.
    b. fields are far from the smoke-filled cities.
    c. they have a large labor supply and plenty of rainfall.
5. Australia is good for raising sheep because:
    a. there is plenty of grass throughout the country.
    b. the warm northern lowlands are ideal for raising sheep.
    c. much of the country is dry and sheep need little water.
6. A good reason why Australia has been able to develop industries is that:
    a. there is a large supply of workers.
    b. mineral resources are in good supply.
    c. oil is its most important resource.
7. An *artesian* well is:
    a. dug on the side of a mountain.
    b. a spring in which water is pumped to the surface.
    c. dug deep in the soil through a layer of rock.
8. The word *station*, as used in this chapter, refers to:
    a. land and buildings used in raising sheep and cattle.
    b. a position in line.
    c. a regular stopping place on railroads.

Photograph Study

This photograph should help you to recall parts of the chapter you have just read. What is the main idea of the photograph?

Tell whether these statements are true or false. The underlined words make the statements true or false. If a statement is false, what word or words would you place in it to make it true?
1. The chief export of Australia is <u>sugar</u>.
2. Tropical fruits are grown in <u>northern</u> Australia.
3. Wheat farmers in Australia use mainly <u>simple hand tools</u>.
4. <u>Pineapples</u> are raised by some Australian farmers.
5. Many Australians work on <u>sheep stations</u>.
6. Many <u>cattle</u> ranchers are found in the "outback."
7. <u>Water</u> is an important source of power in New Zealand.
8. New Zealand exports <u>dairy products</u>.
9. Australia and New Zealand carry on most of their trade with <u>countries of Europe</u>.
10. <u>Rabbits</u> are one of the pests that bother Australian ranchers.

Reviewing Chapters 1 through 4. Choose the item that *does not belong* with the others in each group.
1. Important animals of Australia: sheep, cattle, hogs, kangaroos.
2. Mineral resources of Australia: coal, oil, copper, iron ore.
3. Climates of Australia: desert, savanna, humid subtropical, taiga.
4. Cities of Australia: Auckland, Melbourne, Sydney, Perth.
5. Events in Australian history: colonies in Africa, discovery of gold, voyage of Capt. Cook, World War II.
6. Farm products of Australia: wheat, sugar cane, citrus fruits, peanuts.

5 LIFE ON THE ISLANDS

Reading For A Purpose: What is life like on the Pacific islands?

1. The great world of the Pacific Ocean is made up of thousands of islands. You will not be able to find most of them on a map. All of these islands are located in the tropics, north and south of the equator. The islands are divided into three parts: *Melanesia* or "black islands"; *Micronesia* or "small islands"; and *Polynesia*, which means "many islands."

2. The islands of Melanesia lie south of the equator and northeast of Australia. They extend southeastward as far as New Caledonia and the Fiji Islands. The largest island in the group is New Guinea, which covers about 300,000 square miles. Most of the people in Melanesia are Negroid or dark-skinned. None of these volcanic islands is independent. Great Britain, France, Australia and Indonesia each govern some of them.

3. Micronesia lies north of Melanesia. This group of islands is made up chiefly of coral atolls, barely above sea level. Their total land area is smaller than that of the state of Delaware. The chief island groups in Micronesia are the Marianas, the Carolines, the Marshalls and the Gilberts. All of these islands were the scenes of battles during World War II. Except for the Gilberts, the islands are a United Nations trust territory cared for by the United States. A Congress of Micronesia has been formed. The islands may soon become the newest nation in the world. Guam, an old possession of the United States, is part of the Marianas. It has one of the finest harbors in the Pacific area.

4. The eastern part of the Pacific World is known as Polynesia. Its total land area is not as large as that of the state of West Virginia. The largest island groups are Hawaii, Samoa, the Society Islands and the Marquesas. Hawaii, of course, is one of our states. Great Britain, New Zealand and France own other islands in this group. The Samoan islands are divided between the United States and Western Samoa, a new nation. Pago Pago, the capital city of American Samoa, has a very fine harbor.

5. All of the Pacific islands are near the equator. This means that the climate is warm throughout the year. The waters tend to keep the temperatures even, so that there is little change in temperature from one season to another. The average temperature on most of the islands is near 80°. There is plenty of rainfall. The winds blow from the east. If there are mountains on the islands, the eastern or windward side is the part that receives the heaviest rain. This part of the Pacific often has severe storms called *typhoons*.

6. The Pacific islands fall into two groups, the "high" islands and the "low" islands. The "high" islands are usually larger. They are either the tops of underwater mountains or volcanoes that have been built up from the ocean floor. These islands contain more fertile land and support more people. The tribes that live on them have a higher standard of living than their "low"-island neighbors.

7. There are several reasons for this. First of all, "high" islands get more rainfall because

their mountains can catch the winds. The rainy hillsides are covered with forests that are used to build boats and houses. Because of the rain and the fertile soil, a great variety of crops are grown: rice, yams, corn, coconuts, bananas, tobacco and taro (a starchy root made into a paste-like food called *poi*). The natives live in the valleys. Each valley supports a village. Many of the natives also raise pigs or cattle to use for food along with fish and fruit. Whatever they grow is needed for themselves; there is little to be sold.

8. The "low" islands are usually reefs or atolls. Many of them are barely above the surface of the water. The atolls are chains of small coral islands. They have been formed by millions of tiny coral animals that live in the ocean. These animals produce a limy shell that hardens to form the atoll. In the center of the atoll is a lagoon, a body of water like a pond. The coral reefs act as protection for the lagoon, and the heavy ocean waves do not enter it. During World War II, these lagoons were places where hundreds of ships lay at anchor. Because the atolls are hard-surfaced, they have been used as landing fields for airplanes.

9. Life on the "low" islands is much harder than on the "high" islands. There is little or no drinking water. The soil is thin, for it is washed away or broken by wind and waves. People live on their own small farms. They use simple digging sticks to plant their crops. Their chief food crops are coconuts, taro and yams. They also catch fish from the sea.

10. The coconut palm is the chief resource of both "high" and "low" islands. It is grown in special pits free from salt water. It is a source of food, clothing and shelter for the natives. For the outside world, it is a source of *copra*. Copra is dried coconut meat. From the copra, oil is pressed out to make margarine, cooking and salad oils, fine soaps and cosmetics. Coconut-shell charcoal is also exported for use in cigarettes and gas masks as a filter.

11. Along with subsistence farming and fishing, there are also plantations on many islands

A thatched roof house in the Fiji Islands. Judging from what you can see in this photo, which do you think the Fiji Islands are—"high" islands or "low" islands?

A German planter established this coconut plantation in Western Samoa in the late 19th century. Why is the coconut palm such an important resource in the Pacific islands?

called phosphate rock. This phosphate rock is important as a fertilizer. The countries that own these islands export phosphate rock to other lands.

Cutting sugar cane in Fiji. In the 19th century, native islanders provided slave labor on many foreign-owned plantations. The ancestors of this man were brought to Fiji from the Solomon Islands to work on sugar plantations.

that grow crops for export. There are coconut or copra plantations. On New Caledonia, coffee and cocoa are raised; on Fiji, sugar cane; on Hawaii, pineapples. A number of "low" islands use the birds that have flown over them for thousands of years as a natural resource. As the birds fly over, their droppings fall on the islands. These droppings mix with the coral limestone and have changed it to a mineral

UNDERSTANDING
CHAPTER 5

1. Which questions are answered in this chapter?
   a. Why is life difficult on the "low" islands?
   b. What are the many uses of the coconut?
   c. How does the Pacific Ocean affect the climate of the islands?
2. The main idea of *paragraphs 8 through 10* describes:
   a. life on the "low" islands of the Pacific.
   b. export crops of the "low" islands.
   c. the government of the "low" islands.
3. The most valuable resource of the island peoples is:
   a. phosphate rock.   b. pineapples.   c. coconuts.
4. Because they are surrounded by the Pacific Ocean, most of the islands:
   a. are coral atolls.
   b. have plenty of rain.
   c. trade with the nations of Latin America.

5. Few people live on the "low" islands because:
   a. there is little fertile soil.
   b. the Pacific winds are too strong.
   c. the islands are too mountainous.
6. The coconut is important in the life of the island peoples because it is:
   a. a source of oil for machinery.
   b. used in building boats.
   c. a source of food, shelter and clothing.
7. *Copra* is the dried meat of:
   a. the coconut.   b. manioc.   c. sorghum.
8. An *atoll* is built from:
   a. volcanoes.   b. glaciers.   c. tiny sea animals.

DEVELOPING IDEAS AND SKILLS

Photograph Study

This photograph should help you to recall parts of the chapter you have just read. What is the main idea of the photograph?

Tell whether the following items refer to a "high" island or to a "low" island. If the item applies to a "high" island, write H; if it applies to a "low" island, write L.

1. well watered
2. small in size
3. fewer people
4. higher living standards
5. variety of crops
6. volcanoes
7. little fertile soil
8. mountainous
9. more minerals
10. people depend upon the coconut

Agree or Disagree Decide whether or not each of the following statements agrees with what you have read. If the answer is *disagree*, explain why.

1. The Pacific World consists only of islands.
2. All the Pacific islands are made of coral.
3. There are few islands in the Pacific in the high latitudes.
4. All the islands together make up a land area as large as the United States.
5. Most of the Pacific peoples are Negroid or brown-skinned.
6. The United States has had little interest in the Pacific Islands.
7. Most of the people make a living from subsistence farming and fishing.

6 THE PACIFIC WORLD TODAY

Reading For A Purpose: What is the future of Australia and the Pacific islands?

1. Australia is one of the largest countries in the world, and it is one of the driest. A great desert occupies about forty per cent of the land area. There are few important lakes and rivers. The lack of water means that only a small part of the land can be farmed. In order to solve this problem, Australians are doing some remarkable things. One of the important projects under way is to change the course of the Snow River. This river rises in the eastern mountains and flows eastward. Australians are digging a tunnel through the mountains so that the water will flow to the western side where the water is most needed.

2. Parts of the Australian continent have hardly been explored. The great desert has separated the people of the eastern coast from other people in the country. Only one railroad crosses the continent to the city of Perth on the west coast. There is a need for more roads, railways and air routes spanning the continent. (Since air routes are easier to establish than railroads, air travel will probably increase in Australia in the future.)

3. Australia has the problem of defending itself. Before World War II, both Australia and New Zealand felt safe from invasion. They thought they were too far from the rest of the world. However, during the war, Japanese forces came close to the borders of Australia, capturing islands around the continent. Japan bombed the city of Darwin in the north. It was in the Battle of the Coral Sea that the American Navy stopped the advance of the Japanese and saved Australia from invasion.

4. After World War II, Australia and New Zealand realized that they needed allies or friends to help them keep their freedom. The United States joined these nations in a defense treaty in 1952. It was called ANZUS, after the first letters of the three nations. Its members agreed to help each other in case of war in the Pacific. In 1954, the ANZUS nations joined with Pakistan, the Philippines, Thailand, Great Britain and France in forming SEATO (Southeast Asia Treaty Organization). Each of these nations agreed to help the others in case of an attack on any member.

5. There is much to be done in the entire Pacific area, and there are few people to do it. While Australians would like more settlers, they have not welcomed nonwhite immigrants. This is resented by Southeast Asian nations, which are overcrowded. Java, Indonesia, for example, is one of the most crowded places on earth. It is closer to Australia than Puerto Rico is to New York. Yet Javanese are not welcome as settlers. China is not very far away. Many of these nations look to their neighbor to the south for more room for their peoples. They cannot feel too kindly toward a nation that refuses to admit people from their lands as citizens. The policy of not admitting nonwhites has, however, been changing.

6. The lives of the people of the Pacific islands changed greatly during World War II. Many of the islands of Melanesia and Micronesia were occupied by United States and Australian troops. Many of the native people helped to build runways for airplanes and to

load and unload ships. The people also sold food to feed the troops. Many of the island people received more money than they had ever had before. They bought Western clothing, tobacco, chewing gum, canned beef and other goods.

A college chemistry class in New Guinea. What other subjects do you think would be important for these students to learn? Why?

This man beats an old drum to call people to worship at a church. In what way does this show a mixing of island culture with Western ideas and customs?

7. When the armed forces left after the war, the good jobs and good living went too. It was hard to go back to the old ways—to work on plantations for low pay. The people of the islands wanted to share in the wealth of the outside world. Since then, improved air transportation has brought tourists from all over the world to the islands. The same air travel has brought the people of the islands closer together. Micronesians have become more interested in self-government. More and more of them have been to school. Young people are no longer content to live as their parents did.

UNDERSTANDING
CHAPTER 6

1. Which questions are answered in this chapter?
   a. Why did Australia join SEATO?
   b. Why does Australia have some fear of the lands to the north?
   c. How are the Pacific islands prepared for self-government?
2. The main idea of this chapter describes:
   a. how World War II changed the island peoples.
   b. the problem of the peoples of the Pacific World.
   c. the relationship between Asia and Australia.
3. The lands to the north of Australia are:
   a. crowded.   b. small.   c. far away.
4. Both Australia and New Zealand belong to the organization known as:
   a. OAS.   b. NATO.   c. SEATO.
5. Australia joined in a treaty with the United States because:
   a. its population is small.
   b. it has a fear of attack.
   c. it needs to trade for food.

6. Few people have moved to Australia because:
   a. there is no land upon which people can settle.
   b. it is not open to nonwhite peoples.
   c. it is far from the western hemisphere.
7. If a nation works with its *allies*, it is working with its:
   a. neighbors.   b. suppliers.   c. friends.

DEVELOPING
IDEAS AND
SKILLS

Look at the cartoon. Then answer the questions below.

1. What caused the change in people at the left and right sides of the cartoon?
2. What was life like for the left-side people?
3. In what ways have the right-side people been changed?
4. What would be a good title for this cartoon?

SUMMING UP

Fact or Opinion Read each statement carefully. If the statement is a fact, write F in your notebook. If it is an opinion, write O.

1. Most of Australia's problems would be solved if the country were opened to people of all lands.
2. Some day the atolls of the Pacific will be crowded with people.
3. American soldiers brought new goods and ideas to the people of the Pacific islands.
4. The Pacific islands should be given complete freedom to govern themselves.
5. Australia really has little to fear from the countries of Asia.
6. Many of the Pacific islands are too far away to concern the American people.
7. Many of the island people depend upon the sea for a living.
8. Japanese forces came close to invading Australia in World War II.

Tell whether the following items refer to the United States, Australia or both countries. If the item applies to the United States only, write US; if it applies to Australia only, write A; if it applies to both countries, write B.

1. An island country.
2. High standard of living.
3. Modern cities.
4. Near the world's greatest trade routes.
5. Few people live in center of the country.
6. Many large, useful rivers.
7. Cattle-raising is important.
8. Large number of Negro people.
9. Democratic government.
10. Large supplies of oil.
11. Desert region.
12. More sheep than people.
13. Women have equal rights with men.
14. Smaller than China.
15. Took part in World War II.

BOOKS FOR UNIT 10

	Author	Title, Publisher	Description
1.	Borden, Charles	HE SAILED WITH CAPTAIN COOK, Crowell	A very human story of life aboard Cook's ship.
2.	Burchfield, R. W. and E. M.	NEW ZEALAND, Macmillan	The story of the mountains and farmlands of New Zealand.
3.	Cairns, G. O.	THE LAND AND PEOPLE OF AUSTRALIA, Macmillan	The story of animals, sheep stations and mining in Australia.
4.	Fennimore, Stephen	BUSH HOLIDAY, Doubleday	An American visits the bush country of Australia.
5.	Heyerdahl, Thor	KON-TIKI, Rand McNally	The famous account of a voyage across the Pacific on a balsa raft.
6.	Patchett, Mary	CRY OF THE HEART, Abelard-Schuman	Life in the Australian "outback."
7.	Pease, Howard	JUNGLE RIVER, Doubleday	Adventures in the rain forest of New Guinea.
8.	Sperry, Armstrong	CALL IT COURAGE, Macmillan	A young man sets out to prove his courage in Polynesia.
9.	Sperry, Armstrong	PACIFIC ISLANDS SPEAKING, Macmillan	A brief account of the geography of the islands and their military value.

UNIT 11
The World Tomorrow

1 NEW FRONTIERS

Reading For A Purpose: Where are we exploring today?

1. You might think that the entire world has been explored as a result of the great voyages of discovery in the sixteenth century. But this is not so. There are still areas of South America and Africa that are a mystery to us. Also, there are many new frontiers for people who love adventure. These are the polar regions, the deep oceans and the spaces beyond the earth.

2. The polar regions, north and south, have become increasingly important for several reasons. First, the Arctic region in the north lies between the United States and the Soviet Union. Because of the airplane, our two nations are now very close to each other across the North Pole. Second, much of the weather we have in the middle latitudes is caused in part by cold air moving southward from the Arctic Ocean. This cold air sometimes blows as far south as Florida and the Gulf of Mexico. In the Antarctic, the southern polar region, it is believed that there are important mineral resources. As the world population continues to grow, our need for more and more resources is growing with it.

3. The Arctic, the northern polar region, is an ocean surrounded by land. An area of floating ice, it is surrounded by Alaska, Canada, Scandinavia and Siberia. The North Pole is located amid the ice-filled waters of the Arctic Ocean. The first people to explore this region were men looking for a water passage from the Atlantic to the Pacific Oceans. In 1888, a Norwegian explorer named Fridtjof Nansen became the first man to lead a party across the great ice-covered interior of Greenland. In 1909, Commander Robert E. Peary of the United States and his party became the first men to reach the North Pole.

4. In July, 1958, the United States atomic submarine *Nautilus* made one of the most amazing trips in sea history. This submarine, with a crew of 116 men, sailed under the Arctic ice cap all the way from Alaska to Greenland. At times the submarine was 400 feet beneath the surface of the ocean. The submarine traveled a total of 1,830 miles under water on this first voyage across the North Pole.

5. The Antarctic or southern polar region is largely a high, icy plateau 8,000 feet above sea level. This ice cap covers a continent of about six million square miles. (About half the continent is claimed by Australia.) Antarctica is one of the coldest lands on earth. It is colder than the Arctic because of the high elevation of the plateau and because of the thick layer of ice and snow that covers it. If the ice were to melt, the levels of all the oceans would rise and flood every coastal city in the world. Antarctica is really an icy desert. It is empty of people and land animals. The South Pole was first reached

These U.S. engineers helped to survey over 80,000 square miles of Antarctica. Why do you think scientists are interested in surveying this ice-covered land mass?

by man in 1911 when Roald Amundsen of Norway led an expedition there. Another famous explorer of the Antarctic was Admiral Richard Byrd of the United States.

6. One of the newest and most exciting fields for man's exploration is the space above the earth. As early as 1919, an American named Robert Goddard suggested that man could build a rocket to go to the moon. (His doubting neighbors called him "Moon Mad" Goddard.) Later, in the 1930's, Goddard launched liquid-fuel rockets. Rockets were also developed in other countries. During World War II, the Germans fired V-2 rockets on London from across the English Channel. A rocket is a new kind of engine in that it can run without air from the outside. The rocket carries its own air or oxygen in a tank. Thus, with the invention of the rocket it became possible to think of sending men into space, where there is no air.

7. Since the 1950's, scientists have been dealing with the problems of exploring space. In 1957, the Soviet Union sent the first spaceship, Sputnik I, into orbit around the earth. (That is, the spaceship moved around the earth in the same manner as the moon.) This opened up our space age. Shortly thereafter,

the United States orbited its first spaceship or satellite, Explorer I. In 1961, the Soviet Union sent the first man into space, Major Yuri Gagarin. A year later, John Glenn of the U.S. made a successful orbit of the earth. Since then, dozens of manned and unmanned space flights have been launched by the two nations.

8. Space exploration continues. Men from both the Soviet Union and the United States have left their spaceships to take "walks in space." Both nations have landed vehicles on the moon. The Soviet Union has used a woman "cosmonaut" to orbit the earth. United States spacemen have walked on the moon's surface. The pictures they relayed of their "walks" and "rides" on the moon have thrilled viewers all over the earth. Scientists are studying the rocks they brought back to learn more about the age of the moon and how it was formed.

9. Man is also interested in finding out more about the waters of the earth. Three-fourths of our planet is covered by water. Yet this part of the earth is little known and its tremendous riches are hardly touched. The invention of the *bathyscaphe*, a ship that floats under the sea, has made it possible to learn more about our oceans. Two of the great underwater explorers are Henri Picard of Belgium and Jacques Cousteau of France. Because of their work, we are learning more about the earth's oceans, our "silent world."

Exploring the ocean floor. Why is it important for mankind to learn more about the waters of the world?

10. Ocean floors have vast plains and mountain ranges. Some of these mountains "stick their heads above water" and appear as islands. There are also deep trenches in the ocean floor. Near Guam, the Pacific Ocean reaches a depth of almost seven miles. Near Puerto Rico, the Atlantic Ocean is five miles deep.

11. The waters of the world will become more and more important as the years go by. Up to now, the oceans have been a source of food and salt. But soon we will turn to them for other things as well. The available supplies of fresh water must be increased. Scientists are trying to find an easy way to take the salt from sea water. If they succeed, man's supply of pure, fresh water will be almost endless. The demand for minerals is also growing. We are just beginning to realize what a valuable source of minerals the sea can be. Magnesium and oil are already being taken from the waters of the sea.

2 THE WORLD IS YOUR NEIGHBORHOOD

Reading For A Purpose: Why are all people in the world our neighbors?

1. Throughout history, man has been cursed by war. World War II was the most terrible war known to man. More than sixteen million people were killed in battle and millions more died from starvation, bombings, wounds and persecutions. Because warfare has become so horrible, representatives of fifty nations met in 1945 to form a world organization to help keep peace in the world. A charter or constitution was drawn up to form the United Nations Organization. The headquarters of this organizaton is located in New York City. Since it began, the United Nations has been a strong force for peace in the world. The United States has always supported the United Nations in its efforts for peace.

2. Early in 1945, scientists developed a new and terrible weapon, the atom bomb. This bomb was dropped by the United States on the Japanese cities of Hiroshima and Nagasaki in August, 1945. More than 200,000 people were killed or injured in the bombings. Since that time, even more powerful nuclear bombs have been tested. The United States, the Soviet Union, Great Britain, France and China have all tested these newer bombs. Except for China, they all have airplanes and missiles that can carry their bombs to targets thousands of miles away in a matter of minutes. It is within their power to destroy large areas of any nation in just seconds.

3. It is only a question of time before even more nations will be able to make atomic weapons. In 1963, the United States, the Soviet Union and Great Britain signed a treaty agreeing not to explode nuclear weapons under water or in the air. France and China did not sign this treaty. Nevertheless, the treaty may be the beginning of the control of atomic energy. Perhaps people can turn their attention to the use of this energy for the benefit of mankind. The search for peace in a world divided by atomic powers is one of our major problems.

4. Despite war and nuclear bombs, our vast world has still become a single neighborhood. Of course, to think of more than three billion people as your neighbors is not easy. Therefore, think instead of a small land with only 3,000 people. What might we find, if this land represented the world? One thousand of the 3,000 people would be white. They would be living on the best land and making use of its resources. Most of them would have a high standard of living and would look forward to a life of over seventy years.

5. Most of the other 2,000 people would be dark-skinned. More than half would go to bed hungry each night. More than half would not be able to read or write. Because of poor health services, their life span would be only thirty to thirty-five years. Most of these people would be found in Latin America, the Middle East and North Africa, Sub-Sahara Africa, Southeast Asia and parts of Europe. (However, even the United States has areas of great poverty.) We cannot let this poverty around the world continue. People will not accept their poor conditions much longer, and they should not have to. The question facing America and the world is: How can we help poor people everywhere to realize their hopes for a better life for themselves and their children?

6. Many people in the United States believe we should help the developing countries. As you have learned, there are many reasons for doing so. We help people because all of us

Young African woman.   A Hindu swami, or religious teacher.   A Chinese sculptor.

The world is growing smaller every day, many people say. What do they mean by this statement? How may a "smaller world" possibly affect the relationship of each of these people to one another and to you?

are human. Secondly, we do not believe that poverty is necessary in this world. The earth has too many riches for a large number of people to go hungry. Thirdly, when we help others, there are benefits for us—economic, political and social. As the underdeveloped nations raise their standard of living, they are better able to trade with us. And people who are well fed, clothed and housed are better able to resist wars and dictatorial governments.

7. Another problem facing the world is that of the growing population. This increase in population is especially heavy in the Far East, Latin America and Africa. The population of the world passed the three-billion mark some years ago. It is said that if the world keeps growing at its present rate, there will be almost seven billion people in the world in the year 2000. This growth is greatest in the underdeveloped nations, as you might be able to guess.

8. In the past, the population of some countries was kept smaller because so many people were killed in wars or died of disease at a young age. Today, people are taught to care for their health; modern medicines are available to more people. We live longer, yet most of the people of the world are pressed into less than half the land area of the globe! Will there be enough food and resources to provide everyone with a decent standard of living?

9. While more and more resources are needed for the growing population, the world's forest and mineral resources are decreasing. Each year, man digs or pumps more minerals from the earth. Unlike water, these resources cannot be replaced. One wonders how long man can continue taking minerals from the earth. There are limits to the amount of coal, iron ore and oil to be found in the earth's crust. It is time that man thought very seriously about saving or conserving the gifts of nature.

10. Another of the world's problems is the treatment of people of different races. You have learned that people of many races live in

the world. You have learned that there are more nonwhite people in the world than there are white people. Many of the nonwhite people have lived in colonies of Western nations. They have been ruled by white people. In Africa, chiefly, there has been a great deal of bad feeling against white people because they ruled there in years past. Today the whites still hold some of the best land. A question that Americans must answer to the world is this: Does our treatment of people of all races show that we recognize the importance of *each* person as a worthwhile human being, regardless of the race to which he belongs?

THE HORRORS OF WAR

Cost of United States Wars Since 1900

	Vietnam	Korea	World War II	World War I	Total
Killed in combat	45,619	33,629	291,557	53,402	424,207
Wounded in combat	302,393	103,284	670,846	204,002	1,280,525
Direct cost of war	$120 billion	$17 billion	$341 billion	$26 billion	$504 billion

GLOSSARY

The meanings given for the following words are the ones used in this book.

abacá [ab a KA] ● Hemp plant; its fibers are used to make rope.

aborigines [ab o RIJ i neez] ● First people to live in a land, as in Australia.

agriculture [AG ri kul chur] ● Farming; the use of land for raising plants, food crops and livestock.

alliance [a LY ans] ● An agreement among nations to help each other.

altitude [AL ti tood] ● Height above sea level.

aluminum [a LOO mi num] ● Light metal made from bauxite.

Antarctic Circle [ant ARK tik] ● Line of latitude 66½° south of the equator.

apartheid [a PART hyt] ● Policy of separating whites and Negroes in the Republic of South Africa.

archipelago [ar ki PEL a go] ● Any large group of islands.

Arctic Circle [ARK tik] ● Line of latitude 66½° north of the equator.

artesian well [ar TEE zhun] ● Well dug deep in the earth through a layer of rock that causes the water to shoot to the surface.

atmosphere [AT mo sfeer] ● "Blanket" of air that surrounds the earth.

atoll [AT tol] ● Small coral island; most often found in the South Pacific.

atomic energy [a TOM ik EN ur jee] ● Energy released through the splitting of an atom.

automation [aw to MAY shun] ● Use of machines in the manufacture of goods, often to do work once done by men.

axis [AK sis] ● Imaginary line through the earth at its poles, and upon which the earth spins.

basin [BAY sin] ● Low spot in the mountains; lowland area drained by a river.

bathyscaphe [BATH i skayf] ● Diving chamber used to explore the ocean depths.

bauxite [BAWK syt] ● Mineral ore from which aluminum is made.

bay ● Body of water caused by an irregular place in the coastline and protected by the land around it.

bazaar [ba ZAR] ● Marketplace or shopping area in a Middle Eastern town.

Bedouins [BED oo ins] ● Nomadic tribe of the Middle East; herding camels and horses is their chief occupation.

Boers [BORS] ● Dutch settlers in South Africa.

cabinet [KAB i net] ● Group of men specially appointed to advise the head of a government.

cacao [ka KAY o] ● Tropical plant from whose seeds cocoa and chocolate are made.

canal	[ka NAL]	● Waterway made by man to connect two bodies of water.
canneries	[KAN er eez]	● Factories where foods are canned.
capital	[KAP i tal]	● Seat of government in a country; or money and goods used to make more goods.
capitalism	[KAP i tal izm]	● System under which people are free to own and develop their own property in order to make a profit.
cash crop		● Crops raised for sale by a farmer; with profits from this crop he buys the goods his farm does not supply.
cinchona	[sin KO na]	● Bark of a tree that grows in the rain forests of South America and Asia; used in making quinine.
citrus fruits	[SIT rus FROOTS]	● Fruits like lemons, limes, oranges and grapefruit.
civil rights	[SIV il RYTS]	● The rights and opportunities each person has as a citizen and human being, regardless of his race or religion.
climate	[KLY mat]	● Average weather in a given region over a long period of time.
coast		● The edge of land along the sea or ocean.
cold war		● When nations oppose each other without carrying on a shooting war.
collective farm	[ko LEK tiv]	● *Kolkhoz*—large farm owned by the Soviet government; the people work for a share of the crops.
colonialism	[ko LO ni al izm]	● Ownership and governing of distant lands or colonies.
commercial farming	[ka MER shul]	● Raising crops for sale.
Common Market		● An agreement among nine nations in Western Europe to lower tariffs and increase trade with each other.
commonwealth	[KOM un welth]	● A group of nations who govern themselves but still show loyalty to a "mother country"; the British Commonwealth, for example.
commune	[KOM yoon]	● Large state-owned farm in Communist China; the people work for wages as on a Soviet state farm.
communism	[KOM yoo nizm]	● Form of government in the Soviet Union, China and Eastern Europe today. The people are controlled by the state and almost everything is owned by it.
competition	[kom pe TISH un]	● When two or more businesses try to make and sell the same kinds of goods.
conservation	[kon ser VAY shun]	● The practice of saving our natural resources.
constitution	[kon sti TOO shun]	● Written plan of government.
consumer	[kon SOOM er]	● Anyone who buys and uses any product.

574

consumer goods		Products made for people to buy and use, such as food, clothing, automobiles, radios, furniture.
continent	[KON ti nent]	One of the seven largest bodies of land on earth: North America, Asia, Africa, South America, Europe, Australia, Antarctica.
cooperative	[ko OP er a tiv]	Group of farmers who agree to share all their gains and losses.
copra	[KO pra]	Dried "meat" or pulp of a coconut.
country		A nation and its land.
craftsmen	[KRAFTS men]	Workers skilled in making things by hand.
crop rotation	[ro TAY shun]	Growing different crops on a piece of land from year to year in order to keep the soil from "wearing out."
culture	[KUL chur]	Ways of living developed by a people.
current	[KUR ent]	Steady flow of water.
czar	[ZAR]	Former ruler of Russia.
dam		Wall built across a river to hold back the water for conservation or electric power.
degree	[di GREE]	Unit of measurement of temperature and of longitude and latitude.
delta		Area of land at the mouth of a river formed by the deposit of mud washed down by the river.
democracy	[de MOK ra see]	Nation or form of government in which the laws are made by the people or their elected representatives.
density of population	[DEN si tee, pop yoo LAY shun]	Number of people per square mile of land in an area.
desert	[DEZ ert]	Large, dry area where rainfall is less than ten inches each year.
dictatorship	[dik TAY ter ship]	Government ruled by one man or one party in which the people have little chance to choose what they want.
dike	[DYK]	Small mud wall built to control the flow of water in a rice field; also, a wall built to keep out the sea, as in the Netherlands.
distortion	[dis TOR shun]	Made crooked or twisted out of shape.
drift		Weak current or flow of water.
dry farming		Farming in areas of little rainfall. The farmer grows crops every other year, saving the little moisture that is collected in the soil.
dynasty	[DY nas tee]	Rulers of a nation from the same family.
earth	[URTH]	Land or soil; the name of our planet.
earthquake	[URTH kwayk]	Terrible shaking of the ground.
electricity	[ee lek TRIS i tee]	One form of power.
elevation	[el e VAY shun]	Height above sea level or above the surface of the earth.

empire	[EM pyr]	● Group of lands under the rule of one person or one nation.
equal-area map	[EE kwal AIR ee a]	● Map showing the correct size of land and water areas.
equator	[ee KWAY tor]	● Imaginary line around the middle of the earth, halfway between the North and South Poles.
equinox	[EE kwi noks]	● Time of the year when days and nights are of equal length all over the earth. During the equinox, the sun is directly overhead at the equator.
erosion	[ee RO zhun]	● Wearing away of the soil through the action of wind, water or glaciers.
estancia	[es TAN si a]	● Large cattle ranch in Latin America.
evaporation	[ee vap o RAY shun]	● Process by which water is changed into water vapor.
exports	[EKS ports]	● Goods sent out of a country.
extensive farming	[eks TEN siv]	● Farming over large areas with machinery.
fazenda	[fa ZEN da]	● Brazilian coffee plantation.
fellahin	[FEL a heen]	● Peasants or small farmers of North Africa and the Middle East.
Fertile Triangle	[FUR til TRY an gle]	● Rich farming area in the Soviet Union, shaped like a triangle.
feudalism	[FYOO dal izm]	● System in which land is owned by a powerful lord and worked by people called serfs in exchange for the lord's protection.
fiord	[fee ORD]	● Narrow inlet of the sea surrounded by steep cliffs, found especially in Norway.
foreign policy	[FOR in]	● Plan or pattern of relations of one country with others.
Free World		● Countries of the world that are not Communist.
gaucho	[GOW cho]	● Cowboy on the pampas of Argentina.
geography	[jee OG ra fee]	● Study of the earth and how people have adapted to all of its varying conditions.
glacier	[GLAY sher]	● Large mass of ice and snow that moves slowly over the land.
globe		● Round model or true map of the earth.
government	[GUV ern ment]	● Persons who rule, that is, make and enforce the laws of, a country.
grazing	[GRAYZ ing]	● Roaming or wandering over a pasture, and eating the grass.
grid		● Crisscrossing lines on a map that help to locate any place on earth.
growing season		● Length of time from the planting of crops until they are harvested; length of time in which the weather is frost-free.
gulf		● Body of water surrounded by land; usually larger than a bay.
hacienda	[ah see END ah]	● Large plantation or farm in Latin America.

harbor		Body of water caused by an irregular place in the coastline and the land around it.
hardwood		Tough, heavy wood of such trees as oak, teak and mahogany.
heavy industry	[IN dus tree]	Manufacturing that uses heavy materials like iron and steel.
hemisphere	[HEM i sfeer]	Half the earth or globe.
herdsman		One who raises such animals as sheep, goats, cattle and camels for a living.
highland	[HY land]	Area of hills, mountains or plateaus; upland.
high latitudes	[LAT i toods]	That part of the earth between 66½° and 90° north and south of the equator.
hill		Elevated piece of land not higher than 1,000 feet above sea level.
humid	[HYOO mid]	Damp or wet.
humid continental	[kon ti NEN tal]	Climate found inland or on the eastern coast of continents, marked by cold winters, hot summers, and some rain throughout the year.
humidity	[hyoo MID i tee]	Amount of moisture in the air.
humid subtropical	[sub TROP i kal]	Climate on the eastern coast of continents in the middle latitudes, marked by long, hot summers, mild winters, and rain throughout the year.
ice cap		Mass of ice at the Poles that does not melt.
illiteracy	[il LIT er a see]	Lack of ability to read or write.
immigrants	[IM i grants]	People who come to a country from other lands.
imperialism	[im PEER ee al izm]	Rule of one nation over other lands.
imports	[IM ports]	Goods brought into a country.
industrial region	[in DUS tri al REE jun]	Area in which manufacturing is the chief kind of work.
Industrial Revolution	[rev o LOO shun]	The change from the making of goods at home with hand tools to the making of goods in factories with machines.
insecticide	[in SEK ti syd]	Liquid or powder used to kill insects.
intensive farming	[in TEN siv]	Growing crops in a small area with a great deal of hand labor that usually results in high yields.
International Date Line	[in ter NASH un al]	An imaginary north-south line in the middle of the Pacific Ocean; 180° longitude.
investment	[in VEST ment]	Spending of money in the hope of gaining a profit.
Iron Curtain	[KER tin]	A term used to describe the effort of the Soviet Union to close off its lands from communication and trade with the Free World.
irrigation	[ir i GAY shun]	Bringing water to dry land through canals or ditches.
island	[I land]	Body of land entirely surrounded by water.
isthmus	[IS mus]	Narrow strip of land joining two larger bodies of land.

jungle	[JUN gle]	Hot land covered all year with a dense growth of trees and plants.
jute	[JOOT]	Plant fiber used in making rope.
kibbutz	[ki BOOTS]	Farming community in Israel owned by the people who live and work on its land.
kraal	[KRAHL]	Village of an African tribe.
lake		Body of water surrounded entirely by land.
landlocked		Without a coastline or opening to the sea, such as Bolivia or Czechoslovakia.
Lapp		People who live and herd reindeer in the tundra region of northern Europe.
latex	[LAY teks]	Milky fluid from which rubber is made.
leaching	[LEECH ing]	Washing out minerals or nutrients from soil.
League of Nations	[LEEG]	Organization formed after World War I to keep world peace. The United States did not join.
leeward	[LEE ward]	Away from the wind; the dry side of mountains that receives less rain.
legend	[LEJ end]	Key or guide to reading a map.
legislature	[LEJ is lay cher]	Lawmaking body.
light industry		Manufacturing that uses raw materials of light weight, such as fibers.
lines of latitude	[LAT i tood]	Imaginary lines running east and west around the earth and parallel to the equator; they measure in degrees the distance north and south of the equator.
lines of longitude	[LON ji tood]	Imaginary lines running north and south from Pole to Pole. They measure in degrees the distance east or west of the Prime Meridian, which passes through Greenwich, England.
llama	[LAH ma]	Woolly South American mountain animal used by the Indians of the Andes for carrying burdens.
llanos	[LAH nos]	Lowlands of the Orinoco River in South America that are good for grazing cattle.
loess	[LO es]	Fine yellow dust or soil found in the Hwang River Valley in China.
lowland	[LO land]	Flat land near sea level; a plain.
low latitudes	[LO LAT i toods]	That part of the earth between 0° and 23½° north and south of the equator.
maize	[MAYZ]	Indian corn.
majority	[ma JOR i tee]	At least one more than half. For example, in the sentence, "A majority of the 100 members voted for the law," *majority* means that at least 51 voted for it.
mandate	[MAN dayt]	Authorization by the League of Nations to one nation to govern or care for other lands.
manioc	[MAN i ok]	Starchy food of a plant, made into a bread by rain-forest peoples; also called cassava.

manufacture	[man yoo FAK cher]	● Making of raw materials into useful goods by hand or machine.
map		● Flat drawing that represents all or part of the earth by means of a scale.
marine climate	[ma REEN]	● Wet climate on the western side of continents in the middle latitudes, marked by cool summers, mild winters, and rain throughout the year.
market	[MAR ket]	● Anywhere that goods can be bought and sold, or anywhere that there is a demand for goods.
Marshall Plan	[MAR shal]	● Plan to help European nations repair the damage to their homes, factories and farms that resulted from World War II.
mass production	[MASS pro DUK SHUN]	● Method of making large amounts of goods at low cost.
Mediterranean climate	[med i ter RAY nee an]	● Climate marked by hot, dry summers, mild winters, and little rain throughout the year, most of it in winter.
Mercator map	[mer KAY ter]	● Map with straight grid lines, useful as a sailing chart.
merchant	[MER chant]	● Person who buys and sells goods for profit; a trader.
meridian	[me RID ee an]	● Line of longitude.
mesa	[MAY sa]	● Upland with fairly flat top and steep sides.
mestizo	[mes TEE zo]	● Person who is partly Spanish and partly Indian.
middle class		● Group of people, such as professionals and skilled workers, who are in a medium-level income bracket.
middle latitudes	[MID el LAT i toods]	● That part of the earth between 23½° and 66½° north and south of the equator.
migratory farming	[MY gra tor ee]	● Type of farming in which the farmer moves from place to place in search of better soil; practiced by primitive rain-forest peoples.
migratory workers		● Field laborers who move from one farm to another to obtain work. They follow the seasons for harvesting a variety of crops.
mineral	[MIN er all]	● Ore taken or mined from the earth: gold, lead, copper, etc.
missile	[MIS el]	● An object shot into the air by the force of an explosion.
missionary	[MISH un air ee]	● Person who brings his religion to those who are not members of his faith.
money crop		● (See cash crop.)
monoculture	[MON o kul cher]	● Country depending chiefly on its income from the raising of one crop, as in many countries of Latin America and Africa.
monotheism	[MON o thee izm]	● Belief in one God.

Monroe Doctrine	[mon RO DOK trin]	● Policy announced by President Monroe in 1823, warning European nations not to try to regain their colonies in the Americas.
monsoon	[mon SOON]	● Winds that change direction each season. They bring a wet season when they blow from the water and a dry season when they blow from the land.
Moslem	[MOZ lem]	● Follower of the religion of Islam.
mosque	[MOSK]	● Moslem house of worship.
"mother country"		● Country that has colonies.
nationalism	[NASH un al izm]	● Strong feeling of pride in one's nation or government.
NATO	[NAY to]	● North Atlantic Treaty Organization; an alliance of Western nations who have agreed to help each other in case of attack.
natural resources	[NACH er al ree SOR ses]	● Those things given to us by nature in or on the land, such as soil, water, minerals, forests.
nitrate	[NY trayt]	● Chemical used to make fertilizer or explosives.
nomad	[NO mad]	● Person who wanders from place to place in search of better grazing land for his flock or herd.
North Pole		● Northernmost point on earth.
oasis	[o AY sis]	● Desert land where water can be found and some crops can be grown.
ocean		● One of the largest bodies of salt water on the earth.
ocean current	[O shun KUR ent]	● Swift-moving stream or "river" in the ocean.
oil palm	[OYL PAHM]	● Tropical tree. The oil taken from its seeds has many commercial uses.
orbit	[OR bit]	● Path or circle around the sun or around any body in space.
Orient	[OR i ent]	● Countries of eastern and southeastern Asia.
outback	[OWT bak]	● Dry, empty lands of Australia.
paddy	[PAD ee]	● Small rice field, enclosed by dikes of mud.
pampas	[PAM pas]	● Large grassy plains in the southeastern part of South America.
parallel	[PAIR a lell]	● Line of latitude.
parliament	[PAHR li ment]	● Lawmaking body, as in Canada or Great Britain.
peninsula	[pe NIN su la]	● Piece of land almost entirely surrounded by water.
peon	[PEE on]	● Poor farm worker of Latin America.
permafrost	[PERM a frawst]	● Soil just below the earth's surface in the Arctic regions that never thaws or melts.
phosphates	[FOS fayts]	● Salts found in the earth that are used in making fertilizer.
physical map	[FIZ i kal]	● Map showing the land and water features of the earth.
plain		● Broad stretch of level or almost level land.

planet	[PLAN et]	Body in space that revolves about a sun and gives off no light of its own.
plantation	[plan TAY shun]	A large farm on which one chief crop is grown.
plateau	[plat TO]	Large area of level highland, not so rough as mountains.
plaza	[PLAH za]	Public square in a Latin American village or town.
polar map	[PO ler]	Map in which the North or South Pole is the center.
port		Harbor or city around a harbor where ships deliver and pick up goods for trade or people who wish to travel.
prairie	[PRAIR ee]	Dry grassland or steppe.
Prime Meridian	[PRYM ma RID ee an]	First or beginning line of longitude, running through Greenwich, England; 0° longitude.
processing	[PROS sess ing]	Treating food or materials to make them ready for use.
province	[PROV ins]	Political subdivision of a country. Canada has provinces instead of states.
rainfall		Amount of water falling in a given time on a given region, measured in inches.
rain-forest climate		Year-round hot, rainy climate of the low forest lands near the equator.
ranch		Large area of land for raising cattle or sheep.
raw materials	[RAW ma TEER i als]	Natural resources, like wool, cotton, minerals, that can be turned into finished products.
refine	[ree FYN]	To remove the impurities from raw materials such as oil, sugar cane or minerals.
refugees	[REF yoo jeez]	People who flee from a country, usually because of religious or political persecution or war.
reincarnation	[ree in kar NAY shun]	Belief of the Hindu religion in which the spirit is said to take a new form after death.
republic	[ree PUB lik]	Nation in which the people elect representatives to make their laws.
reserves	[ree ZERVS]	Anything not yet used, as oil or mineral ores; or any place set apart, such as Negro settlements in the Republic of South Africa.
reservoir	[REZ er VWAHR]	Place where water is stored.
revolution	[rev o LOO shun]	Sudden change in government or in customs; also, the movement of the earth around the sun.
river		Large stream of water.
river mouth		Place where a river flows or empties into the sea.
river source	[SORS]	Place where a river rises or begins.
rotation	[ro TAY shun]	Turning of the earth on its axis during a whole day; crops planted in turn on the same fields.

rural	[ROOR al]	● Having to do with farms and villages.
satellite country	[SAT e lyt]	● Nation under the control of a larger nation, such as the *satellites* of the Soviet Union.
savanna	[sa VAN a]	● Hot climatic region of two seasons, rainy and dry, found north and south of the tropical rain forests.
scale of miles		● A key that explains distance, or how far one place is from another on a map; also helps to show the size of an area.
sea		● Large body of water, partly surrounded by land.
sea level	[SEE LEV el]	● About the same height as the ocean; low point of land.
serf	[SURF]	● A person who works for a lord or a large landowner, and who is bound to his lord's land and sold with it to any new owner.
sharecropper	[SHAIR krop er]	● One who farms land belonging to another, and receives a share of the crop for his work.
sheik	[SHEEK]	● Head man of a village or a tribe, chiefly in the Middle East.
slum		● Old, crowded, poor section of a city.
South Pole		● Southernmost point on earth.
soviet	[SO vi et]	● Russian word for *council*.
state farm		● *Sovkhoz*—large government-owned farm in the Soviet Union on which farmers work for wages.
steppe	[STEP]	● Large treeless plain that has cold winters and hot summers, and receives from ten to twenty inches of rain a year; called a *prairie* in the United States.
strait		● Narrow body of water that connects two larger bodies of water.
subcontinent	[sub KON ti nent]	● An area of land almost as large as a continent; a land mass separated from the mainland by mountains, such as India.
subsistence farming	[sub SIS tens]	● Farming in which the farmer grows only enough crops to feed himself and his family.
subtropical	[sub TROP i kal]	● Between the temperate and the tropical zones.
surplus	[SUR plus]	● Amount left over after needs are met, as a *surplus* of wheat or clothing.
tableland	[TAY bel land]	● High plain or plateau; a mesa.
taiga	[TY ga]	● Large cold forests of subarctic regions.
tariff	[TAIR if]	● Tax on goods coming into a country.
temperature	[TEM per a cher]	● Amount of heat or cold in the air, measured by degrees on a thermometer.
topography	[top OG ra fee]	● All the features or land forms of the earth's surface: rivers, bodies of water, plains, mountains, valleys, plateaus; the general shape or form of the land.

trade		● Exchange of goods between nations or persons.
treaty	[TREE tee]	● Formal, written agreement between nations about boundaries, trade, etc.
tributary	[TRIB yoo tair ee]	● Branch of a river.
Tropic of Cancer	[TROP ik, KAN ser]	● Imaginary line of latitude 23½° north of the equator; the farthest point north that the sun appears directly overhead.
Tropic of Capricorn	[KAP ri korn]	● Imaginary line of latitude 23½° south of the equator; the farthest point south that the sun appears directly overhead.
trust territory	[TER i tor ee]	● Region placed under the care of one nation by the United Nations.
tsetse fly	[TSET see]	● Insect, found only in Africa, whose bite causes sleeping sickness.
tundra	[TUN dra]	● Level, treeless region of the Arctic that has long, severe winters and short summers. The ground is frozen nearly all year.
typhoon	[ty FOON]	● Violent storm of the western Pacific Ocean.
underdeveloped	[UN der de VEL opt]	● Not making full use of natural resources.
United Nations	[yoo NY ted NAY shuns]	● Organization founded in 1945 to keep world peace.
urban	[UR ban]	● Having to do with towns and cities.
valley		● Lowland between hills and mountains.
veld	[VELT]	● High grassy plain or tableland in South Africa, used for sheep and cattle grazing.
vertical climate	[VUR ti kal]	● Climate of mountainous regions in which temperatures are warmer lower down and cooler higher up.
veto	[VEE to]	● Power to prevent an action by refusing to agree.
Vital Triangle	[VY tal TRY an gle]	● Area extending through Belgium, France and West Germany that is rich in coal and iron deposits and famous for its iron and steel products.
volcano	[vol KAY no]	● Mountain that sometimes pours out smoke, fire and melted rock through a hole in its top.
water power		● Physical force of water used to make electricity or to run machines.
weather	[WETH er]	● Temperature of any area over a short period of time; the day-by-day changes in the condition of the air.
winds		● Currents or streams of air.
windward		● Toward the wind; the rainy or wet side of mountains.
wood pulp	[WOOD pulp]	● Soft wood that has been crushed to make paper.

ARCTIC OCEAN

180°   120°   60°

GREE
(DEN

U.S.S.R.   ARCTIC CIRCLE   Baffin Bay
                            ALASKA

                            Anchorage   Godthaab

60°   Mackenzie R.

            Bering Sea   Hudson
                                              Juneau   Bay

                    Aleutian Is.   CANADA   Newfoundland

                                              Vancouver   Great Lakes
            NORTH   Seattle   Quebec
                                                                      Toronto Ottawa Montreal
            PACIFIC OCEAN   UNITED   Chicago   Boston
                                              San Francisco   STATES   New York
                                                                              Washington
30°   Los Angeles   Bermuda (Br.)   NORTH
            Midway Is. (U.S.)   New Orleans Rio Grande   ATLANTIC OCEAN
                                                                          Gulf of
                            Tropic of Cancer   MEXICO   Mexico
            Honolulu   Hawaii (U.S.)   Havana   Bahamas
                                                      Mexico City   BELIZE   CUBA
                                                                              Belize   HAITI DOMINGO
            Marshall Is. (U.S.)   GUATEMALA   Puerto Rico   WEST
                                                              Guatemala Tegucigalpa Caribbean Sea   INDIES
            International Date Line   San Salvador HONDURAS
            When crossing the date line going west,   EL SALVADOR Managua
            the date is set forward one day.   NICARAGUA COSTA RICA   Caracas
            When crossing the date line going east,   San José Panama   VENEZUELA GUYANA
            the date is set back one day   PANAMA Panama   Georgetown SURINAM
0°   Gilbert Is. (Br.)   Galapagos Is.   Bogotá   Cayenne
                                              (Ec.)   EQUATOR   COLOMBIA   FR. GUIANA
            Ellice Is.   Quito
            (Br.)   ECUADOR   Amazon R.
            SOLOMON IS. (Br.)   Marquesas Is. (Fr.)   SOUTH   BRAZIL
                                                                  PERU   AMERICA
            New Hebrides   Samoa Is.   Society Is.   Lima
                            (Br. & U.S.)   (Fr.)   BOLIVIA   Brasilia
            Fiji Is.   Tahiti   La Paz
            New Caledonia   Sucre PARAGUAY
                                              Pitcairn Is.   Asuncion   Rio de Janeiro
30°   (Br.)   Easter Is. (Chile)   CHILE   São Paulo

            SOUTH   ARGENTINA URUGUAY
                                                                  Santiago   Montevideo
            PACIFIC OCEAN   Buenos Aires

            Auckland
                Wellington   Falkland Is.
                NEW ZEALAND   Strait of   (Br.)
                                                                  Tierra del Fuego Magellan
THE WORLD   Cape Horn
            CAPITALS OF COUNTRIES

INDEX

Buenos Aires (Argentina), 156, 167, 177, 188
Bulgaria, 291, 305, 329, 339
Bunche, Ralph, 384
Burma, 458, 527, 528; freedom, 477, 505; monsoons, 466–467; rice, 496, 501, 529
Burros, 188
Bushmen, 416, 547
Byrd, Richard, 567

C

Cabot John, 92
Cabral, Pedro, 172
Cacao, 188, 217, 218, 422, 450. *See also* Cocoa.
Cairo (Egypt), 361, 388
Calcutta (India), 482, 505, 516
California, 51, 88, 124, 127, 128, 303
Cambodia, 330, 458, 477, 527
Camels, 361, 370, 371
Canada, 3, 35, 40, 43, 48, 51, 52, 53, 67, 266, 566; climate, 86–88; compared with Australia, 548; compared with the U.S., 76–77; education, 97; farming, 122, 141–142; foreign relations, 144–145, 148–149; forests, 137; government, 100, 144; history, 91–93; industries, 136–138, 145; minorities, 148; people, 96–97; problems, 148–149; resources, 136–138, 144; size, 76; standard of living, 97; topography, 81–82; trade, 142; trade with the U.S., 144. *See also* Anglo-America.
Canadian Shield, 136, 138, 141. *See also* Laurentian Shield.
Canals, 39, 40, 127; Egypt, 387; Europe, 230, 248, 249; Far East, 472, 520. *See also* names of individual canals.
Canberra (Australia), 547
Canton (China), 520
Capetown (Republic of South Africa), 412, 444
Capitalism, 110–112
Caribbean islands, 156, 176, 177
Caribbean Sea, 38, 156, 162
Caroline Islands, 555
Cartier, Jacques, 91
Caspian Sea, 294, 299, 316
Caste system, 486, 517
Castro, Fidel, 202–203, 331
Catholics, Anglo-America, 96, 97; Eastern Europe, 339; Latin America, 172, 177, 212, 217; Northern Ireland, 272; Soviet Union, 308; Spain, 277; Western Europe, 238, 243. *See also* Christianity.
Cattle, 124, 127, 128, 141–142, 283; Africa, 408, 425, 426; Anglo-America, 117, 122; Australia, 547, 551, 552; Eastern Europe 339; India, 488, 492, 516, 517; Latin America, 187, 217; New Zealand, 552; Pacific Islands, 556; Western Europe, 254. *See also* Dairying; Grazing.
Caucasian peoples, 6, 481
Caucasus, 34
Caucasus Mountains, 34, 316
Cement, 324
Central America, 156, 171

Central Plains (Anglo-America), 76, 122, 127
Central Treaty Organization (CENTO), 271, 384
Central Valley (California), 82, 128
Ceylon. *See* Sri Lanka.
Champlain, Samuel de, 91
Chao Phraya River, 529
Charleston (South Carolina), 43, 167
Chesapeake Bay, 117
Chiang Kai-shek, 459, 477, 521
Chicago (Illinois), 28, 30, 116, 117
Chile, 28, 29, 51, 52, 157, 167, 171, 176, 191
China, 34, 35, 51, 330, 334, 431, 528, 560; climates, 52, 467–468, 520; communism, 330, 459, 521, 522, 523; education, 504, 522; farming, 493, 497–498, 522; fishing 498; government, 476–477, 521; history, 472–473, 476–478; location, 472, 520; military power, 336, 459, 523, 569; people, 481, 522, 528; relations with Japan, 476 477, 509; with Soviet Union, 336, 521, 523; with U.S., 476, 523; religions, 488, 522; resources, 500, 522; size, 458, 520; topography, 520; transportation, 501, 520, 522. *See also* rivers by name.
Chocolate, 422
Christianity, Africa, 413; Anglo-America, 96, 97; Eastern Europe, 339; Far East, 486, 488–489, 510; Middle East, 346, 357, 393; Soviet Union, 303, 308; Western Europe, 224, 243, 275. *See also* Catholics; Protestants.
Christians, 3, 243, 303, 393, 528
Chromium, 217, 375, 500, 516
Cinnamon, 497
Citrus fruits, 124, 128, 212, 233, 255, 393
Cleveland (Ohio), 30, 116, 117
Climate, 3, 14–15, 17, 18, 23, 35; factors causing changes in, 42–44, 46–48; regions of, 50–53. *See also* countries by name; regions; names of climatic regions.
Coal, 35, 57, 58, 238; Australia, 552; Britain, 248, 271; Canada, 136; China, 500, 520–521, 522; Europe, 248–249, 261; India, 500, 516; Japan 511; Latin America, 192; Poland, 339; Soviet Union, 319, 320, 321; Turkey, 375; U.S., 105–106, 116, 117
Cobalt, 136, 429
Cocoa, 557. *See also* Cacao.
Coconuts, 450, 497, 529, 551, 556, 557
Coffee, Africa, 426; Brazil, 217; Far East, 493, 497, 529; Latin America, 188; Pacific Area, 557
Cold War, 329; spread of, 331
Collective farm, 315–316, 522. *See also* Kolkhoz.
Colombia, 44, 162, 173, 176, 188, 196, 201
Colonialism, 239, 248–249, 265, 269–270, 434. *See also* individual countries.
Colorado Plateau, 127
Colorado River, 81, 127, 128
Columbia Plateau, 127
Columbia River, 81, 106; power project, 136, 144
Columbus, Christopher, 91, 171, 173, 211, 237, 275

Commercial farming, 142, 492. *See also* Plantations.
Common Market, 240, 261–262, 266
Commonwealth of Nations, 270, 271, 444, 449, 548
Communes, 493, 522
Communication, 4
Communism, spread, 149; Africa, 331; Asia, 330–331; China, 330, 459, 477–478, 521, 522, 523; Eastern Europe, 339–340; Europe, 266, 291, 329–330; Latin America, 203, 291, 331; Soviet Union, 290, 304–305, 308, 324, 325; Vietnam, 529. *See also* Communist Party.
Communist Party, 269, 290, 311–312, 325, 334, 459, 521
Confucianism, 486, 488, 522
Congo Republic, 401, 434, 435
Congo River, 39, 404, 413; rain forest, 408
Conservation, 60, 149, 570. *See also* farming in individual countries.
Consumers, 131
Continents, 13–15, 17, 33
Cook, James, 536
Cooperatives, 254–255
Copenhagen (Denmark), 258
Copernicus, 238
Copper, 59; Africa, 401, 429; Australia, 552; Canada, 136; Chile, 191; Finland and Norway, 283; Israel, 393; Japan, 511; Mexico, 207; Soviet Union, 319; Spain, 277; Turkey, 375; United States, 105
Copra, 556, 557
Corn, Africa, 425; Brazil, 217; China, 497; Latin America, 182, 188; Mexico, 207; Pacific islands, 556; Southeast Asia, 529; United States, 122, 124
Corn Belt, 122
Coronado, Francisco de, 91, 249, 275
Cortez, Hernando, 172, 206, 275
Cotton, Africa, 426; Brazil, 217; Egypt, 369, 389; Far East, 497, 500, 501; India, 516; Latin America, 188; Mexico, 188, 207; North Africa, 339; Soviet Union, 299, 316
Cotton Belt, 123–124
Cousteau, Jacques, 567
Crimean Peninsula, 299
Cuba, 156, 157, 176, 201, 291; Fidel Castro, 202–203, 331; freedom, 201, 276; Soviet missile bases, 203, 331; sugar, 187, 196
Culture, 2–4
Culture region, 3
Cuzco (Peru), 171
Czars, 303–304
Czechoslovakia, 291, 305, 329–330, 339, 340

D

da Gama, Vasco, 412, 473
Dairying, Australia, 551; Canada, 141; New Zealand, 552; Puerto Rico, 212; Scandinavia, 283; United States, 123, 128; Western Europe, 254
Damascus (Syria), 361
Dams, 136, 142, 277; China, 522; India, 500;

ACKNOWLEDGMENTS

The photographs included in this text, on the pages indicated below, appear courtesy of the following:

American Airlines, Inc., 3, 82 (top left and right), 87 (right), 91 (bottom), 117 (left), 128, 547, 551, 556
Australian News & Information Bureau, 537, 542, 548, 552, 553
Australian Tourist Commission, 541

Bausch & Lomb Optical Co., 238
The Bettmann Archive, 237 (left)
British Museum, 356

Canadian Industries Ltd., 145
Alexander M. Chabe, 290 (top and bottom), 307 (bottom), 308, 315 (left), 316 (left), 324, 325 (top and bottom)
Collection H. D. D'Allemagne, 413
Commonwealth of Puerto Rico, 211
Coronet Instructional Media, 101, 122, 167, 171 (top and bottom), 172, 176 (left and right), 177, 178, 183 (top), 184, 186, 187, 188, 198, 216, 217, 233, 234, 239 (left and right), 243, 256, 265, 269 (left and right), 281, 339, 340, 400 (bottom), 404 (right), 405, 416 (left and right), 417 (left and right), 421 (left), 422, 423, 425 (top), 435, 439 (left and right), 440, 445, 458 (bottom), 459, 462, 463, 467 (top and bottom left), 473, 481 (left and right), 482 (bottom), 486, 487 (top and bottom), 492, 493 (bottom), 496 (left and right), 497, 499, 500, 501 (top and bottom), 504 (bottom), 510 (bottom), 516, 517 (top and bottom), 536, 557 (left and right), 561 (left and right)

Eva Dukes, 394
Eastfoto, 330 (left)

Ford Motor Company, 111

General Motors, 116
German Information Center, 68 (left), 224, 249 (left and right), 253 (right), 254, 266
Government of India Tourist Office, 4, 64 (top), 482 (top)
The Granger Collection, 304 (left), 305

Leslie Holzer, 570 (center)

Information Service of India, 515
Israel Govt. Tourist Office, 347, 350 (left), 361 (left), 369 (bottom), 393

Japan National Tourist Association, 511
Japan National Tourist Organization, 510 (top)

Mark Kane, 96, 148

Liggett & Myers Tobacco Company, 123 (top)
Lufthansa, 262

National Archives, 476
Canadian Consulate General—National Film Board of Canada, 2 (top and center), 34, 35, 52, 57, 64 (bottom), 76, 77 (top and bottom), 81, 82 (bottom), 86, 93, 97, 100, 132, 137 (top and bottom), 138, 141 (top and bottom)
National Science Foundation, 567 (left)
The New York Historical Society, 91 (top)

Pan American Airways, 276
Puerto Rico News Service, 212

Ruth H. Smiley, 430 (right)

Sovfoto, 294, 303, 311, 312, 315 (right), 316 (right), 320, 325 (bottom), 335 (top and bottom); Novosti from Sovfoto: 298, 304 (right), 319, 320; Tass from Sovfoto: 295
Standard Oil Company (N.J.), 50 (top and bottom), 51, 87 (left), 117 (right), 123 (bottom), 351, 370, 372, 374
South African Information Service, 426

Texaco—S. M. Amin: 350 (right), 360; Joe Brignolo: 430 (left), 431; John Keller: 157, 161, 182 (left and right), 183 (bottom), 192, 225 (top and bottom), 242, 248, 253 (left), 258, 270; J. Rathbone: 361 (right); Robert Yarnell Richie: 193
Trans World Airlines, 2 (bottom), 229, 243 (right), 307 (top), 357, 404 (left), 408 (top), 425 (bottom), 429, 458 (top), 529, 570 (right), 493 (top), 556; Joseph Nethis: 388 (bottom); Pete Turner: 275

Union Pacific Corporation, 105, 106, 107, 127
United Nations, 7, 38, 43 (left and right), 68 (right), 156, 162, 166 (left), 196, 197, 201, 207, 208, 282, 367, 369 (top), 375, 379, 380 (top and bottom), 400 (top), 408 (bottom), 421 (right), 434, 450, 451, 530, 558, 570 (left)
United Press International, 202, 271, 467 (right), 472, 520 (top), 522, 523, 527

Volkswagen, 63

Wide World, 149, 330 (right), 383, 384, 388 (top), 477, 502, 520 (bottom), 521

V. Yakovlev, 317